# REVELATION

# Brian K. Blount

# Revelation

## A Commentary

Hank,
It is so good to be
with you at Sprints 2009 at
in Richmond. God Bless you
in all that you do. And
I hope this is meaningful
for you

**WJK** WESTMINSTER
JOHN KNOX PRESS
LOUISVILLE · KENTUCKY

*First edition*
Westminster John Knox Press
Louisville, Kentucky

09  10  11  12  13  14  15  16  17  18—10  9  8  7  6  5  4  3  2  1

*Book design by Jennifer K. Cox*

**Library of Congress Cataloging-in-Publication Data**

Blount, Brian K., 1955–
   Revelation : a commentary / Brian K. Blount.—1st ed.
      p. cm.—(The New Testament library)
   Includes bibliographical references and indexes.
   ISBN 978-0-664-22121-8 (alk. paper)
   1. Bible. N.T. Revelation—Commentaries.   I. Title.
   BS2825.53.B56 2009
   228'.077—dc22

2008039367

PRINTED IN THE UNITED STATES OF AMERICA

∞ The paper used in this publication meets the minimum requirements
of the American National Standard for Information Sciences—Permanence of Paper
for Printed Library Materials, ANSI Z39.48-1992.

Westminster John Knox Press advocates the responsible use of our natural resources.
The text paper of this book is made from at least 30% post-consumer waste.

# CONTENTS

| | | |
|---|---|---:|
| **Preface** | | ix |
| **Acknowledgments** | | xiii |
| **Abbreviations** | | xv |
| **Bibliography** | | xix |
| **Introduction** | | 1 |
| Justice, Judgment, and Anger: The Theological Focus of Revelation | | 1 |
| Authorship | | 5 |
| Dating | | 8 |
| Social Setting | | 8 |
| Genre: Apocalyptic | | 14 |
| Outline and Structure | | 20 |
| Text | | 22 |

**COMMENTARY**

| | | |
|---|---|---:|
| **1:1–8** | **Prologue and Letter Opening** | **27** |
| 1:1–3 | Prologue: A Chain of Witness | 27 |
| 1:4–8 | Epistolary Greeting: Salutation | 32 |
| **1:9–3:22** | **A Word from the Lord: Ethical Instructions to the Seven Churches** | **39** |
| 1:9–20 | John Introduces Himself and Christ | 39 |
| 2:1–3:22 | Letters to Seven Churches of Asia | 47 |
| 2:1–7 | To Ephesus: You Can Be Too Good | 48 |
| 2:8–11 | To Smyrna: Richer than You Know | 52 |
| 2:12–17 | To Pergamum: At the Foot of Satan's Throne | 56 |

| | | |
|---|---|---|
| 2:18–29 | To Thyatira: Drowning in the Deep End | 60 |
| 3:1–6 | To Sardis: Time to Wake Up | 65 |
| 3:7–13 | To Philadelphia: Open-Door Policy | 72 |
| 3:14–22 | To Laodicea: Lukewarm Vomit | 79 |
| **4:1–22:9** | **A Series of Visions** | **84** |
| 4:1–5:14 | The Model of Heavenly Worship | 84 |
| 4:1–8a | An Opened Door | 85 |
| 4:8b–11 | A Hymn of Counterpraise | 93 |
| **Excursus:** The Hymns of Revelation as Songs of Resistance | | 95 |
| 5:1–5 | Who Is Worthy? | 98 |
| 5:6–10 | The Lamb Is Worthy | 106 |
| **Excursus:** The Lion and the Lamb | | 116 |
| 5:11–14 | Glory to the Lamb! | 119 |
| 6:1–8:1 | The Opening of the Seven Seals | 120 |
| 6:1–8 | The Four Horsemen | 121 |
| 6:9–11 | The Slaughtered Souls | 131 |
| 6:12–17 | Final Retribution | 137 |
| 7:1–17 | An Apocalyptic Intermission | 140 |
| 7:1–3 | Holding Back the Winds | 140 |
| 7:4–8 | The 144,000 | 144 |
| 7:9–17 | An Innumerable, International Multitude | 148 |
| 8:1 | The Seventh Seal: Silence in Heaven | 157 |
| 8:2–11:19 | The Sounding of the Seven Trumpets | 158 |
| 8:2–6 | Introduction to the Trumpets | 158 |
| 8:7–13 | The First Four Trumpets | 166 |
| 9:1–21 | Judgment as Good News | 171 |
| 9:1–12 | The Fifth Trumpet | 172 |
| 9:13–21 | The Sixth Trumpet | 180 |
| 10:1–11:19 | A Pause before the End | 186 |
| 10:1–3 | The Angel and the Little Scroll | 186 |
| 10:4–7 | The Mystery of the Seven Thunders | 192 |
| 10:8–11 | The Little Scroll | 197 |
| 11:1–19 | Measuring the Temple, Commissioning the Witnesses, Executing the End | 201 |

| 11:1–2 | Measuring the Temple | 201 |
| 11:3–13 | The Two Witnesses | 206 |
| 11:14 | A Transition | 218 |
| 11:15–19 | The Seventh Trumpet and the Fourth Antiphonal Hymn | 219 |
| 12:1–14:20 | Visionary Flashback: The Start of the Story | 223 |
| 12:1–17 | The Dragon's War | 223 |
| 12:1–6 | The Woman, the Dragon, and the Son | 224 |
| 12:7–9 | A War in Heaven | 232 |
| 12:10–12 | A Victory Hymn of Praise | 235 |
| 12:13–17 | The Woman, the Dragon, and the Son's Siblings | 240 |
| 12:18–13:18 | Resistance Is Futile | 242 |
| 12:18 | The Dragon Looks for Reinforcement from the Sea | 243 |
| 13:1–10 | The Beast from the Sea | 243 |
| 13:11–18 | The Beast from the Land | 255 |
| 14:1–20 | God Strikes Back: Visions of Judgment | 263 |
| 14:1–5 | The 144,000 | 263 |
| 14:6–11 | The Gospel of Justice | 271 |
| 14:12–13 | Model Behavior | 276 |
| 14:14–20 | Harvest Time | 278 |
| 15:1–22:9 | A Concluding Vision Cycle | 282 |
| 15:1 | Prelude to the Seven Bowls | 282 |
| 15:2–4 | A New Exodus Hymn | 283 |
| 15:5–8 | Introduction to the Seven Bowls | 289 |
| 16:1–21 | The Seven Bowls of God's Wrath | 293 |
| 16:1 | The Command to Pour Out the Bowls | 293 |
| 16:2–4 | The First Three Angels | 294 |
| 16:5–7 | Antiphonal Hymns in Praise of Divine Justice | 295 |
| 16:8–12 | The Fourth, Fifth, and Sixth Angels | 299 |
| 16:13–16 | An Interlude: Envisioning the Final Battle | 302 |
| 16:17–21 | The Seventh Angel | 307 |
| 17:1–19:10 | The Implications of God's Wrath: The Judgment of Babylon | 309 |

| 17:1–18 | Exposing the Great City: Vision of the Woman and the Beast | 309 |
|---|---|---|
| 17:1–2 | Introduction to the Fall of Babylon | 310 |
| 17:3–6a | The Vision of the Whore and the Beast | 313 |
| 17:6b–18 | The Vision Interpreted | 316 |
| 18:1–24 | Prophecies of the Fall of Babylon | 323 |
| 18:1–3 | Fallen, Fallen Is Babylon | 324 |
| 18:4–8 | Judgment for Arrogant Babylon | 327 |
| 18:9–20 | Mourning Babylon | 331 |
| 18:21–24 | An Angelic, Prophetic Sign Act | 336 |
| 19:1–10 | The Hallelujah Chorus | 338 |
| 19:11–21:8 | The Final Battle and Its Aftermath | 348 |
| 19:11–16 | The Rider on the White Horse | 348 |
| 19:17–21 | The Final Battle | 356 |
| 20:1–15 | Aftermath of the Final Battle | 359 |
| 20:1–3 | Satan, Locked Down | 359 |
| 20:4–6 | Witnesses, Reigning with Christ | 363 |
| 20:7–10 | Satan, The Last Stand | 368 |
| 20:11–15 | Witnesses and Everyone Else, Judgment Day | 372 |
| 21:1–8 | A New Creation | 374 |
| 21:9–22:9 | The Implications of God's Victory: The New Jerusalem | 383 |
| 21:9–14 | The Introduction of the City | 383 |
| 21:15–21 | The Measurements of the City | 388 |
| 21:22–27 | The Glory of the City | 392 |
| 22:1–5 | The New Life of the City | 395 |
| 22:6–9 | Transition: Closing 21:9–22:5 and Initiating the Epilogue | 399 |
| **22:10–21** | **Epilogue and Letter Closing** | **404** |
| **Index of Ancient Sources** | | **419** |
| **Index of Subjects** | | **447** |

# PREFACE

When I was first approached by editorial team members of the New Testament Library about writing a commentary on the book of Revelation, I must admit that I was somewhat apprehensive. Though I had long enjoyed a fascination in both teaching and publication with apocalyptic literature, I had never before engaged the Apocalypse. Although I had served as a solo pastor in a local church, preaching almost every Sunday for over six years, I rarely preached on *this* book. And the two sermons I did deliver from the text came from two relatively *easy* sections, the ethical exhortation in one of the seven letters to the seven churches in chapters 2–3 and the testimony of hope in the new heaven and new earth section at the book's close. Like many Christians, I watched with fascination as different groups espoused various forms of millennial proclamations and prophecies that they believed were inspired and directed by the book's content. Also like many Christians, particularly those in so-called mainline denominations and churches, I held the book at a theological and exegetical arm's length, ceding its interpretation to those whose theological perspective and social agenda tend to be very different from my own.

Because I believe that apocalyptic literature can have a historically as well as spiritually transformative agenda, I was intrigued by the commentary invitation. While most lay readers of apocalyptic material intuitively approach these texts as though they are exclusively preoccupied with otherworldly travels and exploits, I have spent much time engaged in the study of historical apocalypses like the book of Daniel and the Gospel of Mark. Both pieces of literature, the former Jewish and the latter Christian, are deeply interested in the way God's revelations to individuals or groups can transform the social and political landscape in which God's people find themselves. I do not believe that it is a coincidence that one of John of Patmos's primary bibliographic resources is the book of Daniel. John's Revelation, too, is interested in how people respond historically, socially, politically, as well as liturgically to the palpable spiritual presence of God in the world. His risen Christ is also a natural follow-up to the earthly Jesus; both are provocative figures who demand a discipleship willing to bear a cross. While Mark's Jesus asks his disciples to take up their crosses and follow, John's Christ demands that they witness to the same testimony to which Jesus testified, the very declaration of lordship that took Jesus to his own cross. Both are asking the Jesus/Christ followers to emulate their Lord's defiant belief that he, and not any human power, was master and Lord of human history. All the many visions of the Apocalypse testify to this single revelation, which was declared by Jesus and demanded by Jesus of his followers: Jesus Christ is Lord! That declaration of faith has powerful implications for the construction and maintenance of social and political life. In other words, what is revealed in and from heaven dramatically alters how humans should expect to conduct life here on earth.

There is a problem, a paradox: how can Christ, and the God he represents, be Lord of history when God's people suffer persecution (i.e., the cross) for making that very claim? Revelation intends to reveal the answer. John begins by introducing metaphors, such as a dragon in chapter 12. The dragon is the representation of satanic power that infests the hearts of humans and the governments they wield. The moniker "beast from the sea" applies to the Roman Empire. In order to reach Asia Minor (present-day Turkey), where John and the seven churches to whom he wrote were based, Rome had to cross the Aegean Sea. The third enemy, the beast from the land, also called the false prophet, was John's way of representing the bestial puppet governments in Asia Minor, which cooperated with Rome's military, political, and economic agenda.

Recent scholarship has concluded that there was no systematic persecution of Christians when John of Patmos wrote. The Romans, generally tolerant of indigenous religions, allowed locals to worship their own gods and goddesses as long as they also paid proper allegiance to the deities of Rome and the divine nature and human historical lordship of Rome's emperor. They generally operated by what one today might call a "Don't ask, don't tell" policy. During Domitian's reign, the time during which the Apocalypse was most likely written, imperial forces did not go looking for persons who would not show proper veneration of Roman divinity and therefore lordship. However, if someone brought such lack of fidelity to their attention, the Asia Minor authorities, on Rome's behalf, were bound to act.

Christians intolerantly held to the view that there was only one God, one Lord. When a Christian was so charged, he was brought before government leaders and punished. The sentence could result in loss of social standing, or reputation, or property—even life. John did not want his followers to wait for such a charge to be brought against them. He demanded that the Christ-believers tell on themselves by publicly witnessing to their exclusive belief in the lordship of God and God's Christ.

Christ-believers who followed John's counsel suffered. To stake its own claim to lordship, the empire executed many of these believers the way it had once executed their Christ (see Rev 20:4). And so they cried out, "Sovereign Lord, holy and true, how long will it be before you judge and avenge our blood on the inhabitants of the earth?" (Rev 6:10 NRSV).

Eschewing vengeance, God brought justice. The violence connected with the seven seals, trumpets, and bowls occurred as a direct result of the movement of justice into a defiantly unjust world. Christ-followers were not raptured out of the devastation; they were caught up within it (Rev 7:13–14). Shockingly, they were neither asked nor expected to fight back—at least not violently so. Christ-believers would conquer imperial oppression "by the word of their witness" (Rev 12:11). Long before Mahatma Gandhi in India or Martin Luther King Jr. in the American South, John of Patmos asked his people to engage in a testimony that was tantamount to active, aggressive, nonviolent resistance. Their witness to the world would transform the world.

For modern readers, the book of Revelation remains a call to nonviolent arms against any and every human person or people who would position themselves as lord over the destinies of others. In our own troubled times, when so many people seek spiritual direction and guidance, those who turn to the book of Revelation should not expect to find a blueprint for constructing a spiritual escape hatch to heaven. John's focus is not on running away from the world but on changing the world by standing up to humankind's most draconian impulses and tendencies and witnessing against them. Revelation is about resistance.

This is the book of Revelation that I found during my scholarly journey, and the book of Revelation that I enjoy teaching and from which I delight in preaching. It is the book of Revelation to which I hope to introduce you now.

BRIAN K. BLOUNT
RICHMOND, VIRGINIA

# ACKNOWLEDGMENTS

I am very grateful to the many persons who were helpful to me during my research and writing of this commentary. John Carroll and Beverly Gaventa were the two editors of the New Testament Library who invited me to engage this project and offered a great deal of support throughout the process. As chair of the Department of Biblical Studies at Princeton Theological Seminary, along with my wonderful colleagues in that department, Professor Gaventa helped ensure that I had both encouragement and opportunity to teach several courses on the book of Revelation as a way of introducing myself to the material. The department and the school also provided sabbatical opportunity for me to do research and write articles and an earlier book on the Apocalypse. John Carroll, now a departmental colleague at Union Theological Seminary and Presbyterian School of Christian Education, as well as dean of the seminary, has been an indefatigable editor as I have moved the manuscript to its latter stages. One of the best editors I have ever witnessed, he gives exquisite attention to the work at the most detailed of levels and helps ensure the finest of technical quality for the finished product. To be sure, any errors that remain are due to my own inadequacies, not his. He has certainly done all he could have done to help me shape the strongest manuscript possible.

I also want to thank the Board of Trustees at Union Theological Seminary and Presbyterian School of Christian Education. Art Ross, board chair, and John Kuykendall, chair of the presidential search committee, are to be singled out for appreciation. When the search committee extended an April 2007 call to me to become president of Union-PSCE on July 1, 2007, I confided to them that my manuscript was close to being finished, but several more months of undivided attention were needed for me to conclude the work. After their consultation with the trustees, the board magnanimously allowed me to spend the first three months of my presidency at my desk in Princeton. When I arrived on the Union-PSCE campus in August 2007, I was able to bring the draft of my commentary with me. Revisions to that draft have been possible during this first year of my presidency; I knew that original research and writing would not be. I am grateful for the board's understanding.

I also thank two individuals whose work was also instrumental. During the draft revisions of the past year, I have been immensely appreciative of the copy-editing work done by Kathy DuVall. Princeton Theological Seminary Ph.D. candidate Matthew Novenson deserves special recognition. Matt was my final teaching assistant as I finished my time as the Richard J. Dearborn Professor of New Testament Interpretation at Princeton Theological Seminary. And although revisions to the manuscript took place after my move to Union-PSCE, Matt continued his support by contributing final evaluations and interpretations, especially of my commentary translations. His work has been immensely valuable.

I am also indebted to the collegiality offered by two different departments of Bible, one at Princeton, the other at Union-PSCE.

Finally, I want to say a word of thank-you to my family—my daughter Kaylin, my son Joshua, and my wife Sharon. The three of them have always given me the space I need to study and reflect and the encouragement upon which I have depended to work through the difficult times that come with the writing of such a long-term project. It is to their love and faith that I dedicate this volume.

# ABBREVIATIONS

| | |
|---|---|
| AB | Anchor Bible |
| ACCS | Ancient Christian Commentary on Scripture |
| *ANRW* | *Aufstieg und Niedergang der römischen Welt: Geschichte und Kultur Roms im Spiegel der neueren Forschung.* Edited by H. Temporini and W. Haase. Berlin: Walter de Gruyter, 1972– |
| ANTC | Abingdon New Testament Commentaries |
| *AUSS* | *Andrews University Seminary Studies* |
| BECNT | Baker Exegetical Commentary on the New Testament |
| *Bib* | *Biblica* |
| BDAG | Bauer, W., F. W. Danker, W. F. Arndt, and F. W. Gingrich. *Greek-English Lexicon of the New Testament and Other Early Christian Literature.* 3d ed. Chicago: University of Chicago Press, 2000 |
| BIS | Biblical Interpretation Series |
| BMW | Bible in the Modern World |
| *BSac* | *Bibliotheca sacra* |
| *BT* | *The Bible Translator* |
| BZNW | Beihefte zur Zeitschrift für die neutestamentliche Wissenschaft |
| *CBQ* | *Catholic Biblical Quarterly* |
| CC | Continental Commentaries |
| ColBC | Collegeville Bible Commentary |
| *CurBS* | *Currents in Research: Biblical Studies* |
| DRLAR | Divinations: Rereading Late Ancient Religion |
| EdF | Erträge der Forschung |
| ESEC | Emory Studies in Early Christianity |
| *Hor* | *Horizons* |
| *HTR* | *Harvard Theological Review* |
| IBC | Interpretation: A Bible Commentary for Teaching and Preaching |
| ICC | International Critical Commentary |
| *Int* | *Interpretation* |
| ITSRS | Italian Texts and Studies on Religion and Society |
| *JBL* | *Journal of Biblical Literature* |

| | |
|---|---|
| *JSNT* | *Journal for the Study of the New Testament* |
| JSNTSup | Journal for the Study of the New Testament: Supplement Series |
| JSPSup | Journal for the Study of the Pseudepigrapha: Supplement Series |
| *JTS* | *Journal of Theological Studies* |
| LCBI | Literary Currents in Biblical Interpretation |
| LNTS | Library of New Testament Studies |
| LXX | Septuagint, as in *Septuaginta*, Rahlfs, 7th ed. |
| MBS | Message of Biblical Spirituality |
| MT | Masoretic Text, as in *Biblia Hebraica Stuttgartensia*, 4th ed., emended |
| NA$^{27}$ | *Novum Testamentum Graece*, Nestle-Aland, 27th ed. |
| NCB | New Century Bible |
| NCBC | New Cambridge Bible Commentary |
| NICNT | New International Commentary on the New Testament |
| NIGTC | New International Greek Testament Commentary |
| NIVAC | New International Version Application Commentary |
| *NovT* | *Novum Testamentum* |
| NRSV | New Revised Standard Version |
| NTC | The New Testament in Context |
| NTM | New Testament Message |
| NTR | New Testament Readings |
| NTT | New Testament Theology |
| PTMS | Princeton Theological Monograph Series |
| RSV | Revised Standard Version |
| SBL | Studies in Biblical Literature |
| *SBLSP* | *Society of Biblical Literature Seminar Papers* |
| SCMPC | SCM Pelican Commentaries |
| SemeiaSt | Semeia Studies |
| SNTSMS | Society for New Testament Studies Monograph Series |
| StABH | Studies in American Biblical Hermeneutics |
| StBL | Studies in Biblical Literature |
| Str-B | Strack, Hermann, and Paul Billerbeck, eds. *Kommentar zum Neuen Testament aus Talmud und Midrasch* |
| *TDNT* | *Theological Dictionary of the New Testament*. Edited by G. Kittel and G. Friedrich. Translated by G. W. Bromiley. 10 vols. Grand Rapids: Eerdmans, 1964–1976 |
| TNTC | Tyndale New Testament Commentaries |
| *TynBul* | *Tyndale Bulletin* |
| UBS$^4$ | *The Greek New Testament*, United Bible Societies, 4th ed. |
| WBC | Word Biblical Commentary |

| WBComp | Westminster Bible Companion |
| WH | Westcott, B. F., and F. J. A. Hort. *The New Testament in the Original Greek.* 2 vols., with Hort's "Notes on Select Readings" in vol. 2. New York: Harper & Bros., 1881 |
| WUNT | Wissenschaftliche Untersuchungen zum Neuen Testament |
| ZNW | *Zeitschrift für die neutestamentliche Wissenschaft und die Kunde der älteren Kirche* |

# BIBLIOGRAPHY

Achtemeier, Paul J. "Revelation 5:1–14." *Int* 40 (1986): 283–88.

Adams, Edward. *The Stars Will Fall from Heaven: Cosmic Catastrophe in the New Testament and Its World.* LNTS 347. New York: T&T Clark, 2007.

Aland, Kurt, and Barbara Aland. *The Text of the New Testament: An Introduction to the Critical Edition and to the Theory and Practice of Modern Textual Criticism.* 2d ed. Translated by Erroll F. Rhodes. Grand Rapids: Eerdmans, 1989.

Alexander, Loveday, ed. *Images of Empire.* JSNTSup 122. Sheffield: Sheffield Academic Press, 1991.

Aune, David. "Following the Lamb: Discipleship in the Apocalypse." Pages 269–84 in *Patterns of Discipleship in the New Testament.* Edited by Richard N. Longenecker. Grand Rapids: Eerdmans, 1996.

———. *Revelation.* Vol. 1, *1–5.* WBC 52a. Dallas: Word, 1997.

———. *Revelation.* Vol. 2, *6–16.* WBC 52b. Dallas: Word, 1998.

———. *Revelation.* Vol. 3, *17–22.* WBC 52c. Dallas: Word, 1998.

———. "The Apocalypse of John and the Problem of Genre." *Semeia* 36 (1986): 65–96.

Aus, Roger D. "The Relevance of Isaiah 66:7 to Revelation 12 and 2 Thessalonians 1." *ZNW* 67 (1976): 252–68.

Barr, David L. "The Apocalypse as a Symbolic Transformation of the World: A Literary Analysis." *Int* 38 (1984): 39–50.

———. *Tales of the End: A Narrative Commentary on the Book of Revelation.* Santa Rosa, Calif.: Polebridge, 1998.

———. "Towards an Ethical Reading of the Apocalypse: Reflections on John's Use of Power, Violence, and Misogyny." Pages 358–73 in *SBLSP 1997.* Atlanta: Scholars Press, 1997.

Bauckham, Richard. *The Climax of Prophecy: Studies on the Book of Revelation.* Edinburgh: T&T Clark, 1993.

———. *The Theology of the Book of Revelation.* NTT. Cambridge: Cambridge University Press, 1993.

Beale, G. K. *The Book of Revelation: A Commentary on the Greek Text.* NIGTC. Grand Rapids: Eerdmans, 1999.

Beasley-Murray, G. R. *Revelation*. Rev. ed. NCB. Grand Rapids: Eerdmans, 1981.

Blount, Brian K. *Can I Get a Witness? Reading Revelation through African American Culture*. Louisville, Ky.: Westminster John Knox Press, 2005.

———. "Reading Revelation Today: Witness as Active Resistance." *Int* 54 (2000): 398–412.

———. *Then the Whisper Put On Flesh: New Testament Ethics in an African American Context*. Nashville: Abingdon, 2001.

Böcher, Otto. *Die Johannesapokalypse*. 4th ed. EdF. Darmstadt: Wissenschaftliche Buchgesellschaft, 1998.

Boesak, Allan A. *Comfort and Protest: The Apocalypse from a South African Perspective*. Philadelphia: Westminster, 1987.

Boring, M. Eugene. "Narrative Christology in the Apocalypse." *CBQ* 55, no. 4 (1992): 702–23.

———. *Revelation*. IBC. Louisville, Ky.: John Knox Press, 1989.

Boxall, Ian. *Revelation: Vision and Insight*. London: SPCK, 2002.

Brasher, Brenda E. "From Revelation to the X-Files: An Autopsy of Millennialism in American Popular Culture." *Semeia* 82 (1998): 281–95.

Caird, G. B. *The Revelation of St. John the Divine*. San Francisco: Harper & Row, 1966.

Carey, Greg. *Elusive Apocalypse: Reading Authority in the Revelation to John*. StABH 15. Macon, Ga.: Mercer University Press, 1998.

Charles, R. H. *A Critical and Exegetical Commentary on the Revelation of St. John*. 2 vols. ICC. Edinburgh: T&T Clark, 1920.

Collins, Adela Yarbro. *The Apocalypse*. NTM 22. Wilmington, Del.: Michael Glazier, 1979.

———. "The Book of Revelation." Pages 384–414 in *The Origins of Apocalypticism in Judaism and Christianity*. Edited by John J. Collins. New York: Continuum, 1998.

———. *Cosmology and Eschatology in Jewish and Christian Apocalypticism*. Leiden: Brill, 2000.

———. *Crisis and Catharsis: The Power of the Apocalypse*. Philadelphia: Westminster, 1984.

———. "Numerical Symbolism in Jewish and Early Christian Apocalyptic Literature." In *ANRW*, Part 2, *Principat*, 21.2:1221–87. Berlin: Walter de Gruyter, 1984.

———. "The Political Perspective of the Revelation to John." *JBL* 96 (1977): 241–56.

Collins, John J., ed. *Apocalypse: The Morphology of a Genre*. SemeiaSt 14. Atlanta: Scholars Press, 1979.

———. "From Prophecy to Apocalypticism: The Expectation of the End." Pages 129–61 in *The Origins of Apocalypticism in Judaism and Christianity*. Edited by John J. Collins. New York: Continuum, 1998.

————, ed. *The Origins of Apocalypticism in Judaism and Christianity*. Vol. 1 of *The Encyclopedia of Apocalypticism*. New York: Continuum, 1998.

————. "Towards the Morphology of a Genre." *Semeia* 14 (1979): 1–19.

Comay, Joan. *The Temple of Jersualem*. New York: Holt, Rinehart & Winston, 1975.

deSilva, David A. "Honor Discourse and the Rhetorical Strategy of the Apocalypse of John." *JSNT* 71 (1998): 79–110.

————. *An Introduction to the New Testament: Contexts, Methods and Ministry Formation*. Downers Grove, Ill.: InterVarsity, 2004.

————. "What Has Athens to Do with Patmos? Rhetorical Criticism of the Revelation of John (1980–2005)." *CurBS* 6, no. 2 (2008): 256–89.

Ehrman, Bart D. *The New Testament: A Historical Introduction to the Early Christian Writings*. New York: Oxford University Press, 2000.

Elliott, J. K. *A Bibliography of Greek New Testament Manuscripts*. 2d ed. Cambridge: Cambridge University Press, 2000.

————. "The Distinctiveness of the Greek Manuscripts of the Book of Revelation." *JTS* 48 (1997): 116–17.

Elliott, Keith, and Ian Moir. *Manuscripts and the Text of the New Testament: An Introduction for English Readers*. Edinburgh: T&T Clark, 1995.

Eusebius. *The Ecclesiastical History*. Translated by Kirsopp Lake. New York: G. P. Putnam's Sons, 1927.

Farrer, Austin. *The Revelation of St. John the Divine*. Oxford: Clarendon Press, 1964.

Ford, J. Massyngberde. *Revelation*. AB. Garden City, N.Y.: Doubleday, 1975.

Friesen, Steven J. *Imperial Cults and the Apocalypse of John*. Oxford: Oxford University Press, 2001.

————. "Revelation, Realia, and Religion: Archaeology in the Interpretation of the Apocalypse." *HTR* 88 (1995): 291–314.

Frillingos, Christopher A. *Spectacles of Empire: Monsters, Martyrs, and the Book of Revelation*. DRLAR. Philadelphia: University of Pennsylvania Press, 2004.

Garrow, A. J. *Revelation*. NTR. New York: Routledge, 1997.

Gilbertson, Michael. *God and History in the Book of Revelation: New Testament Studies in Dialogue with Pannenberg and Moltmann*. SNTSMS 124. Cambridge: Cambridge University Press, 2005.

González, Catherine, and Justo L. González. *The Book of Revelation*. WBComp. Louisville, Ky.: Westminster John Knox Press, 1997.

Hanson, Paul D. *The Dawn of Apocalyptic: The Historical and Sociological Roots of Jewish Apocalyptic Eschatology*. Rev. ed. Philadelphia: Fortress, 1979.

Harrington, Daniel J. *Revelation: The Book of the Risen Christ*. Hyde Park, N.Y.: New City Press, 1999.

Heil, J. P. "The Fifth Seal (Rev 6, 9–11) as a Key to the Book of Revelation." *Bib* 74 (1993): 220–43.

Herms, Ronald. *An Apocalypse for the Church and for the World.* Berlin: Walter de Gruyter, 2006.

Hernández, Juan, Jr. *Scribal Habits and Theological Influences in the Apocalypse: The Singular Readings of Sinaiticus, Alexandrinus and Ephraemi.* WUNT 2/218. Tübingen: Mohr Siebeck, 2006.

Horn, Stephen Norwood. "The Author's Use of Hymns as Summaries of the Theology of the Book of Revelation." Ph.D. diss. New Orleans: New Orleans Baptist Theological Seminary, 1998.

Howard-Brook, Wes, and Anthony Gwyther. *Unveiling Empire: Reading Revelation Then and Now.* Maryknoll, N.Y.: Orbis, 1999.

Huber, Lynn R. *Like a Bride Adorned: Reading Metaphor in John's Apocalypse.* ESEC 10. New York: T&T Clark, 2007.

Humphrey, Edith McEwan. *The Ladies and the Cities: Transformation and Apocalyptic Identity in Joseph and Aseneth, 4 Ezra, the Apocalypse and the Shepherd of Hermas.* JSPSup 17. Sheffield: Sheffield Academic Press, 1995.

Johns, Loren L. *The Lamb Christology of the Apocalypse of John: An Investigation into Its Origins and Rhetorical Force.* WUNT 2/167. Tübingen: Mohr Siebeck, 2003.

Justin Martyr. *Dialogue with Trypho.* Translated by Thomas B. Falls. Washington, D.C.: The Catholic University of America Press, 2003.

Kampen, John. "The Genre and Function of Apocalyptic Literature in the African American Experience." Pages 43–65 in *Text and Experience: Towards a Cultural Exegesis of the Bible.* Edited by Daniel Smith-Christopher. Sheffield: Sheffield Academic Press, 1995.

Käsemann, Ernst. *New Testament Questions of Today.* Philadelphia: Fortress, 1969.

Kealy, Seán P. *The Apocalypse of John.* MBS 15. Wilmington, Del.: Michael Glazier, 1987.

Keener, Craig S. *Revelation.* NIVAC. Grand Rapids: Zondervan, 2000.

Keller, Catherine. *Apocalypse Now and Then: A Feminist Guide to the End of the World.* Boston: Beacon, 1996.

Koester, Craig R. *Revelation and the End of All Things.* Grand Rapids: Eerdmans, 2001.

Kovacs, Judith, and Christopher Rowland. *Revelation: The Apocalypse of Jesus Christ.* Blackwell Bible Commentaries. Oxford: Blackwell Publishing, 2004.

Kraybill, J. Nelson. *Imperial Cult and Commerce in John's Apocalypse.* JSNTSup 132. Sheffield: Sheffield Academic Press, 1996.

Lambrecht, J. "The Opening of the Seals (Rev 6,1–8,6)." *Bib* 79 (1998): 198–220.

Louw, Johannes P., and Eugene A. Nida, eds. *Greek-Lexicon of the New Testament: Based on Semantic Domains.* 2 vols. New York: United Bible Societies, 1988.

Lupieri, Edmondo. *A Commentary on the Apocalypse of John.* Translated by Maria Poggi Johnson and Adam Kamesar. ITSRS. Grand Rapids: Eerdmans, 2006.

MacLeod, David J. "The Fourth 'Last Thing': The Millennial Kingdom of Christ (Rev. 20:4–6)." *BSac* 157 (2000): 44–67.

Maier, Harry O. *Apocalypse Recalled: The Book of Revelation after Christendom.* Minneapolis: Fortress, 2002.

Malina, Bruce J., and John J. Pilch. *Social-Science Commentary on the Book of Revelation.* Minneapolis: Fortress, 2000.

Mayo, Philip L. *"Those Who Call Themselves Jews": The Church and Judaism in the Apocalypse of John.* PTMS 60. Eugene, Ore.: Pickwick, 2006.

Mazzaferri, Fred. "MARTYRIA IĒSOU Revisited." *BT* 39 (1988): 114–22.

McDonald, Patricia M. "Lion as Slain Lamb: On Reading Revelation Recursively." *Hor* 23, no. 1 (1996): 29–47.

Metzger, Bruce M. *Breaking the Code: Understanding the Book of Revelation.* Nashville: Abingdon, 1993.

———. *The Text of the New Testament: Its Transmission, Corruption, and Restoration.* 3d, enlarged ed. New York: Oxford University Press, 1992.

———. *A Textual Commentary on the Greek New Testament.* London: United Bible Societies, 1971.

Moore, Stephen D. *Empire and Apocalypse: Postcolonialism and the New Testament.* BMW 12. Sheffield: Sheffield Phoenix Press, 2006.

Morris, Leon. *The Book of Revelation: An Introduction and Commentary.* TNTC. Grand Rapids: Eerdmans, 2007.

Morton, Russell S. *One upon the Throne and the Lamb: A Tradition Historical/Theological Analysis of Revelation 4–5.* StBL 110. New York: Peter Lang, 2007.

Mounce, Robert H. *The Book of Revelation.* 2d ed. NICNT. Grand Rapids: Eerdmans, 1998.

———. "Worthy Is the Lamb." Pages 60–69 in *Scripture, Tradition, and Interpretation: Essays Presented to Everett F. Harrison by His Students and Colleagues in Honor of His Seventy-Fifth Birthday.* Edited by W. Ward Gasque and William Sanford LaSor. Grand Rapids: Eerdmans, 1978.

Moyise, Steve. *The Old Testament in the Book of Revelation.* JSNTSup 115. Sheffield: Sheffield Academic Press, 1995.

———, ed. *Studies in the Book of Revelation.* Edinburgh: T&T Clark, 2001.

Murphy, Frederick J. *Fallen Is Babylon: The Revelation to John.* NTC. Harrisburg, Pa.: Trinity Press International, 1998.

O'Donovan, Oliver. "The Political Thought of the Book of Revelation." *TynBul* 37 (1986): 61–94.

O'Rourke, John. "The Hymns of the Apocalypse." *CBQ* 30 (1968): 399–49.

Osborne, Grant R. *Revelation*. BECNT. Grand Rapids: Baker, 2002.

Pattemore, Stephen. *The People of God in the Apocalypse: Discourse, Structure and Exegesis*. SNTSMS 128. Cambridge: Cambridge University Press, 2004.

Perkins, Pheme. *The Book of Revelation*. ColBC 11. Collegeville, Minn.: Liturgical Press, 1983.

Pilch, John J. *What Are They Saying about Revelation?* New York: Paulist Press, 1978.

Pippin, Tina. *Death and Desire: The Rhetoric of Gender in the Apocalypse of John*. LCBI. Louisville, Ky.: Westminster/John Knox Press, 1992.

Rapple, Eva Marie. *The Metaphor of the City in the Apocalypse of John*. SBL 67. New York: Peter Lang, 2004.

Reddish, Mitchell G. *Revelation*. Macon, Ga.: Smyth & Helwys, 2001.

Resseguie, James L. *Revelation Unsealed: A Narrative Critical Approach to John's Apocalypse*. BIS 32. Leiden: Brill, 1998.

Rhoads, David, ed. *From Every People and Nation: The Book of Revelation in Intercultural Perspective*. Minneapolis: Fortress, 2005.

Richard, Pablo. *Apocalypse: A People's Commentary on the Book of Revelation*. Maryknoll, NY: Orbis, 1995.

Rogers, Cornish R., and Joseph R. Jeter Jr., eds. *Preaching through the Apocalypse: Sermons from Revelation*. St. Louis: Chalice, 1992.

Roloff, Jürgen. *The Revelation of John*. CC. Translated by John E. Alsup. Minneapolis: Fortress, 1993.

Rossing, Barbara R. *The Rapture Exposed: The Message of Hope in the Book of Revelation*. Boulder, Col.: Westview Press, 2004.

Rowland, Christopher. "The Lamb and the Beast, the Sheep and the Goats: 'The Mystery of Salvation' in Revelation." Pages 181–91 in *A Vision for the Church: Studies in Early Christian Ecclesiology in Honour of J. P. M. Sweet*. Edited by Markus Bockmuehl and Michael B. Thompson. Edinburgh: T&T Clark, 1997.

———. *Revelation*. Epworth Commentaries. London: Epworth, 1993.

Royalty, Robert M., Jr. *The Streets of Heaven: The Ideology of Wealth in the Apocalypse of John*. Macon, Ga.: Mercer University Press, 1998.

Ruiz, Jean Pierre. "The Politics of Praise: A Reading of Revelation 19:1–10." Pages 374–93 in *SBLSP 1997*. Edited by Eugene Lovering. Atlanta: Scholars Press, 1997.

———. "Revelation 4:8–11; 5:9–14: Hymns of the Heavenly Liturgy." Pages 216–20 in *SBLSP 1995*. Atlanta: Scholars Press, 1995.

Sánchez, David A. *From Patmos to the Barrio: Subverting Imperial Myths*. Minneapolis: Fortress, 2008.

Sanders, E. P. *Judaism: Practice and Belief, 63 BCE–66 CE.* Philadelphia: Trinity Press International, 1992.

Schüssler Fiorenza, Elisabeth. *The Book of Revelation: Justice and Judgment.* 2d ed. Minneapolis: Fortress, 1998.

———. "The Followers of the Lamb: Visionary Rhetoric and Social-Political Situation." *Semeia* 36 (1986): 123–46.

———. *Invitation to the Book of Revelation: A Commentary on the Apocalypse with Complete Text from the Jerusalem Bible.* Garden City, N.Y.: Image Books, 1981.

———. *The Power of the Word: Scripture and the Rhetoric of Empire.* Minneapolis: Fortress, 2007.

———. "Revelation." Pages 407–27 in *The New Testament and Its Modern Interpreters.* Edited by Eldon Jay Epp and George W. MacRae. Philadelphia: Fortress, 1989.

———. *Revelation: Vision of a Just World.* Minneapolis: Fortress, 1991.

Shea, William H. "The Parallel Literary Structure of Revelation 12 and 20." *AUSS* 23 (1985): 37–54.

Smalley, Stephen S. *The Revelation to John: A Commentary on the Greek Text of the Apocalypse.* Downers Grove, Ill.: InterVarsity, 2005.

Smyth, Herbert Weir. *Greek Grammar.* Revised by Gordon M. Messing. Cambridge, Mass.: Harvard University Press, 1956.

Stein, Stephen J., ed., *Apocalypticism in the Modern Period and the Contemporary Age.* Vol. 3 of *The Encyclopedia of Apocalypticism.* New York: Continuum, 1998.

Stevenson, Gregory. *Power and Place: Temple and Identity in the Book of Revelation.* BZNW 107. Berlin: Walter de Gruyter, 2001.

Stuckenbruck, Loren. *Angel Veneration and Christology: A Study in Early Judaism and the Christology of the Apocalypse of John.* WUNT 2/70. Tübingen: Mohr Siebeck, 1995.

Sweet, J. P. M. *Revelation.* SCMPC. Philadelphia: Westminster, 1979.

Swete, H. B. *The Apocalypse of St. John.* London: Macmillan, 1906.

Talbert, Charles H. *The Apocalypse: A Reading of the Revelation of John.* Louisville, Ky.: Westminster John Knox Press, 1994.

Thompson, Leonard. *The Book of Revelation: Apocalypse and Empire.* Oxford: Oxford University Press, 1990.

———. *Revelation.* ANTC. Nashville: Abingdon, 1998.

Tonstad, Sigve K. *Saving God's Reputation: The Theological Function of Pistis Iesou in the Cosmic Narratives of Revelation.* LNTS 337. New York: T&T Clark, 2007.

Trites, Allison A. "*Martus* and Martyrdom in the Apocalypse: A Semantic Study." *NovT* 15 (1973): 72–80.

Vassiliadis, Petros. "The Translation of *MARTYRIA IĒSOU* in Revelation." *BT* 36, no. 1 (1985): 129–35.

Volf, Miroslav. *Exclusion and Embrace: A Theological Exploration of Identity, Otherness, and Reconciliation.* Nashville: Abingdon, 1996.

Wainwright, Arthur. *Mysterious Apocalypse: A History of the Interpretation of the Book of Revelation.* Nashville: Abingdon, 1993.

Ward, Ewing. "Babylon the Great and the New Jerusalem." Pages 189–202 in *Politics and Theopolitics in the Bible and Postbiblical Literature.* Edited by Henning Graf Reventlow, Yair Hoffman, and Benjamin Uffenheimer. Sheffield: JSOT Press, 1994.

―――. *The Power of the Lamb: Revelation's Theology of Liberation for You.* Cambridge, Mass.: Cowley Publishers, 1990.

Weinrich, William C., ed. *Revelation.* ACCS 12. Downers Grove, Ill.: Inter-Varsity Press, 2006.

Weiss, Johannes. *Die Offenbarung des Johannes: Ein Beitrag zur Literatur-und Religionsgeschichte.* Göttingen: Vandenhoeck & Ruprecht, 1904.

Witherington, Ben, III. *Revelation.* NCBC. Cambridge: Cambridge University Press, 2003.

# INTRODUCTION

## Justice, Judgment, and Anger: The Theological Focus of Revelation

I have heard it said that a person should not make critical decisions when angry. Generally speaking, this is good advice. Anger clouds the mind and twists whatever judgments that mind conceives. Anger makes the cause for which the victimized was angered a righteous one. That righteousness militates against mercy and gravitates toward meanness, hovering like a stalled hurricane that lashes out furiously until every enemy is completely and utterly destroyed.

In the literary storm that is the book of Revelation, John writes in anger. Teleported into its passion by the Holy Spirit, he is caught up in it like a broken kite jammed into the limbs of an avaricious tree. His fanciful flight of faith aborted by what he sees as evil projecting out in every direction, he fortifies himself while he holds on for the God he believes is coming to his rescue. Equally furious, this God will not climb the tree to release him; this God will rip the tree from the ground, tear out its roots, topple it to a certain doom, and take a vindicated and liberated John by the hand so as to lead him safely and comfortably away.

Revelation is a mean book; it is not, however, mean-spirited. The line between those two points on the human emotional scale is admittedly razor thin. John's meanness is the effect of a sure cause. It derives from the anger he feels about the injustices that have been imposed upon him and his people, and the even greater injustices that he is sure will soon arise if his people live out their faith in the way that he hopes they will. It is this causal connection to an evil that has been and surely will be perpetrated against his people that separates his anger from a spirit of meanness existing irrespective of the circumstances that surround it. A spirit of meanness will greet even a gift with hostility, yet John awaits God's gift of a new heaven and a new earth with a boundless hopefulness and generosity of spirit. That gift is available to all, even to those who currently persecute and sometimes kill his fellow believers. John not only allows for repentance; he also encourages it, begs for it, and pleads with those who have joined forces hostile to God's world-transforming intent to come back to God's way of being and doing in the world. Those who do will find themselves gifted with an eternal relationship with God that has already been reserved for the people whose names are written in the Lamb's Book of Life.

John's meanness is responsive. He is not mean to every person or force he meets, but only to those who act against him and his people, or those of his people who act against the God who has given them a new spiritual life and social identity. For those who either cause the persecution of God's people or abide an accommodation to their persecutors, John's anger mirrors what he believes to be God's own. He envisions a God who means the business of judgment and justice.

Revelation is therefore a violent book. Some interpreters argue that because of its violence, it does not belong in a New Testament canon that takes its direction and energy from a Jesus who extended forgiveness to sinners and counseled love even for one's enemies. A decision about the work's canonical inclusion is not ours to make. Our decision, rather, concerns what should be done with the book that is already in the canon: how to interpret it, how to read it, how not to abandon it to the devices of those who are not only angry but also mean-spirited, who will surely use John's ultimately constructive vision for the most destructive of purposes.

God is the author of what John clearly understands to be constructively oriented violence. Where destructive acts that John presents through the lens of justice are concerned, John's presentation in the form of (divine) passive verbs demonstrates his understanding that the agent behind the violence is God. It is violence meant to frighten those who are persecuting God's people so that they will cease their hostilities. It is violence done on behalf of a people who are being persecuted so as to ensure them that God has heard their cries and is responding swiftly and convincingly. It is violence meant to scare those who are evil straight back to the ways of a good God, and to warn those who already stand with God to maintain their place lest they find themselves in the same crosshairs as their intractable enemies. This violence is, then, like the furious fire of a kiln, which burns away all impurities until what is pulled from the furnace emerges unblemished and pristine.

The violent fires of Revelation appear in the form of plagues and catastrophes that wipe out entire swaths of earthly landscape and human beings. They do not burn down, though, as much as they tear *up*. The cataclysms are like the plow that must break the ground, tear it up, if a farmer is to prepare it for the seeding that is necessary for a productive harvest. The direction is always up, back toward God's mythological staging point in the heavens, to where John is lifted and the hearers and readers of John's narrative are called. The divinely orchestrated destruction is God's way of shepherding human traffic in the direction of eschatological salvation. Those who refuse to follow are pushed. Those who are following are often caught up in the maelstrom. Because there is no rapture in the book of Revelation, believers also find their way to God through the terror that those opposed to God inflict on the earth and the terror that God wields in what John sees as a just response. The conflict in heaven, having spilled onto the earth, catches up everyone and everything in creation.

John justifies God's violence by staging it as a just response to the cries of God's people (6:9–11). When the Hebrew people cried out to God for just and liberating intervention, God sent Moses. Moses secured their freedom by wielding for God the very same violent, cataclysmic plagues that God reprises in John's visions. God's regional move against a hard-hearted Egypt becomes a universal move against a hard-hearted world. The violent form of the move is the same. John's God, like Moses' God, is a violent God.

Can such a God be justified in a twenty-first-century context? It is a difficult issue, to be sure. It is the book's binary (either/or) dualism that almost ensures a need for God's violence. At every turn, good is threatened by great and powerful evil. If there is to be justice, such evil must be eradicated by the good at whatever cost. God therefore meets fire with apocalyptic fire.

Writing from the perspective of a South African black man terrorized by the plague of apartheid, Allan Boesak writes a commentary that, while not seeking to justify God's violence, clearly aims to explain it. Boesak knows not only that violence is practiced against God's people, but also that God's people cry out for a matching recompense from the Lord. The text's meaning is meaningful in and specifically for this particular way of life:

> At the moment of detention; in the long dark hours of incarceration; as the footsteps of your interrogators come down the passage to your cell; above the harsh voices and scornful laugh; through the blows of fists on tender flesh, the blinding pain of electric shocks; through the hazy, bloody mist of unwanted tears; above the roar of guns and tanks and armoured vehicles; in the nauseating sting of tear gas and the tearing, searing burn of the bullet through your body—these words are shouted, or whispered: "How long, Lord?" (69)

Boesak reads the call, and the attendant divine actions that go along with it, as a call for and an acting out of necessary justice: "People who do not know what oppression and suffering is react strangely to the language of the Bible. The truth is that God *is* the God of the poor and the oppressed. . . . Because they are powerless, God will take up their cause and redeem them from oppression and violence. The oppressed do not see any dichotomy between God's love and God's justice" (72). Boesak seems impatient with Christians who chastise John for not being more careful with his language, more selective with his imagery, so that it would come across as less violently oriented, so that its binary nature might be toned down from the harshness of moral black and white to the ambiguity of a more sophisticated and acceptable gray. Perhaps he even finds that such Christians stand more on the immoral ground that must be overturned than on the side of those who must overturn it. "Christians who enjoy the fruits of injustice without a murmur, who remain silent as the defenceless are slaughtered, dare not become indignant when the suffering people of God echo the prayers of the psalms and pray for deliverance and judgment" (72–73).

More than a decalde later, Miroslav Volf reads Revelation's violent language, but he does so out of a similarly haunted context, that of the war-devastated Balkans (he himself is Croatian), and comes to a similarly nuanced conclusion. For him, Rome is the purveyor of a tyrannical system that threatens both human and cosmic life. It is a killer creature with a malevolent instinct to destroy anything that fails to worship its nature and participate in its political and economic exploitation. Does God respond with violence to horrors perpetuated by this beastly force? To be sure. Can it be justified? From his reading angle, through his reading lens, apparently so: "Without such judgment there can be no world of peace, of truth, and of justice: terror (the 'beast' that devours) and propaganda (the 'false prophet' that deceives) must be overcome, evil must be separated from good, and darkness from light" (296).

Volf knows about the trust many place in the power of nonviolence and the belief that there is some spark of good in every power that pulls it toward proper response to a nonviolent call for transformative justice. Volf, though, is not so sure. "In this belief," he writes, "one can smell a bit too much of the sweet aroma of a suburban ideology, entertained often by people who are neither courageous nor honest enough to reflect on the implications of terror taking place right in the middle of their living rooms!" (296). Too often, he grieves, nonviolence not only fails to break the grip of evil, its engagement with the powers of this earth often also brings down horrific suffering upon the very heads of those who unleash it. In the worldview of Revelation, this is precisely the scenario he finds; there is no power great enough to stop the beasts from wanting to be beasts. In both John's world and our own, "This is where God's anger comes in" (279). That anger, he argues, is consistent with the sacrificial love God shows on the cross. And so we have what Volf calls a polarity within the heart of Christianity, a crucified Lamb who turns out to be the Rider on the White Horse: "After all, the cross is not forgiveness pure and simple, but God's *setting aright the world of injustice and deception.* The polarity is there because some human beings refuse to be 'set aright'" (298). Can the Christian accept such a premise, endure such a polarity, and remain a disciple of a crucified Lord? Apparently so. "For the sake of the peace of God's good creation, we can and must affirm *this* divine anger and *this* divine violence, while at the same time holding on to the hope that in the end, even the flag bearer will desert the army that desires to make war against the Lamb" (299).

Like Boesak, Volf harbors little patience for Christians who upbraid John's chronicling of what he sees as God's necessary acts of judgment and justice. The ones who refute such a position have not seen as Volf himself has seen, do not read as Volf himself reads, through the cultural lens of a people who have been raped and pillaged by the bestial power of a force like the one John fights against in Rome. "They deem the talk of God's judgment irreverent, . . . crude. And so violence thrives, secretly nourished by belief in a God who refuses to wield the sword" (303).

> To the person who is inclined to dismiss [this thesis], I suggest imagining that you are delivering a lecture in a war zone (which is where a paper that underlies this chapter was originally delivered). Among your listeners are people whose cities and villages have been first plundered, then burned and leveled to the ground, whose daughters and sisters have been raped, whose fathers and brothers have had their throats slit. The topic of the lecture: a Christian attitude toward violence. The thesis: we should not retaliate since God is perfect noncoercive love. Soon you would discover that it takes the quiet of a suburban home for the birth of the thesis that human nonviolence corresponds to God's refusal to judge. In a scorched land, soaked in the blood of the innocent, it will invariably die. And as one watches it die, one will do well to reflect about many other pleasant captivities of the liberal mind. (304)

Nevertheless, an attentive mind will reach the conclusion that John never sees God's people operating with violence in the book, not even in response to the evil that is perpetrated continuously against them. Even the Lamb, operating like a lion of war at 19:11–21, wields a sword that John images more like a rapier tongue than a killing saber. The word he proclaims is the word of his own lordship, which cuts against the lordship assertion broadcast by Rome. Throughout his presentation of the Christ figure, who is a virtual child of humanity, representing the hopes and dreams of humankind, John has in mind cutting, world-transforming, evil-decimating words (1:16; 2:12, 16; 19:15, 21). This Lamb's ultimate victory against evil comes in the form of self-sacrifice (5:9; 12:5). When he is faced with the ultimatum of ceasing his faith proclamations or losing his life, he refuses to capitulate. He continues to testify. Because of that stubbornness, his life is ripped from him on a Roman cross. It is in this nonviolent resistance to evil in the form of testimony to the exclusive lordship of God and his own re-presentation of that lordship in human history (cf. 1:5; 3:14) that he becomes the behavioral faith model for the believers in John's Asia Minor churches (cf. 1:2, 9; 2:13; 6:9; 11:17; 12:11, 17; 20:4). It is in the understanding of that lordship claim and the nonviolent testimony to it that one comprehends the meaning and purpose of John's work.

## Authorship

Identifying the John behind this work is a daunting and, in the end, impossible task. We call him John because he gives himself that moniker (1:1, 4, 9; 22:8). Because apocalyptic literature was often pseudonymous, written in the name of an important figure from the past (see the comment on 22:10), one cannot even be certain that the author's real name was John. It is unlikely, however, that an author would have mislabeled himself when writing so openly to church communities that could easily have identified him and thereby challenged his pseudonymous claim. The name John was likely the author's real name.

Knowing which John he was is the problem. Given the authority with which he writes, one can assume that he was a John of some stature in the Asia Minor Christian community. Two such figures come immediately to mind. As early as 155 C.E., Justin Martyr was the first to identify the most famous of these two, one of Jesus' twelve apostles, the son of Zebedee, as the book's author (*Dialogue with Trypho* 81.4):

> Moreover, a man among us named John, one of Christ's apostles, received a revelation and foretold that the followers of Christ would dwell in Jerusalem *for a thousand years*, and that afterwards the universal and, in short, *everlasting resurrection and judgment* would take place. To this our Lord himself testified when he said, *They shall neither marry, nor be given in marriage, but shall be equal to the angels, being sons of God, being of the resurrection.* (Justin, trans. Falls, 127; emphasis original)

Writing in the fourth century, Eusebius quotes Papias of Hierapolis who around 120 C.E. penned thoughts that Eusebius took to give authorship to a different John. This other John was also an authoritative figure in nascent Asia Minor Christian circles:

> But if anyone came who had followed the presbyters, I inquired into the words of the presbyters, what Andrew or Peter or Philip or Thomas or James or John or Matthew, or any other of the Lord's disciples, had said, and what Aristion and the presbyter John, the Lord's disciples, were saying. For I did not suppose that information from books would help me so much as the word of a living and surviving voice. (*Hist. eccl.* 3.39.4)

Eusebius understood Papias to mean that the first John mentioned was one of the apostles, and thus the evangelist. The other John was an elder or *presbyter*. Eusebius's conclusion, on Papias's authority, was that the second, presbyter John, was the one responsible for authoring Revelation.

> It is here worth noting that he twice counts the name of John, and reckons the first John with Peter and James and Matthew and the other Apostles, clearly meaning the evangelist, but by changing his statement places the second with the others outside the number of the Apostles, putting Aristion before him and clearly calling him a presbyter. This confirms the truth of the story of those who have said that there were two of the same name in Asia, and that there are two tombs at Ephesus both still called John's. This calls for attention: for it is probable that the second (unless anyone prefer the former) saw the revelation which passes under the name John. (*Hist. eccl.* 3.39.5–7)

No doubt Eusebius was also working from evidence he recorded in the name of Dionysius of Alexandria. Writing in the third century, Dionysius had approached the problem from a literary angle. He operated from the assumption that the apostle had written the Gospel and the three Johannine Letters. Because the literary style and expression of Revelation is so distinct from the aforementioned works, it was clear to him that the apostle could not have written Revelation.

> But I should not readily agree that he was the apostle, the son of Zebedee, the brother of James, whose are the Gospel entitled According to John and the Catholic Epistle. For I form my judgment from the character of each and from the nature of the language and from what is known as the general construction of the book, that [the John mentioned] is not the same. (*Hist. eccl.* 7.25.7–8)

Eusebius goes on to quote Dionysius as saying that John had plenty of opportunity in Revelation to identify himself as the apostle John and thereby claim apostolic authority for his work. He never did, no doubt because he was not the apostle. Dionysius subsequently muddies the waters of author recognition even further when he admits that there were so many people who named their sons out of respect for the apostle that there were a multitude of Johns circulating throughout Asia Minor.

> I hold that there have been many persons of the same name as John the apostle, who for the love they bore him, and because they admired and esteemed him and wished to be loved, as he was, of the Lord, were glad to take also the same name after him; just as Paul, and for that matter Peter too, is a common name among boys of believing parents. (*Hist. eccl.* 7.25.14)

The author also could not have been the famous John Mark, since he did not accompany Paul and Barnabas to Asia (Acts 13:13). In the end, Dionysius came to the same conclusion that a responsible contemporary reader must: the work was written by a mostly unidentifiable man named John who was not the same John credited with authoring the Fourth Gospel (see the comment on 1:1–2).

Two things, however, can be ascertained from the work itself about the John who authored Revelation. First, he considered himself a prophet. He calls his work a word of prophecy (1:3; 22:7, 10, 18, 19) and in developing this work depends heavily on the efforts of Hebrew prophetic figures like Moses, Isaiah, Jeremiah, Ezekiel, and Daniel. John apparently belonged to a prophetic community that gave itself responsibility for directing the communal lives of the Asia Minor churches (see the comment on 22:16). It was no doubt the conflict between his own view of God's revelation in the community and that proclaimed by other, competing prophets—like those whom he nicknamed Jezebel and Balaam—that heightened the intensity of his own vision-inspired proclamations. Though the future orientation of the visions gets all of the notoriety, it is secondary to their prophetic intent. The visions service the prophecy; the prophecy is not determined by the visions. The present is also not overshadowed by the future. The references to the future are meant to influence a person's behavior in the present. "Therefore, the book's 'prophecy' includes divine precepts for living in the present, about which the readers must make a decision. This understanding of 'prophecy' is consistent with the OT idea, which emphasizes revealed interpretation of the present together with the future, demanding ethical response for the present audience" (Beale 555).

Second, as his heavy dependence on Hebrew biblical material implies, John was most likely a Palestinian Jew who had come to the conclusion that Christ was God's messianic agent charged with the task of ushering in God's reign. He writes in a kind of Semiticized Greek that suggests someone whose native language was not Greek but the Aramaic spoken by Palestinian Jews. He also appears very knowledgeable about the topography of Jerusalem, the design and cultic practice of the Jerusalem temple, even prior to its destruction in 70 C.E., and the broader landscape of Palestine itself.

## Dating

Dating the book of Revelation can be as challenging a task as identifying its author. Based largely on the external evidence of Irenaeus (ca. 140–202 C.E.; *Against Heresies* 5.30.3) that John's visions were witnessed at the end of the reign of the emperor Domitian (81–96 C.E.), the book is most commonly dated at 95 C.E. Commentators rightly point to two primary internal reasons that support such a dating. First, there is the obvious assignment of the name Babylon to the city and empire of Rome. John clearly intends a critical correspondence between the two imperial forces: the sacking and destruction of Jerusalem. Babylon's devastation occurred in 587 B.C.E. Rome ruined the city in 70 C.E. The connection between the two names and empires would not have made sense unless John wrote after 70 C.E. A second internal factor adds at least two decades (from 70 C.E.) to the probable writing time of the work's final edition. In chapters 13 and 17, John works from an apparent preoccupation with a belief current during the latter years of the first century that Nero (d. 66 C.E.) would return to power and wreak vengeance upon the Roman west that had rejected him. "The legend of Nero *redux* or *redivivus*, upon which the author-editor of Revelation seems to depend, is attested as early as A.D. 69, though a later date for the widespread currency of this legend seems required" (Aune 1:lxix–lxx).

## Social Setting

In Roman-occupied Asia Minor in the last decade of the first century, during the reign of the emperor Domitian, there existed a strong motivation to accommodate. In Rome's ideological infrastructure, religion and politics were quite intentionally mixed. Worship often mutated into politics; politics was often exercised through religion. Worship of Roman deities not only demonstrated a cultic devotion and communal piety; it also signaled loyalty to the Roman state, which was mythologically connected to and practically founded upon them. It is not surprising, then, that the mother goddess would savor the name *Roma*, or that the messianic hopes for the empire should be bound up in the person of the emperor. This blending of politics and worship was especially evident in Asia Minor, where John and his seven churches were located. There, particularly during the last decade of the first century, emperor worship flourished. "Under the Flavians, especially Domitian, the imperial cult was strongly represented in the Roman provinces. Domitian demanded that the populace acclaim him as 'Lord and God' and participate in his worship. The majority of the cities to which the prophetic messages of Revelation are addressed were dedicated to the promotion of the emperor cult" (Schüssler Fiorenza, *Justice*, 193).

Thyatira was an illustrative case in point. The city was caught up in the throes of idol and emperor worship. Here, in fact, cultic propaganda went so far as to declare the Roman emperor to be the incarnation of Apollo and therefore a son of Zeus. This religious-political alliance heightened the risk for persons who tried to opt out of the Greco-Roman cultic infrastructure; rejection of the gods implied resistance to the state. Complicating matters even further was the fact that Thyatira hosted a large number of trade guilds that had strong cultic affiliations. Especially important were industries of wool, textile, and the manufacture of purple dye (cf. Acts 16:14–15). Beale believes that "since the guilds had patron deities, Christian guild members would be expected to pay homage to pagan gods at official guild meetings, which were usually festive occasions often accompanied by immoral behavior. Nonparticipation would lead to economic ostracism" (261). Socially, economically, and politically, then, Christians in Thyatira had every reason to accommodate themselves to the expectations and practices of Greco-Roman religion and culture.

So did the Christians in Pergamum. Because they clearly did not believe in the reality or lordship of pagan deities, their participation at the cultic festivals and other social gatherings where elaborate meals and rituals were prepared to honor those deities was socially, economically, and politically motivated. Their complicity in artisan, trade, and funeral associations allowed for upward social and economic mobility. They passed themselves off as Roman cultic devotees in order to avail themselves of Roman resources. Unlike the believers in Smyrna, who apparently opted out of such accommodating activities and thereby found themselves impoverished and persecuted as a result, many Pergamum Christians blended in and therefore moved up socially, politically, and economically.

While John was exiled on Patmos, the prophets he named Jezebel and Balaam, and Balaam's Nicolaitan colleagues, offered some Christian counsel.

They taught the people that it is permissible to eat meat that has been sacrificed to idol gods at these guild, quasi-cultic functions.[1] For John, though, persons who eat meat that has been sacrificed to foreign gods give credence to the reality and lordship of those gods; those persons have therefore prostituted themselves to a foreign faith.[2] Where Paul had, in his Corinthian correspondence (1 Cor 8–10), offered the very practical advice that strong Christians could eat meat sacrificed to idols unless their behavior offended the spiritual psyche of weaker Christians for whom such activity seemed sinful, John theologically overrules the behavior outright.

Jezebel, Balaam, and the Nicolaitans, like Paul, were probably trying their best to help their fellow Christ-believers adapt their faith to the new circumstances in which they found themselves. John's very conservative, intolerant attitude disallowed any kind of compromise; Jezebel, Balaam, the Nicolaitans, and those who followed their teaching were guilty of spiritual prostitution. The backside of Christ's double-edged sword (1:16; 2:12, 16) was therefore meant for them. Christ was coming soon; if they did not repent of their accommodating behavior, his Pergamum coming would not be salvific, but judgmental. John's rhetorical move is a complex endeavor that recognizes the problem of accommodation, understands its practical motivation, but simultaneously argues that the evil of believing in the lordship of a human force as more powerful than the lordship of God requires such accommodation. He then showcases the role his accommodating believers unwittingly play in sustaining that evil.

The evil that John fears is so manipulative and seductive that his only parallel for it is the seductive evil of the prostituting whore. His demonization of women in his effort to keep his people from accommodating themselves to Greco-Roman cultic, social, economic, and political expectations is one of the most regrettable side effects of his prophetic effort. But it is helpful to know what he is doing and why he is doing it. Though he clearly sees a problem with what Christians are doing in accommodating themselves to Greco-Roman life, his agenda ranges far beyond a critique of the Christians themselves. He wants the Christians to see that they are caught up in a draconian, prostituting system. The only challenge to that system resides in the will of those who refuse to par-

---

1. Although some commentators argue that the term John employs, *eidōlothyton*, refers to the meat that was sacrificed and then eaten later, after the sacrificial ceremonies had concluded, Beale contends that the term refers to the eating of the contraband meat as a part of the ceremony itself. He therefore argues that John is concerned not just about eating leftovers, but the actual participation in foreign cults (248). The narrative itself does not offer enough evidence to answer the question about John's specific concern either way. In any case, the impact of his concern is the same since John apparently sees the eating of the meat, whether as part of the service or afterward, as worthy of the fullest measure of condemnation. Either timing suggests an appreciation for and tacit acknowledgment of the lordship claims of the involved cultic or imperial figures.

2. See 2:22, where he likens such eating to adultery.

ticipate in its many social, economic, and political benefits. Whatever it costs them, those Christians must find a way to stand up and then opt out. That, in essence, is his prophetic charge.

A final appeal to the social location of John and his Asia Minor Christians brings further clarity to his prophetic urgency. In a historical reconstruction that represents today's prevailing scholarly thinking, Loren Johns argues that there was no wholesale persecution of Christians during the time of Domitian's reign (Johns 122). In fact, applicable source material from the period suggests only sporadic mistreatment that targeted specific persons who were charged with being Christ-believers, and only when they either refused to deny the allegation or would not repent of their delusion. A letter (ca. 112 C.E.) from the governor of the Asian province of Bithynia, Pliny the Younger, to the Emperor Trajan (98–117 C.E.) is indicative of the official thinking that was no doubt in vogue during the reign of Domitian just a few years prior. Boring's translation of Pliny's letter is so compellingly rendered that I offer it here at length, including a very helpful parenthetical remark that links the concerns of Trajan's time to similar concerns that existed in Domitian's.

> I have never been present at the interrogation of Christians. Therefore, I do not know how far such investigations should be pushed, and what sort of punishments are appropriate. I have also been uncertain as to whether age makes any difference, or whether the very young are dealt with in the same way as adults, whether repentance . . . and renunciation of Christianity is sufficient, or whether the accused are still considered criminals because they were once Christians even if they later renounced it, and whether persons are to be punished simply for the name "Christian" even if no criminal act has been committed, or whether only crimes associated with the name are to be punished.
>
> In the meantime, I have handled those who have been denounced to me as Christians as follows: I asked them whether they were Christians. Those who responded affirmatively I have asked a second and third time, under threat of the death penalty. If they persisted . . . in their confession, I had them executed. For whatever it is that they are actually advocating, it seems to me that obstinacy and stubbornness must be punished in any case. Others who labor under the same delusion, but who were Roman citizens, I have designated to be sent to Rome.
>
> In the course of the investigations, as it usually happens, charges are brought against wider circles of people, and the following special cases have emerged:
>
> An unsigned placard was posted, accusing a large number of people by name. Those who denied being Christians now or in the past, I thought necessary to release, since they invoked our gods according to the formula I gave them and since they offered sacrifices of wine and incense before your image which I had brought in for this purpose along with the statues of our gods. I also had them curse Christ. It is said that real Christians cannot be forced to do any of these things.
>
> Others charged by this accusation at first admitted that they had once been Christians, but had already renounced it; they had in fact been Christians, but had

given it up, some of them three years ago, some even earlier, some as long as twenty-five years ago. [Note that this would be in the time of Domitian.] All of these worshipped your image and the statues of the gods and cursed Christ.

The emperor responded with praise for the governor's actions.

My Secundus! You have chosen the right way with regard to the cases of those who have been accused before you as Christians. Nothing exists that can be considered a universal norm for such cases. Christians should not be sought out. But if they are accused and handed over, they are to be punished, but only if they do not deny being Christians and demonstrate it by the appropriate act, i.e., the worship of our gods. Even if one is suspect because of past conduct, he or she is to be acquitted in view of repentance. (Pliny, *Ep.* 10.96–97, trans. Boring, *Revelation*, 14–15)

Such evidence suggests that John was writing more about the "*expectation* of persecution rather than the present *experience* of persecution" (Johns 122; Johns points to 2:10–11; 7:13–14; 11:7–9; 12:11; 16:6; 17:6; 18:24; 19:2; 20:4–6). The problem lay with the imminent conflict he knew *would* erupt if his hearers and readers lived out the kind of nonaccommodating Christianity that he himself professed and refused to back away from the faith when Asia Minor officials demanded that they do so.

Extensive trouble, however, had not yet arisen. This peaceable reality is the historical proof that validates John's literary claim: the Asia Minor Christians were passing themselves off as every other emperor-worshiping, meat-sacrificed-to-pagan-gods-eating Greco-Roman. According to Johns, "the resistance called for was an *offensive* maneuver as John tried to unmask the spiritual powers at work behind the churches' compromising involvement in the empire, in its commerce, and in its imperial cult" (Johns 127; emphasis original). John was unyielding; there could be no compromise with any activities that gave credence to the idea that Caesar, Rome, or Rome-sponsored divinities held title to the allegiance due only God and the Lamb. No matter what the cost.

But if all this is correct, if there was only sporadic persecution, if John's people were not vulnerably standing out because they were finding ways comfortably to blend in and accommodate, then the seer's immediate problem was, as Johns points out, more spiritual than social and historical. The social-historical crisis would not arise *unless* John's people actually started living by the ethical mandate of witness that his apocalyptic prophecy demanded. And so Johns concludes: "The resolution of that spiritual crisis would ironically induce a very real and dangerous *social* crisis as the churches began faithfully to resist the imperial cult and to face the consequences of their allegiance to Christ" (Johns 127; emphasis original).

Here is where both John's prophetic call and a consummate prophetic problem arise. If John was indeed asking his people to stand up and stand out in a world they had accepted and that had accepted them, a world into which they had covertly and successfully passed, he was essentially telling them to go out and pick a fight! No matter the consequences! He was ordering his people to self-identify, to declare that they were now nonaccommodating Christians who could no longer participate in a world that had not really noticed them since they had heretofore been accommodating to it. In a classic "Don't ask, don't tell" (that I'm a Christian) kind of environment, John was essentially ordering his Christians to be about the business of telling on themselves, with full knowledge of the repercussions such telling might bring (recall Pliny's letter). He was asking them to come screaming out of the Christian closet, knowing that it could well solicit the same consequence it had attracted to the Lamb: slaughter.

John's visions operate in support of his effort to incite his followers to self-identify and then stand behind that self-declaration, that revelation, no matter what the consequences. There are many visions; there is only one Revelation, and it is hiding in plain sight. Many claim that there is some great mystery behind the secret of Revelation. Many claim that one needs proper methods of translation and computation to break the code of Revelation. Many believe that the primary message of Revelation was not for John's church in John's time, but for the universal Christian church in some future time. They are wrong. Revelation's one revelation is the same revelation revealed by the Gospel writers, Paul, and the many disciples who followed each of them. Revelation's revelation is that Jesus Christ is Lord. It is that simple and that straightforward. Jesus Christ is the Lord of human history, the director of human destiny, the controller of human fortune. Jesus is Savior, Redeemer, transformer, and Lord.

Why does John need so many complex, frightening visions to support such a single, clear point? John is like a great sports coach who tries to rally his team before the most important game of their season. He wants to whip up a frenzy that will lift them to physical and emotional highs where confessing a subversive allegiance to Christ before hostile forces that promote the lordship of Rome becomes not only a possibility but also an imperative.

His confessional witness (*martys*) language is, then, his prophetic language. *Martys* is a word of active engagement, not sacrificial passivity. A believer's witness might provoke such a hostile response that it leads to the believer's death, but always, at least in the first-century mind-set, it seems, the transformative focus was on the provocative testimony that had to be given, not a passive life that had to be extinguished. When someone in John's turn-of-the-first-century environment said "witness," she meant witness, not martyr.

John meant witnessing to their identity, self-declaring in a world that previously did not care about them because previously they had blended into it. They had allowed their world to believe that they were as Greco-Roman as everybody else. John wants them to self-declare that they believed not in the lordship of Rome, its gods, its social, political, and economic infrastructure, nor its emperor, but in the lordship of Jesus Christ, and that they would now fight to make that religious lordship of the future the governing principle of social, political, cultic, and religious practice in the present. Knowing what vicious response such a seditious claim would provoke, John nonetheless *demanded* that his followers make it.

John himself was their forbidding, prophetic role model. He makes it clear that his banishment to Patmos was a direct result of his witnessing to the lordship of Christ. Even knowing the dangers, he wants them to stick their necks out and partner with him in both the witness and the tribulation it will surely bring (cf. Boring, *Revelation*, 82; Aune 1:clxxvii–clxxviii).

## Genre: Apocalyptic

Revelation is apocalyptic literature. In fact, it bears the title *apokalypsis* (apocalypse). In a 1979 *Semeia* volume, John J. Collins offered the now-classic definition of both this genre and John's literary effort:

> "Apocalypse" is a genre of revelatory literature with a narrative framework, in which a revelation is mediated by an otherworldly being to a human recipient, disclosing a transcendent reality which is both temporal, insofar as it envisages eschatological salvation, and spatial insofar as it involves another, supernatural world. ("Morphology," 9)

An apocalypse intends to reveal a long-anticipated truth of prophetic significance about the end time. Unfortunately, that truth defies the logic of human language. There is much more to the truth than words can convey. Poetic and sometimes cryptic imagery must therefore be used instead. John's Revelation operates in just this literary way. It intends to reveal the truth about the future, a truth that enables its hearers and readers to see the present in a new light. But that truth is so powerful, so overwhelming, that John's words cannot properly convey it. He therefore appeals to symbols and codes that must bear the weight his language cannot. John seems to believe that a person must viscerally feel what cannot be linguistically conveyed. That belief prompts the crafting of the odd and frightening imagery that prevails throughout his apocalypse. The imagery is odd for a reason: it represents John's understanding of the future. Future hope, particularly in the case of the spiritually distraught and politically dispossessed, does not agree with present reality. They are contrary and combustible, so hostile to each other that the images related to each seem to ignite upon narrative contact. Whenever the future hope that is the inbreaking of God's eschatological reign and present reality that is the historical truth of the Roman Empire encounter each other in John's presentation, the results are explosive images of global war, natural catastrophe, and human death on a scale so massive as to be almost incomprehensible. It is this explosion that John wants to narrate. The truth behind the explosion (the lordship of God and the Lamb) is the truth that his Revelation intends to reveal. Because there are no words capable of revealing the power of that truth, he resorts to symbol.

The symbols' roots are grounded in Hebrew prophecy. John J. Collins argues that thinking on the "end time" goes all the way back to the eighth century B.C.E. and the prophet Amos. In his proclamation that the northern kingdom was doomed, he talked about the "day of the LORD," a day of darkness and not light. While he did not speak of it in terms of the end of the world, he did intend the end of northern Israel's history as a sovereign nation. It was an end orchestrated by God ("Morphology," 129; see Amos 5:18–20; 8:2).

In the same article, John Collins argues for three developmental periods for apocalyptic thinking and writing in Jewish history. (The discussion here will draw much from J. Collins's very helpful discussion.) The first period is that of the postexilic prophets, prophets like Second Isaiah writing in the aftermath of the Babylonian exile. Isaiah 24–27 records prophetic oracles so striking in their vision and tone that they are often referred to as "the apocalypse of Isaiah." Isaiah 24:1 offers an illustrative example: "Now the LORD is about to lay waste the earth and make it desolate, and he will twist its surface and scatter its inhabitants."[3] Just as revealing is 24:19–20: "The earth is utterly broken, the earth is torn asunder, the earth is violently shaken. The earth staggers like a drunkard." The prophet proclaims that God will swallow death (25:7) and punish Leviathan and slay the sea dragon (27:1). And Babylon, that great fortified city and palace of aliens (25:2), will be laid low. These images of Isaiah are the images of John's book of Revelation as well. Isaiah even hints at the very Johannine talk of resurrection for the faithful: "Your dead shall live, their corpses shall rise. O dwellers in the dust, awake and sing for joy! For your dew is a radiant dew, and the earth will give birth to those long dead" (26:19).

Ezekiel deploys an even more vivid resurrection accounting in his chapter-37 vision of the valley of dry bones. Like John's apocalyptic account, Ezekiel also added frightening monster combat scenes. As does Rev 20:8, Ezek 38 and 39 depict God battling Gog, the representation of Gentile power, from the land of Magog.

Third Isaiah, chapters 56–66, are just as intense, so intense in fact that in 1975 Paul Hanson called these chapters *The Dawn of Apocalyptic.* During the time when Israel was trying to rebuild the temple, during a time when the people of Israel felt utterly alienated from God and hopeless regarding their situation as a national entity, Isaiah conjured up the hope for a new heaven and a new earth: "For I am about to create new heavens and a new earth; the former things shall not be remembered or come to mind" (65:17). Revelation 21:1

---

3. Translations in the introduction are from the NRSV. Unless otherwise noted, I have crafted the translations of the Apocalypse in the rest of the commentary.

comes immediately to mind. This is prophetic language where the future looks radically different from the present. It is that future that the people of the present seek.

In J. Collins's second, Hellenistic period, apocalyptic comes into its own. This is the time of literature written pseudonymously. Visionary authors write under the names of important figures in Israel's past so as to give authority to the message of their visions for the present. Works like *1 Enoch* flourish during this period.[4] The book of Daniel also derives from this time. In the first six chapters, the seer/prophet Daniel interprets two dreams for the Babylonian king. As in John's Apocalypse, Babylon is the enemy. In Daniel's case, Babylon stands in symbolically for the Seleucid kingdom and its kings like Antiochus Epiphanes. Daniel interprets the king's dream by showing that there are human kingdoms, one of them Babylon, that will perish, while God's kingdom, which is coming, will endure forever (Dan 2:44).

Daniel's point, much the same point that John's Apocalypse wishes to reveal, is that God is in control of history, no matter how unlikely such a claim appears to be in a present dominated by the Seleucid Empire (Rome in John's case). Despite appearances, God's kingdom and God's people would be vindicated on God's final day. Daniel 7, one of the most influential apocalyptic passages in history, picks up on this theme with imagery that was instrumental for John's crafting of Revelation. Daniel envisions four beasts coming out of the sea, each one more fearsome than the preceding (cf. Rev 13). But he also sees thrones, and a deity, an ancient one, who passes judgment on the beasts. And then one like a child of humanity on the clouds of heaven appears and is given dominion and glory, and a kingdom that will never be destroyed. A battle of epic proportions erupts between God and the forces arrayed against God. The mythological enemy forces use the Gentile powers as their historical representatives. Just as God will defeat the heavenly forces on the mythological level, so God will soon enable the defeat of the earthly enemies and the vindication of God's earthly followers. The Seleucid Empire will be overthrown and the kingdom of God will be lifted up. This is the truth that Daniel's imagery wants to convey.

There is, however, an interesting twist. Daniel does not counsel his readers to join the revolutionary activity of the Maccabees, the historical force that represented God against the Seleucid Empire. Much like John in Revelation, he understands that the role of God's people is a nonviolent one. The difference between his accounting and John's is that Daniel counsels his enduring people

---

4. As J. Collins observes, "The book includes at least five distinct works: the *Book of the Watchers* (chapters 1–36), the *Similitudes* (chapters 37–71), the *Astronomical Book* (chapters 72–82), the *Book of Dreams* (chapters 83–90), and the *Epistle* (chapters 91–105). Within these books, the *Animal Apocalypse* (chapters 85–90) and the *Apocalypse of Weeks* (93:1–10 + 91:11–18) stand out as distinct compositions" ("Morphology," 134–35).

to wait for God to act. Passive, nonviolent waiting, though, is not the only alternative in apocalyptic literature. Daniel's choice is not the only choice. Much of the Enoch material encourages God's people to join the earthly revolution. Through the language of witness, John will also champion action. In his case, it will be the action of nonviolent resistance.

Also important for comparative purposes is the realization that Daniel is the second of two types of apocalyptic literature. One is typified by otherworldly journeys. The imagery is escapist, searching for a future hope beyond this world. Daniel, though, is a historical apocalypse. Its goal goes beyond the envisioning and expectation of an otherworldly transformation; it just as fervently anticipates a transfiguration of the human world and human history. This-worldly transformative hope of this kind is very much on display in John's Apocalypse, too.

John J. Collins's final apocalyptic stage is the Roman era, John's era. Works like *4 Ezra*, *2 Baruch*, and *3 Baruch* derive from this period. The Qumran *Scroll of the War of the Sons of Light against the Sons of Darkness* also stems from this period. While the *War Scroll* focuses on a final, apocalyptic battle that will reveal God's kingdom in power and victory, the *Psalms of Solomon* look to the hope of resurrection and the raising up of a Davidic Messiah. The *Sibylline Oracles*, while attempting to predict the course of history, divide history into periods that lead to a God-directed end. The *Oracles* convey the belief, developed ominously in Revelation, that Nero, the infamous persecutor of Christians, would be revived as a mythical figure who would, in the form of an antichrist, battle God and God's people in the time leading up to the final war (see *Sib. Or.* 4.150–157, 175–77; 5.38–47; 8.88, 193–201). That final war would reveal the truth that God is in charge of the present as well as the future (Rev 17:11).

Even before John put the content of his visions on Patmos into writing, then, an influential worldview that might be called "apocalyptic" had developed. This worldview is characterized by several traits (see J. Collins, "Morphology," 157–59). There is supernatural revelation that is above human understanding. This disclosure clarifies the truth of the present because it can see the present from the perspective of the future. The truth is this: the people who hold power in the present are deluded about the scope of their historical control. God's goals, not theirs, will ultimately be achieved. This truth means that human affairs are in a sense already determined. Because humans do not know what that determination is, they must live as though human choices make a difference. Humans cannot see where the road of the future leads. The path, though, is already ordained. Nothing the powers of the present can do will alter it. God and God's people shall be vindicated. This truth is the hope even in the midst of a horrific present.

This apocalyptic understanding is built upon a dualistic understanding of reality. There are two mutually exclusive eras: the present and the future. Humans must choose between them. The option is either/or, not both/and. To commit to the present and the forces that run the present is to give up on God's future. To commit to the future, even if the forces in the present persecute and kill believers because of that commitment, is to be assured of eschatological relationship with God. God will defeat the forces of Satan in heaven, and God's human agent, the Messiah, the child of humanity, will defeat Satan's human representatives on earth. Divine judgment on a cosmic scale will follow. Entire nations and peoples will be judged. Humans will be held accountable for their decisions. Thus, what humans do and say in the present, they must do and say with an eye always toward that future that has already been determined. The future visions thus serve a very present prophetic end.

Apocalyptic literature, then, has an ethical motivation. It implores people to act in the present in a way that agrees with its understanding of the future. Such an expectation may mean that followers should endure the persecutions of the present, join in battles against the forces of the present, or simply wait for the future in any way they can. In every case, it means that they must choose sides. They must put themselves on God's side, as the apocalyptic writer understands God's side. They must live for God's future in the present, even if making that choice means that they will come into conflict with the leaders of the present, even if the price of that choice is present death. Ironically, with such death comes true life, a resurrected life that will follow God's judgment.

Yet there are a multitude of problems with such an apocalyptic worldview. For many theologians, its view of history is embarrassing. An apocalyptic worldview encounters difficulty with ongoing history because its imminent expectations about the future inevitably go unfulfilled. Apocalyptic dreamers are always, critics say, disappointed.

The deterministic and often pessimistic view of history also makes apocalyptic distasteful to the contemporary believer who wants to believe that history is not planned out, that human behavior can effect changes in the course and direction of human living. Other critics charge that the dualistic worldview of a hoped-for future in competition with a hoped-against present encourages the rejection of the present world in favor of an illusory future that never comes. And, it should be noted, this future is a very patriarchal one, where women are either evil whores or passive madonnas, but not human agents working to inspire and impact the shape of the future.

Indeed, in her fine book *Apocalypse Now and Then*, Catherine Keller argues that while a people poised on critical precipices like ecological collapse or individual destruction cannot escape the impact of an apocalyptic worldview, contemporary humans must reconfigure it. She argues for a counterapocalyptic perspective that draws from the hopeful expectation for the future, but is not based in deterministic, either/or, patriarchal, or escapist categories. I argue that the perspective she seeks exists in a nascent way already in the New Testament apocalyptic materials. The counterapocalyptic presence in New Testament apocalyptic is to be found in its prophetic roots. The Hebrew prophets fervently believed that the choices humans made would influence the direction in which God would choose to move the future. The prophet Jonah is an entertaining example of just this principle. He did not want to serve God, because he knew that God would adjust the course of God's intended future if people repented of their ungodlike behavior in the present. Jonah hated the Ninevites with such passion that he desired a predetermined destruction for them instead. True to God's word, though, when the Ninevites changed their behavior, God changed the course of their future. It is on this ethical expectation—of human behavior that changes until it matches God's desires for human living—that John bases his understanding of the future. He, too, believes that repentance is offered, even for the most egregious offenders (see 2:20–22). When humans choose to change their behavior, God will choose to change the course of their future. For John, then, the future is not all laid out so that some are doomed and others are not (see the comment on 13:8).

There are other Christian legacies of apocalyptic perspective also suggesting that, already in the first century, writers were struggling with the issues that so rightly concern Keller. Paul is fervently apocalyptic. He, too, looks for the triumph of God, but he also realizes the power of God's spiritual activity in the present. Paul never abandons the present. There is room in the present for transformation and ethical activity while humans await God's action in the future. The author of the Gospel according to Mark is another writer with apocalyptic tendencies. He sees Jesus through an apocalyptic lens. Mark finds a way around the destructive either/or dualism by looking forward to God's future in a way that does not give up on the present. Mark already sees the future, represented through the boundary-breaking ministry of Jesus, operating in the present. Mark's Jesus teaches his disciples to do as he himself is doing, to represent in powerful ways the force of God's future kingdom in the present.

For Christian apocalyptic writers, the key event in God's future rule has already taken place in the historical present: Jesus' death on the cross. That death is as significant in Revelation as it is in any other New Testament material (see 5:9; 12:5). This event colors all of history and the expectations of the future and how believers are to live in anticipation of that future. It was key for Paul and Mark; it was key for John in his crafting of Revelation. What does this realization mean? Most important, it means that humans need not wait for God to act. *God has already acted.* Humans only need to find a way of responding appropriately to that past act, which has completely transfigured the future. This expectation for response means that waiting for the consummation of God's future need not be passive. John develops his expectation for active apocalyptic engagement through his witness language.

Finally, Christian apocalyptic encompasses a concern for the world, not just the individual. In his debates with Rudolf Bultmann, Ernst Käsemann recognized that—in order to prevent apocalyptic from devolving into exactly the kind of eschatological enthusiasm that threatened to wreck the church at Corinth, where believers felt themselves already saved through their existential encounter with the living Christ—the church must not lose its focus on the coming of God's "kingdom" as a true objective reality that would transform exterior reality as well as inner hearts (Käsemann, esp. ch. 4, "The Beginnings of Christian Theology," and ch. 5, "On the Subject of Primitive Christian Apocalyptic"). It is this objective expectation that John certainly intends. This is why, in his climactic visions of the end, he connects Christ's coming not with personal confessions of faith but with a tangible, measurable, objective city. The Christ who comes soon comes not just to the human heart but also to the world.

John presents his apocalyptic message in the literary form of a letter. His initial moves follow the conventional norms of Hellenistic correspondence. In his epistolary greeting or salutation (1:4–6), he identifies himself as the sender. Immediately afterward, he points out seven churches of Asia Minor (present-day Turkey) as the recipients (1:11). Like the apostle Paul, he adjusts the Hellenistic letter-writing formula by including an offering of grace and peace (see Rom 1:7; 1 Cor 1:3; 2 Cor 1:2; Gal 1:3; Phil 1:2; 1 Thess 1:1; Phlm 3). John closes the work he began with an epistolary greeting by appealing appropriately to an epistolary benediction (22:21).

## Outline and Structure

1:1–8 Prologue and Letter Opening
1:9–3:22 A Word from the Lord: Ethical Instructions to the Seven Churches
   1:9–20 John Introduces Himself and Christ
   2:1–3:22 Letters to Seven Churches of Asia
     2:1–7 To Ephesus: You Can Be Too Good
     2:8–11 To Smyrna: Richer than You Know
     2:12–17 To Pergamum: At the Foot of Satan's Throne
     2:18–29 To Thyatira: Drowning in the Deep End
     3:1–6 To Sardis: Time to Wake Up
     3:7–13 To Philadelphia: Open-Door Policy
     3:14–22 To Laodicea: Lukewarm Vomit
4:1–22:9 A Series of Visions
   4:1–11:19 An Introductory Vision Cycle
     4:1–11 One Seated on the Heavenly Throne
     5:1–14 The Lamb
     6:1–8:1 The Opening of the Seven Seals
     8:2–11:19 The Sounding of the Seven Trumpets
   12:1–14:20 Visionary Flashback: The Start of the Story
     12:1–17 The Dragon's War
     12:18–13:18 Resistance Is Futile

14:1–20  God Strikes Back: Visions of Judgment
15:1–22:9  A Concluding Vision Cycle
15:1–16:21  The Seven Bowls of God's Wrath
17:1–19:10  The Implications of God's Wrath: The Judgment of
        Babylon
19:11–21:8  The Final Battle and Its Aftermath
21:9–22:9  The Implications of God's Victory: The New Jerusalem
22:10–21  Epilogue and Letter Closing

Two notations about the structure of the book, more fully developed in the relevant commentary sections, should also be introduced here. First, the series of seven visions—the seals, trumpets, and bowls—do not represent a succession of sequentially occurring events. Instead, John intends his hearers and readers to perceive them as happening simultaneously. He has in mind what a contemporary reading might call a three-ring apocalyptic circus. The judgment of God represented in each series of seven events happens only once. All three of the series happen at the same time. From one audience perspective the judgment of God appears in the symbolism of seven broken seals, from another vantage point it looks like the blowing of seven trumpets, and from a third and final angle it has all the symbolic earmarks of seven bowls of wrath. John, then, is intensifying, not repeating, the judgment scenario with his triple-play presentation. He wants to make certain that his hearers and readers recognize just how serious and significant God's act of judgment is.

Second, in terms of real time, John starts his book in the middle of his story. In chapters 2 and 3, he writes to churches that he believes are already under siege. He intends to encourage the members of those churches to continue resisting the lordship claims of Rome even as he implores them to self-declare their allegiance to the exclusive lordship of God and the Lamb. Any reader who comes to this work without sufficient awareness of its overall context would be confused as to how the churches arrived at the precarious situation John describes. How did Satan establish a throne in the affected regions (2:13)? Who is Satan? How is this mythological figure related to the imperial force that is historical Rome? How is Rome related to the regional and local authorities in Asia Minor? Why are believers threatened by them? And where is God and what is God doing in the midst of these troubling circumstances?

In terms of narrative time, John withholds a response to these questions until he inserts the flashback of chapters 12–14. In those texts, he offers the mythological explanation for the circumstance that bedevils his believers. Chapters 12–14 therefore interrupt the judgment and vindication visions with an explanatory set of visions.

Why does he not, then, begin his narrative with these visions? He does not because his primary, prophetic intent is to influence the behavior of the

Christian communities that receive his Apocalypse. He therefore begins with an introduction of himself and their Lord and then moves quickly to the ethical expectations their Lord has for the churches that worship in his name. An apocalyptic letter that the author calls a word of prophecy would most logically begin with prophetic expectations for living rather than mythological combat stories steeped in symbolism. John ultimately turns to the symbolism in order to ratchet up the sense of urgency: to emphasize just how important it is that his hearers and readers abide by the prophetic-ethical expectation to witness to and for the lordship of God and the Lamb. Had he started the letter with material that emphasized the dragon and the beasts from the sea and land, surely his hearers and readers would have been so caught up in the mythological drama that they would have lost sight of ethical expectation. Oddly enough, across the centuries, even with the mythology safely tucked inside the book's midsection, too often even Christian readers have focused on the draconian beasts, their probable contemporary identity, and the timetables for and consequences of war with them, at the regrettable expense of hearing, interpreting, and enacting the prophetic-ethical message of the book.

## Text

Because the translations in this commentary will sometimes discuss manuscript variants and their different formulations of the text of Revelation, and offer hypotheses as to which formulation is the more original, it is helpful here to offer some introductory comments for readers less experienced in matters of textual criticism.[5] Five primary groupings of ancient manuscripts provide the source material for reconstructing the text of the book of Revelation. Kurt and Barbara Aland developed categorizations that appraised manuscript reliability:

- Category I: Manuscripts of a very special quality, which should always be considered when establishing the original text
- Category II: Manuscripts of a special quality, which have alien influences
- Category III: Manuscripts of a distinctive quality, usually important for establishing the original text
- Category IV: Manuscripts of the D text, which has no Revelation material
- Category V: Manuscripts predominantly from the Byzantine text

Papyri comprise the first manuscript grouping. In the New Testament period, texts were primarily written on papyrus, a plant produced mainly in Egypt.

---

5. The material used in this brief discussion can be found in Aland and Aland, *Text of the New Testament*, 106; Metzger, *Text*. Aune 1:cxxxvi, while recognizing the categories, notes that they should not be relied upon indiscriminately.

After its thick stem was cut into thin, vertical strips, the pieces were laid down beside each other and formed into a single layer whose fibers ran parallel to each other. A second layer was laid on top so that its fibers ran at right angles to the fibers of the base layer. The two layers were then moistened, smoothed, dried, and ultimately arranged into a scroll. Five papyrus fragments contain texts of the book of Revelation. $\mathfrak{P}^{18}$ derives from the late third to early fourth century and belongs to category I. The fact that it often agrees closely with the uncials A, ℵ, and C increases its authority. $\mathfrak{P}^{24}$, also category I, derives from the early fourth century and also agrees with A and ℵ. $\mathfrak{P}^{43}$, the late sixth or early seventh century, is category II manuscript. $\mathfrak{P}^{47}$ derives from the middle to latter part of the third century. This second-oldest manuscript witness to the book of Revelation agrees more often with ℵ than any other text, but also shows a great deal of independence. $\mathfrak{P}^{85}$, a fourth–fifth-century text, is also category II. $\mathfrak{P}^{98}$ is the oldest extant witness to Revelation, coming from the second century.

Uncials comprise a second grouping of manuscripts. Of the 301 manuscript witnesses known for the text of Revelation, only 11 are uncials, and only 3 of these (ℵ, A, and 046) are complete texts. These manuscripts are all written in uppercase Greek lettering and are classified with the prefix "0." The codex (book) numbered 01, or ℵ, is the Codex Sinaiticus, from the fourth century, an especially valuable category I manuscript. Codex Alexandrinus (02 or A), one of the most reliable witnesses to Revelation's text, is from the fifth century (category I). Codex Ephraemi Syri Rescriptus (04, or C), is also from the fifth century (category II). The final two to be mentioned here, 025 (9th century) and 046 (10th century), are both category V.

Miniscules comprise a third grouping of manuscripts. Written in lowercase lettering, there are 293 currently known. (For a complete listing, see Aune 1:cxxxix–cxlviii.)

A fourth grouping of manuscripts is comprised of Greek and Latin patristic material. A fifth is comprised of various translations (e.g., Latin, Ethiopic, Syriac) of the text. (For a full discussion of these groupings and text types, see Metzger, *Text*, 67–92.)

Weighing the external manuscript evidence is a delicate enterprise that should always be complemented by internal clues within the text itself. Internal and external clues should be assessed in a balanced way. In addition, the value of external evidence rises as different manuscripts are grouped together in support of various readings.

# COMMENTARY

# REVELATION

## 1:1–8 Prologue and Letter Opening

John's opening chapter establishes the seer's primary theme: witness. His entire work is a witness to the revelation that God has disclosed: God, working through the historical expression of Jesus as the Christ, is Lord. John relays this testimony with a purpose. His hearers and readers must witness to others the truth that John reveals to them, no matter the cost.

### 1:1–3 Prologue: A Chain of Witness

1 This is[a] the Revelation proclaimed by Jesus Christ,[b] which God gave to him to reveal to his servants what must happen soon; he made it known by sending his messenger to his servant John, 2 who witnessed to all that he saw: the word of God, which is[c] the witness proclaimed by Jesus Christ.[d] 3 Blessed is the one who reads and those who hear the words of the prophecy and keep[e] what has been written in it,[f] for the time is near.

a. Because the Greek does not have a verb, one is supplied.

b. The genitive ("of Jesus Christ") is treated here as subjective. That the revelation was something controlled by Jesus is confirmed by the following relative clause, which assumes that Jesus first received it and then passed it along.

c. The *kai* (and) is epexegetical rather than correlative; the second clause clarifies the first.

d. A subjective genitive (see note b above).

e. The plural participle refers back to both the one who reads and those who hear.

f. One might expect that the pronoun here would be plural and masculine, since the structure of the sentence suggests that John should be referring back to "the words," since "prophecy" modifies "the words" and not the other way around. Theologically, though, it is the concept of prophecy that John wants uppermost in the minds of his reader and hearers. For this reason, he forces a gender and number match between the feminine "prophecy" and the feminine form of the pronoun.

[1:1–2] John's single and graphic deployment of the term *apokalypsis* (revelation) conveys the word's abiding narrative importance. Using this ancient word, which would have made his readers think about the disrobing, the *revealing* of a vulnerable virgin on her wedding night, he declares that his work is all about the stripping of Jesus Christ (Keller 1). It is a sexist image that puts a strong man in the position of dominating a powerless woman. And yet, by connecting it to Jesus and making Jesus the subject rather than the object of the action, John tries to redeem it. The revealing of Jesus conjures up the image of his crucifixion, where he was stripped naked and hung out to die. As God's intervening resurrection made clear, however, this revelation ultimately was not something someone did to Jesus; it was what Jesus revealed to everyone else. While being humiliated by hostile authorities and executed on the cross, Jesus stripped world history and human reality bare by clarifying something that was heretofore apparently obscure: his own lordship.

Basing this part of his work on Dan 2:28–47, where King Nebuchadnezzar realizes that God can use humans to reveal even the mysteries of the dream world, John sets up Jesus as the messianic middleman, who takes the stripping (of world history and human reality) that God has given him and passes it on to an angel, who in turn passes it on to John. In v. 2, this chain of transmission (see the commentary on 22:6, 16) develops a functional equivalence between the concepts "word of God" and "witness of Jesus Christ," both of which refer back to "revelation." John is actually defining revelation by connecting it narratively to one clarifying object, not two. The word of God *is* the witness of Jesus Christ. The *kai* (and) that connects the two is epexegetical; that is, the second formulation clarifies and develops the first. In four key places in his text, John dramatically connects "word" and "witness" in this way: 1:2, 9; 6:9; 20:4. The intended clarification actually causes an interpretive problem. John has defined his book of prophecy as the Revelation of Jesus Christ, and has in turn defined that revelation by the formula "word of God, which is the witness of Jesus Christ." The formula is unclear because the defining component is itself undefined. What exactly is the witness of Jesus Christ?[1]

In the phrase "witness of Jesus Christ," the genitive noun is subjective; when John speaks of the "witness of," he means "the witness proclaimed by." So the revelation of Jesus as John defines it in this transmission chain is the revelation—the witness—proclaimed by Jesus Christ.

In the twenty-first century, *martys*, the Greek term for "witness," means something quite different than it did for John and his hearers and readers. The confusion is contextual. When contemporary interpreters transliterate the Greek letters of *martys* into their corresponding Roman letters, we see and hear the word *martyr*. H. Strathmann testifies that for John and his hearers, "The proper sphere of μάρτυς is the legal, where it denotes one who can and does speak from personal experience about actions in which he took part and which

---

1. One could always point to 19:10c, where John declares that the witness of Jesus is the spirit of prophecy, but that clarification only *appears* to help because it tells us no more than what the opening three verses have already revealed: Jesus' revelation is Jesus' witness, which John inscribes as a literary prophecy.

happened to him, or about persons and relations known to him" (Strathmann, *TDNT* 4:476). Allison Trites offers corroboration: "The idea of witness in the Apocalypse is very much a live metaphor and is to be understood in terms of Christians actually bearing witness before Roman courts of law" (72). It is a word of provocative testimony and therefore active engagement, not sacrificial passivity. *Martyr* language, as John introduces (*martyreō*, testify, 1:2; *martyria*, testimony, 1:2, 9; *martys*, witness, 1:5) and develops it, is language preoccupied not with dying, but declaration.

John identifies the *kind* of witness he encourages through key characterizations. At 1:5, he identifies Jesus, *by name*, as *the* faithful *witness*. At 3:14, as witness, Jesus is both faithful and true. Whatever else he might appear to be to his followers (e.g., Lamb), Jesus Christ is first and foremost God's prime witness. Every other characterization must be interpreted in that light, and not the other way around. The question we are narratively driven to ask, then, is this: how are we to understand the spilling of Jesus' blood (1:5) and ultimate killing (5:9) in the light of his role as God's faithful witness? What is it about his witness that connects with and perhaps even causes his killing? The implication from the context of Asia Minor at the end of the first century is suggestive; Jesus, *the* prophetic witness figure, apparently testified to (proclaimed) a truth. He faithfully adhered to that testimony even under the direst of circumstances, at the cost of his own life. As Trites notes, "From the context of the Apocalypse as a whole, it seems probable that *the witness of Jesus* (*hē marturia Iēsou*) in these passages refers primarily to Christ's passion, where he witnessed 'the good confession' before Pontius Pilate (cf. I Tim. vi 13)" (76). What else could that confession be in the narrative of John's Revelation other than the proclamation of cosmic and human lordship that follows directly upon the rhetorical heels of Jesus' introduction as *the* faithful witness (1:4–8)?

According to v. 1, God reveals this deadly testimony to God's servants. According to 1:4, however, the final stop for the revelation was the seven churches of Asia Minor. Did John intend that the servants would be understood as equivalent to the churches, or did he intend a separate group of servants who would then, having received the revelation from John, relay it to John's churches? A relevant passage in Amos 3:7 indicates that God does nothing without first revealing divine intent to God's servants, the prophets. John has a similar way of talking about God's servants as prophets (see 10:7; 11:3, 18; 22:16; cf. 22:6, 9). Servant-prophets (e.g., Jezebel, 2:20–23; Balaam, 2:14) worked as interpretive links between God and God's churches. John sees himself and even God's angelic messengers as such servant-prophets (22:9; cf. 19:10). The servants, then, are prophetic colleagues to whom John reports his revelatory visions. They in turn are expected to broadcast, that is, witness the report to the churches.

Two other stages in the transmission chain also warrant individual reflection. God does not operate directly with humans, but through appropriately designated intermediaries. That presence is symbolized here by the unidentified angel. He bridges the gap between the divine and human so that God's revelation can make its necessary move.

John is another matter. He identifies himself as a link in the revelatory chain because he wants his hearers and readers to recognize his place of authority in their communal lives. John self-identifies on three other occasions: 1:4, 9; 22:8. At both 1:4 and 22:8, the self-references establish John as the writer of the text. Was he the same John identified as the son of Zebedee, one of the twelve apostles of the historical Jesus? Most likely not. Having given himself the prime literary opportunity to lay claim to such an identity and the authority that would go with it, John tellingly demurs. He claims not the authority of a Jesus apostle for his revelation, which would be powerful indeed, but that of a collegial servant-prophet working among other servant-prophets. When he challenges the prophetic work of Balaam and Jezebel in chapter 2, he does not do so on the basis of his personal relationship with the historical Jesus and the knowledge and authority he would have derived from it. Instead, he bases his argument on the truth of the prophetic revelation he has received. In fact, in his single reference to Jesus' historical apostles (21:14; cf. 2:2; 18:20), he speaks of them as though they are historical figures with whom he has had no direct contact. Further, the dramatic difference between the realized eschatology that predominates in the Gospel traditionally attributed to Zebedee's son and the future eschatology of the Apocalypse suggest that this John and the author of the Fourth Gospel come from dramatically different places in theology as well as time.

There are obvious structural parallels between this portion of the prologue and the epilogue (22:10–21). Though it leaves out the transmitting role played by Jesus, 22:6 explains how God sent God's angel to God's servants to "reveal" what must happen soon (see the comment on 22:1). At 22:16, John reinserts Jesus into the chain so that there is no mistaking that Jesus has conveyed the revelation to the angel. Though John uses a noun form (*[en] tachei*) to express imminence only here (1:1) and at the 22:6 parallel (see the comment on 22:6; cf. Dan 2:28), he does express an adverbial sense of imminence throughout (see the comment on 3:11). The expectation of an imminent arrival of God's judgment fits the exhortative mood of the book. Since God is on the way, and right soon, one should act in the ethical manner that the book demands (e.g., see the discussion of the macarism in v. 3, below). These two opening verses already describe that ethic in terms of witness language. The implication is clear: the transmission of God's revelation must not stop with the servants but must carry on to the churches (1:4) and from the churches to the world (see the comments on 6:11 and 12:11).

The theme of necessity is as potent here as the theme of imminence. When John speaks of what "must" take place, he talks in terms of apocalyptic necessity rather than fatalistic determinism. Given the conflict that has developed between God's forces and the draconian forces of empire, which have demanded cultic and political allegiance to its lordship (see chs. 12–13), both the persecution coming to those who testified exclusively to the lordship of God and Christ and God's responding judgment of the imperial forces and saving of Christ-believers are inevitable.

[3] Beatitudes, or macarisms, are formulaic expressions initiated with the word *makarios* (blessed). They exist in two forms: wisdom (e.g., Ps 1: "Happy/Blessed are those who do not follow the advice of the wicked, or take the path that sinners tread, or sit in the seat of scoffers") and apocalyptic (e.g., Dan 12:12–13: "Happy are those who persevere and attain the thousand three hundred thirty-five days. But you, go your way, and rest; you shall rise for your reward at the end of the days"). That the beatitude form is important to John is clear from the fact that he has exactly seven of them (1:3; 14:13; 16:15; 19:9; 20:6; 22:7, 14). Operating from an Old Testament sensibility, where it represents wholeness and completion, the number "seven" is as theological for John as it is numerical.[2] His first beatitude, like the six that follow, is apocalyptic, as are those that occur in Matthew's Sermon on the Mount.

In fact, the forty-four New Testament beatitudes are most often found in the apocalyptic mode. Both modes (wisdom and apocalyptic) recognize that the person who seeks to do God's will is blessed. In that sense they have both indicative and imperative potential. As an indicative statement, the macarism describes the participant who is in right relationship with God. There are also clear indications, however, that *makarios* formulations have an imperative sense. As the Dan 12:12–13 passage demonstrates, the person who performs a particular activity is considered blessed and is subsequently rewarded. By envisioning a proleptic reward, the macarism encourages what is considered to be positive, "salvific" behavior.

By nature, beatitudes are comparative. In the indicative mode, secular blessings are relegated to a position inferior to the joys associated with the reign of God. In the imperative, while some behaviors are considered *makarios*, others are not. What is *blessed* behavior in 1:1–3? The blessed person is the one who witnesses to what Jesus himself testified. The person who reads this witness aloud so that others may hear it and the persons who hear this witness and keep it are also those whom John considers blessed. The implicit ethic is so important that before he closes, he will pronounce the commendation again in the epilogue at 22:7: "See, I am coming soon! Blessed is the one who keeps the words of the prophecy of this book" (cf. Luke 11:28). John encourages his hearers and readers to realize the

---

2. See, e.g., Gen 2:2, 3; 8:4; Exod 12:15–16; 13:6; 16:26–30; 20:10–11; 21:2; 23:11–12; 24:16; 31:15, 17; 34:21; 35:2; Lev 13:5–6, 27, 32, 34; 23:3, 8, 16, 24, 27; Deut 5:14; 15:1, 9, 12; Josh 6:4, 15–16; Jer 34:14.

importance of this "keeping" (see comments on 3:3, 10; 12:17; cf. 3:8; 14:12; 16:15; 22:9); he promises eschatological victory to those who do (2:26–29; 3:10). (On the connection between "hearing" and "keeping" as an ethical combination in Revelation, see the comment on 22:17.)

When John describes his own work as a word of prophecy (see the comment on 22:6), he has a particular point in mind. A prophet is a servant who witnesses to the lordship of God and Christ, even in imperial circumstances where government representatives seek either to co-opt or to annihilate that testimony. The primary objective of prophecy, then, is not to foretell the future, but to model and thereby incite present witnessing behavior that resists imperial attempts to hijack the lordship that belongs exclusively to God and Christ. It is his prophetic exhortation to this kind of witnessing that John wants his people to hear and keep.

John urges Christ-believers to witness because the time (of God's movement for judgment and salvation) is near. In the epilogue, at 22:10, John hears an angel make the same claim. Was John wrong? Given that the twenty-first century has dawned without the onset of God's new heaven and new earth, one would have to say yes. To concentrate on the error of timing, though, would be to miss John's primary theological point. To his credit, he never offers a timetable. Instead, he uses the imminent expectation to craft a sense of urgency that he hopes will foment passionate witnessing for God's exclusive lordship, even in a context where Christ-believers were sure to be persecuted for making such an outrageous claim (see the comment on 22:7).

### *1:4–8 Epistolary Greeting: Salutation*

4 John, to the seven churches that are in Asia. Grace and peace to you from the one who is, who was, and who is coming,[a] and from the seven spirits who are before God's[b] throne, 5 and from Jesus Christ, the faithful witness, the firstborn of the dead, who is[c] the ruler over the kings of the earth.[d] To the one who loves us and liberated us[e] from our sins by his blood, 6 and made us a reign, priests to God, who[f] is his Father: To him be the glory and the power forever.[g] Amen. 7 Indeed, he is coming with the clouds. Every eye will see him, even those who pierced him, and all the tribes of the earth will mourn for[h] him. Amen. 8 I am the Alpha and the Omega,[i] says the Lord God, the one who is, who was, and who is coming, the Almighty.

a. Because the tripartite divine name follows the preposition *apo* (from), John should offer it in the genitive case. As he will do later in presenting the titles for Jesus in v. 5, he instead presents it in the nominative. Some scribes (𝔐 [ar] t; Vic Prim) try to dodge the problem by inserting "God" in the genitive (*theou*) prior to the nominatives in the title.

As in v. 5, John deliberately skews the grammar to make an intertextual point. In this case, the *ho ōn*, in the nominative, recalls the nominative presentation of God's name in Exod 3:14 LXX. It could also be the case that John considered the tripartite name indeclinable.

b. Though the personal pronoun is clearly a masculine reference back to God, where possible a more inclusive translation is to be preferred.

c. The *kai* (and) is epexegetical; the second phrase, "ruler over the kings of the earth," clarifies the first, "firstborn of the dead."

d. The titles describing Jesus Christ are appositions to Jesus Christ and should thus, like Jesus Christ, be in the genitive case. John again skews the grammar to make an intertextual theological point about Christ's kingship.

e. Scribes (TR, following P 1006 1841 1854 2053 1062 𝔐ᴷ lat bo) substituted *lousanti* (washed), but *lysanti* (loosed, liberated) is to be preferred not only because of the stronger manuscript evidence (𝔓¹⁸ ℵ A C 1611 2050 2329 2351 𝔐ᴬ h sy Prim) but also because it fits the exodus emphasis on liberation that John raises here and throughout his work. The alteration is probably an accommodation to the image of washing in the blood of the Lamb in Rev 7:14.

f. The *kai* is epexegetical (see note c above).

g. The words *tōn aiōnōn* (of the ages) are absent in a significant number of manuscripts (𝔓¹⁸ A P 2050 [2344] *pc* bo). This shorter reading is to be preferred given that the longer formula (*eis tous aiōnas tōn aiōnōn*) occurs eleven times in the Apocalypse (1:18; 4:9, 10; 5:13; 7:12; 10:6; 11:15; 15:7; 19:3; 20:10; 22:5). Scribes probably added the final two words here in order to make this occurrence match the others.

h. BDAG (559) identifies the idiom *koptomai epi tina*, "I mourn for someone," citing Rev 1:7; 18:9 in the NT; and 2 Sam 1:12; 11:26 in the LXX. David mourns for Jonathan and Saul (2 Sam 1:12); Bathsheba for Uriah (2 Sam 11:26); and the kings of the earth for fallen Babylon (Rev 18:9). The tribes of the earth do not "wail on account of" the coming Christ, as if they feared his judgment; rather, they "mourn for" the one whom they pierced, expressing contrition.

i. The addition of "first and last" after "omega" in some manuscripts is a scribal attempt to match the statement here with the parallel one at 21:6a.

While vv. 4–6 constitute the letter greeting proper, John's presentation of God as the one who is, who was, and who is coming at vv. 4 and 8 shows that he thought of vv. 4–8 as a unit.

**[4]** As was the case with the apostle Paul, John's initial moves follow the conventional norms of Hellenistic correspondence. Like Paul, though, he does not simply take over the Hellenistic conventions of letter writing; he adapts them to his particular Christian purpose. First, he identifies himself as the sender. Immediately afterward, he points out seven churches of Asia Minor (present-day Turkey) as the recipients (see 1:11 for listing of churches). Since the number "seven" is a symbol of completion for John (see the comment on v. 3), it is probable that the entire church in the region was his target audience. He makes this clear by ending each of the seven letters with a formula that identifies *all* the churches as the target audience. Perhaps he singled out these seven because each of them hosted a Roman law court where believers could be forced to testify about allegations that they were Christ-believers (Boring, *Revelation*, 87).

Like Paul, John further adjusts the Hellenistic letter-writing formula by including an offer of grace and peace (cf. Rom 1:7; 1 Cor 1:3; 2 Cor 1:2; Gal 1:3; Phil 1:2; 1 Thess 1:1; Phlm 3). He repeats the grace sentiment in the benediction at 22:21. Here, as in the benediction, he unleashes an epistolary shot across Caesar's imperial bow. Allegedly, the prosperity of Asian life was owed solely to the emperor's beneficence. According to John, however, that grace and the peace that has developed from it comes from some *ones* else: God, the seven spirits before God's throne, and Jesus Christ. John has twisted the innocuous form of a Greco-Roman letter written for religious intent into what Pablo Richard calls "a liturgical text that amounts to a theological and political manifesto" (40).

Religious rhetoric continues its morph into political counterpropaganda when John provides a descriptive title for this God of grace (on John's skewing of the grammar to make a theological point, see the comment on v. 5). At vv. 4 and 8, he identifies God as the one who is, who was, and who is coming (cf. 4:8; 11:17; 16:5 for altered or truncated uses of the formula). In the Greek-speaking world such a threefold formulation was a commonplace way of celebrating a deity's eternity and immutability. "It was said, for example, that 'Zeus was, Zeus is, and Zeus will be' (Pausanias)" (Boring, *Revelation*, 75). Athena also laid claim to such a testimonial. Plutarch preserves an inscription from the base of one of her statues that reads, "I am all that has been, and is, and shall be" (Aune 1:31). John hijacks the formulation for God. He then adds a direct provocation. His God was also *coming* to bring the reality of supernatural rule to the natural realm. By identifying God as the Alpha and the Omega, as God would do Godself in the second recitation of this threefold formula at v. 8, John claims that God transcends human history and therefore controls it. Rome had already staked that claim by conquering Asia Minor and the people of God who lived in it. It is at just the point of this theological difference of opinion that religious confrontation escalates into political combat. When John records God's second self-reference at v. 8, he uses the very language Moses used to describe the liberator God in the Exod 3:14 account: *Egō Eimi* (I AM). This direct reference reinforces the Exod 3:14 allusion (*ho ōn*, "the one who is") already present in the threefold formulation. The Almighty Lord of Hosts who brought down Pharaoh and set the people of God free was on the verge of unveiling a similar liberating act for the people of God in Asia. In John's historical context that necessarily meant that this Almighty One would be acting against Rome.

This Almighty One was not acting alone. The seven spirits symbolize God's expansive power. They represent the fullness (seven) of God's force in the world through the active presence of the Holy Spirit (see the comments on 3:1; 4:5; 5:6; 14:13; 22:17). Beale sees a connection here with 4:5, where John describes the seven flaming torches burning before the heavenly throne (189).

Interestingly, John also characterizes the churches in 1:12, 13, and 20 as seven lampstands. It does not take much imagination to theorize that the churches (lampstands) are powered by the force of God's Spirit (flames). But if God uses God's power (Spirit) to contest Roman control of human history, *and* God also uses God's power to empower the churches to whom John is writing, then it must also be the case that John's churches will form one of the principal mechanisms through which God will win the fight against Rome. This *Holy* Spirit, then, is very much a *political* Spirit.

[5] John heightens the probability for even more controversy by the way he describes Christ. He does not use proper grammar. John's problems with Greek are legendary; many have argued that his flawed writing can be attributed to the fact that he thinks in Hebrew or Aramaic. Allen Callahan counters that he operates this way intentionally. Because "most of the grammatical rules violated are flawlessly observed elsewhere in the work," he believes that John *chooses* to write in a Greek that is heavily influenced by Semitic principles.[3] He does so because he wants his use of language to be a representation, a working symbol, as it were, of the social and political resistance his people must wage.

Since "Jesus Christ" is in the genitive case, operating as the object of the preposition "from," the titles that follow should also be in the genitive. Instead, John puts "the faithful witness," "the firstborn of the dead," and "the ruler over the kings of the earth" in the nominative case. As Callahan might say, John is not making a mistake; he is making a point. He is following the same pattern he initiated in v. 4, where the threefold formula about God is in the nominative case even though its function as the object of the preposition "from" should have it in the genitive. There, as here, John stays with the nominative because he wants to direct attention to an allusion he is making to Ps 89:37 (88:38 LXX), where the controlling moniker, faithful witness, also occurs in a nominative formulation (Beale 192). But it occurs there with a specific orientation, as does "firstborn" in 89:27 (88:28 LXX). The context of the two references in their Old Testament location is one of kingship, "the unending reign of David's seed on his throne (cf. likewise Ps 88 [89]:30 [29]). John applies the phrase directly to the Messiah's own faithful witness, which led to establishment of his eternal kingship" (Beale 247). Indeed, the reference to "firstborn" in the psalm is directly associated not only with kingship but also with the highest kingship on the earth. That is exactly the kind of kingship John envisions for Jesus Christ here. John has skewed his grammar in order to shepherd his hearers and readers toward this very pointed connection. Now the actual content of the titles can have the force the visionary intended.

Witness is key, not only because of its lead position in the chain of three, but also because it follows up on John's opening three verses, which convey his entire work as the witness—that is, revelation—proclaimed by Jesus (see the

3. Allen D. Callahan, "The Language of the Apocalypse," *HTR* 88 (1995): 453–70.

comments on 1:1–2). The *kai* (and) that connects the two trailing titles is epex-egetical rather than correlative. An appropriate translation would be, "the first-born of the dead, who is the ruler of the kings of the earth." The entire phrase clarifies what it means for Jesus to be a faithful witness; the image of universal kingship clarifies what it means for this faithful witness to be firstborn of the dead. As God is ruler of all, *pantokratōr* (1:8), Jesus is ruler of the entire human realm. *This* is the revelation proclaimed by Jesus Christ.

In a cultural context where Rome already lays claim to ultimate kingship, it is also a revelation bound inevitably for trouble. Christ's kingship, by claiming to be the one abiding and universal kingship, necessarily *resists* any established rule making the same claim. In John's context, that rule would be Rome's.

What does such an interpretive perspective *do*? John's commendation of Jesus as the one who witnesses faithfully, even at the cost of his life (cf. John 18:33–19:16; 1 Tim 6:13), incites emulation. Christ-believers cannot be the firstborn of the dead, nor the ruler over the kings of the earth, but they can, like Antipas (Rev 2:13) and like John himself (1:2), be faithful witnesses to the tes-timony that Jesus himself proclaimed: God is the Almighty One, and Jesus Christ is God's coming king.

John follows up this combative description with an equally combative dox-ology. The first two rationales for human praise of Jesus Christ are his love and his ransoming of humans from sin because of that love. John's verbal use of the concept "love" (*agapaō*: 1:5; 3:9; 12:11; 20:9) is so sparse that one can hardly draw conclusive thoughts about it (even the noun form occurs only at 2:4, 19). Where Christ is the subject of the love (1:5; 3:9), the result is the salvation/vindication of Christ-believers. Where believers are the subject (12:11), John highlights their love for the lordship of Christ above even their own lives. It is this radical love that helps broker the conquest of the dragon. Love, then, as understood from the limited evidence John allows, is a primary motivation for the salvation/vindication and human participation in that victory. The expected goal for all believers is that they become "those who conquer" (2:7, 11, 17, 26; 3:5, 12, 21). Such conquest can only be achieved if humans love life less than the lordship of God and the Lamb.

John goes on to describe the salvation/vindication achieved by Christ as a ransoming from sin (cf. Isa 40:2). This is the only pairing of sin and redemp-tion language in the Apocalypse.[4] One wonders if, even here, redemption is really John's primary concern. He ties the release from sins to one of his most potent images: blood. Blood in Revelation symbolizes not sacrifice and atone-ment but execution and, as 12:11 illustrates, conquest (see the comment on 5:6; cf. 5:9, 12). The executed one ransoms as Moses ransomed Israel from Egypt

---

4. The only other mention of sin occurs at 18:4–5, with reference to Babylon's sins, and has nothing to do with the concept of redemption.

(note the exodus plague imagery, especially in the trumpet and bowl plague cycles), in a liberating rather than atoning sense.

To be sure, John expects repentance from sin. However, his remarks to the churches in chapters 2 and 3 indicate that he desires repentance from a particular kind of sin. He wants those who are accommodating themselves to cultic practices, social affiliations, economic buy-ins, and demonstrations of political loyalty that acknowledge, celebrate, and support the lordship of Rome to repent from such activity. Sin, then, is specifically tied to affiliation with Rome and the Roman imperial cult and its practices. By contrast, conquest behavior witnesses to—that is to say, promotes, celebrates, worships, and extends—the opposition lordship of God and Christ. John's hearers and readers are ransomed, set loose for this witnessing purpose in the same way that the people of Israel were ransomed by Moses so that they could acknowledge Yahweh's lordship. Highlighted here, then, is not atonement, but nonviolent resistance. Jesus looses (ransoms) believers from their sin (accommodation to the lordship of Rome) through a ministry of nonviolent resistance (witness to the lordship of God and his own connection with that lordship) that will become the model for their own witness, that is, ministries of resistance.

[6] The third reason for praise extends the Exodus imagery. Christ establishes believers as a reign of priests to God (cf. Exod 19:6), a theme that is reengaged at the end of the book (22:5). At 5:10, the establishment of this reign is the third reason for acknowledging the Lamb as worthy. Those who are redeemed by Christ's blood have been liberated for a very social purpose. Here on earth, they will be established as a reign that will serve neither Rome nor any Greco-Roman divinity, but God. Where Rome is concerned, any such reign is unauthorized. Any such unauthorized reign is by definition a counterreign and therefore a political provocation that Rome *must* (cf. 1:1) necessarily challenge.

John specifies the relationship between God and Christ as that of father and son. The *kai* (and) that connects "God" and "his Father" is epexegetical; John means to say: God, *who is* his Father. John continues the close relating of God to Jesus Christ with the final refrain of the doxology. The glory and might ascribed rightfully to God (4:11; 5:13) also belong properly to Christ (cf. 5:12).

The concluding "amen" affirms that what has been declared in the doxology about Christ is true and valid (see the comment on 3:14).

[7] The affirmation of the amen in v. 6 is immediately corroborated by the particle *idou* that opens v. 7, a combination of Dan 7:13 and Zech 12:10 that was also celebrated at Matt 24:30 (cf. Mark 14:62; Matt 26:64; Luke 22:69). Aune (1:53) points out helpfully that in the twenty-six occurrences of the particle in Revelation, there are two different, though related meanings. When used in speech (1:7, 18; 2:10, 22; 3:8, 9 [2x], 20; 5:5; 9:12; 11:14; 21:3, 5), the form affirms and validates whatever statement it precedes and should be translated "indeed." When used in narrative (4:1, 2; 5:6; 6:2, 5, 8, 12; 7:9; 12:3; 14:1, 14; 15:5; 19:11), it

draws attention to the material it introduces and is best translated "look" or "behold." Here it follows up the "amen" of v. 6, with an antiphonal affirmation.

Indeed, this Christ, who is the appropriate subject of the 1:5b–6 doxology, will soon demonstrate his eschatological bona fides by coming with the clouds. This highly anticipated event answers the implicit question raised by the comment that the time is near (1:3). What time is near? The time of Christ's coming, his Parousia (see the comment on 19:11–16). In Dan 7:13–14 one like a son of man, a child of humanity, comes to claim a lordship and dominion on earth that, according to Rev 1:5, belongs to Jesus Christ. The cloud reference indicates that the royal coming is for the purpose of judgment (see the comments on 10:1 and 14:14).

With his remark that every eye will see this coming, John alludes to Zech 12:10. In the Old Testament account, the enemy nations would mourn for (*kopsontai ep' auton*, the same idiom that occurs at Rev 1:7) the house of David, which they had pierced, and the people of God would be redeemed after repenting of their "piercing" of God's servant. John's additions of "every eye" and "tribes *of the earth*" are his way of universalizing the account. All the world will participate in the vindicating move to lordship that Christ's coming represents.

Even those who pierced Christ will witness and acknowledge his vindicating lordship (cf. 1:5; 5:9). Once again John's politics rise through his cultic claims. The Romans who pierced him, the Romans who now lay illegitimate claim to cosmic and historical lordship, are hereby forewarned that even they will come to see that true lordship resides in the hands of the very one they thought they had destroyed.

At the end of the verse, John's universalism (addressed in the commentary on 5:9–10; 12:5; 15:3, 4; 21:3, 14, 24, 26; 22:2) pushes him beyond the Romans. Every tribe will mourn on account of this pierced, coming, reigning Christ. While tribes are first mentioned positively in Revelation (5:9; 7:9) as those ransomed by the Lamb, in the latter portions of the narrative (11:9; 13:7; 14:6), they are clearly designated as those who refuse to acknowledge God's and Christ's lordship and are therefore due judgment. If John is alluding, however, to the tribe reference in Gen 12:3 (cf. 28:14), where blessing would accrue through God's servant to the tribes of earth, the mourning in Rev 1:7 may be the genuine distress that motivates and thus precedes repentance, a theme the seer clearly emphasizes throughout the narrative (e.g., 8:7–13; 9:20–21; 11:1, 13; 15:4; 22:11). Indeed, the Zech 12:10 context suggests repentance, as do the contextual implications drawn from John's use of the "tribe" metaphor in the early part of his work. Beale is therefore right to conclude that here "repentant Gentiles are viewed as fulfilling the Zechariah prophecy at the second coming of Christ" (197). To this suggestion, John shouts "Amen!"

**[8]** John closes his salutation by returning to the threefold designation of God that was prominent in the salutation's opening (v. 4). He also makes several notable adjustments. First, he makes the tripartite title part of a quotation from God, one of only two God quotes in the entire work (21:5–8). Second, God's quotation begins with the powerful Exod 3:14 words of self-identifying lordship: "I am" (see the discussion of 1:4). In Isa 41:4; 44:6; and 48:12, these words not only identify God as Lord but also connect this lordship to what is for John an equivalent identifier: "first and last." John builds upon his allusion to Isaiah's claim of "first and last" with his third adjustment. God declares, as God does in the only other place where God speaks in the text of Revelation (21:6), that God is the "Alpha and the Omega" (see the comment on 21:6). These references to the first and last letters of the Greek alphabet symbolize God's role as the one who exclusively exists at the beginning and end of all time. This title, applied in the epilogue also to Christ (22:13), implies that the one who presides at the start and close of time is rightly recognized as the Lord of everything that occurs through time. In the final adjustment, God is the *pantokratōr* (Almighty One). John applies the title to God multiple times: 4:8; 11:17; 15:3; 16:7, 14; 19:6, 15; 21:22 (see the extended discussion at 11:17 and 15:3).

### 1:9–3:22 A Word from the Lord: Ethical Instructions to the Seven Churches

#### *1:9–20 John Introduces Himself and Christ*

9 I, John, your brother and colleague in the persecution and reign and non-violent resistance in Jesus, was on the island of Patmos because of the word of God, which is[a] the testimony proclaimed by Jesus. 10 I was in the[b] spirit on the Lord's Day and I heard behind me a foreboding voice, like a trumpet, 11 saying,[c] "Write what you see in a scroll and send it to the seven churches: to Ephesus, and to Smyrna, and to Pergamum, and to Thyatira, and to Sardis, and to Philadelphia, and to Laodicea." 12 Then I turned to see the voice[d] that was speaking to me, and when I turned I saw seven golden lampstands, 13 and one like a[e] child of humanity[f] was in the midst of the lampstands, wearing a long robe and a golden sash wrapped around his chest. 14 The white hair on his head was as white wool, like snow, and his eyes were like a flame of fire, 15 and his feet were like bronze as refined[g] in a furnace, and his voice was like the sound of many waters, 16 and he had in his right hand seven stars, and out of his mouth went a sharp, two-edged sword, and his countenance shone as the sun in its full force. 17 When I saw him, I fell at his feet as though dead, and he put his right hand on me, saying, "Stop being afraid; I am the first and the last 18 and the living one. I was dead but[h] indeed[i] I am alive forever, and I have the keys of Death and Hades. 19 Therefore, write about what you saw, what is, and what is about to take place after this. 20 As for the mystery of the seven

stars thatʲ you saw in my right hand and the seven golden lampstands: the seven stars are the angels of the seven churches, and the seven lampstands are the seven churches."

a. The *kai* (and) is epexegetical rather than correlative; the second clause clarifies the first (cf. 1:2).

b. Though "spirit" lacks a definite article, classical and later Koine Greek allowed for prepositional phrases that did not use the article but could still presume it (Aune 1:63). John could well, then, have intended the Spirit of God. More likely, he refers to an inspired prophetic trance whose contours were well enough known that he could speak about it in an idiomatic way (as in 4:2; 17:3; 21:10).

c. The participle is in the genitive because of its proximity and relationship to "trumpet," which is in the genitive. Grammatically, though, the participle's referent is "voice," which is in the accusative. The participle therefore should be in the accusative case; $\aleph^2$ makes just this correction.

d. A case of metonymy, where the voice represents the person issuing it.

e. Because *homoios* (like, as) is generally followed by a noun in the dative case, the occurrence of "son" in the accusative is regarded by BDAG (567) as a solecism. Manuscripts A C 1006 1611 1854 2053 2062 2351 𝔐ᴬ; Irˡᵃᵗ provide the more appropriate "son" in the dative. Because the accusative is the more problematic reading, the accusative, supported by 𝕽 1841 2050 2329 𝔐ᴷ is to be preferred. The accusative form of "son" was no doubt caused by an attraction of the noun to the accusative, masculine form of *homoion* before it.

f. While "son of man" is an accurate literal translation, the more inclusive "child of humanity" will be used.

g. The genitive, feminine participle does not match any noun in the sentence and is therefore irregular. This difficult reading (supported by A C), though, is to be preferred, because its existence explains the corrective alternatives: 𝕽 2050 2053 2062 *pc* Irᵃʳᵐ, ˡᵃᵗ ᵛⁱᵈ offer a masculine ending that matches the masculine "furnace"; 𝔐 syʰᵐᵍ offer a masculine plural ending that would agree with the masculine "feet."

h. An adversative *kai*.

i. The particle *idou* reinforces the claim—"first and last"—made prior to it.

j. The relative pronoun agrees with its antecedent, "stars," in gender and number, but not case. In such a phrase, the relative pronoun is often attracted to the case of its antecedent, and 1006 1841 2351 𝔐ᴷ make this adjustment.

**[9]** For the third time in the opening nine verses, John self-identifies. It is particularly intriguing that he names himself at the start of each of the primary units of the chapter (vv. 1–3: v. 1; vv. 4–8: v. 4; vv. 9–20: v. 9). He authenticates the content of each section with his personal authority. Church members can trust his description of revelation and its chain of transmission because it has come to them through him. They can trust the doxological claims about Christ because it is he who praises with them. In offering what amounts to a narrative signature, he vouches for it all. Both he and Christ self-identify in the epilogue for the same authorizing reason (22:8, 16).

Though John is a community leader, he is also one with the Asia Minor Christ-believers. He has already indicated this equality by introducing himself as a servant among many other servants (1:1). John reinforces that collegial relationship with the filial metaphor. He does not use the term *adelphos* (brother/sister) often, but when he does, it is at critical points that indicate a nonhierarchical relationship of witness. At 6:11, all are kin in the faith who suffer because of their witness to the lordship of God and Christ. At 12:10, those same kin-witnesses conquer the dragon because of that testimony. Even angels, when they are operating for God, operate not as powers over believers, but as fellow-servants in the faith (19:9–10; 22:8–9).

These brothers and sisters are colleagues in the persecution (cf. Phil 4:14). The presence of the definite article suggests that "the" persecution was a well-recognized event. Scholars, though, have rightly pressed that there was no longstanding or strategically organized system of persecution during the time of Domitian's reign (81–96 C.E.), when John wrote. What kind of persecution, then, does he envision?

In a reconstruction of the social-historical situation of the Apocalypse that represents today's prevailing scholarly thinking, Loren Johns argues that John was writing about the understandable "*expectation* of persecution rather than the present *experience* of persecution."[5] The members of the churches forestalled that persecution by accommodating themselves to the social, cultural, and religious expectations that centered around Greco-Roman pagan and imperial worship. As long as they did not witness openly for the exclusive lordship of Christ, as long as they blended into a world that did not recognize that lordship, they would be physically, socially, politically, and economically secure. It is no wonder, then, that these believers were "probably succumbing to the temptation not only of maintaining a low profile as Christians in such contexts, but also of paying token acknowledgement to the pagan gods (whether to Caesar or the patron gods of the guilds). As also in the other churches, the motive for this was probably fear of persecution, especially economic ostracism" (Beale 276). The problem therefore lay with "the" imminent persecution John's colleagues knew would erupt if they lived out the kind of nonaccommodating Christianity that he himself professed.

If John was asking his people to stand up (i.e., witness) and thus stand out in a world they had accepted and that had accepted them, he was essentially telling them to go out and pick a fight! He was ordering them to declare that they were now nonaccommodating Christ-believers who could no longer participate in a world that had not previously noticed them since they had heretofore been accommodating to it. In a classic "Don't ask, don't tell" (that I'm a Christ-believer) kind of environment, John was essentially ordering his followers to be

---

5. Johns (122) points to 2:10–11; 7:13–14; 11:7–9; 12:11; 16:6; 17:6; 18:24; 19:2; 20:4–6.

about the business of telling on themselves, with full knowledge of the kind of repercussions such telling would bring. He was asking them to come screaming out of the Christian closet, knowing that it would solicit the same consequence it had attracted to the one true and faithful witness: execution (see the comments on 7:14 and 13:10).

Because John firmly believed that witness would not only draw persecution but also effect conquest (12:11; cf. 2:7, 11, 17, 26; 3:5, 12, 21), it is not surprising that he would offer here the odd pairing of persecution and reign. Christ had made believers a reign of priests (1:6); they consummate that reign, inaugurated by Christ's blood, through the power of their own stubborn witness (12:11) to the lordship of this crucified one. No wonder, then, that John climaxes his enumeration of collegial traits by pointing to their *hypomonē*, a term often translated "endurance," but in John's context has more the sense of nonviolent resistance (see the discussion of 13:10). John is not asking his followers simply to endure the persecution that comes their way; he instead is championing an active response of faith that resists both the belief in the lordship of Rome and the hostile practices Rome wields to propagandize that belief. Though he never asks them to fight with violence, he does urge them, like Jesus and himself, to fight.

John's own location and the reason for it are signs that he practices what he preaches. Patmos is a small island that measures approximately 30 miles in circumference and sits some 37 miles west-southwest of Miletus and 75 miles west of Ephesus. Though it seems clear that the Romans did not use the island as a penal colony (Aune [1:78] argues that there is no historical evidence that anyone was banished there), there is debate as to whether the Romans used it as a place of exile (Boring argues that troublemakers were sent there [*Revelation* 81]). Ascertaining truth in the matter may be neither possible nor necessary. Location is not the seer's crucial point. The issue is that he had been removed from their presence because of his witnessing activities on behalf of the lordship of God and Christ. The location of his exile was not as important for his rhetorical purpose as its reality and its rationale.

He stresses that rationale at the climactic close of the verse. Whenever he uses the phrase "because of" (*dia* with a following object in the accusative case), he does so to refer to the result of an action (Boring, *Revelation*, 82; Aune 1:clxxvii–clxxviii). John has been banished to Patmos as a direct result of his preaching the word of God, which is the testimony proclaimed by Jesus (see the discussion of 1:1–2), that is, the revelation that God and Christ are Lord.

**[10–11]** When John declares that he was in the spirit (cf. Ezek 3:12), he speaks not about an ecstatic experience but a prophetic one. His primary focus is not spiritual fervor but ethical awareness. God's energizing of his human spirit enabled him to comprehend God's revolutionary message of lordship and the behavioral expectations that message raised for him and the people of the Asia Minor churches (see the comment on 4:2–3).

The ambiguous reference to the "Lord's Day" applies to Sunday, the first day of the week, when Jesus was raised from the dead (cf. Acts 20:7; 1 Cor 16:2; *Did.* 14:1). Christ-believers had taken to holding their worship of God and Christ as Lord on this day, a recent custom John defiantly adhered to even while in exile.

The "great voice" John hears registers like a trumpet. "Great voice" is a literary cipher for John: it anticipates an urgent, dramatic message that generally bears the foreboding tone of impending judgment (see the discussion of 7:2). The trumpet comparison brings to mind the theophany of Exod 19:16, where the cloud, thunder, and lightning on Sinai were accompanied by the foreboding blast of a trumpet. Over the centuries, Israel ritualized the trumpet sound in the blowing of the shofar, a ram's horn, in both battle and worship (see the comment on 8:2). A similar trumpet-like voice invites John to come up to heaven for a peek into the throne room at 4:1. In 1:10–12, this voice is identified as that of Christ, the one like a child of humanity.

The voice directs John to write the visions he will see in a scroll (see the discussion of 5:1; cf. Isa 30:8). The command to write occurs often in the work (Rev 1:19; 2:1, 8, 12, 18; 3:1, 7, 14; 14:13; 19:9; 21:5). While the directives in chapters 2 and 3 refer to the specific letters John was to write to each of the seven churches, the command here, like the other remaining ones, probably has in view the entire Apocalypse.

The seven churches, already mentioned as the recipients of John's letter (1:4), are now identified by name.

**[12–13]** The throne room decor, reminiscent of Dan 7:9–10, is illuminating. John first notices the seven lampstands, which symbolize the seven churches (1:20). Clearly, they are crafted from the Exodus image of the stand of seven lamps made from pure gold, designed for placement in the tabernacle of the Lord (Exod 25:31–37; 37:17–24; cf. Num 8:1–4). The prophet Zechariah also envisioned a golden lampstand with seven lamps (4:2). That John also had Zechariah's vision in mind is clear from the use he later makes of the two olive trees that flank the lampstand (Zech 4:3, 14); in chapter 11, John draws directly from this vision for constructing the portrait of his two witnesses. It is unclear whether John intends to say that each of his seven stands has seven lamps, as the Exodus and Zechariah menorahs would have had, or whether each of his stands has a single lamp. Given that he is building from the prophetic images, he probably pictures each stand as a menorah, despite the fact that such a constellation would have confused the numerical point he was trying to make. One thing is clear: John deploys the number "seven" in order to draw an explicit connection between the spirits of God before the throne—that is, God's Holy Spirit (see the comment on 1:4; cf. Zech 4:6)—and the seven churches symbolized by the seven lampstands. The lamps, meaning the churches, are fired by the power of God's Holy Spirit.

One like a child of humanity, a figure obviously drawn from the characteri-zation in Dan 7:13–14; 10:15–21, walks among the lampstands (Rev 2:1). Two points are important about this child of humanity; one is relational, the other concerns identity. Though the identity of Daniel's messianic figure was uncer-tain (the people Israel? the archangel Michael, who represents Israel? a human individual?), for John he is certainly the faithful witness, Jesus Christ. Like the Daniel figure, Christ comes with the clouds (1:7; Dan 7:13) and is the true Lord (1:5–6; Dan 7:14). The relational point is that this child of humanity walks among the lampstands. The symbolism is clear; these churches, who are called to the counterwitness of Jesus' kingship and are therefore destined for perse-cution (1:9), are not alone. Jesus, who is both their priest and their king, is with them. His distinctive dress corresponds to his dual function. The long robe (cf. Dan 10:5; Ezek 9:2, 11) resembles Aaron's priestly garment (Exod 28:4).[6] The golden sash (for priestly implications, see Exod 39:29) worn across the chest (cf. 15:6) is the accoutrement of kings (cf. 1 Macc 10:89).

[14] The child of humanity's hair, which is as white as snow, has the texture of wool. The description reminds hearers and readers of Daniel's description of the Ancient of Days (Dan 7:9; see also *1 En.* 46.1; 71.10; cf. 106.5–6). John's intention is clear: he is indissolubly linking the identities of God and Christ. They, like their lordship, are one. The hair's texture is interesting for another reason. In the cosmopolitan Roman Empire (and no doubt in Daniel's context as well), where people with hair like wool (e.g., Africans), were well known, it is interesting that Christ (and the Ancient of Days before him) is depicted this way, rather than with the straight hair commonly associated with those of Euro-pean descent. The Gospels do not give any physical descriptions of Jesus; Rev-elation gives just this one. It is provocative, to say the least.

His eyes are like flames of fire. Operating from the Dan 10:6 depiction of a child of humanity, and the Dan 7:9–10 accounting of God's fiery presence, John uses this description to cultivate an image of judgment. That concept is rein-forced when he recalls the fiery eyes at 2:18, just before he threatens with judg-ment Jezebel and the Thyatirans who follow her, and again at 19:12, where the rider on the dazzling horse operates as cosmic judge.

[15] Christ's feet of burnished bronze (or copper) have the aesthetic appeal of metal refined in a furnace. The seer continues to work from the Daniel account of a messianic leader who has anything but clay feet (Dan 10:6; cf. Ezek 1:7). At 2:18 and 10:1, similar depictions resurrect the theme of judgment.

---

6. Though the LXX of Daniel uses *byssinos*, an adjective that refers to a garment made from linen, the Ezekiel account uses *podērēs* (long robe), the same term utilized by John to describe the garment worn by the child of humanity. Interestingly enough, however, both the Daniel and the Ezekiel terms refer back to the same Hebrew term: *bad*. The intended garment seems in both cases, therefore, to be a robe.

The powerful, trumpet-like voice (1:10) is said now to have the volume of many waters (cf. Dan 10:6). In Ezek 1:24, the wings of the living creatures that guard the throne produce this same sound effect, as does the movement of God's glory in Ezek 43:2. In John's own work, at 14:2, the voice of heaven carries with the same force, as do the voices crying "Hallelujah!" at 19:6. In each case, the sound is connected to the moving of God's judgment, an event that will also bring salvation to those allied with God.

[16] The earthbound Christ (1:12) holds seven stars in his right hand. According to v. 20, the seven stars are the seven patron angels of the seven churches (vv. 4, 11). Somewhere between 81 and 84 C.E., the emperor Domitian minted coins with the image of his dead, infant son standing astride the earth and playing with seven stars. Since the stars were thought to control human life, the one who controlled the stars had ultimate power (Reddish 42–43). For the Romans, such power lay in imperial hands. John's counterprograming gave the seven stars, and the fullness of cosmic power symbolized by them, to Christ. Human destiny lies with Christ, not with the power of Rome or the grip of astrological fate.

Out of his mouth issues a sharp, two-edged sword. Cutting both ways, it strikes the failures of the faithful (2:12, 16) as surely as it gouges those who would harm them (19:15, 21). The mouth location indicates that this sword is Christ's word of universal, impartial judgment (cf. Heb 4:12). As is the case at 19:15, 21, the imagery builds from the depiction of the sharp prophetic word of judgment in Isa 49:2 (cf. Isa 11:4). Witness language is the cutting, prophetic word of God's lordship. That word is the weapon to be wielded against the powers that tout and enforce the lordship of Rome. The sword, then, is not a literal reference to violence, but a metaphor of nonviolent resistance (see esp. the comment on 12:15, with its discussion of the combat between God's people and the draconian forces as a battle of two opposing "words").

Christ's shining face anticipates the later discussion of the judgment-oriented angel whose beaming face shines like the sun (10:1). Daniel 10:6 pictured a child of humanity's face shining like the sun. At Matt 17:2, Jesus' transfigured face was said to so shine. John clearly escalates eschatological matters here; Christ's entire countenance has a blinding impact.

[17] John is so overwhelmed that he falls to his feet in a trancelike state. The seer has a penchant for going to his knees in the presence of the divine. Later, 19:10 and 22:8–9 will see him consciously falling prostrate before angelic messengers. In those future instances, he will be chided. Here, given that he is responding to Christ, the fear and awe that push him to the ground seem more narratively appropriate (cf. Matt 28:4). Historically, his response is similar to that of the prophet Ezekiel, who fell to his knees at the appearance of God's glory in the sky (Ezek 1:28).

As at Dan 8:18, where Daniel fell to the ground in a trance before the angel Gabriel, John finds his empowerment to rise after he is touched by the figure who induces the faint. Christ explains that he is, like God, the first and the last (1:4, 8; 2:8; 22:13; cf. Isa 44:6; 48:12). (On the use of "I am" in making his case, particularly in reference to "first and last" imagery, see the comments on 1:4, 8.) Knowing Christ's status should relieve John's fears about Roman claims to ultimate lordship and Rome's oppressive enforcement of those claims (cf. 2:10). Rome should not be feared, because Christ is the true Lord. Christ's counsel corresponds to God's advice that Jacob should not fear because the God who forms humans in the womb, and was therefore in charge of history, had chosen Israel (Isa 44:2).

[18] The forceful "I am" declaration that concluded v. 17 runs into and initiates v. 18. John punctuates each of the three descriptors that follow the "I am" with a definite article that signals a functional equality between them. The one who is *the* first and *the* last is also *the* living one. To the witless hearer and reader, the claim seems ridiculously redundant. Christ's "alive-ness" must be understood within the context of resurrection, which John previewed at 1:5 with his claim that Christ is "firstborn of the dead" and immediately clarifies here when he quotes Christ as saying, "I was dead, but indeed, I am alive forever." There are two key points: (1) though dead, he was raised, and (2) he was raised to eternal rather than historical life (on God as one with eternal life, see 4:9; cf. Deut 32:40; Sir 18:1).

The consequence of Christ's resurrection goes beyond his eternal status. Christ also claims now to be uniquely empowered. Death is the force that snatches the essence of human life. Hades is the place where that essence is eternally warehoused (see the commentary on 6:8; 20:13–14). As such, Hades is equivalent to the abyss (see the discussion of 9:1–2). The two forces are presented together because they operate in a grim, caging partnership in the Apocalypse (cf. Job 38:17, which speaks of the gates of death). Through God's power, though, Christ got away. He did not escape empty-handed. He absconded with their keys and now promises to use them as the ultimate ransom tool (1:5b; 20:13). His possession of the keys represents his ability to control the process of judgment and salvation, to decide who obtains eschatological relationship with God and who does not, an ability that parallels his holding of the key of David in 3:7.

Why is this point about Jesus holding the keys of Death and Hades particularly important for John's hearers and readers? John knows that punishment will occur if his followers do indeed witness for the lordship of God and Christ in a world hell-bent on institutionalizing the lordship of Rome. The ultimate punishment would be death (2:13), certainly a potent deterrent to the discipleship behavior John exhorts. Rome's greatest power is its ability to consign Christ-believers to death. John mitigates that power with his declaration, made in the vision by Christ himself, that Christ has the keys that will release persons from death into eternal life.

**[19]** Just as Isaiah was told to declare what he had seen and heard (Isa 48:6), so John is now ordered to publish his visionary accounts. Already, at 1:11, he had been given this same order. It is now reinforced in a more comprehensive way. He is to write about "what you saw," "what is," and "what is about to take place after this."

"What you saw" probably pertains to the visions about Christ and his lordship that have just immediately taken place (1:12–18). The "therefore" that initiates the verse sets vv. 19–20 apart from that vision of Christ's lordship, which is now, though a recent past account, nonetheless a past account. These last two verses subsequently operate as a discussion of the consequences that develop from that lordship symbolism.

"What is" pertains more broadly to the threatening situation that looms over anyone who would dare to proclaim the lordship of God and Christ. As chapter 12 indicates (esp. 12:17), the draconian forces of imperial lordship hunt the churches. This mythical reality comes to historical ground in chapters 2 and 3, which address the circumstances daily faced by the members of the seven Asia Minor churches.

"What is about to take place" pertains to the certain reprisals that will come when Christ-believers "out themselves" as Christ-believers by testifying demonstrably to his lordship. The "after this" that closes the verse, then, does not refer as much to "this apocalyptic age" as it does to the specific circumstances surrounding the aftermath of John's visions of Christ's lordship and the people's testimony to it (for future discussion of this understanding of the limits of the phrase "after this," see the comment on 4:1).

**[20]** This verse is self-explanatory; it refers back to material already presented and clarifies it. The seven stars are explained as the seven patron angels of the seven churches. Most likely, John is building from the traditional Jewish idea that each people or nation had an angel ruling over it as a patron or representative. To address them is a way of addressing the community as a whole (2:1, 8, 12, 18; 3:1, 7, 14). On lampstands and churches, see the discussion of 1:12–13.

### 2:1–3:22 Letters to Seven Churches of Asia

The seven letters of chapters 2 and 3 have a mixed genre background. John clearly draws from the Jewish prophetic pronouncement (cf. his description of his book as word of prophecy: 1:3; 22:7, 10, 18, 19). As the prophets did when they delivered their word from Yahweh, he initiates his Christ messages with an authoritative "Thus says . . . " formula (see, e.g., Gen 45:9; Exod 4:22; 5:1; 7:17; Josh 24:2; Isa 1:24; 3:16; Jer 2:5; Ezek 2:4; 3:11; Amos 1:6, 9, 11; Mic 2:3; 3:5; Zech 1:3, 4, 14, 16, 17; cf. Acts 21:11). Greco-Roman influence is also significant. The "thus says . . ." formula was just as typical of imperial decrees of the period. The feel John inspires by establishing a link between the imperial edict and his own letters is consistent with the combative political tone he strikes throughout. "The author's use of the royal/imperial edict form is part of his strategy to polarize God/Jesus and the Roman emperor. . . . In his role as the eternal sovereign and king of kings, Jesus is presented as issuing solemn and authoritative edicts befitting his status" (Aune 1:129).

The letters' common structural format suggests that they never circulated independently of each other. Each letter begins with the fictive notice that it is addressed to the patron angel of the designated church community. A "write" command always follows. Christ, the sender of the letter, is then introduced via the formula "Thus says. . . ." He is described with one of the characteristics attached to the one like a child of humanity in 1:12–20. John subsequently launches into the body of the letter with an "I know" statement that reveals a critical state of affairs in the church. Christ's knowledge initiates a word of commendation (2:2, 9, 13, 19; 3:8) or one of condemnation (3:1, 15). In only two cases is the message completely laudatory (Smyrna and Philadelphia). John then adds Christ's exhortation, which challenges church members to maintain the endorsed behavior and/or repent of the condemned behavior. Afterward, Christ implores that they listen to the word the Spirit speaks to the churches. Finally (except for the last four letters, where the command to listen comes last and the promise of reward precedes it), Christ offers a reward to the one who "conquers."

### 2:1–7  *To Ephesus: You Can Be Too Good*

1 "To the angel of the church in Ephesus, write: Thus says the one who holds the seven stars in his right hand, the one who walks among the seven golden lampstands: 2 'I know your works, which are[a] your struggle and your nonviolent resistance. Because you cannot bear evil people, you tested the ones who call themselves apostles but are not and you found them to be liars. 3 You demonstrate nonviolent resistance; that is,[b] you bear up[c] for the sake of my name and have not grown weary. 4 But I have against you that you have forsaken your first love. 5 Therefore, remember how far you have fallen and repent and do your former works. If not, I will come against you[d] and remove your lampstand from its place, unless you repent. 6 But this you do have: you hate the works of the Nicolaitans, which I also hate. 7 Let the one who has an ear hear what the Spirit is saying to the churches. I will give[e] the one who conquers permission to eat from the tree of life, which is in the paradise of God.'"

a. The *kai* (and) is epexegetical, i.e., explanatory.

b. The *kai* again is epexegetical.

c. The fact that the aorist form of *bastazō* operates in conjunction with and under the linguistic supervision of the present tense of *echō* (translated "[you] demonstrate" here) indicates that it should be taken as denoting a continuing state.

d. A dative of disadvantage.

e. The verb *dōsō*, used similarly at 2:10, 17 and 3:21, indicates divine prerogative.

Ephesus was one of the most important cities of Asia Minor. Municipally, it housed the residence of the Roman governor. Commercially, though it now sits some six miles inland, at the end of the first century it was a productive port. Religiously, it was a hotbed of pagan worship. The apostle Paul first visited the city briefly in the company of Priscilla and Aquila, whom he left there (Acts 18:19–21). Later, according to Acts 19:8–10, he operated in the city for close to three years (cf. 20:31). It was during this stay that he wrote his Letters to the Corinthian congregation. The apostle encountered difficulty because of conflicts with artisans crafting images of the Greek goddess Artemis (19:23–41). The Roman imperial cult was also influential; the divination of Julius Caesar had been established in 29 B.C.E. at the direction of his heir, Octavian: Caesar Augustus. Cities granted the privilege to build temples to patron deities were given the title *neōkoros*, or "temple keeper" (19:35). Ephesus received this honor four times, on one significant occasion (ca. 90 C.E.) for the right to honor Domitian, the emperor who ruled when John wrote (Aune 1:139).

[2:1] As he does at the beginning of each of the letters, Christ orders John to write to the church's patron angel (see the comment on 1:20). The letter must begin with "thus says . . . ," a Hebrew prophetic formula that directly links Christ with Yahweh, the formulation's rightful subject. Christ next describes himself as the one holding the seven stars (see 1:16, 20) and walking among the seven golden lampstands (see 1:12, 13, 20).

[2] Works are an important concept in Revelation. John uses the term 20 times; 12 of those occurrences are crammed into chapters 2 and 3. On almost all of those occasions, works are connected to judgment (cf. 2:23; 18:6; 20:12, 13; 22:12). One's eschatological relationship with God (or lack thereof) depends on the number and caliber of one's works.

John connects and therefore identifies works with the activity of witnessing to the lordship of God and Christ (see the commentary on 3:1, 2–4, 5, 7–8; 6:11; 9:20–21; 10:4; 14:13; 22:14). Christ develops this connection here by associating the word with two clarifying terms: *kopos* (struggle) and *hypomonē* (nonviolent resistance; see the discussion of 1:9). The *kai* ("and," translated here "which are") that links the clarifying terms is epexegetical; it operates as a clarifying connective. Christ means to say: "I know your works, which are your struggle and your nonviolent resistance. . . ." The packaging suggests that struggle and nonviolent resistance, like works, refer to witnessing activity. John's later use of the terms confirms this thinking. In his only other use of "struggle," he places it in a context where works and the concept of witness are integrally related (see the comment on 14:13). At 1:9 and 13:10, the work of nonviolent resistance and the concept of witnessing are also linked. This same packaging occurs in the opening of Paul's First Letter to the Thessalonians (1:3). Perhaps the grouping indicates, as scholars suggest, that John and Paul are operating from a traditional understanding about the relationship of the terms.

Christ praises the witness work of the Ephesians because it materializes in an important way: they do not tolerate the evil ones who call themselves apostles. Having tested them (cf. 1 John 4:1), the Ephesians recognized them for the liars that they were. John does not use the term "apostle" often. It occurs here, at 18:20, and at 21:14. Revelation 21:14 refers to the twelve historical apostles of Jesus. Clearly, they are in view here, though John more likely intends communal leaders, like servants and prophets (see the discussion of 18:20). The apostle, too, is an authority figure whose words are worthy of obedience, and whose lifestyle is worthy of emulation. These "apostles" no doubt were prophetic figures who entered the community in the same manner that false (according to Paul) apostles entered Corinth following Paul's departure and preached a different gospel than the one he had himself taught (2 Cor 11 and 12; esp. 2 Cor 11:13, where Paul uses the term "false apostle").

How would the Ephesians have tested them? The contextual stress on witnessing suggests that they evaluated communal leaders by judging whether they accommodated themselves to the lordship claims of Rome or defiantly proclaimed the lordship claims of God and Christ. Prophetic leaders like Balaam (2:14), Jezebel (2:20–23), and others who followed the ways of the Nicolaitans (2:6, 15) might claim apostolic status. Nevertheless, because they counseled accommodation with economic, social, political, and cultic activities that either implied or declared outright the legitimacy of imperial lordship, their self-assertions were a lie.

[3] The Ephesians have demonstrated nonviolent resistance, which is to say (another epexegetical use of *kai* [and]), they stood behind Christ's name—that is, his lordship (on John's connection of "name" with the act of witnessing, see the comments on 2:13; 3:8; 13:6)—despite the consequences (persecution; cf. 6:9–11). Christ makes his very serious point in an almost entertaining way with two wordplays that cross over from v. 2 to v. 3. In v. 2, using the verb *bastazō* (bear, "endure"), he has already announced that the Ephesians do not tolerate false prophets. Appealing to the same verb, he now celebrates that the people who *do not* bear with evil persons *do* bear up for Christ. The wordplay climaxes in the second half of the verse with the verb *kopiaō* (grow weary, work hard) which is tied to the noun *kopos* (labor, struggle) in v. 2. The Ephesians do not grow weary in their wearying struggle to testify to the lordship of God and Christ.

[4] Despite his praise of the Ephesians, Christ is concerned, for they have abandoned their first love. The loss of love should be interpreted within the broader context of the letter's primary theme: witness to the lordship of God and Christ. Given that the only other time John uses "love" (2:19), he also connects it to "works" and therefore makes it a defining characteristic of resisting

witness, one might reasonably conclude that Christ was annoyed because the church had developed some sort of "works litmus test" to determine which efforts of resistance, such as a love for Christ's lordship, were worthy and which were not. Faithful believers were to be celebrated because of the work of witnessing; false apostles were to be tested against it. Apparently, the Ephesians became *too* discerning. Preoccupation with the work of love for the lordship of Christ overwhelmed an allegiance to the first love they had once demonstrated toward each other. In the same way that a healthy cell can metastasize into a cancerous one, their commendable insight degenerated into discrimination. They segregated those who were deemed workers of appropriate righteousness from those determined to be unrighteous. Once known as a loving community, they had suddenly become a policing one. Ephesian faith had become a matter of Ephesian quality control. Assessment became more important than love.

[5] Christ's counsel could not be clearer. Using the same command he will again issue at 3:3, he orders the Ephesians to remember what they were doing when they demonstrated their first love. Here and at 3:3, repentance is preceded by and no doubt based upon this remembrance. Only after the Ephesians remember both the witnessing *and* the loving behavior that stood them in right relationship with their fellow church members, and therefore with Christ, can they turn back to it. At 2:16, the command to repent occurs without being introduced by the exhortation to remember, but there it is followed up, as are the repent commands here and at 3:3, with the threat of judgment. That judgment is expressed through the imagery of the lampstands that Christ used to open his remarks in v. 1. The one who walks in the midst of the lampstands and cares for them will remove this one, this Ephesian church, from its place with the others, and thus its place of eschatological relationship with God and Christ, unless the people whom it represents repent. Repentance is a key theme throughout Revelation (see 1:7; 8:7–13; 9:20–21; 11:1, 13; 15:4; 16:9, 11; 22:11); it is a response to God's forgiving love, the kind of love the Ephesians no longer demonstrate toward one another.

[6] Christ returns to a mood of praise when he commends the Ephesians for hating the works of the Nicolaitans (see the discussion of 2:14–16).[1] Psalm 139:21 expresses a similar sentiment of joy at the people's hatred of an evil that God hates. By definition, hated works must be the opposite of the witnessing works, which Christ favors. They are acts of accommodation to economic, social, political, and cultic practices that promote the lordship of Rome or give direct testimony to that lordship.

[7] Christ closes with a rare statement that recalls the Jesus of the Gospel tradition. The exhortation, "Let the one who has an ear hear [cf. Matt 11:15;

---

1. Acts 6:5 references a certain Nicolaus, listed with Stephen, as one of a select group of deacons. Whether he has any relation to this group is impossible to determine.

13:9, 43; Mark 4:9, 23; Luke 8:8; 14:35] what the Spirit says to the churches," repeats at the close of each of the seven letters (2:11, 17, 29; 3:6, 13, 22; cf. 13:9). In the Synoptic Gospels, Jesus uses this phrase to encourage an appropriate response to the message he has just conveyed. In Revelation, Christ endorses the ethic of defiant witness. God's Spirit is the medium through which Christ continues to speak.

A statement of reward begins with another address that is used at the close of each of the letters: "to the one who conquers" (2:11, 17, 26; 3:5, 12, 21). To conquer is to witness resistantly. Such conquest, however, does not mean that a believer "wins." Jesus, after all, was executed because of the revelation he proclaimed (5:6, 9, 12); John is exiled on Patmos (1:9); Antipas was executed (2:13), as are many like him (6:9–11; cf. 11:7; 13:7). Conquest does, however, mean that ultimately the believer will, like Christ, through the very act of witnessing, overwhelm the bestial forces of draconian Rome (12:11; 15:2; 17:14) and obtain eschatological relationship with God. That relationship is symbolized here by the tree of life and paradise, two direct references to the garden of Eden (Gen 2–3; cf. Ezek 31:8–9). John's Christ is initiating a thought here that he will fully develop at 22:2 (see the discussion there). In the Genesis account, humans were forbidden to eat from the tree of life for fear they would obtain eternal life (Gen 3:3, 22–24). Here, eternal life is precisely the reward!

## 2:8–11  *To Smyrna: Richer than You Know*

> 8 "And to the angel of the church in Smyrna, write: Thus says the first[a] and the last, who was dead and lived: 9 'I know your persecution and your poverty (though you are rich), and the slander from those who call themselves Jews, but[b] are not, but are a synagogue of[c] Satan. 10 Fear nothing[d] that you are about to suffer. Indeed, the devil is about to throw some of you[e] into prison so that you might be tested, and you will have[f] persecution for ten days. Be faithful until death, and I will give you the crown of life. 11 Let the one who has an ear hear what the Spirit is saying to the churches. The one who conquers will certainly not be harmed by the second death.'"[g]

a. The reading of A (*prōtotokos*, firstborn) appears to be an assimilation to 1:5, where Jesus is the *prōtotokos tōn nekrōn* (firstborn of the dead; cf. Col 1:18); all other manuscripts have *prōtos*, which here completes the formula "the first and the last" (1:17; 22:13). In light of the formula, *prōtotokos* has a claim to being the *lectio difficilior*; but external evidence, which in this case is quite strong, favors *prōtos*.

b. An adversative use of the conjunction *kai*.

c. A genitive of possession: the synagogue belongs to Satan.

d. The more difficult, and therefore more likely original reading, *mēden* (supported by ℵ 𝔐 sy), a neuter singular pronoun, presents readers with a grammatical problem; it does not agree with the neuter plural relative pronoun (*ha*) that operates with it. Several manuscripts (A C 046 2050 *pc*) therefore substitute the syntactically more appropriate negation *mē* (not).

e. The construction *ex hymōn* ([some] of you) is a partitive genitive, intensified by the preposition, that follows a verb whose action affects its object only in part.

f. The introduction of the future indicative *exete* (you will have), following *kai*, is an indication that the clause it initiates operates independently of the *hina* clause immediately prior to it. Some manuscripts (A P 1854 2344 *pc*) attempted to force the verb "have" to operate with the *hina* clause by giving it a subjunctive form (*echēte*).

g. The preposition *ek* follows the passive form of *adikeō* to locate the source from which the harm comes and also to demonstrate instrumentality from that source.

Smyrna was a wealthy city. Its harbor made it a strong commercial port center. Located approximately thirty-five miles to the north of Ephesus, it also sat at the end of a lucrative Asia Minor trade route. The city was also well known for its dedication to Rome and Greco-Roman cultic religion. As early as 195 B.C.E., the city built a temple dedicated to the worship of the goddess Roma, patron divinity of the empire. In 26 C.E., the emperor Tiberius, who had already allowed the people of Smyrna to dedicate a temple in honor of the deceased Augustus, and the Roman Senate established Smyrna as a *neōkoros*, "temple keeper" (Acts 19:35), for the cult of Tiberius. Despite its devotion to the imperial cult and its construction of numerous pagan temples, like that to the healing god Asclepius, the city also developed a strong Christian presence. Polycarp, the bishop of Smyrna, is a well-chronicled figure. Ignatius, bishop of Antioch, stopped in the city when he was being escorted to Rome for execution (ca. 107 C.E.). Before his death, he wrote letters of encouragement both to the church at Smyrna and to Polycarp, who would suffer a similar fate (ca. 155 C.E.).

[8] As he does at the beginning of each of the letters, Christ orders John to write (see the comments on 1:11, 19) to the church's patron angel (see the discussion of 1:20). The letter again begins with "thus says . . . ," a Hebrew prophetic formula that directly links Christ with Yahweh, the formulation's rightful subject. Christ next describes himself as "the first and the last" and as the one who was dead, but came back to life (see the comments on 1:17, 18).

[9] Christ claims to know both their persecution and their poverty. Though he speaks about the two together, he does not equate them. Their persecution is not their impoverishment. At 1:9, John testifies that his persecution occurs as a direct result of his witnessing to the lordship of God and Christ. The fact that he and Christ-believers are partners in this grim reality implies that their persecution, too, is a direct result of their comparable witnessing.

Persecution is also a by-product of the hostility that erupted between the Smyrna church and its Jewish neighbors. Like its six sister cities, Smyrna was a hotbed of imperial cultic worship. Because Greco-Roman culture did not separate the sacred and secular realms, spiritual activity had dramatic political implications. Citizens were required by law to sacrifice to the emperor on various special occasions, and "those refusing to participate were seen as politically disloyal and unpatriotic" (Beale 241). Apparently, Smyrna's Jewish community took advantage of this situation. Being an ancient religion with an established tradition, Judaism had achieved sufficient status to broker concessions with regard to the worship of other deities. Jews were not required to participate in the imperial and Greco-Roman cultus in ways that compromised their monotheistic beliefs. The Romans were not so accommodating to newer religions. Fortunately for Christ-believers, the Romans, before the Neronian persecutions, were either unable or did not care to distinguish between Christians and Jews. Following that transitional moment in history, however, Christians lived a much more precarious existence *if* the Romans were able to identify them and require from them recognition of their gods' and their emperor's divinity, and instead encountered resistance. According to *The Martyrdom of Polycarp*, "[Polycarp] was told by the Roman governor that he would be executed if he did not give a public, token acknowledgement to Caesar as Lord. He died for his faith" (Beale 243).

John apparently believed that in Smyrna the Jewish community did the Romans' investigative work for them. Knowing that the Christ-believers, many of whom were themselves probably Jews, would not acknowledge Caesar's lordship, synagogue members pointed them out and thereby offered them up to persecution. It is for such scandalous squealing that John labels their fellowship a synagogue of Satan. The epithet is not so much an anti-Jewish denunciation as it is a reference to an intra-Jewish conflict that leads to betrayal.[2] The witness to the lordship of Christ rankled Smyrna's synagogue community as much as it did the Romans, if for quite different reasons.

It is important to speak carefully about John's "synagogue of Satan" language. John lashed out against one minority community that tried to protect its religious turf by seeking approval and status from the powerful majority community and subverting the status of a similarly situated minority group. The harsh language is, however, incredibly unfortunate. Taken out of its social and historical context, it can be and has been used to incite virulent forms of anti-Judaism. When teaching or preaching from this text, or the comparable one in the Philadelphia letter (3:7–13), the contemporary interpreter must focus on John's intent rather than his words. The seer's condemnation applies to any minority community that would sell out another for reasons of doctrinal difference or social standing. The enduring issue, then, is one of ethics, not ethnicity.

---

2. A similar contextual circumstance of intra-Jewish debate probably lies behind a corresponding situation in John 8:30–47, where persons who refer to themselves as children of Abraham are rejected as such because of their rejection and condemnation of Jesus. At v. 44 Jesus says that they are of the devil and they are liars, two themes that also surface here. Acts 18:12–16 recounts a scene between Paul and Jewish leaders that is likewise portrayed as intra-Jewish hostility.

Context is also crucial for understanding John's comment about the church's poverty (cf. 3:17). Smyrna was a wealthy city. The church's impoverishment was an indication that its members did not participate in the life of the city in ways that would move some of that wealth in its or its members' direction. "Indeed, the imperial cult permeated virtually every aspect of city and often even village life in Asia Minor, so that individuals could aspire to economic prosperity and greater social standing only by participating to some degree in the Roman cult" (Beale 240). Their impoverishment was an indication that they had not bought in or, one might more appropriately say, sold out.

[10–11] The malevolent circumstances plaguing the church are a direct result of the satanic behavior that John describes in chapter 12 (cf. esp. 12:17). This behavior lives itself out through the activities of the synagogue (2:9), which John believes is, like Rome (cf. Rev 13), acting at Satan's behest. The resulting imprisonments (like John's own exile on Patmos?) will be a time of testing. John's description of this imprisonment as persecution (see the comments on 1:9; 2:9) indicates that witnessing, even if such witness was compelled because of the blasphemous slander of synagogue members, triggers the hostility. The testing language also reminds John's hearers and readers of Christ's commendation of the Ephesians for testing false apostles (2:2). Those who are castigated and those who are praised are tested on the same content: witness.

To encourage the Smyrnaeans, Christ reveals that their time of trial will be brief. The ten days, reminiscent of a short period of trial in Dan 1:12–15, can and will be endured, even to the death. Christ surely means even to the first death. It is the second death, the one that separates humans from God forever, that the Smyrnaeans should fear (see the comment on 9:6 with its discussion on the cosmology of first and second deaths; cf. Matt 10:28). A first death that occurs because of one's faithful witnessing is not the end, but the sure beginning of eschatological relationship with God. The Lord who engaged death and through resurrection conquered it offers this people who populate a portion of the reign of priests (1:6; 5:10; 20:6) a crown (see the discussion at 3:11 and 4:4), not of kingship or valor, but of eternity (cf. Zech 6:11, 14, where a crown is bestowed upon the high priest). At 20:6, John reiterates with direct language what he pictures here through the symbolism of the crown: these conquering priests will escape the destruction that is the second death. The Smyrnaeans were much richer than they had ever known; their impoverishment, or more correctly the witnessing behavior that led to their impoverishment, had already bought them eternal life.

Christ closes this letter as he does the others, with a call for those in the churches with an ear to listen to what the Spirit says and a promise for those who conquer (see the discussion of 2:7). The actual content of the promise, freedom from the second death, is unique to the Smyrna congregation.

## *2:12–17 To Pergamum: At the Foot of Satan's Throne*

12 "And to the angel of the church in Pergamum, write: Thus says the one who has the sharp, two-edged sword: 13 'I know where you live, where the throne of Satan is. Yet[a] you hold fast to my name and you did not deny my[b] faith in the days of Antipas,[c] my faithful witness, who was executed[d] among you, where Satan lives. 14 But I have a few things against you: you have some there who hold to the teaching of Balaam, who taught Balak to throw a stumbling block before the people of Israel, so they would eat[e] meat sacrificed to idols and commit the sexual offense of prostitution. 15 Thus you also have some who hold to the teaching of the Nicolaitans as well. 16 Repent therefore; if not, I will come against you[f] soon and wage war against them with the sword of my mouth. 17 Let the one who has an ear hear what the Spirit is saying to the churches. To the one who conquers I will give some of[g] the hidden manna, and I will give that one a white stone, and on the stone is written a new name that no one knows except the one who receives it.'"

a. An adversative use of *kai* (here, "yet").

b. The construction is a subjective genitive. The voice refers to the faith that Jesus himself bore, not faith in Jesus (objective genitive). See the comments below and on 14:12.

c. Readers expect that "Antipas" would appear as a genitive construction like *satana* earlier in the verse. Perhaps John takes *Antipas* as an indeclinable noun and intends a genitive understanding. Unfortunately, if this is the case, he confuses the issue by presenting the appositional phrase that follows, "my faithful witness," as a nominative. Antipas, therefore, also appears to be a nominative. Reference to 1:5 may produce clarity. There, John offered "Jesus Christ" correctly in the genitive, but then followed up with a nominative apposition. Here, he may well intend an indeclinable name to be a genitive that is likewise oddly followed by a nominative apposition.

d. When connected to judicial proceedings, *apokteinō* (kill, put to death) has the sense "execute," a rendering that parallels the sense of *sphazō* (see the discussion at 5:6).

e. An infinitive of purpose.

f. A dative of disadvantage.

g. Here, the object of the verb *dōsō* (I will give) appears in the genitive case, a partitive genitive: "*some of* the hidden manna."

Though the governing Roman proconsul may have officially resided in Ephesus, the seat of Roman administration for all of Asia Minor was Pergamum. This large and vibrant city housed one of the most celebrated libraries in the ancient world, even rivaling the grandeur of the more acclaimed library in Alexandria. The worship of Greco-Roman deities flourished in the city. Pergamum boasted not only a great temple to Zeus and an entire complex dedicated to Asclepius, but also temples to divinities like Athena, Dionysus, and Demeter. There were also powerful ties to the Roman imperial cult. In 29 B.C.E., the emperor Augustus allowed the city to become the first municipality in Asia Minor to build a temple honoring the emperor's deified status.

[12] As he does at the beginning of each of the letters, Christ orders John to write to the church's patron angel. The letter must begin with "thus says . . . ," a Hebrew prophetic formula that directly links Christ with Yahweh, the formulation's rightful subject. Christ next describes himself as the one who has "the sharp, two-edged sword" (see the comment on 1:16).

[13] Christ confides that he knows where the church members live (*katoikeō*). The verb is so important that Christ repeats it at the close of the verse. John consistently uses it (3:10; 6:10; 8:13; 11:10; 13:8, 12, 14; 17:2, 8) to designate the inhabitants (dwellers) of the earth who have accommodated themselves to Rome's domination and the lordship claims that arise from it. Such inhabitants necessarily contest both the witness to the exclusive lordship of God and Christ and anyone testifying to such a rebellious claim (see the discussion of 14:6). Perhaps John alludes here to Ezek 12:2, where the prophet was warned by God that he was living in a dangerous, rebellious place. John's Christ so irrevocably connects Pergamum with such rebellion against God that he labels it the abode of Satan's throne.

There are several plausible reasons why the city may have earned such a deleterious moniker: (1) it was the seat of Roman administration for Asia Minor; (2) it hosted a great temple to Zeus; (3) it boasted a plethora of pagan temples; and (4) it reveled in its celebrity as the first Asia Minor municipality to build a temple deifying an emperor. Probably some combination of these factors led to the dubious designation. John had in mind the opposition to the lordship of God and Christ that the categories represented.

Despite their precarious location, the Pergamum Christ-believers hold fast (*krateō*, 2:25; 3:11; cf. 14:12) to Christ's name and do not deny Christ's faith. A similar formulation occurs at 3:8, where Christ commends the Sardis church for keeping his word and not denying his name. Though the verb he uses there for "keeping" (*tēreō*) is not the same one used here, 3:11 follows up with the same verbal formulation, so as to suggest that Christ is thinking in the same thematic terms. These are the same terms of praise that Christ offers the Ephesians who bear up Christ's name (see the discussion of 2:3). The name of Christ is a euphemism for the reputation of Christ as the true Lord. "Christ's faith" is not faith "in Christ," but the very faith that Christ himself bore, the faith in his own lordship, to which he testified and for which he died on the cross (see the comment on 14:12). The Pergamum Christians emulate the faith that Christ himself demonstrated. This is how they witness faithfully.

The poster child for "faithful witness" is the executed Antipas. Except for this salutary recognition here, he is an unknown figure. Christ describes him with the same terminology that is used to describe Christ himself at 1:5 (see the discussion there; cf. 3:14; 19:11).[3] Antipas is the ultimate representative of non-violent resistance.

**[14–16]** Just as Christ tempered his initial praise of the Ephesians with chastisement (2:4), so here, after extolling the Pergamum believers for their faithfulness, he declares that he has a few things against them. He really has one primary concern. Perhaps he speaks about it in the plural because the single concern involves two false prophetic entities: Balaam (cf. 2 Pet 2:15; Jude 11) and the Nicolaitans. He calls up Balaam first. The fact that some believers "hold to" (*krateō*; cf. 2:15) the teaching of Balaam rather than Christ's name indicates that Balaam was a prophetic leader respected (by some) in the community. Though the Pergamum believers have stood fast before external inquisition, they have not been so successful at resisting internal forces that lure them away from a proper witness to Christ's lordship.

Balaam could well have been the historical name of John's opponent at Pergamum. It is more likely, given John's penchant for symbolism, that the name was chosen for paradigmatic reasons. It has a colloquial Hebrew meaning, "one who consumes the people," which partners well with John's other opponent group in the city, the Nicolaitans (cf. 2:6). Their name, in Greek this time, means "one who conquers the laity [people]." Even more likely, John is, as he will do with the so-called Jezebel of Thyatira, crafting a cunning scenario of guilt by association. He applies to his historical opponents the names of people who are well known as traditional enemies of God's people. The Balaam of Num 22–24 and 31:16 was a seer sent by Balak, a king rivaling the Israelites, to curse the people of God. Overwhelmed by God's power, Balaam blessed the people instead. And yet, his story's narrative connection with Num 25, where Israelite men became sexually involved with foreign women and therefore cultically involved with their deities, and the explicit condemnation in Num 31:16, led tradition to charge Balaam with leading the people idolatrously astray.

Pergamum's Balaam teaches the people that it is permissible to eat meat that has been sacrificed to idol gods and to commit the sexual offense of prostitution. In reality, both offenses are the same. For John, persons who eat meat that has been sacrificed to foreign gods give credence to the reality and lordship of those gods; those persons have therefore prostituted themselves to a foreign faith (see 2:22, where the same behavior is likened to adultery; cf. 17:2, 5; 18:3, 9). While some commentators argue that the term John employs, *eidōlothyton*, refers to the meat that was sacrificed and then eaten later, after the sacrificial

---

3. As at 1:5, the description "my faithful witness" (*ho martys mou ho pistos mou*) appears in the nominative when grammatically the description, like the noun "Antipas" it modifies, should be in the genitive case. The warping of the grammar here could well point the reader back to the warping of the grammar in 1:5, where the "mistake" served as a grammatical nod toward the interpretation John wanted his readers to apprehend (see the discussion of 1:5).

ceremonies had concluded, Beale contends that the term refers to the eating of the contraband meat as a part of the ceremony itself. He therefore argues that John is concerned not just about the leftover eating, but the actual participation in foreign cults (248). The narrative does not itself offer enough evidence to decide the matter. Either way, the impact of the concern is the same. John sees the eating of the meat, whether as part of the service or afterward, as worthy of the fullest measure of condemnation. Where Paul, in his Corinthian correspondence (cf. 1 Cor 8–10), had offered the very practical advice that strong Christians could eat meat sacrificed to idols unless their behavior offended the spiritual psyche of weaker Christians for whom such activity seemed sinful, John overrules the behavior outright. He does so no doubt knowing that the members of his church in Pergamum do not believe in the reality or lordship of such deities. Their participation was exclusively social and economic. The sacrificial ceremonies and meals were as much communal as religious affairs. Artisan, trade, and other business associations aligned their groups with patron deities. Funeral associations often did the same. Participation in such groups, which allowed for upward social and economic mobility, often included the obligatory participation in such a group's cultic activities. Unlike the believers in Smyrna, who apparently opted out of such activities and thereby impoverished themselves as a result, many believers in Pergamum wanted to participate, wanted to move up socially, and therefore wanted assurance that their behavior was not problematic. Balaam provided that assurance with his teachings. Since the Nicolaitans are mentioned as operating similarly to Balaam, it is probable that they provided the same assurance. The "thus" which opens the Nicolaitan discussion (v. 15) intentionally refers hearers and readers back to the concern about Balaam (v. 14) as though they were in reality the same concern. Indeed, given John's close narrative association of the two, it is likely that Balaam was an identifiable leader within the Nicolaitan movement. There is little doubt that both were trying their best to help their fellow Christ-believers accommodate their faith to the new circumstances in which they found themselves. However, John's conservative, intolerant attitude disallowed any kind of compromise; Balaam and the Nicolaitans and those who followed their teaching were guilty of spiritual prostitution.

Christ heightens the stakes by declaring that he is coming soon (see the comment on 3:11). For unrepentant, accommodating church members, his coming would not be salvific, but judgmental. The backside of the two-edged sword was meant for them. The language of repentance in Revelation has this consistent sense of turning back to the kind of committed faith that church members first exhibited, presumably when John was teaching in their midst (see the discussion of 2:5). Of the twelve occurrences of *metanoeō* (repent) in the Apocalypse, eight occur in the letters to the seven churches (Rev 2–3), and six of those target the infamous eating of meat sacrificed to idol gods (cf. 2:16, 21 [twice], 22; 3:3, 19).

[17] Christ closes this letter as he does the others, with a call for those in the churches with an ear to listen to what the Spirit says and a promise for those who conquer (see the discussion of 2:7). In Pergamum, Christ promises to give the conquerors the hidden manna and a white stone with a secret name. The hidden manna was a stroke of rhetorical brilliance; to a people starved for idol food, he offered food delivered directly from the one true Lord and God (cf. Exod 16:31–35; Num 11:6–9; Deut 8:3, 16; Ps 78:24). According to the tradition that surrounded the destruction of Jerusalem by the Babylonians (586 B.C.E.), the prophet Jeremiah hid the ark of the covenant, which contained some of the Exodus manna, so that it would not be captured (2 Macc 2:4–8). The ark's location was lost and was promised to remain a secret until the final age. For the Pergamum Christ-believers, this final age would no doubt appear as a messianic banquet feast (cf. Mark 14:25; Matt 22:2–9), as opposed to an idol feast, where the served food would be (eternal) life affirming. The meal choices were clear: seek false satisfaction now or be granted true satiation upon Christ's imminent return.

The other victory symbol was a white stone. Though such stones were often used as magical amulets, given this context of entrance into the eschatological meal, it is likely that John was borrowing from the tradition of the white stone used in antiquity to acquit a person of a crime or enable a person's entrance into a coveted affair. "Either of these explanations could apply, the former indicating that the faithful are acquitted in the final judgment, the latter symbolizing their entrance into the messianic banquet" (Reddish 62). The new name that no one knows (cf. 19:12), except the one who receives the stone, was no doubt Christ's new name, which Christ later says he himself will write on the person of the believer (3:12). In chapter 3, too, the inscription of the name is tied to the metaphor of entrance into God's eschatological life (cf. 14:1; 22:4). In essence, John is declaring that even now Christ is engraving tickets to Christ's own messianic banquet.

### 2:18–29 To Thyatira: Drowning in the Deep End

18 "And to the angel of the church in Thyatira, write: Thus says the Son of God, the one who has eyes like a flame of fire and whose feet are like burnished bronze: 19 'I know your works and your love and your faith and your service and your nonviolent resistance, and your last works are greater than your first. 20 But I have against you[a] that you tolerate the woman[b] Jezebel, who calls herself a prophet[c] and teaches and deceives my servants to commit the sexual offense of prostitution and to eat meat sacrificed to idols. 21 And I gave her time to repent, but[d] she does not wish to repent of her prostitution. 22 Indeed, I am throwing her into a sickbed,[e] and I am throwing[f] the ones who commit sexual offense with her into great distress unless they repent of her works;[g] 23 I will even kill her chil-

dren with the plague.[h] Then[i] all the churches will know that I am the one who examines minds and hearts, and I will give to each of you according to your works. 24 But I say to the rest of you in Thyatira, as many as do not hold this teaching, who do not know the (as they say) deep things of Satan: I do not throw another burden upon you. 25 Only hold fast to what you have until I come. 26 And, as for the one who conquers[j] and keeps my works until the end, I will give authority over the nations, 27 and that one will shepherd them with a rod of iron as when clay pots are shattered. 28 Just as I have received from my Father, so I give to him the morning star. 29 Let the one who has an ear hear what the Spirit is saying to the churches.'"

a. *Poly* (much) is added in ℵ 2050 𝔐^A gig (it) sy^ph; *oliga* (small, few) is added in *pc* vg^cl. The original text likely included neither word. Both additions represent a kind of commentary on the severity of the accusation, albeit in two different directions. *Oliga* is an apparent assimilation to 2:14, while *poly* probably contrasted the minor sin of Pergamum with the presumably more grievous sin of Thyatira.

b. The phrase *gynaika sou* (your woman) appears in A 1006 1841 2351 𝔐^K sy; Cyp Prim. All other manuscripts lack the possessive pronoun (*sou,* your). *Gynē* has the semantic idiosyncrasy of denoting sometimes a woman generally and at other times a married woman (BDAG 208–9), concerning which the presence of a possessive pronoun can be decisive. If the pronoun is present, then *gynaika* is not "woman" but "wife," which might then suggest that the *angelos* of 2:18 could be interpreted as a human bishop rather than an angel (Metzger, *Textual Commentary*, 734–35), which would otherwise be unnecessary. The witness of A and 𝔐^K notwithstanding, external evidence favors reading *gynaika* without the possessive pronoun *sou*.

c. The feminine form and thus equivalent of *prophētēs*.

d. An adversative use of *kai*.

e. The manuscript tradition witnesses to a debate over the severity of Jezebel's punishment (related, perhaps, to a debate over the severity of her offense; see note a above): *phylakēn* (prison) in A; *klibanon* (furnace) in 2071 arm; *astheneian* (weakness) in 1597 sa; and *klinēn* ([sick]bed) in ℵ C P 046 1 1006 1611 1854 2053 2344. *Klinēn*, being by far the best attested, is surely right. That *phylakēn* is found in A is impressive, but is probably best explained as an assimilation to the use of the same term in 2:10.

f. The verb *ballō* (throw) governs both accusatives ("her" and "the ones who commit prostitution").

g. The reading *ergōn autōn* (their works) appears in TR, following A 1 1854 2081 2344 it[61] sy^ph arm eth Cyprian *al*; *ergōn autēs* is attested by ℵ C P 1006 1611 2053 gig vg sy^h sa bo Tertullian *al*. The external evidence is divided in this case, but *ergōn autēs* (her works) is certainly the *lectio difficilior*, since it presents the problem that "they" are to repent of someone else's behavior (cf. the similar problem in 2:23). It is also possible that *ergōn autōn* simply represents an unintentional repetition of the genitive plural ending. But whether intentional or not, the plural reading seems to be secondary.

h. *Thanatos* (death), according to context, can mean the manner of death, such as fatal illness or plague (BDAG 351). Presuming here a dative of means, operating with the preposition *en*, plague would be a natural fit, given the prevalence of plagues in the forthcoming seals, trumpets, and bowls cycles.

i. The conjunction *kai* here introduces the result of a preceding action (BDAG 392).

j. The participle acts as a nominative absolute (cf. 3:12, 21). See also the following participle: *tērōn*.

In Thyatira, cultic propaganda went so far as to declare the Roman emperor the incarnation of Apollo, and therefore a son of Zeus. This religious-political alliance heightened the risk for persons who tried to opt out of the Greco-Roman cultic infrastructure; rejection of the gods implied resistance to the state. Complicating matters even further was the fact that Thyatira hosted a large number of trade guilds with strong cultic affiliations. Especially important were industries of wool, textile, and the manufacture of purple dye (cf. Acts 16:14–15).

[18] As he does at the beginning of each of the letters, Christ orders John to write to the church's patron angel. The letter must begin with "thus says . . . ," a Hebrew prophetic formula that directly links Christ with Yahweh, the formulation's rightful subject. At this point, Christ offers something unique, the titular designation of Christ as the Son of God. Unlike the other designations for Christ at this point in each of the letters, this title does not refer back to the description of Christ at 1:12–20. In fact, it occurs nowhere else in all of Revelation. There is a metaphorical connection to Christ as "son" at 12:5. Even here, however, the title Son of God is not deployed. It does, however, reinforce the presentation of Christ offered at 1:12–20: it acts as a kind of confirming identification. Christ is even more than what 1:12–20 revealed him to be; he is not just an emissary for God, but God's own Son. The designation of sonship contributes to the political polarization. Emperors often proclaimed themselves as "sons" of the deceased and deified emperor whom they had succeeded. The point could not be missed: Christ's sonship is the true one, established in relationship to the true Lord. Having made this provocative point, Christ returns to the pattern of connecting to the character traits revealed at 1:12–20. He describes himself as the one whose eyes are like a flame of fire and whose feet are like burnished bronze (see the comments on 1:14–15).

[19] Christ knows about the work of witness (see the discussion of 2:2) in the Thyatiran community. Their witness is exemplified by love, something the Ephesians no longer were demonstrating (see 2:4). In celebrating their faith, Christ alludes to the kind of witness that refuses to deny the name and thus the lordship of Christ (see the comment on 2:13). Such defiant witness performs a great service (a term John uses only here) in bolstering the larger mission of testimony to the lordship of God and the Lamb. Such work is a nonviolent resistance to claims of Roman imperial lordship (see the comments on 1:9; 2:2–3; 13:10). In fact, some of their more recent acts of defiant witness were the most noteworthy of all.

**[20]** As he did in his comments to the churches of both Ephesus and Pergamum, Christ chastises the community after concluding his initial salutary remarks (cf. 2:4, 14). The problem is simply stated: the community tolerates the woman Jezebel.

Jezebel's name, and the connection made between this name, fornication, and the eating of idol meat (see the discussion of 2:14), clarifies the problem. Like Balaam, who, as an apparent member of the Nicolaitans (2:15), counseled a "gospel" different from John's, this Jezebel operates as a prophetic leader in the church (see the discussion of rival servant/prophet groups at 2:14 and 22:16). Since the objectionable message she proclaimed was the same message proffered by Balaam and the Nicolaitans, it is probable that she, too, was a Nicolaitan. The name "Jezebel" was doubtless not her real name but an epithet that John attached to this rival charismatic leader for the same reason that he attached the legendary name of Balaam to his Pergamum prophetic rival. It is demagoguery by association. John undermines her counsel by discrediting her person; he associates her and her teaching with the work of the infamous person from Israel's past (cf. 1 Kgs 16:31; 18:4, 13; 19:1–3, where she even tries to kill the prophet Elijah; ch. 21; 2 Kgs 9).

The first Jezebel was immortalized as the manipulative foreign wife of the Israelite king Ahab. The queen used her influence to prop up her native Baal cult, discredit and destroy the prophets of Yahweh, and lead the people idolatrously astray. The rival woman prophet of Thyatira was correspondingly influential. Christ therefore describes her evil in exactly the same way that he described Balaam's offense (see the discussion of 2:14–16). Though the sequence shifts slightly, the words themselves are the same; she approves the eating of meat sacrificed to idols, an act that causes a believer to prostitute one's faith in Christ. She assured John's charges that it was perfectly acceptable to participate fully in the imperial and pagan cult activities of one's trade guild, given that one knew the guild's patron deities to be nothing more than empty idols. Her counsel allowed Christ-believers to integrate themselves into the social, political, and economic life of the city and thereby prosper from the connections they made.

**[21–23]** The theme of repentance recurs (cf. vv. 5, 16). Interesting here is the fact that God's gracious offer extends not only to the people who have been led astray but even to the person intentionally misguiding them. Jezebel, however, rebuffs God's overture. In punishment, John's Christ promises to throw her onto what is most likely a sickbed. Even her children would be struck dead. This discomforting image is metaphorical. John is no more speaking about literal children than he is speaking about the literal, historical Jezebel. Her children are the "offspring" of her activities, which commend accommodation to the lordship of Rome; they emulate Jezebel's idolatrous ways, live them, and subsequently teach them to others. They will therefore be struck down as she herself will be struck down. They *must* be struck down, lest they continue leading God's people astray.

As a result of Christ's intervention, all the churches will know that Christ is indeed the Lord who is responsible for executing eschatological judgment. The "I am" establishes Christ's connection with God (see the comment on 1:4) and thus authorizes his activity. The theme of judgment continues with the clarification that Christ examines hearts and minds as if they are open books and, on the basis of what he finds, gives to each what their works of either witness or accommodation deserve (see the comment on 20:12–13; cf. 18:6). This discerning activity also connects Christ integrally with God. In the Hebrew Scriptures, God is the one who judges hearts and minds (Prov. 24:12; Jer 11:20; 17:10); Paul confirms this assertion at Rom 8:27.

[24–25] All Christ wanted was that his people stand fast for their faith. Jezebel apparently claimed some deeper insight into how God was operating in the world. These "deep things" were probably the rationales she used to endorse idol cult participation. She no doubt intended some deep knowledge from God; Christ mocks it as "of Satan." Many Thyatirans were drowning in this so-called deep way of thinking. Christ therefore endorses and celebrates those who recognized the truth and saw her teaching for the evil that it was. He refuses, however, to substitute his own countercomplexities of (deep) mystical thinking. Christ's only burden is a simple one (cf. Acts 15:28–29): until his imminent return (see the discussion of 3:11), the people must hold fast (see the discussion at 2:13) to the work of resisting imperial lordship claims, a resistance symbolized here by their refusal to eat meat sacrificed to idols.

[26–28] A statement of reward begins the address at the close of each letter: "to the one who conquers" (see the comment on 2:7). Here, Christ promises authority over the nations. Unfortunately, that authority is already held by the Romans. If John's believers are to have it, God must, on their behalf, take it away from others. Indeed, just after God promises universal authority to the people of God at Ps 2:8–9, God warns the kings of the earth that if they do not submit to this new reality, they will be destroyed (Ps 2:10–11). John's spiritual vision has a potent and threatening *political* implication. The threat operates through the imagery of the iron rod. The symbol mimics Christ's own rule at 12:5 and 19:15 as one of shepherding. Such symbolism provides not only for the reality of the nations' judgment but also for the possibility and even hope of repentance (see the comments on 2:5, 16, 21–23). The warning, then, if people properly receive it, should guide them back into the proper work of witnessing to the lordship of God and Christ.

The eschatological portion of the promise resides principally in the image of the morning star. Used again at 22:16, where Christ is himself identified as the star, and appealing to Num 24:14–20 (esp. v. 17), the symbol refers to Christ's messianic status and future rule. Christ's promise that he will convey this star to the believers in Thyatira is a powerful testimony that he will give them a prized place in his messianic reign. Ironically, in the Numbers account it is none other than Balaam who declares the oracle that, according to the interpretation here, establishes Christ's eschatological status. While the present Balaam, the Nicolaitans, and Jezebel lead the people astray, the past Balaam, in spite of himself, proclaimed the word and the circumstance to which the people should hold fast: Christ, and only Christ, is Lord.

[29] Christ closes this letter as he does the others, with a call for those in the churches with an ear to listen to what the Spirit says (see the discussion at 2:7).

### 3:1–6 To Sardis: Time to Wake Up

1 "And to the angel of the church in Sardis, write: Thus says the one who has the seven spirits of God and the seven stars: 'I know your works; you have a name for[a] being alive, but[b] you are dead. 2 Wake up[c] and strengthen the remaining things that are about to die, for I have not found your works complete in the sight of my God. 3 Therefore remember what you have received and heard;[d] hold to it, and repent.[e] If, therefore, you do not wake up, I will come like a thief, and you will not know at what hour I will come to you. 4 But you have a few people[f] in Sardis who have not soiled their clothes; they will walk with me in dazzling splendor,[g] because they are worthy. 5 Thus[h] the one who conquers will be clothed in dazzling clothes, and I will cetainly not blot his name out of the Book of Life; I will acknowledge his name before my Father and before his angels. 6 Let the one who has an ear hear what the Spirit is saying to the churches.'"

a. An explanatory use of *hoti* (that); see Louw and Nida 91.15.

b. An adversative use of *kai* (here, "but").

c. A periphrastic construction whose literal imperative sense is "be watchful."

d. While "received" occurs in the perfect tense, "heard" is an aorist. Both verbs, though, as the succeeding imperative verb *tērei* (hold, keep) would indicate, have a perfect sense. John expects that what has been received and heard maintains (keeps) its effect in the lives of the Sardis believers. "Received" is therefore not only primary in terms of sentence location; it also sets the grammatical-interpretative agenda for the verb that immediately follows it.

e. Once again John mixes verbal tenses. The present imperative from *tēreō* implies that the Sardis believers already perform some of the works expected of them; the aorist imperative of *metanoeō*, however, implies that on some crucial issues they do not yet act appropriately. John wants them to turn away from the inappropriate behavior.

f. Though *onomata* literally means "names," it operates figuratively here (cf. 11:13).

g. Though the literal term is "white," John intends not color but ethical quality.

h. *Houtos* appears in TR, following אᶜ P 046 and most minuscules; *houtōs* in א A C 1006 2344 it^{gig, 61} vg sy^{ph, h} sa bo arm eth *al.* Neither word is syntactically necessary, and either one makes sense in the context. Nevertheless, *houtōs* thus can claim superior manuscript support and should be preferred (with NA[27]).

Sardis was the proverbial fortified city set on a hill. Thought by its inhabitants to be impregnable, it cultivated a reputation of invulnerability. As the capital of the kingdom of Lydia, Sardis was the seat of Croesus, a king whose legendary wealth derived from two primary sources: the gold in the river running through the city and the export trade of woven textiles. Ironically, the city was also renowned because of the infamous collapses of its acclaimed defenses. In 549 B.C.E., Croesus, engaged in a conflict with Cyrus of Persia, retired to Sardis, convinced that Cyrus would not engage him there. He was mistaken. Cyrus attacked but after two weeks bogged down in his siege. The offensive prevailed through an act of stealth. Like a thief in the night, one of Cyrus's soldiers stole into the city through an unguarded spot in the fortifications. Centuries later, in 195 B.C.E., the Seleucid King Antiochus III also claimed control of the city because of the negligence of its protectors. "The moral lessons derived from this series of events (one must avoid pride, arrogance, and overconfidence and be prepared for unexpected reversals of fortune) became a *topos* for later historians and moralists" (Aune 1:220).

[3:1] Christ begins by reminding the Sardis faithful that he is the one who has the seven spirits and the seven stars. He is, in other words, the same Lord identified at 1:16, 20; and 2:1. As in those earlier cases, so here the stars are the angels who represent the churches. At 5:6, Christ's vision operates through the metaphorical lens of these seven spirits, who are in fact the Holy Spirit (see the comments on 1:4–8; 4:5; 5:6; 14:13).

Christ knows their works (see the discussion of "works" and "witness" at 2:2). Heretofore this declaration of knowledge has been a prelude to commendation for some positive aspect of a church's ministry (cf. 2:2, 9, 13, 19). Hearers and readers are therefore caught by surprise when Christ, as he does later in the message to Laodicea (3:15), goes immediately on the attack. There is a regrettable parallel between the (witness) works of the church and the history of the city that hosts it. Sardis squandered its name, its reputation of invulnerability, because its benefactors did not stay alert to the dangers around them. The members of the Sardis church, while likewise reveling in their past reputation for witness, were also frittering that reputation away. This is why John plays with the word "name" by using it four times in this short letter. "This word-play . . . emphasizes the problem. . . . They have become a church in name only" (Reddish 72).

To make his contrast between living and dead, Christ does not pit one adjective (alive) against another (dead); he balances a kinetic verb (*zaō*, being alive) against a static adjective (*nekros*, dead). Every time the evangelist uses the verb *zaō* in relationship to a witness (whether Christ [1:18; 2:8] or the believers in the seven churches [20:4–5]), he does so in a context where eternal life trumps death.[1] The adjective *nekros* is also used primarily in a context where someone dead lives again (cf. 1:5, 17, 18; 2:8; 3:1; 11:18; 14:13; 16:3; 20:5, 12, 13). John's point becomes grammatically clear whenever the adjective and verb are used together (1:18; 2:8; 20:5). It is because of their costly witness to the lordship of Christ that believers can cheat death by springing to eternal life. In every case other than 3:1, "dead" gives way to "being alive."[2] Surely, this is a pattern no believer would want to see reversed. Unfortunately, that is precisely what has happened; though having a name for "being alive," the Sardis believers are really "dead." Because they only maintain an appearance of resistant witness, their eschatological prospects are grim.

[2] Christ demands that the Sardis church resurrect itself from the lethargy that holds it captive. It is time for it to wake up (*grēgoreō*; see the discussion of 3:3). He then issues the mysterious injunction that the believers must strengthen the remaining things that are about to die. In recording this demand, John offers his only neuter use of the adjective "remainder."[3] In every case other than 8:13, where John uses the term, he does so to refer to a human remnant. There are therefore two options for interpreting the term. It could be that Christ wants the Sardis believers to strengthen the remaining human witnesses who are about to die because of their testimony. This interpretation would fit John's predominant use of "remainder" to refer to human subjects. The problem, though, is obvious. The neuter form indicates a unique intent. A second option is thus more likely. The Sardis believers must strengthen the remaining (i.e., incomplete) *works* that are about to die.

The final thought of the verse, "for I have not found your works complete in the sight of my God," is a clarification that operates from the thought already conveyed at the end of 3:1. There, Christ describes the works (i.e., resistant witness) of the Sardis church as being alive in name only. Here, Christ restates the same thought with different language when he declares that their works are incomplete before God. They are performing *acts* of witness that do not fulfill

---

1. One could go even further and make the case that every use of the verb has a connotation of eternal life. Used adjectivally, it describes the eternally living God or the eternal creatures in God's employ: 4:9, 10; 7:2; 10:6; 15:7. Even when used in connection with the reviled beast, it has the sense of resurrection; at 13:14, the beast, who was mortally wounded (13:12), overcomes the lure of death and lives. Even at 19:20, where the beast and false prophet are said to be thrown into the unquenchable fire alive, the implication could well be that their living in the fire will go on eternally.

2. See 1:18: "I was dead but indeed I live forever"; 2:8: the one "who was dead and lived." At 20:4–5 the believers who were beheaded because of their witness live again.

3. See 2:24; 8:13; 9:20; 11:13; 12:17; 19:21; 20:5. At 8:13 the term refers to the final blasts on an angel's heavenly trumpet. Even here, however, the form is not neuter but feminine.

the *obligations* of witness.[4] In other words, they are engaged in a witness facade. While flamboyant, their effort has absolutely no transformative effect.

This interpretation fits well with the presumed historical situation of the Asia Minor churches in general and the Sardis church in particular. Like the churches mentioned in chapter 2, Sardis is infested with cultic affirmation for pagan deities and for the Roman imperial regime. The temple of Artemis, constructed by Antiochus III after he refounded the city in 213 B.C.E., was "the fourth largest Ionic temple known to have been constructed in the ancient world" (Aune 1:218). Temples dedicated to Augustus and possibly Vespasian were also on grand display. Believers were invited to accommodate themselves to the lure of social and economic progress that was promised to those who participated cultically in these religious systems. Still, even in those churches where many were following the lead of Balaam, the Nicolaitans, and Jezebel and eating meat sacrificed to idols in order to blend themselves into the Greco-Roman social world, appropriate witnessing was also no doubt taking place. Christ does, after all, except in Sardis and Laodicea, find much to praise. Even in Sardis (v. 4) there is a faithful remnant. One should suppose, then, that even in the most reckless situations, believers were doing more than eating meat sacrificed to idols. That was the *problem* activity. Apparently, there were many corporate faith activities that expressed a genuine Christian commitment and therefore were not a problem for John and Christ. Christ celebrates some of these activities (e.g., 2:2, 3, 6, 9, 13, 19) and no doubt leaves others out. Such praiseworthy works were, however, incomplete. They needed to be shored up before they, too, died out.

One might suspect, for example, that John's Sardis believers were worshiping together every Lord's Day. Yet they were not doing the other necessary work of resisting the lure of Greco-Roman cultic-social life by witnessing transformatively to the lordship of Christ. Cultic correctness, while necessary, was insufficient. Unless they upgraded their remaining work of cultic observance by adding acts of transformative resistance, it too would soon wither and die. The church's death would then be complete; it would be as dead in name as it was already in resistant witness.

This interpretation allows the more dynamic verb "be alive" to match up ironically with the static adjective "dead" at the conclusion of verse 1. They are dead as a community, but their works still have a chance to live (i.e., become complete) and perhaps in their living revitalize the community as well. Like a drowned man whose vital organs still struggle to function while they await the

---

4. This interpretation fits the definition of the term "fulfill" found in Gerhard Delling, "πλήρης, πληρόω, κτλ." (*TDNT* 6:297). Delling notes that it has a temporal sense of completion. It means to finish, to execute a commanded action: "almost always [it is] God's commission which is to be fulfilled." What is God's commission in chapters 1–2, thus far, except that believers do the witnessing works of resistant endurance?

return of oxygen that flooded lungs cannot without help provide, they have died. And yet, for a brief moment at least, they hope for resuscitation.

[3] Christ desires a selective memory. He wants believers to remember the life strategy they saw and heard from *him*, while they forget the egregious teachings of those who have said that accommodation with Greco-Roman cultic-social life is acceptable. Having recalled this more rigorous way, they must hold to, that is, keep (*tēreō*) it. The verb *tēreō* is a primary ethical term for Revelation, and it is integrally connected to the language of witness. At 3:8, Christ celebrates those witnesses who *hold to* his word and thereby resist every opportunity to deny his name. Then at 3:10, he promises eschatological reward for those witnesses who *keep* resisting the lure of Greco-Roman cultic, social, and political success. At 12:17, the dragon fights those who resist his demands by *holding to* their word, and at 14:12, eschatological reward is implied for those who resist the threat of persecution and *maintain* their witness. At 22:9, John's mediating angel declares satisfactorily that he is in the good company of those who have *kept* the witness demanded by Christ in the book. Indeed, John declares in three of his seven macarisms that the blessed person is the one who *keeps* to the resistant witness that the book demands (1:3; 16:15; 22:7).

If the Sardis believers do not rouse themselves to the kind of resistant witness Christ has taught and modeled (cf. 1:5, 9; 2:13), he will come to them like a thief in the night.[5] The imagery is familiar. Several other New Testament texts highlight the coming of the end time as the surreptitious movement of a night bandit (Matt 24:42–44; Luke 12:39–40; 1 Thess 5:2–4; 2 Pet 3:10). Revelation, though, is the only text to identify this thief as Christ (Aune 1:227). Already, Christ promised the church at Ephesus that he would come in judgment if they did not *remember* and turn back (*repent*) to the witness that they offered at first (see the comment on 2:5).[6] Given the thematic parallel with 2:5, one might imagine that the thief would do here what Christ threatened to do in Ephesus: take the lampstand, the church, and remove it from its place of relationship with God.

Thus far in the text of Revelation, Christ's judgment against the churches occurs for only one reason: *not* enduring, *not* resisting the temptation to accommodate oneself to Greco-Roman cultic, social, and economic expectations.

---

5. The connection between repentance and turning away from accommodating behavior is encouraged by the way John uses the verb *metanoeō*. Six of its 10 occurrences in the book fall in the two chapters that include the letters to the seven churches (2:5, 16, 21, 22; 3:3, 19). The other four occurrences all detail situations where evil persons refuse to repent (9:20, 21; 16:9, 11). The implication is that there is hope that the church will repent of its accommodating behavior. At 2:16, 21, 22, John makes explicit the link between the verb and accommodating to the practice of eating meat sacrificed to idols.

6. John's only other use of the verb *mnēmoneuō* (remember) in an imperative form addressed to believers occurs at the parallel 2:5, where it also operates in conjunction with the verb *metanoeō* (repent).

Being awake and alert must therefore be a euphemism for resisting those expectations. This understanding is corroborated by John's only other use of *grēgoreō* (wake up) in 16:15, where it is the key vocabulary in one of the seven macarisms or blessings. First, there is a familiar warning: Christ is coming like a thief in the night. Who will be blessed when that circumstance unfolds? Only those who are awake—who have not shamed themselves by throwing off their clothes. As 3:4 demonstrates, John forges a strong link between clothing (*himation*) and the behavior of resistant witness.

This particular coming, related as it is specifically to this church's behavior, is not the ultimate coming of the end time that is prophesied in other sections of the book. When Christ describes his coming as conditional, as based upon the behavior of believers, it is a specific revelation of punishment within history (cf. 2:5, 16). The unconditional coming, though also imminent, will occur regardless of human behavior and will bring with it the end of the historical era (see 1:3; 2:25; 3:11; 22:7, 10, 12, 20).

[4] Christ defines the remnant as those who have not soiled their clothing (*himation*) and who thus walk with him wearing clean, white garments. Appealing to Daniel and the Synoptic Gospels, many commentators observe that "white" appears as a divine color. In Dan 7:9, it is the color of God's attire. In Matt 28:3 and Mark 16:5, it is worn by heavenly beings, and at Jesus' transfiguration, his clothing transforms to a white that no launderer could match (Mark 9:3; Matt 17:2; Luke 9:29; cf. Reddish 72). For believers, there is a connection between the color of clothing and an eschatological relationship with the divine: "It was customary in the ancient church, when believers came out of the waters of baptism, to dress them in a new, white garment to indicate the beginning of a new life of purity and victory" (González and González 33). This historical observation matches the literary implication that resides in Christ's plea that the Sardis believers remember their former work of witness and return to it (repent). As defiant witnesses to Christ's lordship, they once wore the color of eschatological acceptability; they have soiled that clothing, however, by accommodating themselves to the cultic and social expectations associated with Greco-Roman pagan and imperial lordship. Only a few have held on to their earlier commitment to bear witness to the lordship of God; they, and thus their garments, remain in their pristine state. They alone are worthy.

In John's religious and ethical vision, worthiness is earned through endeavor. God is worthy because God created all things (4:11). Christ is worthy because he witnessed so aggressively to the lordship of this Creator God, and indeed to his own related lordship, that he was executed (5:2, 4, 9, 12).[7]

---

7. This formula works even for the enemies of Christ. In the only other appearance of the adjective (16:6), the people who shed the blood of the saints are "worthy" (i.e., they have earned the right) to be given only blood to drink.

*The* faithful and true witness (1:5; 3:14) is therefore adorned in the quintessential clothing of resistance (dipped in blood, 19:13; inscribed with the name "King of kings," 19:16). It makes sense, then, when John explains that believers are made worthy to wear the clothing of eschatological victory only if they too witness to that lordship. In their dazzling dress, they will stand out in a filthily clad crowd.

Dazzling is the right word. Though *leukos* does translate literally as "white," its emphasis in Revelation is more on qualitative essence than on exterior pigmentation. Too often the color has been connected uncritically with ethnicity and race. Biblical affirmation of the color has therefore often been taken incorrectly as a biblical affirmation of the white race. It is clear, however, that for John the term is an ethical (not an ethnic) one. It is an earned salutation. One is not *born leukos*; one *becomes leukos*. Black people, brown people, people of any ethnicity and hue can become *leukos*. All one needs to do is heed the command that Christ issues to the Sardis believers: wake up and witness relentlessly to the lordship of Christ, no matter how much it costs. That is how a believer, any believer, can "dazzle."

[5–6] Christ has already established those who conquer as persons who resist accommodation to Greco-Roman cultic, social, and economic expectations (see the discussion of 2:7, 11, 17, 28). In connecting the language of conquest with the metaphor of the dazzling clothing, he thereby reestablishes it as triumph over the beastly machinations of imperial Rome (see also 6:9–11; 7:9, 13). It makes sense, therefore, that the twenty-four elders, who were presumably model witnesses and conquerors, are so clothed at 4:4. As a negative example, the church at Laodicea is warned that it must do a better job of resistant witnessing if its members are to earn this glorious attire (3:18).

Two specific rewards await the "dazzlingly" clad believer. First, Christ declares that he will not blot the name of such a person from the Book of Life. The Book of Life (cf. Exod 32:32–33; Ps 69:28; Isa 4:3; Dan 12:1–2; Phil 4:3; cf. Luke 10:20; Heb 12:23; *1 En.* 108.3) registers those who enjoy an eternal relationship with God. Those whose names are not written in it have lost their connection with God (Rev 17:8) and are due eschatological punishment (13:8; 20:15). On the surface it might first appear, given the ethical context in which the term arises in the Sardis letter, that believers are expected to earn their way into the book. Nothing could be further from the truth. Through improper (cultically and socially accommodating) behavior, one can cause one's name to be stricken from the ledger.[8] One cannot, however, cause one's name to be *entered*

---

8. See Aune for a Greco-Roman parallel: "In Athens, whenever any citizen was sentenced to be executed for a crime, his name was first erased . . . from the roll of citizens (Dio Chrysostom, *Or.* 31.84)" (1:225).

there. Entries had already been made from the moment God created the world (13:8; 17:8).[9]

John is working out a fundamental tension that resides still in contemporary Christianity. God determines who has relationship with God. It appears that God graciously decides in favor of everyone—at least at the start. John presumes that even those in the majority at Sardis, the ones whom Christ indicts, have had their names inscribed in the Book of Life. Why else would he threaten them with a blotting out? Works, therefore, do not enable eschatological entry. Appropriate works (witnessing), though, do affirm entry, while inappropriate works (accommodation) negate it. This bit of literary dexterity allows grace and works to stand together in a firm, if very tense, relationship.

As a second reward, Christ declares that he will confess the name of the "dazzling" believer before God and God's heavenly entourage. John uses the term *homologeō* (confess) only here. By placing it in this context, where he encourages a witnessing to (or confession of) Christ in a hostile environment, John is building upon the tradition of the historical Jesus (Luke 12:8; Matt 10:32; cf. *2 Clem.* 3:2) who demanded similar behavior from his followers.

On verse 6, see the comment on 2:7.

### 3:7–13 To Philadelphia: Open-Door Policy

7 "And to the angel of the church in Philadelphia, write: Thus says the holy one, the true one, the one who has the key of David,[a] who opens and no one will shut, who shuts and no one opens. 8 'I know your works. Indeed, I have set before you an opened door, which no one can shut, because you have little power and yet kept my word and did not deny my name. 9 Indeed, I will make[b] those of the synagogue of Satan who call themselves Jews, and are not but are lying—indeed, I will make them come[c] and grovel before your feet, and they will understand that I have loved you. 10 Because you have kept my word of nonviolent resistance, I will keep you from the hour of trial that is about to come upon the entire inhabited earth to test the inhabitants of the earth. 11 I am coming soon; hold fast to what you have, so that no one may take your crown. 12 As for the one who conquers,[d] I will make him a pillar in the temple of my God,

---

9. Rev 17:8 confuses the issue as it suggests that God's enemies, described characteristically as the inhabitants of the earth (see 6:10; 13:12–17), never had their names in the Book of Life. Given the two strikingly different impressions, there is every likelihood that John envisions two categories of people. The first category, which appears to contain the majority, would have their names written in the book and could only find themselves purged from its pages if they do something (e.g., accommodation) to warrant expulsion. The second category would be those whose bestial behavior indicated that they never had a relationship with God to lose. It is difficult to understand how John could fit this perspective into his larger view of God's benevolent genesis and guidance of creation.

and he will never leave it. Moreover, I will write on him the name of my God and the name of the city of my God, the new Jerusalem, which comes down out of heaven from my God, and my new name. 13 Let the one who has an ear hear what the Spirit is saying to the churches.'"

a. *Tou David* in ℵ B P; *David* in A C 1 1611 1678 1778 1854 2020 2053; *hadou* (of Hades) in 104* 218 336 459 620 2050 2051 2057 2067*; *tou thanatou kai tou hadou* (of death and Hades) in 111 1893; *tou paradeisou* (of paradise) in arm^ms. The primary question is whether *David* should be read with or without the article. Because proper names in Revelation are generally anarthrous (Metzger, *Textual Commentary*, 736), it is better to read *David* without the article (so NA^27). The other readings, none of which has a strong claim to being original, seek to provide specific content about the realm the key would unlock.

b. On the verb form *didō* as an alternate form for *didōmi* (give), see BDAG 192. Aune makes a good case for the form operating as a Hebraism, since the Hebrew form *nātan* can mean both "give" and "make" and is translated in the LXX with *didōmi* (1:229–30). John confirms such a reading by pairing *didō* with *poiēsō* (I will make) in the second half of the verse.

c. Literally, "make to come." Operating with *poieō* and the finite verb *agō, hina* introduces a phrase that has the nuance of an infinitive (BDAG 681).

d. The participle acts as a nominative absolute.

Philadelphia, the city of brotherly (*adelphos*) love (*philos*), housed the only church other than Smyrna to receive exclusively positive remarks. While the Smyrna church witnessed in spite of its impoverishment (2:9), the Philadelphia community sustained its work despite the fact that it was powerless before hostile communal forces. The city's name, then, did not represent the circumstance of the believers living in it. It was derived instead from the legends of two royal figures. According to one tradition, the city was named for Attalus Philadelphus, an Attalid king who ruled from 159 to 138 B.C.E. His legendary love for his brother, who preceded him as king from 197 to 159 B.C.E., was the alleged foundation of the moniker. A competing tradition gave credit to the founding efforts of Ptolemy Philadelphus (308–246 B.C.E.). Yet John was not preoccupied with the city's foundational history. He was concerned instead about the city's role in hosting a caustic feud between his followers and the synagogue community, from which they had likely emerged. The city's name was therefore bitterly ironic. In this municipality of "brotherly love," two communities of kindred Jewish roots, one witnessing to Jesus the Christ, the other opposing any such proclamation, found absolutely no love lost between them.

[7–8] The situation in Philadelphia was uncomfortably similar to the one John's believers had experienced in Smyrna. There, too, the Christ community was enduring conflict with some portion of the city's Jewish community. In both cases, Christ uses the derogatory appellation "synagogue of Satan" to describe the churches' opponents (see the discussion of 2:8–11). In Philadelphia, one gets the impression that members of the specified synagogue were not only betraying Christ-believers' identities; they were also teaching that those who had been expelled from the synagogue had forfeited any chance to be a part of God's eschatological community. This is why Christ describes himself to the church in the way that he does and presents them with the particular message that he delivers.

Christ is, first of all, the holy and true one. Isaiah, whom Christ will quote momentarily, conspicuously identified God as the Holy One (1:4; 5:19; 40:25), and a number of Old Testament texts affirm that God is the true one (LXX: Exod 34:6; Num 14:18; Isa 65:16). Christ is so integrally identified with this God that he speaks with and for God as the holy and true eschatological judge. Revelation 6:10 is the only other place where John employs this title. There, souls who have been executed for presenting the very witness these seven letters have been advocating cry out to the holy and true Christ for an avenging judgment against their persecutors. The implication is that this Christ, who is himself also the true witness to the lordship of Christ (3:14), will execute judgment against all who defy that testimony and torment those who profess it.

Christ now strategically enters his Isaiah quotation. Appealing to the prophet's testimony at Isa 22:22, he maintains that he (Christ) holds the key of David. In the Isaiah text, the steward Eliakim is given the key to the historical house of David and thereby the power to determine who can and who cannot enter the king's presence. Christ, however, wields his apocalyptic version of the key for the purpose of exclusively opening and closing the door to David's *eternal* kingdom. In the celebrated instance of Matt 16:19 (cf. 18:18), after Jesus gives Peter custody of the heavenly keys, it is Peter who has permanent power to bind and loose authoritatively both in heaven and on earth. In Revelation, Christ retains key ownership for himself. Christ, in other words, is the keeper of the eschatological gate.

At 9:1 and 20:1, an angel is handed the key to the bottomless pit. At his discretion, he can open its door and consign the guilty to its punishing judgment. Jesus' key, by contrast, opens the lock on the promise of heaven. Perhaps it is related to the keys of Death and Hades he has pocketed in 1:18. He uses those keys to free himself from the captivity of death. He displays them before his followers so that they know he can release them from the death to which any human person or force might consign them. They can therefore witness, no matter what the punishing consequence, knowing that Christ has the wherewithal to set them free from it. Once Christ is freed, with heavenly key in hand he can open the door to heaven and usher them in. No one else has the power to shut that door and, presumably, keep them out.

This would have been an especially welcome message in Philadelphia, where the synagogue community claimed to be the only door to a relationship with God. By excommunicating the Christ-believers, the community claimed to have shut that door on them forever. The picture of Christ holding the key of David is a striking statement to the contrary. It would not have been lost on John's hearers and readers that Christ speaks about the heavenly realm in *Davidic* language. Surely it would not have been lost on the members of the offending synagogue community either. Christ has taken charge of the door to *their* eschatological future. He is ready to open it not for them but for those whom they have thrust aside.[10]

The positive emphasis on the ethically loaded verb *tēreō* (keep; see the discussion of 3:3) is a clear indication that the Philadelphians maintained the primary exhortation of the book. They kept "my word." Given that God and Christ are indissolubly linked, Christ's word is indistinguishable from God's word. John has equated God's word with the testimony proclaimed by Jesus (1:2, 9; see also 6:9; 12:11; 20:4), which is the same testimony desired of Christ's followers. Christ made the connection specific for the Philadelphians when he restated that the community *kept* his word (3:10). This time, however, he used another of his synonyms for witness: nonviolent resistance (see the comment on 2:1–7). Christ is therefore celebrating here what he has been demanding all along; the Philadelphia believers have endured in their witness in spite of the arduous circumstances that have plagued them. He is also celebrating their confession of his name. Confession, too, is identified with witnessing. He makes the point negatively. By saying that they refuse to deny his name, he acknowledges their confession of it. That refusal, at least as it is expressed in relationship to Antipas and the other faithful members of the Pergamum church, is the very essence of witness (2:13; see the discussion of 13:6). It retains that sense in Philadelphia.

For this reason, this witness, Christ has opened the door of the eschatological future to them (cf. 4:1). "I know your works," he declares. "Indeed, I have set before you an opened door, which no one can shut, *because [hoti]* you have little power and yet kept my word and did not deny my name." This reading sets up the parallel causal clause in v. 10, where once again historical witness yields eschatological reward.

[9] Christ's charge that the opponents of the Philadelphians comprise a synagogue of Satan, whose members call themselves Jews but are liars, is intentionally reminiscent of the allegation earlier leveled against the opponents of the Smyrna church (2:9). Though he uses descriptive language that is almost exactly the same, in this latter case he does not focus on the resulting persecution. Instead, he spotlights the actions he will take to vindicate the church's

---

10. The connection between the metaphor "open door" and an eschatological connection with God is affirmed by John's use of the same language in 4:1 (*thyra ēneōgmenē*, though in the nominative case to reflect its use there as a predicate nominative), where the open door leads directly into the heavenly throne room.

position as the eschatologically favored entity. In doing so, he maintains the mocking tone he established in v. 7, where he declared that he would use the Davidic key to open up the Davidic kingdom exclusively to those whom the alleged people of David persecuted. This time, he takes a vision of eschatological vindication that was supposed to operate on behalf of the synagogue and uses it deliberately against those who populate it. Isaianic prophecy (Isa 45:14; 49:23; 60:14) declared that the people of Israel would be vindicated when God forced the Gentile nations who had persecuted them to kneel in submission before them (see also Ps 86:9). As it turns out, at least as far as Philadelphia was concerned, the synagogue had become the tormenting, ungodly force. God would therefore force its members down upon their knees instead. Though Christ does use the language of worship (*proskyneō*), it cannot be his intention that the synagogue members are actually made to worship the members of the Philadelphia church. Only God and Christ are worthy of worship (Rev 4:10; 5:14; 7:11; 11:1, 16; 14:7; 15:4; 19:4, 10; 20:8).[11] Christ is mocking them. In their humiliation, they would be forced to genuflect, to grovel at the very feet they had sent running for cover.

[10] Christ reminds the Philadelphians of the eschatological promise he made with the metaphor of the open door in v. 8. This time he uses the language of ethics. As they have "kept" his word of nonviolent resistance through a singular witness that refused to acknowledge any claim to lordship by pagan deities or Roman emperors, so he will "keep" them. There is considerable debate regarding the translation of the phrase *ton logon tēs hypomonēs mou*. Following the interpretive decisions of the RSV and NRSV, I argue that the possessive "my" should operate with the entire phrase, so that it would read, "my word of nonviolent resistance" instead of "the word of my nonviolent resistance." Christ is not concerned whether they will or will not maintain their hold on some facet of doctrinal content. "Keeping" in this context has the ethical connotation of application; the Philadelphians have applied Christ's witness to their own lives. The language of "keeping my word" therefore operates in tandem with the identical language offered at the end of 3:8. There the Philadelphians were celebrated for "keeping my word" as a witness that lived itself out in confession of Christ's name. Here that same "keeping my word" is described as an enduring witness of nonviolent resistance. The two explanatory phrases are metaphorically synonymous. Resistant witness endures precisely because it maintains the confession of Christ's lordship in an environment hostile to such a claim.

The believer who lives up to this ethical standard can expect Christ's eschatological reward. He will keep them "out of" the hour of testing or trial that is about to come upon the entire inhabited earth to test the inhabitants of the earth.

---

11. See also 9:20 about improper worship of idols, and 13:4, 8, 12, 15; 14:9, 11; 16:2; 19:20 about improper worship of the dragon and its accompanying beasts.

Christ is not speaking here against the entire world, but the part that is "organized and controlled" by the Roman Empire, the part that is determined to celebrate a lordship other than Christ's (Richard 61). The "inhabitants of the earth" are those who in their affirmation of this imperial control find themselves necessarily in opposition to Christ and his followers (see the comments on 2:13; 14:6; see also 6:10; 8:13; 11:10; 13:8, 12, 14; 17:2, 8). As a moment of judgment, the hour is aimed squarely at them. Their testing then is actually a convicting trial. It is "a period of great distress and suffering that early Judaism (Dan 12:1; *T. Mos.* 8.1; *Jub.* 23.11–21; *2 Apoc. Bar.* 27:1–15) and early Christianity (Matt 24:15–31; Mark 13:7–20; Rev 7:14) expected would immediately precede the eschatological victory of God" (Aune 1:239). As a time of apocalyptic woe, it is also a moment of eschatological poetic justice. The tribulation that the inhabitants of the earth brought upon Christ's followers will now be brought upon them instead.

Though Christ vows to keep the Philadelphians out of the hour of testing, he does not say that he intends to spare them from it. Indeed, at the only other New Testament combination of the verb *tēreō* (keep) and the preposition *ek* (out of), Jesus does not ask that God rapture believers out of the difficult moment; he instead asks God to strengthen them so that they might endure and conquer it (John 17:15). Here, as in the Gospel, persecution is something that believers will endure (2:10). Their witness matters as much as it does because they give it in the circumstances of such duress, just as Christ himself did on the cross. That is no doubt why in the end the hour is described in terms of a testing rather than a judgment; believers, too, will have an opportunity to make the grade. They will have the opportunity to witness.

[11] Once again Christ heightens the urgency of loyal witness by testifying that he is coming soon. While the opening and close of the text assure its hearers and readers in a general way that the time is near (1:3; 22:10), there are several specific declarations by Christ that mimic the one made here. At 22:7, 12, and 20 he proclaims, "I am coming soon." And in each case the proclamation is made in the context of his role as judge. At 22:7, the one who is coming soon rules that only the one who "keeps" the words of the book's prophecy/witness (see 1:1–3 on prophecy) is blessed. Speaking more provocatively at 22:12, the one who is coming soon acknowledges that he will repay everyone according to their work/witness (see the discussion of works in 2:1–7). At 22:18–20, the one who is coming soon says that he will remove the eschatological reward of the person who adds to or takes away from the words of prophecy/witness contained in the book. In the references to the churches at Ephesus (2:5) and Pergamum (2:16), Christ's imminent coming is also directly connected to a theme of judgment. The sure implication is that the believers in Philadelphia must prepare themselves for this impending moment lest it dawn upon them as one of judgment rather than celebration. This is why the one who is coming soon

closes the verse by challenging them to "hold fast to" what they have (cf. 2:13, 25), to maintain their witness in spite of the social and political turbulence (part of the testing) such witness causes, so that they might not lose the crown they already wear. The connection between imminence and judgment is even more sharply drawn with the impending woe language of 11:14.

Given the context of Christ's imminent coming and the implication that if the Philadelphian believers are not prepared, that coming will be a moment of judgment rather than celebration, it is reasonable to presume that the someone who might confiscate the crown is the same Christ who would, if the circumstances warranted, blot a believer's name from the Book of Life. The crown is a symbol of eschatological life just as it was in 2:10. It is probably no accident that there, too, the wearing of the crown is connected with a successful engagement with the moment of testing. The assumption that believers already possess the crown fits with the discussion surrounding the Book of Life in 3:5. While they cannot earn their way into the book, they can earn their way out of it by accommodating to the lordship of Rome (i.e., failing the test) rather than witnessing for the lordship of Christ. Here, too, there is no suggestion that one could or would need to earn the crown of life. God's bestowal of it is an apparent given. They need only fear Christ's taking it away when he returns, if they are not ready, if their witness has not been "kept," if their witness has not met the test.

[12–13] For the conqueror, though, for the one who "holds fast" and witnesses in the harsh circumstances of testing and trial that the Philadelphians face, there will be a specific eschatological reward. Christ will make of them a permanent pillar in the heavenly temple of God. Translation difficulties arise when one considers that, later in his work, John declares that God's new Jerusalem will have no temple (21:22). Yet these two apparently opposing realities are not really in conflict with each other. At 21:22 John goes on to say that there will be a temple, but that the temple will be the Lord God and the Lamb (see the comment on 21:22). It would therefore be appropriate here to have any translation reflect this complex reality: Christ will make the conquering witness a pillar in the heavenly temple, *which is* God and the Lamb. The relationship with God and the Lamb will be an intimate one (see the comments on 19:7–8; 21:2; cf. Beale 1091).

To be sure, commentators are correct who suggest that this image of firm placement in God's presence and care would have been particularly relevant for the Philadelphia believers given the city's history of earthquake instability. But there is a deeper relevance here that relates directly to the circumstance narrated in the "synagogue of Satan" phrase at vv. 8–10. The tone of irony and mocking that Christ instituted at 3:8 with the metaphor of the open door makes an encore appearance here. Catherine and Justo González point out helpfully that no one outside of the people of Israel could enter the Jerusalem temple (34). Whether Jew or Gentile, John's hearers and readers were no doubt thought to be exiled from the presence of God experienced in the gathering of the community and the temple privileges that went with presence from the moment the synagogue forced their leave upon them. If the earthly temple of God had still existed in Jerusalem, these Christ-believers would therefore not even have been allowed to enter it. And yet here they were, because of the very witnessing that earned them their exile, promised to be the pillars that held up God's heavenly temple and kept it secure. Kicked out of Israel by God's alleged people, they were planted firmly in God's eschatological future, and therefore God's heaven, by God's holy and true Christ.

Christ adds to his pillar promise a vow to scratch on it the eschatological graffiti of three names: the name of my God (see the discussion of 14:1), the name of the new Jerusalem coming out of heaven, and his own new name (see the discussion of 2:17). How appropriate that "the ones who did not deny Christ's name, even in the face of opposition," are in the end inscribed with Christ's name (Reddish 78; cf. 14:1). All of the names certainly signal the intimate eschatological relationship that the Philadelphians will have with God in God's future. The Isaiah connection that has been important throughout this letter comes to a kind of climax here. In Isa 62:2 and 65:15, the prophet declares that the people of God shall be given a new name by God. Just as important, the Isaiah passages affirm that this new name will come as a way of vindicating the people before those (the nations) who had tormented them. Now, reversing the design one final time, Christ bestows this triple new name—and the identification as the people of God that goes with it—upon his followers as a way of vindicating them before the synagogue community that has surely thought that the Isaiah promise was meant exclusively for them. To push the point even further, Christ implies that God has been the architect of this momentous reversal of fortune. Wealthy patrons of temples often had their names inscribed on the pillars of such edifices to show their support. In the case of the heavenly temple, the columns "will bear the inscription that will tell all that they were placed there by none other than God!" (González and González 35).

For treatment of v. 13, see the comment on 2:7.

### 3:14–22 To Laodicea: Lukewarm Vomit

14 "And to the angel of the church in Laodicea, write: Thus says the Amen, the faithful and true witness, the origin of God's creation: 15 'I know your works; you are neither cold nor hot. I wish you were either cold or hot. 16 So, because you are lukewarm and neither hot nor cold, I am about to vomit you out of my mouth. 17 Because you say, "I am rich and I have become wealthy and I need nothing," but[a] you do not know that you are miserable and pitiful and poor and blind and naked, 18 I counsel you to buy from me gold refined by fire so that you might be wealthy, and dazzling

garments so that you might be clothed and the shame of your nakedness might not be revealed, and salve to anoint your eyes so that you might see. 19 I reprimand and discipline those whom I love; therefore, be earnest and repent. 20 Indeed, I stand at the door and knock; if someone should hear my voice and open the door, I will come in to that person,[b] and I will dine with that one and that person with me. 21 As for the one who conquers,[c] I will allow[d] that one to sit with me on my throne, just as I also conquered and sat with my Father on his throne. 22 Let the one who has an ear hear what the Spirit is saying to the churches.'"

a. The *kai* here is adversative.

b. For the purposes of gender inclusivity, the masculine pronouns are translated as neutrally as possible.

c. The participle acts as a nominative absolute (cf. 3:12).

d. The verb *dōsō* (I will give [allow]) is used to demonstrate divine prerogative just as it does in 2:7, 10, 17.

Christ is as consistently negative toward the Laodiceans as he was invariably positive toward the Philadelphians. He cannot find even a tiny remnant within the community upon whom he might render the slightest offering of praise. The better one understands the history of this city and the place of the church community within it, the better one understands and perhaps appreciates the divine hostility. Laodicea—colonized by the Seleucid King Antiochus II between 261 and 246 B.C.E., and named for his wife, Laodice—was the richest city within the region of Phrygia. It was so wealthy that after it was utterly destroyed by an earthquake in 60 C.E., the city proudly refused imperial disaster assistance and rebuilt itself completely with its own resources.

Located six miles south of Hierapolis, ten miles northwest of Colossae, and a hundred miles east of Ephesus, the city sat at a major intersection, which enabled it to operate as a hub on a lucrative trade route. Its main highway was an east-west thoroughfare that connected the port of Ephesus with the western region of Asia Minor. Its other primary passage connected Pergamum, Thyatira, Sardis, and Philadelphia to the north with cities like Colossae and Perga and the regions of Pisidia and Pamphylia to the south. The city was also well known and well endowed by its textile, banking, and medical industries. Its signature commercial items were a shiny black wool and a so-called Phrygian powder, from which a medicinal eye salve was made. The city also had a signature water problem. It had no water source of its own but had to pipe water in from the hot medicinal springs of Hierapolis. Unfortunately, "by the time it arrived there, its tepidness and mineral content made the water nauseating" (González and González 36). People were prone to spit it from their mouths.

This wealthy Asia Minor city also had an apparently long-standing church community that interacted with nearby church communities. Five times the church is mentioned in the Letter to the Colossians (2:1; 4:13, 15, 16 [twice]). At one point (4:12–13) the letter acknowledges a certain Epaphras as a missionary whose endeavors linked him to the churches in Colossae, Laodicea, and Hierapolis and thereby connected those churches with each other.

**[14]** Christ is the *Amēn*. In the Hebrew text of Isa 65:16, "amen" is applied specifically to God (cf. Aune 1:255). Its use here establishes an integral relationship between Christ and God. Why else was the term used? "In both Judaism and the early church, 'amen' was used as a way of signifying what was true and valid" (Reddish 80). "Amen" was introduced in Revelation at 1:6 and again at 1:7 as an affirmation of the testimony about Christ that had just been proclaimed. Later in the book, it is a closing hymnic response (5:14; 7:12; 19:4): heavenly beings (angels, four creatures, and twenty-four elders) antiphonally affirm the praise of God and Christ that has just been sung. At 22:20, it occurs at the close of the entire book as an affirmation of its primary promise: Christ is coming soon.[12] By identifying himself here as the "Amen," Christ indicates that he is the affirming, closing proclamation of praise in response to all that God has previously done in God's role as Creator. This is why the definitive self-identifier speaks specifically to Christ's role as the origin of God's creation. If the Laodiceans were familiar with the Hebrew understanding of wisdom and particularly the portrait of it in Proverbs, they would no doubt have discerned in this self-reference a connection between Christ and the power of wisdom that God used to construct the world (Prov 3:19; 8:22–31). Moreover, if they were familiar with the Letter to the Colossians, they were already comfortable with the idea that Christ was the firstborn, the beginning of God's creation (Col 1:15). He is also the affirmation of that creation, the antiphonal Word that God utters in response to what God has done.

Even more specifically, Christ is the "Amen" to all that has been said thus far to challenge the seven churches. It is as though a preacher had concluded a sermon or finished a prayer with the immodest declaration "I am the guarantor of all that I have just proclaimed. It is I who certify its validity and its importance for your lives." Christ "amens" himself because he is himself *the* "Amen." He is not just the response; he is also what makes the response truthful and faithful to God's intent. This is why he is also recognized as the true and faithful witness (see the discussion of 19:11; cf. Jer 42:5, where Yahweh is described as a true and faithful witness).

---

12. Indeed, following a host of manuscripts, the NRSV and RSV include "Amen" as the literal last word of the entire book. In those manuscripts it stands as the ultimate affirmation of all that John has witnessed to in his prophetic word.

[**15–16**] The faithful and true witness knows about the lackluster witness of the Laodiceans (see the discussion of works as witness at 2:2). Lukewarm, they are neither hot nor cold. The adjectives "hot" and "cold" should not be taken to represent different kinds of Christian witness, so that, for example, the cold Christian does not witness properly, whereas the hot one maintains the zeal and fire that Christ demands. Christ opposes the hot *and* the cold to the lukewarm. He wishes that they were one or the other, but not one *as opposed to* the other. He intends simply that, knowing definitively where they should stand, they stand there. They should surely stand where all other witnesses should stand, against any form of accommodation to Roman imperial or pagan lordship. The lukewarm believer is therefore the accommodating Laodicean believer. The hot or cold Laodicean is the one who has made a decision to identify oneself with the lordship of Christ. "Declare yourselves! Be hot *or* cold! Be clear! Witness for my lordship alone!" Otherwise, Christ will respond by doing to them what the oft-nauseated Laodiceans did to the lukewarm mineral water piped in from Hierapolis; sickened, he will vomit them from his mouth. The warning sounds eerily familiar to the threat Christ issued to the Ephesians, when he promised to throw their lampstand from its place if they did not repent (2:5).

[**17**] The Laodiceans do not recognize the precarious nature of their situation. Laodicea was a wealthy, self-sufficient town, and the Laodiceans have apparently incorporated this secular perspective into their ecclesial self-understanding. They are a wealthy, self-sufficient community of faith. They are the opposite of Smyrna, which was described as materially destitute but rich in witness (2:9). Though rich in possessions, Laodicea is poor in doing works of enduring, resistant witness. Indeed, their very wealth suggests that they have been accommodating themselves to the social and economic expectations of the Greco-Roman society in which they live. By attending the festivals, trade gatherings, cultic ceremonies, and other social situations where upward financial mobility could be bought at the high price of eating meat sacrificed to idols and acknowledging in other ways imperial and pagan lordship, the Laodiceans have enriched their historical circumstance at the expense of their eschatological one. Christ piles up the adjectives so that they will not miss the point; they are wretched, pitiable, poor, blind, and naked. Commentators have well recognized how Christ's last three metaphorical points operate directly from the social circumstance of the Laodicean community. This city of wealthy bankers would feel chagrined at being labeled poor. This city of medical schools that pioneered pharmaceuticals for the betterment of sight would not appreciate an insult that labeled their entire municipality blind. This city full of merchants who outfitted the Greco-Roman world in the finest textiles, particularly their famous black wool, would not be amused to hear someone call them naked. Clearly, though, at least as far as Christ is concerned, they are fooling themselves. Though they think they have it all, they actually have nothing.

[18] After scolding them by using imagery they would uniquely appreciate, Christ now offers the Laodiceans a way forward by reconstituting and thereby revaluing that same imagery. Though he appeals to the last three adjectives of v. 17 in a different order (1, 3, 2), it is clear that he has the same metaphors in mind (wealth, clothing, and restoration of sight). He advises them first to buy gold that has been refined by fire so that they might become truly wealthy. Refined gold was a symbol of a purified life (Beale 305; see Prov 27:21; Mal 3:2–3; *Pss. Sol.* 17.42–43). Perhaps, too, Christ has in mind the Smyrna church that already was rich and had obtained their wealth through the "fire" of persecution that came as a result of their obstinate, resistant witness (see the discussion of 2:9). The text of Revelation offers two ways to become rich. One can become rich through the refinement of fire, as in 3:18, or one can become rich through accommodation (18:3, 15, 19). The opposing of fired wealth as a positive trait and accommodated wealth as a negative one suggests that the fire is indeed the persecution that occurs as a result of nonaccommodating, resistant witness. Christ, then, is suggesting that the Laodicean believers gain their wealth in the same way that Smyrna gained it, by being hot or cold, by standing up for the lordship of Christ in a context virulently hostile to that message.

Christ ended v. 17 by advising the Laodiceans that they were naked. Now, in v. 18, that nakedness is described as their shame. They can cover their shame by clothing themselves with the dazzling garment of the witness-induced victory they are now offered (see the comment on 3:2–4).

The eye salve to end their blindness is yet one more phase of redundancy on the same theme. Their blindness is their lukewarmness, their accommodation to Greco-Roman lifestyle and authority. The salve is the witness that can cure it. Christ offers the opportunity for that witness now.

[19–22] The Laodiceans must repent. This is why Christ has been so harsh on them in this letter. He is only harsh toward those whom he loves, and his harshness is meant not to destroy but to teach. The point of instruction here is simple: witness for the lordship of Christ!

Though the Laodiceans are not where Christ wants them to be in terms of witnessing discipleship, they do form a community of faith and apparently practice all the ritual expressions of that faith, evidently even the Lord's Supper. Because of their lukewarmness, though, they do so without Christ's approval and presence. This is why Christ likens himself to someone standing outside their door and knocking. In vv.18–19, Christ offers them an opportunity to rectify the disastrous situation they have created for themselves. They can do that only if they pay attention to what he has said in this letter to them. That is how they will "hear" his voice. If they "hear" it and respond to it, if they become hot or cold, then and only then will Christ enter and share supper with them. Only at that point will they eat the Eucharist in his presence instead of tricking themselves into thinking that they do, just as they have tricked themselves into believing that they are rich when they are poor, perceptive when they are blind, and dressed in victorious garb when they are in truth naked.

To the person who conquers in this fashion, who witnesses in spite of the risks, Christ will issue the same reward God gave Christ as a result of his testimony. He will give them a seat on his heavenly throne. One final time in the seven messages to the churches of Asia, John's hearers and readers are invited to join ranks with those who, with attentive ears, hear and heed the words of prophetic encouragement and warning that the Spirit is addressing to all the churches (on v. 22, see the discussion of 2:7).

## 4:1–22:9 A Series of Visions

### 4:1–5:14 The Model of Heavenly Worship

Chapters 4 and 5 were intended to be read as a unit. While chapter 4 focuses on God and chapter 5 highlights the Lamb, the grammatical presentation of the two characters is essentially the same. Both texts open with a nod to the glory of each protagonist (4:2b–8a, God; 5:5–7, Lamb). Because of that glory, each should be worshiped (4:8b–11, God; 5:8–12, Lamb). That worship takes shape in the form of an initial hymn (4:8b, to God; 5:9–10, to the Lamb), which is followed by an explanatory narrative (4:9–10, God; 5:11–12a, Lamb), and antiphonally acknowledged by a concluding hymn (4:11, to God; 5:12b, to the Lamb) (Talbert 26–27; cf. Reddish 92).

Commentators hypothesize that the parallelism results from the debt both chapters owe to the visionary, otherworldly throne room material of Dan 7 and Ezek 1–2. The Daniel material is primary. "Revelation 4–5 thus repeats fourteen elements from Dan. 7:9ff. in the same basic order, but with small variations resulting from the expansion of images" (Beale 315; see 314–15 for a detailed outline of the 14 comparative points).

Like the Daniel text, Rev 4–5 recounts an otherworldly experience. In chapters 1–3, John is on the island of Patmos, where Christ comes to him. By chapters 4–5, Christ has returned to heaven. He invites John to join him by way of a spiritual journey. In these two different travel scenarios, John makes use of both primary forms of apocalyptic mediation. In 1:9–3:22 he showcases the first type, which includes dreams, visions, and direct discourse. Through a vision, the child of humanity speaks directly with John and the seven churches in his charge. In chapters 4–5 and indeed throughout most of 4:1–22:5, the seer employs a variation of the otherworldly journey, even if he does not fully carry the journey motif through (Reddish 89). John sees, but John does not actually travel. The emphasis, then, is less on his movement than on what he sees.

As Schüssler Fiorenza has argued, "The central theological question of chapters 4–5 as well as of the whole church is: Who is the true Lord of this world?" (*Vision of a Just World*, 58). The reader knows that God and Christ are Lord because the heavenly court positions and worships them as such. The reader is to take a liturgical clue from these celestial beings. Heavenly worship becomes the model for the kind of adoration humans must craft on earth. God, and no other, is to be celebrated in word and song as the one true Lord of cosmic and human history. In John's Asia Minor context, this liturgical expectation is also a politically potent ethical directive. The call to worship only God conflicts with Rome's demand that its caesar and its deities be recognized as the true sovereigns. Worship of God alone becomes the resistant witness that Christ exhorted in the seven letters, the kind of witness that resists accommodation to the claim of Roman lordship and obstinately offers a provocative counterclaim in its place. The combined theme of chapters 4 and 5 is a powerful example of the way in which an otherworldly religious experience can have a decidedly this-worldly social and political impact. In John's presentation, the ethics of religio-political witness develop directly from the expectation of proper eschatological devotion.

### 4:1–8a  An Opened Door

1 After this I looked, and behold,[a] a door was opened in heaven, and the first voice, which I had heard as a trumpet speaking[b] with me, said:[c] "Come up here, and I will reveal to you what must happen after this." 2 Immediately I was in the spirit, and behold there stood a throne in heaven, and one seated on the throne. 3 And the seated one was like jasper stone and carnelian in appearance,[d] and around the throne was a rainbow like emerald in appearance. 4 And around the throne were twenty-four thrones, and twenty-four elders, clothed in dazzling clothes, sat on the thrones, with gold crowns on their heads. 5 And lightning and rumbling and thunder went out from the throne, and seven flaming torches, which are the seven spirits of God, were burning in front of the throne. 6 And in front of the throne there was something like a sea of glass, like crystal. And in the midst of the throne and around the throne were four living creatures, covered with eyes in front and behind. 7 And the first creature was like a lion, and the second creature was like an ox, and the third creature had a face like a human, and the fourth creature was like a flying eagle. 8a And the four living creatures, each of whom had six wings, were covered with eyes all around and inside, and without ceasing they sing[e] day and night.

a. On the choice of translating *idou* as "behold" instead of "indeed," see the commentary on 1:7.

b. The genitive participle *lalousēs* (speaking) should be either in the nominative case, if it modifies the nominative *phōnē* (voice; cf. Aune 1:269), or in the accusative, as a match with the relative pronoun *hēn* (which; cf. Beale 318). In fact, textual witnesses offer both nominative and accusative forms of the participle for just such reasons. Aune theorizes that John has attracted the participle to the genitive form of the word "trumpet," which occurs just before it, so that he can call to the knowledgeable reader's mind a parallel with the LXX version of Ezek 43:6: "and behold a voice from the house speaking to me." There, too, the participle "speaking" was attracted to the genitive form of "house" when it should have occurred in the nominative, as did its antecedent "voice." For Beale, the irregularity alludes to Exod 19:16–19.

c. As *legōn* (said) is modifying *phōnē* (voice), it should occur as a feminine participle rather than in the masculine form that John offers. This is an instance of construction according to sense: "the one whose voice is heard to say."

d. A dative of respect (Smyth §1516), repeated at the end of the verse.

e. Though John uses *legontes* (speaking), singing is clearly his intent because he follows with a hymn.

[4:1] The opening phrase, "after this I looked, and behold . . ." (*meta tauta eidon, kai idou*) is a grammatical indication that John has shifted to another topic. Though he uses the phrase in this exact way only once more (7:9), it is clearly a loosely developed, formulaic way of initiating a new narrative line of thought. Similar constructions occur at 7:1; 15:5; 18:1; and 19:1 (though the sensory emphasis there is on hearing rather than sight). The key words are the first two: "after this" (*meta tauta*). They occur without the rest of the formulaic expression at the end of 4:1 and at 1:19; 9:12; and 20:3. Although they certainly indicate that new information is breaking, the prepositional emphasis ("after") refers back to what has come before. This does not mean that John is working chronologically, so that what is about to happen in the rest of the book occurs sequentially right after the events chronicled in chapters 1–3.[1] John is instead emphasizing a thematic connection between the themes of chapters 1–3 and the imminent revelation about to occur. The coming disclosures are meant to be understood with the charge to the churches in mind; they clarify and intensify the need for John's hearers and readers to make the right witnessing choice. After being told to witness to the lordship of Christ in a context hostile to such a witness, it is encouraging to be shown that the witness will be vindicated and avenged.

John sees an "opened door." The passive construction is important; God has invited John inside the heavenly throne room. The opened door also symbolizes earned access to God. In Ps 78:23, God graciously opened the door of heaven despite the fact that the Hebrews did not maintain proper faith. John, though, first connects the language to the steadfast witness of the Philadelphi-

---

1. For discussion contesting a chronological reading of the phrase, see William Baird, *History of New Testament Research* (Minneapolis: Fortress, 1992), 316.

ans (3:8).[2] It is because they kept the word and did not deny Christ's name, and therefore his lordship, that the heavenly door is opened to them. John, too, despite the physical cost, has been faithful to the word of God, which is the lordship of Jesus Christ (1:9). For this reason he is offered this special opening. Note, too, how the two witnesses at 11:12 are invited into heaven after the demonstration of their faithful testimony. Though the opened-door metaphor is not applied, the witnesses are solicited with the same words that greet John in 4:1: "Come up here."[3] The overall ethical implication for the reader should be clear: faithful witness to Christ's lordship may well provoke hostility from human powers, but it will guarantee direct access to God.

The trumpet-like voice John first heard at 1:10 directs him to the opened door. Revelation 1:12–13 identified the source of that voice as the child of humanity. This makes sense given the child of humanity's assertion at 3:8 that he is the one who makes the opened door available to believers and believing communities. After telling John to "come up here," Christ explains why he should: he will reveal to him the things that must necessarily occur after this.[4] This promise is Christ's personal follow-up to the narration John used to open his text. At 1:1, he described his entire writing effort as the revelation proclaimed by Jesus Christ to reveal the things that must necessarily occur soon. He repeats this narration almost verbatim at 22:6.[5] After accounting for the differences mandated by the fact that 1:1 is the introduction to the book and 22:6 is moving quickly toward its conclusion, one finds that the grammatical presentation is almost the same.

There are only two key differences between those two occurrences and Christ's use of the same language at 4:1. The infinitive construction ("to reveal") of 1:1 and 22:6 changes to a first-person verb ("I will reveal") in 4:1. That is understandable given the fact that in 4:1 Christ is speaking directly. The other change is in the timing. What was necessarily to happen "soon" in 1:1 and 22:6 must happen "after this" in 4:1. One could argue that "after this" is synonymous with "soon." If that were the case, however, why does John not simply repeat the phrase for which he has already demonstrated fondness in 1:1 and to which he will return in 22:6? The change in wording suggests a change in

---

2. The word choice, order, and passive construction are the same. The only difference between the two constructions is the accusative case in 3:8 and the nominative case in 4:1. The difference can be easily explained since in the former case the construction acts as an object and in the latter as a subject.

3. The only difference is the plural imperative form used at 11:12 because in that case there are two recipients of the invitation.

4. Cf. Dan 2:29 for a comparable phrase, "the things that must happen" (*ha dei genesthai*).

5. Moreover, 1:19 is a close parallel. There, though, John is directed toward what "is about" to happen. The necessity (*dei*) is absent.

intent. The change in timing suggests a specificity that can occur because of what the hearers/readers now know that they did not know at 1:1. That can only be the information acquired in chapters 1–3. Christ wants to show John what must happen after the initial vision of his lordship (chap. 1) and the ensuing ethical mandate to witness to that lordship (chs. 2–3). In view of the fact that what will happen after all this *must* happen, one necessarily assumes that the events of chapters 1–3 in some way trigger everything that follows in the rest of the book. In other words, if believers witness to the lordship that has been revealed to John in chapter 1 in the ways he exhorts in chapters 2–3, tribulation will *necessarily* result. Nature will suffer alongside human beings as a result of the ferocious reprisals that will be unleashed against those who would testify against the lordship of Rome. In such a context of apocalyptic conflict, the "necessity" is not surprising. If Rome indeed believes in its own lordship and prosecutes that belief through conquest, empire building, and self-deification, it has no alternative but to eliminate any force within its realm that witnesses to a contrary belief. If Rome truly is lord, Rome cannot countenance the obstinate testimony that someone else is Lord. Rome *must* fight back. God, though, cannot allow Rome's resistance to God's own true lordship to stand. God, too, *must* therefore engage. Through the activities of the Christ, God will oppose the enemy, destroy him, and vindicate God's people.

[**2–3**] Immediately after seeing the opened door, John is caught up "in the spirit." The phrase "in the spirit" occurs three other times in Revelation (1:10; 17:3; 21:10). Allusion to Old Testament prophecy is strong (cf. 1 Kgs 22:19; Isa 6:1–13). Of particular note, the phrase is "a reflection of the prophet Ezekiel's repeated rapture in the Spirit" (Beale 318; cf. Ezek 11:24). John, though, has much more than a spiritual high in mind. In the cases where he speaks about being in the spirit, he appears to be describing circumstances where he has been enabled to see things that are crucial to God's plan and God's expectation for God's people. John has not been caught up in the spirit of ecstasy, but the spirit of prophecy.

At 1:10, the first occurrence of the phrase, using the same language that he deploys in 4:2, John declares, "I was in the spirit" on the Lord's Day. The result of this encounter is a command to write what he sees and send it on to the seven churches as chronicled in chapters 2–3. Moreover, 1:3 has already clarified that John writes prophetically to encourage appropriate ethical behavior; the letters of chapters 2–3 make that ethical purpose explicit. At 17:3, an angel carries him away in the spirit, not so that he can become ecstatically charged but so that he may see the whore of Babylon drunk on the blood of God's witnesses, and therefore know how egregious any act of compliance to her lordship claims must be. Finally, at 21:10, the angel's presentation of the holy city Jerusalem coming down from God is a powerful inducement for John and his hearers/readers to maintain their testimony on Christ's behalf. It is not surprising, then, that at

19:10, under the guise of an angelic interpreter, John explicitly connects that testimony to the spirit of prophecy. John's hearers and readers are expected to act "in the spirit" in as prophetic a manner—a witness—as John himself.

This prophetic reading reveals that the ensuing throne-room language is much more than a flaunting of the heavenly decor. For John's hearers and readers, the language should be as prescriptive as it is descriptive. What they see should influence what they do. They see, first of all, a throne. John so desperately wants them to see it that he packs throne references into seven of the eleven verses that make up this chapter. Throne-room imagery is common to biblical and apocalyptic texts.[6] Psalter texts like 103:19 establish that God has established God's throne in heaven; John follows up on that supposition by describing that throne in a manner similar to the depictions rendered in Ezek 1:4–28 and Dan 7:9–14. Clearly, the one sitting on the throne in v. 2 is intended to be God. The God whom John's audience sees enthroned is the God for whom they should exclusively witness.

Then, there are the special effects. The key terms—"throne" and "the one sitting on it"—are repeated, but this time in more glowing terms. The one sitting on the throne shines like a vision of illuminating jasper and carnelian; the throne itself is lit up by an emerald rainbow.[7] The accents highlight God's glory and majesty. In heaven, the place of royal recognition is reserved only for God. In heaven, God rules. That realization should temper the fear that John's hearers and readers have about the historical rule of Rome. It should overcome the hesitancy they have about proclaiming the lordship of God and God's Christ in the Roman world. Despite the pretensions to control asserted by Rome, ultimate power belongs to God. God is therefore due ultimate and singular witness.

**[4]** The heavenly council models the ethic that the throne room images: all glory is due to God. Just as the rainbow surrounds the throne and therefore illuminates it, so do the twenty-four lesser, encircling thrones. In fact, John uses the same preposition, *kyklothen* (surround), to describe the positioning of both the rainbow (v. 3) and the twenty-four thrones (v. 4). He will use the same word only once more, at 4:8 as an adverb, when depicting the eyes that envelop (surround) the four living creatures. A similar preposition, *kyklō* (around, surrounding), occurs at 4:6; 5:11; and 7:11. It describes the positioning of the four living creatures and later the angels who also attend God's throne. The suggestion here is one of concentric circles (Aune 1:286). Just beyond the perimeter of the emerald bow sit the attending chairs of God's divine congress. Just as the power of a great leader of the ancient world was magnified through the attentiveness of the

6. See Reddish 93, who cites 1 Kgs 22:19; Isa 6:1–13; Ezek 1:4–28; Dan 7:9–14; *1 En.* 14.8–16.4; 39.1–40.10; 71.1–17; *T. Levi* 5.1.

7. The three stones mentioned will resurface during the description of the new Jerusalem: jasper in 21:11, 18–19; carnelian in 21:20; emerald in 21:19.

lesser leaders who courted him, so the magnificence of God's throne is enhanced by its relationship to subordinate figures whose heavenly stature suggests that they nonetheless wield great power.[8] The implication is that the subordinates' thrones are all facing God's throne. They are thereby offering, by their very posture and position, a kind of narrative, celestial salute. It is a pose humans would do well to reproduce.

Though they apparently do not comprise the ring of honor closest to God's throne (see the discussion of 4:6), the 24 elders who occupy the 24 lesser thrones are mentioned first. There is great debate and no consensus regarding their identity. A heavily subscribed position contends that the 24 represent the combined presence of the 12 tribes and the 12 apostles. In them, the wholeness of the people of faith is represented. Those who find the representation of entire tribes in single thrones too unwieldy opt for a variation of this proposal. Just as each of the seven churches is represented by an angel in chapters 2–3, so too are the tribes and the apostles represented on the heavenly throne by surrogate angels. There are numerous other hypotheses. The 24 elders alternately represent the 24 star gods of the Babylonian zodiac; the 24 courses (i.e., shifts) of either the priests or Levites who served the Jerusalem temple before its destruction (see 1 Chr 24:1–19); or the 24 hours of the day, and thus the fullness of time, which should be spent praising God.

In the end, John is more interested in narrating the significance of the elders than he is in identifying them. The symbolism is indeed all about wholeness. He takes the number "twelve" (a figure of wholeness) and doubles it. Here in this heavenly worship scene, believers find the complete and sure picture of how humanity is to orient itself in faithful repose before God.

The narrative also clarifies how these 24 earned the privilege of worshiping in such close proximity to God. Through their dress, they are revealed as complete witnesses. Their dazzling robes (see the comment on 3:4) are a reward bestowed because the 24 have witnessed to the lordship of Christ in spite of the hostile response they had expected and in turn did receive from the imperial force of Rome (see the discussion of 3:2–4). At 3:4 and 7:9–13, the imagery of dazzling clothing is directly linked to the act of resistant, obstinate witnessing that provokes hostile Roman response. At 19:14, the believers who make up the armies of heaven are suggestively attired in dazzling linen. And at 6:11, following the clear statement that the believers in question were slaughtered because of their testimony to the lordship of Christ (6:9), dazzling garments *are*

---

8. Aune writes, "All such descriptions of God enthroned in the midst of his heavenly court are based on the ancient conception of the divine council or assembly found in Mesopotamia, Ugarit, and Phonecia as well as Israel" (1:277). See also Reddish, who posits that the imagery is "drawn from ancient royal courts in which a variety of personal and official attendants surrounded the ruler and his throne" (97). On the background of the imagery surrounding the heavenly council, he points to Gen 1:26; 1 Kgs 22:19–23; Job 1:6; 2:1; Ps 89:7; Isa 6:1–13; Dan 7:10.

explicitly tied to resistant witness. Witnessing—washing oneself in the blood of the Lamb—is the gory enterprise that ironically brightens one's apparel (7:9–14) and simultaneously maintains its dazzling appearance (3:4).

If the dazzling robes have any other meaning, it is that of conquest. At 3:5, Christ declares that they are the proper payment for those who conquer by witnessing faithfully in a hostile context. The crown reference (see the discussion of 4:10) picks up this language of victorious commendation and extends it (see the comments on 2:8–11; 3:11). At 6:2, the description of the rider on the dazzling horse connects the images of conquest and crown.[9] Nowhere, though, is this linkage more dramatic than in 14:14, where a child of humanity, the ultimate conqueror, is said also to be capped with a golden crown. How impressive have been the exploits of these twenty-four? They have earned them the same headgear as the Christ! Their witness has conquered indeed. What they have done is more important to John than who they are. Humans who are encouraged to emulate their praise of God are invited through John's presentation to mimic the behavior that enabled their praise to take place where it does.

**[5]** The shock and awe of the throne room theophany add to the splendor that the throne and its room decor already exude. The imagery builds from a wealth of Hebrew Bible sources where this kind of heavenly activity signals God's cosmic prominence. Key among them is the Sinai theophany at Exod 19:18–21. There are many others, however, among them Job 36:30–32; Pss 18:7–19; 77:17–18; Ezek 1:4, 13, 14, 24, 26–28; and Dan 7:9–10. John effectively returns to these dramatizations at 8:5 (see the discussion there); 11:19; and 16:18–21. Perhaps just as important is the recognition that the imagery has a competitive edge. Lightning and thunder were used in association with Greco-Roman deities and emperors.[10] John's presentation presumes a more natural and longstanding association with God instead.

The seven flaming torches further increase the sense of grandeur. Their presence, though, is more than a special effect, for they recall the lampstand of Zech 4:2 and the seven flames that burn upon it. For the prophet, the stand and its lamps represented the presence and vision of God throughout all creation. Also reminding the reader of the lamps that burned before the ark of the covenant, they expand on the discussion that John introduced at 1:4. The spirits at 1:4 represented the fullness (the number "seven") of God's force in the world through the active presence of the Holy Spirit. The all-seeing nature of that Spirit is declared in 5:6.

---

9. One might also point to the two other crown occurrences. At 9:7 the locusts are depicted as conquering hordes and also wear crowns. So, too, does the woman clothed with the sun at 12:1. By 12:16 it becomes clear that, with the help of the earth, she too overcomes the attempts of the dragon to slay her.

10. Aune remarks, "The thunderbolt was closely associated with the Greek god Zeus, as it was with his Roman counterpart Jupiter, and was consequently used as a symbol suggesting the divinity of several Roman emperors including Domitian" (1:295).

[6–8a] The sea of glass appears to be an allusion to the heavenly dome of crystalline ice at Ezek 1:22 (Beale 327). In John's mind, it threatens the access to God that the opened door represents. The sea is the site of chaos in the Bible (Job 26:12–13; Pss 74:12–15; 89:9–10; Isa 27:1; 51:9–11). The raging sea represents resistance to God, God's people, and the future of God's people. Before God can create and secure the world, God must first seize control of the sea.[11] John repeats at 13:1 the belief that Daniel initiated (7:2–3): great beasts of terrible destruction are fomented in and from the sea.

Remarkably, in the staging that John envisions, the sea appears closer than the twenty-four elders to the throne. Indeed, that portrait fits Revelation's witness theme. To gain access to God, believers must cross over the chaos of the sea. That is, they must find a way to witness to the lordship of Christ by pushing past the torrential forces that demand celebration of Rome's lordship.

God has made the crossing easier by freezing into place the sea and the hostility it represents. God has not, however, realized the goal that John's vision ultimately promises: the complete destruction of the sea (21:1). In fact, the sea now exists with God. It sits in heaven, next to the throne. God harboring the sea in the throne room is like the president of the United States stashing an unstable, active, Soviet-era nuclear bomb on the credenza behind the desk of the Oval Office. Indeed, the sea is glassed over like a cosmic throw rug. It is, however, still there, waiting to break open and flood away the hopes and dreams of heaven itself. Locked down is not thrown out. When John sees the sea through the opened door, he therefore knows that the future, even God's future, is still a very dangerous place.

Back closer to the throne (it is as if John's enraptured eyes are flashing back and forth, seeing erratically, certainly not in sequence), John now glimpses what he had apparently missed before: four oddly appointed, living creatures—the cherubim. The use of the preposition *kyklō* (surrounding) indicates that they represent another of the concentric circles ringing the throne. They are so close to the throne, in fact, that John also says that they are in the midst of it. This odd description most likely means that they are right up against the throne. Their placement, then, would make them the first of the attendees to God's presence. The rainbow, the seven flaming spirits, the sea, and the twenty-four elders would all apparently follow them in turn.

Clearly, these four living creatures are a composite picture drawn from the visionary recollections of Ezek 1:5–25 and Isa 6:1–4.[12] While Ezekiel's creatures had four wings, John's, like Isaiah's, have six. The match with Isaiah, however, is not a perfect one in this regard. In Isaiah's presentation, the wings are paired together as they perform certain functions. In Revelation they appar-

---

11. In the Synoptic Gospels, before Jesus can quiet the storms, he must first tame the watery tempest (see Mark 4:35–41; 6:47–51; Matt 8:23–27; Luke 8:22–25).

12. Reddish (99) points to variations of the cherubim in Gen 3:24; Exod 25:18; Num 7:89; 1 Sam 4:4; 2 Kgs 19:15; Pss 80:1; 99:1; Ezek 10:1–22.

ently operate individually. The creatures are also positioned differently. Isaiah situates them above the throne; in Ezekiel, they appear to bear the throne (with the assistance of their adjoining wheels) from a position below. John sees them stationed right next to the throne. They are also described differently. In Ezekiel, each creature has four faces; however, Revelation presents four different creatures with four different faces. In Ezekiel, the creatures move but do not speak; in both Revelation and Isaiah, they introduce a worship of God that begins with a resounding cry of "Holy, Holy, Holy." The echo reminds John's audience that his vision is an accurate prophetic rendering, but with a new clarity and emphasis that comes in the wake of the identity of God's Christ being revealed.

Building from the parallels with the creatures in both the Ezekiel and Isaiah accounts, John describes and thereby characterizes the cherubim he sees. As in Ezek 1:18 and 10:12, they are filled (or "covered") with eyes. This description characterizes them as all-seeing. The wings suggest that they are completely mobile. Indeed, their very number symbolizes their omnipresence. They are themselves the representation of the four compass points and thus personify the entirety of the cosmos (cf. Rev 7:1).

The creatures' omnipresence suggests that they may well be a metaphor for all of living creation, as so many commentators take them to be. Yet I argue instead that their divine character traits link them more closely to God than to humanity. Reddish is therefore more likely correct to associate them with angelic rather than human being. He maintains that they represent the "highest order of angels, those who stand closest to the throne of God" (100). Such a connection makes literary sense; it agrees with the later portrait of four angels standing at the four corners of creation (7:1).

Whoever they are, their function is clear: they exist to praise God (cf. 4:9; 5:8, 11, 14; 7:11; 14:3; 19:4). They are paired with the twenty-four elders as models of appropriate worship behavior. This makes them divine witnesses to the lordship of God and God's Christ. These omniscient creatures, who see everywhere and who personify the expansiveness of the cosmos, are in the perfect position to recognize true power. They are genuflecting before God, not before Caesar. They are therefore modeling and exhorting appropriate witness behavior. No matter the circumstances, whether one is lifted to the highest reaches of the heavens or crushed beneath the foot of Rome, one's primary duty is to praise God. The one true Lord will soon intervene in human affairs and set history right (cf. 1:3; 3:11; 22:7, 10, 12, 20).

### 4:8b–11 A Hymn of Counterpraise

8b "Holy, holy, holy,[a]
   Lord God, the Almighty,
      the one who was, who is, and who is coming."

9 And whenever the living creatures give glory and honor and thanks to the one sitting on the throne, who lives forever and ever, 10 the twenty-four elders fall before the one sitting on the throne, and they worship the one who lives forever and ever, and they throw their crowns before the throne, singing: 11 "You are worthy, our Lord and God, to receive glory and honor and power, because you created all things, and by your will they existed and they were created."[b]

a. The adjective *hagios* (holy) appears seven times in Andr *l*[1678], eight times in ℵ*; nine times in 𝔐[K], and three times in other manuscripts. The threefold *hagios*, which agrees with the Old Testament text being quoted (Isa 6:3 LXX) and has superior manuscript support, is to be preferred. The variants arose either for numerological reasons or by conflation of the various numbers mentioned in the passage.

b. *Ouk* (not) is added in 046 *pc*; the phrase *kai ektisthēsan* (and they were created) is omitted in A. Neither variant has strong external evidence in its favor. The addition in 046 and omission in A were two different ways of eliminating the ambiguity and communicating more straightforwardly the traditional idea of creation.

**[8b–11]** Playing the role of heavenly liturgists, the four creatures initiate a hymn that praises God's holy and glorious lordship. As did their Isaiah counterparts (Isa 6:3), they jump-start the singing with the *trisagion*, a threefold declaration acknowledging the holy nature of the Almighty. John transforms the *trisagion*, however, by adding the information that was so well highlighted in chapter 1 (vv. 4, 8): the one who was, who is, and who is coming. Here, the creatures corroborate the testimony offered by John (1:4) and then declared in God's own voice (1:8). By using this formula which was often attributed to human leaders, and attaching it to the title "Almighty," the creatures turn their worship into an act of political counterpraise (see the comment on 1:4–8). They therefore model exactly the kind of witness John expects from his hearers and readers in Roman-occupied Asia Minor.

This worship of the creatures is affirmed antiphonally by the twenty-four elders. In John's description of the ongoing heavenly choreography, the creatures initiate an act of praise to which the elders respond. The pattern repeats forever. Having fallen before the one who sits on the throne and rules forever, they worship. In the process, they cast at God's feet the crowns (see the discussion of 4:4) for which they have expended so much effort—bearing their courageous witness—to earn. The gesture that kings used to demonstrate their fidelity to Caesar was performed by these heavenly authority figures toward God.[13] The

13. Schüssler Fiorenza comments, "According to the Roman writer Tacitus, the Parthian [Armenian] King Tiridates placed his diadem before the image of Nero in order to give homage to the Roman emperor" (*Vision of a Just World*, 59). And Aune observes, "Gold crowns were frequently presented to Roman emperors for a variety of reasons; this practice was inherited from Hellenistic kingship tradition. The Roman emperor was presented with gold crowns by the senate and delegates from provincial cities on such varied occasions as accessions, consulships, victories, and anniversaries" (1:308).

ethical implications are clear. Given that the elders represent the faithful community of believers in its entirety, John's hearers and readers know they must emulate them. They, too, must respond to the praise of the four creatures by bowing and giving exclusive allegiance to God.

The elders, however, do more than simply respond; they also expand the rationale for worship. While the creatures celebrate God's holy, almighty status, the elders attribute God's worthiness to God's role as Creator (for discussion of the adjective "worthy," see the comments on 3:4 and 5:2). Despite their connection with titles like *dominus* (Lord), *deus* (God), and *despotēs* (Master), no Roman Caesar could claim the power to create cosmic and human being. He could never credibly claim to have brought into existence the world he so desperately wished to control. That prowess is God's alone. Knowing that the ultimate power lies with God, believers ought to feel empowered to resist any claim to lordship tendered by Rome.

### Excursus: The Hymns of Revelation as Songs of Resistance

Revelation is a dangerous blend of memorable music and recalcitrant rhetoric. Its liturgical hymns witness to the promise that God is relieving Rome of its historical command. Right now.

Of the nine hymnic units in the Apocalypse, seven (4:8–11; 5:9–14; 7:9–12; 11:15–18; 16:5–7; 19:1–4; 19:5–8) are antiphonal in form. Call and response between God, angels, cherubim, executed believers, and even the inanimate heavenly altar cascade down to earth and rise back up to the heavens in worshipful celebration of God's identity and God's purpose for human- and heaven-kind. It all begins at 4:8–11, a celebratory declaration of God's transcendent and historical lordship that sets the tone for the hymns that follow. Paced by their threefold testimonial to God's holiness, the four cherubim who guard the throne sing to the majestic status of the Almighty One who is, who—unlike human kings—has always been, and who will soon be coming with great and transformative power. It is no accident that they use the same descriptors (Almighty; the one who was, is, and will be) assigned the duty of communicating either Caesar's or a Greco-Roman god's magnificence. It is no accident that these descriptors are found several times in close relationship with each other, and on almost all of those occasions as integral parts of these forceful hymns.[14] It is no accident when the cherubim start, no accident when the twenty-four elders finish, by casting down their crowns before God's throne, and declaring God not only ruler but also Creator of all. They sing clearly so they can be heard forcefully: "You, Lord God, are worthy." What they mean is, *only* you!

Thus 4:8–11 makes the point for God, and 5:9–14 establishes the same point for God's messianic regent, the Lamb. Maintaining the same themes, in many cases with

---

14. Aune observes, "The phrase κύριε ὁ Θεὸς ὁ παντοκράτωρ, 'Lord God Almighty,' is a formula found 5 times in Revelation (4:8; 11:17; 15:3; 16:7; 21:22). . . . It is particularly significant that the full title occurs in Revelation several times in close association with the title ὁ ὢν καὶ ὁ ἦν (καὶ ὁ ἐρχόμενος), 'who was and is (and is to come)': 1:8; 4:8; 11:17" (1–5, 642).

the same language, though in a reverse order of presentation, this hymn sings of the Lamb's worthiness:

| A  | 4:8  | 5:14    | four creatures (cherubim) praise              |
|----|------|---------|-----------------------------------------------|
| B  | 4:9  | 5:12–13 | glory, thanks (4:9), honor, power (5:12–13)   |
| C  | 4:10 | 5:11    | worship                                       |
| B′ | 4:10 | 5:10    | crowns/kingdom                                |
| A′ | 4:11 | 5:9     | worthy                                         |

If, as most critics agree, the seven-sealed scroll holds the details about the plan and purpose of human history, then the one charged to open and read it is the one given charge of that history. It is no accident that the Lamb and not any human ruler is the one being, the *only* being, worthy of such responsibility. It is not Caesar who sets the course of human life and gives it meaning; instead, the Lamb does so, by his blood. "According to Roman law, those prisoners of war who were ransomed were brought back home and reintegrated into their own nation. In the same way, those who were ransomed by Christ for God were liberated in order to constitute here and now a 'kingdom of priests'" (Schüssler Fiorenza, *Vision of a Just World*, 61). Where Rome is concerned, any such kingdom is unauthorized. Any such unauthorized kingdom is by definition a counter-kingdom and therefore a provocation to be challenged. By singing this song, the twenty-four elders dare Rome to bring the challenge on. Backing them up are the responding voices of myriads of heavenly hosts, who reaffirm the singular worthiness of the Lamb and thereby initiate the bowing down of every creature in heaven, on the earth, and even under the earth (thereby comprising all three tiers of the three-tiered mythological universe) before the Lamb rather than Caesar. Is that the right move? According to the four cherubim, it is. After opening the initial hymn with their deafening "Holy, holy, holy," they salute the combative claims made in this hymn with a resounding "Amen."

Even where the hymnic language seems to be the benign stuff of spiritual salvation and praise, the theme of opposition to the Roman regime rears its resistant head. At 7:9–12, an innumerable soul multitude of every tongue, tribe, and nation stands before the heavenly throne and the Lamb, uniformed in dazzling robes and armed with fronds of palm. This vast chorus cries out: "Salvation belongs to our God . . . on the throne and the Lamb." Problems? First, according to Roman imperial rhetoric, every tongue, tribe, and nation owes its peace and salvation exclusively to Caesar. Second, salvation is imaged as a transformative, historical victory. Over whom? For John, there is only Rome. The dazzling robes have already been established as a symbol of victorious conquest over the beastly machinations of imperial Rome (3:4; 4:4; 6:9–11; cf. 7:13). The palm fronds represent victory in a broader historical sense: "The frequency with which palm fronds occur on Jewish coins together with the name of the current ruler suggests that they symbolize, like the wreath, an ascendant ruler."[15] But if Rome *is* the rule, how can this "salvific" language about an *ascendant* ruler be heard as anything other than political taunting? Appar-

---

15. Citing 2 Macc 14:4, Aune (1:468–69) points to an ex–priest named Alcimus, who gave the Syrian King Demetrius I Soter (187–150 B.C.E.) a gold crown and a palm, which were most likely symbols of a victorious ruler. Similar gifts were given with the same probable effect to Demetrius II Nicator (161–125 B.C.E.) by Simon the Hasmonean (1 Macc 13:36–37).

ently on the rise is a new human victory/rule, this apparent kingdom of priests, backed up by this cheering, heavenly throng. Even the heavens believe it. When the angels, twenty-four elders, and four cherubim hear this heavenly call to rhetorical arms, they fall on their faces before God and worship with another resounding Amen.

Indeed, the fourth antiphonal hymn (11:15–18) clarifies what the third one left implicit. Not only do boisterous heavenly voices declare victory; they also thank God for making it so. The kingdom of the world—it has to be Rome—becomes the kingdom of God and the Lamb instead. They, not Caesar, will reign forever. Once again the twenty-four elders respond. They fall before God and the one true Almighty who, unlike every historical king, both was and now is. No need any longer to add the proclamation that the Almighty is coming; as the trumpet fanfare attests, by this hymnic moment God is already here.

It is all about justice now. In the fifth antiphonal hymnic unit (16:5–7) the angel of the waters sings accompaniment to the Almighty's destruction of Rome and its political and economic minions. The devastation is the righteous effort of a holy and just God. The one who is again identified as having championed both past and present history gives back to the evil ones the very wickedness they have perpetrated on others. The bloodthirsty are made to choke on the very blood they shed. Elated, the altar that had once served as shelter for the souls of those slaughtered for their historical witness to the lordship of Christ (6:9–11) responds in hymnic affirmation.[16] God's devastating blow is so fiercely appropriate that even the furniture is compelled to sing.

So, apparently, is everyone else. The sixth (19:1–4) and seventh (19:5–8) hymnic units erupt in a hallelujah chorus of affirmation. How thankful are John's choral witnesses to God's judgment? This is the only place in the New Testament where "Hallelujah," "praise Yahweh," occurs (4 times here). The Almighty God, not Rome, is the ultimate historical judge: "God has reversed Rome's judgments against the Christians in a higher court" (Boring, *Revelation*, 192). The Almighty God, not Rome, reigns supreme. The hallelujahs rain down in the first hymnic unit as the heavenly multitude twice praises God's salvation as a historical/political liberation that follows immediately from the utter decimation of bloodthirsty, oppressive, and imperial Roman power. The twenty-four elders and four cherubim respond with a corroborating "Amen" and "Hallelujah" of their own. This is the very essence of *political* worship.

The scene celebrates the relationship that now may freely develop between the Lamb and his church. Heretofore the threat of Roman lordship had stood in the way. John feared that his followers would align themselves with Rome's imperious claims and accommodate themselves to Rome's political and economic prowess in the same way that a weak person might be lured into the sin of prostitution. But now that Rome and its claim to lordship have been justifiably removed, God's people have the freedom to witness properly, which is to say defiantly. The reward for that witness is symbolized by the imagery of fine linen, bright and pure.

---

16. Beale notices the intentional connections between this hymnic unit and the narration about the slaughtered souls beneath the altar following the opening of the fifth seal at 6:9–11. He points out that the hymnic use of the Holy One (*ho hosios*) and the verb "to judge" (*krinō*) "reflects virtually the same description of God in 6:10, which is the persecuted saints' prayer to God that he will vindicate himself and them by judging their persecutors" (818).

The other two hymnic units (12:10–12 and 15:3b–4) celebrate the same primary themes: while resisting the lordship of Rome, they worship the lordship of God and the Lamb. Nowhere is this slap in the Roman imperial face more evident than at the Lamb's victory hymn in 15:3b–4. As a shameless appeal to the song of victory sung following the exodus from Pharaoh (Exod 15:1–18), it champions the great and marvelous present deeds of the Almighty as a recapitulation of the legendary earlier one. The difference: while Israel's song focuses on the decimation of Pharaoh's army, the song of those who conquer the beast rivets attention on the awesome power of God (Boring, *Revelation*, 173). This God, not Rome, is the one Universal Sovereign. All nations knew it long ago. All nations will know it now.

They will know it not only because of God's actions but also because of the conquering behavior, the resistant witness, of the Lamb's followers. A heavenly voice sings of their efforts in 12:10–12. They join in God's conquest of Rome by assisting in demolishing the demonic foundation upon which Rome was built. By the power of the Lamb's blood and by their own testimony, not only do they witness to the contrary lordship of the Lamb; their very witness also helps effect the Lamb's lordship.

The hymns of Revelation, then, are a celebration of confrontational resistance. John's hearers and readers live in an oppressive climate where they will be punished for standing up and standing out against the lordship of Rome. These hymns incite them to respond to the eschatological worship call of angels, cherubim, elders, and a heavenly multitude of souls with their own politically charged worship and witness to history's sole sovereign—to the Almighty God and to the Lamb.

## 5:1–5 Who Is Worthy?

1 Then[a] I saw in[b] the right hand of the one seated on the throne a scroll written inside and on the back,[c] sealed with seven seals. 2 Then I saw a mighty angel preaching in a great voice: "Who is worthy to open the scroll by[d] breaking its seals?" 3 And no one was able in heaven or on the earth or under the earth to open the scroll or look into it. 4 And[e] I wept profusely, because no one was found worthy to open the scroll or look into it. 5 Then one of the elders said to me: "Stop weeping. Behold the lion from the tribe of Judah, the root of David, has conquered, so that he is able to open[f] the scroll and its seven seals.

a. The *kai* (here, "then") operates as a coordinating conjunction (also beginning 5:2, 5).

b. Instead of choosing the clearer preposition *en* (in), John here opts for *epi*, followed by "the right hand" in the accusative case. The preposition can therefore reasonably be translated as "on," "upon," or "in." John knows how to be more precise. At 1:16; 10:2, 8, when he locates objects similarly in someone's hand, he deploys the more exact *en* (*en tē cheiri*). At 1:16, when he locates the stars in the right hand of the child of humanity, he clearly means "in." When he speaks about the location of those stars again at 1:20, he uses the preposition *epi* instead of the *en* he had used earlier. This grammatical turn of events suggests that John is using the terms interchangeably and that in 5:1 he intends to say that God holds the item of concern *in* God's right hand.

c. NA²⁷, following A, reads *esōthen kai opisthen*, "inside and behind." A majority of Greek manuscripts, though, read *esōthen kai exōthen*, "inside and outside." This variant appears to be a window into codicological history in early Christianity. Metzger comments, "After the Church began to use codices for its sacred books, the terminology appropriate for scrolls seemed to be strange" (*Textual Commentary*, 737). Copyists accustomed to using codices rather than rolls would have naturally thought of a *biblion* as having *esōthen kai exōthen*; hence the variant. The idiosyncratic reading of ℵ, *emprosthen kai opisthen*, "in front and behind," is probably an assimilation to Ezek 2:10 LXX.

d. The connecting *kai* (and) is epexegetical; the second formulation clarifies the first: "Who is worthy to open the scroll and to break—that is, by breaking—its seals?"

e. The great Codex A, which is generally regarded to be the single best manuscript of Revelation, lacks v. 4 altogether. In all likelihood, this is a simple case of haplography due to homoioteleuton. That is, the copyist has inadvertently leapt from *blepein auto* (to look into it) at the end of v. 3 to the same phrase at the end of v. 4 (so Metzger, *Textual Commentary*, 737).

f. Because the infinitive *anoixai* (to open) completes the meaning of *enikēsen* (has conquered), it should be construed as an infinitive of result (Aune 1:323).

**[5:1]** "Then I saw" (*kai eidon*) appears at 5:1 because John's vision shifts now from a general appraisal of the throne room and God, the one seated on the throne (see the comment on 4:2–3), to a more specific concern with an item located in God's right hand.[1] Biblically speaking, the right hand is a symbol of prestige and power.[2] In the eschatological reign, it is the coveted place to sit next to God (Matt 22:44; Mark 12:36; Luke 20:42; Acts 2:34; Heb 1:13). Jesus himself declares that when even his enemies see him so positioned, all will recognize him as God's messianic agent (Matt 26:64; Mark 14:62; Luke 22:69). No wonder, then, that the disciples seek a seating at Jesus' right hand when he comes into his reign (Matt 20:21; Mark 10:37). The image of salvation itself is positionally determined. At the moment of judgment, when the wheat is separated from the chaff or, to use another popular metaphor, the sheep are distanced from the goats, the ones favored by God (wheat, sheep) end up on the right (Matt 25:33–34). Numerous other references demonstrate the positive symbolic value of being located on the right (see Mark 16:5; Luke 1:11; Acts 2:25, 33; 5:31; 7:55–56; Rom 8:34; Col 3:1; Heb 1:3, 13; 8:1; 10:12; 12:2; 1 Pet 3:22).

1. After analyzing all of John's 33 uses of the *kai eidon* construction, Aune concludes that one of its three primary functions was the introduction of "a major scene within a continuing vision narrative" (cf. 6:1; 8:13; 13:11; 15:2; 19:19; 21:2, 22). He also points to Ezek 2:9. Another function of the construction is the introduction of "a new or significant figure or action that occurs within a continuing vision narrative" (1:338). John uses the formula in this way several more times at 5:2, 6, and 11 (cf. also 6:2, 5, 8, 12; 7:2: 9:1; 16:13; 17:3, 6).

2. According to Aune, "The 'right hand' of God is . . . a common metaphor frequently found in the OT and Judaism signifying his power and authority (Exod 15:6, 12; Pss 18:35; 20:6; 63:8; Isa 41:10; 48:13)" (1:340).

John clearly holds the right hand in high esteem. When the child of humanity secures the seven churches, he cradles their seven representative angels (stars) in his right hand (1:16, 20; 2:1). When an angel raises a hand to swear, it predictably is the right hand (10:5). When John pictures the mythological marking of the dragon showing up on a person's body at a place that represents a person's identity and life choices, he mentions the forehead and the right hand (13:16). And when the child of humanity wants to encourage John and calm his fears, he intentionally places upon the seer his right hand (1:17).

The object in God's right hand is a *biblion*. John's word use is imprecise. *Biblion* could easily denote the flat codex-type book with cover and bound leaves that was a precursor to contemporary books. It could just as easily intend a rolled-up scroll, more commonly found in the early and middle decades of the first century. Although the codex began to be used more frequently in Christian communities toward the end of the first century, one cannot appeal to the historical context as a way of clearly determining what kind of "book" John has in mind. At the end of the first century, it could have been either.

The higher probability, however, is that John intends a rolled-up scroll. The metaphor he applies to the heavens just a chapter later (6:14) is suggestive. He describes the horrific vision of the sky rolled up like a *biblion* (cf. Isa 34:4). There he clearly means "scroll." It is likely that John was operating with the same image throughout since he never feels a need to explain it differently. This interpretation gathers further corroboration from the background imagery drawn from Ezek 2:9–10. Like Rev 5:1, the Hebrew text speaks of a scroll written on the inside and back. Ezekiel's volume is clearly a scroll, and the LXX uses *biblion* to refer to it.

There remain two even more pertinent questions. How many scrolls does John include in the course of his writing? And if there are more than one, to which one is he referring here? I argue that one can build a credible argument that John is working with either four, three, or two scrolls. His use of *biblion* is just that imprecise. If one argues that John is working with four scrolls, one could appeal to (1) John's own scroll of prophetic visions (1:11; 22:7, 9, 10, 18, 19); (2) the heavenly scroll of chapter 5 (5:1, 2, 3, 4, 5, 8, 9); (3) the little scroll of chapter 10 (10:2, 8, 9, 10); and (4) the Scroll(s) of Life/judgment (3:5; 13:8; 17:8; 20:12, 15; 21:27). One could make a strong argument that each of these scrolls has its own unique identity and, moreover, that John speaks about each of them in closed blocks of material in a manner suggesting that he only speaks about a new scroll after he has closed discussion on the one that came before it. The only exception to this rule is an understandable one. He introduces his own scroll at 1:11, when he clarifies what he is writing and why he is writing it. He then refrains from speaking about it again until he reaches the closing chapter, where he explains the scroll's relationship to the believing community.

Yet one could also make the case that John operates with three scrolls. On this reading, one would collapse the second and third categories above so that the little scroll of chapter 10 is identified with the heavenly scroll of chapter 5.[3] The many critics of this view point out immediately that the scroll in chapter 10 is described diminutively as a *biblaridion*, or "little scroll" (vv. 2, 9, and 10). Again, though, John is imprecise. While speaking of that little scroll at the critical moment of 10:8, he writes *biblion*. One therefore cannot make a determination on the basis of the diminutive use in vv. 2, 9, and 10. In fact, the evidence suggests that John has the same scroll in mind in the two chapters. At 10:8, he is ordered to take the scroll, which is open, from the hand of the mighty angel who was introduced at 10:1. One recalls that at 8:1, after the loosing of the seventh seal, the scroll John discusses in chapter 5 was fully open. There is also the matter of the presence of the mighty angels. There is one on hand at 5:2 to announce the appearance of the scroll and another on hand at 10:1 to handle the scroll that John is to take at 10:8. The mighty angels played leadership roles in the mythical cosmos. It is not surprising that they would be tasked with the shepherding of a scroll of such obvious importance that its natural place of residence is in the right hand of God.

Once again the background of Ezek 2:9–10 comes into play. In the third chapter of Ezekiel, the prophet is commanded to eat a scroll that has been given to him. When he does, he finds that it is as sweet as honey, even though its fulfillment will mean judgment for the people. John clearly foregrounds the scroll of 5:1 against the texts from Ezek 2–3. It is interesting, then, that John is also commanded to eat the scroll that he has taken from the hand of the mighty angel (10:8–9). Like Ezekiel, he finds it sweet as honey to the taste, but ultimately bitter to the stomach, since the realization of its words will bring about divine acts of justice and judgment. If Ezekiel was talking about the same scroll and John was operating directly from Ezekiel's imagery, it is not improbable that in the two different chapters, John also intended to speak about the same scroll.[4]

It would be difficult to make a convincing case that John intended a discussion of only two scrolls, his own and the one mentioned here in 5:1. That would mean that the scroll of 5:1 is to be identified with both the scroll of chapter 10 and the Lamb's Scroll of Life. The telling argument against this intriguing possibility is the fact that the Scroll of Life is only opened at 20:12, a late stage in John's visionary prophecy. John is clear that the scroll of chapter 5 is fully opened with the breaking of the seventh seal (8:1). Additionally, John digests the "little scroll" (10:9). Thus, if indeed, as I think is the case, the scroll of chapter

---

3. For a recent critique of the assertion that the scrolls in 5:1 and 10:2 are the same entity, particularly as it challenges Richard Bauckham's proposals for identifying the two, see Herms 142.

4. In 10:2, 9, and 10 multiple variants also recognize the possibility that John is speaking of the same scroll. In order to build consistency, the variants substitute *biblion* for *biblaridion*.

5 is the same scroll described in chapter 10, that scroll cannot be the Lamb's Scroll of Life, which is opened intact at 20:12. John is therefore working with three scrolls.

The second scroll is closed with seven seals (5:1). The number "seven" indicates a complete and total binding. The seals are themselves suggestive: "In antiquity, wet clay or wax was applied to secure the closures of containers or documents. Seals were then used to make an impression in the clay or wax to identify the source of a document or object to guarantee the work's authenticity or to safeguard the document from tampering" (Reddish 108). John uses the noun "seal" (*sphragis*) throughout chapters 5 and 6, right up until the moment when the final scroll seal is broken at 8:1 (cf. 5:1, 2, 5, 9; 6:1, 3, 5, 7, 9, 12; 8:1). In its only other occurrences in Revelation, 7:2 (cf. also 7:3) and 9:4, the term refers to the seal of God that ultimately marks the identity of those who have been faithful, which in John's language means that they have witnessed (i.e., have not accommodated). Those who are so sealed are marked with the name of God on their foreheads (7:3; 9:4; 14:1; 22:4). They are marked as God's authentic property. If the seven scroll seals were likewise God's seals, then they too would designate God's property.

Many scholars have tried to clarify this particular property by analyzing John's description of it. Exodus 32:15 states that the tables bearing the Ten Commandments were written on both sides, front and back. This observation has led some to conjecture that perhaps the scroll contained either the commandments or the entire Old Testament, whose proper interpretation was only realized in and through the life of Christ. As objecting scholarship has pointed out, however, John's book, like Ezekiel's, upon which it depends, is more a metaphor of salvation and judgment than it is a clarification of the Hebrew Bible.

Beale focuses on the seals, which he claims represent "witnesses" on a legal document (343). This is an intriguing proposition, given all the attention John pays to witness language. Could the seals themselves be doing precisely what John wants his hearers and readers to do? That is, could they be testifying to God's lordship? In their case, they would be doing so by refusing scroll entry to anyone except God's own authorized, messianic agent. Only someone uniquely empowered by the true Lord could open the Lord's scroll. Beale argues that a legal document like a testament or will would fit such a literary mold. The testament was a document generally inscribed on both sides. It was also generally secured with seven wax or clay seals, on which were imprinted the stamp of an authorizing agent. In some cases, each seal, as a witness, gave an abbreviated testimony of the scroll's contents. In other cases, the testament was constructed so that only some parts of the scroll were revealed with the breaking of each seal. "Either understanding of the seals in 5:1–2 would mean that parts of the book's contents would be progressively revealed with the breaking of each seal and would not have to await the breaking of all the seals"

(Beale 343). Beale therefore concludes that John's scroll should be interpreted as a "covenantal promise of an inheritance," a testament whose will for humankind was enacted by God's messianic executor as he loosed the seals that had once secured it (340–41).

Reddish is unimpressed: while he agrees that testaments were indeed written on and sealed in a manner like the one Beale describes, he maintains that "the presence of scrolls or books in other apocalyptic writings suggests those traditions as the source for John's imagery (cf. Dan 10:21; *1 En.* 81:1–3; 93:1–3; 103:1–3; 106:19)" (108). Aune takes his cue from the awkward way in which John describes the scroll; it was written on the front and the back. There are clear textual problems with John's description. John does not choose antonyms as one would expect. Aune (1:338) points to Luke 11:40, which appropriately parallels outside and inside (*to exōthen kai to esōthen*), and Rev 4:6, which justifiably opposes front and behind (*emprosthen kai opisthen*). Indeed, the Ezekiel text (2:9–10 LXX) upon which the scroll in Rev 5:1 is surely based correctly opposes the antonyms back and front (*ta opisthen kai ta emprosthen*). John's use of inside and back (*esōthen kai opisthen*) is therefore so puzzling that some textual variants try to correct the anomaly by making the language read either "inside and outside" or "front and back." Though the NRSV renders the correct translation, "inside and back," it tries to cope with the textual ambiguity by offering an improbable, alternative translation, "written on the inside, and sealed on the back." Aune solves the problem by arguing that John was writing with an *opistograph* (*opisthographos*)—a "papyrus roll written on both sides"—in mind: "There is no compelling reason to reject the notion that the *biblion* is an *opistograph* modeled after Ezek 2:9–10, with the writing on both sides primarily representing the fullness of the prophetic message given to Ezekiel, as well as the fullness of God's eschatological plan for the world in the scroll of Rev 5:1" (1:342–43). There is also no compelling reason not to think of the seals binding the *opistograph* as "witnesses," whose summary information testifies to the lordship of Christ. As seals, they would also prevent unauthorized access to the content and the power represented by that content.

The closed scroll no doubt reminds John's readers of the sealed scroll in Isaiah that contained God's vision for humankind, which the people could not read (Isa 29:11). Jeremiah speaks of a similar instrument (32:10). Daniel writes about a scroll whose information about human destiny was so complete that God ordered it shut until the end of time, which would be preceded by days of great struggle (12:4, 9). In John's vision, that end time, complete with days of preparatory struggle, had come. In such a time, humans might take encouragement from knowing whether humankind was destined for obliteration or restoration. That knowledge was apparently secured in the scroll. Revelation 4:1 promises that John would have access to this knowledge, that is, see all things to take place "after this." The scroll is the realization of that promise. "After this" refers to what is to happen in the remainder of John's "book." History's destiny is to be revealed during just this period.

[2] After signaling the start of a new throne room scene with the *kai eidon* (then I saw) construction of 5:1, John opens 5:2 in the same way. This time, though, the formula does not start a new scene but flavors the same scene with the introduction of a novel theme: worthiness.

Initially, though, John's focus is on "a mighty angel preaching in a great voice" (see the discussion of "great voice" as a judgment metaphor at 7:2). This powerful messenger bears a striking resemblance to Daniel's holy watcher sent from heaven (Dan 4:13–14, 23 LXX). Both figures evoke the symbolism of judgment. This judgment focus continues in Revelation with the appearance of mighty angels at 10:1 and 18:21. Notably, the second mighty angel is also associated with a scroll.

John's enduring focus is on the angel's question: "Who is worthy to open the scroll by breaking its seals?" The hymn that begins at 5:9 supplies the answer. The continuation of the worthiness theme throughout the chapter is also an indication that John is much more preoccupied with this question than he is with any mere angel sighting. Up to this point he has seen many great sights. All of those sights, including this angelic one, take a back seat to the gradually clearing message about someone's worthiness to open the scroll.

Worthiness itself is earned through endeavor (see the comments on 3:4; 5:9, 12). John connected the worthiness of the remnant at Sardis to their refusal to accommodate themselves to the social, economic, political, and spiritual expectations of Greco-Roman pagan and imperial lordship. They combined their refusal to accommodate with the contrary declaration of Christ's lordship. Indeed, their very witness to that lordship was a manifestation of its reality. By testifying to it, they participated in bringing it about. In order to stop their testimony and the result it threatened, the representatives of pagan and imperial lordship could be counted upon to respond in a reactionary manner. Worthiness was thereby integrally connected with both the work of witness and the suffering such work would inevitably bring about.

[3–4] John's narration assures his readers that there are no witnesses worthy enough to open the scroll. Picking up on the three-tiered mythical understanding of the universe as a heavenly upper region, an underworld region comprising the Old Testament sense of Sheol and the New Testament understanding of hell, and earth in between (cf. Exod 20:4; Deut 5:8), John declares that no one can be found anywhere in all the cosmos who meets the standard. For all his world power and domination, not even Caesar has attained the requisite stature. Not even Caesar, therefore, has the kind of control over human destiny that his rule pretends to exert.

Perhaps the even greater tragedy is that the Christ-believers who have been worthy witnesses have not earned sufficient standing to accomplish this monumental task. At 1:9, John describes himself as one who has witnessed to the lordship of Christ and suffered exile as a result. Still, John cannot presume to open the book. At 2:13, he reminds his readers about Antipas, a witness so faithful that he was killed because of his testimony. Yet he, too, did not earn the right to open the book. At 3:4, John describes the Sardis remnant that witnessed and suffered together as a believing community. They, too, were insufficiently worthy. Witnessing alone, even being slaughtered because of one's witnessing, is not enough.

Apparently the mighty angel wants to know if there might exist some second-level, more radical version of witnessing than has been narratively demonstrated thus far. Only such a witness would be worthy to open the book. John has offered a clue. On two separate occasions (1:5; 3:14) he went out of his way to identify Christ as the one faithful and true witness.

Verse 4 adds little in the way of new information. John repeats the tragic announcement of 5:3; no one was found worthy enough to open and read the scroll. He adds only the notice of his own mournful response to this bitter news. Profusely, he wept.

[5] The throne room attendants, however, know of a possibility that has to this point eluded John. One of the twenty-four elders (see the discussion of 4:4) tasked with heavenly worship (see the discussion of 4:8b–11) confides to the grief-stricken seer that there is someone worthy enough to open the scroll. After telling John to cease crying, the elder describes the candidate by using two messianic descriptors that would be as recognizable to John's readers as they are to him. The worthy one is first of all described as the lion out of the tribe of Judah, an image that builds upon accounts at Gen 49:9–10; *T. Jud.* 24.5; and *4 Ezra* 12.31–32. His second attribution is the "root of David," a symbol that draws its intertextual strength from accounts like Isa 11:1, 10; Jer 23:5; 33:15; and Zech 3:8; 6:12 (cf. Rom 1:3). Both images suggest great strength; the lion is a feared predator that rules whatever domain it occupies, as no doubt Israel hoped, with God's help, to do in the future. That rule would be instigated by and established through a leader of David's messianic lineage, someone from the great king's roots, who would have David's close relationship with God (see the comment on 22:16).

Clearly this messianic figure is a powerful force. To describe the results of his work, John uses the verb "conquered." This messiah conquered. It is on the basis of that conquest that he has acquired sufficient worthiness to break the seals and open the scroll. John writes awkwardly at this point, following up his indicative verb, "conquered" (*enikēsen*), with an infinitive "to open" (*anoixai*). The narrative context suggests that the infinitive initiates a result clause. John intends to say that the lion out of the tribe of Judah, the root of David, has conquered; as a result, he is worthy to open the scroll.

The understanding that John intends a result clause comes from the connections he has drawn between the terms "witness," "conquer," and "worthy." For John, a faithful *witness conquers* by testifying to the lordship of Jesus Christ. The seer makes this clear in chapters 2 and 3, where he exhorts the seven churches to live by a witness code demanding that they not accommodate themselves to the expectations of pagan and imperial lordship. John describes witnesses who are successful resisters as conquerors. As a result of their conquest, witnesses are worthy of an eschatological relationship with God (15:2; 21:7). He makes the case to each of the seven churches at 2:7 (Ephesus), 2:11 (Smyrna), 2:17 (Pergamum), 2:26 (Thyatira), 3:5 (Sardis), 3:12 (Philadelphia), and 3:21 (Laodicea). Still, a believer does not witness in order to gain an eschatological relationship. That relationship is a by-product of the witnessing act. The goal of witnessing is the declaration of the lordship of Christ in an environment hostile to such testimony. There are many possible responses to that testimony. Opposing powers will persecute and punish the witnesses. God, however, will count their witness, even if it results in the ultimate punishment of death, as a conquest worthy of eschatological relationship.

Nowhere is this connection between witnessing and conquering made more explicitly than at 12:11, where John declares that those who conquer do so by the blood of the Lamb and the word of their witness. By conquering in this way, John's believers mimic the actions of the Lamb, who himself is the faithful and true witness (1:5; 3:14) who conquers (17:14).

Because worthiness is an attribute earned by the work of witness (see the comments on 3:4; 5:9, 12), the connection between worthiness and conquest is also narratively secured. The conquering witness is a worthy witness. The conquering believer who testifies to the lordship of Christ is worthy of an eschatological relationship with God. The conquering lion from the tribe of Judah, the root of David, is apparently exceptional. He already has an eschatological relationship with God; he is God's messianic emissary. His conquering testimony makes him worthy of something else: he can open the scroll sealed with the seven seals.

### 5:6–10  The Lamb Is Worthy

6 Then I saw among the throne and the four living creatures and the elders a Lamb, standing as though executed, having seven horns and seven eyes, which are the seven[a] spirits of God sent out into all the earth. 7 And he went and took the scroll[b] from the right hand of the one seated on the throne. 8 And when he took the scroll, the four living creatures and the twenty-four elders fell before the Lamb, each holding a harp and golden

bowls filled with incense, which represent the prayers of the saints. 9 And they sing a new song:

> "You are worthy to take the scroll
>     and open its seals, because you were executed and by your
>         blood you ransomed for God[c]
>     people from every tribe and
>         tongue and people and nation.
> 10 And you made them, for our God, a kingdom and priests,
>     and they will rule on the earth."

a. The brackets placed around *hepta* (seven) in NA[27] indicate doubt about the adjective's presence in the original text. Though the external evidence is fairly evenly distributed for its presence ($\mathfrak{P}^{24}$ ℵ 1854 2053 2329 2344 2351 $\mathfrak{M}^{K}$ it vg[cl] sy; Ir[lat] Hipp Cyp) and for its absence (A 1006 1611 1841 2050 $\mathfrak{M}^{A}$ ar vg; Ir[arm]), it is more likely that it was added by later copyists to build consistency with the presentation of seven spirits at 1:4; 3:1; and 4:5.

b. Several witnesses (1006 1841 2050 *pc* it vg[cl] sy[ph.h**] co; Cyp Prim) insert *biblion* here, no doubt because the sentence makes more sense with it. I have added it in translation for the same reason. The context indicates that the scroll must be the object the Lamb secures.

c. The pronoun *hēmas* (us) is substituted for (1 *pc* vg[ms]; Ir[lat vid]) or added to (ℵ and $\mathfrak{M}$) *tō theō* (A). Whom did the Lamb purchase, and for whom did he purchase them? The problem here seems to be that *ek pasēs phylēs* (from every tribe) is not a proper direct object, though Aune (1:325) notes that a partitive genitive, accentuated by a preposition like *ek*, often acts as a verb's object in Revelation. It would be no surprise, then, that a copyist should supply an object, and this seems to have happened with *hēmas* here (so Weiss 108). Codex A, albeit a single manuscript, is a formidable witness in Revelation. In this case it is best to follow it in reading *tō theō* (God) without *hēmas*.

[6] The *kai eidon* (then I saw) of 5:6 introduces yet another novel element to the ongoing throne-room scene centered on the scroll in God's right hand. Having introduced the character who is worthy enough to open the scroll, John now identifies both his person and the conquering witness that gave him such lofty eschatological stature.

The "lion from the tribe of Judah," the "root of David," is awkwardly positioned. John claims that he is "in the midst" of the throne and the four cherubim and "in the midst" of the twenty-four elders. John used this awkward phrasing ("in the midst") before when he described the location of the cherubim as "in the midst of the throne and surrounding the throne" (see the discussion of 4:6–8a). He meant that they are right next to the throne, so close to it in fact that they are the most intimately located attendees to God's presence. He means the same thing here; the one who is "worthy" stands so close to both the throne and the four cherubim that he is right next to them. The problem with this stated location is that John also locates him "in the midst" of the twenty-four elders. When we appeal to John's chapter 4 narration about the location of the attendees to God's heavenly presence, we find that their positions fall away from the throne in the following order: the cherubim, the rainbow, the seven flaming spirits, the sea, and the twenty-four elders. But if these elders represent the outer ring of throne room attendees and the cherubim the innermost ring, the messianic figure John sees cannot be in the midst of both groups at the same time. John's language therefore suggests movement.[5] The one who is worthy is, in effect, "working" the throne room. He is on the move, next to God, as one might expect God's eschatological representative would be, and yet also in the midst of the representative believers, who witness to God's lordship. What appears to be impossible physically, John establishes kinetically by his awkward phrasing. In his envisioning, the one who is worthy to open the scroll is with God *and* with those who witness to God because he is moving between them.

Matters become stranger still. The scene appears to shift character focus. Without warning, John distances himself from the lion and focuses on what, in terms of strength anyway, is its polar opposite: a Lamb, standing as slaughtered. This is a striking turn of events. Why does John set the reader up to expect a text about a messianic, conquering lion, and then, after the dramatic notice of a topical shift ("then I saw"), cut immediately to a scene whose protagonist is a slaughtered Lamb? Is he using the latter figure to subvert the former?

John will use the term "Lamb" (*arnion*) some twenty-eight times in the book as a metaphor for the Christ. Though the word appears to be a diminutive Greek form, most commentators agree that by the end of the first century, when John was most likely writing, it had lost any diminutive sense and was synonymous with the word "sheep" (*probaton*) (cf. Beale 354). The term *arnion* appears elsewhere in the New Testament only once (John 21:15), and in that case it refers not to Jesus but to his followers. In the only four New Testament texts where "Lamb" does refer to Jesus (John 1:29, 36; Acts 8:32; 1 Pet 1:19), a different Greek word (*amnos*) is deployed.

At least on the surface, the intertextual history of the term appears to be more significant than the nomenclature in ascertaining why John so radically shifts his focus. John could have had in mind any of four possible "lamb" figures from Jewish history when he envisioned this messianic Lamb: (1) the *tamid* lamb (*tāmîd*, Exod 30:38–42), sacrificed at the Jerusalem temple in the mornings and evenings; (2) the Passover lamb, symbolizing God's deliverance of the people from Egyptian bondage; (3) the sinless lamb of Isa 53 (see esp. 53:2, 7, 9), whose sacrifice has atoning significance; and (4) the conquering lamb of *1 En.*

---

5. This suggestion fits the understanding of 5:7, where the Lamb works his way back to the throne.

89–90. Reddish is right to argue that John probably draws elements from each of these figures in creating his own portrait of the slaughtered Lamb: "Rather than seeing the lamb imagery in Revelation as being drawn from one source or having only one meaning, a better approach is to acknowledge the multivalent character of this powerful symbol" (109).

The key interpretive question is this: what might all this multivalence mean? Reddish argues that the Lamb becomes a "victorious figure who conquers by self-sacrifice, who willingly gives up his life to become the 'faithful and true witness'" (109). Aune (1:32) believes that John has purposely joined the theme of Christ as conquering Messiah (v. 5) with that of Christ as atoning sacrifice (v. 6). The implication seems certain: John wants his hearers and readers to recognize that Christ's conquest comes by way of his sacrificial, atoning death on the cross.

I offer an alternative explanation. Christ conquers by his actions as the faithful and true witness, which in his context resulted in—though it need not always require—death. In other words, I recognize the same variables of witness, conquest, and slaughter. I contend, however, that John has packaged those variables toward a different interpretive end. The Lamb does not conquer by self-sacrifice and thereby become the faithful and true *atoning* witness. The Lamb already *is* the faithful and true witness who selflessly sacrifices concern for his own well-being in order to carry out his testimony to his God's and his own lordship in a hostile Greco-Roman, Palestinian world.

The research of Loren Johns is instructive. Johns focuses exclusively on what he calls the rhetorical force of the Lamb symbolism in the Apocalypse. He asks a pertinent question: how, in their particular social-historical setting, will John's readers appropriate his Lamb language? After an exhaustive survey of lamb imagery in early Judaism, he reaches the conclusion that "there is no evidence at this point to establish the existence of anything like a recognizable redeemer-lamb figure in [its] apocalyptic traditions" (106). John therefore would not have expected his apocalyptically oriented readers to connect his Lamb's suffering and slaughter to their own redemption. A survey of the Hebrew Bible affords no better warrant. In a study that offers the most relevance for our particular concern about the redemptive efficacy of the Lamb's slaughter, Johns explicitly rules out an agenda of transformative suffering. After comparing texts that associate lambs with atonement for sin to the Lamb language in Revelation, he concludes that "the terminology used in the Apocalypse does not fit well with the lambs of the sacrificial system" (129). In fact, he points out appropriately that John does not even restrict slaughter language to the Lamb (cf. 6:4, 9; 13:3; 18:24). His conclusion: "In none of these other cases is the 'slaughter' considered expiatory, reducing the possibility that the rhetorical force of the 'slaughter' of the Lamb in 5:6 is primarily expiatory" (129). Johns then broadens his conclusion even further. Given that only two verses (1:5–6) have even any remote expiatory themes connected to them, and given that they occur well outside the central section of the conflict visions (chs. 4–19), he argues that "there is little in the Apocalypse of John to support this understanding of Jesus' death as Atonement" (130).

We can, however, support an understanding of his death as an act of witness. Well before John characterizes Jesus as the Lamb, he identifies him, *by name*, as *the* faithful *witness* (1:5). At 3:14, still before any mention of the Lamb, comes linguistic reinforcement: as witness, Jesus is both faithful and true.[6] There is no need for interpretation; John has made his point clearly. Whatever else he might appear to be to his followers, Jesus Christ is first and foremost God's prime witness.

The question we are narratively driven to ask, then, is this: how are we to understand the Lamb's slaughter in the light of his role as God's faithful witness? That is to say, what is it about his witness that connects with and perhaps even causes his killing? From the context in Asia Minor at the end of the first century, the implication is suggestive: Jesus, *the* prophetic witness figure, apparently testified to a truth. He faithfully adhered to that testimony even under the direst of circumstances, at the cost of his own life, on the cross.[7]

Because of this witness, Christ, "the Lamb," was slaughtered. Because of the sacrificial overtones implicit in the language of slaughter, "executed" would be a better descriptive term. John may well be making such a linguistic distinction when he chooses the Greek term *sphazō* (slaughter), rather than the "slaughter" term with stronger sacrificial associations, *thyō*, to describe the fate of Christ and those who follow him. Except for the anomaly of 1 John 3:12, "slaughter" (*sphazō*) is found in the New Testament exclusively in the Apocalypse. Though the more sacrificially oriented term (*thyō*) is prevalent elsewhere in the New Testament (see Mark 14:12; Luke 22:7; Acts 14:13, 18; 1 Cor 5:7), it does not occur in the Apocalypse at all.[8] If John does think of Christ's slaughter as an atoning sacrifice, why does he avoid the very vocabulary that would help make that connection more explicit?

Instead, throughout his narrative, John develops the vocabulary in a way suggesting that witness may well lead to execution not because it is redemptive but because it is resistant. Witness is the kind of nonaccommodating (resistant), provocative behavior that John exhorted his followers to practice in chapters 2 and 3. Antipas, the attentive reader will remember, paid the price of his life because of his obstinate witness (2:13). Perhaps this is why John describes the

6. John even speaks of the testimony or "witness" of Jesus (1:2, 9). Johns (162) points out that before Jesus is identified as the Lamb, John uses some *thirty* other terms to describe him.

7. Trites observes, "From the context of the Apocalypse as a whole, it seems probable that *hē marturia Iēsou* [the testimony given by Jesus] in these passages refers primarily to Christ's passion, where he witnessed 'the good confession' before Pontius Pilate (cf. I Tim. vi 13)" (76).

8. Cf. Louw and Nida 236, 534.

Lamb as "standing." While the *tamid* lamb was apparently killed as it was standing, the symbolism need not be reduced to that literal historical meaning.[9] Standing, particularly as John uses the language, also has a provocative implication of resistance. He appears to mean something like "standing up" or "standing fast." At 3:20, the only other time prior to chapter 5 where John uses the verb *histēmi*, the risen Christ is said to be standing and knocking. In lukewarm Laodicea, where no one heeds Christ's call to witness, Christ resists rejection by seeking entrance even in the face of their closed door. This subtle verbal emphasis continues throughout the narrative. At 6:17, after the opening of the sixth seal, the great ones of the earth ask who can stand (i.e., stand up to, resist) the wrath of the Lamb. At 7:9 and 15:2, those who have resisted the lure of accommodation and have witnessed to the lordship of Christ stand up before the throne and the Lamb. At 14:1, the Lamb, the epitome of resistance, stands with them on Mount Zion. And in chapter 11, two great witnesses stand in determined opposition to all those who would challenge their testimony to the lordship of Christ (11:4, 11). Though mortally wounded, they, apparently like the Lamb, are still standing, still resisting.

This metaphorical correlation between standing/resistance and execution becomes a causal connection at 6:9, where John declares that the souls under the altar have been executed *because of* their nonaccommodating witness. Jesus is the faithful and true witness; it makes good narrative sense to connect his execution to his witness as well (5:9). In making such a linguistic move, John can celebrate the power of the Lamb's enduring witness even as he laments the slaughtering the Lamb had to endure because of it. The Lamb is (still) standing, as (even though) slaughtered. Though he carries with him forever the marks of his destruction, he remains victoriously alive. Executed because of his witness, he maintains the living, resistant force of that witness (since he stands) nonetheless. His posture is itself a sign of resurrected defiance—a powerful, hopeful message for a people who fear that their own witness may provoke a hostile government to persecute them (6:11). Even if they should fall in death, they, like the Lamb, will still stand as defiant, victorious witnesses.

What does this language do? Ethically speaking, it encourages the kind of behavior highlighted by its showcased character, the Lamb. The saints are described as those who follow the Lamb wherever he goes (14:1–5). This obviously means that they imitate the Lamb by acting as he has acted. This is why it

---

9. Cf. Sanders: "Here we should explain that pagan and Jewish methods of slaughtering were similar, and that all or most males would know how to do it. The animal's throat was cut, or the carotid arteries were opened, ordinarily while it was standing. In Jewish slaughter, because of the prohibition of consuming blood, one had to be especially careful to slit the throat in such a way that the animal lost most of its blood; that is, the windpipe was not to be cut through, lest the animal choke on its own blood. A deft stroke would sever the carotid arteries relatively painlessly, the blood would gush out, and the animal would soon lose consciousness" (107).

is so important to be clear about one's interpretation of the slaughter/execution language. Did Christ conquer through his suffering and slaughter? Or did Christ conquer in spite of suffering and being executed? If indeed the Lamb conquers by being slaughtered, then an emphasis on discipleship calls for believers, too, to suffer on their own way toward eschatological relationship with God. If, however, the Lamb conquers by a provocative witness that might indeed provoke a hostile response from the powers threatened by that testimony, then the summons to discipleship would have believers engage in their own acts of nonaccommodating witness despite any suffering that might result.

In describing the Lamb, John showcases his strength. He possesses seven horns. The horn is a symbol of power in key pieces of Jewish literature (Deut 33:17; 1 Kgs 22:11; 2 Chr 18:10; Pss 22:21; 89:17; Ezek 34:21; Dan 7:8, 20, 24; 8:3, 6, 8, 20; Zech 1:18–21; *1 En.* 90.6–12, 37). It is also a metaphor for great power in John's narrative (Rev 9:13; 12:3; 13:1, 11; 17:3, 7, 12, 16). Like the beast in Dan 7, the great red dragon and the beasts who operate in its employ sport ten horns fashioned to foment shock and awe. The Lamb, though, is unimpressed. While he carries three fewer horns in number, his power over the dragon and its beasts is incalculable. The number "seven" symbolizes wholeness, fullness, and completion. While the dragon has more horns, the Lamb has more power. His power is complete.

So is his vision. The Lamb's seven eyes represent complete, perfected perception in the same way that the seven horns represent complete power. As spirits, they also symbolize a consummate relationship with God. Prior to 5:6, whenever John used the plural term "spirits" (1:4; 3:1; 4:5), he was referring to the seven spirits of God. He was figuratively speaking about God's Holy Spirit (see the discussion of 1:4–8). The reference is dependent upon Zech 4:2, 10, where seven mysterious lamps are revealed as the seven eyes of the Lord, whose perceptive powers range throughout all the earth and whose identity is "associated with Yahweh's omnipotent Spirit" (Beale 355).

[7] Though the ensuing action is described sparingly, much happens in this next narrated moment. The Lamb approaches "the one seated on the throne" (cf. Dan 7:9–10; see the comment on 4:2–3). In Dan 7:13, when the one like a child of humanity approaches God's throne, dominion, glory, and kingship are bestowed upon him. Something very similar is happening in John's vision. After the Lamb arrives at the throne, he removes the scroll from God's right hand. God allows the withdrawal because the Lamb is worthy (see the discussion of 5:5).

[8] The Lamb's special status is confirmed by the behavior of the cherubim and the twenty-four elders. Tasked with the eternal worship of God (ch. 4), they now fall to their knees and shower their praise upon the Lamb.[10] Twice, after

---

10. For the connection between the language of falling (*piptō*) and worship in Revelation, see 1:17; 4:10; 5:14; 7:11; 11:16; 19:4, 10; 22:8.

John falls to his knees before them in worship, angels chastise him and redirect his praise toward its proper object: God (19:10; 22:8–9). The Lamb is as proper an object for worship as God.

In their praise of the Lamb, the cherubim and elders come equipped with two special props: harps and golden bowls filled with incense. The harps (particularly in the hands of the twenty-four elders) remind John's hearers and readers of the Levites, who like the priests worked in twenty-four orders or shifts in the Jerusalem temple. One of the Levitical tasks was the presentation of music. They "were commissioned to 'prophesy in giving thanks and praising the Lord' by 'singing' to the accompaniment of 'lyres, harps, and cymbals' (1 Chr 25:6–31)" (Beale 357).

More important to the overall meaning of the scene are the golden bowls, whose incense represents the prayers of the saints. Saints—literally, "holy ones"—is simply John's euphemism for the people of God, more particularly the people who demonstrate their relationship with God through their witness to God's and the Lamb's lordship (see the discussion of 21:2). Incense had a special place in the rituals of the Jerusalem temple. Each morning and evening, at the sacrifices that signaled the opening and close of daily worship, incense was burned on the small golden altar that stood inside the sanctuary, near the door to the holy of holies.[11] Psalm 141:2 not only recognizes incense as a key component in the liturgy of worship, but also connects incense metaphorically with prayer.

While John does not specify the content of those prayers, the location of the text is suggestive. The prayers would seem to be less an offering and more a challenge to God to begin the process of vindicating God's people. In the only other significant text where the terms "prayer" and "incense" occur together in the book of Revelation (8:3–4), they are also metaphorically linked.[12] There the prayers of the people rise with incense to the heavens. As a result of that rising, the angels sound their seven trumpets and thereby initiate God's judgment upon those who have persecuted the saints. Revelation 5:8 is just as provocatively positioned. It precedes the Lamb's opening of the seven seals, which also brings about catastrophic acts of judgment that vindicate the lordship of God and the Lamb and, perhaps just as importantly, those who witness to that lordship. Seen in this way, the metaphorical prayers in 5:8 may well anticipate the under-the-altar calls for vindication from those who had been executed because of their witness to God (6:9–11).

**[9–10]** The cherubim and elders certainly seem to think that the prayers in 5:8 are calls for God to act in judgment and vindication. They follow up those

---

11. Comay 175. Cf. Exod 30:34–38.

12. The term "incense" does appear again at 18:13, but there it is simply one more item in a cataloguing of cargo. Prayer appears only in 5:8 and 8:3–4.

prayers with a *new* hymn of praise. "In the OT a 'new song' is always an expression of praise for God's victory over the enemy" (Beale 358; Pss 33:3; 40:3; 96:1; 98:1; 144:9; Isa 42:10).

The song is also contextually new because the object of praise has shifted. The singers who glorified God in chapter 4 sing the praises of the Lamb in chapter 5.[13] Subsequent *new* songs follow the narrative pattern established here. They demonstrate a shift of either focus or content from the songs that occurred before them. The new hymn at 14:3 is sung not by the cherubim and elders but by the 144,000, and its mysterious lyrics can only be learned by the 144,000. Those who conquer the beast sing the final new hymn at 15:3. This hymn is the "Song of Moses" and the "Song of the Lamb." Its very learnable lyrics are then played out in the ensuing text. The one thing that each of these new hymns has in common with the others is something they also hold in common with the hymns of the Old Testament: they anticipate God's impending judgment against those who have persecuted God's witnesses, and they celebrate God's vindication of those witnesses, who have been persecuted.

This particular new song at 5:9–10 also addresses the central concern of the chapter's first 5 verses. Who is worthy to open the scroll that contains God's historical design for judgment and vindication? The narrative answered the question at 5:5 by showcasing the "lion of Judah," "the root of David." It then has inexplicably shifted focus in the next major scene (5:6–10) by switching attention to the Lamb. The move would have been disorienting for a first-time reader, who would not have been sure why John was suddenly talking about the Lamb when he had led them to expect further discussion on the "lion." Only in v. 9 does it become clear that the Lamb and the lion are the same character. The language of worthiness that belonged to the lion also belongs to the Lamb. Only one was worthy. The lion and the Lamb must therefore be the same entity.

The lion/Lamb is worthy. After making that clear, v. 9 uses a causal formulation to explain exactly how the Lamb earned the worthiness for which he is so acclaimed (see the discussion of worthiness as an earned endeavor at 3:4; 5:2). There are three reasons. First, the Lamb is worthy *because* he was executed. This surely confuses the identity issues even further. The lion, which usually conquers by might, earns its heavenly credentials in this apocalyptic case by being slaughtered like a lamb.

Second, the Lamb is declared worthy because he used the blood of his execution to ransom/purchase people. The universalism of the vision is on full display as John explains that those who are ransomed/purchased represent every ethnicity, tongue, people, and nation. No group is left out.

---

13. For a comparison of the similar structures of the two hymns, one lauding God and the other praising the Lamb, see the excursus "The Hymns of Revelation as Songs of Resistance" (above, after ch. 4).

The economic nature of the language is equally clear. "This metaphoric language most probably refers to the ransom of prisoners of war who were deported to the countries of the victors and could be ransomed by a purchasing agent from their own home country. The image also alludes to the exodus tradition. As the blood of the paschal lamb signified the liberation of Israel from the bondage of Egypt, so has the death of Christ made possible the liberation of Christians from their universal bondage" (Schüssler Fiorenza, *Vision of a Just World*, 61).

This is not, however, a matter of expiation. In the narrative design that John has laid out before us, Christ's witness and the death he endures because of that witness enable an eschatological relationship with God (cf. 14:3–4). At 3:18, Christ instructs the Laodiceans to buy into that relationship by purchasing gold, dazzling robes, and salve from him. In the ethical context of chapters 2 and 3, the items for purchase are metaphors for the kind of nonaccommodating witness that will lead to eschatological relationship with God. Witness and purchase have a natural, narrative relationship for John. That relationship continues in a negative way at 13:17, where one can only buy and sell in the Roman economy by accepting the mark of the beast (see also 18:11). Just as one buys into a relationship with God by the risky act of nonaccommodating witness, so one buys into a relationship with the beast by acts of compliant, self-protecting accommodation.

Purchase for John, then, is more political than it is expiatory. As Johns points out, only 1:5 connects Christ's liberating activity to the theme of ransoming humans from sin (130). In every other significant text that mentions blood in a manner that relates to the eschatological relationship believers hope to have with God (i.e., "purchase"), blood draws its most potent meaning from the metaphor of witness.[14] At 19:11–13, the Lamb, who is the faithful and true witness (cf. 1:5; 3:14), exemplifies in his person the strategic connection between his identity as a living testimony to the word of God and the blood that was shed on account of that identity. At 6:10–12, slaughtered believers cry out for vengeance upon their blood, spilled because of their witness. Read through the clarifying lens of 3:2–4, the text of 7:9–14 instructs that clothes washed in the blood of the Lamb are the due of those who have witnessed to the lordship of Christ. The link becomes clear in 12:11: believers conquer by the blood of the Lamb *and* the word of their witness. The Lamb's blood and the believer's witness are indissolubly linked. It is by appealing to both—one as received gift, the other as engaged act—that believers find themselves in the purchase of an eschatological relationship with God. Blood and purchase are indeed linked in Revelation, but they are linked through the theme of witness, not that of expiation.

Like the faithful believers in Daniel (7:18, 22, 27) and those who followed Moses (Exod 19:6), John's Christ-believers would also find themselves to be a

---

14. There are numerous uses of blood language in the Apocalypse. Most of them refer more generally to traditional notions of the bleeding that comes as a result of combat, suffering, or both.

reign of priests (cf. Rev 1:6). This is the third reason why the Lamb is found worthy. By his powerful witness, and the sacrifice he makes in proclaiming that witness, he establishes God's believers as a reign of priests on earth. Revelation 20:4–6 clarifies the believer's role. Believers who refuse to accommodate to the expectations of Rome, the satanic beast, are executed because of that witness. These martyrs become the reign of priests (cf. 22:5). While John does not make the connection causal so that their witness causes their rule, he does make the connection explicit. Witnessing and reigning go together for believers just as they went together for the Lamb. It was the Lamb's witness that purchased the reality of that rule; it is the believers' witness to the lordship of the Lamb that apparently will procure—that is to say, enable—their connection with and participation in that rule.

The rule itself is an oppositional one. It personifies the very life and language of resistant witness that brought it into being in the first place. "Insofar as John utilizes sociopolitical language in 5:9–10, he transforms the anthropological understanding of redemption expressed in the traditional baptismal formula of 1:5–6 into a sociopolitical one. Just as the exodus of Israel resulted in the election of Israel as a special nation and kingdom for Yahweh, so does the redemption of the Lamb's followers who were elected from the nations constitute a new alternative kingdom or empire whose members are priests" (Schüssler Fiorenza, *Vision of a Just World*, 62). No wonder Allen Boesak can say of this material: "It is dangerous, heady stuff, this song. It is a freedom song" (60).

## Excursus: The Lion and the Lamb

John's witnessing Lamb is hardly a vulnerable figure. He is a conquering lion (5:5), armed with the fullness of God's power (symbolized by the seven horns, 5:6), who deposes the dragon Satan (12:10), and having taken up the sword of God's word, rides out to meet Satan's forces on the field of apocalyptic battle (2:16; 19:11–16). In the visionary world that John inhabits, the Lamb's victory depends on his power. And yet, even in victory, the Lamb carries in his person the visage of slaughter. How is one to hold these opposite dramatizations of vulnerability and conquest together in a believable narrative tension?

I believe that this emphasis on the necessity of power is the reason John finds it necessary, before he introduces Christ as the slaughtered Lamb, to announce him as a mighty lion (5:5). There is every narrative indication that John thinks the two titles belong together. In the end, neither subverts the other. The lion reveals a Lamb; the Lamb remains a lion. Patricia McDonald advises that John hints at his intention by the way he uses his language: "There is, on the whole, a distinction between what John sees and what he hears. . . . Hearing tends to give the inner reality of what is seen."[15] Perhaps it

---

15. McDonald 33. See also Bauckham: "Jesus Christ *is* the Lion of Judah and the Root of David, but John 'sees' him as the Lamb. Precisely by juxtaposing these contrasting images, John forges a symbol of conquest by sacrificial death, which is essentially a new symbol" (*Climax of Prophecy*, 183).

is no coincidence, then, that John *hears* the moniker "lion," but *sees* a Lamb. Whenever hearers/readers *see* the Lamb in the remainder of the narrative, the staging of this character profile in chapter 5 suggests that they *hear* the footsteps of a lurking lion. Robert Mounce, after observing that John has retrofitted this particular Lamb with the symbolism of perfect power (seven horns) and complete wisdom (seven eyes), agrees: "The *arnion* of Revelation is not a dramatic contrast to the figure of the Lion but an extension of the same powerful figure" (Mounce, "Worthy," 68). The slaughtered Lamb is a powerful conqueror (5:5–6; 12:11; 17:14). Yet there is something unique about this lion/Lamb's modus operandi: "Although [John's] lion of Judah 'conquers,' . . . it does so not in a lion-like way, by tearing its prey to pieces and devouring it, nor even in the military way that the imagery surely implies" (McDonald 37). Instead, it conquers through predatory weakness.

Does this kind of description hold? It did for Martin Luther King Jr. In his very capable hands, nonviolent, peaceful protest was nevertheless a will-to-power. The Civil Rights leader was quite specific: "Power without love is reckless and abusive and . . . love without power is sentimental and anemic."[16] An observer of his nonviolent, active, engaged, and acerbic resistance would not have been wrong to describe him as a "lion" for justice and equality. Neither would an observer of John's executed Lamb be wrong thus to characterize the Lamb. Perhaps this is precisely why, after his initial introduction of the Lamb in chapter 5, John no longer feels it necessary to continue the lion language. The hearer/reader no longer needs it; he/she has the executed Lamb, which is the appropriate narrative interpretation of the lion. The slaughtered Lamb is *how* the lion manifests itself in the world. In other words, the predatory way of the lion *is* the slaughtered lamb. "Slaughtered Lamb," then, is not so much a descriptive, static noun as it is a paradoxical, action verb. Though John's lion is a powerful conqueror, it would not be right to say that this lion "*hunts* its prey." The more appropriate language would be something like "this lion *slaughtered-Lambs* (*sLambs*) its prey." This lion *slaughtered-Lambs* (*sLambs*) the dragon and the beasts that historically represent it.[17] The weak Lamb, then, does not subvert the powerful lion; the Lamb's weakness, its slaughter, is precisely the way the lion works out its power. The lion *sLambs* God's opposition.

It does so on its own active, preemptive terms. Johns's survey of the social-historical situation of the Apocalypse reveals a tantalizing interpretive clue. In a reconstruction that represents today's prevailing scholastic thinking, he argues that there was no wholesale persecution of Christians during Domitian's reign (81–96 C.E.), the time John was most likely writing. The evidence suggests that John was writing about the "*expectation* of persecution rather than the present *experience* of persecution."[18] The problem lay with

16. Quoted in Anthony B. Pinn, *Why, Lord? Suffering and Evil in Black Theology* (New York: Continuum, 1995), 77. See Martin Luther King Jr., *Where Do We Go from Here: Chaos or Community?* (Boston: Beacon Press, 1967), 37.

17. Indeed, this lion also *slaughtered-Lambs* God's people. Jesus' death on the cross, after all, is as much a judgment as it is a victory. That is a point John tries desperately to get across in his letters to his wavering churches in chs. 2–3. For further discussion on the "sLamb" interpretation, see Blount, *Can I Get a Witness?* 69–90.

18. Johns (122) points to 2:10–11; 7:13–14; 11:7–9; 12:11; 16:6; 17:6; 18:24; 19:2; 20:4–6.

the imminent conflict he knew would erupt if his hearers and readers lived out the kind of nonaccommodating Christianity that he himself professed. He was concerned primarily about the claims of lordship declared by Rome and Caesar and the witness to those claims made in the local municipalities where his churches were located. Johns paints a historical picture of local leaders pitched in feverish competition to land the rights to build temples praising the divinity of the emperor and the lordship of Rome. In order to fit in socially, politically, economically, and religiously in these communities, John's followers would have to accommodate themselves to the demands of these localized cultic affections. Resisting those demands would invite trouble.

Trouble, however, had apparently not yet arisen. That might well mean that John's believers were all too occupied in the business of accommodation: "The resistance called for was an *offensive* maneuver as John tried to unmask the spiritual powers at work behind the churches' compromising involvement in the empire, in its commerce, and in its imperial cult" (Johns 127). His concern that other Christians' prophets, whom he calls Jezebel, the Nicolaitans, and Balaam, were approving of such behavior raised his hackles even further. John was unyielding; there could be no compromise with any activities that gave credence to the idea that Caesar, Rome, or Rome-sponsored divinities laid claim to the allegiance due only God and the Lamb.

But if all this is correct, if there was only sporadic persecution, if John's people were not standing out, vulnerable, because they were finding ways comfortably to blend in and accommodate, then the seer's immediate problem was, as Johns points out, more spiritual than social and historical. The social-historical crisis would not arise *unless* John's people actually started to live by the mandates his apocalyptic prophecy demanded: "The resolution of that spiritual crisis would ironically induce a very real and dangerous *social* crisis as the churches began faithfully to resist the imperial cult and to face the consequences of their allegiance to Christ" (Johns 127).

This recognition is precisely what makes Lamb-like behavior active and aggressive, even as it remains "weakly" nonviolent. If John was indeed asking his people to stand up and stand out in a world they had accepted, a world that had accepted them, he was essentially telling them to go out and pick a fight! He was ordering them to declare that they were now nonaccommodating Christians, who could no longer participate in a world that had not really noticed them because they had heretofore been accommodating to it. In a classic "Don't ask, don't tell" (that I am a Christian) kind of environment, John was essentially ordering his Christians to be about the business of telling on themselves, with full knowledge of the kind of repercussions that such telling would bring.

However, as we can plainly see, slaughter was *not* the goal. The goal was an active ministry of resistance that would witness to the singular lordship of Jesus Christ. Ironically, just as Jesus' death led to his empowered life, the slaughtering would help lead to the transformative goal of eternal life in a new heaven and new earth where that lordship was on full display (12:10–12). This is how the power of the Lamb works. For those who are slaughtered because they stand up for Christ and therefore cause themselves to stand out to Rome and its Asia Minor vassals, defeat is conjured to victory, death is conjured to life. Like the dragon and the imperial power that worships it, even death itself is *sLambed.*

*5:11–14  Glory to the Lamb!*

11 Then I saw and I heard the sound of many angels surrounding the throne and the living creatures and the elders (and their number was myriads of myriads and thousands of thousands), 12 singing with a great voice,

> "Worthy is the Lamb who was executed
> to receive power and wealth and wisdom and strength
> and honor and glory and blessing."

13 Then I heard every creature in heaven and on earth and under the earth and upon the sea, and everything in them, singing:

> "To the one seated on the throne and[a] to the Lamb
> be blessing and honor and glory and might
> forever."

14 And the four living creatures sang, "Amen." And the elders fell down and worshiped.

a. The conjunction *kai* (and) is absent in ℵ[1] A 1611 2344 *pc* and present in all other manuscripts. In question is the phrase *tō kathēmenō epi tō thronō [kai] tō arniō*, which is either "to the one seated on the throne *and* to the Lamb" or (if we do not read a *kai*) "to the Lamb seated on the throne." Impressively, Codex A lacks *kai*, and the first corrector of ℵ actually strikes it from his text. But the stronger manuscript evidence for its inclusion, together with the christological motive for a copyist to identify the Lamb with the one seated on the throne (cf. 5:7, where the two are distinguished), compels us to read *kai* here.

[11–12] John introduces the second hymn to the Lamb with his fourth use of the scene-shifting narrative formula "then I saw" (*kai eidon*). Before identifying the poetic shift in emphasis, he sets up the hymn with a narrative prelude. He sees a throng of angels crowding the throne room. There are so many present that they cannot be numbered (cf. Dan 7:10). They are readying themselves to respond antiphonally to the psalm previously sung by the cherubim and elders.

The angels open their song by echoing the thought of the cherubim and elders: the slaughtered Lamb is worthy. Then the angels shift the focus. In their song, they do not explain *why* the Lamb is worthy. Instead, they emphasize *what* the Lamb is worthy to receive. It is just here, though, that there is a great deal of similarity in the two worship refrains. Before the cherubim and elders explain why the Lamb is worthy, they too declare what the Lamb is worthy to receive. In their thinking, the Lamb is worthy to receive and open the scroll. Using the same verb of reception (*lambanō*), the angels now observe the Lamb's worthiness to take power, wealth, wisdom, might, honor, glory, and blessing. The parallel formulations suggest that there is a relationship between the scroll and power, wealth, and wisdom, and so forth. With knowledge and control of history (i.e., the opened scroll) comes massive power. Because Caesar has been shown to be incapable of opening the scroll, he can no longer justifiably lay claim to such power. Only the Lamb is worthy to take the scroll and open it. Therefore, only the Lamb is worthy of the formidable rights that go along with that capability (cf. Dan 7:14).

[13–14] A cascading praise effect erupts, like dominoes falling, where the singing of one group ignites the responsive singing of another. Once the heavenly chorus finishes its choral response to the song of the cherubim and elders, the voices of every creature in creation rise up in yet another antiphonal reply. John appeals again to the three-tiered mythical construct of the cosmos (see the comment on 5:3) to make certain that his hearers and readers understand the universal range of his vision. He hears voices from every realm of the created order, and he hears them singing a song of praise both to God on the throne and to the Lamb. They are *both* due the blessing and honor and glory and power mentioned in 5:12. And they are due them forever. The hymn of 4:11 has explained the reason why the cherubim and elders believed God was worthy of such accolades: God is worthy because God created all things. In the hymn of 5:9–10 the cherubim and elders explained the three reasons why the Lamb is worthy. Creation is now apparently affirming those declarations with a responsive chord of acclamation. Fittingly, the cherubim and elders finish both worship scenes by sealing those affirmations with a confirmation of their own. The cherubim cry out "Amen" (see the comment on 3:14) while the elders acknowledge the truth of the hymns by falling before the throne in worship.

### 6:1–8:1 The Opening of the Seven Seals

John is the master of a three-ring narrative circus. The seven seals (6:1–8:1), the seven trumpets (8:2–11:18), and the seven bowls (16:1–21) stage the same preparatory build-up to the Last Judgment. They do so, however, from different perspectives. Hearers and readers watch three different versions of the end time unfold simultaneously at three different places on the narrative set. That explains why the scenes, while loosely similar, differ in detail. Like any good rhetorician, John hammers home his single message by rearticulating it in a variety of ways. The message is simple: God will execute a cosmic verdict that will judge those who have set themselves up as lord and save those who have witnessed to the alternative lordship of God's Lamb-like Christ.

When the world *appears* to be spinning wildly, madly, and violently out of control, even then God is firmly in charge. While it is difficult to reconcile the New Testament image of a kind, benevolent God with the chaos and destruction associated with the seals, trumpets, and bowls, there is a kind of intertestamental continuity in John's presentation. The Old Testament God is most violent and destructive when acting as cosmic and historical judge. In Revelation, the violent executors of God's judgment are based on Zechariah's presentation of patrolling, colored horses (Zech 1:7–17; 6:1–8) who operate by divine decree. The four forces of sword, famine, wild animals, and pestilence in Ezekiel likewise prefigure John's presentation (Rev 6:8; cf. Ezek 14:12–23, esp. 21). Because God is consistently just, John trusts that God must act decisively, even harshly.

## 6:1–8 The Four Horsemen

6:1 Then I saw when the Lamb opened the first[a] of the seven seals, and I heard one of the four living creatures say, as with a voice of thunder: "Come!"[b] 2 And I looked,[c] and behold a dazzling horse, and its rider had a bow, and a crown was given to him, and he went out conquering in order to conquer even more. 3 When he opened the second seal, I heard the second living creature say: "Come!"[d] 4 And another horse, fiery red, went out; its rider was allowed to take peace from the earth so that humans might slaughter one another. A great sword was given to him. 5 When he opened the third seal, I heard the third living creature say: "Come!"[e] And I looked,[f] and behold there was a black horse. Its rider held a balance scale in his hand. 6 And I heard something like a voice in the midst of the four living creatures say: "A liter of wheat for a denarius and three liters of barley for a denarius, but[g] do not harm[h] the oil and the wine!" 7 When he opened the fourth seal, I heard the voice of the fourth living creature say: "Come!"[i] 8 And I looked,[j] and behold a pale greenish-gray horse. The name of its rider was Death, and Hades followed with him. They were given authority over a quarter of the earth to kill with sword, famine, and plague, and by the wild beasts of the earth.

a. Appealing to Maloney, Aune notes that "cardinal and ordinal numbers are usually distinguished, except when the cardinal number εἷς is used to enumerate the first in a series of things when the subsequent items in the series are named" (2:379). This is the case here ("one" = "first"). John operates similarly at 9:12.

b. The imperative *erchou* (Come!) is supported by A C P 1 1006 1611 1854 2053 vg sa bo *al*, but ℵ 2329 2344 M$^K$ it vg$^{cl}$ sy$^{ph, h**}$; Vic Prim Bea add *kai ide* (and see!). The added singular imperative suggests that the cherub speaks directly to John rather than to the first horseman. Such a reading has the theological benefit of separating the devastating work of the first horseman from the command of one of God's agents; however, it is clearly secondary, as also in vv. 3, 5, 7.

c. Though *kai eidon* (and I looked) is omitted in 2329 2351 𝔐$^K$ ar; Prim Bea, stronger manuscript evidence (ℵ A C [*idon*] P 1 1006 1611 2053 2344 gig vg sy$^h$ bo arm *al*) argues for its inclusion. The same text-critical problem recurs in vv. 5, 8.

d. As was the case at the end of v. 1, though *erchou* (Come!) is supported by strong external evidence (A C P 046 1006 1611 1854 2053 vg sy[ph, h] sa bo *al*), other witnesses (א 2344 *pc* it vg[cl] bo[ms] ; Prim Bea) add *kai ide* (and see!).

e. See note b above.

f. See note c above.

g. The conjunction *kai* has adversative force here: "but."

h. An ingressive aorist, commanding that the prohibited action not even begin.

i. See note b above.

j. See note c above.

**[6:1]** The sequence of *kai eidon* ("Then I saw"; see the discussion of 5:1) and *ēkousa* (I heard) signals John's turn to a new visionary scene that sets up an apocalyptic theology of opening. "Opening" language, even when neither God nor the Lamb is its subject (3:20; 9:2; 12:16; 13:6), is always salvation and/or judgment language. At 3:7–8, the child of humanity has the keys of David. This clear image of salvation/judgment is bolstered by the subsequent declaration that what the Son opens no one can shut, and what he shuts, no one can open. At 3:20, Christ begs the Laodiceans to open their door so that he may enter and bring salvation with him. At 4:1, a door apparently opened by God represents the portal into the heavenly throne room and the eschatological relationship with God connected to it. At 9:2, the angel opens the shaft of the abyss in preparation for the acts of judgment that follow the blowing of the fifth trumpet. At 12:16, the earth opens its mouth to save the woman clothed with the sun. At 13:6, the beast opens its mouth to offer the blasphemies that justify its judgment. The other occurrences of the verb in Revelation, following the opening of the seventh and final seal in 8:1, are all presented as divine passives. The implication is that either God or the Lamb is the subject of the saving and/or judging behavior. At 10:2 and 10:8, the "opened" little scroll recalls Ezekiel's bitter scroll of judgment (10:9; cf. Ezek 2:10). At 11:19 and 15:5, the "opened" heavenly temple and tent of meeting respectively bring to mind an image of salvation. Then 19:11 chronicles the "opened" heaven, which reveals the faithful and true Word of God. This Word rides into the narrative armed with the power of salvation for those who witness for God and with the assurance of judgment for those who do not. Finally, 20:12 registers the presence of "opened" books of the dead (judgment) sitting alongside an "opened" Book of Life (salvation).

The opened seals likewise symbolize judgment and salvation. Eschatological woes (i.e., acts of judgment) are unleashed each time the Lamb breaks a seal. These woes will be as destructive and judgmental for those who oppose God as they will ultimately be salvific for those who witness faithfully for God. Key to this interpretation is the understanding of the child of humanity's earlier promise that he will keep the Philadelphians who conquer from the coming trials (3:10). The vow does not mean that believers will be "raptured" out of the trials (see the comment on 3:10). The tribulation that accompanies the breaking of each seal is something that believers, too, will endure (2:10). Their faith-fulness will matter as much as it does because they will perform it in the cir-cumstance of such duress, just as Christ himself did on the cross. That is no doubt why, in the end, the hour is described as a testing rather than a judgment; believers, too, will have a chance to make the grade. They will have the oppor-tunity to witness. Seen in this light, the eschatological moments of destruction and disturbance that follow the "opening" of each seal will likewise be God-initiated and God-directed opportunities for believers to demonstrate the met-tle of their faith and the witness that continues from it. Believers may live *through* these times and be strengthened *by* them.[19] By contrast, those who per-secute the believers will be judged by and crushed beneath them.

It is therefore appropriate that when one of the cherubim (see the discussion of 4:6–8a) acknowledges the opening of the first seal, his response registers as thunder. In John's moving, vision picture, thunder is the background music that precedes and therefore prefigures cataclysmic, transformative action. After the first peals of narrative thunder (4:5), John introduces his hearers and readers to the seven flaming spirits before the throne of God, the sea of glass, and the flanking cherubim who launch the first of the book's magnificent antiphonal hymns. At 8:5, thunder explodes as the first of seven angels prepares to blow the first of the seven trumpets. Then, at 10:3–4, seven thunders erupt as the heavenly voice speaks and John prepares a bitter prophecy of apocalyptic judg-ment. Thunder heralds the opening of the heavenly temple (11:19), the cries of the 144,000 (14:2), the horrors of the seventh bowl (16:18), and the hallelujah of the heavenly chorus (19:6) when the marriage of the Lamb and his bride occurs just before the binding of the satanic dragon. The thunder that carries the voice of the cherub here at 6:1, therefore, intends much more than aesthetic effect. Something awe-ful is about to "come."

**[2]** With a lengthened introductory formula, *kai eidon, kai idou* (and I looked, and behold), which he will deploy several more times (6:5, 8; 14:1, 14; 19:11), John warns his hearers and readers that something new is about to occur. Attention shifts from the cherub who thunders the "Come!" command to the horse and rider who obey. The description of the rider and the consequence of his actions are oddly familiar. In the chapters that preceded this one, John char-acterized Christ-witnesses as conquerors in dazzling/white clothing (see the discussion of 3:2–4). Now he turns both the color and the conquest on their head

---

19. Cf. Beale: "As in Ezekiel 14, the trials here not only affect nations in general but [also] have the dual purpose within the covenant community of purifying the faithful and punishing those dis-loyal to Christ. It is striking that in Sir. 39:25–40:9, which presents early Jewish exegetical tradi-tion based on Ezek. 14:21 (and Lev. 26:18–28; Deut. 32:24–25; Jer. 15:1–4; 16:4–5; Ezek. 5:16–17), where the four judgments occur, there is also emphasis on these calamities affecting both the righteous and the wicked" (384).

by attributing them to this first rider on a *dazzling/white* horse, who comes fiercely armed with a bow so that he may *conquer.*

The Messianic Rider of 19:11 also rides a dazzling/white horse. In fact, John's description of the two matches verbatim: "and behold a dazzling/white horse, and the one seated upon it." The rider in 19:11 is an instrument of God's judgment. The rider in 6:2 appears to symbolize the same reality. There are, however, significant problems with equating the two riders. In 19:11 the rider is the Lamb. Here in chapter 6, the Lamb is tasked with breaking open the seals, not riding out on horseback. In addition, the Lamb specifically targets Satan and his bestial allies, while the horseman's wrath in 6:2 is globally and cosmically indiscriminate. In this way, the horseman functions as part of a "woe package" with the three who succeed him in vv. 3–8. Each horseman breeds the one that follows: "Nevertheless, a logical pattern repeatable throughout the age is discernible: conquest (the first rider), together with civil unrest (especially for persecuted Christians, the second rider), leads to famine (the third rider) and death (the fourth rider)."[20] Finally, the riders in 6:2 and 19:11 are also outfitted differently. In 6:2 the horseman sports a bow for his weapon and wears a crown, while in 19:11 the figure wields a sharp, two-edged sword from his mouth and is bedecked in diadems. The rider in 19:11 deploys as his arsenal a spoken word, but the rider in 6:2 fires lethal arrows.

There is a more logical explanation for John's matching descriptions of these two riders. Because the rider in 6:2 is the first, his appearance indicates that the initial opposition to God will be one of confusing mimicry. By setting himself on a dazzling horse and laying claim to the Lord's language of conquest, this satanic emissary tries to wreak havoc in God's own image. In this way, the first horseman would be the prelude to the many false christs who would eventually appear in Christ's name and image.[21] Even so, he and the ones who follow him do not act independently of God's design. One of John's primary theological tasks is assuring his readers that, no matter how chaotic and destructive world affairs appear to be, God as just judge is in control. That reasoning leads to the rather uncomfortable conclusion that God's control extends even to the work of the four devastating horsemen. They act within God's direct sphere of influence. Indeed, it is God's elite cherubim who ignite their activity with the thundering "Come!" commands.[22] John believes that when the horsemen go to work, they have been put to the job by God.

---

20. Beale 371. Reddish likewise understands the four as a kind of narrative-package presentation: "For John, the four horsemen are not messengers of assurance or world order, but rather they symbolize the cataclysmic destruction that will precede the end" (125).

21. Cf. Boring: "Further, the resemblance of this first figure to Christ is another expression of John's view that the destructive power unleashed in the world is only a pale imitation, a parody in fact, of the true power of God/Christ" (*Revelation*, 124).

22. Beale comments, "This is confirmed from Zech. 6:7–8a, where an angel of the Lord commands the four groups of horses to 'go' and to execute divine judgment. The phrase has the same meaning in Rev. 6:4a, 4b, and 8" (378).

The first rider is the first case in point. His crown, the symbol of his authoritative victory, was given (*edothē*) to him. The divine passive assumes God's agency.[23] The rider also wielded a bow. According to classical historians, as fearsome as Rome was as a military power, its legendary legions never mastered the use of the bow. Archers from the ranks of client kingdoms were employed as auxiliary troops. The bow was, however, a primary weapon of several of Rome's principal enemies. In fact, it stood as a metaphor for the kingdom Rome feared the most: Parthia. Just in case the bow by itself was an insufficient prompt for any Roman reader, John has placed the archer prominently on a white horse. The Parthians were renowned not only for their archery skills but, even more impressively, for their ability to fire their bows accurately while mounted on galloping, white horses. The Parthian calvary had engaged and defeated the Romans on several memorable occasions.[24] The thought of them running roughshod across the human landscape at God's command would certainly have stirred a loathing fear in the spirit of every Roman. And that is precisely the seer's point. John is writing as much now for the Romans as he is writing to his own believing community. He wants Rome to fear this inaugural equestrian moment as the first act in God's judgment against it.

The intersection of the dazzling color with crown and conquest instructs hearers and readers on the motivation for judgment. With the opening of the fifth seal, Christ-witnesses, described via the symbolism of dazzling/white, crown, and conquest, will cry out for God's justice and judgment. The trappings of their identity (dazzling/white, crown, conquer) also characterize the force that is already answering their call on God's behalf. The chaotic situation erupting in their world is therefore the working out of God's justice. Because of their plight, God has unleashed the scourge that is the first horseman. The child of humanity (seated, dazzling/white, crown), who relates so poignantly to the conquering witnesses (dazzling/white, crown), bears an eerie resemblance to the first horseman (seated, dazzling/white, crown). Sickle at the ready in 14:14, the Son is clearly the messianic agent of God's fierce judgment. Chapter 6 not only chronicles that judgment (see vv. 16–17) but also, in the scene depicted in vv. 6:9–11, presents the rationale for it. The child of humanity may not be the first rider, but he is in charge of the circumstance that sets him loose. In the process, he gives to the rider just enough of his characteristic bearing

---

23. John uses this same form of the verb a multitude of times to express this divine passive sense: 6:4, 8, 11; 7:2; 8:3; 9:1, 3, 5; 11:1–2; 13:5, 7, 14–15; 16:8; 19:8; 20:4.

24. Schüssler Fiorenza's discussion is helpful: "The image of the royal, conquering, mounted archer evokes the memory of the Parthian victory over the Romans, who were defeated three times (in 53 B.C.E, 35 B.C.E., and 62 C.E.) by the Parthian cavalry. Moreover, according to Jer 51:56, Babylon's warriors were taken captive and their bows were broken. In the symbolic discourse of Revelation, the rider with the bow reveals that the expansionistic military power of Babylon/Rome will be overcome. If that is the case, the first rider functions as the precursor of the victorious parousia-Christ" (*Vision of a Just World*, 63).

and dress so that all who see the rider will realize that he advances under the authority of the Lamb.

The problem with this scenario is that the faithful witnesses are as plagued by the actions of the rider as are those who persecute them. John apparently believes that in these times of trial, believers will have the opportunity to demonstrate their faithfulness under duress. Because they are not raptured out of the moment but forced like everyone else to endure it, they have the unique opportunity to demonstrate their ability to witness for God in the midst of tragic circumstances, just as Christ witnessed for God from the cross. Appealing to John's dependence upon Ezek 14:21, Beale makes a similar point: "The purpose of the trials is to punish the majority of the nation because of its sin and simultaneously to purify the righteous remnant by testing their faith (cf. [Ezek] 14:14, 16, 18, 20, 22–23)" (372).

**[3–4]** Though the second cherub is now the principal actor, v. 3 repeats the narrative content of v. 2a. The color of the second mount is flaming red, the shade of slaughter. The only other time John uses this color is in his description of the fiery red (*pyrros*), satanic dragon (12:3; scarlet red—*kokkinos*—is used at 17:3, 4; 18:12, 16). The implication is that even the destructive force of the devil is harnessed under God's control. Like the first rider, this one enters the cosmic and historical fray only after it is summoned forth by cherubic command. When he acts to depose the Pax Romana and install anarchy in its place, he does so with a sword bestowed by God (see the discussion of *edothē* at 6:2). John taunts any Romans among his readers by using their own imperial imagery against them. "What this second rider carries is the heavy sword that was used for swinging and cutting rather than for stabbing. It was also a symbol of imperial authority—in particular, the emperor's authority to decree the death penalty, which was called 'the right of the sword' and which could also be exercised by provincial governors" (González and González 47–48). John sees God snatching Rome's symbol of power, handing it over to the red rider, and allowing him to use it to stir up a bloodbath.

There is nothing redemptive about the slaughter that ensues (see the comment on 5:6). The term "slaughter" indicates horrific carnage. John uses it to refer either to the execution of the Lamb (5:6, 9, 12; 13:3, where the killing of one of the bestial heads is really a mimicking of the Lamb's execution) or to the butchering of his followers (6:9; 18:24). Here it refers to global holocaust. Later, John declares that those who kill *with* the sword shall likewise themselves be killed *by* the sword (13:10). The second rider uses his weapon to set that tragic circumstance into motion. The Romans, who used the sword to create their self-interested peace, now find the sword being used to cut them down and shred their serenity to bits. The irony is eschatologically delicious. They not only receive the justice they deserve; their own symbolic tool of pitiless oppression is used to deliver it.

**[5]** Familiar language abounds. Once again, the Lamb initiates the action by breaking open a seal. And once again, John declares that he heard a cherub pronounce the command "Come!" Once again, John appeals to the visual formula (*kai eidon, kai idou*, "and I looked, and behold") that announces a shift in the setting of the scene. He sees a black horse. He will refer to this color once more in his narrative, when he confides that the sun turns as black as sackcloth (6:12). The connection between sackcloth and judgment is explicit throughout the Bible.[25] The link with black and, by extension, sackcloth therefore implies that the third seal's opening will ignite the fury of divine judgment. The nature of that judgment is symbolized by the balance scales that the rider holds in his hand.

In biblical literature, particularly the book of Daniel, which often serves as a direct background to John's thinking and writing, scales also have an integral connection with the theme of divine judgment (Prov 16:11; Isa 40:12; Dan 5:27). Ancient balance scales "consisted of a crossbeam suspended by a hook or cord with a pan suspended from each end of the crossbeam. Weights placed in one pan were used to determine the weight of commodities placed in the other pan" (Aune 2:396). John is not so much interested in how the scale works as in what its presence represents. "In the ancient world food was distributed by rationed amounts (using scales) when it became scarce (see the metaphorical use of scales indicating famine also in Lev 26:26; 2 Kgs 7:1; Ezek 4:10, 16)" (Beale 381). Famine has followed naturally upon conquest and slaughter. Famine is the third seal's form of judgment.

**[6]** If there was any doubt about God's association with the scales and the famine they represent, John erases it with his claim to have heard a voice from within the midst of the four creatures. Given the close proximity of the cherubim to the throne, the voice must belong to God. God issues instructions on the use of the scales: to weigh the value of the scarce food that remains. There is an immediate problem for which the text never accounts. Scales measure weight, yet the values John records are in volume. The seer rides roughshod over such details in his attempt to reach his primary point.

The primary point is that famine has caused the price of the remaining food to soar. The going rates became "a *choinix* of wheat for a denarius and three *choinikes* of barley for a denarius." "The term 'liter' is used as an equivalent to the Greek dry measure called a χοῖνιξ (*choinix*, pl. *choinikes*), roughly equal to a day's ration of wheat for one person" (Aune 2:397). The three "liters" of barley were equivalent to a day's rations for a person's horse or mule. Though barley was less attractive than wheat as the main ingredient for a meal, three "liters" of it could also serve as a small family's daily food ration. The denarius, according to Matt 20:2, was the expected daily wage. If John's accounting

25. See, e.g., 1 Kgs 20:31–32; 21:27; 2 Kgs 19:1–2; 1 Chr 21:16; Isa 3:24; 37:1–2; Jer 4:8; 6:26; 48:37; 49:3; Amos 8:10; Jonah 3:5–8; Matt 11:21; Luke 10:13.

is correct, a person's entire daily wage was committed solely to food. Aune sets the inflationary rate as 8 times the normal price for wheat and 5⅓ times the normal value for barley.[26]

While staple foods were being destroyed, there was a cruel and mostly inexplicable culinary twist. The marauding rider on the black horse was ordered not to harm (*mē adikēsēs*) the olive oil and the wine. The singular number of the verb "harm" indicates that God is speaking directly and only to the rider; its aorist tense (aorist of prohibition) specifies that the rider had not yet touched the oil and wine and was therefore being ordered not even to start. Why did God demand the protection of the oil and wine when wheat and barley rations had taken such a hit?

Several explanations have been offered. The first and most often argued is that God did not want the olive oil and wine touched because the vineyards that produced them took much too long to regrow.[27] The thinking here is that God intended to curb the extent of the famine. Once the war and chaos subsided, wheat and barley could be regrown quickly. Since the vineyards had not been touched, oil and wine would then have been even more readily available. This picture fits the image of a just God, who punishes in order to correct rather than to destroy. The problem with this theory, however, is that John has to this point portrayed the God of the four horsemen as the executor of apocalyptic devastation. The cataclysms initiated by the riders are not restrained punishment; they are judgment acts of cosmic proportions.

A second explanation calls to mind the edict of Domitian following the great famine of 92 C.E. Wealthy Roman landowners had determined that if they devoted their lands to oil and wine rather than grain, they could build greater profits. The end result, particularly during a food shortage, was devastating. While oil and wine continued to flow in abundant quantities, wheat and barley became frighteningly scarce. To ameliorate the effects of this catastrophe and ameliorate the possibility of future ones, Domitian ordered that all the vineyards, particularly those in Asia Minor, be cut back by half. In this case, the voice of God would speak with this recent imperial action in mind (cf. González and González 48–49; Beale 381).

A connection with Domitian's edict would be an interesting one indeed, particularly since this would tie John's symbolic narrative to an actual historical event. There would also be interesting literary implications. Domitian's edict

---

26. Aune 2:397. Beale (381) estimates that the values are about 8 to 16 times the normal average prices. Catherine and Justo González (49) argue for an astounding 1,200 percent inflationary rate for wheat and 800 percent for barley.

27. Cf. Aune: "Most commentators have argued that the intent of the prohibition is to lessen the severity of the famine (i.e., an olive tree must be cultivated five years before fruiting, and fifteen to twenty years to mature; vineyards also take several years to establish); i.e., the scarcity of wheat and barley is a partial judgment" (2:398).

was apparently rescinded only after the aristocracy bitterly complained. Since John does not mention that historical detail, it could well have been his narrative intent to demonstrate that the victorious opposition to the imperial command came from God. While the emperor demanded that half the vineyards be chopped down, God commanded that they not be touched. That would mean that at the singular moment when God's desire for judgment actually matched the goal of one of Caesar's edicts (i.e., massive destruction, in this case, of vineyards), God changed course. The end result would have been a human emperor humiliated by a heavenly countermand of his orders. God would have vetoed Caesar's order at the one time when accommodating to Caesar's order would have furthered God's stated plan of judgment, as that plan was embodied in the work of the first, second, and third riders. This illogical, almost fanatical opposition to Roman intentions would certainly fit the overall presentation of a narrative that begs its hearers and readers not to accommodate to Roman expectations for daily social and cultic life under any circumstances.

The problem with this explanation, however, is that the narrative itself never connects God's command to the imperial edict. It is difficult and risky to attempt such a speculative connection between historical events and John's eschatological work unless one can find a specific literary link to that event. None exists.

This brings us to a third possible explanation: John has an ironic point to make by demonstrating a divine intent to spare luxuries like oil and wine while destroying staples like wheat and barley. "[The oil and wine] symbolize the luxury and extravagant lifestyle of the wealthy. John envisions the final days as a time when the poor are starving while the rich are unaffected by the shortages" (Reddish 127). Pablo Richard agrees: "Only the wealthy enjoy the economic prosperity for which the empire is known, just as only they enjoy the *Pax Romana*" (Richard 69).

Here, too, there are problems. In the ancient world, one would be hard-pressed to tag olive oil and wine as luxuries; they were as common a part of everyday meals as grains. Whether one could find enough sustenance from them alone to sustain life in the midst of a famine is, however, another question. On the other hand, one might metaphorically associate oil and wine with parties and feasts (cf. Matt 25:1–13; Luke 7:33–34; John 2:1–10; Eph 5:18; 1 Tim 3:8). Is it possible that John's message here is an ironic one that fits with his overall theme of witness and nonaccommodation? In chapters 2–3, he showed particular concern that his hearers and readers not accommodate themselves to Greco-Roman social and cultic expectations by eating meat sacrificed to idols at celebratory social gatherings. If indeed wine and oil carry the same symbolic association with such gatherings and John is still pressing his point of nonaccommodation, which I believe he does throughout the book, then it may well be that he offers God's order to leave the oil and wine in place as ironic sarcasm. Caught in the midst of a famine where they can find neither wheat nor

barley, people still have before them the option of an accommodating participation in the cultic rituals that celebrate pagan and imperial lordship. They will
have enough oil and wine to carouse but not enough food to survive. They can
party themselves to an accommodating, starving death. Perhaps this is the judgment the third horseman brings. He renders to the idolatrous, accommodating,
famished world exactly what it wants: oil and wine.

[7–8] Though the fourth cherub is now the principal actor, v. 7 repeats the
narrative content of vv. 2a, 3, and 5a. The familiar formula *kai eidon, kai idou*
(and I looked, and behold) announces yet another scene shift. The fourth horseman will be the worst yet. John describes the color of the animal he rides as
*chlōros.* Chlorophyll is the green coloration in leaves. It is also, according to
New Testament narratives, the coloration of the green grass (Mark 6:39; Rev
8:7; 9:4). In the larger Greco-Roman world, it connotes a "pale green" or "pale
greenish gray," the color associated with sickness, death, and dying. The association is a fitting one since, by the time this horseman is through, one-quarter
of the world's population will be dead.

It is not surprising, then, that this rider's name is "Death." There is a logis-
tical problem of having Hades follow along with Death even though only one
horse is mentioned. John, though, is not concerned with such details. He means
to connect the personification of death with the equally fearful personification
of Hades so that his readers may be assured that the peril now confronting them
in the narrative is total. Death is the force that snatches up the essence of human
life. Hades is the underworld place where that essence is eternally enslaved.
The two form a partnership of grim reaping, which is why John often pictures
them working together (1:18; 6:8; 20:13–14).

Should the marauding presence of Death and Hades also be attributed to the
execution of God's judgment plan? Yes. At 1:18, John declares that the resurrected
child of humanity holds the keys of Death and Hades. Since he holds the keys, he
must be the one who has unlocked the gates that have set them loose. To be sure,
the inference from the narration at 1:18 is that in his resurrection Jesus has used
the keys to free himself from death. Did he unlock the door to Death and Hades
and allow Death and Hades to slip out while he was making his own escape? Or
did he intentionally open the door so that they could move through it? The overall judgment motif of chapter 6 suggests the latter (cf. 20:2–3, 7). For those who
might flinch at the prospect of God wielding death as a weapon against the enemies of God's people or even against the believers who have accommodated
themselves to the cultic and social practices of those enemies, there are instructive texts like 18:8 and 2:23. At 18:8, God brings death to the whore of Babylon
as a judgment against her, and according to 2:23, God will consign Jezebel's children to death as a judgment against them (see the discussion of 2:18–29).

Equally persuasive is the presence of the divine passive of the verb "to give"
(*edothē*), which also accompanied the actions of the riders on the dazzling (6:2)

and red (6:4) horses. The fourth rider's power, too, has apparently been furnished by God.

The judgment theme gains further credibility when readers recognize the prophetic background against which John is writing. The closest parallel to 6:8 is Ezek 14:21, which recounts the same four harbingers of death (sword, famine, pestilence, and wild animals) in almost the same order.[28] Though no wild animals are mentioned in Ezek 5:12, one-third of the population will be wiped out by sword, pestilence, and death. Jeremiah 14:12 is equally striking. An angry God will consume the people by sword, famine, and pestilence (cf. Jer 15:2; 21:7). The destruction caused by wild animals is likewise a recurring Old Testament theme.[29] The common denominator in each of those scriptural cases is God's judgment. God *intends* that these catastrophes take place as punishment for a particular offense. "Most of these references mention idolatry as the cause of judgment, which enforces the suggestion . . . that idolatry was part of the reason for the afflictions on unbelievers in [Rev] 6:2–8" (Beale 383). It is probable that this judgment was also intended against those in John's congregations who had accommodated themselves to the idolatrous behavior of the unbelievers around them in an attempt to benefit from the social and economic opportunities such an association would bring.

## 6:9–11 The Slaughtered Souls

Verses 9–11 provide narrative motivation for God's judgment. This text, along with 12:10–12 and 20:4–6, contains a provocative intersection of some of the Apocalypse's most engaging images—*psychē* (soul), *martyria* (witness), and *logos* (word)—as well as the revelation that word and witness are causally linked to key narrative activity involving the souls (execution, 6:9–11; beheading, 20:4–6; conquest of the dragon who instigates the killings, 12:10–11). In both 6:9 and 20:4a, the souls of those who have not accommodated themselves to the social and cultic benefits of Greco-Roman society find themselves executed because of their resistant witness to the word (i.e., the lordship) of God. Revelation 12:10–11 explains, however, that their deaths have not been in vain. Their witness, along with the blood of Christ, provided the ammunition to conquer the great red, satanic dragon. Then 20:4b–6 explains how witnesses will be rewarded for their death-defying participation in that combative endeavor. They will participate in the messianic reign. It is 6:9–11 that provides the initial rationale for

28. The reference to death (*thanatos*) in the second half of the verse has the more descriptive sense of pestilence, whereas in the first half, in its connection with Hades, the term clearly has a more personalized nature and function.

29. Cf. Aune: "Several OT prophetic oracles of doom predict that wild animals will devour both domesticated animals and people as a punishment (Lev 26:22; Deut 28:38, 39, 42; 32:24; Jer 5:6; 8:17; Ezek 5:17; Hos 13:7–8; Lam 3:10–11)" (2:403).

God's activity of judgment, sets up the witnesses' successful participation with God, and prefigures the messianic celebration by chronicling the dead witnesses' passionate and ultimately irresistible call for just judgment.

9 When he opened the fifth seal, I saw under the altar the souls of those who had been executed because of the word of God, that is,[a] because of the witness they had given. 10 And they cried out with a loud voice, saying: "Master,[b] holy and true, how long will it be before you judge and avenge our blood on[c] the inhabitants of the earth?" 11 Then they were each given a dazzling robe and told to rest a little longer, until the work of[d] their fellow servants, who are their brothers,[e] who were about to be killed as they themselves had been, would be complete.

a. "Word of God" and "witness" are narratively equivalent. John connects them with *kai* (and) at both 6:9 and 20:4. The *kai* in these cases should be read epexegetically, in an explanatory way, rather than as a conjunctive (see the discussion of 1:2).

b. The articular noun functions here as a vocative (Aune 2:383).

c. The preposition *ek* designates the persons on whom the vengeance is taken (BDAG 238).

d. I have supplied "the work of"; for discussion of this translation, see the comment on v. 11 below.

e. The *kai* that joins servants and brothers is epexegetical, or explanatory. Cf. 1:9, where John describes himself as a fellow worker and brother with an epexegetical *kai*. Clearly, there, since he is referring to himself, he cannot be designating two different people.

**[9]** John refers to the resurrected remains of nonaccommodating witnesses as "souls" for the first time here. The term "soul," as John uses it, can only be fully understood when read in light of the semantic domains in which the seer places it. In one set of texts it operates in a limited way as a reference to living, animate creatures (8:9; 16:3; 18:13). According to the other set of texts, the soul is the force that animates them (12:11; 18:14; 20:4). Particularly at 6:9 and again at 20:4, that animating force lives on after the human being it once occupied meets an earthly death.

These particular souls have made their way to heaven in a most noteworthy fashion. The human beings whom they once animated were executed on earth *because of* their nonaccommodating commitment to the word of God, which is the witness to the lordship of Christ (see the comments on 1:2, 9). The language of execution connects these souls to the Lamb, whom John also has described as executed (see the discussion of 5:6). In his introduction of the Lamb, John clarifies that the execution is not an act of redemption but the result of the Lamb's witnessing to a truth that resisted the claim of Roman rule and lordship. Those who follow the Lamb by testifying to the witness that he himself bore will meet a similar fate (1:9; 2:13).

In heaven, the souls who have met this fate are crammed into the crawl space beneath the heavenly altar of sacrifice. Two altars are presented in the Apocalypse. The heavenly altars were understood to be the cosmic prototypes for their earthly counterparts in the Jerusalem temple. The Jerusalem temple had two distinct altars. The outer one, located in the court of the priests, was the sacrificial altar of burnt offering. The inner altar, also known as the golden altar of incense, was located just in front of the curtain that marked off the holy of holies from the rest of the sanctuary. It is the sacrificial altar that is imaged here and again at 11:1; 14:18; and 16:7. The explicit mention of incense or being golden indicates that the references in 8:3, 5 and 9:13 are to the altar of incense (Comay 161; Sanders 62). It is from the cramped space beneath the altar of sacrifice that the souls cry out for God's justice. Their presence under the altar is an indication to some scholars that John has in mind sacrificial, martyr imagery (e.g., Reddish 130; Boring, *Revelation*, 125). These scholars refer to Lev 4:7, where the blood of a sacrificial bull is poured out at the base of the altar. Since the life or soul was thought to be in the blood, John was symbolically representing the souls as the blood of the altar poured out. In this case, these slaughtered souls sacrificed themselves so that their bloody deaths would provoke God's final intervention into human history.

I instead argue for the primacy of another aspect of the altar's meaning potential: justice and judgment. It is, in fact, the imagery of justice and judgment that has been the unifying theme throughout the first eight verses of the chapter. John extends it here with his focus on the altar. Just as the heavenly throne is a symbol of God's rule, "altar" characterizes God's judgment. John does not picture a sacrificial slaying on the altar; the slaying, presumably with all the accompanying bleeding, takes place on earth. John images the altar to picture what will now happen *as a result* of the slaying. In other words, the altar does not represent killing; it personifies the divine response to it. At 16:7 the altar is so focused on this objective that it miraculously comes alive and voices the opinion that all God's judgments are true and just. Even though it is apparently a reference to the altar of incense, 8:3 offers helpful corroboration. In that altar reference, though the prayers of the saints are understandably offered without any mention of blood or suffering, the connection to the coming judgment is clear. Indeed, all of John's representations of the heavenly temple's two altars fit this symbolic mold (8:3, 5; 9:13; 14:18; 16:7); they point to divine recompense, not saintly suffering. By connecting both pieces of furniture to the common theme of judgment, he has given "altar" a uniform narrative characterization (see further the discussion of 8:3, 5). Even the slaughtered souls are convinced of this connection. Apparently certain that God will act, their question concerns only the timing of the event. They are asking when, not if. The altar symbolism assures them that transformative, liberating justice is coming. This is why John locates them there; he wants his readers to be focused more on God's justice than on their own sacrifice.

**[10]** The souls' passionate "How long?" no doubt reminds John's hearers and readers of similar prophetic calls for divine engagement (e.g., Zech 1:12; cf. Ps 79:5).[30] In those cases, however, a contrite people asked how long God would keep punishing them.

The souls address God as their *despotēs* (master, lord), a Greek translation of the two Latin terms for emperor, a point that would certainly not have gone unnoticed (Aune 2:406; cf. Acts 4:24). In hijacking this designation for God, they were rhetorically slapping Caesar in the face. Even in lament, they witnessed.

In describing their *despotēs* as holy and true, the souls voiced their faith that God would engage Rome and judge it. The adjectives are echoes of the self-descriptors used by the child of humanity in his opening address to the Philadelphians (see the comment on 3:7). Though the adjectives acted as substantives (nouns) in that case, the essence of their relationship to Christ and God is the same. There the child of humanity, as the holy and true one, holds the key of David and, like a judge beyond whom there is no appeal, has the power to close what no one can shut and open what no one can close. He would make the enemies of God's witnesses bow before their feet even as he prepared the coming trial that would judge the inhabitants of the earth (a Johannine euphemism for those who oppose God and God's people; see the comment on 2:13; 3:10). The souls of the slaughtered echo this appeal to the holy and true one for judgment against the inhabitants of the earth. In so doing, they also echo the cries of Old Testament figures who seemed assured that God would avenge the blood of God's people (Deut 32:43; 2 Kgs 9:7; Ps 79:10; cf. Rev 16:6; 17:6; 18:24; 19:2). The specific term for avenge (*ekdikeō*) appears only one other time in the Apocalypse, at 19:2, which provides a direct narrative answer to the petition made by the resurrected souls (6:10). God justly obliterates "the great whore of Babylon" for spilling the blood of God's people. The other key term, "judge" (*krinō*), appears more often but operates similarly. God's judgment will bring destruction to the great city that has persecuted and killed God's witnesses (11:18; 16:5; 18:8, 20; 19:2, 11). Revelation 20:12–13 implies that this judgment, even when destructive, is just; every person will receive proper due for one's deeds.

This clarification does not dissuade contemporary commentators from rightly flinching at John's depiction of the harshness of God's punishment. Many contend that God's hyperviolent judgment in Revelation is unchristian, certainly not Christlike.[31] Other scholars point out that the violence God displays in the book should be understood as a necessary evil since it operates in the realm of public justice rather than private vengeance. "Justice must not only

---

30. Cf. Pss 3:1–2; 6:3; 35:17; 74:9–10; 79:5; 80:4; 89:46; 90:13; 94:3; *4 Ezra* 4.33–37.

31. See, e.g., Keller, who suggests the need for a counterapocalypse that sustains Revelation's intensity, drive for justice, and desire to face insurmountable odds while at the same time disarming its commitment to misogyny, binary dualism, and extreme violence.

be done; it must be seen to be done" (Caird 85). God was caught up in a war of lethal cosmic force. Rome, the power representing Satan, had no compunction about acting with extreme violence. John apparently believed that, if cosmic and historical justice were to be served, God would need to respond in kind. This expectation of violence to bring about justice is a theological premise with an impressive Old Testament pedigree. Though pointing most specifically to the imprecatory psalms (Pss 7, 35, 55, 58, 59, 69, 79, 83, 109, 137, 139), Aune observes that there are large swaths of Old Testament and other Jewish materials that indicate God's need and right to respond appropriately to human violence (2:407–11). Lincoln and Mamiya point out that Christians in the black church tradition have long identified with this Old Testament view of God, and that "this notion of God as an avenging, conquering, liberating paladin remains a formidable anchor of the faith in most black churches."[32] Speaking from the black church tradition in South Africa, Boesak even asserts that by denying this reality, white Christians not only desecrate the faith but also do so in a way that helps to perpetuate the very evils their Christian God supposedly deplores.

> Why is there this division between the God of the Old Testament and the God of Jesus? Why, on this point, does white Western Christianity go back to the heresy of Marcionism? God takes up the cause of the poor and the oppressed precisely because in this world their voices are not heard—not even by those who call themselves Christians. God even has to take up the cause of the poor *against* "Christians." Christians who enjoy the fruits of injustice without a murmur, who remain silent as the defenseless are slaughtered, dare not become indignant when the suffering people of God echo the prayers of the psalms and pray for deliverance and judgment. (Boesak 72–73)

[11] The same God who gave destructive power of judgment to the four horsemen (see the discussion of *edothē* [it was given] at 6:2, 4, 8) rewards the souls of the executed witnesses with dazzling clothing (see the comments on 3:2–5, 18; 4:4). The dazzling robes mark the souls as defiant witnesses who actively engaged in testimony to the lordship of Christ. As J. P. Heil (231–32) points out, their dress ties them to other key characterizations in the text. The multitude standing before the Lamb and the heavenly throne in 7:9 are similarly dressed. So, interestingly enough, are the figures of 7:13–14. These figures, presumably the same as the slaughtered souls of 6:9–11, achieved their high laundry marks only after washing their robes in the blood of the Lamb. According to 12:10–12, this high-powered plasma detergent is the cleansing force that enables God and God's people to wipe out the stain of Rome's oppressive, satanic power. The dazzling robe is thus the symbolization of this conquering witness.

---

32. C. Eric Lincoln and Lawrence Mamiya, *The Black Church in the African-American Experience* (Durham, N.C.: Duke University Press, 1990), 3.

In other words, the dazzling robe, metaphorically speaking, is not a noun; it is an action verb. The robe signifies the paradoxical washing in the blood as bringing about the transformative justice that God's people have been seeking. They have therefore not just been "given" dazzling robes; they have earned them by washing, that is to say, acting in the way of the Lord that incites Rome and its agents to spill their blood. Surely this active witness is what John had in mind when he declared that the remnant at Sardis have earned their dazzling dress because of their ongoing and victorious witness (3:4–5). Who, finally, are the ones whom John considers blessed and worthy of the liberating salvation that God will bring? Who else but those who act, who "wash" their robes. According to John, the only mechanism that makes this "washing" possible is the courageous act of witnessing to the very truth that Rome has deployed all its power to contest.

In John's narrative, there is dissonance between the social body (the expectation of emperor worship) and the witness body or "soul" (which symbolizes resistance to that expectation). The Roman system promotes a celebration of the physical body and physical life lived in accommodation to Roman religious and political interest. Revelation, though, symbolizes a rejection of that holding on to the physical body. It is not the body but the redressed and eternal soul (*psychē*) that is key. This spiritual body is certainly in extreme dissonance with the Roman social one. By definition, it is therefore resistant, and actively so. A believer must make an active choice, given the social context of Asia Minor at the end of the first century, to be one type of body or the other. John dramatizes his preference with the description of slaughtered souls clothed in dazzling robes. He has essentially reconfigured the dress of execution into the clothing of defiance and change. He takes even the worst, this slaughter, and linguistically connects it as closely to Christ's resurrection as to his death. The executed Lamb, every hearer and reader will remember, was still standing. So too are the believers who take the wardrobe of Christ's slaughter upon themselves. Though huddled beneath the heavenly altar, they are well dressed and, figuratively speaking at least, still standing. Suddenly what some might view as a martyr's attire has become the fine, dazzling linen of active, subversive, and transformative witness. These dead souls, all dressed up, are a soul force.

The answer that the heavenly voice speaks to this soul force is one that on the surface appears to cause a problem for the thesis I am suggesting. After all, the respondent directs that the pleading souls should wait just a short time until the appropriate number of their brothers (and sisters) had, like them, been killed. Actually, the Greek says no such thing. Although the NRSV and many other translations report that a sufficient *number* of witnesses first had to be slaughtered before God would move, John himself actually says nothing about numbers. He simply writes that first the brothers and sisters must be fulfilled. Admittedly, this odd response is ambiguous. It is not surprising that translators and interpreters have sought clarification from the historical context. Commentators observe that apocalyptic texts like *1 En.* 47.4 and *4 Ezra* 4.35–37 expect a certain quota of slaughtered righteous to be filled before God will act.[33]

Reddish agrees that John probably has this apocalyptic concept in mind, but he is not so sure that John wants to use it to the same effect as his literary forebears. He writes: "Whether John took literally this idea of a fixed number of martyrs who must die before God intervenes is not clear. The freedom he exhibits elsewhere to adapt and modify ancient traditions and to cast ideas in symbolic form leads one to suspect that here also he is using a traditional apocalyptic idea in a nonliteral way" (131). I agree—especially since John, whose idea of a martyr is that of a witness, left out any talk of a "number" at all. John's concentration is focused on the term "fulfill" (*plēroō*). Gerhard Delling explains that "fulfill," particularly when associated with the term "time" (*chronos*), has a temporal sense of completion. In other words, it means to finish, to execute a commanded action; "almost always [it is] God's commission which is to be fulfilled" (*TDNT* 6:297). That broader use of the term fits quite nicely with the way John uses the term in 3:2, the only other time he deploys it. There, it is works that are fulfilled. The Lord is angry because the works of the believers have not been "accomplished" in the Lord's sight. All this would suggest that when John uses the verb "fulfill" in 6:11, particularly in connection with rest (from works; see the comment on 14:13) and time, he is speaking about the works of the surviving colleagues of the slaughtered souls. The spotlight falls on that ongoing work of defiant, provocative witness, which must still be accomplished, in whatever manner it is to be done. Doing that work is the way believers operate in synergy with God to bring about the liberating transformation of history.

Corroboration comes from John's closing remark about the brothers and sisters who would be killed just as the souls under the altar had been. We already know that these souls were executed because of their witness; John is clarifying here that their brothers and sisters will be executed for the same reason. Nonetheless, they evidently are to keep witnessing until their *work*, too, is complete.

### 6:12–17  Final Retribution

The eschatological events that follow the opening of the sixth seal are a direct narrative response to the souls of the slaughtered in 6:9–11. Verses 12–17 are the end frame of an intercalation. With the help of vv. 1–8, they bracket the appeal for justice and judgment (vv. 9–11) around which the whole of chapter 6 pivots.

---

33. E.g., Aune 2:391; cf. Reddish: "The answer that Ezra received in [2 Esd] 4:35–36 is, 'Did not the souls of the righteous in their chambers ask about these matters, saying, "How long are we to remain here? And when will the harvest of our reward come?"' And the archangel Jeremiel answered and said, 'When the number of those like yourselves is completed'" (130).

12 Then I looked when he opened the sixth seal, and a great earthquake
occurred, and the sun became as black as sackcloth, and the full moon
became as red[a] as blood, 13 and the stars of heaven fell to the earth as a
fig tree shaken by a fierce wind drops its unripe figs, 14 and the sky vanished like a rolled-up scroll, and every mountain and island was shaken
from its place. 15 And the kings of the earth and the important people and
the generals and the wealthy and the powerful and every slave and free
person hid themselves in the caves and in the mountain rocks, 16 and they
said to the mountains and to the rocks: "Fall on us and hide us from the
presence of the one seated on the throne and from the wrath of the Lamb,
17 because the great day of their[b] wrath has come, and who is able to withstand it?"

a. Though John does not use the word "red" here, it is clear from his comparison with
the changed color of the sun that his intention is to describe a shocking change in the
moon's hue.

b. Although A 𝔐 sa[ms] bo; Prim attest the singular *autou* (his), the plural *autōn* (their),
supported by ℵ C 1611 1854 2053 2329 2344 *pc* latt sy, is to be preferred. The easier
singular reading is an attempt to bring agreement with the singular *orgē* (wrath) of the
preceding v. 16.

[12] The Lamb's opening of the sixth seal is followed immediately by a great
earthquake. "In biblical tradition, earthquakes are often expected to occur in the
end time as one effect of the presence or coming of God (Joel 2:10; 3:16 [4:16
MT]; Isa 24:18–23; 29:6; Mic 1:4; Nah 1:5)" (Beale, 413). Earthquakes were
also integrally related to the theme of judgment (Jer 10:22; Ezek 38:19). At 8:5,
an earthquake is part of the theophany that introduces the acts of judgment
accompanying the blowing of the seven trumpets. All this takes place, just as
the earthquake of 6:12 follows the appeal in vv. 6:9–11, after the prayers of the
people rise up before God with the smoke of incense (8:3–4). One gets the sense
that at 8:5, too, the judgment is a direct result of a prayerful appeal for intervention. Similarly, earthquakes are associated with God's acts of judgment in
11:13, 19; 16:18.

In the second phase of this initial act of eschatological travail, the sun
becomes as black as sackcloth. The strong connection between God's acts of
judgment and the color "black" were previewed with the presentation of the
rider on the black horse at 6:5 (cf. Isa 50:3). The addition of sackcloth heightens the emphasis on judgment. At 11:3 the two witnesses are said to be outfitted with sackcloth before they enact prophetic judgment on God's behalf.

Finally, there is an accompanying bloody moon. The presence of this odd
celestial combination in Acts 2:20 suggests that a blackened sun and blood-red
moon may well have been understood as traditional precursors to the coming
of the Lord's Day.

**[13–14]** With the stars falling out of the heavens like winter fruit shaken from a fig tree by a great wind, John is building from traditional Old Testament imagery. In Isa 34:4 the heavens rot away like fruit withering on a fig tree just as God is about to render judgment. In Isa 13:10; Ezek 32:7; and Joel 2:10, the stars darken as a prelude to God's coming judgment. No doubt this is also the image Mark builds upon when he records Jesus' claim that the child of humanity's return in judgment would also be prefaced by falling stars and darkened heavens (Mark 13:24–25; Matt 24:29; Luke 21:26). John uses this imagery to great effect not only here but also repeatedly in his text. The connection between falling stars, tribulation, and coming judgment is reiterated narratively at Rev 8:10–12; 9:1; and 12:4.

The influence of Isa 34:4 extends from the image of a rotting heaven in Rev 6:13 to the rolling up of the heavens like a scroll (v. 14). John also wants to make it clear that everything is happening by God's command. Each of the three primary verbs in the verse parses out in the passive voice (*apechōristhē*, vanished; *elissomenon*, being rolled up; *ekinēthēsan*, were moved). These divine passives presume God to be the controlling agent. At Heb 1:12, as well, God's judgment begins with a divine rolling up of the cosmos.

**[15–17]** Having seen the signs of God's coming judgment, the great ones and those who serve them (cf. Rev 19:18) appropriately run for cover (v. 15). "In the OT, the major reason for fleeing from the presence of God is to avoid judgment (Gen 19:17; Ps 68:1; Hos 5:3; Zech 14:5)" (Aune 2:420). In Mark 13:14 (cf. Matt 24:15–16; Luke 21:20–21), Jesus advises that once the signs of the end began occurring, people should act in just such a manner. The lengthy enumeration of the fleeing powerful people and the servants and free ones connected with them reads like a laundry list of persons who would either run the political and economic infrastructure of the Greco-Roman world or accommodate themselves to it (on "kings of the earth" as representing rulers hostile to God, see the comment on 17:2). Like the disobedient people chronicled in Isa 2:10, 19, 21 and Jer 4:29, they have become refugees who seek asylum from God's justice under the cover of nature.[34] They exist as a direct narrative contrast to the executed witnesses of 6:9–11.

In v. 16, John finally reveals his belief that everything that is happening in chapter 6 occurs as a result of God's judgment. Appealing directly to Hos 10:8 (cf. Luke 23:30), he recounts that the refugees beg the mountains and rocks to shelter them from the face of God and from the wrath of the Lamb. The Lamb, too, executes judgment. Here, as elsewhere in the text (11:18; 14:10; 16:19;

---

34. Cf. Aune (2:419–20): "During times of invasion or siege, residents of cities and towns would often flee to the mountainous regions to hide from their enemies (Judg 6:2; 1 Sam 13:16; 14:11; Job 30:6; Ezek 33:27; Jer 13:4–6; 49:30; Jos. *Ant.* 6.99, 116; 12.272–75, 421; 14.429; *J.W.* 1.307; 6.370."

19:15), divine wrath occurs as a just recompense for evil that has been perpetrated against God and God's people.

The refugees now declare what John's text has already revealed: the breaking of the sixth seal has inaugurated the Great Day of the Lord (v. 17). It falls like a Great Day of Wrath upon those who have resisted Christ's lordship and have persecuted those who witnessed to that lordship. Once again, John builds from Hebraic tradition. Joel 2:11; Nah 1:6; Zeph 1:14–15; and Mal 3:2 all record God's final day as one filled with so severe a judging, eschatological wrath that no one is able to withstand it.

### 7:1–17 An Apocalyptic Intermission

Chapter 6 closes with a question: who is able to withstand the wrath of God and the Lamb? Chapter 7 opens with the answer: the constituent members of two groups. First, a relatively small number will be sealed on the forehead with the name of God and the Lamb. Just as lambs' blood protected the firstborn Hebrews by directing God's angel of death to "pass over" their homes (Exod 12), so the imprint of God's seal will protect this believing remnant. Second, an innumerable horde of believers will stand before the throne of God and sing, despite the fact that they have not been sealed and therefore protected. Caught in the apocalyptic cross fire between God and the forces of Satan (see esp. 6:12–17), though cut down, they nonetheless also stand. The sealed remnant is enabled to stand on earth. Having fallen on earth, the unsealed horde makes its stand in heaven.

### 7:1–3 Holding Back the Winds

> 7:1 After this, I saw four angels standing at the four corners of the earth, restraining the four winds of the earth so that no wind could blow on the earth nor on the sea nor on any tree. 2 Then[a] I saw another angel, who had the seal of the living God, ascending from the rising of the sun, and he cried out with a foreboding voice to the four angels who were given power to damage the earth and the sea, 3 saying: "Do not damage the earth or the sea or the trees until we have marked the servants of our God with a seal on their foreheads."

a. The *kai* (here, translated "then") operates as a coordinating conjunction.

[7:1] The words "after this, I saw" (*meta touto eidon*) indicate that John is working in a new subject area (see the comment on 4:1). John is not saying that the events in 7:1–3 take place at a later time than the events recorded in chapter 6. The preposition "after" has a narrative rather than a chronological sense.

While John's vision in 7:1–8 explores a new topic, the material contained in the topic relates directly to the earlier visions. It is only "after" John has shared the visions of chapter 6 that he can emphasize the importance of being exempted from the horror they represent.

God works via angelic proxy. Four angels have been stationed at the four compass points of a mythically conceived flat earth (cf. Isa 11:12; Ezek 7:2); the entire world is under their regulatory purview. Their charge is to hold back the four winds that blow out across the entire earth (cf. Dan 7:2). This blowing is a euphemism for angelic action that will damage (*adikeō*) the entire global landscape.

Given the destructive potential of these four winds, many commentators identify them with the four horsemen of 6:1–8. It is intriguing that the four horsemen of Zech 6:1–8, upon whom John's horsemen are obviously based, are also characterized as the four winds (Zech 6:5). We will perhaps never be able to determine whether John is also recasting his horses in this way. What is clear is that he envisions widespread desolation in both accounts, and in both accounts the executors of that desolation operate as God's agents.

Repeatedly, in 6:1–8, the seer claimed that the horsemen's destructive power was given (*edothē*) to them by God. He makes the same claim about the winds at 7:2 (cf. Jer 49:36; Dan 7:2). The association of the four winds with God is heightened by the fact that angels control them. To this point, angels have played an exclusive role as God's divine agents and messengers (Rev 1:1, 20; 2:1, 8, 12, 18; 3:1, 5, 7, 14; 5:2, 11). The association continues through John's use of the verb "to damage" (*adikeō*), which is strongly tied to the theme of judgment (cf. 2:11; 6:6). Particularly at 9:4 (see also 9:10, 19), destructive locusts operate by God's direction. The connection to God's authority seems clear when the locusts are ordered not to harm those who have the seal of God, just as in 7:1–3 the winds are prevented from harming those who have been so sealed. The association between God and the winds climaxes in 7:2, when John explains that the power to wield the destructive winds was not something the angels acquired on their own; it was given (*edothē*) to them by God.

The point John made in chapter 6 is therefore made anew, via different imagery, here in chapter 7: despite how chaotic many things look, God is in control. Even the desolation of the apocalyptic woes is a part of God's creative final plan. Like the fury of birth pangs, they presage the hope for new and sustained life in God's coming kingdom.

**[2]** John opens the second verse by appealing to yet another familiar narrative device: *kai eidon* ("Then I saw"; see the discussion of 5:1). As he did frequently throughout chapters 5 and 6, he uses the term here to indicate a shift in staging within the same scene. While keeping his hearers and readers focused on the four angels and the winds they hold at bay, John now introduces a fifth and strategically critical angelic messenger. This angel's message, though, is for neither John nor his followers. He addresses his four colleagues.

The imposing fifth angel ascends from the place of the sun's rising, the east (cf. 16:12; 21:13). It is not inconsequential that in Isa 41:25, the Lord God stirs up one who will come from the rising of the sun to trample on rulers in much the same way rulers and their patrons are trampled at Rev 6:12–17. This fifth angel, then, is the executor of God's judgment. John reinforces the judgment theme when he characterizes this angel as speaking in a "great voice." John is less interested in volume than he is in tone. In earlier texts, the great voice is a cipher for urgent, dramatic messages. John was told by a great voice to write his visions (1:10). Great voices celebrated in song the worthiness of the Lamb (5:2, 12; also 7:10). The remaining "great voice" citations share another common theme; they all convey the tone of judgment. After the souls under the altar cry out in a great voice to God for a just judgment against those who shed their blood (6:10), one great voice after another confirms the judgment to come (8:13; 10:3; 11:12; 12:10; 14:7, 9, 15, 18; 16:1, 17; 19:1, 17).[1] In fact, judgment imagery is so consistently related to the "great" voice that a better translation would be "foreboding" voice.

The fifth angel's gear is even more interesting than his origin and tone. He carries a key piece of eschatological equipment: the seal of the living God, which is to say, eternal God.[2] Unlike the seven seals mentioned in chapter 5, six of which were opened in chapter 6, this seal is most likely a type of signet device for embossing an imprint upon the seals that acted as binders for the apocalyptic scroll. Worn either as a cylinder hung on a cord around the neck or as a seal mounted like a stone on a ring, the device would have been immediately recognizable in either Jewish political or Greco-Roman magical circles. "By possessing God's seal, the angel acts with God's authority" (Reddish 143).

[3] The fifth angel orders the other four not to harm (*adikeō*) the earth, sea, or trees that have been positioned squarely in their sights since v. 1. Critical, though, is the nature of the command; it is a stay of the action, not an end to it. The destruction is to be abated until (*achri*) we have sealed the servants of *our* God upon their forehead.

The first-person plural pronouns are curious. The fifth angel appears to be acting alone. Could it be that he expects God and the Lamb to join him in the sealing process? But if that is the case, why did God surrender control of the signet device and apparently delegate the task? In fact, God has delegated the task. The fifth angel refers instead to his four colleagues. The angels whose actions will unleash the judgment and the angel whose orders control the timing and scope of that judgment are working in concert.

If the sealing is anything like the sealing that takes place in the story of Ezek 9:4–8, upon which 7:1–3 is surely based, then its function is to afford divine

---

1. See also 18:2. Although the adjective strong (*ischyros*) is used with the word "voice," the emphasis on judgment remains.

2. Note the participial use of *zaō* (live) in relation to God at 4:9–10; 10:6; 15:7, and to the child of humanity at 1:18.

protection.[3] In Ezekiel's account, God commissioned six executioners to slaughter the idolatrous inhabitants of Jerusalem. At just the moment when the reader expected the bloodbath to begin, however, there was an intermission. Before commencing the kill, God ordered that all those who grieved the abominable behavior be branded with a mark upon their foreheads. When an executioner saw the mark, he was to pass by the persons who bore it, leaving them unharmed. Precisely the same scenario plays itself out here. God's fierce and final judgment awaits the Lamb's breaking of the seventh seal. At just the moment when the reader expects God to act, the fifth of God's agents calls time-out so that certain believers can be branded with a protective mark on the forehead. A similar branding took place in the Genesis account where the mark God placed upon Cain acted as a seal of protection from future harm (4:15). One might argue similarly that the Hebrews in Exod 12 sealed themselves with the mark of lambs' blood on their doorposts. That "seal" protected them from the destructive force of God's death angel, who eventually killed all of Egypt's first-born males. Other commentators note the similarity to *Pss. Sol.* 15.6, 9, where the righteous are marked so that they may be saved.[4] Indeed, later in John's own story, the locusts, who are also obviously executing a portion of God's judgment, are specifically ordered to harm only those who do not sport God's protective seal on their foreheads (Rev 9:4).

The seal identifies the branded persons as God's possessions; John describes them as God's slaves/servants.[5] Later, when this select group of God's slaves/servants is again mentioned, John explains that the branding is God's own name (14:1–5). To mark someone with one's name is clearly to mark them as one's possession (see 9:4; 13:16; 14:1, 9; 17:5; 20:4; 22:4).

The seal, then, secured the possession (see John's use of the term *sphragizō*, "to seal," in 10:4; 20:3; 22:10), that is, protected it.[6] The scroll of chapter 5 was sealed and thereby protected from being opened by anyone but the worthy

3. Aune (2:452) points out that the concept of sealing is well known in apocalyptic circles; cf. *4 Ezra* 2.38, 40; 6.5.

4. Beale writes, "In both Ezekiel and *Pss. Sol.*, faithful Israelites are protected from the temporal harm of the plagues. The destruction of the plagues affects only those who are unfaithful and openly demonstrates their unbelieving identity" (410).

5. Aune writes, "The combination of the notions of sealing or tattooing with the term δοῦλοι, 'slaves, servants,' indicates that this metaphor is derived from the Eastern practice of tattooing secular and religious slaves" (2:455). Aune is right to argue further that any attempt to develop sealing as a metaphor for baptism or the reception of the Holy Spirit is unwarranted; cf. Reddish 143. Boring, though, points out that "incorporation into the body of Christ by baptism (I Cor 12:13) was sometimes pictured in Pauline churches as the seal which stamped the new Christian as belonging to God (II Cor. 1:22; Eph. 1:13; 4:30)" (*Revelation*, 129).

6. Reddish comments, "to be marked with the seal of God signifies divine protection. It is this idea that is primary here. Placing a seal on a document or a container guaranteed the authenticity of the contents. They could not be altered or removed without breaking the seal. Thus the contents were secure" (143).

Lamb. God's people, or at least a select portion of them, will be similarly sealed and thereby protected against the onslaught that will come with the setting loose of the four destructive winds.[7] Here, then, is the answer to the critical question asked at 6:17: who will be able to stand? Only those who are sealed, which is to say, are secured, protected, by God's angels.

### 7:4–8 The 144,000

4 And I heard the number of those who were sealed, one hundred forty-four thousand, sealed out of every tribe of the people of Israel: 5 from the tribe of Judah twelve thousand sealed, from the tribe of Reuben twelve thousand, from the tribe of Gad twelve thousand, 6 from the tribe of Asher twelve thousand, from the tribe of Naphtali twelve thousand, from the tribe of Manasseh twelve thousand, 7 from the tribe of Simeon twelve thousand, from the tribe of Levi twelve thousand, from the tribe of Issachar twelve thousand, 8 from the tribe of Zebulun twelve thousand, from the tribe of Joseph twelve thousand, from the tribe of Benjamin twelve thousand sealed.

[4] At this point John's vision turns abruptly into an audition. He stops seeing and begins hearing. No doubt there is a certain amount of practicality involved in this shift; the witnessing of 144,000 individuals being sealed would have taken an inordinate amount of time. Narratively, the act transpires so quickly that it does not even require any descriptive space. The sealing takes place offstage, in the literary gap between vv. 3 and 4. A report summarizing the action is then released.

The report is brief. The angels have sealed 144,000 of God's servants, 12,000 from each of Israel's twelve tribes. Brevity, though, does not mean simplicity. The short report raises a long list of important narrative and theological questions. Why does God choose only 144,000 when there are surely many more faithful servants across time? Who are the 144,000? Does the fact that they are taken from the tribes of Israel mean that they are Jews? Are they to be understood as the multitude standing before the heavenly throne in 7:9–17? What is their role in God's grand strategy of eschatological judgment and salvation?

---

7. Schüssler Fiorenza argues that "the vision of sealing appears not to refer to eschatological salvation but to divine protection during the turmoil of the Last Day" (*Vision of a Just World*, 67). Beale proposes a more spiritualized understanding of the protection offered by the sealing: "The nature of this protection is spiritual. This is apparent from the fact that believers and unbelievers suffer similar physical afflictions (see on 6:1–8). But, whereas these trials purify God's servants, they harden the ungodly in their response to God (so 9:19–21)" (409–10).

The 144,000 are the human wing of God's cosmic army. To be sure, God has heavenly armies (9:16; 19:14); this human force on earth is tasked with the assignment of reconnoitering and then campaigning for—witnessing to—the lordship of God and the Lamb. That testimony is the weapon they wage in the victorious battle against the satanic belief that Rome and its Caesar are lord (12:11).

Grammatical and thematic hints offer clues to the identity of the 144,000. First, the phrase "out of every tribe of the people [lit., 'sons'] of Israel" is controlled by the partitive genitive introduced by the preposition *ek* (out of). John understands each grouping of 12,000 to be part of a larger number that would make up an entire tribe. The collective 144,000, then, is the remnant of a much larger company of God's people. Second, John's handling of the 144,000 and the innumerable multitude of 7:9–17 indicates that they are two different groups. The clearest distinction is that the 144,000 are specifically numbered while the multitude is not. At this point in the narrative, the 144,000 also operate on earth prior to the period of the end-time eschatological woes. By contrast, the innumerable multitude is located in heaven. In addition, they have already gone through the "great tribulation" for which the 144,000 are bracing. Third, the 144,000 in 7:4–8 are to be identified with the 144,000 in 14:1–5. Besides the fact that both groups comprise the same number of persons, there are several reasons for equating them. The members of both groups are marked on their foreheads. In 7:1–8, the marking is God's seal, and 14:1–5 then explains the content of that seal as the names of God and the Lamb. In both cases, moreover, the symbolism of a remnant community abounds. While 7:4–8 speaks of 12,000 out of the larger number of each tribe, 14:4 speaks of the firstfruits of what will ultimately be an abundant harvest. The 144,000 of 7:4–8 are secured with the mark of God for the coming eschatological conflict, and the 144,000 of 14:1–5 then prepare themselves for eschatological combat in the ancient way of the holy war. They maintain themselves as virgins who do not engage in sex in order that they will be pure as they follow the Lamb wherever he goes. According to 19:11–15, he goes out to war. Finally, the remnants in 7:4–8 and 14:1–5 occupy the same historical moment. In 7:4–8 the sealing from the coming wrath indicates a time prior to the judgment and the eschatological woes that go along with it. Similarly, the fact that the remnant in 14:1–5 symbolizes the firstfruits of those to be redeemed suggests that the redemptive process has only just now gotten under way. They, too, stand in anticipation of God's judgment day.

Who, though, are these 144,000? Are they Jewish? John does refer to them with the term that Jews of the period used to identify themselves: "Israel." There is also the obvious appeal to the twelve tribes, and then the awkward listing of those tribes in vv. 5–8. In this scenario, the 144,000 would comprise the Jewish component of God's followers, while the innumerable multitude of 7:9–17 would comprise the Gentile portion. There is, however, a problem with this reading. The

144,000 of 7:4–8 are the same as the 144,000 of 14:1–5. That latter group, whose members are marked with the name of the Lamb on their foreheads, is clearly Christian. The 144,000 of 7:4–8 must therefore also be Christian.

Could it be that John took an earlier Jewish source about Jewish martyrs and turned it into a text about Christian martyrs? Unlikely. The sealing offers protection against the very tribulations that create martyrs. If 7:4–8 ever was a Jewish source about a Jewish remnant, John has certainly revised it so that its protagonists have become Christians who most decidedly do not suffer martyrdom.

This does not mean, however, that John intends to exclude Jews from the company of this sealed remnant community. The number "144,000" is clearly not to be taken literally: it symbolizes wholeness. John has taken a figure representative of completion, the number "12," multiplied it by itself and then extended the total in a millenarian way: 12 x 12 x 1000 = 144,000. In its representation of the "whole" or "complete" remnant people, the double use of 12 signifies both the 12 tribes of Israel and the 12 apostles of the Lamb. John will later confirm this inclusive reading of the two twelves in his description of the new Jerusalem (21:12–14). The city has a great wall with 12 gates. On each gate is inscribed the name of one of the 12 tribes. The great wall also has 12 foundations, on each of which is inscribed the name of one of the 12 apostles. The number "144,000" symbolizes the same Jew/Gentile inclusiveness implied in the description of the new Jerusalem's great wall.

John has in mind a remnant group of Christians from both Jewish and Gentile backgrounds; what does he believe is their role in this eschatological scenario? Why are they set apart and protected from the coming eschatological woes? They are set apart as the human regiment of God's apocalyptic army. Military imagery is present throughout the narrative depiction in 7:4–8. The listing of groups of 12,000 implies a census with military objectives in mind. "The census is a specific form of list that occurs with some frequency in the OT, where it is used for purposes of taxation (Exod 30:11–16; 2 Kgs 15:19–20), for labor conscription (2 Chr 2:17–18; cf. 1 Kgs 5:13–18), for determining the cultic duties and social structure of members of the tribe of Levi (Num 3:14–4:49), for determining Israelite descent (Ezra 2 and par. in Neh 7 and 1 Esdr 5), but most commonly as a means for determining military strength (Num 1:2–46, esp. vv 2–3; 26:1–56, esp. vv 1–2; 2 Sam 24:1–9 [and par. 1 Chr 21:1–6]; 1 Chr 27:1–24)" (Aune 2:43). Once again, the identification of the groups in 7:4–8 and 14:1–5 is illustrative. The holy war imagery of soldiers keeping themselves sexually pure before battle reinforces a military identification and purpose for the 144,000 (Bauckham, *Climax of Prophecy*, 215–29).

When John describes this army as composed from the people of Israel, he is speaking symbolically. At the close of the first century when he writes, the twelve tribes no longer exist. His mythical rendering of Israel's past encourages a similarly mythical or, one might say, eschatological expectation for Israel's future.[8] In this case, Israel would refer not to ethnic Jews, but to all those who exhibit the primary Israelite character trait of belief in the lordship of God and now God's Lamb-like Christ. "Israel" would thus signify the Christian church. In this way, John can envision an eschatologically restored Israel composed of both Jews and Gentiles.[9] The presentation of the 144,000 as the restored remnant of Israel's twelve tribes is, then, John's way of eschatologically imaging the universal church.

[5–8] When John informs his hearers and readers that 12,000 persons are chosen from each tribe to be sealed, four points deserve notice. First, even though John is apparently working from Old Testament tribal listings, he offers his own unique list by beginning not with Reuben (whose name tended to head most Old Testament lists) but with Judah.[10] While some earlier lists presented the tribes in geographical order from south to north and thus started with Judah (Num 34:19–28; Josh 21:4–7; 1 Chr 12:23–37), John no doubt chooses to list Judah first because he believes that Judah is the originating tribe of the Lamb (5:5). John emphasizes the tribe's placement by attaching the term "sealed" to Judah's 12,000. Even though he always implies such a sealing, he refrains from using the key term again until he comes to the final listing: the announcement of Benjamin's 12,000 at the close of the census. The term, then, not only highlights the selection of Judah but also serves to bracket the census material off from the rest of the material in the chapter.

A second oddity in the presentation is the inclusion of the names Manasseh and Joseph in the same listing (vv. 6, 8). In most traditional lists, Manasseh and Ephraim were generally mentioned together, but not Joseph, since the former two were sons of Joseph. A probable explanation for this apparent anomaly comes from a third observation: Dan is absent. Dan was apparently replaced by Manasseh because Dan was thought to have been connected with egregious

8. Boring writes, "Judaism knew that the original unity of twelve tribes had been disrupted by the Assyrian deportation (II Kings 17; Jer. 16:10–15; Ezek. 47:13–48:29; Bar. 4–5; II Bar. 63; 67; Test. Mos. 2:3–9) and had never been restored, but at the eschaton God would reassemble the full complement of all Israel (Ps. Sol. 17:28–31, 40; 1QM 2; T. Sanh. 13:10; II Esdr. 13:40–47; II Bar. 78–87; cf. Matt. 19:28; Luke 22:30). John declares that the eschatological hope for Israel is realized in the church" (*Revelation*, 129).

9. Such a vision would have been in line with the way other Christian writers of the time envisioned the symbolic future of Israel. As Boring explains, "The key argument for identifying the 144,000 as intended to represent the church as such, however, is the theological understanding of the church as the continuation of Israel. This view was widespread in early Christianity (e.g., Matt. 10:5–6; Luke 1:68–79; 2:29–32; John 1:47; 5:43–47; 11:52; Acts 2:14–21; 26:14–23; James 1:1), but was particularly strong in the Pauline tradition to which John belongs (1:6; 5:10; cf. Rom. 9–11; Gal. 3:29; 6:16; Eph. 2:11–22; I Pet 2:9)" (*Revelation*, 129).

10. See Gen 49; Num 1:16–54; Deut 33; Judg 5. For a comparative enumeration of these accounts, see Reddish 146.

activities like idolatry (Judg 18; 1 Kgs 12:25–33). John insisted that his readers and hearers maintain their fidelity to the lordship of God and the Lamb. He persisted with this demand even though his followers lived in an environment that rewarded accommodation and punished faithful witness. It is therefore not surprising that he would omit the names of tribes associated in Jewish tradition with idolatry, the very essence of accommodation. Given Manasseh's presence, John may well have written "Joseph" when he intended to write "Ephraim." In any case, it is Joseph's tribal lineage that is intended.

Fourth, Levi's inclusion is odd. Because the tribe was not given a portion of land and its members were exempt from military service, the name Levi was generally omitted from such listings (Num 1:49; 2:33; Deut 10:8–9; 18:1–5; Josh 13:14, 33). Interestingly enough, however, Levi was included in the accounts of 1QM 1.2; 2.2, where the tribes were gathered together in anticipation of an eschatological war (Aune 2:463). Since John has put his census of the tribes in just such an eschatological setting, it is, in the end, unremarkable that Levi is included.

### 7:9–17  An Innumerable, International Multitude

9 After this I looked, and behold a great multitude that no one was able to count, from all nations and tribes and peoples and tongues, standing before the throne and before the Lamb, dressed in dazzling robes and with palm branches in their hands, 10 and they cried out in a foreboding voice, saying:

> "Salvation belongs to our God who is seated on the throne
>     and to the Lamb!"

11 And all the angels stood around the throne and around the elders and the four living creatures, and they fell on their faces before the throne and worshiped God, 12 singing,[a]

> "Amen! Blessing and glory and wisdom
> and thanksgiving and honor
> and power and might
> belong to our God forever and ever! Amen!"

13 Then[b] one of the elders answered, saying to me, "Who are these who are clothed in dazzling robes, and where did they come from?" 14 I said to him, "Sir, you know." Then he said to me, "These are the ones who came out[c] of the great tribulation; they washed their robes and made them dazzling (white) in the blood of the Lamb.

15 For this reason they are before the throne of God
  and worship him day and night in his temple,
  and the one seated on the throne will shelter[d] them.
16 They will hunger no more, and thirst no more;
  the sun will not strike them,[e]
  nor any scorching heat.
17 Because the Lamb in the center[f] of the throne will be their shepherd,
  and he will guide them to springs of the water of life,
  and God will wipe away every tear from their eyes."

a. John uses *legontes* (speaking), but because he follows with a hymn, singing is clearly his intent.

b. The *kai* (then) operates here as a coordinating conjunction.

c. Literally, "who are coming out." For discussion of this translation of the present participle, see the comment on v. 14 below.

d. Though *skēnoō* means to live or dwell, particularly as in a tent (*skēnē*), this verb also, in conjunction with the preposition *epi* (over, above), has the sense of sheltering, as, no doubt, with a sheltering edifice like a tent (BDAG 755).

e. Literally, "will not fall upon them": the phrase *piptō epi tina* has the nuance of causing harm. See Louw and Nida 24.93.

f. Literally, "in the middle (midst)": the phrase *to ana meson* has the nuance of being centered. See BAGD 49.

[9] Once again, John opens a new subject area with the introductory phrase "after this I looked, and behold" (*meta tauta eidon, kai idou;* see the discussion of 4:1). As has been the case with his past uses of this phrase, the preposition "after" is not a chronological marker. He does not mean to say that the events chronicled in vv. 9–17 occur immediately after the events described in vv. 1–8. He instead means to say that after having seen the vision of the sealing of the 144,000, he saw another vision that dealt with a different though related topic. Having conveyed the sealing scene that took place prior to God's intervening acts of judgment and justice, he now feels obliged to relate the vision that relays the ultimate fate of all believers, both those who were sealed *and* those who were not. In order to do so, he must jump forward rather than backward in time. In fact, he vaults so far forward that he finds himself looking beyond the very end of time. The vision assures his hearers and readers who are presently suffering—and have therefore most assuredly not been sealed—that all who are knocked down because of their witness for the lordship of the Lamb will stand eternally tall in heaven. This futuristic, spiritual vision ends up having a real-time social and political discipleship effect: it encourages the members of the seven churches to resist relationship with Rome.

The object of John's sight was a vast crowd (*ochlos polys*; on the difference between the 144,000 and this crowd, see the discussion of 7:4), a legion of people so great that no one could possibly have counted it. At this point hearers and readers could not be blamed for remembering God's great promise to Abraham. The pledge that the patriarch's seed would one day grow as innumerable as the sands of the sea and the stars of the heavens (Gen 13:16; 15:5; 22:17; 26:4; 28:14; 32:12; cf. Heb 11:12) has been accomplished in two significant ways. The first is the count; as God had promised, the numbers are titanic. The second is the vast crowd's universal nature; they represent every nation, tribe, people, and tongue. This means that Jews, Abraham's literal descendants, *and* Gentiles, who have been metaphorically grafted onto Israel's family tree through the gift of the Christ Lamb (cf. Rom 11:13–26; Gal 3:7, 29; 6:16), stand together in their worship, praise, and identification as the people of God. According to this second vision in chapter 7, Abraham's light has indeed drawn all the nations, or at least representatives from each of them, to the worship and into the glory of God.

John notices two important things about the constituents of the great crowd. First, each one of them is dressed in white. By now, John has so vigorously stressed the connection between dazzling (white) clothing and conquering witness to the lordship of Christ that it would be impossible for any hearer or reader to miss it here (see 3:2–5, 18; 4:4; 6:11). The fact that they are so dressed is an indication that they have been faithful witnesses and that their witness has contributed to the destruction of satanic rule as well as the liberation of those enslaved to it. Earlier, John declares that the Lamb is worthy because he redeemed (i.e., liberated) every tribe, tongue, people, and nation (5:9). Though John orders the elements differently in 7:9, he clearly has the same universal, believing congregation in mind. The crowd now gathered is the same gathering that the Lamb liberated through his execution (i.e., his blood). The Lamb, though, did not act alone. At 12:11 John articulates a human-divine partnership. Human witness worked alongside the Lamb's slaughter/blood to bring about the conquest of satanic rule. The members of the multitude earned their dazzling robes through their nonaccommodating, conquering witness. Their reward is the eschatological relationship with God and the Lamb that John now envisions.

The second thing John notices is that the constituents of the great crowd hold palm branches (*phoinikes*) in their hands. Though the term does occur in the Gospel of John, when the crowd greets Jesus' entry into Jerusalem with the acclamation, "Hosanna! Blessed is the one who comes in the name of the Lord—the King of Israel" (12:13), this is the only time it appears in Revelation. In 1 Macc 13:51 and 2 Macc 10:7, palm branches were used to celebrate great feats like the victorious purification of the temple. Indeed, the Greek pronunciation of the plural form (*phoinikes*) reminded hearers of the victory (*nikē*) for God that they sought. Given the eschatological context of praise for the victorious God and Lamb, it is clear that the John who authored Revelation also intended the palm branches to be a symbol of adulation. The great crowd celebrates the conquest of satanic Rome.

The presence of the universal crowd standing worshipfully before the throne also encourages a complementary explanation. Zechariah 14 chronicles the vision of the nations trekking into the new Jerusalem for an eschatological Feast of Booths. Given the connection of the palm branches and this festival (Lev 23:40, 43; Neh 8:14–18; 2 Macc 10:6–7), not to mention John's vision of an innumerable, *international* horde, it may be that he also wants to evoke the image of an apocalyptic Feast of Booths. It is not surprising that John may be thinking simultaneously of conquest and festival images since the author of 2 Maccabees, too, brings those images triumphantly together (10:6–7).

**[10]** In v. 10, the assembled multitude belts out a hymn of praise to God (see the discussion of the one who sits on the throne at 4:2–3) and to the Lamb (see the comment on 5:6). They, like the angel at 7:2, make their declaration in a foreboding voice. John's characters are still broadcasting the judgment that will occur at the last day. Here, though, the seer emphasizes the reverse side of the end-time coinage. At the very moment that those who persecuted the Lamb's witnesses are being brutally judged (see 6:1–8, 12–17; 7:1–3), the witnesses will be saved. The direct connection between the salvation of believers and the judgment of those who persecute them is explicitly declared by foreboding voices at 12:10 and 19:1–2. Both groups earn the end to which they come. Death and destruction will greet the satanic, oppressive forces of Rome; dazzling robes of conquest, on the other hand, will adorn the souls of the resurrected witnesses (see the discussion of 7:9).

It is not coincidental, then, that the only times John uses the word "salvation" (*sōtēria*), he narrates its proclamation through a foreboding heavenly voice in the context of God's apocalyptic judgment (7:10; 12:10; 19:1–2). These three salvation texts form a sort of narrative progression: 7:10 makes the opening declaration that salvation belongs to God and to the Lamb; 12:10 then develops the thought by explaining exactly how God and the Lamb brought about the circumstance of salvation. They obliterated (i.e., judged) the one who had tormented believers and had enlisted Rome's institutional assistance in the effort. Finally, 19:1–2 clarifies the rationale: God has toppled satanic Rome as an act of ultimate judgment.

The connection with Rome is important. It makes the attribution of salvation to God and the Lamb as political as it is spiritual. To be sure, the picture of a robed throng in heaven encourages John's hearers and readers to think of a heavenly, spiritual reward for their active, nonaccommodating, rebellious witness. But the contemporaneous understanding of salvation as an imperially guaranteed commodity also reminds John's hearers and readers that a competition for global affection is being waged. Both God/the Lamb and Rome claim to be the sole providers of "salvation": the peace and security of a life freed from oppression and harm. When John makes that claim exclusively for God, as he does here at 7:10, he is not only making a positive statement about God and the Lamb; he is also making a pejorative one about Rome. He is claiming that Rome cannot live up to its own hype. It does not hold the power of salvation that it alleges. John wants his hearers and readers to recognize Rome for the false pretender that it is. So educated, they will be less likely to accommodate to Roman social and religious practices in hopes of gaining the social, religious, and economic security that Rome claims to offer. They will seek such security, such salvation, from God and the Lamb instead. John's message of salvation is therefore every bit as political as it is spiritual. Though it is a vision about the end time, it maintains an ethical message commending politically active, nonaccommodating behavior in the present moment of the churches in Asia Minor. This is what Schüssler Fiorenza means by writing that "the time of eschatological tribulation is coextensive with the everyday troubles of the Asian communities" (*Vision of a Just World*, 68). Despite the persecution that promises to follow upon rebellious witnessing to the lordship of the Christ Lamb, believers should stay the course, knowing that what Rome offers as salvation and punishment is transitory. God's judgment and salvation are eternal. It is God's judgment that believers should therefore avoid, God's salvation that they should seek.

[11] The angels who encircle the throne and the elders and the cherubim (on this positioning of heavenly attendants, see the comments on 4:4, 6–8a; 5:6, 11) prepare for antiphonal affirmation by falling on their faces before the throne in a classic pose of worship (cf. 1:17; 4:10; 5:8, 14; 11:16; 19:4, 10; 22:8). The scene is reminiscent of the one at 5:11–12, where countless angels respond antiphonally to the song of the cherubim and twenty-four elders. Here, surrounded by the cherubim and twenty-four elders, they react to a heavenly and apparently redeemed multitude. The earlier praise scene (5:11–12) has cycled back upon itself. The key thought remains the same: salvation, and therefore praise, belongs to God and the Lamb.

[12] "Amen" to that, exclaim the responding angels. This affirmation brackets the angelic worship refrain. "Amen" signifies what is true and valid (see the discussion of 3:14). When used as a personal referent, it typically applies to God. At 3:14, it applies to Christ, who appears as the living validation of the lofty claims made about God's blessings and glory. Here, operating as the opening and closing angelic commentary, it affirms the validity of the interior statement's claims about God. Seven key attributes, six of which were earlier mentioned in relation to the Lamb at 5:12, are noted. Blessing and glory and wisdom and thanksgiving and honor and power and might belong eternally to God.[11] Why? Because, as the context implies, God has brought about a just and

___

11. At 5:12 most of the same seven descriptors appear, though in different order, in relation to the Lamb: power and wealth and wisdom and might and honor and glory and blessing. In 7:12

fair conclusion to history, where the evil are judged and the faithful are saved. How can John's hearers and readers be sure? They have the angels' "Amen" word on it.

[13] John apparently looks puzzled. That would explain why one of the twenty-four elders (see the discussion of 4:4) answers even though John has not asked a question. Helping John frame his thoughts, the elder offers a rhetorical question to which he, but evidently not John, knows the answer. "Who," the elder asks, "are these dressed in dazzling (white) robes, and where did they come from?" The elder knows that who (they are) and why (they are here) are John's main concerns.

[14] Like the prophet Ezekiel, who tells God, "Lord, you know," after God asks whether the dry bones before him can again live (37:3), John turns the question back to the elder. In this case, though, the moniker *kyrios* (sir) is a title of respect rather than divinity ("Lord"). Still, he presumes that the elder's heavenly status gives him access to information that John does not have.

John is not disappointed. The verbal tenses the elder deploys in his answer are as important as the content those verbs convey. This horde of people whom John sees beyond the end of time are those who *went* through the great tribulation that was described at 6:1–8, 12–17; and 7:1–3, and that was anticipated in the letters to the seven churches (chs. 2–3). They were unsealed and therefore unprotected. The 144,000, too, will go through the great tribulation. They, however, will navigate it unscathed. John poetically explains the very different circumstance of the innumerable multitude by declaring that they washed their robes and made them dazzling (white) in the blood of the Lamb. Though the participle *hoi erchomenoi* (lit., "the ones who are coming"), which explains their movement through the tribulation, is in the present tense, it must, because of its clausal relationship to the aorist main verbs "washed" and "made dazzling/white," be translated with a past sense (Smyth 419). Its present form refers not as much to a sense of time as it does to its structural relationship with the main verbs. Their movement through the tribulation was contemporary or "coincident" with the washing and making dazzling/white. Like the washing and making dazzling/white, both the tribulation in question and the movement through it have been long over.

---

thanksgiving is cited instead of wealth. At 4:9 only three such attributes are mentioned; the cherubim give glory, honor, and thanks to God. At 4:11, the twenty-four elders respond by also extolling three attributes: glory, honor, and power. It is suggestive, however, that even though the listings in 4:9, 11 are much shorter, they have the symbolism of completion because each has three of the consistent seven attributes. John has three numbers for completion: 12, 7, and 3. These lists of lofty credentials belonging to God (4:9, 11; 7:12) and the Lamb (5:12) use two of them: 7 and 3. In either case, then, God and the Lamb receive the full acclamation of which they are worthy. In all four listings (4:9, 11; 5:12; 7:12), glory and honor are present as belonging either to God or to the Lamb.

When the elder says that these are the people who *went* through the great tribulation *and* in so doing washed their robes *and* made them dazzling/white in the blood of the Lamb, the two uses of *kai* (and) employed to link the three primary clauses should be treated epexegetically.[12] That is to say, they not only connect the clauses but also identify the material in the trailing clause as a clarification of the information revealed in the preceding clause (see the discussion of 1:2). One should therefore translate: "These are the ones who went through the great tribulation, which is to say, they washed their robes; that is, they made them dazzling/white in the blood of the Lamb." Though they deploy different symbolism, each of the three clauses says essentially the same thing. They are narratively equivalent.

An identification of the key phrase *tēs thlipseōs tēs megalēs* (the great tribulation) is critical to understanding the meaning of 7:14. The combination of the article and the adjective "great" suggests that this is not just any tribulation but the great time of distress that would accompany the ushering in of God's Day of Judgment and Salvation (see Dan 12, esp. vv. 1–4). Early Christian writers tended to view historical afflictions as a preamble to that apocalyptic moment. The Synoptic Gospel declarations (see Matt 24; Mark 13; Luke 21) attributed to Jesus indicate that the response of hostile Roman and Jewish leaders to acts of faithful discipleship comprised the Great Tribulation's opening act.[13] The connection Jesus made between acts of discipleship and present tribulation is critical for John. His use of the term *thlipsis* (tribulation, affliction) at 1:9; 2:9, 10 betrays his belief that the struggles of his hearers and readers indicate that the great struggle of the end time is already under way. It is equally intriguing that, like Jesus in the synoptic accounts, he connects the believers' affliction to their discipleship behavior. John uses the language of witness to bring discipleship behavior to narrative life. Their witness triggers the affliction that sets the stage for the even greater tribulation to come. This is the warning John tried to deliver in his letters to the seven churches in chapters 2 and 3, as he exhorted his churches to even more vigorous expression of that witness. Later, John emphasizes the point through the language of slaughter (6:9). It is precisely because of their determination to reject accommodation to Roman lordship and the economic, political, and religious benefits associated with it, and their effort to proclaim the alternative lordship of the Lamb—that is, their witness—that his people suffer as they do.

Witness, then, not martyrdom, is John's focus with his tribulation language. The Daniel text upon which he is surely building also emphasizes faithful witnessing more than self-sacrificial martyrdom. As Beale observes, "In Daniel's

---

12. "These are the ones who went through the great tribulation." "They washed their robes." "They made them white in the blood of the Lamb."

13. Similarly, Beale: "The trial has already been set in motion in John's day" (434).

tribulation, the eschatological opponent persecutes the saints because of their covenant loyalty to God (cf. Dan. 11:30–39, 44; 12:10)" (433). The tribulation, whether in its early, historical or its final, apocalyptic stage, is to be connected not with martyrdom, but with witness and the sacrifices (martyrdom included) that go along with it. In John's narrative world, then, "washing" and "making dazzling/white" are, like "conquering," euphemisms for witness (see the comments on 3:4–5).

Even John's pointed reference to the blood of Christ is not a reference to martyrdom.[14] John's later narrative language will not allow for such a reading. At 12:11 he does not tie Jesus' blood to the imagery of human self-sacrifice but to the language of conquest and Christian witness. Both Jesus' blood and Christian witness are necessary for realizing the conquest of satanic Rome. Jesus' blood, which is significantly attached to the witness he bore (see the discussion of 1:1–3), is the component given exclusively by God. The part that believers can control is their own witness. That is why the ethical exhortations of chapters 2 and 3 are targeted toward the endeavor of witnessing. John does not want his believers to think, however, that their witness is alone sufficient for the task. Only when they work in concert with God's own work will their effort have the victorious result that they seek. That witnessing effort, euphemistically pictured as a washing and making dazzling/white, takes place in concert with, and therefore in direct relation to—one might even say, as John does, *in*—the blood of the Lamb. In other words, a believer washes one's robes in the blood of the Lamb by testifying to the lordship of that executed Lamb. It is witness, not dying, that is ethically preeminent.

**[15]** Having explained who the crowd is, the elder now clarifies why they have been awarded such lofty status. It is because of (*dia touto*) their witness. Revelation 22:14 confirms that those who wash their robes will procure an eternal eschatological relationship with God.

The eternal nature of the eschatological relationship is celebrated in two principal images. The first is that of perpetual worship. At the Jerusalem temple, worship began with the initial morning sacrifice (*tamid*) and ended with the closing sacrifice at the end of the day. Not so in the heavenly realm. There would be neither a beginning nor an ending in the cycle of worship. The faithful would have the perpetual opportunity to stand in God's temple and celebrate God's lordship and God's rule.

The presence of the temple appears at first sight to be problematic. After all, this scene takes place in heaven in the future following God's Day of Judgment and Salvation. Later, however, John will declare that no temple exists in

---

14. For various discussions of washing, particularly as related to the symbolism of blood and images of redemptive sacrifice, atonement, and martyrdom, see Aune 2:474–75; Reddish 151; and Beale 423, 435–37.

the new Jerusalem, because the Lord God and the Lamb are themselves now the temple. What appears at first to be a contradiction is in reality complementary. Far from disputing the affirmation of 7:15, the vision of the new Jerusalem in 21:22 essentially agrees with it. From the very beginning of his work, John has maintained that there would be some type of temple in God's future kingdom (3:12). Both 7:15 and 21:22 understand that God and the Lamb will themselves be that presence. As Beale argues, "Rev. 7:15 does not portray a literal 'temple' in which the saints serve God (so 21:22). Rather, as the second part of the verse reveals, the temple now consists in the presence of the lamb and of 'the one sitting on the throne, who tabernacles over his people' (so also 21:22)" (441).

When John asserts that God will dwell with the people and so shelter them,' the accent is once again on perpetuity. John's shift to the future-tense verb is intended to convey that the future already envisioned will itself be further extended, into forever. In this forever, God will dwell with God's people. Clearly building from Ezek 37:26–28, John reclaims the Festival of Booths imagery that he implied with his mention of palm branches in 7:9. God will tabernacle (*skēnoō*) with the people (21:3) even as the people tabernacle in tents to celebrate God's lordship and rule. Forever.

**[16–17]** In what many call the longest allusion to an Old Testament passage in the book of Revelation, John draws upon the vision in Isa 49:10 to assure his hearers and readers that those who faithfully witness, who resist accommodating themselves to Roman lordship and the benefits that go with it, will never again, even in the extended future that progresses beyond the end of time itself, experience hunger or thirst, or the heat of wandering and separation that their forebears once experienced in the postexodus wilderness and the post-Babylonian exile.

John's hearers and readers can be assured of this promise because the Lamb himself will shepherd the people (v. 17). The vision of a lamb operating as a shepherd is not as paradoxical as it first appears. It is the Lamb whose witness and execution helped to establish the peoples' eschatological relationship with God. In delivering that witness, in enduring and rising beyond the accompanying execution, the Lamb has shown them the way of witness that leads to God. In that sense, even as executed Lamb, he has been their shepherd, their guide. That shepherding role will continue unabated in the future. And so, appealing once again to well-known Old Testament images (Ps 23:1–2; Isa 25:8; 49:10; Jer 31:16; cf. Ezek 34:23), John declares that those who witness shall never again know want or distress. They shall know only the joy and praise that come from eternal relationship with God. The fruit of that relationship is symbolized in two important ways that will be dramatically developed in the eschatological visions of chapter 21: springs of the water of life or living water (21:6), and the wiping away of every tear (21:4).

*8:1　The Seventh Seal: Silence in Heaven*

1 When the Lamb[a] opened the seventh seal, there was silence in heaven for half an hour.

a. Though John uses the impersonal third-person singular, it is clear from context that the acting agent is the Lamb (cf. 6:1).

**[8:1]** Verse 1 is the natural conclusion to the visionary recounting of the first six seals (cf. 6:1–17). After the narrative interlude of chapter 7, where the seer flashed back to the past that preceded the seals episode (7:1–8) and then envisioned the future that would occur after it (7:9–17), John's hearers and readers are now ready to witness the final judgment that would accompany the Lamb's opening of the seventh seal. John uses the language of "opening" (see the discussion of 6:1) as a verbal metaphor for the eschatological opportunity humans have to perform the kind of witness that would lead to salvation. In this case, the opening (of that opportunity) is associated with the time unit of a half hour. The half hour is a metaphor, not a literal measurement. It is a momentary break, a respite in the horror of judgment that immediately followed the opening of each of the past six seals. Humankind has been given this brief time-out for a reason. Though they now live on the proverbial edge of time, they have a final opportunity to operate in ways that will either invite salvation (witness) or demand judgment (accommodation).

John amplifies the judgment theme with the declaration of silence.[1] Though the seer only uses the word *sigē* (silence) here, in both Old Testament and Jewish contexts the term conjured images of divine judgment.[2] John enhances and broadens this emphasis with his specification of the time unit as *one-half* of an hour. Each of his later uses of the concept "half" occurs in a context that highlights either the judgment/destruction of those who have persecuted God's people (11:9, 11) or the salvation of those whose witness endures (12:14).[3]

1. Silence is not a narrative device that allows God to hear the forthcoming prayers of the saints (8:3–5). It is unlikely that an all-seeing, all-knowing countenance (cf. 1:4; 3:1; 4:8; 5:6) would require quiet in order to hear the concerns of the people.

2. Though the term *sigē* rarely appears in the LXX, the theme of silence, particularly as related to manuscript texts, is prevalent and related to the theme of judgment. Beale points to Pss 31:17–18; 115:17; *4 Ezra* 7.30; Isa 47:5; Ezek 27:32; Amos 8:2–3; Lam 2:10–11; 1 Sam 2:9–10, as well as Hab 2:20 and Zech 2:13. "IQpHab 13.1–4 interprets the silence of Hab 2:20 as 'the day of judgment [when] God will destroy all those [among the nations] who serve idols'" (446–48).

3. Note, though, the difference in terminology. As relating specifically to time in 8:1, John employs *hēmiōrion*. The later uses employ *hēmisu*. There is also thematic development of the image of "half" with the designation "one thousand, two hundred sixty days," which represents one-half of a seven-year period. This transitory period also symbolizes a period of short duration and occurs in contexts of either explicit judgment (11:3) or salvation (12:6). For a direct connection between the themes of judgment and "half," see also Wis 18:14–16.

The relationship between the moment of silence and the breaking of the seventh seal is reminiscent of the silence that preceded God's creation of heaven and earth. In this case, following the cataclysms of the final judgment, God will create a new heaven and a new earth. As at the beginning (cf. *4 Ezra* 6.39; *2 Bar.* 3.7), so here at the end (*4 Ezra* 7.26–44), the creative moment is set up by quiet.

Some commentators counter that this claim would be more compelling if the silence in 8:1 were actually followed by the creation of a new heaven and new earth instead of eschatological woe (e.g., Reddish 159). A key point bears consideration. John is playing with narrative time, employing the techniques of flashback and anticipation. It only *appears* as if the moment of new creation does not follow directly upon the period of silence narrated at 8:1. The pleas of 8:3–5, together with the trumpet woes that follow, are not new (chronologically later) events but a dramatic retelling of the petition in 6:9–11 and the seals judgment, for which it forms the centerpiece. The position of 6:9–11 was described through the lens of the sacrificial altar; in 8:3–5 John again appeals to incense altar imagery. When the narration of the trumpets recapitulates the breaking of the seals, John's hearers and readers find reassurance that God has indeed heard the cries of the faithful and has intervened. In other words, the narration that follows 8:1 recapitulates the events that have already happened (the seals episodes) from a different eschatological perspective (trumpets). Time itself has not moved chronologically forward. Just as John separated the movement from the opening of the sixth seal (6:12–17) to the opening of the seventh (8:1) with the flashback of 7:1–8 and the flash forward of 7:9–17, he separates the creative silence that follows the opening of the seventh seal from the eschatological creation that begins at 21:1. The next chronological step (after John finishes relating God's intervening acts of judgment) will be the creation of the new heaven and the new earth. The silence of 8:1 is therefore properly positioned (in real time) just before that moment. Only because of John's method of narrating his visions does the silence seem to be separated from the new creation. That separation is a literary fiction that gives John more narrative "time" to make his point. As far as eschatological real time is concerned, 8:1 moves chronologically right to 21:1. Everything in between is either a recapitulation of events already narrated or an anticipation of events yet to be narrated.

## 8:2–11:19 The Sounding of the Seven Trumpets

### 8:2–6 Introduction to the Trumpets

The acts of judgment that accompany the blowing of the trumpets by the seven archangels structurally and thematically parallel those associated with the Lamb's breaking of the seven seals. In John's narrative chronology, then, the breaking of the seals and the blasting of the trumpets occur simultaneously.

They are the same set of events, encountered from different perspectives (see the introduction to ch. 6).

2 And I saw the seven angels who stand[a] before God, and they were given seven trumpets. 3 And another angel with a golden censer came and stood at the altar; he was given a great quantity of incense to offer[b] with the prayers[c] of all the saints on the golden altar before the throne. 4 And the smoke of the incense went up with the prayers of the saints before God, from the hand of the angel. 5 Then the angel took the censer and filled it with some fire[d] from the altar and threw it on the earth; and there were thunders and rumblings and flashes of lightning and an earthquake. 6 And the seven angels who had the seven trumpets prepared to blow them.

a. The verb *hestēkasin* is a durative use of the perfect tense, which indicates an ongoing circumstance: "[who] stand."

b. Here occurs the unusual circumstance of a future indicative following *hina* (to, in order to, so that) instead of the more normally expected subjunctive.

c. Dative of advantage; see the commentary below.

d. A partitive genitive construction.

[2] The formula *kai eidon* (and I saw) distinguishes 8:2 from the material that precedes it. The hearer/reader remains a spectator in the seer's three-ring apocalyptic circus (see ch. 6 introduction). Having shifted perspective, one no longer sees God acting in the first ring through the metaphor of a Lamb breaking seals. In this second ring, God's preliminary acts of judgment operate through the image of seven angels blowing seven trumpets.

The angels are a subset of the larger group of angels whom John sees standing with the elders and cherubim at 7:11. The definite article implies that his audience is already familiar with them. John has, after all, mentioned a grouping of seven angels before: the seven guardians of John's seven churches (1:16, 20; 2:1, 8, 12, 18; 3:1, 7, 14); and the seven spirits located before God's throne (1:4; 4:5). Three observations support the view that the earlier angels/spirits are the same ones understood to be standing before God's throne in 8:2. First, John introduces the seven angels in 8:2 as though the reader has met them before. Second, he has heretofore only mentioned such a grouping in regard to the seven angels/spirits from chapters 1–4. Third, the seven spirits and seven angels are both located before the throne. John returns to them later at 15:1 and 16:1 (see also 17:1; 21:9) when he reimagines the breaking of the seals for the second time as the pouring out of God's bowls of wrath upon the earth.[4] These archangels, then, initiate the action in both the second and the third of the three

4. Cf. Schüssler Fiorenza: "They are probably identical with the angels who in 15:5–19:10 pour out the bowls of the wrath of God" (*Vision of a Just World*, 70).

apocalyptic rings. The fact that they are doing so simultaneously is not a problem given the fact that John is describing a single event with symbolic and poetic license. The normal constraints of time and place do not apply.

These seven are the archangels mentioned in the Jewish literature of the time.[5] John mentions only one of them by name. At 12:7 he credits Michael with ousting the dragon from heaven. If Michael's function and capability are any indication, these angels represent the awesome power of God to punish and thereby judge wrongdoing. It is no wonder, then, that John connects them so integrally to the eschatological judgment of the trumpets and bowls.

The seven archangels wield seven trumpets. Most often associated with the advance of an army in battle (Josh 6:5), the trumpet was also used as a signal of warning (Ezek 33:3–6; Joel 2:1), as accompaniment to religious ritual (Lev 23:24; 25:9; Joel 2:15; cf. the blowing of the shofar as signal to open and close the daily temple worship), as part of theophany scenes (Exod 19:16; cf. the depiction of one like the child of humanity speaking with the sound of a trumpet in Rev 1:10 and 4:1), and as an image of eschatological judgment (Zeph 1:16). Perhaps the most celebrated account of the trumpet call in connection with warfare, particularly warfare in which God was directly engaged, occurs in Josh 6. In this story, seven priests were assigned seven trumpets and ordered to blow them successively for seven consecutive days. On the seventh day, at the seventh trumpet blast, the walls of Jericho fell. The parallel to John's vision of the seven trumpets is difficult to miss. Similarly, "in the Qumran War Scroll seven Levites carry seven rams' horns into the eschatological conflict (1QM 7.14)" (Aune 2:510). Given this background, it is no wonder that both Jewish and New Testament writers associated the sounding of the trumpet with the engagement of God's final eschatological battle (Zeph 1:14–16; Zech 9:14; *Apoc. Abr.* 31.1; *4 Ezra* 6.23; *Gk. Apoc. Ezra* 4.36; Matt 24:31; 1 Cor 15:52; 1 Thess 4:16; *Did.* 16.6).[6]

John picks up on this eschatological emphasis and highlights it. The noun form for trumpet (*salpinx*) at 8:2 and 6 brackets a text where God responds to the prayers of the people by pouring an avenging and judging wrath upon the earth. This word reappears at 8:13, where the blasts of trumpets are connected to three dire eschatological woes; and at 9:14, where the sixth angel's trumpet unleashes a punishing force that kills one-third of all humankind. Interestingly enough, this image of the trumpet sound is balanced with the earlier instances where a trumpet blast issues from the child of humanity or the throne of God

5. See Aune 2:509; Reddish 160; González and González 61; Beale 454. These and other commentators point to a host of Jewish materials, such as Tob 12:15; *1 En.* 20.1–7; ch. 40; 54.6; 71.8–9; 81.5; 90.21–22; *T. Levi* 3.5; 8.2; *Jub.* 1.27, 29; 2.1–2, 18; 15.27; 31.14. The archangels are identified as Uriel, Raphael, Raguel, Michael, Saraqa'el, Gabriel, and Remiel.

6. Aune 2:519. Cf. Schüssler Fiorenza: "They herald the Day of the Lord (Zeph 1:14ff), announce the day of judgment (4 Ezra 6:23), or proclaim the resurrection of the dead and the dawn of a new order (1 Thess 4:16; 1 Cor 15:52; Matt 24:31)" (*Vision of a Just World*, 70).

and is both revelatory and salvific (1:10; 4:1). The verbal form (*salpizō*) has the same emphasis. Throughout the trumpet scenes (8:6, 7, 8, 10, 12, 13; 9:1, 13; 10:7; 11:15), this verb is applied both to God's preliminary acts of judgment and to the final act of judgment at the last day. Revelation 11:15 is illustrative. Its larger context (11:15–18) also includes an image of salvation that is as potent as the theme of judgment most often associated with the sound.

This dual focus on judgment and salvation makes sense because God is the figure who directs the trumpet blasts and orchestrates the events that respond to them. John demonstrates God's control here in the same way that he demonstrated God's control over the judgment events that took place after the Lamb's breaking of each of the seals; he deploys the divine passive construction *edothē* ("it was given"; see the comments on 6:1–8; 7:2). The trumpets, and thus the acts of judgment and salvation that follow their blowing, belong not to the angels but to God. God controls them, distributes them, and no doubt directs when and to what effect they are to be blown. Depending on how one has responded to God through either witness or accommodation, the sounding of God's trumpets will signal either the dawn of salvation or the coming of judgment.

[2, 6, 3–5] Even the casual observer notices how redundant 8:2 and 8:6 are. Verse 6 adds little new content to the information already revealed in v. 2. Hearers and readers would have assumed that the instruments were issued in order to be played. Verse 6 is important, though, because it works with v. 2 to bracket vv. 3–5. Verses 3–5 are so different from the rest of the chapter that many commentators believe they were inserted here either by John or by some later editor. They certainly disrupt the otherwise smooth narrative flow of trumpet distribution and trumpet playing. Once the trumpets have been given to the seven angels (v. 2), hearers and readers are ready for the sound of the horns and the preliminary acts of God's judgment that will accompany them. Instead, there is a lengthy diversion, as another angel at the altar offers incense mixed with the prayers of the saints. If indeed this is a late textual insertion, John, or the final editor who added it, apparently recognized the problem. Diverted attention would have to be reengaged; v. 6 would therefore be needed to remind the hearers and readers of the situation left hanging at the end of v. 2.

Since I am more interested in a literary/narrative reading than one preoccupied with questions of source and redaction, I prefer to engage the material as we have it before us. If indeed the trumpet scene is a replay of God's acts of preliminary judgment, depicted earlier in the Lamb's breaking of the seals, but from a different perspective, then one would expect some structural parallels between the two scenes. The obvious parallel is that the preliminary acts of judgment take place in six stages, leading to a final and consummatory seventh stage. There is also a parallel presentation of the stages in bundles of four, two, and one. In both scenes, the first four catastrophic acts of judgment occur together. The second pair occur as a separate and more troubling set. And then the seventh and final episode is set apart from the other six by intervening narrative occurrences (ch. 7 separates the seventh seal from the first six; 10:1–11:14 separates the seventh trumpet from the first six). Even more dramatic, though, is the parallel way in which John provides narrative motivation for God's acts of judgment. In the seals episode, John strategically framed 6:9–11 so that hearers and readers would recognize that God's acts of judgment were motivated by the cries of the executed souls. John fashions a similar narrative framing in chapter 8. Verses 3–5 are strategically positioned so that hearers and readers will understand early on what motivates the destructive behavior God undertakes through the archangels. Once again, the prayers of the witnesses compel God to act.

If John is indeed presenting the same scene (God's acts of preliminary judgment) from three different perspectives (seals, trumpets, bowls), one would expect that these structural parallels would hold to form in the presentation of the seven bowls. Indeed, chapter 15 will introduce the bowls with a literary structure similar to the introduction of the trumpets in chapter 8. In this case, the introduction of the seven angels with seven plagues (15:1, 5–6) frames material that gives a hymnic rationale for the judgment (15:2–4). In all three cases, John employs a framing technique to assure his hearers and readers that the judgment to be narrated is an appropriate response to the cries of God's people and a just recompense for the evil perpetrated against them.

[3] Verse 3 introduces yet another angel, an eighth one. He has a priestly assignment. Golden censer in hand, he comes before the golden altar of incense (cf. 9:13; Exod 30:1–10), which John locates before the heavenly throne.

The seer is operating from the layout of the Jerusalem temple. There, after moving through the court of the priests where the altar of sacrifice resided, on the way to the holy of holies, a priest encountered the golden altar of incense. During his approach, the priest ascended the twelve steps from the court of the priests and entered a vestibule whose large opening was flanked by columns. A double doorway covered in gold opened into the *Hechal*, or main chamber. Inside the *Hechal* were a shewbread table; a golden, seven-branched menorah; and a small, golden incense altar. Incense was burned twice daily, at the morning and evening *tamid* sacrifices (Comay 161; Sanders, *Judaism*, 62–63). Moreover, "when the high priest entered the Holy of Holies once a year on the Day of Atonement, he bore with him a censer of incense."[7]

---

7. Comay 175. Sanders describes a controversy over the use of the censer and the incense as regards the Day of Atonement: "The Sadducees thought that when the high priest enters the Holy of Holies on the Day of Atonement, he should put incense on the coals before he opens the curtain. The Pharisees thought that he should hold the censer in one hand and the incense in the other, somehow managing to carry them separately past the curtain (perhaps by going past it backwards, hoping that the heavy folds would not knock the censer and incense out of his hands). Here the Pharisees are closer to the text of Leviticus, while the Sadducees show prudent common sense. They, after all, supplied some of the high priests" (335).

There were several ways to offer incense in ancient Israel. First, while there is no clear evidence that it was sprinkled on animal sacrifices, it could be burned with grain offerings (Lev 2:1, 15; 6:15). Second, instead of being placed on an altar, it could be offered in a long-handled censer (Lev 10:1; Num 16:6). Censers were either an upright vessel or a long-handled, ladle-like vessel; the fire was placed into the censer in the form of live coals secured from the sacrificial altar in the court of the priests. Third, a special recipe was used for incense offered twice a day in connection with the daily sacrifices (Exod 30:34–38). After live coals were taken from the sacrificial altar and spread on the incense altar, the incense would be added. A fourth and special case involved the use of incense in the holy of holies on the Day of Atonement (Lev 16:11–14).[8]

John appears to envision some form of the third type. The angel pours the incense onto the altar, where the hot coals are already in place. The smoke of the incense then rises up as it no doubt once had during the morning and evening sacrifices in the Jerusalem temple. The altar imagery is important because of its symbolic implications for John. The term appears only once (Rev 6:9) before John's use of it here. Although John uses altar imagery sparsely in his work, he makes certain to include it in each of the scenes that chronicle God's preliminary acts of judgment: the seals (6:9); the trumpets (8:3–5; 9:13); and the bowls (16:7). This careful positioning of the term is one more reason for understanding the narratives of the seals, trumpets, and bowls as three distinct different viewings of the same eschatological events.

Equally important is the thematic significance that John attributes to the altar imagery. "Altar" symbolizes God's eschatological judgment. That is evident in the seals, trumpets, and bowls texts, given the preoccupation those texts have with God's judgment. John's other uses of the term are equally oriented to the judgment theme. The occurrence at 11:1 takes place during the interlude between the sixth and seventh trumpet blasts. There God instructs that the temple be measured so that it will not be harmed when the punishing hostilities begin. Later an angel comes out from the altar armed with a sickle, ready for the winnowing of the eschatological harvest (14:18). To be sure, in these passages John jumps between the sacrificial and incense altars, often without informing his hearers and readers which one he has in mind.[9] Perhaps that kind of specificity was not important to him. His main goal, after all, was not to identify a particular altar but to clarify what "altar" in its essence meant: God's judgment.

The connection with the altar in 6:9–11 is particularly interesting. Because this is an altar of sacrifice, it would be easy for a hearer or reader to interpret the imagery in chapter 6, and by way of association also in 8:3–5, through the

8. See the sketch in Aune 2:513–14.
9. Still, it should be noted that both the golden altar of incense (8:3, 5; 9:13) and the altar of sacrifice (6:9; 11:1; 14:18; 16:7) can be clearly identified in John's text.

notion of atonement. In that case, the incense would be seen as a sacrifice to God, in the way that the "martyrdom" of believers was often understood sacrificially. Incense, however, rarely carried the sense of atonement.[10] It certainly has no such sense for John. His mention of the altar identifies it with prayer (5:8). John develops that thematic connection here at 8:3–5. While he is careful to keep prayers and incense as distinct entities that both rise up from the incense altar, he relates all three elements (prayer, incense, and altar) to God's avenging, judging activity. The motivation for divine action thus rests with the content of the prayers that accompany the incense, much as it earlier rested with the prayerful cries of the slaughtered souls (6:9–11). As a consequence of those prayers, the altar's fire is thrown down in judgment against the earth. Here at 8:3–5, then, with the angel in the role of priest, the human prayers that rise up with the divine-priestly incense are not offerings of sacrifice or pleas for redemption but appeals for God's intervention. God answers with fire and the acts that accompany the sounding of the trumpets, just as God answered earlier with the acts of judgment that accompanied the breaking of the seals.

God is in control. God gives (*edothē*, "it was given," is a divine passive; see the discussion of 6:1–8; 7:2) the angel the combustible materials that spark the people to cry out in intercessory prayer and trigger the judgment. God thus scripts the situation that ends up providing the motivation for God's own action.

The angel packages the incense with the prayers of the saints, that is, people of God (see the comment on 5:8). John uses a dative construction (*tais proseuchais*), which is repeated at 8:4, to show relationship between the incense and the prayers. Some ambiguity exists because the construction can be translated in multiple ways. As a dative of respect or reference, the phrase can mean that the angel was given the incense in order to give or offer it as a symbol of the prayers. That might have been the intent at 5:8, where the incense and prayer are identical, but it is clearly not the case here, where John strives to keep them separate. As a temporal dative, it could mean that the incense was offered at the same time as the prayers. That is obvious; an aspect of this category surely is in play. As a dative of association, the incense would simply be rendered with the prayers but have no real connection to them. The strong relationship between the two, however, argues against such a reading. As a dative of advantage, the incense would be given as a supplement to make the prayers more acceptable to God. In this case, the prayers would be somewhat like a burnt offering whose often rank smell needed to be "adjusted" so that it would be con-

---

10. Aune (2:511) can find an atoning emphasis only in Num 16:46–47 and *T. Levi* 3.5–6. To be sure, at Exod 30:1–10 the altar of incense, complete with horns (cf. Rev 9:13), is used as a site for atoning sacrifice once a year. However, it is the blood of the sin offering, not the incense, that is the mechanism for this action.

sidered suitable for the Deity.[11] Given that these prayers are not only pleas but also direct challenges for God to intervene, one could understand that they would need to be presented in the best possible light.[12] They are, in effect, acts of worship, and worship operates by ritual prescriptions that allow the presentations to God to be acceptable in God's sight. The incense performs that ritual, liturgical function here.

**[4]** When the incense hits the hot embers on the altar, it flashes into smoke that rises up with the prayers. Because this scene (like the corresponding one at 6:9–11) is taking place in heaven, the smoke and the prayers do not have far to travel before they reach their intended audience.

Smoke, even when connected with God's glory, bears an unmistakable aura of wrath and judgment. Here the angel is about to pour out the fire that has produced this smoke as a punishment against the earth. In every subsequent use of smoke (9:2, 3, 17, 18; 14:11; 15:8; 18:9, 18; 19:3), John makes its relationship to God's judgment clear. There is probably no more poignant a vision in Revelation than the smoke of Babylon's burning climbing into the sky (18:9, 18; 19:3).

**[5]** Having sent the smoke and prayers on their way, the eighth angel captures some of the fire from the altar by scooping up some burning coals into his censer (cf. Lev 16:12). He subsequently throws live fire onto the earth. There can be no clearer image of divine wrath.[13] Then, as if to confirm God's eschatological role in the affair, signature signs of theophany close out the scene.

In the Old Testament, thunders, rumblings, flashes of lightning, and earthquake not only indicate God's presence, but also confirm God's judgment against God's enemies and God's salvation on behalf of God's people (e.g., Exod 19:16–18; Ps 77:18–19; Isa 29:6). John narrates theophanies with the same intent. There are four key passages in Revelation: 4:5; 8:5; 11:19; and 16:18. Not only is 4:5 the first occurrence; it also is the only one of the four that omits mention of an earthquake, probably because the finality of judgment associated with the simultaneous occurrence of all four events is not yet on display. The lightning flashes, rumblings, and thunders are tasked with introducing God's majesty,

---

11. See Comay 174. What was pleasing to humans was supposed to be pleasing to the deities as well, not only food and wine but also sweet odors. In a hot climate, with worshipers crowding the temple area, "the carcasses of the slaughtered animals and the lack of sanitation together produced smells that were uncomfortable and regarded as injurious to health." Reddish writes, "One of the purposes of incense was to provide a sweet aroma that would be pleasing to God and render God more accepting of human pleas. Here, the mingling of incense with the prayers of the people assures their reception by God" (162; cf. Beale 456; Ps 141:2).

12. See, for example, Wis 18:21, where a petition is said to have been presented with incense: "For a blameless man was quick to act as their champion; he brought forward the shield of his ministry, prayer and propitiation by incense."

13. Gen 19:24; 2 Kgs 1:10, 12, 14; Job 1:16; Ps 11:6; 2 Thess 1:8; cf. Aune 2:516.

not God's judgment. John attaches the final three theophany scenes to presentations of God's judgment. Revelation 8:3–5, then, not only explains why judgment takes place but also shows how that judgment plays out: fire.[14]

## 8:7–13 The First Four Trumpets

The seven-stage judgment John sees is the same pattern of judgment he narrated at 6:1–8:1 (seals) and the same one he will revisit at 16:1–20 (bowls). He conveys that wrath here through familiar exodus imagery. Though the book of Exodus remembers ten plagues (Exod 7:8–12:36), in two separate accounts in the psalms there are seven (Ps 78:43–51) and eight (Ps 105:27–36). The Psalter accounts follow the Yahwistic version of the plagues, as opposed to the Priestly account's enumeration of ten (Aune 2:506). John works from the Yahwistic perspective.

Exodus implies liberation. Liberation as a theme is appropriate to John's overall ethical intent. John asks the people to remain faithful, to refuse accommodation, no matter the threats or promises. God will respond. "Each plague is God's challenge to the power of the Caesar. Each trumpet blast is a ringing command from the Liberator God: 'Let my people go!'" (Boesak 76).

As in the case of the exodus plagues, even during the chaos and destruction, God is firmly in control. John narrates this point with a long train of divine passives. Hail and fire *was mixed* with blood. That mixture *was thrown* onto the earth. One-third of the earth *was burned*. One-third of the trees *were burned*. All the green grass *was burned*. A great, burning mountain *was thrown* into the sea. A third of the ships *were destroyed*. One-third of the waters *was made* bitter. A third of the sun, moon, and stars *were struck* so that their light *was darkened*. God is not only acting but acting more intensely from this trumpet perspective. Where John had first envisioned targets destroyed in quarters (cf. 6:8), from his trumpet angle he sees decimation by the thirds.

Many scholars seem convinced that the destructive judgment unleashed by God's angelic representatives with the blasts of their trumpets is an act of punishment, not a call to repentance.[15] Clearly the plagues associated with the trumpets were punishing events. However, John's entire visionary effort has operated under the ethical premise that those who hear and read will respond by either witnessing or at least curtailing their accommodations to the lordship of Roman imperial rule and religions. For those who are presently accommodating, the ethical expectation would certainly be one of repentance. John's

---

14. As opposed to flood waters in Noah's time: Gen 6–8.

15. Beale, e.g., comments, "Therefore, the trumpet plagues are better viewed primarily as actual judgments on the majority of earth's inhabitants, though secondarily they are warnings for only a remnant" (466–67).

account of the devastating acts of judgment would not only report the coming desecration but also, since they are *coming* desecrations, spur those who take the visions seriously to use what little intervening time they have to change their ways. That certainly seems to be the spirit behind John's exhortations in the letters to the seven churches in chapters 2 and 3. It also seems to be John's expectation in 9:20–21 (cf. 16:8–9), where he laments the fact that many did not repent, thereby implying that some did. And while scholars do correctly observe that the Egyptian plagues upon which the trumpet plagues seem to be based were intended not to garner Pharaoh's repentance but to harden his heart further, it is clear that many later Jewish writers understood the plagues as inducements to repentance (Amos 4:10; Josephus, *Ant.* 2.14.1; Philo, *Mos.* 1.95).

7 The first angel[a] blew his trumpet, and there came hail and fire, mixed with blood, and the mixture was thrown to the earth; and a third of the earth was burned up, and a third of the trees were burned up, and all the green grass was burned up. 8 The second angel blew his trumpet, and something like a great mountain burning with fire was thrown into the sea, and a third of the sea became blood, 9 and a third of the living[b] creatures in the sea died, and a third of the boats were destroyed. 10 The third angel blew his trumpet, and a great star, burning like a lamp, fell from heaven, and it fell on a third of the rivers and on the springs of water. 11 The name of the star is Apsinth, and a third of the waters became wormwood,[c] and many people died from the waters because they were made bitter. 12 The fourth angel blew his trumpet, and a third of the sun was struck and a third of the moon and a third of the stars, so that a third of them were darkened and a third of the day would not appear and likewise the night. 13 Then I looked, and I heard an eagle[d] flying in midheaven, crying with a foreboding voice: "Woe, woe, woe to the inhabitants of the earth because of[e] the remaining trumpet blasts of the three angels who are about to blow!"

a. Though the external evidence supports the omission of the word "angel," John so obviously intends to say "angel" here that a clear translation is obligated to supply it.

b. John breaches grammatical felicity. The phrase *ta echonta psychas* (the living ones/spirits) modifies *tōn ktismatōn* (creatures). Since "creatures" is in the genitive case, "the living ones/spirits" should be also. John places it in nominative apposition instead.

c. The star's name and "wormwood" are the same Greek word.

d. While most manuscripts substitute "angel" for "eagle," the stronger support lies with the latter (א A 046 et al.). A scribe would have been more likely to change the word to "angel" than the reverse—particularly since the figure is said to speak—to conform this passage to 14:6, where an angel does fly in midheaven with an eschatological message. In a narrative where an altar can speak, however (16:7), surely an eagle can too.

e. The preposition *ek* with the genitive as a marker of cause or reason; see Louw and Nida 89.25.

[7] The plague of hail and fire, mixed with blood, that accompanies the sounding of the first angel's trumpet is based on the exodus plague where hail rains down upon the Egyptians (Exod 9:22–26). It is also based loosely on the account at Ezek 38:22, where an avenging God threatens an outpouring of hail, fire, pestilence, and blood (cf. Joel 2:3, 30; Sir 39:29). John will use hail as a symbol of God's judging wrath twice more at strategic points in the text (11:19; 16:21). The emphasis on judgment is heightened by the fact that the hail is mixed with fire and blood. At 16:6, John is as clear as he possibly can be that blood is God's way of responding directly to the shedding of the saints' blood. Rome wants blood: God will rain it down until its people drown in it.

Perhaps an even more fearsome judgment image is that of raining fire: it burns up one-third of the earth, one-third of the trees, and all the green grass. It is unclear why the fire destroys grass completely, while burning only one-third of the trees and the earth.[16] The discrepancy probably demonstrates God's freedom to act as God pleases. Once again, the seer builds from Old Testament imagery, principally the account of Ezek 5:2, 12, where three different judgments are meted out, each punishing one-third of the people (cf. Zech 13:9; Wis 16:22).

[8–9] There is thematic consistency with the punishment that ensues at the blast of the second trumpet; it, too, wipes out its target by thirds, and it mobilizes the weapons of fire and blood. Divine passive constructions—a burning mountain was thrown and ships were destroyed—credit the action to God.

Verse 8 is a virtual doublet of v. 10, where a burning *star* rockets out of heaven and burns one-third of the rivers and springs as a complement to the one-third salt water destroyed in v. 8. A similar parallel exists with 16:3, where the second angel's bowl of divine wrath is poured out. The object of the bowl's fury is also the sea. In keeping with the escalation of intensity from one end-time viewing to the next (seals to trumpets to bowls), in the case of the second bowl *all* of the sea turns to blood and *all* of the sea's creatures are killed. The destruction maintains John's exodus connection. At Exod 7:17–21, operating by God's command, Moses orders Aaron to stretch out his staff and hand over (i.e., against) the waters of Egypt. When he does, the great river of Egypt turns to blood and all of its fish are killed. In Revelation, sea vessels are added to the casualty count. One could argue that because in John's vision only one-third of the fish and one-third of the ships were destroyed, the magnitude of the punishment was greater in Egypt, where the waters and fish were destroyed completely. Such an argument would miss the more important point that in Revelation all the seas on earth, not just those in a single country, were targeted.

---

16. The argument that all the grass is destroyed since it grows back more readily than the earth and the trees is not convincing since John expects that these preliminary acts of judgment are leading to a final and complete judgment. There will not be an "old" earth upon which the grass might grow back.

The method of destruction was the hurling of a great burning mountain into the sea. Although one cannot with certainty connect Revelation's symbolic imagery to any historical event, there are suggestive possibilities. Surely the narration of burning mountains catapulted into the sea would have conjured the searing memory of the eruption of Mount Vesuvius (August 24, 79 C.E.). "Debris from Vesuvius fell into the bay, making it impossible to land boats (Pliny, *Ep.* 6.16.11), though no streams of lava were emitted from the crater" (Aune 2:519). According to the Roman historian Dio, trumpets were heard blaring just before the disaster took place (66.23.1; see Aune 2:520).

**[10–11]** When the third angel blows his trumpet, a flaming star explodes out of heaven (cf. 9:1) and lands on one-third of the rivers and all the springs, destroying them. Obviously, John is working symbolically here; it would be impossible for a single star literally to land simultaneously on one-third of all the rivers and all the springs on earth. His point, though, is not literal. He wants to convey God's complicity. The home of the star, a term John uses euphemistically to refer to angels (1:20; 9:1; 22:16), is heaven. God has launched it as another instrument of punishing judgment (cf. the burning mountain in 8:8–9).[17] The parallel with the inanimate mountain in vv. 8–9 suggests that the burning star, too, is an inanimate missile.

While there is no parallel this time to one of the exodus plagues,[18] there is a strong thematic connection with the pouring out of the third bowl of wrath (16:4). While one-third of the rivers and springs of water are destroyed in chapter 8, the dramatically heightened intensity of the bowl episode in chapter 16 pictures the rivers and springs completely decimated.

John personalizes the destruction by giving the offending star a name that he uses only here: Apsinth. The more colloquial term would be "wormwood." According to Reddish, "Wormwood is the popular name of several related plants. The wormwood mentioned several places in the Bible (Deut 29:18 KJV; Prov 5:4; Jer 9:15; 23:15; Lam 3:15, 19; Amos 5:7) is probably a small shrub with hairy, gray leaves that was known for its extremely bitter taste" (166). The herb was so caustic that physicians used it medicinally to root worms from a person's intestines. John uses the plant's reputation for bitterness to great narrative effect. The impact on the waters is so ruinous that the seer likens it to a poisoning, even though wormwood was not technically a toxin.

According to Jer 9:15 and 23:15, wormwood was also an appropriate punishment for the crime of idolatry. Punishing the impurity of seeking after false gods with an agent that made drinking water impure is thus an act of divine

---

17. One could argue that the dragon also coaxes fire out of the heavens at 13:13. The interesting point there is that the dragon does this in order to mimic God. It is precisely the awareness that God can send fire from heaven that makes the mimicry work.

18. Beale (478) contends that Exod 7:15–24, which was the background for the second trumpet blast (Rev 8:8–9), remains in focus. Cf. also Ps 78:44.

poetic justice that would most certainly have intrigued John. After all, he was preoccupied with those who accommodated themselves to the attractions and threats of Rome. One of the most visible methods of such idolatrous—that is, "impure"—accommodation was the eating of meat sacrificed to idols (cf. Rev 2–3). The angelic "poisoning" of the waters is a deliciously ironic way of punishing a people who have so poisoned their faith.

[12] The destruction by thirds now expands to the cosmos. When the fourth angel blows his trumpet, John witnesses the darkening of one-third of the sun, moon, stars, and therefore the extinguishing of one-third of the day and night-time light they provide. The preponderance of divine passives ("was struck," "was darkened") once again indicates that everything is happening according to God's design. This is the darkness of judgment. (See Reddish 167; cf. Isa 13:10; Joel 3:15; Amos 5:20; 8:9; Matt 24:29; Mark 13:24–25.) It parallels the plague God visited upon Egypt (Exod 10:21). Perhaps John also has in mind Amos 8:9, where God punishes the evil of the people by darkening the sun. The most striking connections, though, are found in John's own text. During his accounting of the end-time judgment that occurs with the breaking of the sixth seal (6:12), John describes the darkness through the metaphor of the sun blackened like sackcloth and the moon covered in blood. At 16:8–9, the angel with the fourth bowl pours its contents on the sun, no doubt darkening it. The sun responds by punishing the people with a vicious, searing heat.

[13] John's appeal to the short formula *kai eidon* (then I looked) once again signals a shift to a different scene within the same narrative act (cf. 8:2; see the comment on 5:1). For a moment he suspends his recital of the actions taken by the trumpeting angels, as he anticipates the even more fearsome events that will attend the blowing of the final three trumpets. These will be true eschatological woes.

John sees and hears an eagle flying in midheaven. The term for eagle (*aetos*) is also used for vulture (e.g., Luke 17:37). Either way, the image is particularly disturbing, reinforcing the theme of judgment. The eagle is a bird of prey; its hovering above the inhabitants of the earth would imply that their destruction is imminent.[19] The vulture feeds on carrion; its presence affirms the deathly destruction that is, through the work of the first four angels, already under way. The image of judgment is amplified through an appeal to two of the eagle's characteristics. First, it cries out in a foreboding voice (see the discussion of 7:2). Second, its flight path confines it to midheaven. For John, midheaven is a divine dais from which the word of God's judgment and salvation are intoned (14:6; 19:17).

---

19. See Beale 490. He points to multiple instances where the eagle is used in the Old Testament as a metaphor for judgment: Deut 28:49; Jer 4:13; 48:40; 49:22; Lam 4:19; Ezek 17:3; Hos 8:1; and Hab 1:8. Hosea 8:1 and Jer 4 (vv. 5, 21) also have trumpet imagery, and Job 9:26 has an eagle hovering over prey.

Many commentators have noted John's use of onomatopoeia when describing the content of the eagle's cry. The words, when sounded out, bear the essence of a bird of prey's call: *ouai, ouai, ouai*. Each woe will find itself attached to one of the final three trumpet blasts. While the first two woes are given explicit content (see 9:12; 11:14), the third and final one is not. It was probably John's intent that it be linked with the third and final trumpet blast (cf. 12:12), which, like the seventh seal, was not fully laid out.[20]

### 9:1–21 Judgment as Good News

Though the catastrophes associated with the first four trumpets targeted nature, trumpets five and six set their sights on human beings. Before this preliminary stage of judgment is through, all but a tiny remnant of humankind (144,000) will have experienced unspeakable torment; one-third of humanity will die. In describing the devastation, John appeals to a familiar narrative device, the divine passive (see the comment on 6:2). One-third of humankind *was killed* (9:18). He reinforces the effect by deploying his favorite passive construction, *edothē* ("it was given"; cf. 6:2, 4, 8, 11; 7:2; 11:1–2; 13:5, 7, 14, 15; 16:8; 20:4). With it, he expresses his belief that a being's or an object's power comes from (is given to it by) God. A fallen, apparently evil angel, perhaps Satan himself, is given the keys to the abyss so that he may open it and free all of the destructive chaos once locked inside it (9:1–2). Locusts are given the authority to torment but not to kill (9:3–5; cf. 2 Chr 7:13). John understands that God controls human destiny. He therefore believes that even when his visions relay massive destruction and unimaginable terror, God is working out a judgment plan that ultimately leads to a benevolent though just end. As incredible as it seems, God is using the horror to realize God's purpose of judgment/salvation.

In fact, in John's portrait the horror harbors good news. There are three indications of it. First, despite the apparently chaotic way in which history is unfolding, God remains in charge. Second, because the trumpet catastrophes constitute an act of preliminary and not final judgment, there is opportunity for repentance. The visions are intended to produce more than shock and awe; their purpose is to encourage the kind of behavior that leads to an enduring eschatological relationship with God: witnessing to the lordship of God and the Lamb. Third, these destructive acts are God's just and *liberating* intervention in the world. John encourages such a reading by intentionally linking the trumpet plagues with the exodus plagues unleashed by Moses. As Schüssler Fiorenza

---

20. Aune, however, writes: "It is also possible to argue that, since no plague is unleashed by the seventh trumpet (but rather a scene of victory in the heavenly court is presented), the author understands the third 'woe' to consist of the judgment of Babylon in 17:1–19:8, where the phrase 'Woe, woe, you great city' is repeated three times (18:10, 16, 19)" (2:524).

argues, "Just as God had inflicted the Egyptian plagues in order to make possible the exodus of Israel from Egypt, so the cosmic plagues of the trumpet series and the bowl series execute the judgment of God over the cosmos, enabling the liberation of the Christian community from the oppression of Babylon/Rome" (*Vision of a Just World*, 70).

## 9:1–12 The Fifth Trumpet

**9:1** Then the fifth angel blew his trumpet, and I saw a star that had fallen from heaven to the earth, and he was given the key to the shaft of the abyss. **2** He opened the shaft of the abyss, and smoke rose from the shaft like smoke from a great furnace, and the sun and the air were darkened by the smoke from the shaft. **3** Then from the smoke came locusts on the earth, and they were given authority as the scorpions have authority over the earth. **4** But[a] they were ordered not to harm the grass of the earth nor any green plant nor any tree, but only the people who did not have the ·seal of God on their foreheads. **5** They were not allowed to kill them, but to torture them for five months, and their torture was like the torture of a scorpion when it stings a person. **6** And in those days people will seek death, but[b] they will not find it; they will long to die but[c] death will flee from them. **7** And the appearance of the locusts was like horses prepared for battle. And on their heads were what appeared to be crowns of gold, and their faces were like human faces, **8** and they had hair like women's hair, and their teeth were like lions' teeth. **9** They had scales like iron breastplates, and the noise of their wings was like the noise of many chariots with horses rushing into battle. **10** And they have tails like scorpions, and stingers, and in their tails is their power to harm humans for five months. **11** They have over them as king the angel of the abyss; his name in Hebrew is Abaddon, and in Greek he has the name Apollyon. **12** The first woe has passed; behold, two woes are still to come after this.[d]

a. The *kai* operates as an adversative.
b. The *kai* operates as an adversative.
c. The *kai* operates as an adversative.
d. Since *meta tauta* (after this) generally begins sentences in the Apocalypse (see the comment on 4:1), some manuscripts join it to v. 13. Others either move or drop the *kai* that opens v. 13 so as to smooth the transition. The text has strong external support, however, and the Apocalypse also uses the phrase to close sentences (cf. 4:1; see Metzger, *Textual Commentary*, 743).

**[9:1–2]** When John opens with the verb *esalpisen* (blew the trumpet) he immediately invokes the theme of God's judgment (8:6, 7, 8, 10, 12, 13; 9:1, 13; 10:7; 11:15). The trailing *kai eidon* (and I saw) introduces a new dramatic scene in the continuously unfolding act (see the discussion of 5:1). John is still caught up in the vision of the seven trumpets, but now he sees a shift in both target and intensity. Human beings rather than inanimate objects of nature are being singled out for destruction, and an angel rather than a natural event has been dispatched to carry the catastrophe out.

This angel/star, unlike the astral object of 8:10–11, is a living entity who can take possession of a key and use it to open the door to the great *abyssos* (abyss). John has used stars as metaphors for angels before. At 1:16, the child of humanity holds seven stars in his right hand, which later turn out to be the seven angels who represent the seven Asia Minor churches (1:20; cf. 2:1; 3:1). On two important occasions John likens the child of humanity himself to the bright morning star (2:28; 22:16). In building this metaphorical connection, John operates from Jewish interpretive links between stars and angels (cf. Judg 5:20; Job 38:7; Dan 8:10; *Sib. Or.* 5.158–61).

Particularly significant are the connections between fallen stars and disgraced and deposed angels (Rev 12:7–9, 13; cf. Isa 14:12; *1 En.* 86.3; 88.3).[1] The fallen angels' identification means that this angel is not the same one mentioned at 20:1. Though both hold the key to the abyss, the second angel, who is not introduced as "fallen," locks Satan in the pit. The "fallen" angel of 9:1 uses the key to open the pit and release its demonic forces. In fact, the naming in 9:11 suggests that this angel is the dragon whom John later identifies as Satan. Tradition records that Jesus saw Satan fall like lightning (like a star?) from heaven (Luke 10:18). As a result, Jesus' followers were able to walk safely across snakes and scorpions (Luke 10:19). It is probably not a coincidence that the witnesses who were sealed with God's mark upon their foreheads (Rev 9:4) found themselves protected from the terror unleashed by the demon locusts that operated specifically with the authority of scorpions.

John does not see the angel fall. Apparently, though, he does see when God gives him the key to the shaft of the great abyss (another divine passive: *edothē*, "it was given"). Technically, *abyssos* means without (*a*) depth (*bythos*). Following the mythical understanding of a three-tiered universe (see the comment on 5:3), the abyss was the underworldly/hellish region below both heaven and earth. John introduces it here at 9:1–2 and quickly mentions it again in v. 11. The fact that on both occasions the angel is the authority figure of the abyss is strong evidence that John is referring to the same angel.

---

1. Reddish traces the concept of fallen angels back to the story about the angelic beings who came to earth and caused humans to sin (Gen 6:1–4). The "Book of Watchers" in *1 Enoch* is a commentary on the tradition that developed from this brief text: "'Watchers' is the name used in this work (as well as in other Jewish writings) for the disobedient angels who came down to earth, took wives from among the earthly women, and taught them practices and ideas that corrupted the earth. As a result of the angels' disobedience, God imprisoned them in a place full of fire that 'had a cleft reaching to the abyss' (*1 En.* 21:7)" (176).

The abyss is a place filled with fearsome, fiendish forces. At 11:7, a great beast emerges from the abyss, makes war on God's great witnesses, and kills them; then the beast upon whom the great whore (Babylon/Rome) rides rises from the abyss (17:8). The prelude to the final judgment will find the dragon, Satan, locked in the abyss for a thousand years, only to be let loose when that millennium has ended (20:1, 3). John's portrait is in keeping with wider Jewish understanding: The "abyss" is synonymous with the concept of Hades (Job 38:16; Ezek 31:15; Jonah 2:6) and is the realm of suffering (Ps 71:20) and death (Exod 15:5; Isa 51:10; 63:13; Wis 10:19). Isaiah 24:21–22 says that God will punish angels and evil kings, and "they will be gathered together as prisoners in the pit [*bôr*], and will be confined in prison and after many days will be punished" (Beale 493). The abyss is a bad place. The eschatological version of a maximum security prison, it is home to the worst cosmic offenders. Knowing this, God still gives this fallen angel the key.

The image of a key is important for John. Here, and again at 20:1, the abyss is locked behind a closed door. In both cases, a character uses a key to open the door and swing it open. In both instances, too, destruction immediately ensues. God is the ultimate keeper of this key. At 1:18, God's child of humanity introduces himself as the one who controls the keys to death and Hades, forces that are narratively synonymous for John with the place he calls the abyss. The implication is that the child of humanity, who was exiled to the abyss by way of the crucifixion, had laid claim to the key and used it to open the door and set himself free. According to 3:7, the child of humanity also possesses the key of David, a key that symbolizes the Son's ability to open the eschatological realm of salvation, understood as a heavenly, Davidic reign. The child of humanity's control of these two keys indicates that he secures both salvation (key of David) and judgment (keys of death and Hades). At 9:1 and 20:1, God entrusts to other divine emissaries the key that opens the door to judgment. While the angel in good standing at 20:1 recognizes that he is operating in concert with God's judgment/salvation plan, the angel in 9:1 does not. Not realizing that his effort to set his forces free is actually part of God's salvation plan, he eagerly unlocks the door and throws open the shaft of the abyss.

It is God who decides if satanic forces are to be given the ability—the key—to open their realm and gain access to earth and the humans who inhabit it. It is God who decides when that access comes and how long it will last. It is God who decides the purpose of the destruction that access enables. In John's handling, God purposes to intervene on behalf of those who cry out for justice (6:9–11; 8:3–5), and God will use the very force of evil itself to obliterate the humans (i.e., the Romans and all who accommodate to their claims of imperial lordship) who operate under evil's employ. Here is the irony: evil will be unleashed, but evil will be made to act as God's judgment tool. The demonic, bestial forces that rise up from the bottomless pit will target and destroy the very humans who do evil's satanic, beastly bidding. While both God's witnesses and those who persecute them will die in the cataclysms that ensue, only the persecutors and those who accommodate them will die forever.

When the door finally opens, dense smoke pours out. The seer appeals to Exod 19:18, where the people at the foot of Mount Sinai see smoke go up from the mountain when the Lord descends upon it in fire. Interestingly enough, all of this occurs at the sounding of trumpets. John likens the smoke he sees to the thick exhaust from a raging furnace. It is as though evil and those who perpetrate it are combustible agents whose perpetual blaze powers the infamy thriving inside the bottomless pit. It is the smoke of this villainous burning that rushes out when the door opens. Like the door itself, though, smoke moves under God's control. When John uses the term, he envisions God's judgment. Smoke is unmistakably linked with the prayers of the saints who request God's intervention (8:3–5). Surely John's account would have prompted his hearers and readers to recall the story of Abraham gazing out at the rising smoke of Sodom and Gomorrah's ruin (Gen 19:28).

The smoke pollutes the air. As was the case in the book of Joel, its darkening of the sun is an explicit indication of God's judgment (see Joel 2:10, 31; 3:15). John makes the case by putting the key verb in the divine passive voice (see the comment on 6:2). When he says that the sun and the air are darkened, he means that God has darkened them. Throughout his narrative, John appeals to the sun as a glorious force (1:16; 7:16; 10:1; 12:1; 21:23; 22:5), but he also connects it to God's judgment (6:12; 8:12; 16:8; 19:17). In two other instances besides 9:2, that judgment is imaged as a darkening (6:12; 8:12).

[3–5] Before the smoke can clear, another source of darkness emerges: locusts. Locusts are different from grasshoppers; they swarm and migrate in large numbers, usually plundering any and all vegetation in their path. This apocalyptic horde arrives with the smoke and, like it, shrouds the earth in darkness.

As in Joel 2:1, 15, a trumpet calls the locusts forth. The prophet Joel reflects on the plague where locusts darkened the land of Egypt (Exod 10:5, 15). John's reference to the exodus account by way of the allusion to Joel is yet another association of the end-time judgment with the plagues against Egypt. The manner of the locusts' attack is different, though. In Exodus, the locusts devoured the vegetation and so caused a famine. Here, at the blowing of the fifth angel's trumpet, they are specifically ordered not to touch the vegetation.[2] Instead, they are to attack humans. Having gone from voracious to vicious, they are more like the locusts of Wis 16:9, which, along with a legion of flies, inflicted bites from which there is no healing.

---

2. Beale makes the point that in John's mythical worldview, there is no contradiction with the notice in 8:7 that all of the green grass was burned up: "The emphasis here is that the trumpet woe is directed against rebellious humanity and not nature" (496).

Because of their affiliation with the abyss, the locusts also have an unmistakably demonic nature (see Rev 9:11). Even so, they operate according to God's plan. They are given (by God) the authority of scorpions on the earth. They operate very much like the locusts of Wis 16:9 and Sir 39:30, whose bites are instruments of God's judgment.[3]

The similarity of John's locusts to scorpions suggests that their power is related to a sting rather than a bite. Their job is to inflict pain upon every human who has not been marked with the seal of God upon their forehead (see the comment on 7:3). Since the trumpets and bowls are recapitulations of the judgment acts associated with the seals, but from a different eschatological perspective, it makes sense that the device that provided the 144,000 protection from the seal judgments would also provide protection from the acts of judgment associated with the trumpets and bowls.

Good news for the sealed saints is ambiguous news for the rest of them. The saints at 7:9–17 were not sealed and therefore were not protected from the ravages that accompanied God's preliminary acts of judgment (see the discussion of 3:10; 6:1; 7:9–17). This means that there will be many saints who will also be tormented by the scorpion stings of the demon locusts. As 3:10 explains, the child of humanity will keep them, enable them to endure, but will not rapture them from the circumstances that surround the coming of the end.

John clarifies that the demon locusts are given the authority (by God) not to kill humans, but to torture them for five months. Does God operate this way? John's hearers and readers would know that the answer is yes. According to Job 2:6, God gave Satan the authority to torment and torture Job, but not to kill him.

John's, and Job's, theological presentation is troubling. In depicting the simultaneous beliefs that evil exists in the world and that nothing exists outside of God's control, John finds himself locked into the uneasy presentation of a God who is an accomplice to a practice as hellish as torture in order to obtain a heavenly design.

Why five months of torture? Some commentators argue that five months is the typical life cycle of a locust, and thus the time of torment agrees naturally with the actual time that locusts would have lived and swarmed. Since John is rarely this literal, there is little reason to believe that he would have been so literal here. More likely the time is just a round number that indicates a specified and limited time for the work of the locusts. Believers could therefore know that an end would come and that it would come relatively soon.[4] According to Mark 13:19–20 (cf. Matt 24:21–22), if God does not cut short the calamities

---

3. For other texts that picture scorpions as instruments of punishment, see 1 Kgs 12:11, 14; 2 Chr 10:11, 14.

4. Aune (2:530) points to several biblical texts in which "5" appears as a round, limited number: Lev 26:8; Jdt 7:30; 8:9, 15; Matt 14:17–19 = Mark 6:38–41 = Luke 9:13–16; 12:6, 52; Acts 20:6; 24:1; 1 Cor 14:19.

associated with the acts of judgment that prefaced the end time, no one will be able to endure it. Because of the faithful, who are apparently, as in John's account, caught up in the maelstroms, God does indeed cut the time short.

[6] John's opening line in v. 6, "in those days," is a euphemism for the period when the preliminary acts of judgment that lead up to the final judgment are taking place (see 2:13; 10:7; cf. Joel 2:29; 3:1). This is precisely the time that is presented from three different eschatological perspectives by the seals, trumpets, and bowls.

John means to say, then, that during this preliminary judgment period, the torment will be so horrific that humans will prefer death to life. Job 3:21 and Jer 8:3 present Old Testament examples where, because of the horrible circumstances associated with living, death becomes preferable to life (cf. Rev 6:12–17).[5] At 1:18, John pictured the child of humanity holding the key to Death and Hades. Even death lies within his control. Here though, knowing that death is the only escape from the pain and torment being inflicted by the demon locusts, the child of humanity either actively locks Death away from the suffering peoples' grasp or passively allows Death to scurry uselessly away. The judgment associated with the scourge of the demon locusts must be endured.

For John, death is a state of being like life. Indeed, death allows a measure of control that life does not. One cannot choose to live. One simply finds oneself alive. One can, however, choose to die, especially in a circumstance where life becomes torturously unbearable. Even then, though, persons may be more likely to choose death if they believe that death does not end all sensibility, but only alters the state and place of being.

A study of the noun *thanatos* (death) and the verb *apothnēskō* (to die) reveals that John understands "death" to have two distinct layers. First, death ends earthly existence. We might call this Type A death. This is clearly the kind of death John alludes to in 9:6. It is the type of death associated with the preliminary acts of judgment that follow the opening of the first six seals, the sounding of the first six trumpets, and the pouring out of the first six bowls. Type A death brings a merciful end to the preliminary judgment acts of God. It is Type A death to which John refers at 2:23, when the child of humanity warns that he will strike the children of Jezebel dead. It is Type A death that the fourth apocalyptic horseman brings at 6:8. Babylon's death at 18:8 is Type A death.

John's hearers and readers know that Type A death is not final because the narrative presents multiple occasions where the seer implies that there is life beyond it. When John talks about the death wound of the beast, he refers to the Type A death, from which even the beast can resurrect into a new life (13:3, 12).

---

5. Beale (498) lists several texts where "severe suffering causes a desire for death in place of a life of torment," including 1 Kgs 19:1–4; Job 3:1–26; 6:8–9; 7:15–16; Jer 8:3; 20:14–18; Jonah 4:3, 8; Luke 23:27–30.

Similarly, the death mentioned at 20:13 is one that allows its captives new life. At 2:10, the child of humanity voices a paradox: "Be faithful until death, and I will give you the crown of life." Apparently one not only lives beyond Type A death but can also receive gifts in that new life, rewards for honorable behavior in the old life. The presumption is that the new life, connected as it is to the metaphor of the crown, is better than the old one. John offers a corroborating portrait in 12:11. A voice from heaven honors living witnesses who did not cling to life even in the face of death. Indeed, the souls whose cry to God sets into motion the acts of preliminary judgment (6:9–11) have endured Type A death because of their faithful witness. They now enjoy the reward of eschatological life in relationship with God. So do the witnesses mentioned at 14:13. One of the benefits for those who enjoy that relationship will be the complete cessation of Type A death (21:4).

Just as there are two lives in John's cosmology, so too are there two deaths. According to 2:11, those who have been faithful witnesses in their first life will not endure a second death. This second death, which we may call Type B death, is for John a permanent cessation of existence. It is the death that follows a guilty verdict at the final judgment. Type B death, then, is the death one should fear. Revelation 20:13 indicates that at God's final judgment a decision will be made as to whether those who have died a Type A death will be given life in eschatological relationship with God or given Type B death. God makes this ruling on the basis of how a person has lived one's first life. Given the ethical program of John's narrative, it is a life lived in witness to the lordship of God and the Lamb that will earn eschatological relationship with God (cf. 14:13). A life lived either in witness to Roman imperial and pagan lordship or in accommodation to those who did advance such idolatrous claims would merit Type B death. It is Type B death to which John refers in 20:6, 14; 21:8.

At 9:6, though, the people who seek escape from the torture of the demon locusts surely long not for a permanent cessation of existence but for the transient reprieve of Type A death. This death is so transitory that it is preferable to earthly struggle and torment. Just as those who witness to the lordship of Christ should not fear this death, so those who are caught up in the fury of the scorpion-like locusts, believers and nonbelievers alike, do not fear it. Instead, in such a circumstance as this, they try their best to embrace it.

[7–10] Unable to summon any other common reference point, John characterizes the locusts as horses arrayed for battle. His hearers and readers may well have been aware of the Old Testament comparisons between the two creatures in Jer 51:27 and Job 39:19–20. In the Job text, it is God who claims to have empowered the horse to leap like a locust. God, in other words, just as John imagines here, is in control of this bizarre mammal-insect crossbreeding. But it is Joel to whom John is indebted here the most. The prophet warns of a marauding army whose numbers are so massive that they extend like a blackness across the horizons (Joel 2:2). At 2:4 he likens the foot soldiers to warhorses prepared for a charge.

John continues with a loathsome description that becomes more appalling every time he adds a new descriptor. These demonic forces wear golden crowns. Beneath the crowns, warhorse-locusts sport human faces framed by women's hair. The odd reference to female hair is an indication that their hair was long and possibly unkempt. According to legend, the dreaded Parthian warriors wore their hair long. John may well be trying to kindle the paranoia associated with Rome's famed adversaries in his description, just as he tried to do when speaking earlier about the threat of the first horseman (6:2).

Weird turns to fearsome when John depicts the warhorse-locusts with the teeth of lions in their mouths. The invading army that Joel describes also deploys lionlike teeth (Joel 1:6). Protecting their bodies are breastplates or scales of iron. When they move their wings, the noise they make is that of the army Joel foresaw, the sound of innumerable horse chariots rumbling ominously into battle (2:4–5).

**[11]** John's hearers and readers know that this is an army of demons, not mutant insects, because they are organized under the rule of a king. According to Prov 30:27, locusts in nature have no monarch, but John immediately identifies their king as *the* angel of the abyss. The fact that "angel" is modified by the definite article suggests that John believed his hearers and readers would be familiar with him. That familiarity follows from the description of the angel as a fallen star in 9:1–2. Luke 10:18 describes Satan in just this way.

John's name for the demon locust ruler also indicates a connection with Satan. The Hebrew form of the name is Abaddon (*Abaddōn*): destruction. The term surfaces in several significant Old Testament passages (Job 26:6; 28:22; 31:12; Ps 88:11; Prov 15:11; 27:20). John follows the lead of these Old Testament authors in building a relationship between the realm of death, which is Sheol, and the name "Abaddon." In other words, Abaddon is a literary personification of the loss and destruction that are integral to death. In the narrative world of Revelation, the power most closely allied with death is Satan (see Rev 12).

The Greek form of the angel's name is Apollyon (*Apollyōn*, destroyer). The name is a play on the Greek verb *apollymi* (to destroy). It may also be a play on the name of the pagan god Apollo. Interestingly enough, the locust was one of Apollo's symbols. Domitian, likely the Roman emperor during the time of John's writing, had a particular fondness for Apollo and liked to suggest that he was himself an incarnation of that deity. If indeed Domitian through this identification was expressing an implicit divine foundation for his imperial lordship, then John's attribution of satanic implications to the name makes perfect narrative sense. John wrote to exhort his readers to embrace a life of witness to the lordship of God and the Lamb. He charged that accommodation to any competing claims of lordship amounted to the kind of perverse and satanic (2:13) idolatry that he linked with the names Balaam (2:14) and Jezebel (2:20–21). As the patron god of emperor worship, Apollo—and Domitian, as his alleged human incarnation—would, like Balaam and Jezebel, have been responsible for destroying the hope of eschatological relationship with God for anyone who accommodated to the social, political, religious, and economic expectations of imperial lordship.

[12] The preliminary act of judgment associated with the blowing of the fifth trumpet comes to an end with the identification of Satan as the destructive king of the locusts whom God uses to exact judgment in 9:1–11. The terror and torture of the demon locusts was the first woe. Though it has ended, there is no eschatological relief in sight. John confides that "after these things" (*meta tauta*) two more woes are yet to come. (For "after these things" as a narrative and not chronological marker, see the comment on 4:1.)

## 9:13–21 The Sixth Trumpet

13 Then the sixth angel blew his trumpet, and I heard a[a] voice from the four[b] horns of the golden altar before God, 14 saying to the sixth angel who had the trumpet: "Release the four angels who have been bound at the great river Euphrates." 15 Then the four angels who had been prepared for the hour and the day and the month and the year were released to kill a third of humankind. 16 And the number of the soldiers of cavalry was 200 million; I heard their number. 17 And this was how I saw the horses and their riders in my vision: they had breastplates that were fiery red and sapphire blue[c] and sulfur yellow. The heads of the horses were like the heads of lions, and out of their mouths spewed fire and smoke and sulfur. 18 A third of humankind was killed by these three plagues, by the fire and the smoke and the sulfur that spewed from their mouths. 19 For the authority of the horses is in their mouths and in their tails, for their tails, which are like snakes, have heads, and with them they inflict harm. 20 The rest of humankind, those who were not killed by these plagues, did not repent of the works of their hands, so that they did not stop worshiping[d] the demons or the idols made of gold and silver and bronze and stone and wood, which can neither see nor hear nor walk. 21 And they did not repent of their murders nor their sorceries nor their idolatry nor their thefts.

a. The numeral "one" acts as an indefinite article (see BDAG 231).

b. The balance of external evidence for including "four" (𝔐 vg^cl sy^ph) and excluding it (𝔓^47 א^1 A 0207 1611 2053 2344 *pc* lat sy^h co) is inconclusive. Because it is difficult to determine the reason for its addition (perhaps to match the four angels of v. 14), it is included in the translation here. One manuscript (א*) omits *mian ek tōn tessarōn keratōn* (one from the four horns) altogether.

c. The term translated here as sapphire is *hyakinthinos*. According to Reddish, "In antiquity, *hyakinthos* could denote one of several varieties of flowers or a precious stone (either the jacinth, a yellow-red stone that is a form of zircon, or the sapphire, a dark blue stone)" (182).

d. The literal phrasing, "so that they will not worship," carries John's hope that repentance would lead them to stop the idolatrous worship in which they are engaged.

[13] When v. 13 opens with the sounding of the sixth angel's trumpet, the change in trumpets is matched by a change in sensory perception. (For the connection between the verb "sounded" [*esalpisen*] and John's judgment theme, see the discussion of 9:1.) John *hears* a voice coming from the horns of the golden altar before God.[6] The description "golden" suggests that John is thinking about the altar of incense in the Jerusalem temple. It was upon the heavenly version of this altar that the prayers of the saints were mixed with incense (8:3–5). Those prayers, which most likely contained the same kind of petition as the cries of the slaughtered souls beneath the heavenly sacrificial altar (6:9–11), motivated the acts of judgment associated with the trumpet blowing. It is only natural that John would recapture the emphasis of those altars in the context where one-third of humankind is killed, thereby reminding his hearers and readers why he believed God was acting so ruthlessly.

In this new altar scene, the speaker and the speech are quite different from the previous ones. The voice here comes from the altar that is before God; therefore, it is unlikely that God is the one speaking. And since John, who quite freely draws upon the talents of angels when he so desires, does not position an angel in the narration, it is also unlikely that an angel is speaking. It is more likely that John hears the altar, through its horns, speak up for itself. Later it is clear that in his worldview, altars have the ability to speak their inanimate minds (16:7).

[14–15] The altar orders the sixth angel to participate in the judgment that his trumpet playing ignites. He must release the four angels who have been bound by the great river Euphrates. There are two significant points here. The first is that the action takes place only upon orders from God. As God was in control during the events surrounding the demon locusts in 9:1–12, so God controls the timing and shape of these events. The second point concerns the modification of "four angels" with the definite article ("the"). John's use of the article suggests that his hearers and readers would be familiar with these divine emissaries. It is unlikely, though, that these are the same four angels who held back the four winds from the four corners of the earth (7:1–3). Unlike the previous angels, these have been bound. John's use of yet another divine passive construction indicates that God has restrained them. The binding suggests that

---

6. For instructions regarding the golden altar of incense, complete with horns, see Exod 30:1–10; 40:5. Exodus 27:2 speaks of altar horns positioned on the four corners of the sacrificial altar. For further mention of altar horns, see Exod 37:25–26; 38:2; Ps 118:27; Ezek 43:15.

they, like the four winds of 7:1–3, are a destructive force that if not properly directed would not act in accordance with God's intent. It appears, then, as Boring argues, that "the 'bound angels' at the edge of John's world is another allusion to the mythical pattern of fallen angels discussed above (9:1–12)" (*Revelation*, 138). The four angels at 7:1–3, by contrast, were related positively to God and appeared willing to do God's bidding. They were also dispersed among the four corners of the earth, while the present four angels are positioned together at the Euphrates River.

The involvement of the Euphrates River is important. Later, the angel of the sixth bowl will release the contents of his bowl upon the Euphrates River and dry it up (16:12). Marauding kings from the east will use the resulting riverbed to come across and wreak devastation.

John's hearers and readers would have sensed the dread associated with the symbolic Euphrates even without a premonition of the sixth-bowl angel's exploits. For the Jewish people, the Euphrates River had always marked the outer geographical boundaries of their existence (Gen 15:18; Deut 1:7; Josh 1:4). The peoples who lived beyond this boundary were unknown and feared. The prophets declared that God would use them to punish the people of Israel whenever they refused to repent from their sins. No doubt the presence of fallen angels standing at this river rekindled thoughts of those disturbing prophecies.[7]

In the first century C.E., the river played a more international role. The Euphrates marked the literal and metaphorical boundary between the Roman and Parthian Empires (see the discussion of the Parthians at 6:2).[8] Given the history of conflict between Rome and Parthia, Parthia's ability to defeat Roman legions in key combat situations, and the unsettling legend that the disgraced emperor Nero would one day resurrect and lead a Parthian army to destroy Rome, it is easy to understand how John's hint that a hostile force massed at the river, incited by fallen angels, would have fomented fear in the minds of his hearers and readers.

The seer's use of yet another divine passive construction (*hētoimasmenoi*, having been prepared) indicates God's involvement in the work of these fallen ones. The same God who bound them at the Euphrates now orders them released (*elythēsan*, they were released). Though it is the sixth trumpet angel who performs the physical loosing, God is responsible.

This means that God is also responsible for the killings the four fallen angels subsequently commit. John clarifies the point when he follows up the notice of

7. E.g., see Isa 5:26–29; 7:20; 8:7–8; 14:29–31; Jer 1:14–15; 4:6–13; 6:1, 22; 10:22; 13:20; 25:9, 26; chs. 46–47; 50:41–42; Ezek 26:7–11; 38:6, 15; 39:2; Joel 2:1–11, 20–25; Amos 7:1 LXX; *As. Mos.* (= *T. Mos.*) 3.1. For further detail, see also Aune 2:506; cf. Reddish 181–82.

8. Aune (2:507) points to *1 En.* 56.5–8; *2 Bar.* 6, which both depict the Parthian threat from beyond the Euphrates as an updating of the Old Testament tradition. According to those texts, the invasion was to be triggered by angels.

their release with a relative clause that defines the purpose of that release. The four are released (by God) in order to do what they have been prepared (by God) to do: kill a third of humankind. Good news? One certainly has to search for it. No doubt John wanted his hearers and readers to discern positive value in the belief that, despite what sounded like global massacre, the world had not spun out of control. God remained in charge.

John's hearers and readers would have to trust, as John apparently himself trusted, that God had a plan that would make the high cost of this judgment sound not only reasonable but also preferable to whatever other options for living were available at their eschatological moment. Such trust was possible only because of the perspective on death that John counseled his readers to take. Yes, one-third of humankind would die. That death, though, was a justifiable response to the cries (6:9–11) and prayers (8:3–5) of those who had reached out to God through the vehicles of the sacrificial and incense altars (9:13). That death, also, need neither be feared nor considered final. It was Type A death (see the discussion of Type A death at 9:6).

Beyond Type A death was complete and certain opportunity for revival. It did not signal an end to being but an introduction to another kind of being, where humans would have yet another opportunity to make account of themselves before the divine. It must be stressed that John is not speaking about the final judgment, but about the preliminary acts of judgment that lead up to it. It must only be because he understands God's involvement to be with the Type A death naturally associated with these preliminary acts of judgment that he can relay such involvement without so much as a theological flinch.

**[16–19]** Throughout the next four verses, John explains how the massive killing introduced in v. 15 will take place. John reveals what he has heard about the Euphrates River force that the four now unbound angels are poised to unleash. He reports their numbers as a double (two times) myriad of myriads. The term "myriad" symbolizes, as it does at 5:11, a number so immense that it is incalculable. Many commentators equate the term with the number "10,000." For this reason the NRSV, apparently using the calculation 2 times 10,000 times 10,000, arrives at a figure of 200 million. At a time when armies numbering 50,000 or 100,000 would have been considered invincible, the appearance of an army 200 million strong would have had a staggering effect.

Though John is unable to count and perhaps even see the entire battle force because of its massive size, he apparently is able to make out the way its troops are dressed. Perhaps because he is so overwhelmed, the seer's grammar is a little confusing at this point. He sees horses and riders on the horses. It is unclear, though, whether only the horses or both the horses and the riders are equipped with breastplates. Because the horses and not the riders appear to be the instruments of imminent killing, one is right to wonder whether John is preoccupied with them and is describing their breastplates. However, the noun *hippous* (horses) stands farther from the participle "having breastplates" than does the substantival participle *kathēmenous* (riders). Following the description of the breastplates, John resumes explicit depiction of the horses by writing "the heads of the horses." This placement suggests that the breastplate phrase belongs with either the riders or both the riders and the horses.

Like the locusts of the fifth trumpet, these killing-machine horses are mutant instruments of divine destruction. They have the heads of lions.[9] This image again reminds John's hearers and readers of the demon locusts that had the teeth of lions in their human faces (9:8). With the horses, though, John focuses not on the teeth but on the exhaust that surges from their mouths. The chemicals that make up this exhaust are represented by the colors of their breastplates: the plagues of fire (red), smoke (sapphire blue), and sulfur/brimstone (yellow). These are the elements that cause such massive human casualties. Fire and sulfur are complementary agents of judgment to which John will return later in his work (14:10; 19:20; 20:10; 21:8). Biblically, the three elements appear together in Gen 19:24–28 as the forces of God's judgment against Sodom and Gomorrah. It is this theme of justifiable judgment that John wants to stress.

Although the mouths of these fire-, smoke-, and sulfur-vomiting horses are ominously toxic, their tails wreak an equal amount of havoc. Their tails are serpentlike appendages that have lethal mouths. Apparently many humans who survive the plagues of fire, smoke, and sulfur as the massive army advances will be bitten to death by the rearguard action of the horses' tails as they pass. Once again, the imagery is precisely calculated to instill maximum panic. "The Parthians were renowned archers on horseback. Not only did they shoot their arrows as they advanced toward their enemy, but as the archers went past, they turned around backwards on their horses and fired a volley of arrows from the rear" (Reddish 183).

**[20–21]** Despite the ravages they have witnessed as a result of the plagues, the two-thirds of humans who survive refuse to repent from the works of their hands. The emphasis on repentance is suggestive. The seer's mention of repentance gives a clue to his understanding of God's motivations. From the very start of his narrative, John has made the case that the primary focus for writing has been ethical. He has exhorted the members of the seven Asia Minor churches to witness to the lordship of Christ. For those who are afraid of the consequences such witnessing will bring, he encourages resistance. For those who have so feared the loss of status, privilege, economic success, political stature, or even life that they have accommodated themselves to the expectations of Roman imperial and pagan lordship, he exhorts repentance. It is no

---

9. Many commentators argue that the creature was based on the legendary Chimaera: "The Chimaera is consistently described as having the head of a lion, the tail of a dragon or serpent, and the body of a goat and belching fire ([Homer,] *Iliad* 6.181–82; Hesiod *Theog.* 319–24)" (Aune 2:539).

accident that the verb "repent" occurs most often (and prior to 9:20 only) in chapters 2 and 3 (2:5, 16, 21, 22; 3:3, 19). Indeed, as much as John detests Jezebel for misleading the people, he maintains that there is hope for repentance even for her (2:21).

"Works of their hands" is a suggestive phrase. Employing a *hina* clause as a result clause this time, John declares that their lack of repentance—their refusal to recognize God's lordship—results in their continuing to attribute divine lordship to demons and the "works of their hands" instead. Clearly, John is referring to idols, which are traditionally represented in Jewish literature by works of gold, silver, bronze, stone, and wood (see Deut 32:17; Pss 115:4–7; 135:15–17; Isa 2:8, 20; 17:8; 44:9–20; Jer 10:1–16; Dan 5:4, 23; Wis 13:10–19). Demons were often associated with these gods and the works that portrayed them (e.g., Deut 32:17; 1 Cor 10:19–20). Those objects were just that, objects of human creative activity. They had no power, no capability, no life separate from that which fallible humans gave them. They were therefore incapable of directing the very human lives on which they were themselves dependent for existence.

Entities that could not shape their own destinies could not be expected to shape the destinies of others. Surely those who believed in such creations of their own hands must have realized, when the acts of judgment accompanying the seven trumpets began, that those creations were incapable of stopping the acts or even lessening their intensity. That recognition alone should have caused people to repent of placing trust in works of their own hands. Still, though, they refused. Even when humans did finally admit that God was the author of the judgment acts associated with the seals, trumpets, and bowls (16:9, 11), those who resisted God's lordship steadfastly persisted in their refusal to honor God.

Instead, they fall into a pattern of social disruption and evil that is a direct result of their idolatry, which is itself a result of their failure to repent. The four offenses John now mentions are prominently associated in other biblical texts with the sin of idolatry[10] (see also the discussion of vice lists at 21:8).

Revelation 9:13–21 is a troubling text. Yet the combination of the liberation theme, which reverberates throughout this chapter, with the repentance theme that concludes the section infuses the text with a hint of good news.[11] It is good

---

10. Aune (2:519) points to 2 Kgs 9:22; Isa 47:9–10; 48:5; Jer 7:5–11; Hos 3:1–4:2; Mic 5:12–6:8; Nah 1:14; 3:1–4; Wis 12:3–6; Acts 15:20; Rom 1:24–31; Gal 5:19–21; Eph 5:5; Col 3:5.

11. Other commentators sense good news in this text of judgment. Richard writes, "The aim of this judgment of God in history, or the realization of the Exodus in the bosom of the Roman empire, is the conversion of the oppressors and idolaters and the liberation of the holy ones. Repeating the Exodus, God attempts to rein in the Roman empire's rush to destroy the world and itself. Hence the Exodus is the good news of God's judgment (see [Rev] 10:7 and 14:6–7)" (86). Schüssler Fiorenza comments, "The concluding verses 9:20–21 indicate, however, that John writes this grotesque and brutal vision not for cruelty's sake but rather for the sake of exhortation to repentance" (*Vision of a Just World*, 72).

news that God hears those who have lifted their cries (6:9–11) and their prayers (8:3–5) upon the altars of sacrifice and incense (9:13). It is good news that God's judgment, as massively destructive as it is, even during the final preliminary stage of the sixth trumpet, intends not to destroy but to reprove. Even at the approach of the end of time, there is still time to turn back to God and find the life that is eschatological relationship with God and the Lamb.

## *10:1–11:13 A Pause before the End*

An interlude now separates the first six trumpet blasts from the seventh and final one. Because the trumpets vision parallels the seals vision, it is no surprise that there is also a parallel between their intermission scenes. Corresponding to the two-part seals interlude (7:1–8, 9–17) is a two-part trumpets interlude (10:1–11; 11:1–13).

The strategy for the trumpets interlude is twofold. First, John encourages his readers to continue believing that despite how frightening the times are, everything is happening according to God's design. Though the surrounding circumstances are a mystery to human understanding, God has planned the tragic events like a carefully plotted book focused on the themes of punishment and reward. Second, John will use the second half of the interlude, 11:1–13, to showcase for his hearers and readers the kind of witnessing behavior that is worthy of God's reward.

## 10:1–3 The Angel and the Little Scroll

> **10:1** And I saw another mighty angel coming down from heaven, wrapped in a cloud, with a[a] rainbow over his head, and his face was like the sun, and his feet like columns of fire. **2** He held in his hand a little opened scroll. He placed his right foot on the sea and his left on the land. **3** Then he cried out with a foreboding voice, like a lion roaring. And when he cried out, the seven thunders sounded their own voices.

a. Though the Greek supplies the definite article for "rainbow," it is not translated here because it refers back several chapters to the occurrence of the word in 4:3. Several manuscripts (ℵ[1] 2053 𝔐[A] sa) omit the article, no doubt for this reason.

**[10:1]** After using the phrase *kai eidon* (and I saw) to introduce this section as a new scene within the ongoing trumpet narrative (see the comment on 5:1), John shifts his spatial focus. To this point he has envisioned all the critical activity from what appears to be a heavenly perch. Having been invited up to the heavenly throne room (4:1–2), he sees everything that happens from that lofty perspective. By the time he opens his chapter 10 narration, however, this traveler in the spirit has apparently been grounded. When he catches his glimpse of the mighty angel, his vantage point is from below. Looking up, he sees the angel coming down (*katabainonta*).

John's use of the verb *katabainō* is instructive. His first and last applications narrate the descent of the new Jerusalem as a kind of eschatological reward, a temporal realization of eternal salvation (3:12; 21:2, 10). Yet John makes clear, right from the start, that a person's citizenship in this eschatological city is conditioned upon one's exercise of the appropriate witnessing behavior (3:12). Those who refused to witness and instead chose a path of accommodation to Roman legal, economic, political, and cultic expectations should instead expect that this city's gates would afford them no entry. The implication of judgment becomes explicit in John's other uses of the descent motif. At 16:21; 18:1; and 20:1, 9, God's judgment rains down. In three of those four occurrences, judgment is mediated by an angelic presence.[12] John's use of the descent metaphor throughout the narrative suggests that he intends something specific when he records the "coming down" of another mighty angel (10:1). While he does not specifically mention the complementary themes of judgment and salvation, their presence must surely be felt.

That presence, particularly judgment, becomes more explicit as John rivets attention on the mighty angel. The characterization is surely drawn from Dan 12:5–9. In the Hebrew text, during a time of great eschatological angst, Daniel sees two angelic figures by a stream. The two angels stand on the opposing banks. One of them asks a question of a man clothed in linen, who is introduced in Dan 10:5 with traits that for John must have identified him as the one like a child of humanity.[13] One of the angels asks the man how long it will be until the end of the envisioned wonders. The man raises his right and left hands to heaven and swears by the one who lives forever that it will be a time, two times, and a half a time—apparently three and a half years—until God accomplishes God's purposes. When Daniel asks for clarification, he is sent away with the instruction that the words he has heard are to remain sealed and therefore secret.

Though in Daniel's case there were two great angels, John envisions only one. This one angel plays the role of Daniel's two angels as well as the one

---

12. At 13:13, it is the beast from the earth that makes fire come down from heaven. In this case, though, the beast is clearly trying to imitate the manner in which God executes judgment. Thus, even this situation of descent, not orchestrated by God, can only be understood against the backdrop of God's descending acts of judgment. A bit more unusual is 12:12. Here it is the devil, the serpent, who comes down. The narration indicates, though, that the serpent is driven down to the earth after being cast out of heaven (12:7–9). According to John's broader narration, the devil can only act on earth because God allows it (see, e.g., 20:7). The implication is that everything happening, even the evil, happens under God's control (see further the discussion of divine passives at 6:1–8; 7:2; 9:1–2).

13. On a face like lightning, see 1:16; on eyes like flaming torches, see 1:14; on arms and legs like burnished bronze, see 1:15; on his sound as the roar of a multitude, see 1:15.

clothed in linen. He answers John's questions and provides the overall instruction the seer craves. But first he represents the image of God's power to effect the end time and the judgment that comes with it.

John quickly builds that representation in several ways. First, he uses the suggestive adjectives *allos* (another) and *ischyros* (mighty). Prior to 10:1, he has spoken of "another angel" only twice (7:2; 8:3). Both of those occasions were saturated with the theme of judgment. At 7:2 another angel ascends from the east and orchestrates the sealing of the 144,000 from the great damage that will accompany God's preliminary acts of judgment. Then at 8:3, another angel stands at the heavenly incense altar and throws down the fire of God's judgment upon the earth. Anyone hearing and reading carefully would, at the precise moment of encountering "another" angel at 10:1, feel an appropriate sense of foreboding. It is a sense of dread that John maintains. With similar phrasing ("I saw another angel"), 14:6 kicks off a series of presentations in which "another" angel six times operates in a manner that delivers some measure of God's judgment (14:6, 8, 9, 15, 17, 18). That judgment activity reaches a climax when, for the seventh time, at 18:1–2, "another" angel comes down (*katabainō*) from heaven and seals Babylon's fate.

The angel in 10:1 is also "mighty."[14] The seer reports only two other sightings of a mighty angel (5:2; 18:21). By chapter 18 the narrative atmosphere is thick with judgment and doom. John attributes this punishing outcome to the fact that the city ("Babylon") and its associates have so viciously persecuted those who witnessed to the lordship of God and the Lamb (18:24). Perhaps even more provocative is the fact that the first appearance of a mighty angel (5:2) occurs in direct connection with the scroll that John saw sitting in the right hand of the one who sat on the heavenly throne, that is, God (5:1). Surely the mention of another mighty angel in 10:1 would remind John's hearers and readers of the seven-sealed scroll that was subsequently opened in 6:1–8:1. Can it be coincidence that the scroll held by the mighty angel in chapter 10 has already been opened? Clearly, John is not talking about the same angel; this one is surely *another* mighty angel.

The chapter 5 scroll is so significant that only the Lamb can handle it. Similarly, only a very special divine figure can handle the scroll in chapter 10. This is no ordinary angel. John clothes his characterization with regal traits. He

14. Commentators often speculate on the name of the angel by appealing to the history of the term "mighty." For example, Reddish writes, "The angel in the book of Daniel after whom this mighty angel of ch. 10 is modeled is named Gabriel. Some commentators have suggested that John intended a wordplay on the name Gabriel since in Hebrew the name Gabriel is related to the Hebrew word *gibbôr*, which means 'mighty'" (192). Reddish also argues that the mighty angel has a great many of the characteristics of Gabriel in Dan 8:15–17; 10:2–9; 12:5–13. For an extrabiblical comparison to the Colossus of Rhodes, a famous bronze representation of the sun god Helios, see Aune 2:556–57.

appears in the divine dress of a cloud. In Exod 16:10 and 1 Kgs 8:10, clouds are a metaphor for the presence of God. A halolike rainbow (*iris*) hovers over his head. John uses *iris* one other time, to describe the glowing form that fills the air around the heavenly throne (Rev 4:3). His face shines like the sun. The only other time John uses the brilliance of the sun to describe someone's face, he refers to the child of humanity (1:16; cf. Matt 17:2, where Jesus' transfigured face is said to shine like the sun). Finally, though the text uses the term for feet, since John envisions them as columns of fire, he clearly intends to speak of the mighty angel's legs. Once again the imagery recalls the presentation of the child of humanity in chapter 1. His eyes are like flames of fire (1:14; cf. 2:18), and his feet have the appearance of bronze burnished in a fiery furnace (1:15; cf. 2:18). Exodus 13:21 speaks of God leading the people of Egypt out of bondage via a pillar of fire by day and a pillar of cloud by night (cf. Dan 10:6; Ezek 1:27). The specific implication here is thus assurance of liberation and salvation for those who witness to this God, even as the wider language connects with judgment.

[2] The little scroll lies opened in the hand of the mighty angel. Since 10:5 pictures him raising his right hand to heaven, he must be holding it in his left. After John has given such prominence to the scroll the Lamb unsealed in 6:1–8:1, one could not fault John's hearers and readers for wondering if the two scrolls of chapters 5 and 10 are the same. The Lamb opened the first scroll (ch. 5) to an escalating series of judgment events; the second scroll (ch. 10) is already opened and surrounded on both narrative sides by escalating acts of judgment.

The adjective *ēneōgmenon* (opened) is a helpful identifier. The Greek participle occurs in the perfect tense, implying a past action that has enduring narrative effect. Such a description hints at a connection between the scroll of 5:1–8:1 and the one that appears in 10:2. Opened in the past (in the course of 6:1–8:1?), the scroll now plays a significant role in the ongoing prosecution of God's judgment (see 10:8–10) that began with the breaking of the first of the seven seals.

The participle's voice is passive. From chapter 6 forward, John has relied heavily on passive constructions to indicate the agency of either God or the Lamb in acts of both judgment and salvation (see the comments on 6:1–8; 7:2; 8:2; 9:1–21). It would be unremarkable here, then, if John used the passive construction to indicate that either God or the Lamb opened this scroll. This consideration is bolstered by the fact that John explicitly identifies the Lamb as the one who opens the scroll in 5:1–8:1. It seems appropriate, therefore, to presume that the scroll in 10:2 must also have been opened by the Lamb.

Yet another observation speaks to the possibility of a close link between the two scrolls. If the seals and trumpets episodes are indeed John's recounting of the *same* set of events from different eschatological angles (see the comment on 8:1–6), it would be logical to expect that John's hearers and readers are also encountering the *same* scroll.

There is also a potent intertextual reason for considering a strong relationship between the two scrolls. Both are foregrounded against Ezek 2:9–10 (see the discussion of 5:1; 10:8–10). Like the Ezekiel scroll, the one in 5:1–8:1 was written on the inside and back. Apparently the Ezekiel scroll, like the one in 10:2, had already been opened; Ezekiel could make out words of lamentation and woe. Ezekiel was eventually commanded to ingest that scroll, just as John is commanded to eat the scroll in 10:9.

There is a major problem with the theory that John speaks of a single scroll: he uses different terminology for them. He calls the first scroll a *biblion*; the second he labels a *biblaridion*. The latter is translated "little scroll" since it is a diminutive for *biblos*, the term for scroll. On its own, this significant observation would seem to doom any presumption that the two scrolls are one and the same. However, there are significant caveats to the observation. First, *biblion* is itself a diminutive form. By the time John writes, it no longer requires the adjective "little," because it is a so-called "faded diminutive." That is to say, it was used so often in general speech that it came to be accepted as a stand-alone noun in its own right, not a diminutive descriptor of another noun. Second, John seems unsure that any significant linguistic difference exists between the two diminutive forms. While he does introduce the scroll with the form *biblaridion* (10:2), and follows up with the same noun form in vv. 9 and 10, at the critical point when the scroll takes narrative center stage, he describes it as a *biblion* (v. 8). The usage in vv. 2 and 8 suggests that John treats the two words as though they are synonymous. As many commentators point out, in this regard John would not be unlike the *Vision of Hermas* (2.1.4; 2.8.1–2), which treats *biblaridion* and *biblion* as though they are synonyms (e.g., Beale 530). There is every reason to believe that John envisioned one and not two different scrolls (see further the discussion of 5:1).

John's focus on the scroll does not last very long. He can probably introduce it so briefly and with such little discussion without fear of either distracting or losing his audience because his hearers and readers are already familiar with it. Its mention recalls its prior appearance and its association with the theme of judgment. He can therefore move quickly to what principally occupies him: the behavior of the mighty angel. Echoing Dan 12:5, where two angels occupy opposite banks of a stream, John envisions this one great figure straddling all of earthly creation, with his right foot on the sea and his left on the land.[15] The implication is that the angel has control over both sea and land.

**[3]** The mighty angel roars like a lion with a foreboding voice that portends judgment (see the comment on 7:2). The metaphor intends an image of sovereign, destructive power. In the animal world, the history of Hebrew Scripture

---

15. Beale (529) points out that use of "sea and earth" alone generally designates the totality of God's creation (Job 11:9; Ps 146:6; Prov 8:29; Isa 42:10; Jonah 1:9).

(Jer 25:30; Hos 11:10; Joel 3:16; Amos 1:2; 3:8), and John's narrative, the lion is a force to be feared. The first of the four awesome cherubim is described in lionlike terms. The Lamb of God is introduced first as the lion of Judah, a force thought to bring destruction upon the foes of Israel even as he delivered salvation for Israel's people. Even more significantly, two trumpet blasts correlate lionlike characteristics with divine judgment (9:8, 17).

Seven thunders voice antiphonal affirmation of the mighty angel's foreboding roar. John is working here from Hebrew scriptural references. His introduction of thunders with the article is an indication that he believes his hearers and readers are well acquainted with the imagery. At Ps 29:3 the glory of God's voice thunders for all to hear. At 1 Sam 7:10, this thundering is the mighty voice of God that confounds and then routs the Philistines.[16] For John, too, the thunders are a part of a theophany package that illustrates God's majesty. Thunders occur first in his narrative at 4:5, with the lightning and rumbling that emanate from the throne. In the ensuing three theophany presentations, where thunders, rumblings, and lightnings are joined by earthquake (8:5; 11:19; 16:18) and hail (11:19), there is also an unmistakable emphasis on the theme of divine judgment.

Even when the other theophany elements do not accompany thunder, it operates as a metaphor for the movement of God's justice. After the Lamb breaks the first of the seven seals, the first of the four cherubim calls out "Come!" in a thunderous voice (6:1). The wave of vicious judgment that follows is unmistakable (see the comment on 6:1–8). Thunderous voices also sound in 14:2 and 19:6. In both of these cases, though, God's justice begins with an emphasis on salvation. At 14:2, hearers and readers are reminded that the 144,000 have been sealed from the acts of judgment that preface the final judgment. Thundering multitudes later praise God for the salvation that comes in the metaphor of marriage to the Lamb (19:6). In each of those occasions of celebration, though, judgment is not far off. God's punishment of those who oppress God's witnesses and accommodate to social, political, economic, and cultic expectations is quickly reasserted (14:6; 19:11).

Thunder is thus a thematic metaphor for the glorious execution of God's justice in both judgment and salvation. The number "seven" indicates that John is picturing that justice in its most complete and potent form (see the discussion of seven as wholeness at 1:4–8). The thunders, then, signal total affirmation of the judgment/salvation that the foreboding voice of the mighty angel implies. If one takes into account the Old Testament echoes, this thundering affirmation may well be God's own voice.

---

16. Cf. 1 Sam 2:10; 2 Sam 22:14; Job 37:2–5; Ps 18:13; Isa 29:6. Beale draws the connection to the Sinai theophany: "In Jewish tradition God's voice of thunder at Sinai (Exod. 19:16–19) is referred to as 'seven voices' or 'sounds'" (535).

10:4–7  The Mystery of the Seven Thunders

4 When the seven thunders spoke, I was about to write, but[a] I heard a voice from heaven saying: "Seal up what the seven thunders said; do not write it down." 5 Then the angel whom I saw standing on the sea and on the land raised his right hand to heaven, 6 and he swore by[b] the one who lives forever, who created heaven and everything in it, and the earth and everything in it,[c] and the sea and everything in it:[d] "There will be no more time, 7 but in the days when the seventh angel is to sound his trumpet, then the mystery of God will be completed, as he announced to his servants, the prophets."

a. The conjunction *kai* is adversative here: "but."
b. There is strong textual evidence ($\mathfrak{P}^{47}$ ℵ* 1854 2329 2344 2351 $\mathfrak{M}^{K}$) for omitting the preposition *en*, which clarifies that the angel is swearing "by God" and not "to God." Aune therefore argues that *en* was a later insertion, added for clarity (2:550).
c. No doubt the omission in A $\mathfrak{M}^{A}$ of the phrase "and the earth and everything in it" was accidental, due to the repetition of the form.
d. Similarly, the omission in ℵ* A 1611 2344 (et al.) of the phrase "and the sea and everything in it" probably came from a copyist's mistake.

**[4]** John's hearers and readers are not surprised when he informs them that he is ready to write down the judgment message that he heard the seven thunders convey. After all, throughout the narrative he has been commanded to transcribe his visions (1:11, 19; 2:1, 8, 12, 18; 3:1, 7, 14; cf. 14:13; 19:9; 21:5). The many previous orders to write make this subsequent command to abort the writing effort all the more intriguing—especially since the order comes directly from heaven.[17] Given the overall narrative intent to reveal God's designs for ultimate justice, why in this particular case would a heavenly agent suddenly require John to halt his revelatory efforts?[18]

While it is impossible, given John's lack of specificity, to determine the answer to that important question, there are related matters that can be clarified. First, since John was specifically ordered to relay his visions in the writing of this book, his hearers and readers know that the message of the thunders does

17. Cf. 2 Cor 12:2–4, where Paul speaks of a person who was not to write the things he had seen when caught up into paradise.
18. The source of the voice is not specified; given John's wider use of the writing command, this might suggest that it is the one like a child of humanity, the Lamb, who demands that John stay his pen. Unfortunately, such a view cannot be confirmed. John speaks specifically about a voice (which does not issue a command to write) out of heaven on four other occasions (11:12; 12:10; 14:2; 18:4); 12:10 actually places the voice "in" heaven. In only two of those occasions could one hope to identify the speaker with the one like a child of humanity. Both 1:10–13 and 4:1–2 clearly depict the one like a child of humanity speaking in heaven, but not with the particular construction used in 10:4.

not include the content of John's overall narrative. Indeed, using the same verb that is so puzzling here, an angel specifically warns John at 22:10 *not* to seal up the words of this book. John's visions must be conveyed; the thunders' message must not be. Second, since the scroll of 10:2 is a virtual "open book," whose content will later be internalized and then presumably proclaimed (vv. 8–11), its message also cannot be the same message as that which John hears from the seven thunders. If this scroll is the scroll of 5:1–8:1, which contains the shape, plan, and destiny of human history (see the comment on 5:1), then the seven thunders are not speaking exclusively about that plan. Through his visionary writing, John is already in the process of laying bare the direction and meaning of that plan.

At the very least, the similarity between John's recounting of the "seal" command and the order given to Daniel that he seal up the vision given to him at Dan 8:26 (cf. 8:19) is instructive. Daniel's classified vision is about the happenings that will take place at the very end of time. Given John's overall focus on the end time, it takes no leap of the imagination to conclude that the thunders, too, are speaking about final events. The context here suggests that the arrival of those final events is imminent.

**[5–6]** Verse 5 refocuses attention on the mighty angel first introduced in v. 1. John reminds his hearers and readers that the angel is a colossus; while his right foot occupies the land, his left covers and therefore controls the sea. With his left hand apparently clutching the little scroll (v. 2), he raises his right hand to heaven in what v. 6 shows to be an oath-swearing gesture (on the significance of the right hand, see the comment on 5:1).

The lifting of one's hand toward heaven as an oath-swearing gesture had a long history in Israelite tradition. Deuteronomy 32:40, in the context of judgment against those who have persecuted God's people and mocked God's lordship (see esp. vv. 35–39), records such an instance.[19] More to the point, though, is the relationship with Dan 12:7. There a divine figure dressed in linen lifted both hands to heaven and swore by the one who lives forever that it would be a time, two times, and a half (i.e., three and one-half) before God would accomplish all things.

The parallel with the mighty angel in Rev 10:5 is intentional. He, too, swears on the one who lives forever, already identified by John as the one seated on the heavenly throne: God (4:9). He secures this identification by drawing upon other unforgettable characteristics that are exclusive to God. The one upon

---

19. Aune, however, cautions against too quickly reading Deut 32:40 as an instance of oath swearing. He points out that the Hebrew text mentions only the lifting of the hand: "There is danger, however, that the modern practice of raising the right hand when taking oaths has unduly influenced the exegesis of Deut 32:40 and similar passages" (2:564). The context, however, does imply the swearing of an oath, and the LXX translators read the circumstance as one of oath bearing since it narrates not only a swearing but also one using the right hand.

whom the angel swears created heaven and every divine thing in it. This part of the oath is reminiscent of Gen 14:19, where King Melchizedek of Salem blesses Abram by the God who made heaven and earth. Abram responds to the king of Sodom by swearing upon this same God, who has made heaven and earth (14:22). Obviously, the emphasis upon the earth echoes in the second phase of the mighty angel's declaration. His oath operates with the Creator of the earth and all the things in it in mind. He also declares this God to be the Creator of the sea and all within it. Numerous biblical texts corroborate this testimony about God's authorship of heaven, earth, and sea (Exod 20:11; Neh 9:6; Ps 146:6; Acts 4:24). That the angel swears upon so mighty a God assures the validity of his forthcoming statement. Indeed, his very posture helps build the credibility that his name-dropping intends. The one who swears upon the God who created heaven, earth, and sea has descended at God's apparent direction from heaven and now stands simultaneously upon the earth and sea as he delivers his oath. He represents the very reality upon which he swears; there can be no greater assurance of his credibility and the viability of his oath than that.

It is the content of his oath that is critical. In Dan 12 the figure dressed in linen declared that God's final accomplishment (i.e., judgment) would take place in three and one-half times. Three and a half, half of the complete number of seven, also used by John (Rev 11:2, 3, 9, 11; 12:6, 14), is a euphemism for a temporary, short duration of time. John makes that point here by transcribing the angel's message as there will be no more time.

The phrasing is odd, to be sure. The NSRV translates the angel's words as "There will be no more delay." *Chronos*, the key term in the text, can be translated "delay" as well as the more customary "time." At this stage of the text, the translations are practically synonymous. After the sounding of the sixth trumpet, with the expectation of the seventh trumpet's imminent sounding, John has brought his hearers and readers to a critical turning point. The first six trumpet calls beckoned preliminary acts of judgment in response to the cries (6:9–11), or prayers (8:3–5), of the persecuted witnesses. The seventh trumpet, like the seventh seal and the seventh bowl, will bring the preliminaries to an end by ushering in God's final act of judgment. The mighty angel, scroll in hand, swears now that this end point has finally come. Time itself has come to completion. By definition, then, there can be no more delay before the arrival of God's final judgment act.

This interpretation makes sense if the little scroll in question is the same scroll that in chapter 5 contained the plan of human history.[20] With the scroll

---

20. As Reddish points out, this is not the usual interpretation of the content of the little scroll. Those who see it as distinct from the scroll in chapter 5 argue that it has a more limited historical content. "The usual interpretation is that the little scroll of 10:2 contains the events described in 11:1–13. The larger scroll of 5:1 is seen to contain either all of God's eschatological plans or specifically the events of 6:1–8:5" (197).

now open, the angel can plainly see when the end will be, and he can apparently see that it is now. He can swear confidently on the God who lives forever and who created all things because he has this God's scroll. He can see the timeline of history and where he and the rest of creation are on it. They are at the point where time will be no longer because it has reached the objective God has set for it. While "There will be no more delay" therefore is an accurate representation of what the angel has to say, the translation "There will be no more time" is more eloquent and appropriate. In this visionary scenario, it is time itself that has run out.

In every other case where *chronos* is used in Revelation, there is a little time left. Only a little time remains, but it is there. There is time to repent (2:21), time to rest (6:11), and time to rule (20:3). The first two occurrences seem natural because, narratively speaking, they occur prior to the declaration in 10:6 that there will no longer be time. The last, though, since it occurs at the end of the narrative, appears out of place. Although the angel declares in chapter 10 that there will be no more time, Satan is loosed for yet a little more time in chapter 20. How can Satan have more time at 20:3 when the angel swears here that there will be no more time?

Clarification lies with an understanding of John's unorthodox presentation. He is not presenting events chronologically. He is jumping back and forth in real time as he renders his narrative presentation. One can sense this time-displacement phenomenon when considering John's presentation of the seven seals, trumpets, and bowls. Though they represent the same end-time events, viewed from different eschatological perspectives, John's narrative presentation implies that they occur in chronological order: first seals, then trumpets, and finally bowls. His apparent narrative progression forward in time actually represents a double reconsideration of the same set of moments in time that describe God's preliminary acts of judgment (see the comment on the introduction to the trumpets at 8:1–6).

In like manner, the events narrated at 20:3 take place, in real time, before the declaration by the angel in chapter 10, even though in the narrative itself those events occur well after the angel's declaration. If both 10:6 and 20:3 are true, John has given us a glimpse of the end of time at 10:6, while still intending to explain the progression of events in time, such as what has happened in 20:3, that has led up to this end. He continues in the narration in order to remind his hearers and readers about events that have occurred prior to this almost-final moment. The release of Satan at 20:3 is one such prior event.

Recognition of John's calculated time displacement has an important bearing on the way hearers and readers approach the remainder of his narrative. One can never be sure that just because events follow one another narratively, they are also envisioned by John to occur that way chronologically. John is intentionally presenting his visions out of chronological place. In order to maximize dramatic effect, he pictures the end moment (e.g., 10:6) before he narrates the events (e.g., 20:3) that have led up to and shaped it.

[7] John opens v. 7 by describing the days of the final trumpet blast (on the connection of *salpizein*, "to blow a trumpet," to judgment, see the comments on 8:2; 9:1–2). With the realization that time's purpose has been achieved, the mystery that God conveyed as good news to the prophets will be brought to its point of completion.[21] What is that mystery? Traditionally, one would try to answer that question by initiating a query of the Old Testament prophetic records. Was there a common promissory thread that ran through all of the Hebrew prophetic writings? This is a difficult question to answer in John's terms, since the Hebrew prophets tended to seek realization of God's promises for freedom, land, the establishment of a vast people, and a return to the land following exile *within* history. John clearly anticipates the actualization of God's ultimate promise at the end of history. When he talks about the promise to the prophets, he therefore must be speaking metaphorically. He is not speaking about a literal promise per se. He is instead focused on the idea that God will be as faithful to God's promises regarding judgment and salvation as God was faithful to the promises God proclaimed to the prophets.

John suggests a starting point for deciphering the mystery that God revealed as good news to the prophets: his narration of the seventh trumpet's inauguration of God's reign at 11:15–19. The key verse is 11:18. John speaks specifically about the time of judgment that registers as salvation for God's servants, the prophets. He then goes on to add the saints and all who fear God's name—that is, those who testify to the lordship of God and the Lamb—to the list of those who are saved. The clarification of any mystery at the end seems to revolve, then, not around a promise of freedom, land, life, or nationhood within history, but the promise of life in eschatological relationship with God. More particularly, it involves an identification of the categories of people who will be saved. John reminds his hearers and readers of the categories to which they must belong if they would hope for an eschatological relationship with God: servants, prophets.

John has based the critical phrase "his servants, the prophets" (10:7 and 11:18) on actual prophetic statements. The phrase is highlighted in Jer 7:25–26, where it is noted that God sent the prophets in order to urge righteous and ethical behavior from the people of Israel. Moreover, like John (Rev 10:3), Amos speaks of the heavenly message issuing forth in the sound of a lion roaring (3:8). Even more significantly, Amos speaks of that roar in the context of the Lord's message to his servants, the prophets (3:7). As with the Jeremiah text, the focus is on the ethical behavior God expected from the people. Because they failed

---

21. See Beale (543): "Therefore, 'of God' in 'the mystery of God' (τὸ μυστήριον τοῦ θεοῦ) is best taken as a genitive of source or a subjective genitive, since God is the revealer of the mystery in Daniel."

time and time again to demonstrate it, they were subject to judgment. Zechariah maintains this focus on the ethical behavior that God's servants, the prophets, expected from the people (1:6). In his case, however, there was a glimmer of salvation. The prophetic word had a positive impact: the people repented. God therefore promised to punish the nations that had persecuted them and to bring them victory. This emphasis on the expectation of ethical behavior as a response to God's call for righteous living is present on almost every occasion when the phrase "his servants, the prophets" occurs in the prophetic literature.[22]

The most telling case comes from Daniel, who speaks of God's servants, the prophets, in a context explicitly concerned with the failure of the people to heed God's prophetic call for righteous and ethical behavior (9:6, 10). As a result, God's judgment was rightly executed. John's own focus on the connection between judgment or salvation and God's expectation for righteous and ethical (witnessing) behavior provides a natural bridge to these Hebrew prophetic themes. It must be this emphasis upon the expectation of righteous, ethical behavior, and God's reward of salvation for those who meet that expectation and judgment against those who do not, that John has in mind when he calls upon God's proclamations to God's servants, the prophets.

### 10:8–11 The Little Scroll

The final four verses of chapter 10 operate in concert with the first two of chapter 11. In the complete six verses John narrates two mutually supportive scenes. In the first scene the seer receives a recommissioning of his original call to disclose God's purpose and goal for human history (10:8–10). The opened scroll represents the presentation of that history. By taking it from the angel's hand, John lays claim to it. By eating it, he internalizes it and makes it his own.

The recommissioning is followed in 10:11 with John's orders to declare the prophecy he has just internalized. It will be a destructive word of judgment that will nonetheless operate as a word of protective security, and therefore salvation, for those who witness to the lordship of God and the Lamb (11:1–2).

8 Then the voice that I heard from heaven spoke with me again, and said: "Go, take the scroll which lies opened in the hand of the angel who stands on the sea and on the land." 9 Then I went to the angel and told him to give me the little scroll. And he said to me, "Take it and eat it; it will be bitter to your stomach, but in your mouth it will be as sweet as honey." 10 So I took the little scroll from the hand of the angel and I ate it, and it was sweet as honey in my mouth, but when I ate it, it turned my stomach

22. See 2 Kgs 9:7; 17:13, 23; 21:10; 24:2; Ezra 9:11; Jer 25:4; 26:5; 29:19; 35:15; 44:4; Ezek 38:17; Dan 9:6, 10.

bitter. 11 And they[a] said to me: "You must again prophesy against peoples and nations and tongues and many kings."

a. Although 1611 1854 2053 𝔐[A] it (vg[cl]) sy sa bo[mss]; Tyc Prim substitute the third-person singular verb *legei* (he said), the more difficult plural construction is surely the original. The singular construction is an attempt to match the single speaker from 10:8 with the speaker here.

**[8]** The scroll is the same one mentioned at 10:2. John refers to it with the definite article because his readers are already familiar with it. He also describes the 10:2 and 10:8 scrolls in almost duplicate fashion in vv. 2 and 8. As in v. 2, the scroll in v. 8 has already been opened, and it rests in the hand of the angel who stands with one foot on the sea and the other on the earth.

John's redundant and therefore emphatic effort to link the scroll (*biblion*) of v. 8 with the "little" scroll (*biblaridion*) of v. 2 and vv. 9–10 is all the more interesting since he does not use the diminutive form *biblaridion* in v. 8. Apparently, for John the terms, while distinct, are interchangeable here and refer to one and the same scroll. It is, moreover, the same scroll introduced at 5:1 and opened by the Lamb over the course of 6:1–8:1 (see the comments on 5:1; 10:2). The scroll's content therefore presents God's plan and purpose of eschatological justice for human history.[23]

John's attention is refocused on the scroll by a voice from heaven. His use of *palin* (again) indicates that this voice is the same heavenly voice that denied him permission to write down what the seven thunders had said. This time the order is an affirming one.

**[9–10]** When John asks for the scroll, he is told, in what sounds like eucharistic language, to take and eat it (cf. Matt 26:26). It is at this point that allusions to Ezek 2:8–3:3 become unmistakable (see the discussion of 10:2). At his prophetic commissioning, Ezekiel is given a scroll written on both front and back and told to eat it. The description of the scroll clearly calls to mind the scroll introduced by John in Rev 5:1. Ezekiel explains the content of his scroll as words of lamentation and woe. Those who do not live up to God's expectations for righteous and ethical behavior will be sorely judged. This description

---

23. Cf. Aune 2:571–72. Aune surveys the various explanations of the scroll's content offered by scholars who distinguish between the scrolls of chapter 5 and chapter 10. While the consensus view is that it refers to the events of 11:1–13, others suggest 11:1–15:4 (Elisabeth Schüssler Fiorenza, "Composition and Structure of the Book of Revelation," *CBQ* 39 [1977]: 363); 12:1–22:5 (Wilhelm Bousset, *Die Offenbarung Johannis* [6th ed., 1906; repr. Göttingen: Vandenhoeck & Ruprecht, 1966], 312); Rev 12 or 17 (Adela Yarbro Collins, *The Combat Myth in the Book of Revelation* [Missoula, Mont.: Scholars Press for *HTR*, 1976], 26); 1:1–2:9 (C. H. Giblin, "Revelation 11:1–13: Its Form, Function, and Contextual Integration," *NTS* 30 [1984]: 455); or chs. 20–22 (Beasley-Murray 82).

fits precisely the Rev 10 scroll as well. Chapter 10 consistently emphasizes God's coming justice as a word of judgment.

Ezekiel is ordered to eat the scroll, thereby internalizing its words of lamentation and woe, and then to go and prophetically deliver it. He does eat it and finds that, despite its harsh message, it is sweet as honey in his mouth. As Aune observes, "The metaphor 'sweet as honey' is occasionally used of the commands of God in the OT (Pss 19:10; 119:100–103) and is a metaphor used for agreeable speech (Prov 16:24)" (2:572; cf. Jer 15:16). The parallels with Rev 10:9–10 are striking. After telling John to take the scroll and eat it, thereby internalizing its content, the angel explains that it will embitter his stomach even though it will be like honey in his mouth.

Verse 10 repeats the content of v. 9 by narrating John's actual consumption of the scroll. Working backward, though, John speaks about how bitter the scroll made his stomach feel, despite its sweet taste in his mouth. Though he revels in the knowledge that he is interacting so closely with God's word of justice for human history, his stomach apparently turns when he realizes how much destructive and devastating judgment that justice will necessarily bring.

**[11]** John is now recommissioned to the task of prophecy (cf. 1:3). Since he has been operating prophetically throughout the course of his work, the command intends that he recommit himself to the effort. That recommitment is necessary because the effort will become even more difficult. His judgment oracle becomes universal, and if chapter 11 is any guide, his witnessing and the witnessing of those who heed his call will provoke vicious resistance.

The clarification that it is necessary for John to *prophesy* again is instructive. The mandate begins oddly. Up until this point, John's primary conversation partner has been the mysterious voice from heaven (cf. 10:4). Given that *voice* occurs in the singular, it appears that the speaker is a single person or entity. Yet v. 11 opens with the narration that "*they* [spoke] to me." Commentators have offered several somewhat plausible options as to why the narration shifts to the plural. It could be that the mighty angel and the heavenly voice, both interlocutors with John during the course of chapter 10, take this unsolicited opportunity to speak to John in unison. Other commentators suggest the even more unexpected possibility that the mighty angel and the "fictive *angelus interpres*" (cf. 22:8–9), who has guided John throughout, take this opportunity to speak together. There is, unfortunately, no warrant in the text to expect such a joint appearance. Finally, several commentators take the grammatical route in the quest for clarity. They "understand the plural pronoun to be an example of 'the plural of indefinite statement,' which according to R. H. Charles is 'an idiom sometimes found in Hebrew, and frequent in Biblical Aramaic'" (Reddish 200, citing Charles 269; cf. Aune 2:573).

There is another option that develops from the narration of the text itself. Even though *they* apparently represent the singular presence of God's voice and direction (see the comments on 10:3–4), the thunders operate as a plural entity. More simply and naturally, John may intend that the same thunders issued God's directive to seal up what he has heard (to, in effect, stop what he was doing) and are now reengaging him in his more appropriate task. His job is not to reveal the end-time mystery, at least not yet. His job is to prophesy about God's coming judgment against those who, out of loyalty to Roman lordship, have persecuted witnesses to the lordship of God and the Lamb.

No doubt, *they* have in mind the same kind of prophetic mandate issued to prophets like Ezekiel (Ezek 25:2) and Jeremiah (Jer 25:30). In both of those illustrative cases, the prophet was ordered to prophesy against the enemies of God and God's people. Though John is working thematically from Ezekiel in this Rev 10, it is the Jeremiah text that is especially illuminating here. Jeremiah was given the specific mandate to speak as a voice of judgment against the nations (Jer 1:10). Then, in a passage that more closely parallels Rev 10:11, Jeremiah is commanded to prophesy against the inhabitants of the earth and to declare that the Lord will vent anger from on high with the fury and violence of a mighty roar (Jer 25:30).[24] John's hearers and readers would no doubt recall the lion's roar in Rev 10:3. Even more significant is Jeremiah's listing of the kings, starting at 25:18, against whom the prophet is specifically commissioned at this point to prophesy. Before it closes, John's universal charge (peoples, nations, languages), also mentions the category of monarchs. John will be particularly concerned about the obstinacy of the kings as his narrative progresses (cf. Rev 16:12, 14; 17:1–2, 12, 18; 18:3, 9; 19:18–19).

Up to this point in his narrative prophecy, John has twice mentioned similar groupings of nations, tribes, languages, and people (5:9; 7:9; cf. Dan 3:4). On both occasions, the groupings are mentioned positively. The Lamb sheds his blood in order to redeem them. The effort of redemption, however, morphs into a prophecy for judgment when the nations, tribes, languages, and people fail to live righteously and ethically as a result of the Lamb's redemptive effort. In this heavenly address to John, "they" make certain that the kings of the earth also realize that they, too, are included in this message of judgment.

On every subsequent occasion—until the consummation of God's reign as represented in the final chapters of the book—when peoples, tribes, languages, and nations are either specifically or euphemistically mentioned, the prophet speaks in negative terms (11:9, 18; 13:7; 14:6, 8; 17:15; 18:3, 23; 19:15). Although the kings are not explicitly named in those passages as they are in 10:11, John continues to make clear that the judgment language is truly universal. Moreover, he does include a separate flurry of specific prophecies against the kings (see the passages listed just above). It is for all these contex-

---

24. Note that it is the Hebrew, not the LXX, that operates with the verb form for "roar" (*šā'ag*).

tual and intertextual reasons that translators who render the ambiguous preposition *epi* "against" are translating correctly.[25] John's order, as with Jeremiah and Ezekiel, is to prophesy against (*prophēteusai epi*) them.

## 11:1–19 Measuring the Temple, Commissioning the Witnesses, Executing the End

In chapter 11, John illustrates the prophetic witness he expects from his hearers and readers. The story of the two witnesses is meant to be their story, too. As representatives of the entire church, these two characters live out the prophetic recommissioning that John received at the end of chapter 10 (vv. 8–11).

### 11:1–2 MEASURING THE TEMPLE

Just as the prophetic commission symbolized by the scroll of chapter 10 had a two-stage progression from sweetness to bitterness, so is the chapter 11 enactment of that commission conceived in two distinct phases. In phase one, John measures and therefore shields a select portion of the temple and those who worship there.[1] In phase two, John does not measure and therefore leaves vulnerable to destruction the greater part of the temple infrastructure and those who symbolically inhabit it.

---

25. Beale notes: "[*Prophēteuō epi*] appears in the LXX only twice in Jeremiah, twice in Amos, and twenty-one times in Ezekiel. The expression typically refers to a prophecy 'against' sinful Israel or some other nation (so eighteen times); only three times, all in Ezekiel, does the phrase refer to a prophecy of blessing" (554).

1. Since John was most likely writing in the closing decade of the first century, well after the temple had been destroyed by the Romans in 70 C.E., why would John go through the motions of recording a command to measure and thus protect it? The easiest argument both to make and to refute is that John actually wrote before the temple fell. Given that the weight of scholarship so highly discounts this possibility, one might alternatively turn to the supposition that John is working here with the contents of a Jewish Zealot prophecy that did indeed surface before the temple's destruction. According to this theory, the Zealots, who had holed up in the temple in their doomed battle against the Romans, believed right up until the end that God would enable them to prevail. Besides the fortunate happenstance that the content of John's command can be read in such a way that it fits the historical account of the Zealots' dire circumstances, there is no credible historical, archaeological, or literary evidence that John operates here from such a source. Caird calls the idea of John working from a Zealot oracle "improbable, useless, and absurd" (131). John writes well after the destruction of the temple and therefore almost certainly has a different perspective on the measurement/protection of the temple than did the desperate Zealots of 70. He would not be thinking about the literal, physical temple since it no longer existed, but a spiritual one whose shape and form, while predicated on the Jerusalem temple, were eschatological. The more appropriate task is to interpret this eschatological imagery in the light of a prophetic call to witness to which John so strenuously exhorts his hearing and reading audience.

11:1 I was given a measuring reed, like a rod, and I was told:[a] "Arise and measure the temple of God and the altar and those who worship there. 2 But[b] exclude the courtyard outside[c] the temple; do not measure it, because it has been given over to the nations, and they will trample the holy city for forty-two months.

a. The syntax of the sentence is garbled. Though "reed" is a match in gender and number, it obviously cannot be the subject of the participle *legōn* (saying). The speaker operates instead from 10:11 (see the comment on v. 1 below).

b. The conjunction *kai* is adversative here: "but."

c. The reading "outside" (*exōthen*) has a stronger external claim ($\mathfrak{P}^{47}$ A P 046 1006 1611 1854 2053 it[61] vg sy[h] sa bo arm *al*) than "inner" (*esōthen*), supported by ℵ 2329 *al* vg[s] sy[ph]; Vic, which probably resulted because scribes considered "outer courtyard" to be a puzzling construction (see Metzger, *Textual Commentary*, 746).

[11:1] When John opens the chapter with yet another formulaic appeal to the divine passive construction *edothē* (lit., "it was given" [to me]; cf. 6:2, 4, 8, 11; 7:2; 8:2; 9:1–21), he means to say that God provides the tool that makes his prophetic activity possible. God operates by proxy. The singular participle *legōn* (saying) refers most likely to the "they" who spoke for God at 10:11. The indefinite plural "they" represents there and here the singular voice of God (see the comments on 10:3, 4, 11). This continuity of speaker makes sense given that God's expectations for John's prophecy, narrated at the close of chapter 10, are enabled by God as chapter 11 opens. With that continued contextual emphasis from chapter 10, the hearer/reader should also presume that an intermediary, not God, places the measuring reed in John's hands. God spoke through the thunders and acted through the mighty angel in chapter 10 (vv. 1, 5, 10). The reader is meant to presume the same mediating activity here. In 21:15–16, the only other place in Revelation where the term "reed" occurs, an angel who has been charged to measure the holy city is specifically outfitted with a reed to accomplish the task (cf. Ezek 40:5).[2] In both Ezekiel (40–48) and Zechariah (2:1–5), there are similar angelic measurements of the city of Jerusalem. Particularly in Zechariah, the act symbolizes God's protection (2:5).[3]

John indicates his broader theological understanding of the measuring reed by pairing it with *rabdos* (rod). At 2:27 he affirms that all who conquer because

2. Cf. Reddish 206. According to Reddish, the measuring reed was "a bamboo-like cane whose woody-jointed stems are hollow." Such cane grew to a height of 4–10 feet and ½–1 inch thick.

3. Aune observes, "'Measuring' can be a metaphor for destruction (2 Sam 8:2a; 2 Kgs 21:13; Amos 7:7–9; Isa 34:11; Lam 2:8) as well as for preservation (2 Sam 8:2b; Ezek 40:1–6; 42:20; Zech 2:[1–]5), though the latter is obviously intended here" (2:604). Pointing specifically to Ezek 40–48, Beale comments, "There the sure establishment and subsequent protection of the temple are metaphorically portrayed by an angel measuring various features of the temple complex (in the LXX of this section διαμετρέω and μέτρον each occur about thirty times)" (559).

of their witnessing will be rewarded with an iron rod, which they will use to rule the nations in the same way that a shepherd watches over, guides, protects, and disciplines his flock. The same construction occurs at 12:5. There, the woman clothed with the sun gives birth to a child, who will shepherd the nations with an iron rod. The child is clearly Christ. In his letters to the churches (chs. 2–3), it was clear that Christ shepherds his flock in a caring but disciplinary way. It is not coincidental that at both 2:27 and 12:5, the shepherding rule is over the nations. Notably, John's prophecy at 10:11, the same prophecy that he now enacts in 11:1–2, is against the nations. This nuance suggests a shepherding, watchful, though disciplinary role for his prophecy even where the disobedient nations are concerned. The final occurrence of the term "rod" offers confirmation (19:15). The Lamb, having struck down the nations, will shepherd them with a rod of iron. The terminology suggests that the judgment is reconstructive, not punitive.

Like the witnesses in the churches who conquer (2:27) and Christ (12:5; 19:15), John is to prophesy in a way that will shepherd with discipline. Although his measurement will protect, it will also chasten in the same way that Christ's letters promised both protection and judgment. The measurement here, then, is not simply a reward, but another complex stage in John's exhortation to his hearers and readers. They are set apart not so that they can exult in their saved, meaning safe, status but so that they, like John himself, can be directed toward more witnessing (and therefore conquering) behavior. Even the nations are not given up for lost. They, too, are being shepherded—toward repentance.

The object of measurement is the *naos*, the inner temple sanctuary, and two components, the altar and those who worship. The inner temple sanctuary most likely referred to the court of women, the court of the Israelites, the court of the priests, and the highest point, the holy of holies into which only the high priest entered once a year to sacrifice on behalf of the sins of the people. Despite the fact that on every other occasion when he mentions *naos*, John is referring to the heavenly sanctuary, one gathers the sense that he is speaking here of the earthly one (see 3:12; 7:15; 11:19; 14:15, 17; 15:5, 6, 8; 16:1, 17; 21:22). First, he puts himself, a historical being, in direct proximity to it. In his heavenly citations, he relates the infrastructure to resurrected witnesses, angels, or a heavenly voice. Second, in 11:2, the nations will trample the outer part of the temple and will apparently also target the inner sanctuary. Only John's protecting measurement will keep them at bay. The earthbound nations would not have destructive access to the heavenly temple. Third, at 11:19, John clearly puts the heavenly sanctuary in opposition to this one.

John similarly considers the sacrificial altar (or the room in the court of the priests that housed it) that stood in the sanctuary of the Herodian temple (see the comments on 6:9; 8:3, 5), not its heavenly counterpart (Aune 2:606). Although all his other altar references depict heavenly attendees (resurrected souls, 6:9;

angels, 8:3, 5; 9:13; 14:18; 16:7), he puts himself in direct historical relationship to this one. Likewise, though the nations target it, they cannot get at it.

Since John envisions the earthly sanctuary and sacrificial altar, when he speaks of worshipers he has in mind human celebrants. In this narrative setting, these can only be the faithful believers in his seven churches. John's prophetic activity will measure, that is to say, shepherd and protect them.

John writes well after the Roman destruction of the Jerusalem temple, and yet there is every narrative indication that he has in mind here the historical sanctuary. How can he measure what has already been destroyed? The prophecy only works on an imaginative level. John can resurrect the temple by figuratively re-creating it (over and over? note the present tense imperative "arise") in the imaginations of his hearers and readers. Then he can populate it with them as its worshipers. In John's visionary imagination, the sanctuary can become the figurative representation of the people of God. In chapters 2 and 3, he raised that representation through the myth of seven churches that stood for the entire church, that is, the whole people of God. He remakes that figurative move with new casting here.

[2] A contrast is drawn with the figurative outer court. For those familiar with the Herodian temple, this image would most likely bring the court of Gentiles to mind. Because it is not measured, and therefore protected, it is trampled. What does this mean for the people who occupy it? The outer court is, after all, still part of the temple. Believers come to all parts of the temple to worship God. One must conclude, then, that the outer court is also populated by believers.[4] But which believers would be left unprotected?

The easiest answer would be that those in the sanctuary are believers of Jewish origin, while those in the outer precincts are Gentile believers. John, however, makes no such ethnic-religious distinctions anywhere else in the narrative. For him, relationship with God is based on witness, not ethnicity. A better solution can be found in John's narration. The only distinction among believers that John has thus far made (other than between those who do and those who do not witness) occurs at 7:1–8 (cf. 14:1–5) and 7:9–17.

The inner sanctuary and the worshipers who populate it correspond to the invulnerable believers of 7:1–8 and 14:1–5.[5] This company is comprised of

---

4. See Reddish 209. Reddish argues for three possible identifications for what the outer court-yard represents: (1) Christians for whom the time of suffering is redemptive; (2) the church in its engagement with the world; (3) the unbelieving world that will feel the full effect of God's punishment and eschatological woes. Reddish thinks the third is the most likely option. As will soon become clear, I press for something more like his option number 2.

5. Richard writes, "John's prophetic action of protecting the community is not different from God's action of sealing the elect in 7:1–8" (90). See also Aune 2:598–605. But both Reddish (208) and Boring (*Revelation*, 143) see the shielding of the community in 7:1–8 as a shielding from spiritual rather than physical calamity.

both Jewish and Gentile believers (see the comment on 7:4); those in 7:9–17 are also of both Jewish and Gentile pedigree (see the discussion of 7:9–17). These believers in 7:9–17 correspond to the unmeasured and therefore unprotected outer courtyard. It is clear from the narration that they, like the souls of 6:9–11, were trampled and slaughtered. Indeed, the souls in 6:9–11 are probably a subset of this larger group in 7:9–17. The correspondence with John's language of measured and unmeasured here at 11:1–2 works because, while the believers of 7:1–8 are protected from both the physical and spiritual savageries that engulf John's apocalyptic visions, the believers of 7:9–17 are not. Though they are not spared the horror, they are no less faithful believers. Because they are engaged with the world, *in* the world, they share in the fate of the nations, as does John who suffers in exile, even though they suffer for different reasons. They suffer because of their witness. The persecution imposed by the nations elicits the divine anger that erupts as both cosmic and natural disaster. Though the believers are not responsible for this disaster, neither are they raptured out of it. Theirs is a double portion of distress. They are persecuted by the nations who trample them; because they live in the world of those nations, they must also endure the retribution the unjust nations deserve. This is why John figuratively describes them as the temple's unmeasured outer courtyard. They remain part of the community of faith, just as the outer courtyard remains part of the temple. They will not, however, be protected. Like Jesus just after his baptism (Mark 1:12), they are cast directly (*ekballō*) into harm's way.

Why? Their struggle provides an even greater opportunity for witness; they witness to the nations even though the struggles they experience are a direct result of the hostility and injustice those nations impose against their witness. Here John uses the matter of theodicy as a teaching tool. Nonbelievers who see the suffering of the faithful (the unprotected outer courtyard), and who wonder if their God can truly be God, will nonetheless see these believers maintaining their witness to the lordship of that God. After all, God really is in control. Through yet another strategic use of the divine passive formulation *edothē* (it was given), John makes his case. The nations have the power to trample the outer courtyard only because God gives it to them. This knowledge is power. Knowledgeable believers, though physically vulnerable, witness through the horror. Their faith is not based on the historical circumstance of a troubled present, but on trust in the secure future that God promises.

That future will not suffer a long delay. The trampling will last only forty-two months. One-half of seven years indicates a time of transience, not long duration (see the comments on 10:5–6; 12:6, 14; cf. Dan 7:25; 12:7). The fact that John raises the same half-of-seven metaphor for transience when describing the tribulation endured by the people of faith in 12:6, 14 reinforces the contention that here, too, the seer has in mind a temporary tribulation. The people of faith will endure; the destructive force of the nations, powered by Rome, will not.

11:3–13  THE TWO WITNESSES

If vv. 1–2 present John's renewed call to witness through a prophetic sign act, vv. 3–13 contain a renewed call for witness from the believers. It is particularly a message to the unmeasured and therefore unprotected believers of v. 2. These are the believers who engage the world, pay a severe price, and yet are called to maintain their prophetic activity. What John promised in v. 2 he therefore reaffirms in v. 3: the time of such tribulation, though devastating, will be short lived. Endure it. Outlast it. Witness through it. In the two witnesses, John's hearers and readers find the model for such enduring prophetic behavior. Their story is the story of every faithful, unprotected, world-engaging witness.

3 And I will grant authority[a] to my two witnesses to[b] prophesy for 1,260 days, wearing sackcloth. 4 These are the two olive trees and the two lampstands that stand[c] before the Lord of the earth. 5 And if anyone wishes to harm them, fire streams from their mouths[d] and devours their enemies; and if anyone wishes to harm them, he must be killed in this way. 6 They have the authority to shut the sky, so that no rain would fall during the days of their prophecy, and they have authority over the waters to turn them into blood and to strike the earth with every plague whenever they wish. 7 When they have completed their testimony, the beast that rises from the abyss will wage war with them and he will conquer them and he will kill them. 8 And their corpses[e] will lie[f] in the street of the great city, which is prophetically[g] called Sodom and Egypt, where also their Lord was crucified. 9 And members of the peoples and tribes and tongues and nations[h] will see their corpses[i] for three and a half days, and they will not allow their corpses to be placed in a tomb. 10 And the inhabitants of the earth will rejoice over them and celebrate and exchange gifts with one another, because these two prophets had tormented the inhabitants of the earth. 11 But[j] after the three and a half days, the spirit of life from God entered them, and they stood on their feet, and great fear overwhelmed those who saw them. 12 Then they heard a foreboding voice from heaven say to them: "Come up here!" And they ascended into heaven in the cloud, and their enemies saw them. 13 In that hour there was a great earthquake and a tenth of the city fell; seven thousand people were killed in the earthquake, and the rest became terrified and gave glory to the God of heaven.

a. Though the term *exousia* (authority) is not used, its presence is clearly implied (cf. 9:3, and note the mention of *exousia* in 11:6).

b. *Kai* (and) operates here as a consecutive particle (Aune 2:578).

c. John's grammatical infelicity is impossible to miss. He pairs the masculine participle *estōtes* ([that] stand) with two feminine nouns that act as the subject: *elaiai* (olive trees) and *lychniai* (lampstands). No doubt he makes this error because he thinks of the two witnesses, for whom these feminine metaphors are used, as male (i.e., Moses and Elijah).

d. Though the noun is in the singular, John intends that the fire comes from both their mouths.

e. Though he uses a singular noun, he clearly intends to speak of both witnesses. Indeed, many manuscripts ($\mathfrak{P}^{47}$ $\aleph$ 1611 1854 2329 $\mathfrak{M}^A$ latt sy$^{ph}$ [sa bo$^{pt}$]) shift to the plural *ptōmata* (corpses) to correct the grammar. The more difficult singular noun is preferable.

f. Because there is no verb, one that makes sense in the context is supplied.

g. The literal sense is that it is "spiritually" called Sodom and Egypt. This spiritual-metaphorical sense is understood in the larger context to be another instance of prophetic recognition of a truth not seen by all.

h. John has constructed the string of four partitive genitives together so that they function as the subject of the verse.

i. Again, the singular noun refers to both witnesses (cf. v. 8).

j. Another adversative use of the conjunction *kai* (but).


**[3]** Grammatically, John introduces this new section by stating declaratively what he has only alluded to passively before: God is in charge. At 11:1 he made his case with a passive formulation of the verb *didōmi* (to give); he makes it here by appealing to a future formulation of the same verb. The future form *dōsō* (I will grant) indicates that the two witnesses (like John himself: 11:1) are given their task as a result of divine prerogative. It does not matter whether God is speaking directly or speaking through a proxy.

Thematically, John only uses the verb "to prophesy" twice in the entire narrative (10:11; 11:3). He saves it specifically for this context. The witnesses' charge to prophesy is the very same task issued to John in 10:11. As prophets, they are charged to mimic John's witness to the lordship of Christ. That witness marks out the boundaries of their belief, identifying them as part of the Lamb's community. Their identification leaves them vulnerable, like the unprotected outer courtyard of the temple.

John further establishes in vv. 6–7 the synonymous relationship he implies here between witness and prophecy. The prophecy of v. 6 finds content in the witnessing to the lordship of Christ in v. 7. Likewise, the two witnesses of v. 3 are identified as prophets (v. 10). The prophetic role of these two witnesses is, like John's own prophetic role, defined by their testimony to the lordship of Christ. In John's narrative world, one prophesies by testifying. The parallel statements at 19:10 and 22:9 are illustrative. In both cases, John is chastised for bowing down to worship an angelic figure instead of God or the Lamb. In the first case, the divine figure tells John that he must not do that because the divine figure is a fellow servant of John and of John's brothers and sisters who bear witness to Jesus. In the latter case, the divine figure tells John the same thing.

This time, however, instead of pointing redundantly to John's brothers and sisters, the witnesses, he identifies them as prophets. He means the same brothers and sisters. As witnesses, they are prophets. As prophets, they testify. Since such testimony in a context so resistant to it will inevitably lead to persecution, it is perhaps encouraging to know that one need only endure that persecution for a temporary period of 1,260 days, the same length of time the believers symbolized by the outer courtyard will be persecuted (11:2, 3; 12:6, 14; 13:5).

In symbolizing both his own prophetic work and the prophetic witness of the church, John has made the odd choice of narrating two witnesses. Commentators have connected the two with a range of prophetic figures. To be sure, the priestly and Davidic lay messiahs of Zech 3–4 and 6:9–14 are in the back of his mind. Yet in view of John's declaration that the two witnesses can redeploy plagues associated with Moses and Elijah (Rev 11:6), those two prophets are obviously also important for his presentation. Other commentators offer Elijah and Jeremiah, Peter and Paul, Jesus and John the Baptist, the Old Testament and the New, and so forth. Though he is certainly working from a Moses and Elijah connection, John is also thinking broadly. According to Luke 10:1, when Jesus sends his disciples out to witness to his gospel message, he dispatches them in teams of two. Luke 10:19 clarifies that Jesus' teams are as protected from harm as John's two witnesses initially are here (see Schüssler Fiorenza, *Vision of a Just World*, 78). John 8:17 is equally illustrative. Jesus there appeals to the Jewish tradition that required two corroborating witnesses before any testimony was to be considered valid (see Num 35:30; Deut 19:15).[6] The number of witnesses in Rev 11 thus validates the testimony of their prophetic activity: Christ is Lord.

The negative response to that testimony heightens the connection between the work of these two witnesses and the prophetic work of the now-exiled John. When they prophesy/testify, two results occur: protection and destruction. They are protected (measured) by God so that they can finish their prophecy (11:7). Only then is their destruction allowed. In other words, they play both the measured and unmeasured roles from 11:1–2 at different stages in their prophetic-witnessing tour. The narrative point?

The sackcloth hints at the two witnesses' prophetic intent. John has already used sackcloth to symbolize God's judgment (see the comments on 6:5, 12). Here, too, judgment is an important theme. The plagues directed by the two witnesses (vv. 5–6) and the retribution exacted by God for their deaths (v. 13) are acts of judgment. So are the events of woe that accompany the blowing of the seventh trumpet (vv. 15–19). In this immediate context, then, their prophecy,

---

6. Cf. Beale (575): "The number two is from the OT law requiring at least two witnesses as a just basis for judging an offense against the law (Num. 35:30; Deut. 17:6; 19:15). The legal principle is continued in the NT on the basis of Deut. 19:15 (cf. Matt. 18:16; Luke 10:1–24, where there are thirty-five groups of two witnesses each; John 8:17; 2 Cor. 13:1; 1 Tim. 5:19; Heb. 10:28). Therefore, the emphasis is on a just or valid legal witness."

cloaked as it is in the attire of sackcloth, is a word of judgment. Bauckham is right to point out, however, that there is also a hint of the theme of repentance.[7] In the Hebrew tradition, the wearing of sackcloth could signify repentance.[8] In Matt 11:21 and Luke 10:13, sackcloth ties in directly with repentant mourning. It seems to do so in the narrative context in Revelation as well. Through the use of the shepherding "rod" imagery (see the discussion of 11:1), John describes his own work as that of harsh but correcting rebuke. The witnesses' work acts much like an extension of that figurative iron rod. Their prophetic testimony is by its very nature as much an invitation to belief as it is a condemnation of the opposing belief in the lordship of Rome. Their prophetic activity, then, like a shepherd's firmly applied staff, not only strikes a blow of judgment against reckless wandering (toward belief in and loyalty to the lordship of Rome) but also simultaneously provokes redirection.

[4] John narrates the close connection between these two witnesses and Christ by describing them as standing before the Lord of the earth (cf. Zech 4:14).[9] In introducing them, he applies definite articles. These are *the* two olive trees and *the* two lampstands. He clearly expects familiarity from his readers as he builds from the narrative scenario of Zech 4, particularly vv. 2–3 and 11–14. There, two anointed ones stand before the Lord of the whole earth as two olive trees positioned at the left and right of a golden lampstand. If the lampstand represents the destroyed Solomonic temple (cf. Zech 1:16), then the two olive trees represent the priestly (Joshua) and Davidic (Zerubbabel) messianic hopefuls (cf. Zech 3:8) who would guide the temple's postexilic reconstruction and, further, the apocalyptic restoration of the entire people. It is fascinating that God initiates this restoration by appointing an angel to measure and thus protect Jerusalem from hostile, satanic intent (Zech 2–3), just as in Rev 11:1–2 John measures and thereby protects.

John keeps the metaphors but mixes them. First, there is no need to identify the temple as a lampstand since no temple will exist (21:22). Second, he alternately envisions the anointed two as either olive trees *or* lampstands. Their functions are also different. They are no longer messianic figures who will usher in God's reign; the Lamb plays that role in the Apocalypse. They operate instead as exemplary witnesses who, like John, model the prophetic practice that John desperately exhorts from his church(es).

---

7. Bauckham 278.

8. Beale comments, "The OT refers to sackcloth primarily with a view to mourning over judgment, though sometimes repentance is also in mind; 27 of about 42 OT occurrences refer only to mourning, and an additional 13 refer to mourning together with repentance" (576). Beale, however, does not think the symbolism has anything to do with repentance in Rev 11:3.

9. According to Beale, "In Jewish writings 'standing before the Lord' connoted an eternally secure relationship of the faithful with God" (576). He points to *Jub.* 30.18–20; 1QH 4[12].21; 18.24–29 [21.9–14].

[5] The work of these witnesses is so important that God will take extreme measures to ensure its execution. The use of fire as the witnesses' weapon is instructive. John uses fire as a metaphor for God's Spirit (4:5; cf. 2 Kgs 1:10). Their weapon, in other words, is of God. More often, though, fire is described as a part of the heavenly armament that God deploys as a weapon of judgment (Rev 1:14; 2:18; 3:18; 8:5–8; 9:17–18; 14:10, 18; 16:8; 18:8; 19:12, 20; 20:9–10, 14–15; 21:8; cf. 2 Sam 22:9; Ps 97:3; Jer 5:14; *4 Ezra* 13.25–38). Even when John associates fire with the dragon (13:13) or forces of evil (17:16), the connection is meant to showcase their desperate attempt to mimic God's power. At a climactic moment, fire comes down from heaven to destroy the satanic forces trying to overthrow God's people (20:9), just as here fire issues from the mouths of the two witnesses to defeat the same surreptitious agenda. It is no accident that the fire, like their testimony, comes from the orifice of speech. Their testimony is the ultimate weapon; it not only declares Christ's lordship but obliterates (*katesthiō*) those who oppose it and, in so doing, establishes it (cf. 12:11). In this way, too, the witnesses, and through them the church, are like Christ. God's power operates as a testimony so forceful that it issues from Christ's mouth as a judging, obliterating sword (1:16; 2:16; 19:15, 21). Whether John uses the metaphor of sword or fire, his poetic appeal to the mouth and the testimony that issues from it to envision, establish, and protect the apocalyptic community suggests that he believes the witnesses (i.e., the church) are most in sync with the victorious and transformative power of God when they proclaim the lordship of Christ. The church can best protect itself from the persecutions inflicted against it not by hiding from or accommodating to the satanic forces that claim to control the world, but by directly engaging those forces with the opposing testimony that Christ is Lord. The offense of that witness is the church's best defense.

In the second half of the verse, John affirms his position by redundantly declaring that anyone who wishes to harm the two witnesses before they conclude their objective (cf. the use of *teleō* in v. 7a) *must* die. In this world of apocalyptic mortal combat, either God's forces (the witnesses, i.e., the church) or Satan's forces (Rome) will win. Since there is no conceivable compromise, there can also be no peace. Because for these witnesses identity and work are synonymous, they *must* witness. The only way to stop them is to destroy them (*adikeō*). To prevent that destruction from happening, the opposition *must* itself be destroyed.

[6] The plagues connect the two witnesses with Moses and Elijah. The only nuance is that "the powers of both Moses and Elijah are attributed to *both* the two witnesses equally, and not divided among them. They are identical prophetic twins" (Beale 575). Notably, they also represent the very two prophetic figures who were expected to usher in the eschatological age. By linking Moses and Elijah with the church through the metaphor of the two wit-

nesses, John implies yet again that through its witness the church helps to usher in God's coming reign (cf. 12:11).[10]

Like Elijah, who shut the sky for three years (1 Kgs 17–18), the two witnesses have the power to bring drought for a particular period, in this case the time of their prophecy. Like Moses, they have the ability to turn water into blood and strike the earth with plague. John's description yields several key points. First, his description of their work as prophecy highlights yet again the fact that John holds witness and prophecy to be synonymous (cf. 11:7). A prophet is one who witnesses to the lordship of Christ. Second, the connection between prophecy and the phenomena of drought, blood, and plague is an explicit indication that the witness to Christ's lordship brings judgment upon those who testify to the lordship of Rome. Picking up on broader biblical allusions to drought (Deut 11:16–17; cf. Luke 4:25; Jas 5:17), water transformed into blood (Exod 7:17–25), and plague (1 Sam 4:8), John narrates blood (Rev 6:12; 8:7, 8; 16:3–4) and plague (9:18, 20; 15:1, 6, 8; 16:9, 21; 18:4, 8; 21:9; 22:18) as judgment imagery. Third, because the work of these two witnesses is a work of prophecy that follows and emulates John's own prophetic endeavors (11:1–2), one might reasonably understand the drought, blood, and plagues to be an extension of the shepherding rod of iron that intended both the disciplining and the redirection of the human flock (see the discussion of 11:1). Indeed, biblical drought allusions also entertain a theme of repentance. Though the promise of drought at Deut 11:16–17 is a judgment warning, it is also a threat whose ultimate goal is to turn the people back to God. Moreover, when the Epistle of James addresses drought, the climactic stress falls upon the theme of repentance (5:17, 19–20). So also, Exod 7 contains the commonsense expectation that even Pharaoh himself, having seen the Nile bloodied, would have to concur with the testimony that God is Lord. Like Moses and Elijah, then, the two witnesses (i.e., the church) use their prophecy as a weapon (rod) that will simultaneously judge and redirect, even if the primary weighting is toward judgment.

[7] Bad times are coming, but not until the two witnesses complete their work. Indeed, John's description of their prophecy as *martyria* (witness) is a hint that the bad times will ultimately be overturned. To be sure, *martyria* is inextricably linked with disaster. At 1:9, Christ is executed (cf. 5:6) and John is exiled because of it. At 6:9, resurrected souls are executed because of it. Though the murder of the two witnesses occurs after they finish their testimony, the causal link between that testimony and their murder is just as clear. This is the

---

10. Boring offers a similar interpretation: "Early Christianity had to come to terms with the Jewish view that the eschatological times could not dawn until Moses and/or Elijah had returned, and did so in a variety of ways (Mark 9:2–13; Luke 1:15–17; 4:25–26; 7:11–17). *John meets this condition by casting the faithful church in the role of Elijah and Moses*" (*Revelation*, 146, emphasis orig.).

last time, however, that John uses witness in such a disquieting way. In its very next use *martyria* is a conquest tool (12:11), and 20:4 offers climactic affirmation.[11] There, the same *martyria* that brought destruction also ensures a victorious reign with Christ. John's point is one of encouragement. Though witnessing may well bring immediate persecution, it will, as vv. 11–13 make clear, yield an ultimate, eschatological victory. The appeal, therefore, is to keep witnessing despite the temporary cost.

Even this short-term bestial conquest—as opposed to the bestial persecution that is ongoing even as he speaks—will not be allowed to occur until the work of witness is complete (*teleō*; see the discussion of *edothē* at 6:1–8; 7:2).[12] John is narrating the interlude between the sixth and seventh trumpets. The apocalyptic end point has not yet arrived. Having done their victorious work, having helped to usher in God's victory (12:11), the witnesses will see the beast resurface just before the final victory. John describes this resurfacing as a bestial rising up (*anabainō*) from the abyss. The rising, completion, and fire imagery connect this verse with the apocalyptic combat imagery in chapter 20. There it is only after the victorious reign of God is finished (*teleō*) that the dragon is given its due (20:7). At 20:9, John portrays the vindictive movement of the bestial, satanic force as a conquest-minded rising up (*anabainō*). How are these forces stopped in chapter 20? Fire. A historical weapon blazing as an unrelenting testimony out of the mouth of the two witnesses in 11:5 transforms into the ultimate eschatological weapon when deployed from heaven in 20:9. The point is reaffirmed: what the witnesses (i.e., the church) do historically is mimicked and supported by God eschatologically. Ultimate victory, even during this premonition of current defeat, is assured.

The language of the abyss taints the beast with an evil, draconian sensibility (see 9:1, 2, 11; 20:1, 3). At 17:8, John reaffirms this destructive rising (*anabainō*), but immediately consoles his hearers and readers with his suspicion that any such rising will be short lived; the beast rises to its destruction. Just as helpful is the close identification between the dragon and the beast that John draws at 17:8. While he is clearly speaking about the beast, the language he uses—"it was and is not and is to come"—is the kind of language he reserves for God (see the comments on 1:4, 8). In his apocalyptic war of images, John typically pits God language against dragon language since, mythologically speaking at least, these are the two supernatural and therefore best-matched combatants. His use of imagery may seem more appropriate to the dragon, for his narration of the beast suggests a close identity between the two. There is also a similarity in mission: the beast's work is authorized by the dragon (13:4).

---

11. The ensuing use of *martyria* in 12:17 describes a time prior to the moment envisioned at 12:11; yet 19:10 is a descriptive use unrelated to this particular thematic concern.

12. Note the similar emphasis at 10:7; 15:1, 8; 17:17; 20:3, 5, 7.

Like the dragon, the beast is consigned to and must arise from the abyss (see 20:1, 3). For John's narrative purposes, then, the dragon and the beast are functionally synonymous. Thus, when at 20:7 John narrates yet another resurfacing as the escape of the dragon from the pit and the unleashing of its fury against the church, he is reimaging the rising of the beast in chapter 11.

Beast is an apocalyptic cipher for the historical Rome. Using the same vocabulary that is so important in 11:7, John declares in 13:7 that the beast who comes from across the sea (13:1; cf. Dan 7:3) was allowed to make (*poieō*) war (*polemos*) against believers and conquer (*nikaō*) them (cf. Dan 7:21). At Rev 17:14 this same beast (note the ten horns: 13:1; 17:3, 7, 12, 16; seven heads: 13:1; 17:7, 9; and link to waters/sea: 13:1; 17:15) even has the audacity to make war (*polemeō*) directly against the Lamb. The linguistic correspondence is so close that it can hardly be unintentional. Rome, the city on seven hills (17:9) that comes from across the sea, becomes the historical symbol for the mythical abyss (see the discussion of 4:6–8) as it makes war against—that is, persecutes—the believing Asia Minor churches for testifying to the lordship of Jesus Christ (see the comment on 13:1–3). The "war" is Rome's reaction to and programming against the testimony to Christ's lordship that John exhorts from his churches. Rome demands worship of its lordship instead (20:4). With the military and police power of the imperial state behind it, bestial Rome will win the lordship campaign, at least in the short term (vv. 7–10; cf. Dan 7:21).

One final note about the identity of the beast: Though "beast" has not appeared before as a mythical figure in the Apocalypse,[13] John's use of the article ("*the* beast") suggests that his readers are narratively familiar with it. At 13:1, however, he does not employ the article. The depiction in chapter 13 suggests that readers have not yet been introduced to the beast when, in fact, that introduction occurs already in 11:7. This apparent discrepancy is resolved when one understands how John has designed the actual visionary presentation. Chapters 12 and 13 are part of a narrative flashback that sets the scene and motivation for everything that occurs prior to the opening of the book. In other words, although chapters 12 and 13 follow chapter 11 in the narrative, they actually precede chapter 11 in the story that John's visions are relating (In the introduction to 12:1–17, see the discussion of the literary technique of time displacement in the Apocalypse). Chapter 13, then, is in a real sense the introduction of the beast. In chapter 11, using the metaphor of the two witnesses, John links the hostility of that beast to the witnessing of the church and explains why the beast's apparent success is in reality the prelude to God's ultimate victory. This is why the conflict between the two witnesses and the beast is envisioned as the moment immediately before the climactic blowing of the seventh and final trumpet.

---

13. In 6:8 the term applies to actual wild beasts.

**[8]** Having been conquered and killed, the corpses of the two witnesses (i.e., the executed believers of the testifying church) lie in the street of the great city. It is strange that John literally speaks of a single corpse (*ptōma*) when he is referring to two dead witnesses. The confusion most likely results because the two witnesses act symbolically for the one church. It is the witnessing church's suffering and destruction that he really has in mind. Because John refers to the resting place of the corpse with a definite article, he probably believes that his hearers and readers knew precisely which street was "the street" in question. The ultimate scorn for the two witnesses can be inferred from the fact that no one came forward to bury them.[14]

Because John often refers to Rome as the great city (16:19; 17:18; 18:10, 16, 18, 19, 21) and to Jerusalem as the beloved or holy city (11:2; 20:9; 21:2, 10, 14–16, 18–19, 21, 23; 22:14, 19), initially there is some question as to which "great" city he envisions. Here, the great city is Jerusalem, as John indicates when he identifies it as the city where the Lord of the two witnesses was crucified. The identification reinforces the relationship that John elsewhere establishes between the suffering of Christ and the suffering of believers by describing both their ordeals as a slaughtering (5:6, 9, 12; 6:9; 13:8; 18:24). Now, both the Lord and the church (i.e., the two witnesses) suffer and die in the same great city. Perhaps John's literary bridge was Ps 79:2–3, which identifies Jerusalem as the city where the servants of God were killed and their corpses lay unburied on the streets. John's references to Sodom and Egypt are also instructive. Egypt maintained a traditional image as a place of resistance to God. Though the seer refers to Sodom only here, he probably has in mind Old Testament texts where a disobedient Jerusalem is mentioned in municipal relationship to that prototypically evil city (Isa 1:9–10; Jer 23:14; Ezek 16:2, 46, 49).

John wishes to make the point that not even in the holy city (cf. 11:1–2) will someone stand up for those who have courageously borne witness that Christ is Lord. This tragic turn of narrative events mirrors the historical concern John conveys in his letters to the seven churches. He worries that believers have so accommodated themselves to the styles and expectations of Greco-Roman life that they not only are afraid to witness, but even refuse to offer assistance or comfort to those who do.

**[9]** Through the metaphor of three and a half days (cf. 11:2–3), John implies that the time of disgrace for the witnesses will be brief. He reinforces the intensity of the disgrace with his reminder that their corpses (this time, at least in the second half of the verse, he remembers that there are two witnesses) lie in the

---

14. Beale observes that "nonburial was an indignity in the biblical world" (590) and points to 1 Sam 17:44, 46; 2 Kgs 9:10; Ps 79:1–5; Isa 14:19–20; Jer 8:1–2; 9:22; 16:4–6; 22:19; Tob 2:3–8; *Pss. Sol.* 2.30–31 [26–27]; *Sib. Or.* 3.634–46; *Jub.* 23.23; Josephus, *J.W.* 3.376–78, 380–84; 4:314–18; 5.33; Philo, *Joseph* 25.

streets unburied. He then adds a subtle nuance. The believers in the city, at least some of them, apparently want to give the corpses a proper burial. The narration now clarifies that members of the peoples, tribes, tongues, and nations will not allow proper burial. The peoples, tribes, tongues, and nations are the very ones against whom John was directed to prophesy in the recommissioning that ended chapter 10 (10:11) and opened chapter 11 (11:1–2). They are hostile to the work of prophetic witness. Some believers may want to assist either in the witnessing or in the care of those who do so, but fear of this opposition has paralyzed them.

**[10–11]** John reconfirms the opposition as the inhabitants of the earth. This is a term he consistently applies to those who reject the testimony to Christ's lordship and persecute persons who maintain it (6:10; 8:13; 11:10; 13:8, 12, 14; 17:2, 8). It is therefore used here as a synonym for the hostile peoples, tribes, tongues, and nations of v. 9.

Restoration begins with resurrection. In this case, John does not want to rely upon a divine passive to imply God's control (see the discussion of *edothē*, "it was given," at 6:1–8; 7:2); he chooses an active verb instead (*eisēlthen*, entered) to describe the entrance of God's spirit/breath of life into the dead witnesses to revive them. God's action has sanctioned their testimony even as it has rejuvenated them; God and Christ are indeed Lord.

God and Christ control even the experience of death. For their followers, its duration will not be long. The two witnesses are down for only three and a half days before they are raised to an eternal eschatological relationship with God (v. 12; on three and a half as a number symbolic of transience, see 11:2–3; 12:6, 14; 13:5).

They were raised by a spirit of life that came from God. It is notable that John does not give "spirit" a definite article here. When he intends to speak of the Spirit(s) of God, he consistently employs the article (1:4; 2:7, 11, 17, 29; 3:1, 6, 13, 22; 4:5; 5:6; 14:13; 22:17). To be sure, there are prominent instances where John alludes to the Spirit of God without using the article (1:10; 4:2; 17:3; 21:10). In each of these cases, however, he speaks more about a human condition—being "in the spirit"—than about the divine person. It is likely that in 11:11, too, he is speaking less directly about the person of God's Spirit than about a particular quality, the empowering force of that Spirit. The language is metaphorical; it denotes the breath of God that would be very much like the breath that animates human life in the Genesis accounts (1:30; 2:7; 6:17; 7:15, 22) and resurrects life in Ezekiel (37:5, 10). Oddly, the bestial forces also deploy a breath of life. At Rev 13:15 the beast from the land breathes into the image of the beast from the sea so that it can come to life. John is suggesting that the Roman and local officials in Asia Minor (the beast from the land) breathe life into the worship of the imperial cult. In this way, the beast from the land mimics the power of God so as to animate those to whom it wishes to peddle its interests and proclaim its name.

Like the once-dry bones of Ezek 37, the spirit-raised witnesses stand on their feet. "Standing" for John has theological implications. It is a metaphor for resistance (see the comment on 5:6). Though they were knocked down even to death, the witnesses remain defiant about the lordship of Christ.

"Fear" is the final important component of the verse. The fear refers back to the peoples, tribes, tongues, and nations (v. 9), who are then described as the inhabitants of the earth (v. 10), and who celebrate the deaths of the two witnesses for three and a half days. In Old Testament accounts fear falls upon the enemies of God's people when God moves to vindicate the people (see Exod 15:16; Ps 105:38). This is the kind of fear that does not lead to faith but simply springs from acute alarm.[15] In this case, the fear arises as a result of (1) the resurrection of the two witnesses, (2) the knowledge that their God is the agent of this resurrection and will avenge the death that made it necessary, and (3) realization that the defiant message of Christ's lordship was resurrected with them.

[12] The fear generated in v. 11 is compounded when the enemies of God's people witness their elevation on "the cloud" into heaven. In the Apocalypse, cloud conveyance is reserved for Christ (1:7), a mighty angel (10:1), and a child of humanity (14:14–16).[16] The presence of the definite article here indicates that this is the same cloud John saw draped around the mighty angel at 10:1. The mechanism that brought the angel down now carries the witnesses up. The visual corroborates John's claim of vindication. The foreboding audio sounds the tone of judgment (see the discussion of "great voice" at 7:2). Cosmic justice is about to be enacted.

Prior to the commencement of judgment, the foreboding voice gives the two witnesses the same command ("Come up here") that was given in the singular to John when he was invited to enter the heavenly throne room (4:1). In fact, the only two places where the verb *anabainō* (Come up) is used in the imperative in the Apocalypse are 4:1 and 11:12. In 4:1 it was apparently Christ's own voice that summoned John; it was identified as a voice like a trumpet (cf. 1:10–13). Christ invited John into God's eschatological presence. Is John implying that Christ is also personally inviting the two witnesses, and through them, the faithful, witnessing church? To be sure. As for John, so for the church: while faithful witness to Christ's lordship will provoke hostility from bestial

---

15. Aune explains that "the phrase 'great fear fell on them,' is a Semitic expression for a collective response of awe, either because the Israelites or Jews seem invincible (Exod 15:16; Deut 11:25; Esth 8:17; 9:2; 1 Macc 3:25; 7:18; 2 Macc 12:22) or as a reaction to a display of supernatural power (2 Macc 3:24; Luke 1:12, 65; Acts 5:5; 19:17)" (2:624).

16. See also 2 Kgs 2:11; Dan 7:13 and the interpretations or imitations of Dan 7:13 in Matt 24:30; 26:64; Mark 13:26; 14:62; Luke 21:27; 24:51; Acts 1:9. Also note 1 Thess 4:17, where at the moment of God's consummation of the divine reign, all who are faithful will be caught up in the clouds to meet the Lord.

human powers, it will guarantee direct access to God. Indeed, Christ himself will call you up! *That* is motivation.

[13] An implicit summons to repentance resurfaces in the final act of divine judgment against the great city and the inhabitants of the earth who populate it. When John uses the language of "hour," he intends the imminent arrival of God's judgment (3:3, 10; 9:15; 14:7, 15; 18:10, 17, 19). Of particular note are 14:7 and 14:12, where a voice speaks in a foreboding voice, as one does also in 11:12, about the coming of God's judgment. In the three occurrences of the term in chapter 18, one hour is all the time necessary for the destruction of the great city of Babylon.

This particular moment of judgment, which anticipates the consummate moment of judgment that will come with the imminent blowing of the seventh trumpet (11:15–19), begins with an earthquake. As part of a theophany package (6:12; 8:5; 11:19; 16:18), Revelation's earthquakes signal both the presence of God and the reality of judgment, which often attends that presence. In making this connection between the quake and judgment, John follows in the theological footsteps of Ezekiel (38:19–23). It is especially interesting that John has crafted the scenario so that in both seals and trumpets episodes, the initial earthquakes at the penultimate stage of judgment (i.e., the sixth seal, 6:12; the sixth trumpet, 11:13) act as a premonition of the fuller slate of theophanic events that will occur with another earthquake at the seventh and ultimate stage of judgment (8:5; 11:19). Richard is right to point out that in seeing the metaphorical connection to judgment, we should also not miss the social and political connotations that bind earthquake and witness language together: "As in all apocalyptic literature, the cosmic earthquake is mythical and symbolic in nature. It represents the disturbance and historical subversion brought about by the testimony of the martyrs and prophets. . . . The martyrs bring about true social, political, spiritual, and ecclesiological earthquakes at the heart of empires" (Richard 92).

This penultimate stage of judgment also includes the destruction of a tenth of the city of Jerusalem (see the discussion of v. 8). This physical decimation results in the killing of seven thousand people. The number "seven" surely figures rhetorically as a symbol of completion. The repetition of the verb *apokteinō* (to kill) is intentional. The beast has killed the two witnesses, who represent the whole church (v. 7). Now a complementary number of named souls who live in loyalty to that beast and its declaration of lordship will be killed in judgment for that earlier homicide.

John seems more interested, though, in those who are not killed. They respond in fear. John has already established that fear need not have anything to do with repentance. In v. 11, the human associates of the beast are terrified when they witness the resurrection of the two witnesses. But this fear has no positive value; it is merely terror. Something happens, however, in the intervening moments. The beast's associates observe both the elevation of the two witnesses on the cloud into heaven (v. 12) and the theophany and destruction that follow (v. 13a). It is not coincidental that fear is accompanied this time by glorification not of the beast but of the God who resides in heaven. There is every indication that for John this glorification amounts to repentance.

No doubt John is aware that there are times in the tradition when fear of God's presence can produce something more positive than awe, such as repentance or faith (cf. Gen 15:12). Indeed, the formulation "give glory to God" has a traditional association with repentance and conversion.[17] With obvious literary links to chapter 11, Rev 14:6–7 narrates an angel flying through midheaven with the obvious intent of eliciting repentance. Here, at the critical judgment hour, the same opportunity for repentance opens up for the members of every nation and tribe and language and people.

John has hinted at the possibility of repentance throughout chapter 11 (see the comments on 11:1, 3, 6). More broadly, he has declared all along, in the critical ethical chapters containing the letters to the seven churches (2:1–3:22) and at other key narrative moments, that God expects repentance not only from the faithful (2:5; 3:3, 19; see esp. the discussion of 3:7–13), but also from notable recalcitrants like Jezebel (2:21; see the comment on 9:20–21; cf. 14:6–7; 16:9, 11). Unfortunately, sometimes it takes an earthquake, massive destruction, and unimaginable death to bring it about. When repentance does occur, however, it brings fulfillment to the prophetic charge of 10:11. Prophetic witness brings not only judgment but also repentance. That is the good news.[18]

### 11:14 A TRANSITION

14 The second woe has happened; behold, the third woe is coming soon.

[14] Revelation 8:13 initiated the woe sequence. Verse 14 is a transitional verse, completing the narration of the second woe and inaugurating the story line of the third. The first woe was associated with the blowing of the fifth trumpet (9:1–12). The second woe is associated with the blowing of the sixth trum-

---

17. On this response of glorifying God, Aune observes: "This is somewhat surprising, however, since it is the only instance in Revelation of people turning to the true God as a result of a punitive miracle. Yet there is strong evidence that διδόναι δόξαν τῷ Θεῷ is an idiom for *conversion*" (2:628–29). As comparative texts, Aune points to Dan 4:34 LXX, where the conversion of Nebuchadnezzar is described as giving God glory, as well as 1 Esd 9:8; Acts 13:48; Herm. *Sim.* 6.3.6; 8.6.3.

18. Cf. Schüssler Fiorenza: "It is crucial to recognize that Revelation's rhetoric of judgment expresses hope for the conversion of nine-tenths of the nations in response to Christian witness and preaching. Otherwise, one will not understand that the author advocates a theology of justice rather than a theology of hate and resentment" (*Vision of a Just World*, 79).

pet (9:13–11:13). Though it is never actually narrated, the third woe appears to accompany the blowing of the seventh and final trumpet (11:15–19). The language of woe highlights the emphasis on judgment that has been significant throughout the trumpet narration.

11:15–19 THE SEVENTH TRUMPET AND THE FOURTH ANTIPHONAL HYMN

Two observations highlight any discussion of 11:15–19. First, it appears that although v. 14 announces the coming of the third woe, the woe itself never appears. Verses 15–19 instead contain for the most part (and this is the second observation) an antiphonal hymn of praise (see the excursus on "Hymns of Revelation" after ch. 4). For this reason, some commentators argue that the third woe should actually be found elsewhere in the book, perhaps in chapters 15 and 16, which recount the catastrophes associated with the pouring out of the seven bowls. Because I see the bowls as a recapitulation of the seals and trumpets in another guise (see the "apocalyptic three-ring circus" in the introduction to 6:1–8:1), I maintain that chapters 15 and 16 reprise rather than conclude the judgment themes contained in the trumpet scenes. Chapters 12 and 13 follow chapter 11 in the narrative sequence, yet they actually represent flashbacks, recounting circumstances that took place before the events narrated in the seven trumpets. Therefore, they also cannot be the narration of the seventh and final woe. The seventh woe is located instead right here in vv. 15–19. The celebration contained in the antiphonal hymn of praise is merely the flip side of the judgment. What those opposing God (i.e., the beast, v. 7; the peoples, tribes, tongues, and nations/inhabitants of the earth, vv. 9, 10) experience as judgment, those faithfully following God experience as joy. Since vv. 15–19 represent the final movement in God's eschatological act of judgment (as did the narration of the seventh seal), praise is an appropriate response.

15 And the seventh angel blew his trumpet; there were foreboding voices from heaven, saying:

"The kingdom of the world has become the kingdom of our Lord
and of his Messiah,
and he will rule forever and ever."

16 And the twenty-four elders who are seated before God on their thrones fell on their faces and worshiped God, 17 saying:

"We give you thanks, Lord God Almighty,
who are and who were,
because you have taken great power
and begun to rule.[a]

18 The nations raged, but[b] your wrath has come, and the time for the dead
to be judged, and to give the reward to your servants, the prophets, and
to the saints and those who fear your name, the small and the great, and
to destroy those who destroy the earth." 19 And the temple of God which
is in heaven was opened and the ark of his covenant was seen in his temple, and there were flashes of lightning and rumblings and peals of thunder and an earthquake and great hail.

a. The aorist tense has an ingressive nuance here: "have . . . *begun* to rule."
b. An adversative use of *kai*: "but."

[15] When the seventh angel sounds his trumpet, a chorus of "foreboding
voices" breaks out in heaven. If the presence of a single foreboding voice was
an omen of judgment (see the comments on 7:2; 11:12), the increased volume
from multiple foreboding voices must quantitatively heighten the perceived
impact of the imminent reckoning.

If it has not been clear before, John clarifies it now: the seventh trumpet blast
inaugurates the reign of God and Christ. Connected as it is with the foreboding
voices and the language of woe, it is a rule built upon the premise and expectation of judgment/justice. The lordship to which the witnesses testified has
become reality. The prophecy of Dan 7:14 that all peoples, nations, and languages would serve God comes to fruition now, as the remnant of peoples,
tribes, tongues, and nations, having glorified God and repented (Rev 11:13),
find themselves a party to the realization of the divine reign where that service
will endure forever (cf. Ps 10:16; Dan 2:44). If the scenario that plays itself out
in chapter 11 is to be taken seriously, even those who were among the ones
mocking the two witnesses (i.e., the church) have an opportunity to participate
in this rule.

[16–17] The antiphonal response to the declaration by the foreboding voices
that the reign of God has arrived comes from the twenty-four elders on their
twenty-four thrones (see the discussion of 4:4). Repeating an earlier act of gen-
uflection, they fall on their knees and worship in response to the good news they
hear (see the comment on 7:9–11, esp. at v. 11). Falling to one's knees is a formulaic posture of worship for both John (1:17; 4:10; 19:10; 22:8) and the elders
(5:8, 14; 19:4).

John identifies the hymn as one of thanksgiving (v. 17). Here, for the only
time in his work, he deploys the verb *eucharisteō* (to give thanks).[19] The elders
declare the reason for their praise with a litany of key theological titles that have
been used before in anticipation of God's rule but now signal its triumph. The
Lord God is first of all *ho pantokratōr*, "the Almighty" (cf. LXX: 2 Sam 7:8; Amos

19. John uses the noun form *eucharistia* (thanks) at 4:9 and 7:12.

3:13; 4:13). In the two occurrences prior to this one (Rev 1:8; 4:8), "Almighty" was also packaged with the descriptive title "the one who is and who was and who is to come." In 4:8, the packaging occurs, as it does here, in a hymnic context. In both the previous and the ensuing uses of the title, John offers a reason why it is an appropriate designation for God. Status as almighty is connected with God's role as creator (4:8), ruler (1:8; 19:6; 21:22), and judge (15:3; 16:7, 14; 19:15).

The Almighty One is not bound by time but transcends it; this is highlighted through the designation "the one who is and who was" (here, "[you] who are and who were"). Heretofore, the title has always had a threefold formulation, "the one who is and who was and who is to come" (see the comments on 1:4, 8; 4:8). John even applies a similar formulation to the beast; it portrays the beast's pitiful, failing attempt to mimic God's transcendence of time (17:8). Though negative, even that threefold formulation has a concluding future premonition: "about to rise." John drops the future sensibility here and in subsequent citations that relate to God (16:5), however, because it is no longer applicable. According to the praise song of 11:15, the God who was (recognized as ruler of all) now is (recognized as Lord of all). The revelation has been realized. John, therefore, appropriately changes the titular designation. In place of the phrase "who is to come," he adds an entire clause, "because you have taken great power and begun to rule." In other hymns, too, John uses comparable clauses to explain why praise for God is appropriate (4:11; 5:9; 12:10). The perfect-tense verb formulation, "you have taken," signals both the accomplishment and the expected long-term endurance of the powerful reign God has accomplished. The aorist verb for rule operates with the controlling perfect "[you] have taken" in an ingressive grammatical sense ("[have] begun to reign") that agrees with the narrative assessment of v. 15: the rule is under way, but it is only just under way. It has just begun. In this sense, 11:17 has close affinity with 19:6. In that hymn, too, the worship song, employing a similar *hoti* (because) clause, declares that the Almighty has begun to rule and is therefore worthy of praise.

[18] The twenty-four elders are the only ones to respond positively to the news of God's inaugurated reign. The nations also respond, not with praise but with rage. The allusion to Ps 99:1 (98:1 LXX) could hardly be clearer. In the psalm, using an aorist formulation of *basileuō* (to rule) similar to the one used in Rev 11:17, the writer declares that the people rage in retaliation. There is a similar pattern in Exod 15:14; although the verb "rule" is not used, the context indicates that God's rule, through the defeat of Pharaoh's army, elicits rage among the nations.

God's response to the nations' rage is divine wrath. Every time John uses the term "wrath" in his work, it harbors this thematic sense of judgment (6:16–17; 14:10; 16:19; 19:15). John sees it as an appropriate instance of *lex talionis*: the punishment fits the crime (Beale 615).

The connection between God's wrath and judgment is made evident in the first of the three stanzas that follow the declaration that the wrath has come. Each of them is controlled by an infinitive that operates from the primary verb *ēlthen* (came). When God's wrath came, it spawned a new season: a time to be judged, to give reward, and to destroy. The judgment of the dead refers to those who have died the first, physical, mortal death, but who await a ruling regarding the second death (cf. Dan 12:2). All humans are mortal and therefore all will experience the first death. Even the two witnesses experienced it (Rev 11:7). While that death may be punishing, it is ultimately not a judgment. The judgment refers to those who have lived in such isolation from God and the expectations God has for the living that they will be consigned to the second death, which will wipe away any possibility for eschatological relationship with God (cf. 2:11; 20:6, 12–14; 21:8).

The flip side of the judgment is life—not long, physical, mortal life, but eschatological life lived in relationship with God. This "second" life is the proper reward for the servants, the prophets (see the comments on 10:7 and 11:3), who have faithfully testified to the lordship of God and Christ. The synonymy between prophets and witnesses (see the comments on 11:3, 6–7, 10) suggests that John has in mind the two witnesses who were emblematic of the believing church. It is for them that judgment time is the time of eschatological relationship with God.

[19] There is one more antiphonal response: God's. Using a divine passive construction, John indicates that God opened the temple sanctuary (*naos*). In contrast to the earthly sanctuary mentioned earlier in the chapter (vv. 1–2), John with a clarifying attributive clause specifies that this is the sanctuary located in heaven. At 15:5, when he again narrates the opening of the heavenly temple, John sees seven angels with seven bowls filled with the wrath of God. When the heavenly temple opens, one thinks not of invitation but judgment.

Again, there is a flip side of judgment (see the introduction to 11:15–19). In the second key movement of the verse, John sees the lost ark of the covenant. The mentioning of the ark confirms that John's visual object is the temple sanctuary, and in this case, even more specifically, the most sacred part of the sanctuary. According to 1 Kings, the ark was remanded to the holy of holies on Solomon's orders (8:1, 6; cf. Heb 9:1–4). According to 2 Macc 2:4–8, however, the ark was led out of the temple by Jeremiah and hidden. "A likely possibility is that the ark was destroyed or taken as a spoil of war by the Babylonians when they captured Jerusalem and the temple in 587 BCE" (Reddish 218). Though absent from the Herodian earthly sanctuary at its destruction in 70 C.E., therefore, its mythical counterpart apparently remained in place in the parallel heavenly universe. Traditionally, this wooden chest or box, overlaid with gold, housed the tablets of the Ten Words (the Decalogue). Additionally, it served as a representation of both God's throne and God's presence. John's sighting of it at the moment of the inauguration of God's reign suggests that the promise of the ark is now to be realized: God's presence will reside in the midst of God's people (cf. Rev 21:22). In other words, the ark is a metaphor for eschatological relationship with God: salvation.

The final movement of the verse chronicles the unleashing of a series of theophanies. The theophany package climaxes the theme of judgment that has been on prominent display throughout the chapter (see the comments on 4:5; 8:5; 10:3; 16:18).

### 12:1–14:20 Visionary Flashback: The Start of the Story

Why does Rome claim a lordship that belongs exclusively to God? Why cannot Rome recognize the true lordship of Christ? Why does Rome with such unmitigated violence resist those who witness to Christ's lordship? Why are the witnesses not protected by God? What set of circumstances has brought history to this point of apocalyptic conflict? As the attention of John's hearers and readers flickers between the perspectives of the seals and the trumpets, before he allows his narrative to flash over to the bowls, he pauses so he can answer those critical questions. He inserts the visions of 12:1 to 14:20. John takes the time to do what he should perhaps have done at the very beginning: provide the narrative rationale for the movement of his visionary plot.

### 12:1–17 The Dragon's War

Within chapter 12, John also tells the story in a nonsequential manner so that his hearers and readers can recognize the chapter's meaning from its structure. Five primary plot movements form two outer frames around a core central message. (1) Verses 1–6 introduce a celestial woman and a dragon as competing signs in the sky and then detail both the dragon's attempt to destroy the progeny of the woman and God's rescue of the woman and her son. This confrontation in heaven is balanced at the end of the chapter by a confrontation on earth. (2) Verses 13–17 re-present the conflict between the woman and the dragon, the woman's rescue, and the dragon's futile attempt to destroy her progeny. (3) The first inner frame (vv. 7–9) details the result of the war: the dragon's defeat in heaven. (4) A matching inner frame (v. 12) presents the result of the war in terms of heavenly joy and earthly woe. Inside the frames is (5) a liturgical hymn of praise (vv. 10–11) that clarifies exactly how the dragon was brought down. The force of the chapter lies here, with the twin weapons of the Lamb's blood and the believer's witness. John's narration encourages thanksgiving for the blood and continuation of the witness (Richard 98).

12:1–6  The Woman, the Dragon, and the Son

12:1 Then a great sign appeared in heaven: a woman clothed with the sun; the moon was under her feet, and a crown of twelve stars was on her head. 2 She was pregnant, and cried out in labor, in the agony of childbirth.[a] 3 Then another sign appeared in heaven: behold, a great red dragon with seven heads and ten horns, and seven diadems on its heads. 4 Its tail swept down a third of the stars of heaven and threw them to the earth. Then the dragon stood before the woman who was about to give birth, so that it might devour her child when she gave birth. 5 And she bore a son, a male child,[b] who will shepherd all the nations with an iron rod. But her child was snatched away to God and to God's throne. 6 And the woman fled into the wilderness, where she has a place prepared by God, so that there she might be nourished[c] for 1,260 days.

a. The awkward phrase literally translates "being tormented to give birth." The infinitive explains the reason for the struggle.

b. John stumbles into a grammatical infelicity when he crafts "male child" as a matching apposition to "son." The two nouns should therefore be in grammatical agreement. The noun *arsen* (male child), however, occurs as a neuter accusative adjective when one expects the masculine form *arsena*, which would match the masculine accusative noun *huion* (son). Several manuscripts have tried to eliminate the incongruity by rewriting *arsen* in the masculine form, *arsena* ($\mathfrak{P}^{47}$ $\aleph$ 051 $\mathfrak{M}$). A and C contain the more difficult and therefore preferred neuter construction.

c. The Greek literally reads "so that there they might nourish her." See the commentary on v. 6 below for explanation of the third-person plural.

**[12:1]** Revelation 12:1–14:20 is held together by the bracketing phrase *sēmeion en tō ouranō* (sign/portent in heaven). In his only three uses of this terminology (12:1, 3; 15:1), John introduces the interlude of chapters 12–14 and then closes it off with the presentation of the seven bowls.[1] He reinforces his structural intentions by linking the signs together with the adjective *allos* (another). The second (12:3) and third (15:1) signs are distinctly related to the first (12:1). The second sign introduces the antagonist who will oppose the protagonist showcased in the first sign. The third sign signals the end of their narrated conflict.

In 12:1, 3, as in 11:19, John conveys his vision with an awkward aorist passive construction, *ōphthē* (was seen). Since the visions are his alone, he clearly means to say, "I saw." The ark of the covenant in the heavenly sanctuary and now the appearances of the cosmic woman and the dragon in the sky are so sig-

1. In the other four plural uses of "signs," John refers to activities perpetrated by the false prophet/beast from the land to deceive God's people (13:13, 14; 16:14; 19:20). In none of these cases is the sign referred to as a singular "heavenly portent."

nificant, though, that they and not he must be highlighted. He speaks this way because he wants attention to be focused on those objects, not on himself.

Who is the cosmic woman? Some connect her with figures in Israel's or the church's past or future: Eve, the mother whose seed would bruise the head of the dragon/serpent (Gen 3:1–16); Mary, the mother of Jesus; or the heavenly Jerusalem as bride of the Lamb (19:7–8; 21:9–10). Others suppose a pagan or astrological connection: a queen of heaven like the Egyptian Isis, or the constellation Virgo. Still others hypothesize a corporate representation of God's people: Israel, who escapes the dragon/Pharaoh into the wilderness on wings of eagles (Exod 19:4; cf. Ps 74:12–15); or Zion, the mother of the persecuted people of God (Isa 66:7–9; *4 Ezra* 13.32–38). It is unlikely that John has in mind an individual woman, historical or otherwise. Mary, the mother of Jesus, did not give birth to the entire people of God as this woman will (Rev 12:17). Eve gives birth to all humans, not specifically the believing community. Though the "sign" language clearly intends to guide hearers and readers to look to the heavens in the way that they seek out constellations, John cannot have had Virgo exclusively in mind since she is the sixth sign of the zodiac and this woman (12:1) is connected integrally with the number "twelve." It is even more unlikely that John, who cannot tolerate having people eat food sacrificed to foreign gods (chs. 2–3), would compose the progenitor of the believing people from the sole image of a pagan deity. It is much more likely that he has combined a great many themes from historical and mythical woman/mother images in Israel's and the church's past, present, and future and fashioned them thematically into a representation of the church's corporate existence.

We can gain a better sense of what John intends by his "woman" representation when we look at the way he puts it to narrative use. He deploys the word *gynē* (woman) nineteen times. He is preoccupied with several primary roles for women in first-century society: wife (19:7), mother (12:4, 13, 17), and sexual threat (Jezebel's false teachings conveyed through symbolism of fornication, 2:20; sexual intimacy that defiles holy warriors, 14:4; harlotry of Rome, 17:3, 4, 6–7, 9, 18). A more comprehensive study reveals that John has oriented his use of *gynē* around competing images. Most notable, though the images do not come into play directly in chapter 12, is the thematic opposition between the *wife* and the *harlot*. This woman is as directly associated with her *children* (12:17) as the harlot later is with *Rome* (17:18). The most intriguing opposition is the one between the competing signs of the *woman* in 12:1 and the *dragon* in v. 3. To be sure, war breaks out in heaven between Michael and the dragon (v. 7), but that later conflict is based upon the enmity that already exists between the dragon and the woman. God's intentions, as they operate through the characterization of the woman, are already being opposed by the dragon, according to vv. 1, 3. If it is not an outright hot war, it is certainly a hypertense cold one.

The important question is why John does not see God fighting directly. Instead, Michael (v. 7) and subsequently the Lamb and "they" (v. 11) are pressed into service. John's point is a simple one: for all of the dragon's great strength, it is never, even narratively, on a par with God. God need not engage the battle directly because God's representatives are sufficient for the task; they handle the eschatological "light work." Though the woman is not God, she is, like Michael and the Lamb (symbolized in ch. 12 as the woman's son), a representation of God's intention in and for humankind. The Lamb represents God's saving power, which can defeat the dragon by bringing the people into eschatological relationship with God (v. 11; see the treatment of the Lamb in ch. 5). Michael represents God's capacity directly to thwart the dragon's ability to deceive and unmercifully accuse God's people (vv. 7–10). The woman, on the other hand, represents God's procreative capability. The dragon desires to eliminate God's capacity to birth a son who will shepherd all the other children who will follow him (v. 17).

The woman's attire reveals much about her identity. She is, first of all, clothed with the sun. Clothing in Revelation is more than mere outer wear; its type and color illustrate important qualities or character traits of the person wearing it. Sackcloth indicates mourning and judgment. A purple and scarlet dress symbolizes Rome's harlotry and opposition to God (17:4; 18:16). Christ's bloody robe indicates the slaughter he and his followers have endured for their witness (19:13). Yet John then declares that the followers' robes are dazzling (19:14); this is precisely because they have washed them in the Lamb's blood (7:14). The dazzling robe takes on a quality of particular significance; it signals a successfully established eschatological relationship with God. The mighty angel of 10:1 is robed in a dazzling white cloud. Dazzling robes are worn by those who witness victoriously to the lordship of Christ (3:5, 18; 4:4; 7:9, 13). The bride's (i.e., the church's) intimate relationship with the Lamb is indicated partially through her dazzling attire (19:8). Even more dazzling would be the brightness of the sun. Though John uses "sun" most often in reference to the physical star around which the earth orbits (even if he did not himself understand it in this way), in two other places besides 12:1 he connects the quality of the sun's color or shining with a character who populates his prophecy. At 1:16, the child of humanity has a face that shines like the sun. The face of the mighty angel clothed in a cloud at 10:1 shines similarly. In both those cases, their sunshine indicates that they are representatives of God. According to the psalmist, it is God who is apparently so adorned (Ps 104:1–2). This woman's relationship with God and her identity as a representative for God are highlighted by the fact that she, too, is cloaked with the sun. All of her shines like the sun! Clearly, she must represent something extremely important about how God expresses God's self in the life of God's people. I have already argued and will maintain subsequently that she represents God's procreative ability to birth a people of faith.

The "moon under her feet" signals elevated status; as a cosmic being she stands far above the human followers who trace their faith existence through her. But it is the *stephanos* (crown) of stars on her head that best complements the sun-cloak that robes her. Like the dazzling robe, the crown is an accoutrement awarded the believer who conquers by witnessing faithfully to the lordship of Christ (2:10–11; 3:11–12). The twenty-four heavenly elders whose perpetual worship is highlighted in the hymnic sections are outfitted with crowns (4:4, 10), as is the one like a child of humanity himself (14:14). Interestingly, the child of humanity also holds a symbolically complete 7 stars in his hand (1:16, 20; 2:1; 3:1). This woman's crown possesses stars in another symbolically complete number: 12. Though the number of the stars no doubt operates from the cosmological understanding that there were 12 stars of the zodiac, John integrates its use into his narrative as a number representing completeness in terms of rapport with God (7:5–8; 21:12, 14, 16, 21; 22:2). Beale argues that the number represents both the 12 tribes (7:4–8) and the 12 apostles, who formed the leadership of the nascent church (626–29). This interpretation gains strength from the fact that earlier in his prophecy John equates stars with angels, who in turn represent churches (1:16, 20). The 12 stars, then, represent the completeness of the church that finds its foundation and indeed its genesis in this woman.

**[2]** The woman is so intimately involved with God that she turns out to be pregnant with God's Lamb/Messiah (v. 5). Reverberations from Hebrew prophecy emphasize the point. Isaiah 7:14 LXX speaks of the *sēmeion* (sign) of a pregnant young woman (*en gastri*) who will give birth (*tiktō*) to a son (see Rev 12:5). The close linguistic parallels indicate John's dependence on that Isaianic prophecy as he introduces the celestial woman and her eschatological role. Interestingly, at Isa 26:15 God is seen as the one who propagates the believing community. That procreation is metaphorically portrayed two verses later as the people giving birth during a very difficult labor. In describing the hard labor of the celestial woman in Rev 12:2, John picks up on the same Greek vocabulary used in Isa 26:17 LXX: *ōdinō* (to suffer birth pangs); *tiktō* (to give birth); and *krazō* (to cry out). In Isa 27 God wages victorious war against the serpent Leviathan, just as here in Rev 12 God's forces fight victoriously against a great red satanic serpent. At Isa 66:7 LXX, the prophet declares, again using the same vocabulary that John stresses in Rev 12:2 (*ōdinō* and *tiktō*), that Zion gives birth first to a messianic son and then to a multitude of children.[2] The prophet Micah also employs this vocabulary (*ōdinō* and *tiktō*) to reaffirm the picture of Zion writhing in childbirth but being promised, as is the woman in Rev 12:2–6, rescue by God (LXX: 4:9–10; 5:3; cf. Rev 12:6, 14).

These Old Testament texts and Rev 12 emphasize the same key themes. Faced with hostile opposition, God's ability to create a people of faith, symbolized in

2. See also *4 Ezra* 9.38–10.57, which is based on the Isaiah texts.

the agonizing labor process of the celestial woman/Zion, will prevail. The woman in extreme labor pain, then, is both the Israelite and apostolic (the 12 stars of v. 1) people of faith (who in turn represent God's procreative capability), who groan before their persecutors (cf. 6:9–11) as they await the birth of the Messiah, who will shepherd them toward a place in God's victorious reign.

Is the figure of the woman as passive as some critics contend?[3] I think not. In contemporary terms, I am reminded of the Vietnam War, the so-called helicopter war. One of the primary troop-carrying strategies employed by the United States during that war was to drop soldiers into hostile combat zones. They were ferried in and out by helicopter. To be sure, the active agents in the circumstance were the soldiers dispatched to fight and die. The helicopter itself exited the combat zone as soon as its human payload had been discharged. But it returned to retrieve the wounded, bring in reinforcements, and facilitate either retreat or a postvictory exit. Each and every one of those ingresses and egresses was made under either the threat or the reality of hostile fire. Metaphorically speaking, the helicopter's job was to give birth to a combat force amid an agonizing labor of enemy fire. Its role, too, was an active and desperate one. John's cosmic woman, laboring against the pain of impending birth that symbolizes the persecution of God's people as they await the deployment of God's messianic son and the forces who will follow him, is, metaphorically speaking, God's lead helicopter. Hers is a dangerous and active role. Without the successful completion of her mission, there can be no movement of God's people into human history. Unless she successfully delivers both God's son and the community that follows him, there can be no victory (cf. 12:11).[4]

[3] The parallelism John intends between the woman and the dragon is drawn through his introduction of the dragon as *another* heavenly sign. Using the same aorist-passive construction ōphthē (was seen), John demonstrates that he regards this sign as a natural countersign to the woman. The woman represents the power of God to birth and build up the believing community; the dragon represents the power to destroy that community at any point from its inception onward.

3. See, e.g., Pippin.
4. By making this unprecedented and awkward move of comparing John's metaphor with one of my own, I run many risks. Chief among them might be the perception that I intend to place God on the side of the United States and the Vietnamese people on the side of the dragon in the context of the war. I do not. I use the image only in the restricted sense of the helicopter's role, which could apply to a dropping of firefighters into a forest fire, or a ferrying of emergency medical personnel to a crisis event. In using the example above, I only choose this particular war setting because (1) a war setting fits John's understanding of the people's plight and (2) this particular war made explicit and intentional use of the helicopter strategy. It is only that strategy and not the politics of the war itself that I wish to use as a metaphorical reference point.

In his first use of the term *drakōn* (dragon), John introduces the character without a definite article. Every subsequent reference is to "the" dragon.[5] The lack of the article here suggests that this is not a character with whom John expects his hearers and readers to be familiar. They should, however, be familiar with the general concept of the dragon. The dragon is a metaphor for historical powers, like Egypt, that assailed God's people.[6] I have already noted in the commentary on 12:2 that Isaiah follows up his account of God's people being birthed through an agonizing labor (26:15, 17) with an account of God slaying the sea dragon Leviathan (27:1). Ezekiel 29:3, using the same description of a great dragon, identifies the prosecuting force explicitly with Egypt. Other Old Testament texts reinforce God's successful rescue of the people from Egypt with the metaphor of a dragon defeated in the sea (Ps 74:13–14; Ezek 32:2–3). Rome, for John, has become the new Egypt and therefore the contemporary incarnation of the dragon. Rome will pursue the people just as Pharaoh once did. The ultimate promise of chapter 12 is that God will defeat the dragon's Roman manifestation as surely as God defeated its Egyptian one. The new exodus will be from Rome.

John's description of the dragon reinforces its hostile nature. It is red, a color that symbolizes destruction. In its only other appearance, it stains the horse whose representation is slaughter (6:4). The dragon is the shade of slaughter. This is a powerful realization in a narrative context where the protagonist is a slaughtered (i.e., executed) Lamb.

In a display of fierce power, the dragon also sports seven heads and ten horns. Upon each head is a diadem. This description connects the dragon immediately with the beast who will soon emerge from the sea (13:1–10; 17:3, 7, 9, 12, 16), who flaunts seven heads and ten horns but places its ten diadems on its horns. Because John will identify the beast from the sea as a metaphor for Rome in chapter 13, the dragon is best understood as the satanic force behind the imperial power. This fits with John's portrayal of the dragon as a metaphor for the evil that has animated historical powers like Egypt.

Rome is not the only character whose attributes resemble those of the dragon. The Lamb was also outfitted with horns (5:6). Horns represent power. Daniel's fourth beast, too, had ten horns (Dan 7:7). Daniel went on to describe its horns as powerful and disruptive earthly kingdoms (7:20, 24). The dragon's pretense to historical power is also represented by the diadems that adorn each

---

5. See 12:4, 7, 9, 13, 16, 17; 13:2, 4; 16:13; 20:2; in 13:11 the term "dragon" is used adverbially ("was speaking like a dragon").

6. Beale writes, "'Dragon' (δράκων) is another OT word for the evil sea monster that symbolizes evil kingdoms who oppress Israel" (631). And Caird comments, "Jeremiah had compared Nebuchadnezzar to a dragon which had gulped Jerusalem down whole (Jer. li. 34); Ezekiel had pictured Pharaoh as 'the great dragon lying in the midst of his streams' (Ezek. xxix. 3); and in the Psalms of Solomon (ii. 25) the dragon seems to be Pompey" (150).

of its heads and symbolize a claim of kingship that opposes any lordship claims of the Lamb. By similarly outfitting these principal combatants, John compares and contrasts their relative strengths. Quantitatively, the dragon has more horns (10). Qualitatively, since the Lamb has the perfectly complete number of seven horns, it has more power. John knows, though, that those who look with eyes of logic will fear allying themselves with the woman and her son (the Lamb) against the dragon and its minion from the sea. On first view the Lamb, because he has fewer horns and is in fact a lamb, does not look the part of one who could successfully engage a great red dragon with 7 heads, 7 diadems, and 10 horns. Faith that sees beyond the evidence of sight is required.

[4] Part of the celestial woman's magnificence is the crown of twelve stars that she wears on her head. The dragon is unimpressed. It has the power to sweep a third of the stars from the sky with a flick of its tail. The arrogant, powerful beast of Dan 8:10 had the same capability.

Having described the dragon, John sets out to convey its hostile intent. It takes up a position before the celestial woman so that it can devour her child as soon as it is born. One would think that since the woman is in a vulnerable position, the dragon's logical move would be to eliminate her. By terminating the woman, the dragon will terminate her even more dangerous baby. But the dragon waits. Is this because it cannot murder the woman since she, too, is a mythical figure, a metaphor for God's procreative capability that gives birth to a tangible, historical thing that *can* be slaughtered?

[5] Fulfilling an Isaianic vision (Isa 7:14; 66:7), the celestial woman gives birth to a messianic son. The son's identity and role, as well as his relationship to the woman's other children (Rev 12:17), can be determined through consideration of the verse's key vocabulary. *Poimainō* (shepherd), *rabdos* (rod), and *sidērous* (made of iron) operate as a narrative package in 2:27; 12:5; 19:15. The son will shepherd not just believers but also all the nations with an iron rod. The implication is that he will institute a rule of discipline that will turn people in the proper direction, toward faith in the lordship of God and God's Christ. (On reading this language as oriented toward repentance, see the comments on 2:27 and 11:1.)[7] The imagery refers back to the language in Ps 2:9 about the leadership of the Messiah. Revelation 19:15 clarifies that the one who shepherds with an iron rod is none other than Christ. There the connection is unmistakable with the rider on the white horse. At 7:17, John's only independent use of *poimainō*, he specifically identifies the Lamb as the one who shepherds toward springs of living water.

At 2:27 this shepherding ability also relates to believers who conquer, that is to say, who successfully witness to and for the lordship of Christ. (See also

---

7. Cf. Boring's point that "John (like the Septuagint) changes the Hebrew Bible's 'break' to 'shepherd' ('rule' in RSV), transforming what might still seem like a harsh picture of the Messiah's rule into his characteristic 'Lion into Lamb' christological terms" (*Revelation*, 153).

11:1, where the only independent use of *rabdos* [rod] pictures the seer's leadership.) Their testimony appears to be the rod of discipline that corrects and turns (cf. 12:11). It is not surprising that the image of shepherding is used of both the Lamb/Son and those who witness to him. John has already linked them by a similar language of witness and slaughter (see the comments on 5:6 and 6:9). What the Lamb does, the people are called to do as well.

The verb *mellō* (is about to) suggests that the leadership of the son will soon take place. No doubt that leadership is part of the apocalyptic moment when God's reign occurs. But John's hearers and readers know that the seventh trumpet has already sounded (see 11:15–19). The reign has already begun; the presence of the verb *mellō* here, then, is either wrong or further evidence that chapter 12 is a flashback to what occurs before the opening of the seals and the blowing of the trumpets.

Having described the child, John also indicates why he would be a threat to the dragon. He would shepherd the people toward a belief in God's power and rule and therefore away from allegiance to the dragon. Because the conjunction *kai* (and, but, also) that introduces the second half of the verse details God's action against the dragon's intent, it should be read adversatively. The dragon is poised to devour the child, *but* the child is snatched up to God and God's throne. The aorist-passive construction *hērpasthē* (he was snatched by force) is another of John's divine passives that should be read with God as the active agent. God snatches the child to God's self and God's throne. This is precisely the location where the Lamb/Son is found in Rev 5:6–7, 13; 7:9–10, 17 (cf. 22:1). Once again, via flashback, chapter 12 provides the background and rationale for earlier character placement. It is only after we read this passage that we know how the Son/Lamb arrived at the throne in chapter 5. We are also in a better position to understand the connection between his location at the throne and his shepherding of the people (7:17).

The violence implied in the verb "to snatch by force" gives John's hearers and readers a clue to the seer's point of reference. History and myth merge in John's effort to clarify the human eschatological situation. One might wonder why John presents the child's birth and then moves right to his ascension to the throne of God without even mentioning his death. Such a query misses the power of myth. The birth *is* the death. The child is begotten on the cross. The cross is also the mechanism of his leadership, his shepherding of the people. The dragon seeks to destroy him. And like the two witnesses of chapter 11, he is killed. He is crucified. And yet, as was the case for the two witnesses, this death turns out to be the road through which he finds his way to God. Death becomes the means to the child's glory and the people's future. Do not be afraid of dying for the witness of God, therefore. This is the mythic exhortation. In dying, you rise to a place of power with God (cf. 6:9–11). That is the historical truth the myth wants its hearers and readers to comprehend.

[6] Although John will later clarify that it is God who facilitates the woman's escape from the dragon after the birth and ascension of her son (12:14), here John only notes her flight into the wilderness. John uses *erēmos* (wilderness) only three times (12:6, 14; 17:3). At 17:3, he describes it as a refuge where he is carried away *in the spirit* (see the comment on 4:2–3) to view the destruction of Babylon. John is working from traditional images. Uppermost in his mind no doubt is the account of Israel's exodus from Egypt into the wilderness, where the people were nurtured and disciplined by God (Exod 16:32; Deut 2:7, 15–16; 29:5; 32:10; Josh 24:7; Neh 9:19, 21; Pss 78:15, 19; 136:16; Isa 40:3; Jer 31:2; Ezek 34:25 RSV; Hos 13:5). There are also thematic connections. Moses flees to the wilderness to escape Pharaoh (Exod 2:15). At 1 Kgs 17:1–7, Elijah is nurtured and protected by God in what clearly appears to be a wilderness setting. Matthew records Joseph's flight with Jesus to escape the threat of Herod the Great (2:13–15; cf. Hos 11:1). God has once again prepared the wilderness as a place of refuge and nurture for the people, who are symbolized here by the woman through whom they are given existence. Notice how the symbols are allowed to shift in reference in the slippery, dreamlike world of myth. The woman who has up to this point represented the *genesis* of the people now takes on the *identity* of the people. In this new guise she is apparently vulnerable to the dragon in a way that she was not before (see the comment on 12:4).

The duration of the woman's stay in the wilderness is obviously symbolic. The 1,260 days is the same temporary period of time that marked the outer temple's trampling and immediately afterward the duration of the two witnesses' traumatic preaching tour (see 11:2–3). It is also the same period that the dragon was allowed earthly authority (13:5). The time of the woman's hiding corresponds, therefore, to the time when the dragon will seek out and persecute the people of God (12:17) because of their witness (cf. Dan 7:25; 12:7). Since the figure represents exactly half of seven years, John in each case means to suggest that it is a temporary period. The time of victory and vindication, by contrast, will be eternal.

The tie-in to the end of chapter 10 and the work of the two witnesses in chapter 11 can be seen through John's odd appeal to the third-person plural presentation of the verb "nurture." Who is the "they" who will care for the woman? One would have expected a singular reference to God, who is obviously the active agent behind the passive formulation "a place was prepared." "They" most likely recalls the "they" of 10:11, the plural representation of God's singular intent (see the comment on 10:11). The key is that God intends to shelter the woman—that is, the church—from the devastation the dragon is plotting.

### 12:7–9 A War in Heaven

7 And war broke out in heaven. Michael and his angels had to fight[a] with the dragon. The dragon and his angels fought back, 8 but they were

defeated, and there was no longer a place for them in heaven. 9 Then the great dragon was thrown down; the ancient serpent, who is called devil and Satan, who deceives the whole world, was thrown down to the earth, and his angels were thrown down with it.

a. The articular infinitive explains the purpose of the war that was introduced in the previous sentence. The war apparently breaks out at God's initiative.

[7] When war breaks out, it begins in heaven between the dragon and those who represent God. The comments on 12:1 show what John has clarified through his positioning of the dragon against the woman, rather than against God. The same conclusion reached there applies here: John does not put God and the dragon in opposition; instead, the dragon's character is balanced against Michael. Michael represents God's combat capability in the same way that the woman represents God's procreative potential. God far surpasses the dragon and therefore need not engage him directly. God's subordinates can do the job. And so, in this case, God delegates the task of battling the dragon to the archangel Michael.

Michael is another mythical figure. In Revelation his name occurs only here. In his one other appearance in the New Testament (Jude 9), he disputes with Satan over the body of Moses. Most likely, John is working more closely from the presentation of Michael in the book of Daniel, where he is a princely defender of the faithful people (10:13, 21; 12:1).[8] He fulfills that protective role here by battling the dragon and its angels.

The language of war (*polemos*) clarifies what is happening. John deploys the term in chapters 11–13 three key times. Once the two witnesses have finished their testimony, John explains that the beast from the abyss will make war with them and kill them (11:7). The description of the beast suggests that this is the same enemy who will be described in chapter 13 as Rome, the beast from the sea. Indeed, John reaffirms that this beast is allowed to make war on the saints and conquer them (13:7). At 12:17 John summarizes these events as the earthly war against the church that develops because the heavenly war is going so badly for the dragon and his angelic minions. The war is the (Roman) persecution (imaged in 12:2 as the agony of the celestial woman's labor pains) that the people must endure on account of their witness to the lordship of Christ. If the dragon cannot rule in heaven, he is determined to destroy God's people on earth.

A more comprehensive look at the war language, along with the presentation of the woman and the successful snatching of her son in 12:1–6, suggests a parallel mythological/historical timeline. At stage one, the celestial woman is prepared to give birth. She represents God's procreative power to deliver a faith

8. See also *1 En.* 54.6, where Michael helps cast the fallen angels into the fire on judgment day.

people/community through a firstborn son who will then shepherd the woman's other children, his figurative brothers and sisters. It is no doubt at this mythological point that John would place the historical ministry of Jesus. Stage two finds the dragon plotting to stop this communal hope by destroying the son who is so crucial to it. Stage three brings the snatching of the son, which is contemporaneous with the heavenly war that erupts between Michael and the dragon. The dragon makes the first move with the cross. It is this historical attack on Jesus' life that triggers Michael's mythical response. This scenario helps explain why the messianic son is not fighting for God in heaven along with Michael. His fight is the historical one. His charge is to engage the dragon on earth, and he does so on the cross (12:11). At the very moment that Jesus is dying historically on the cross, Michael and his angels are fighting mythically with the dragon in heaven. The snatching of Jesus to the throne—that is, the resurrection—is the historical cipher for the event of Michael's expelling the dragon from heaven. As Jesus rises into the mythical realm of heaven, the dragon is thrown down into the historical one. Stage four finds the dragon now fuming in history and taking his anger out on the people of God. Here is where John positions the 1,260 days or 42 months of persecution, the transitory time when the bestial forces of the dragon (described in Rev 13) will persecute God's people because of their witness to the lordship of Christ. In the language of myth, John describes it as the time of the woman's nurture in the wilderness (12:16), which happens historically at the same time as the dragon's bestial pursuit of her other, earthbound children (12:17). It is the time in and for which John sees himself now writing.

[8] With the dragon's defeat comes the recognition that there is no longer a place for him and his supporting angels in heaven. Just as there was a place of nurture prepared (*ētoimasmenon*) for God's procreative potential (12:6), so has one of punishment been prepared (*ētoimasmenon*, so Matt 25:41) for the dragon and its bestial supporters (20:10–11).

[9] Verse 9 highlights two points about the dragon, reaffirming that the dragon has been cast out of heaven and detailing the dragon's identity. John deploys the aorist passive of *ballō* (to throw [or cast]) no less than three times in this single verse. The passive indicates God's agency. The repetition ensures that the point is heard: God, through representation both angelic (Michael, v. 7) and historical (the son and the witnesses, v. 11), is ultimately responsible for removing the dragon from his heavenly perch.

Before celebrating his defeat, John wants to make sure that his hearers and readers know clearly who the dragon is (see 20:2). It is *the* ancient serpent. John uses the definite article because he assumes his hearers and readers will recognize this figure from their traditions. The ancient serpent was the deceiver of the entire world. His deception of Adam and Eve in the garden of Eden led to the sinful separation of the entire world from its intended relationship with God

(Gen 3). As punishment for that deception, God promised perpetual enmity between the seed (*sperma*) of the woman and the seed of the serpent. This explains why, when John chooses to describe the hostility between the dragon and the woman's children (12:17), he surprisingly refers to her children with the same term (*sperma*) that is primarily used to designate a male's offspring. The battle between the church and the dragon is the eschatological result of the primordial conflict initiated by the serpent's deception.

Both narratively and historically, John's image of the serpent as deceiver connects the dragon to the bestial forces of Rome and those who accommodate themselves to it. As Aune observes, "Subjects of the verb [*planan*] in Revelation include 'Jezebel' (2:20), the devil (12:9; 20:3, 8, 10), the beast from the land (13:14), also called the false prophet (19:20), and Rome (18:23)" (2:698). Richard Bauckham adds that in Asia Minor serpents were often used in the pagan cults of Asclepius, Dionysus, Sabazius, Cybele, and Zeus to symbolize divinity. "These associations cannot be easily dismissed as irrelevant, for in the image of the snake John appears to have selected precisely the most pervasive image of pagan divinity in the area of his churches and he cannot have been unaware of the fact. . . . The serpent symbol of pagan divinity therefore adds significant local dimensions to the Dragon" (Bauckham, *Climax of Prophecy*, 196). John will develop this local flavor when he aligns the serpent with the beast from the land in chapter 13.

Traditionally, the ancient serpent had been associated with the devil, who is also called Satan. John now makes that connection explicit. Satan is the ultimate deceiver of humankind. Just as he has operated in Israel's past (e.g., 1 Chr 21:1), so now he operates deceptively in the life of the Asia Minor churches (slander, 2:9; deep things, 2:13, 24; lying, 3:9).

## 12:10–12 A Victory Hymn of Praise

Highlighted at the center of the chapter, these three verses are a liturgical hymn that explains God's victory and acknowledges the identity of God's historical accomplices.

10 Then I heard a foreboding voice in heaven, saying: "Now have come the salvation and the power and the kingdom of our God, and the authority of God's Messiah, because the accuser[a] of our brothers and sisters was thrown down, who accuse,[b] them night and day before our God. 11 And they conquered him through the blood of the Lamb and through the word of their testimony, because[c] they did not love their life even to the point of death. 12 Therefore rejoice, you heavens and those who dwell in them. But[d] woe to the earth and the sea, because the devil has come down to you with great wrath, for he knows that he has little time."

a. Codex Alexandrinus offers here the only occurrence of *katēgōr* (accuser) in the entire New Testament, while $\mathfrak{P}^{47}$ ℵ C 051 𝔐 all prefer the more usual Greek term *katēgoros*. Because it is less likely that a scribe would change *katēgoros* to *katēgōr*, the more difficult reading is to be preferred (cf. Metzger, *Textual Commentary*, 747–48).

b. The participle is present tense. Though thrown down, Satan maintains a prosecutorial role.

c. Because the conjunction *kai* introduces a clause that provides the rationale for the clauses preceding it, it is translated with a causal sense (see Aune 2:655).

d. An adversative sense of the conjunction *kai* is implied through the contrast between the two sentences.

**[10]** John introduces this hymn by declaring that he heard a foreboding, heavenly voice. The "foreboding voice" (see the discussion of 7:2) consistently introduces the theme of judgment (see 5:2; 7:2; 8:13; 10:3; 11:12–13, 15; 14:7, 9, 15, 18; 16:1, 17; 19:1, 17), which certainly fits the preceding narration of Satan being exiled from heaven (vv. 7–9).

The reason for praise is twofold: Satan has been conquered, and the reign of God has come. The reign, as the antiphonal hymn of 11:15–18 has already affirmed, is *arti* (now). Each new stanza of this new hymn adds clarifying detail about the reality of that reign. Salvation (eschatological relationship with God) and power (realized as the defeat of the dragon) act as synonyms for the reign of God. Those synonyms are themselves placed in parallel relationship to the authority of the Christ, the messianic son whose eschatological role has been narrated in 12:1–6 and will be further clarified in v. 11. That authority, that lordship, is now in effect. It is for this reason that John so strenuously exhorts the believers in his letters to the seven churches to witness courageously to that lordship (chs. 2–3).

If chapter 12 is indeed a flashback that sets up the scenario of everything that happens from chapter 1 onward, John has offered an interesting salvific proposition. The Apocalypse is preoccupied with the idea that persecution will occur as a direct result of believers' testimony to the lordship of Christ. John himself, a prisoner on Patmos, is living out this reality. "Now" is a time when believers will be persecuted for witnessing to the lordship (i.e., the sovereign authority) of Christ. But "now" is also the time of God's reign and the time of Christ's earthly lordship (i.e., authority). Apparently, then, the time of persecution overlaps with the time of God's reign. In the only other place where John uses the adverb *arti* (now), that possibility seems certain (14:13). Surely the dead who die in the Lord are blessed from now on because "now" is the turning point where the reign of God pivots into human history. John's hearers and readers are apparently living at that critical juncture. Perhaps this is because in heaven, as the narration of the dragon's expulsion from heaven shows (vv. 7–9), the victory is already won. John reaffirms that point here. It is precisely *because* (*hoti*) Satan has been cast down that the salvation/power/reign/authority of Christ can now be celebrated. What remains is a mopping up of the huge pocket of satanic resistance that the dragon has now initiated on earth (v. 17). Persecution is part of that pocket. Soon, however, that pocket of resistance, too, will be overthrown. The present ("now") accomplishment of God's reign in the mythic imagination (i.e., in the world as only faith can see it) is the guarantee of its future historical realization. It is this guarantee that 12:10 now celebrates.

In reaffirming the cause for celebration, John adds a piece of the dragon's character portrait that he omitted from the description in v. 9. The dragon is also the one who accuses our brothers and sisters day and night before God. "The term [*katēgōr*], 'accuser,' is a literal translation of the Hebrew—cf. *śāṭān*, 'Satan'" (Aune 2:700). Clearly, this is a preexpulsion role of Satan. In heaven, Satan had the divinely approved appointment of divine prosecutor who brought charges against human beings before God (see Job 1–2, esp. 1:9–11; 2:4–5; Zech 3:1). In both the New Testament and rabbinic writings, Satan retained this judicial role and was often opposed by Michael, who would act as counsel for the human defense (Beale 661).[9] Caird points out that as long as there are human sinners to accuse, Satan's presence in heaven is necessary and must be tolerated, for God recognizes the need for justice (154). The problem with Satan as accuser is evidently similar to the problem John perceived with the church in Ephesus (2:1–11). In his narrow, one-sided devotion to the law (he accuses day and night), he misunderstands and misrepresents God. Although the mercy of God is as real as God's justice, the mercy is not only ignored but also fought against. The prosecutor therefore finds himself at odds with God to the point of war (v. 7). It is for this reason that the perpetual struggle between Satan and Michael is as much a courtroom war as it is a battlefield one.

Satan's prosecutory ambitions targets those who might be described as God's faithful people. John calls them "our brothers and sisters." This terminology associates the defendants with John, who describes himself as a brother at 1:9, and with the other "brothers and sisters" who testify to the lordship of Christ (19:10; 22:9). They are all persecuted because of their witness (6:9). In making his case, John deploys both "brothers and sisters" and the personal pronoun "them" as objects of the prosecutor's accusations. Narratively speaking, the two terms operate as synonyms. While this observation at first appears meaningless, in 12:11 it takes on monumental force.

[11] The "brothers and sisters" of v. 10 resurface immediately as referents for the personal pronoun "they," which comprises the primary subject for the verb *nikaō* (conquer). John could make his point with a simple third-person construction of the verb; however, he chooses to emphasize the subject by redundantly

---

9. Regarding accusing or interceding angels, Beale points to *Jub.* 1.20; 17.15–16; 18.9–12; 48.15–18; *1 En.* 40.7; *T. Levi* 5.6; *T. Dan* 6.1–6; cf. Caird (154), who adduces 1 Pet 5:8; Jude 9; 1 Tim 3:6; *b. Ber.* 46a; *b. Yom.* 20a.

deploying the third-person plural pronoun. John pleaded with the hearers and readers in each of his seven churches to testify to the lordship of Christ and thereby conquer the satanic delusion that Rome is lord of human history (2:7, 11, 17, 26; 3:5, 12, 21). Eschatological conquest, he promised, would come through historical witness. In the "now" of God's reign (see 12:10), the aorist construction of *nikaō* (they conquered) indicates that the promise has been fulfilled. The only other place where John deploys an aorist, nonsubjunctive use of *nikaō* is 5:5. That verse describes the completed conquest of the Lamb, which 12:5, drawing from the language of myth, explains as having taken place on the cross. Verse 11 adds the new dimension that this conquest has happened in large part because "they," the perpetually accused and persecuted brothers and sisters (v. 10), have conquered (15:2 also mentions "their" conquest of the beast).

John expresses the instrumental nature of the conquest through his use of the preposition *dia* (because of) followed by the actual conquering instruments in the accusative case (see the comment on 1:9 and 6:9). "They" conquer the dragon with two primary weapons: the blood of the Lamb and the word of their witness to the lordship of the same bloodied Christ Lamb (on word and witness as synonyms, see the comment on 1:1–3).

With the Lamb's blood, they use the dragon's greatest weapon against him, just as Christ himself once did. In Rev 5, John describes how the lion of Judah conquers by becoming an executed lamb (cf. 5:5, 6, 9). Here in Rev 12 John recounts the conquest mythologically through the symbolism of the child being "snatched" to the heavenly throne. The dragon's attempt to kill the child—crucifixion—instead leads to inaugurating the child's reign (resurrection). The child/Lamb conquers by turning the dragon's ultimate weapon, death, against him. It is a mythological picture of nonviolent resistance and revolution inspired by the historical narration of the cross. The Lamb has drawn up a new combat strategy and has used it to surprise and defeat, that is, *sLamb*, the dragon (see the excursus on "The Lion and the Lamb" in ch. 5). John's "brothers and sisters" have followed up by metaphorically throwing that blood victory in the dragon's face. Their testimony about the blood conquest restages and reenergizes the conquest every time they witness to it. It is for this reason that John exhorts them so strenuously to witness in his seven letters (chs. 2–3).

Will they pay a heavy price for "throwing the blood of the Lamb" in the face of the dragon? Indeed, they will. They will suffer persecution and perhaps even death. John has already reminded his hearers and readers, though, that their blood mingles with and is transformed by the blood of the Lamb (7:13–14). The faithful brothers and sisters (i.e., "they" in heaven), dressed in the dazzling garments of victory, earned their distinction precisely because they paid that heavy price. Through them, too, God used the dragon's ultimate weapon against it;

God used the death it imposed to give them the eschatological life with God, the salvation, they had always sought. (On death and life in Revelation, see the comments on 2:10–11 and 9:6.)

John no doubt hopes that this claim and vision of past victory will inspire more contemporary witness. That is why he stresses the testimony of the past witnesses and puts their effort on a narrative par with the blood of Christ as a conquest tool. They wielded both the blood and their own testimony about the transformative, revolutionary power of that blood to establish Christ's lordship in heaven and on earth. The expectation is that his contemporary hearers and readers will do the same, even with the specter of death looming as a draconian response. In such a context, after all, death leads not to separation from God but to eschatological relationship with God. God defeats the dragon by using death to bring life. John makes the point regarding Christ at 12:5. He makes the point regarding past believers here at the end of v. 11 ("they did not love their life even in the face of death"). To put it simply, John tells his hearers and readers that their past brothers and sisters defeated the dragon by testifying to the conquering blood of Christ, because he wants them to go out and courageously offer the same testimony. They have the power and the means, if fear of dying does not get in the way, to defeat the dragon and thereby participate in the inauguration of God's reign. This is the striking news that 12:11 communicates. No wonder, then, that their colleagues are in heaven waiting for them to finish the witness they started (6:9–11).

The repetition of *kai* (and), then, does not so much add new content as it extends what has already been stated. The witness is not different from the blood, and the disregard for their own lives is not new to the blood and the witness. John uses the three different clauses to ratchet up his expectation for the single act of contemporary witnessing. One might therefore more accurately translate what he has said in the following manner: "They conquered Satan through the blood of the Lamb, which is experienced through the word of their witness, which is only expressed if one cares more about proclaiming that witness than about life itself."

**[12]** John has narrated the results of the heavenly war (vv. 7–9). He returns to that task here. This time, however, he uses hymnic language. He makes three quick points. First, heaven should rejoice because there the dragon has been defeated and removed (cf. 18:20). That act deserves praise befitting God's people when God moves victoriously on their behalf (cf. Deut 32:43; Ps 96:11; Isa 44:23; 49:13). Second, heaven's joy is earth's lament. John introduces the catastrophic turn of events with a succinct utterance: *ouai*, "woe." Satan is loose on earth. The chaos he can no longer wreak in heaven, he executes here. Third, Satan is furious for the simple reason that his prosecutorial time on earth, too, is limited (i.e., 42 months; 1,260 days; 3½ years; see 11:2, 9; 12:6, 14).

12:13–17  The Woman, the Dragon, and the Son's Siblings

Verses 13–17 essentially offer a reprise of the information about the combat between the woman and the dragon narrated in vv. 1–6. The new information in this case is that the dragon seeks out the other children of the woman instead of the son who has been snatched away.

> 13 And when the dragon saw that he had been thrown down to the earth, he pursued the woman who had given birth to the male child. 14 But the woman was given the two wings of the great eagle, so that she could fly to her place in the wilderness where she is being nourished for a time, and times, and half a time away from the presence of the serpent. 15 Then the serpent spewed water like a river from its mouth behind the woman, so that he might sweep her away with a flood. 16 But the earth helped the woman; the earth opened its mouth and devoured the river that the dragon spewed from his mouth. 17 And the dragon was angry with the woman and went off to make war with the rest of her seed, those who keep the commandments of God and hold to the witness of Jesus.

[13] As far as narrative plotting is concerned, v. 13 takes up where v. 9 left off. John interrupts the sequence with his vision of the heavenly hymnic celebration. According to v. 9, the devil and his angels were thrown to the earth. Verse 13 describes the devil's reaction to this unwelcome turn of events. In his earlier fixation on the child, he had not tried to take out the woman (12:4); but now that the son is gone, he becomes preoccupied with her elimination.

It is at this point in the slippery, dreamlike world of myth that the woman's identity morphs. In John's earlier telling of combat between her and the dragon, she represented God's procreative ability to bring a believing community to life. In that guise, her natural habitat was heaven. Now, following the hymnic recognition that those who witness to Christ's lordship are under satanic duress (v. 11), John locates her on earth and re-visions her as the church that gives birth to the people of God. She is the same woman who gave birth to the *arsen* (male child) of v. 5, which means that she simultaneously represents both mythical (divine procreative ability) and historical (church) realities.[10]

[14] John has already told his hearers and readers that the woman fled to a wilderness place of nourishment prepared by God, where she stayed for 1,260 days (12:6). Now he tells them again. This time, though, he describes the way in which her flight was facilitated. God took her up as if on the wings of an eagle and carried her away from the dragon into the prepared wilderness place for a time, two times, and a half (i.e., 1,260 days, or three and a half years).

---

10. The fact that "male child" is introduced with the article here but without one in v. 5 indicates that John is referring to the same male child he introduced in v. 5.

John appeals to tradition to make his case for successful sanctuary. In the Old Testament, flight on eagles' wings was a well-regarded image for the secreting away of the faithful under God's care (Exod 19:4; Isa 40:31; Ezek 17:3, 7). (On the significance of "wilderness" as a place of exodus-type refuge, see the discussion above of 12:6.) The length of the stay alludes to Dan 7:25 and 12:7 (see the comment on 12:6).

[15] Just as the primary weapon of the Christ/Lamb is the sword of his mouth (1:16; 2:12, 16; 19:15, 21), so the dragon uses his mouth to initiate his powerful assault. Given that Christ's sword is most likely the word of his testimony to his own lordship (on Christ as God's prime witness, see the discussion of 1:4–8), one might reasonably conclude that the dragon's mouth-weapon is the word he uses to deceive people (12:9; cf. 2:14, 20) into believing in its own lordship and the lordship of its minions like Rome and its Asia Minor vassals (see Rev 13). These two opposing words (see the comment on 16:13) are the swords that the Lamb and the serpent wield against each other in mythical and indeed historical (witness) combat. No doubt John's hearers and readers would also recognize that the dragon, by using water to attempt destruction of God's people, would be trying to undo the order established by God at the creation.[11] There God tamed the sea (Gen 1:2–10; Pss 74:13; 77:16). The image of the sea glassed over in heaven, and ultimately no more, is a testimony to God's present and future ability to thwart the chaos it represents (Rev 4:6; 15:2; 21:1). The dragon thus attempts here to reestablish that mythical chaos through the historical guise of deception, which John depicts as water spewing murderously from his mouth.

[16] All of creation is apparently caught up in the conflict that has erupted between God and Satan (cf. Rom 8:23). All of creation is bound to choose sides. Earth makes its choice and comes to the defense of the woman, opening to swallow that which would destroy God's plans for God's people, just as it had done in the past (Exod 15:12; Num 16:30–34; Deut 11:6; Ps 106:17). If the woman is indeed the church, John's message is that, even in this hostile historical context, God will provide refuge.

[17] The dragon is no doubt angry with the woman for several narrative reasons. In the mythic drama, she represents God's ability to produce a messianic son who will inaugurate and shepherd God's people in the ways of God's, not the dragon's, lordship. In the historical arena, the woman represents God's ability to produce a community of believers who follow the leadership of God's son. Realistically, the dragon cannot destroy her because God has enlisted even creation to protect her.

Because he cannot destroy her, the dragon goes off to make war on the rest of her offspring, the siblings of the messianic son—that is, the church, the same

---

11. In the Noah story, it is God who uses water destructively (Gen 7).

entity symbolized by the two witnesses in chapter 11. John had already noted that the beast that comes up from the abyss makes war on them and therefore on the church (11:7). In chapter 13, John will characterize the beast as the prime minion of the dragon. Apparently, then, it is through the beast that the dragon executes his attack against the church. Even though the woman, as church, will be protected (as 12:6 shows), those who populate the church may well be killed (11:7). The dragon can destroy individual believers, but since he cannot get to the woman, it has no hope of destroying the church itself. John makes this unusual claim in his narration of the two witnesses who are killed and yet survive. He makes it anew here by showing the woman's other children engaged in mortal hostilities with the dragon while the woman's future remains assured. (On John's use of the term *sperma*, "seed," for the children of the woman and the connection to Gen 3:1–16, see the discussion above of 12:9.)

The individual believers at risk are those who keep the commandments of God and bear the witness of Jesus Christ (see 14:12). The last *kai* (and) of (12:17) is epexegetical; the second clause completes the thought of the first. Since for John the commandment of God is that believers should testify to the lordship of Christ, he means to say that the dragon will make war with those who keep the commandment of God, which is to testify to the lordship of Christ.

The second half of the statement identifies the believers as witnesses to the lordship of Christ. It is precisely because of their witness to the word of God, which is the lordship of Christ, that the dragon makes war against them. The first half of the statement is about exhortation. When John uses the verb *tēreō* ("keep," 1:3; 2:26; 3:3, 8, 10; 14:12; 16:15; 22:7, 9), he has primarily an ethical intent. He is encouraging his hearers and readers to hold to the word, that is, the commandments of God, which they have been taught. Because word and witness are functionally synonymous for him (1:2, 9; 6:9–11; 20:4), he is demanding that his followers keep the testimony that Christ has revealed to them. According to 2:26–27, those who keep to this way of witnessing will conquer and thereby find themselves tasked with the same role as that of the messianic son, the shepherding of the people with an iron rod (12:5). In other words, those who keep witnessing will, like Christ himself, be leaders of God's people, even if they may also, like Christ, suffer persecution because of that leadership. They can be assured, though, that like Christ, they too will conquer. Even though they may be killed (11:7), they too will receive eschatological relationship with God: salvation.

## 12:18–13:18 Resistance Is Futile

Unable to destroy the church, the dragon sets his sights on the individuals who comprise the church. To engage them, he summons the services of two historical minions. The two beasts are reminiscent of the legends of the primeval sea monster Leviathan and the primeval land monster Behemoth, who were separated from each other by God on the fifth day of creation.[1] According to legend, on the last day, at the arrival of the Messiah, they will be killed. Their carcasses will become the meat of an eschatological feast. According to Rev 13, that apocalyptic comeuppance, described at 19:20 and 20:10 as their committal to an eternal lake of fire, will not occur until after they have unleashed their chaos in the form of Roman Empire.

The predominant influence on John's characterization of this bestial power is Dan 7. Daniel, too, speaks of an empire and its attempt to claim a lordship that belongs exclusively to God. In asking his people to resist the beasts, John like Daniel is pleading that they reject the imperial reality the beasts represent. John, then, is not just speaking the language of combat myth. This is the narrative poetics of political theology. He is simultaneously asking and answering a very particular question: To whom does the earth, and the allegiance of those who populate the earth, belong? The message of the beasts is clear: all earthly power belongs to the beast from the sea. Accommodate to him. Worship him. Resistance is futile.

## 12:18  The Dragon Looks for Reinforcement from the Sea

18 Then the dragon[a] stood[b] on the sand of the sea.

a. Though the verb form implies an unidentified third-person singular pronoun, the context indicates that the dragon is the subject.

b. While the third-person singular form is well supported ($\mathfrak{P}^{47}$ ℵ A C 1854 2344 2351 *pc* lat sy[h]), 051 𝔐 vg[mss] sy[ph] co attest the first-person singular ("I stood"). The first-person form indicates that it is John, rather than the dragon, standing on the seashore. Both the context and the external evidence argue for the reading "[it] stood." The first-person singular was apparently an attempt to put the verb into agreement with the first-person singular *eidon* (I saw) that follows immediately in 13:1 (Metzger, *Textual Commentary*, 748).

[**12:18**] The visionary narrative of Rev 13 actually begins here. When the dragon stands on the seashore, it is not looking toward land with its back to the sea, as though it is trying to scope out the hiding places of the woman's remaining offspring. It is looking instead for reinforcement. To that end, its back to the land, it searches the sea, awaiting the appearance of two entities that will rise to its aid. Evil finds a way, or a partner, to reinvigorate itself.

## 13:1–10  The Beast from the Sea

13:1 And I saw a beast rising up from the sea, with ten horns and seven heads, and on its horns were ten diadems and on its heads were blasphemous

---

1. See Gen 1:21; Isa 27:1; Job 3:8; chs. 40–41; Pss 74:14; 104:25–26; *4 Ezra* 6.47–52; *1 En.* 60.7–11, 24; *2 Bar.* 29.3–4.

names.[a] 2 The beast that I saw was like a leopard, and its feet were like a bear's, and its mouth was like a lion's mouth. And the dragon gave it his power and his throne and great authority. 3 And one of his heads appeared to have suffered a mortal wound, but[b] its mortal wound was healed. And the whole earth marveled and followed behind[c] the beast. 4 They worshiped the dragon because he gave authority to the beast, and they worshiped the beast, saying: "Who is like the beast, and who is able to fight against it?" 5 The beast was given a mouth speaking haughty and blasphemous things, and it was allowed to exercise authority for forty-two months. 6 It opened its mouth to speak blasphemies against God, to blaspheme God's name and God's dwelling, that is,[d] those who dwell in heaven. 7 And it was allowed to make war against the saints and conquer them, and it was given authority over every tribe and people and tongue and nation. 8 And all the inhabitants of the earth will worship it, everyone whose[e] name was not from the foundation of the world written in the Book of Life of the executed Lamb. 9 Let anyone who has an ear listen. 10 If you[f] are destined for captivity, into captivity you will go; if you are destined to be killed by the sword, by the sword you will be killed. Here is the nonviolent resistance and the faith of the saints.

a. While the plural "names" (*onomata*) in the text is supported by the important manuscript A as well as 051 1611 1854 2053 2344 2351 𝔐ᴷ ar vg syʰ, the singular "name" (*onoma*) is supported by 𝔓⁴⁷ ℵ C 1006 1841 2329 𝔐ᴬ gig vgᵐˢˢ syᵖʰ co; Prim Bea. *Onoma* could have resulted from the letters "ta" being accidentally omitted after the preceding letters "ma," but it is equally probable that a plural form was constructed to match the preceding plural form of "heads." The letters "ta" are thus included in brackets in NA²⁷ as a sign of their contested nature. However, 17:3 offers strong internal evidence for the plural form (see Metzger, *Textual Commentary*, 748).

b. An adversative *kai*: "but."

c. The construction suggests discipleship (see the commentary on 13:3 below).

d. Several copyists (ℵ² 046* 051 2053ᵗˣᵗ 𝔐ᴬ lat co; Irˡᵃᵗ Bea) add an explanatory *kai* (and). Contextual clues support reading the phrase as a relative clause ("those who dwell"). See further the commentary on v. 6 below.

e. John makes a grammatical error by referring back to the plural inhabitants of the earth with the singular pronouns *hou* (whose) and *autou* (his). Several manuscripts try to correct the problem by substituting the plural pronoun *hōn* (whose) and inserting the plural *onomata* (names) with or without the plural *autōn* (their). The shifts align the text here with the more properly composed formulation at 17:8, where John reminds his hearers and readers about the inhabitants of the earth whose names are not written in the Book of Life.[2] The grammatically more difficult reading supported by C 1854 2053 *pc*; (Irˡᵃᵗ) Prim is to be preferred.

f. The impersonal ("someone") is translated as a second-person singular so that the following third-person verb ("he/she goes") can be translated inclusively.

2. At 17:8 John also leaves out the redundancy by only using the initial, relative pronoun.

**[13:1]** The seer Daniel claims sight of a churning sea that spits up four devastating apocalyptic beasts (Dan 7:2–3). He senses that the ultimate strength of the fourth and most fearsome of the set resides in its ten horns (7:7), which he then interprets as ten kings (7:24).

John catches sight of something eerily similar. His first words, *kai eidon* (and I saw), immediately link this new apparition to the revelation of the dragon in chapter 12. John uses the phrase consistently to introduce a new scene in a continuing narrative vision (see the comments on 5:1, 6; 6:1, 8, 12; 7:2, 9; 8:2, 13; 9:1; 10:1). What continues is John's perspective. Looking with the dragon out to sea, he sees what it sees: a roiling sea. The site of primordial chaos, which God first quelled in the creation accounts (Gen 1:2–10), the sea is a symbolic representation of resistance to God (see the discussion of 4:6–8a). The level of that resistance rises exponentially when the sea spits up a beast.

Because John introduces "beast" without the article, one can assume that he thinks he is presenting it to his hearers and readers for the first time. That assumption is correct, even though John has already announced it as "the" beast rising from the abyss (see the comment on 11:7). In chapter 11, John acts as though his hearers and readers already know about "the" beast when in fact it is the first time he is telling them about it, while in chapter 13 he talks about "a" beast as if they have not yet become acquainted. This odd narrative sequencing makes sense when one reads chapter 13 as part of the larger section of chapters 12–14, where John employs the literary device of a flashback. In real time, the events narrated in chapter 13 occur prior to those that take place in chapters 1–11. John therefore properly introduces the beast from the sea here without using the article.

The similar titles and functions identify "the" beast from the abyss (11:7) and "a" beast from the sea (13:1) as the same entity. Mythologically speaking, the sea and the abyss are functionally identical; they represent the lockdown region of chaos and the forces that perpetrate it.[3] Though almost all of John's 22 references to *thalassa* (sea) refer to the physical sea as a great and neutral body of water, he does have five clarifying metaphorical uses. These all show the sea operating either as a repository for the dead or as chaos (4:6; 13:1; 15:2; 20:13; 21:1). Since death chaotically disturbs life, the symbolism has a constant emotional impact throughout all five passages. The word *abyssos* (abyss) functions similarly. For John it is always a place of chaos (9:1, 2, 11; 11:7; 17:8; 20:1, 3). Therefore, when John says, on the one hand, that a beast arises from the abyss and that, on the other hand, a beast arises from the sea, he is talking about the same beast and the same menacing reality. The bestial target and accomplishment are also the same: to make war on the people of the church and to conquer them (11:7; 13:7).

---

3. Caird comments, "In the Greek Old Testament *abyssos* is used as a rendering for the Great Deep, the primaeval ocean of the creation story (Gen. i.2; vii. 11), and for the sea in general (Job xxviii. 14; xxxviii. 16)" (161).

John's mythical presentation has a decidedly historical point. The beast is Rome. "The first monster represents the Roman imperial power which, for the province of Asia, annually came up out of the sea, with the arrival of the proconsul at Ephesus" (Caird 162). In making this historical case, John also makes the most of his mythological connection with Daniel. Daniel, too, used the dramatic presentation of mythical beasts from the sea to interpret the struggles of his people against the forces of historical empire. According to John, this bestial, imperial power is satanic. He therefore immediately associates the beast from the sea with its patron, the dragon (see the comment on 12:3). Like the dragon, the beast has ten horns and seven heads. John will relate these accoutrements directly to Rome (17:3, 7, 9, 12, 16); the seven heads are the seven hills and the seven emperors (17:9). The beast therefore is not one emperor as such but, as seven represents completion, the entire sense of Roman rule: "The beast is a whole system, one that is universal and total (it has power over every tribe, people, tongue, and nation). The beast is the entire empire, in its economic, political, social dimension, and especially its religious, theological, and spiritual dimension" (Richard 114).

Though the dragon's ten horns were uncovered, the beast from the sea wears ten diadems on its ten horns. While the dragon had seven diadems on its seven heads, the beast outfits its heads with blasphemous names. As for the dragon, so for the beast, the horns and diadems signal power and kingship. The ten horns are ten kings (17:12; cf. Dan 7:24). The diadems on the horns represent the beast's claim to be king of kings, a title John and his fellow believers ascribe exclusively to Christ (19:16), who also wears many diadems on his head (19:12). The dragon and the beast parody the Lamb's claim to power by positioning their ten horns against his seven (see the discussion of 5:6 and 12:3). John wants his readers to realize that, since seven represents perfection, the Lamb retains more qualitative power even though he is outnumbered.

The blasphemous names on the beast's seven heads evoke images associated with Roman coinage. John's hearers and readers would regularly have seen the heads of emperors on imperial coins accompanied by titles in Greek like "god," "son of god," "savior," or "lord." Since those titles and the realities behind them belong only to God and the Lamb, John regards their attribution to Roman emperors as blasphemy.

[2] Daniel 7:3–6 provides the inspiration for the next phase of the sea beast's description. It has the general appearance of a leopard, the feet of a bear, and the mouth of a lion. John presents these traits in reverse order from Daniel, who sees a lion, a bear, and a leopard. Daniel witnessed a fourth beast with the ten horns John depicts in 13:1 (Dan 7:7). For Daniel, the four beasts represent empires that had conquered the people of God in a bestial manner. By folding all their attributes into the characterization of a single brute, John presses the narrative claim that this new beast is an imperial force without peer.

[3] John focuses on one of the beast's seven imperial heads. If, as 13:1 and 17:9 indicate, the seven heads symbolize seven Roman emperors, then one of those emperors has suffered a mortal wound. John's description is "as slaughtered." It is precisely the same description he gives for the Lamb, who was standing "as slaughtered" (*hōs* plus the perfect-passive participle of *sphazō*; see 5:6, 9, 12; 13:8). In order to emphasize that this trait is as much a part of the beast's character as it is a part of the Lamb's, John repeats the death imagery twice more within the same chapter (13:12, 14). The beast's hijacking of the Lamb's defining features mocks those who follow the Lamb. While they cry out because they have been slaughtered (6:9–11; cf. 18:24), the beast who has butchered them feigns kinship with them even as it sneers about a slaughtering of its own.

The *hōs* (as) is not hypothetical or illusory. It is no fiction. Since the Lamb's slaughtering is a reference to Jesus' demise on the cross, John is most certainly conveying a brutally real fatality. He makes that clear when he adds that it was a slaughtering "to death" (*eis thanaton*). By specifying the death as a *plēgē* ("plague"; cf. 13:12, 14), John indicates that like the other acts of eschatological destruction connected with that term (9:18, 20; 11:6; 15:1, 6, 8; 16:9, 21; 18:4, 8; 21:9; 22:18), it was an act of God's judgment. Verse 14 then explains that the mortal wounding was with a sword.

The head bounces quickly back. Immediately after narrating its demise, a horrified John reassesses the situation. His adversative *kai* (but) initiates a clause that sees the head healed from its death blow. Two observations are important here. First, John clearly understands this head to be the representative of a larger entity; its regeneration is a revival of the beast (13:12). Second, the verb for healing occurs incredulously in the passive voice: *etherapeuthē* (he was healed). With yet another of his divine passives, John implies that God is responsible for the head's regeneration (cf. 20:7, where God allows the dragon's release from the abyss). John does not explain why God would either allow or directly cause the restoration of a force so hostile to God's own people and church. He is apparently more interested in assuring his hearers and readers that nothing happens in human history that is beyond the realm of God's control. Even the bestial movements of a satanic minion happen within the confines of God's divine orchestration.

The theme here is resurrection: the head died; the head rises from that death just as the Lamb rose from his execution. At 13:14, when John describes the beast's return with the verb *ezēsen* (he lived/came back to life), he employs the same resurrection language he applies to Christ at 2:8. In its continuing parody of the Lamb, the beast, using its head, ridicules any notion that the Lamb is somehow more worthy because of its regeneration. Perhaps just here lies the important point John heard from the hymnic stanza at 5:9. The Lamb's worthiness does not derive from any miraculous events, even one as stupendous as resurrection. The Lamb's worthiness derives instead from the same source as the worthiness of those who follow him. The Lamb's worthiness comes from his willingness to witness to his own lordship and the lordship of his God at the expense of his own life. It is that willingness to witness, that transformative act of witness in the face of whatever loss may come because of it, that sets the Lamb and his followers apart. The head of a Roman beast can indeed come back from the dead and perhaps bring a staggering monster back to life with it. The beast has been allowed that much rein. The beast cannot, however, stop the realization of God's rule that is even now breaking in through the blood of the Lamb and the enduring witness to that Lamb (12:11). The beast cannot stop it because ultimately God is in control.

Because the bestial heads represent Roman emperors, many have speculated about the historical figures John had in mind. Most attention has focused on the one head narrated with sufficient detail to make an educated historical guess, the one whose mortal sword wound was healed. The odds are high that John had Nero in mind. According to Suetonius (*Nero* 49), Nero committed suicide by stabbing himself in the throat with a sword. His death therefore fits the picture John paints in Rev 13. So does the murky legend surrounding an expectation for his return.

The Romans remembered Nero with a great deal of hostility. His scandalous, oppressive rule degenerated to such depths that the Roman senate eventually declared him an enemy of the state. Shortly thereafter, disgraced and fleeing, he took his own life. Unfortunately, because there were few witnesses to either his death or his corpse, various conspiracy theories emerged. They took one of two forms. In the first, Nero did not die but instead escaped to a place of exile. In most versions of this theory, he fled to the East, where he was as revered as he was reviled in the West.

In the East, Nero had always been acknowledged positively for his contributions to the arts. He was particularly honored for crafting a stable diplomatic relationship with the Parthians. Indeed, many believed that he had fostered so strong a friendship with the Parthians that they had provided him refuge. When he had sufficient time to amass even more support among the Parthians, he would lead their armies across the Euphrates to take revenge on the empire that had ousted him.

The second version of the legend took on the name of Nero redivivus. This is the version that appears to lie behind John's vision of the slaughtered head returned to life. In this scenario, Nero did indeed die. However, those who either expected or feared his return believed that it would truly be a return from the dead. Christ-believers would certainly have feared it. They would remember Nero as the first emperor to instigate a widespread and vicious persecution of the witnesses to their faith (in 64 C.E.). According to tradition, key apostolic leaders Peter and Paul were both killed during that wave of terror. Commentators are correct to assert that John does not expect Nero's literal return from the dead, but that he is warning his followers to recognize that evil itself resurrects. Evil, when destroyed in its incarnation in one person, will manage to find other willing and capable hosts to continue its draconian work (cf. 17:11). "The impending confrontation between the beast and the followers of the Lamb would appear to John as an apocalyptic extension and intensification of the Neronian persecution" (Bauckham, *Climax of Prophecy*, 412).

The Nero redivivus version of the legend also fits with John's understanding that the death and resurrection of the bestial head reflects a similarly astounding revival of the empire itself. When Nero died, the empire sank into a quagmire of tumultuous violence. The Julian Dynasty that had been in place since Caesar Augustus died with Nero in 68 C.E. A civil war and perhaps even the dissolution of the empire itself threatened. In 69, no fewer than four men pursued and laid claim to the imperial throne. With the rise to power of Vespasian and his Flavian Dynasty, the empire remarkably rose to new life. Like the head, the beast managed, and thereby mocked, resurrection.[4]

The people of the earth were so impressed with the beast's regeneration that they followed it. The language is that of discipleship (cf. Mark 1:17; 8:34; Matt 4:19; 16:24; Luke 9:23). No wonder Christ and his followers would need rods of iron to shepherd the nations so that they follow God instead (see the comments on 2:27; 12:5; 19:15; cf. 11:1).

[4] The subject switches suddenly and somewhat awkwardly to the plural when John declares that "they" worshiped the dragon first and then the beast. The reference is to the "whole earth" (v. 3) and by implication the nations from the earth (10:11; 11:2, 9, 18). They all worship the dragon, even though John's hymnic visions have made clear that proper worship belongs exclusively to God and God's Christ (4:10; 5:14; 7:11; 11:16; 19:4).

John is making two interrelated points. First, the beast, Rome, has amassed complete historical control. The dragon has created an empire by bestowing its authority upon Rome. This is the second point: Rome is satanic. The nations of the world worship the dragon because they love empire. John wants his hearers and readers to understand this critical point: to participate in the Roman imperial cult is to worship the draconian evil that lurks behind Rome.

The nations of the world are looking at what they can see rather than what John knows to be true. They claim that no one is like the beast, which is to say, no one can make war with it.[5] Once again God is being parodied. The question "Who is like this one, and who can make war with this one?" is a mimicking of the very rhetorical question asked about God in the Hebrew Scriptures (Exod

---

4. For a more detailed discussion of the legends of Nero's return and Nero redivivus, see Bauckham, *Climax of Prophecy*, 410–45. Bauckham sees John's use of the legends as developing from the reference to Nero as the great beast in the *Sibylline Oracles* and especially the *Ascen. Isa.* 4.2–14.

5. I take the *kai* (and) here to be epexegetical, so that the second clause ("Who is able to fight against it?") extends and clarifies the first ("Who is like the beast?").

15:11; Deut 3:24; Pss 35:10; 71:19; 89:6; 113:5; Isa 40:18, 25; 44:7; Mic 7:18). John offers a narrative counter to their imperial taunt. When one tracks his use of war language in both verb (*polemeō*) and noun (*polemos*) forms, his take on the matter becomes apparent. Who can make war with the beast? It is *not* a rhetorical question. God's angel Michael (12:7), the Christ Lamb (2:16; 17:14; 19:11), and the church (11:7; 12:17; 13:7) can all engage not just the beast but also the draconian force that powers it. Even if the dragon takes the initiative and initially appears to win, victory ultimately will belong to God and those who follow God.

[**5**] To stress yet again that the beast's powerful actions, even those that operate against God's interests, are under God's ultimate control, John emphasizes the divine passive in the ensuing section with an almost redundant use of *edothē* ("it was given," twice in v. 5 and twice in v. 7; see the commentary on 6:2; 9:1–21 introduction; 11:1). Here God allows the beast to speak boastful and blasphemous words. The boasts are no doubt an extension of the claims to greatness implied in the rhetorical question of v. 4: "Who is like the beast?" Traditionally, the beasts recall Daniel's narration of Nebuchadnezzar's pretentious claims to singular greatness just before God offered a counterclaim by humiliating him (Dan 4:30–37). The boasts of Antiochus IV Epiphanes are even more specific examples of an oppressive ruler declaring his greatness as he oppresses the people of God (Dan 7:8, 20, 25; cf. 11:36). Like Revelation, these texts from Daniel refer to the king as the appendage (a horn in this case) of a great beast from the sea whose rule was temporary: two times and a half, the functional equivalent of John's 42 months, 1,260 days, or 3½ years (Rev 11:2–3; 12:6, 14). In 13:5, the blasphemies no doubt echo v. 1 (cf. 17:3) and the imperial names and the titles of divinity connected with them. Such imperial images and names were on rich display in cultic temples and on imperial coins.

[**6**] Still operating with Dan 7:25 and 11:36 in mind (cf. Isa 52:5), John specifies the nature of the blasphemies introduced in Rev 13:5. They are directed first toward God's name. John's use of the term *onoma* (name) suggests that one's name conveys one's identity and reputation, particularly as being for or against God (3:1; 6:8; 8:11; 9:11; 13:1, 17; 14:1, 11; 15:2; 17:3, 5, 8; 19:12–13, 16; 22:4). When associated with a supernatural figure, the term signifies not only identity but also worthiness to receive adulation, even if that adulation must be given under duress (2:3, 13, 17; 3:8, 12; 11:18; 14:1; 15:4). The blaspheming of God's name, then, no doubt involves a mocking of God's identity as the Lord who is exclusively due worship. By avowing blasphemous names of lordship for its emperors and inciting its own cultic worship, the Roman beast has done exactly that.

Second, the blasphemies are directed against God's *skēnē* (dwelling). The allusion could work in one of two directions. If John maintains his dependence upon Daniel and links the Roman beast to the atrocities committed by Antiochus Epiphanes, he is perhaps referring to the Roman desecration of the temple that took place in 70 C.E. Aune points out, "Antiochus IV Epiphanes is remembered as having violated, or attempted to violate, several temples (Polybius 31.9; 1 Macc 6:1–5; 2 Macc 1:14–17) as well as the temple in Jerusalem (1 Macc 1:20–24; Jos. *Ag. Ap.* 2:83–84)" (2:745). It is more likely, however, that John is thinking in contemporary terms. By using *skēnē*, which refers to God's act of tabernacling with the people rather than the physical place in which that dwelling occurred (cf. Rev 21:3), John recognizes that what is being ridiculed is the possibility that a presence more forceful than Rome—namely, God—actually participates in the life of Christ-believers.

The strangest part of the statement is the final one, which either clarifies or adds to *skēnē*. Because of the strangeness of the formulation, several copyists added *kai* (and), which would indicate that both God's presence (the *skēnē*) and the ones who reside with God in heaven are being ridiculed. Others take the relative clause that follows *skēnē*, "the ones who dwell in heaven," as a clarification of *skēnē*. The *kai* can be reasonably explained as a scribal attempt to clarify a difficult text. It is more likely that the relative clause develops the preceding statement about God's dwelling in some way. In that case, John would be particularly concerned about the debasement of those who are in God's presence in heaven.[6] John recognizes that what is being ridiculed is the possibility that those who have died have moved into the presence of a force more powerful than the Roman one that killed them. The souls crying out beneath the altar at 6:9–11 come immediately to mind. Why are they crying out to a God who could not prevent their slaughter? The one who slaughtered them is the power they should recognize; its altar is the only one before which they should seek comfort. In mocking them, the beast does the double duty of mocking the God with whom they claim to dwell.

[7] Repeating what he has already said through the symbolism of the two witnesses (11:7), John acknowledges that the beast makes war on the holy ones, or saints, that is, members of the church (see the discussion of "holy ones/saints" at 5:8), and conquers them (cf. Dan 7:21, 25). Still, he persists in his claim that this conquest was allowed (*edothē*) by God. It is important to note, however, that the "saints," not the church itself, are conquered. There is no rapture out of the devastation for believers.

While Christ-believers are being conquered, the beast universalizes its control (cf. Dan 7:14). Once again, there is a mocking of God and of Christ's own claims. Though he presents them in a different order, John lists this fourfold grouping (tribe, people, tongue, nation) elsewhere as the object of the universal reach of both God and Lamb (Rev 7:9; 14:6). Christ has ransomed them

---

6. I agree with Caird (166) that it is doubtful that John has the blaspheming of angels in mind here.

(5:9), but because they did not respond properly, John was commanded to prophesy against them (10:11). Then these "inhabitants of the earth" gloat over the demise of the two witnesses, who symbolize Christ-believers such as John (11:9). They do so, if chapter 13 is indeed a flashback, because before John begins to write, they are under the authority of the beast.

[8] John once again refers to the whole earth (13:3), which marvels behind the beast and worships it (v. 4), with what has become his traditional formula: "the inhabitants of the earth" (see the comments on 2:13; 3:10; 6:10). Though the verb "will worship" is in the future tense, since chapter 13 is a flashback John is no doubt talking about his present eschatological moment, when the inhabitants of the earth are heavily invested in the imperial cult.

The key interpretive problem centers on the prepositional phrase "from the foundation of the world." Since such prepositional phrases are overwhelmingly adverbial, this one can modify two different components in the verse: the writing of the names in the Book of Life, or the slaughtering of the Lamb. It is unlikely that John intends to say that the Lamb was slaughtered from the foundation of the world. Though he speaks about it in mythic terms as a snatching to the throne of God (12:5), it is clear throughout that he understands it to be the historical event of Jesus' crucifixion (e.g., 1:5; 5:6, 12; 12:11). One could suppose that John intends to speak about the planning of Jesus' slaughtering from the foundation of the world, but then that would mean going beyond what the actual text conveys. It is better to read the language of slaughter as an attributive modifier of the Lamb in the way that John uses it throughout the book. He is speaking about the Book of Life of the executed Lamb.

The more appropriate of the two interpretive choices is the one that has the phrase "from the foundation of the world" modifying the writing of the names in the Book of Life. In this case, John would be talking about the inhabitants of the earth whose names were not from the foundation of the world written in the Book of Life. One's salvation was dependent on having one's name written in the Book (20:15; 21:27). In other words, some names were predestined from the beginning to be excluded from the possibility of eschatological relationship with God. This interpretive choice carries the disturbing implication that no matter whether they responded to John's exhortations, their fate was sealed. One wonders, then, why John works so hard to get even the likes of Jezebel, Balaam, and the Nicolaitans to repent, or why he seems to be surprised that even after all the devastating acts of judgment, many who survive them refuse to repent (see the comments on 9:3–5, 20–21; 11:1, 3, 6, 13). He seems to expect that repentance, and the relationship with God that comes with it, is still possible. At 3:5 he indicates that some names are first included in the book, only to be blotted out for refusal to respond appropriately to God's call to witness. This deterministic linking of the phrase "from the foundation of the world" with "not writing the names of the inhabitants of the earth in the Book of Life" may therefore simply reveal an inner tension within John's narrative (if not, indeed, in his mind) on how human relationship with God is ultimately negotiated.

Yet there is also a more intriguing possibility. Later John at the final judgment pictures multiple books being opened prior to the opening of the Book of Life (20:12). Why so many books? The function of the Book of Life is clear; it records the names of those granted eschatological relationship with God. The context of 3:5 implies that those names belong to believers in John's churches. Their only fear is that acts of accommodation to Rome's claims to lordship will blot their names from their recorded place. Apparently, though, as the text here indicates, there are other names that have not always resided in the Book of Life. Here the presence of the other books in chapter 20 becomes significant. Since the names in the Book of Life were recorded there from the foundation of the world, their recording cannot be the result of their proper witness behavior. The recording happened before the people attached to the names were ever born. The other books are therefore the ones that must record the deeds spoken about at the end of 20:12. By their repentant acts of witness, those whose names were not written in the Book of Life from the foundation of the world (i.e., the inhabitants of the earth), can nevertheless earn an inscribing of their names in those other books. If this interpretation is correct, there is no real tension in John's understanding of the manner in which eschatological relationship with God is negotiated. No one is predestined for eschatological judgment. All have an opportunity to be saved. Believers' names are already recorded; all they need to do is witness authentically so that their names will not be blotted out. Others, the "inhabitants of the earth," need only repent and give God glory and their names will be added to the Book of Life, after their recorded works have been duly noted in the other books that are opened first (see the discussion of 20:12).[7]

**[9]** The sentence "Let anyone who has an ear listen" is all about exhortation. John uses it consistently to encourage action. In fact, except for this unique occurrence, John only deploys it at the conclusion of the letters to the seven churches (2:7, 11, 17, 29; 3:6, 13, 22). In those cases he uses it to buttress the preceding ethical mandates. He revives it here for the same reason. This vision scene has the same goal as the more direct exhortations in the letters; John is encouraging appropriate behavior. Once his people know how satanic the Roman beast is, they must reject it.

**[10]** John is not only asking his hearers and readers to "hear" what he *has* said about the beast and to respond appropriately; he also wants them to hear what he *will* say about how they must also be prepared to endure the devastating reprisal with which the beast will answer their rejection. Operating from the background of Jer 15:2 and 43:11, John declares that if someone is destined for

---

7. I am indebted to Professor Shane Berg of Princeton Theological Seminary for observations that have led to this interpretation.

captivity, then that person goes into captivity. The conditional statement squares with John's conviction that everything, even God's allowance of the beast's reign of terror against God's people (see the use of *edothē*, "it was given," in vv. 5 and 7), is scripted. Those who witness to the lordship of Christ can, like the Lamb, who was himself executed, expect—that is, because of their witness they are *destined*—to be taken captive by a beast whose primary goal is to institutionalize its own exclusive lordship.

Still operating with Jeremiah's warning in mind, John turns his attention to death by the sword in the second half of the verse. This second conditional statement is so difficult to decipher in the Greek that it has spurred many textual variants. John uses two aorist-passive infinitives but no main verb. One would expect that after the protasis, "if someone is to be killed by the sword," the apodosis would follow with a primary verb, preferably in the future passive: "he will be killed by the sword." Beale argues that the formulation is part of John's intentional effort to remind his hearers and readers of the message conveyed by the infinitive "to kill" elsewhere in his text: "Infinitive forms of *apokteinō* ('kill') also portray the suffering of believers in 6:8 and 6:11. 13:10 continues the theme and adds an exhortation for the saints to endure faithfully through such persecution" (704–5). If he is right, and I think he is, then John intends to say something very much like what Jesus conveys in Matt 26:52. There, in directing his followers to put away the sword because those who take the sword will perish by it, Jesus demonstrates that the proper response to bestial violence is not more violence but a faithful endurance that witnesses to one's confidence that God is indeed Lord and therefore in control.

John makes exactly this point as he closes out his introduction of the beast from the sea with the third line of v. 10: here is the endurance, which is the faith of the saints. I take the *kai* (and) that connects endurance and faith as epexegetical (see the comment on 1:2). Faith extends and develops the meaning of endurance. In three of his four uses of *pistis* (faith), in fact, John bundles it with *hypomonē* ("endurance," 2:19; 13:10; 14:12). One's ability to endure is a measure of one's faith in the lordship and therefore the ultimate control of God and the Lamb. John uses "endurance" in just this way when writing to his churches (2:2, 3, 19; 3:10).

The two other uses of the term (1:9 and 14:12) are, together with 13:10, even more illustrative. In each case John either models or calls for an enduring witness to the lordship of Christ, even in those circumstances where offering such testimony will provoke persecution. In other words, John is warning his hearers and readers about the risks they will face when witnessing against the beast. Some will be imprisoned; others will be slain by the sword. But hold on. Resist. Yes, resistance does appear to be futile, but if you realize that God is still in control, that nothing is happening without God's leave, then you should also realize that everything that happens is part of God's strategic plan for victory. Not only is resistance *not* futile; resistance is part of God's strategy to humble the arrogant beast by using its own destruction of God's witnesses as the very tool with which God's kingdom action will make its final move (6:9–11; 12:11). Reddish is therefore right to argue that *hypomonē* should not be so lamely translated as patient endurance: "It is in fact closer to absolute intransigence, unbending determination, an iron will, the capacity to endure persecution, torture, and death without yielding one's faith. It is one of the fundamental attributes of nonviolent resistance" (256; see further the discussion of nonviolent resistance at 1:9 above).

Indeed, this kind of obstinate faith in God's direction of human history and the call for humans to respond to that direction were hallmarks of the nonviolent civil rights movement in the United States. Many leaders and followers of the movement endured social ostracism, political persecution, police brutality, and even death with a resolve born of faith to continue the fight against segregation no matter the consequences because of their belief that ultimately God, not the beast of racism, was Lord. Refusal to take up the sword against oppressive evil, and acceptance of imprisonment as the price of one's stubborn (though nonviolent) resistance to an oppressive system, does not mean surrendering to it. Instead, this posture of persistent witness participates in God's transformative work in the arena of human history.

### 13:11–18 The Beast from the Land

11 Then I saw another beast rising up from the earth, and it had two horns like a lamb, but[a] it was speaking like a dragon. 12 And it exercises all the authority of the first beast, on its behalf,[b] and it makes the earth and its inhabitants worship the first beast, whose mortal wound was healed. 13 It performs great signs, even making fire come down from heaven to the earth before people; 14 and it deceives the inhabitants of the earth because of the signs that it was allowed to do on behalf of the beast, telling the inhabitants of the earth to make an image of the beast who was wounded by the sword but lived. 15 And it was allowed to give breath to the image of the beast, so that the image of the beast might even speak, and cause whoever did not worship the image of the beast to be killed. 16 And it causes all, the small and the great, the rich and the poor, the free and the slave, to be marked on their right hand or forehead, 17 so that no one could buy or sell who does not have the mark, which is the name of the beast or the number of its name. 18 Here is wisdom. Let the one who has understanding calculate the number of the beast, for it is the number of a person, and its number is 666.[c]

a. The *kai* is adversative: "but."

b. For this translation, see BAGD 271.

c. The text's calculation of 666 is supported by A $\mathfrak{P}^{47}$ 051 $\mathfrak{M}$, which read *hexakosiai/oi hexēkonta hex*, and by P 1006 1841 1854 2053$^{vid}$ *al*, which read, *hexakosia hexēkonta hex*. This strong external support indicates that 666 was the original text. Additionally, as Aune observes, "it$^{gig}$ vg Beatus syr$^{ph}$ cop arm, $\mathfrak{P}^{47}$ 025 051 Hippolytus (*De Ant.* 48) Andr de f$^{2073}$ n 598 and the Byzantine text have three letters that function as numbers, χξϛ, . . . χ = 600; ξ = 60; ϛ . . . = 6" (2:722). The shift of the single middle letter from ξ to ι would create a total of 616 (χιϛ). This accounting is supported by C; Ir$^{mss}$: *hexakosiai deka hex*. Though the letters could easily be switched by mistake, the fact that the numerical value of Nero Caesar in Latin letters equals 616 suggests that the change was intentional (Metzger, *Textual Commentary*, 752). Even less likely is *hexakosia hexēkonta penta* (665), found in 2344.

[11] With *kai eidon* ("and I saw"; see the discussion of 13:1), John introduces another scene in the continuing narrative vision of beasts rising to meet the dragon (12:18). This second beast rises from the land and is a clear allusion to the male Behemoth whom God separated from the female Leviathan on the fifth day of creation (see the introduction to 12:18–13:18).

This monster is a contradiction in terms. It has the look of a lamb but the mouth of a dragon. It is lamblike because of its two horns. At Dan 8:3, however, a ram with two horns represents opposition to, rather than assistance for, the people of God. This beast clearly represents the same. Given that both the dragon and the beast from the sea have ten horns, however, one gains the immediate sense that this beast is neither as powerful nor as directly related to the dragon as is the beast from the sea. Even so, the mere fact that it has lamblike horns prolongs the parody of God and the Christ initiated by the dragon and the beast from the sea.

Despite its lamblike appearance, the beast's mouth, or at least what comes out of it, immediately gives it away. It speaks like, and is therefore most certainly affiliated with, the dragon. These competing attributes (lamblike looks, dragonlike mouth) must have reminded some of John's hearers and readers of the Matthean Jesus' warning about false prophets who come looking like sheep but in reality are ravenous wolves (Matt 7:15). In fact, only here in v. 11 does John even refer to it as a beast. All further references invoke the title "false prophet" (16:13; 19:20; 20:10).

Scholars have noted two other important points about this figure. First, since it rounds out the complement of mythical and historical enemies arrayed against God's people, it parodies the Trinitarian force of God (4:3, 11), the Lamb (5:6, 12), and the Spirit (1:4; 3:1; 4:5; 5:6). Second, because it is portrayed as lamblike in appearance, it is quite likely that John envisioned it as having a function similar to the Lamb's. The Lamb was the primary model for witnessing to the lordship of God and Christ, suffering on account of that witness, and then being vindicated by God through resurrection. As such, the Lamb is a motivating factor for faith; his life encourages others to believe and to witness to that belief. According to vv. 12–18, the false prophet is the role model for a counterbelief in the lordship of the dragon and its beast.

[12] Though it does not have the strength (only two horns), this false prophet does have the authority of the first beast. The first beast has delegated its authority to the false prophet in the same way that the dragon delegated its authority to Rome (v. 4). "The phrase [*enōpion autou*] literally 'before him, in his presence,' really means 'by his authority, on his behalf' . . . or even 'at his commissioning'" (Aune 2:757).

The false prophet uses this authority for one primary reason, to encourage the inhabitants of the earth (see the comments on 2:13; 3:10; 6:10; 13:8) to worship the first beast. The prophet is therefore by definition false since worship belongs exclusively to God (see the discussion of 13:4). Because John's mythical portraits often have historical referents, this false prophet is likely also a cipher for a prophetlike person or entity who encouraged devotion to the Roman beast. John probably had in mind the people and infrastructure that institutionally embodied Asia Minor's commitment to the imperial cult. Rome, as the beast from the sea, is a foreign force. Land based, the false prophet has a more indigenous feel; he rises up out of the very soil on which John's hearers and readers have built their lives and homes. This beast is local. It represents the native traditions and institutions that nevertheless serve the bestial imperial cult. Rome exercised its rule through just such institutions. In Asia, the imperial cult was in the hands of a body known as the *koinon* in Greek and the *commune* in Latin. The *commune Asiae* was a provincial council that included representatives from the major towns. Such councils were often populated with priests or other political representatives who promoted the imperial cult. "Priests of the imperial cult wore crowns that displayed the busts of the deified emperors and the gods whose cult they served" (Aune 2:756). The Asiarchs of Acts 19:31 may well have been members of just such a commune.

The mixture of political and religious affairs built into the identities of these councils means that the false prophet's role cannot be relegated to an exclusively religious arena. Worship of the emperor and of the Roman deities associated with the imperial cult was as much a sign of political as religious loyalty. The members of the *koinon* were charged with encouraging and fostering belief with the knowledge that such faith would eventually mutate into political loyalty, that is, loyalty to the political, economic, social, and cultic lordship of Rome. (On the healing of the first beast's death wound, see the comment on v. 3.)

[13] As one might expect from a prophet, this false one performs miracles.[8] Signs help convince people about one's professed supernatural status or

---

8. Beale (708) points to Moses' validation of his actions with signs: Exod 4:17, 30; 10:2; 11:10.

connections (16:14; 19:20). Just as the land beast attempts to fool Christ-believers into following it with its lamblike appearance (13:11), so now it tries to link up with one of God's signature prophetic acts: the raining of fire down upon the earth (1 Kgs 18:38–39; 2 Kgs 1:10–14; cf. Luke 9:54; Rev 20:9). Christ-believers had already been warned to expect such false prophets performing such false signs in the hopes of luring them to a false faith (Mark 13:21–23; Matt 24:23–25; 2 Thess 2:9).

[**14**] As with the first beast, so with this one, all that it accomplishes is under God's direction. John makes this point with yet another deployment of the divine passive *edothē* ("it was given"; see the discussion above of 13:5). Still, because of the land beast's signs, the false prophet is able to deceive (cf. 19:20) the inhabitants of the earth into making an image of the first beast. John is working here from the account in Dan 3, where the imperial ruler crafts an image of himself and demands, under penalty of death, that all in his kingdom worship it.

[**15**] God allows (once again John appeals to the divine passive *edothē*, "it was given") the false prophet the charisma to make the imperial cult and its images seem to come alive and even speak. Many priestly types claimed the power to animate images of the gods so that the images might speak and convey oracles about the present and the future: "The specific example of trickery that John mentions, a speaking statue, is mentioned in several ancient sources. Through ventriloquism, through a person hiding in a hollow statue, or through some mechanical device, statues could appear animated and be made to talk" (Reddish 259). This nod to Hellenistic magic is John's metaphorical way of saying that the false prophet has breathed life into a cultic system so that people believe that the images populating the system can actually make a positive economic, social, political, and religious difference in their lives. Those imperial images are supposed to bring them a life of rewards that a reliance upon the lordship of God and Christ could not.

Like Nebuchadnezzar in Dan 3, the imperial image can also threaten death against all those who resist worshiping it. John appears to be reminding his readers of the saying that those who are destined to be killed by the sword for their witness to the lordship of God and the Lamb will indeed be killed (Rev 13:10). He fears that this threat of death will lead many to surrender their testimony to the lordship of Christ and accommodate themselves to the idolatrous expectations of the imperial cult. This is why he pleads so fervently—and sometimes desperately—in his letters to the seven churches (chs. 2–3). He wants his followers to realize that while the Roman beast may have been allowed the ability to impose the first death, they need fear only the second death, from which only their eschatological relationship with God and the Lamb can save them (see 2:11; 9:6). At this point John issues a threat of his own. Those who, fearing the first death, submit to worshiping the image of the first beast may prosper on earth, but they will be sentenced to eternal separation from God and thus the second death when the ultimate judgment comes (14:9, 11; 16:2; 19:20). Those who do not worship this beast will reign with Christ (20:4).

[16] One thing is clear: the false prophet does not discriminate. The land beast targets everyone; it considers neither social standing nor economic status (cf. 6:15; 19:17–18). John knows that even his Christ-believers have been targeted. He also knows that many of them are being persuaded by the false prophet's deceitful tactics. Many are accommodating themselves to the bestial imperial cult, to its claims of lordship, and to the social, economic, political, and cultic ramifications of such a lordship. Unlike Christianity at significant periods in its history, the forces of evil have always had an "open door, come just as you are" policy. Perhaps this is something else the dragon and its beasts have to brag about.

The false prophet issues an identifying *charagma* (mark) on the right hand or forehead of those who respond positively to its invitation to worship the image of the first beast. John is speaking symbolically; there is no literal mark. The "mark" of the beast symbolizes a person's allegiance to and participation in the religious, social, economic, and political rites associated with the imperial cult (13:16–17; 14:9, 11; 16:2; 19:20; 20:4). "Rather, John is saying that those (including people in the church) who participate in the worship of the emperor have, in so doing, 'marked' themselves as belonging to Satan" (Reddish 260).

Once again John's Greek is awkward. Although he has been speaking about the single false prophet, when he speaks of the branding with the mark, he employs a third-person plural formulation. He says, "in order that *they* might give them a mark upon their right hand or forehead." The "they" most likely refers back to the counter-Trinitarian sensibility that John has been trying to establish for the affiliation between the dragon, the beast from the sea, and the false prophet/beast from the land. The action of one reflects the intentions of the triumvirate. When the false prophet acts, he acts not alone but for them all, in the same way that the Lamb's actions reflect the intentions of God and the Spirit. In this subtle way, John again recognizes that evil mimics and therefore mocks the good.

The parody becomes explicit when John's hearers and readers remember that God's followers are also marked with a seal upon their foreheads (7:2; 14:1; 22:4). If chapters 12–14 are indeed a flashback to events and realities that have preceded the visionary narratives in chapters 1–11 and 15–22, then the false prophet's markings took place first. In real time, God's sealing was a retaliatory response. In God's case, however, this action was not for parody but for protection. John has just disclosed that those who do not worship the first beast will be killed (13:15). And he has painfully acknowledged that those destined for captivity and the sword because of their loyalty to the lordship of God and the Lamb will succumb to that destiny (v. 10). There will be no rapturelike escape for the people of the Lamb. Because they do not bear the mark of the beast, they will be vulnerable to destruction by the beast. Although their protection from the second death is guaranteed (2:11; 20:6), their susceptibility to the first death is all but certain (11:7; 13:7). God does, however, desire a remnant, military-like force to engage the forces of the beast. God will seal and therefore protect the 144,000 from the ravages of the beast so that they can provide whatever counter to the beast God intends (see the comments on 7:4 and 11:1–2). Ultimately, in a show of superior strength, God will use even the beast's own mark as a weapon against those whom it was designed to protect. It will become a locating beacon. The mark will make it impossible for the worshipers of the beast to hide from God's coming judgment. Because of the mark, God will easily identify and destroy them (14:9–11; 16:2; 19:20) and reward those who have remained faithful (20:4).

In John's narrative time, however, a different scenario develops. God seals first in chapter 7, and the evil triumvirate appears mockingly to counterseal here (in ch. 13). Through the use of the literary technique of the flashback in chapters 12–13, John can make two very different points simultaneously. He can demonstrate God's ability to protect God's people from the power of the dragon if God so chooses and ultimately punish those who worship the beast, even as he concedes that the draconian forces flaunt their historical power by mocking God and singling out God's people for destruction whenever they can. John's hearers and readers can therefore acknowledge the reality of their tragic historical situation and yet draw upon the belief that ultimately God is the greater power and, despite appearances, still in control.

[17] It is easy to see why some scholars have linked the mark of the beast with imperial coinage, which John associated with bestial blasphemies at 13:1, 5.[9] The mark clearly has a commercial connection. Without it, without an expression of one's loyalty to the beast, a person loses one's ability to engage in commerce. Shut out of the economic system, a person would be hard-pressed to progress socially and politically, perhaps even to survive. The symbolism of the mark, then, is much broader than imperial coinage. It goes back to John's concern about all the enticements that draw his people toward accommodation to imperial cultic practice. John was particularly concerned that his people are so interested in maintaining strong membership in their trade and other guild associations that they will participate in the idolatrous rites, such as eating meat sacrificed to idols, connected with those associations in order to progress

---

9. Cf. Richard: "If the image of the beast is really the depiction of the empire on Roman coins, the meaning would be that Roman money is the visible representation of the empire's spirit. Money is fetishized and becomes an active subject; it has spirit and life, and it speaks and kills. Money becomes the image of the beast being worshiped, the idol being worshiped, the divinity being worshiped. . . . Money is something inert that the false prophet turns into a living subject" (116).

socially and economically (see, e.g., the commentary on Pergamum, 2:12–17; Thyatira, 2:18–29). It is such unholy, idolatrous accommodation that he depicts through the symbolization of the mark that contains the name or number of the first beast.[10]

[18] Wisdom and understanding go together for John. Wisdom belongs initially to the Lamb (5:12) and to God (7:12). In John's only other uses of the term "wisdom," he pairs it with the only occurrences of "understanding" in Revelation (13:18; 17:9). Both 13:8 and 17:9 speak to the same circumstance: the identity and nature of the beast from the sea. This beast is identified with Rome and the emperors who leashed it (17:9). Likewise, in 13:18, the identity of the monster is inextricably tied to one of its most vicious imperial heads. As will be the case when a similar saying appears in 17:9, the emphasis on wisdom to solve the eschatological conundrum looks back at the material that has already been presented. One needs wisdom to be able to decipher what John has just revealed.

Additionally, though, the capably wise person will be able to calculate the number of the beast because it equals the number of a person's name. John is working here from the classical practice of gematria, a riddlelike activity where letters are given corresponding numbers. One adds up the numbers that stand for the particular letters in a name to create a numerical sum for that name (cf. 15:2). According to the *Sibylline Oracles* (1.324–30), the Greek letters of Jesus' name (*Iēsous*) total a numerically perfect 888.[11] In John's time, the practice of matching the beast's name and number was much easier than it is now. John appears to assume that his hearers and readers already have the name and can therefore easily equate it with the number. Thus John was not really giving his hearers and readers a puzzle; he was reinforcing an identification they already knew. However, since many names could produce the same number, it is much more difficult to work back from a given number to a particular name. Therein lies the problem for the contemporary interpreter, who has only a number that could represent a multitude of names.

However, John has graciously offered an important clue. In this chapter he has been preoccupied with the beast from the sea and with the head on that beast that suffered a mortal wound but regained life for itself and the beast. In v. 3 John appears to identify that head with Nero. Nero's reputation as the most vicious of emperors toward Christ-believers would solidify his symbolic identification with the monster that was imperial Rome. Interestingly, when the

---

10. Caird (53), however, argues that the Romans did not punish through economic sanctions but through courts of law.

11. See Bauckham, *Climax of Prophecy*, 385: $\iota = 10$; $\eta = 8$; $\sigma/\varsigma = 200$; $o = 70$; $\upsilon = 400$. So *Iēsous* = 888.

Greek letters for Neron Caesar are transliterated into Hebrew, the Hebrew letters add up to 666.[12] Yet John is writing in Greek to a Greek-speaking audience. Why would his riddle operate with Hebrew letters? Throughout the discussion of chapter 13, we have consistently seen that John depends upon Hebrew tradition to ground his first-century visions. It is not surprising, given his reliance upon Hebrew prophetic tradition to support his narrative, that at a climactic moment in the narrative he would also turn to the Hebrew language. Even textual variants support the choice of Nero as the name of the beast; in Latin, Caesar Nero totals the very 616 that the variants offer. Scholars have more recently pointed out an even more tantalizing reason for choosing Nero. Given that his is the one name in chapter 13 directly linked to the beast from the sea, it cannot be coincidental that when the Greek word for beast (*thērion*) is transliterated into Hebrew letters, those letters also add up to 666.[13] Bauckham points out that the reference to Nero as a great beast in the *Sibylline Oracles* (8.157) may reflect a tradition that remembered him as a monster quite apart from the symbolism of Jewish apocalyptic (*Climax of Prophecy*, 409–10). Nero is the imperial face of the beast that threatens all those who would dare to defy the lordship claims of Rome by obstinately witnessing to the lordship of God and the Lamb instead. For John it would be no coincidence that "beast" and "Nero" add up to the same ominous sum.

John has been working symbolically and not literally; therefore, I do not believe that one can end the interpretive effort with the number/name puzzling of gematria. Given John's focus on the number "seven" as indicating wholeness and perfection, it could well be that the seer is playing the beast's own taunting game against it. Even as he concedes its power, he finds a way to mock it. The repetition of the "six" for its number suggests that the beast keeps trying to approach the level of completeness that is represented in seven, but cannot quite make it. It is as though it is struggling to become something it never can be. In that regard, its own name betrays its limitation. Even as it flaunts its strength, it wallows in weakness. It is always a six, never a seven; 666 on into eternity. It will never have complete power because, like the number that symbolizes it, it will never itself be completely whole.[14]

---

12. קסר נרון: $n = 50$; $r = 200$; $w = 6$; $q = 100$; $s = 60$. When account is made for $2 \times 50$ and $2 \times 200$, the total is 666 for Neron Caesar. Beale warns, however, that this calculation is based on "a defective Hebrew spelling of קסר without a *yodh*," and adds that "a concordance check of the Talmuds, the Mishnah, the Tosephta, and the Tannaitic Midrashim finds only a spelling with the *yodh*" (719). Bauckham counters: "The defective spelling . . . used for Nero himself has now been shown by a papyrus document in Aramaic from Murabba'at, which is dated in the second year of Nero Caesar (נרון קסר)" (*Climax of Prophecy*, 388).

13. תריון: $t = 400$; $r = 200$; $y = 10$; $w = 6$; $n = 50$.

14. See, however, A. Collins, "Numerical Symbolism," 1271–72. Collins makes the argument that six does not function as an imperfect number elsewhere in the Apocalypse and that Philo actually thought the number also conveyed wholeness.

Therein lies perhaps the juiciest part of John's own taunt. People who worship the beast do so by saying its name. They fall down and worship its power, its greatness, its ultimate lordship by calling out its name. But every time they call out that name, they also proclaim what the name itself proclaims: not lordship but limitation. In their worship of the beast, then, they actually mock it.

The hearers and readers of John's work, however, should recognize the number and what it signifies. On the basis of that knowledge, they must find a way to hold on and resist. For the beast's time is as imperfect as its name (13:5). Its power and control will not last forever. Therefore, John admonishes, "Do not buy into its economic schemes or accommodate to its imperial force. Resistance is not futile."

### *14:1–20 God Strikes Back: Visions of Judgment*

John's explanatory flashback concludes. Having raised the dramatic tension in the book to almost unbearable heights with the blasting of the seventh trumpet (11:19), the seer either had to construct a climax or broker a narrative respite that would allow his hearers and readers an opportunity to catch their end-expecting breaths. He was not yet ready to end it all since he had not finished explaining the circumstances that hounded his followers (ch. 13) or sufficiently alerted them to the reality that their resistance would reap a bountiful yield (12:11). In chapter 14, he stakes the claim that God can and will protect God's own.

As the concluding movement in the flashback, chapter 14 introduces figures and themes that are central throughout chapters 1–11 and again in chapters 15–22. The three eschatological protagonists are presented: God the Creator (v. 7); the Lamb (v. 1), one like a child of humanity (v. 14); and the Spirit (v. 13). The exhortations so critical for the letters to the seven churches (chs. 2–3), are echoed in the call to resistance in 14:12 and the apocalyptic macarism of 14:13. God's seven-staged march toward justice/judgment (seals, trumpets, bowls) is triumphantly anticipated through the actions of seven divine agents: six angels and the one like a child of humanity. The destruction of Rome (chs. 17–19) is anticipated in horrifyingly graphic detail in vv. 10–11, 17–20. And God's protection and deliverance of the faithful in chapters 20–22 has its prequel in vv. 1–5, 14–16. In chapter 14, the beginning of the end (chs. 12–14) yet told in the middle, comes to a shocking visionary conclusion.

### 14:1–5 The 144,000

14:1 Then I looked, and behold, the Lamb was standing on Mount Zion. And with him were 144,000 who had his name and the name of his Father written on their foreheads. 2 And I heard a voice from heaven like the sound of many waters and like the sound of loud thunder. The voice that

I heard was like that of harpists playing on their harps. 3 And they sing aᵃ
new song before the throne and before the four living creatures and the
elders. No one was able to learn the song except the 144,000 who have
been redeemed from the earth. 4 These are the ones who were not defiled
with women, for they are virgins. These are the ones who follow the Lamb
wherever he goes. These have been redeemed from humankind as first-
fruitsᵇ to God and for the Lamb. 5 And in their mouth no lie was found;
they are blameless.

a. The external evidence is balanced in support of the inclusion (A C 051 1006 1841
𝔐ᴬ lat syᵖʰ) and the exclusion (𝔓⁴⁷ ℵ P 1611 1854 2053 2329 2344 2377 𝔐ᴷ gig syʰ)
of *hōs* (as). The word could just as easily have been added to imitate its use in v. 2 or
deleted so as to match the use of "new song" in 5:9.

b. The phrase *ap' archēs* appears in 𝔓⁴⁷ ℵ *pc* t; Prim Bea; *aparchē* is attested by all
other witnesses. This interesting variant is apparently an accident of lexicography. *Ap
archēs* and *aparchē*, although distant etymological cousins, have very different meanings, both of which however make reasonably good sense in this context: "They were
redeemed from humanity *from the beginning*" (*ap' archēs*); or "They were redeemed
from humanity *as a firstfruit*" (*aparchē*). 𝔓⁴⁷ and ℵ notwithstanding, the manuscript tradition generally favors *aparchē*. Appearing only here in Revelation, it is also the slightly
more difficult reading.

**[14:1]** John opens with one of his favorite formulas for announcing a new vision:
*kai eidon, kai idou* ("Then I looked, and behold . . ." [see the discussion of 5:1;
6:5, 8; 13:1, 11; 14:14; 19:11]). He then introduces us to the Lamb. The definite
article attached to "Lamb" suggests that John's hearers and readers were already
familiar with this designation as a moniker for Christ. Given the way narrative
flashbacks work, by the time they reached this "introduction" of the Lamb, they
had already been clued into his identity by the "spoiler" scene at 5:6. John chose
not to use a definite article with "Lamb" at 5:6 because he was contrasting Jesus'
depiction as "*a* lamb" with that of his expected presentation as "*the* lion of
Judah," not because 5:6 was the first real-time expression of his identity as
Lamb. The lack of the article grammatically emphasized its comparative weakness. The real-time, initial expression of his identity as Lamb occurs right here
in 14:1, or at least it would have if John had chosen to present chapters 12–14
in chronological sequence (i.e., as chs. 1–3) rather than as a flashback. It is appropriate that "Lamb" be accompanied by the article in this flashback section even
though the term "beast" was not (13:1, 11). First, the hearers and readers have
not had narrative preparation for the beasts. Second and even more theologically
important, beasts, though powerful antagonists, are inferior to *the* Lamb. Once
again John allows his grammar to state his case before he presses it narratively.

John also presses his case visually. The Lamb is standing. As many commentators have pointed out, since the Lamb is clearly the Christ child who was

snatched to the throne of God (12:5), one would expect the seer to portray him as enthroned. His staging, though, fits the central thesis of resistant witness that pervades the book. Standing, for John, is as much about theology as posture (see the comment on 5:6); he means that the Lamb is standing strong against the idolatrous claims to lordship made by the beast from the land on behalf of the dragon and the beast from the sea.

John uses geography to shore up his theological presentation. The name "Zion" originates as the title for a fortress ("stronghold of Zion") in the Jerusalem area before David's conquest of the region (2 Sam 5:7; 1 Chr 11:5). Later the name was given to the ridge that separates the Kidron and Tyropoeon valleys in Jerusalem. Solomon built his temple on the highest point of that ridge, which came to be known as Mount Zion. Eventually the term was used for all of Jerusalem and sometimes even euphemistically for the people of Israel. Central to all of these applications was the understanding that Zion, whether as place, building, or people, was the location of God's presence and God's rule.[15] Eschatologically, Zion came to be known as the gathering place where the Messiah would assemble the people of God and execute God's final judgment.[16] Of particular importance is Ps 2, where God stands the Messiah on Zion in open defiance of the powers that would circumvent God's interests. Zion was ultimately envisioned as a place of refuge and protection during the troubling apocalyptic events that would surround the end time. Of the nineteen occurrences of "Mount Zion" in the Old Testament, nine of them "allude to a remnant being saved" (Beale 731). New Testament writers picked up on these themes and developed them in connection with their Christ portraits (Matt 21:5; John 12:15; Rom 9:33; 11:26; Heb 12:22; 1 Pet 2:6). Despite all appearances to the contrary, the crucified one will gather the faithful and judge the faithless—from Zion, the very stronghold upon which the Lamb now makes his stand.

With the Lamb is a witnessing remnant of 144,000. Though John has narratively introduced them at 7:1–8, because this scene is a part of the flashback (chs. 12–14), he describes them here as if his hearers and readers are encountering them for the first time. And yet, because of the narrative sequencing, there is much about this remnant that the audience already knows. As their location on Zion confirms, they are a protected group. Their protection is symbolized by the seal of God on their foreheads. John now explains the content of that seal: the name of the Lamb and the name of his Father. The seal identifies them as witnesses (cf. 3:12; 22:4) who conquered the dragon (12:11) by resisting its lordship claims. The seal, then, is a direct counter to the beast's mark that was tattooed onto the forehead or right hand of all those who testified to and

---

15. 1 Kgs 8:1; 2 Chr 5:2; Pss 2:6; 9:11 [9:12 LXX]; 14:7 [13:7]; 50:2 [49:2]; 53:6 [52:7]; 84:7 [83:8]; 99:2 [98:2]; 125:1 [124:1].

16. Cf. Ps 2:6–12; Isa 24:23; Mic 4:7; *Jub.* 1.28; *4 Ezra* 13.25–52; *2 Bar.* 40.

participated in its lordship (see the discussion of 13:16). The imagery is that of two marked combatant forces poised before each other, ready for eschatological battle (cf. 19:14).

The significance of the 144,000 is also contemporary. As a narrative construct, they operate somewhat like the transfiguration of Jesus in the Gospel of Mark (9:2–8). That event was a narrative sign that Jesus, and those who followed him, would be vindicated by God. This is the 144,000's function as a remnant community. The revelation of their "protected" witness to the lordship of God and the Lamb demonstrates that God *can* and *will* be able to live up to God's promises to reward with life all those who bear witness, even to the point of death (cf. 13:10; 14:12).

[2] John turns from what he *sees* on earth to a sound he *hears* issuing from *heaven*. The shift in sensory perception and location is similar to the move he narrates at the opening of chapter 7. There, after seeing four angels standing at the four corners of the earth and another ascending from the earth (7:1–3), he hears a voice proclaim, presumably also from heaven, the number of God's sealed servants (7:4). Here John emphasizes the awesome magnitude of the voice. The voice's weight suggests its message and the identity of those who sing. At 19:6 a great heavenly multitude cries out in praise of God with what John describes in almost precisely the same way as a voice of many waters and great thunder.[17] The multitude at 19:6, and apparently here—note the plural pronoun "they" that opens v. 3—sings praises to God for the establishment of God's rule.

This multitude, though related to the 144,000 in 14:1–5, clearly cannot be identified with them. While they are singing from heaven, John's narration locates the 144,000 on earth. In fact, it is not even clear that the 144,000 hear the song; John specifies that its sound registers only with him. This multitude is probably the same throng that cried out from heaven in a great voice at 7:9–17 to celebrate the salvation of God and the Lamb. John described that multitude as the universal assembly of witnesses from every nation and tribe and people and tongue (7:9) that had been redeemed by (cf. 5:9), and had conquered through (7:14; 12:11), Christ's blood. Like chapter 7, chapter 14 has placed the 144,000 and the larger multitude from which they have been culled in an antiphonal narrative relationship. The purpose of that relationship is the same in both texts, to symbolize and then celebrate the realization of God's salvific rule.

John further specifies the multitude's identity by placing harps in their hands. At 15:2 those who conquer the beast stand beside the sea of glass with harps. The sea of glass occupies a position in front of the throne, which is also the location of the multitudes in 7:9 and 14:3. This means that the multitudes in 7:9; 14:3; and 15:2 all stand before the heavenly throne, which suggests that John

---

17. The only difference is the choice of *ischyros* rather than *megas* to describe the "great" sound of the thunder.

is speaking about the same group. The multitude in 15:2 also praises God for the enactment of God's just and kingly rule. In fact, the language of singing as it is connected to songs and harps occurs in only three places in the book, the hymnic sections 5:8–14; 14:2–3; and 15:2–4. In each of these texts the central theme is praise for the realization of God's rule. Even before John tells us about the song, then, we have a very good idea about the message it exclaims.

[3] The fact that it is a new song further clarifies its message. In the Old Testament the new song establishes a theme of ransom or protection and adds to it a corresponding assurance that God will rightly judge those who have persecuted God's witnesses. In Ps 144 the new song, sung on a ten-stringed harp, is chanted in celebration of the one who gives victory to kings and rescues faithful servants like David (v. 9). The theme of justice pervades the singing of new songs at Pss 33:3; 96:1; 98:1; 149:1; and Isa 42:10.[18]

A similar dual emphasis occurs in Rev 14:2–3, where the new song celebrates God as the one whose universal rule materializes in both the judgment of those who reject God's lordship and the ransom/redemption of those who witness to it. At 5:9 the new song was sung in celebration of the Lamb's ransoming/redeeming of every tribe and language and people and nation. Apart from 14:2–3, only one other passage in Revelation presents a similar coherence of song, singing, and harps, and there a universal multitude sings in celebration of God's rule, exemplified through acts connected with Moses and the Lamb (15:2–3). Moses ransomed God's people and implemented God's judgment against Pharaoh through the plagues and the exodus victory at the sea. That political exodus must, for John, have had some bearing on the nature of the ransoming that is accomplished by the Lamb. The celebratory singing occurs in a context where the victory of the witnesses is portrayed as a victory against imperial Rome and its patron Asia Minor cities. The multitude is therefore celebrating more than a redemption from sin; they sing just as fervently on account of the Lamb's ransom from any need to accommodate to the lures and threats of Rome.

The song that is sung before the throne (as euphemism for God; see the discussion of 4:2–3), the cherubim (see 4:6–8a), and elders (see 4:4) can only be learned by the 144,000. This is an odd claim since it seems to exclude even the elders and cherubim before whom it is sung. John apparently has not himself learned it; he hints contextually at the theme but never actually reveals the words as he does in his other hymnic sections. Additionally, it is not even certain that the 144,000 hear the song, at least not in their present earthly setting.

18. Indeed, Bauckham believes that John has based his work here on the psalms in the group 96–100, which are "closely related in language and themes. They all celebrate Yahweh's universal lordship and his coming to judge the world, and they all call on the whole world to worship him" (*Climax of Prophecy*, 289).

The focus, though, is not so much on their present hearing as it is on their future capability; they *can* learn the words of this song.

Scholars are right to note that the verb *manthanō* (learn) can either have an ordinary sense or connote esoteric knowledge (cf. 2 Cor 12:4). John is more concerned with how one learns and whether the learning is tied to resistance (Richard 119). This connection fits the portrayal of the 144,000, who have been singled out because they resisted Rome's lordship claims. Their resistance enabled their learning. John no doubt must also mean that the 144,000 are the only ones *on earth* who can learn the song. Clearly the song has already been learned by the heavenly multitude of victorious witnesses (7:9–17) who sing it. Their past resistance, which clearly cost them their lives, must have earned them their capability.

What John does not make clear is why no other earthly witnesses can learn the song. Perhaps this is a marching song whose cadence can only be comprehended by those who parade with the Lamb on the eschatological battlefield (cf. 19:14). If the content of the song is integrally connected to its cadence, then one would expect that it is only by taking up the march (of nonviolent resistance) that one can learn the lines.

John's statement that these 144,000 have been redeemed from the earth parallels his descriptive statement in v. 4 that they have been redeemed from humankind (see the comment on v. 4 below).

[4] Verse 4 is a compilation of three clauses employing the pronoun "these" (*houtoi*), each of which adds a new character trait to the description of the 144,000. The first clause is also the most puzzling. These are the ones who have not defiled themselves with women; they are virgins. It is unlikely that John intended *molynō* (defile) literally, for "Revelation's language does not function as a cipher with a one-to-one meaning" (Schüssler Fiorenza, *Vision of a Just World*, 88). John enjoys using language figuratively. In his only other use of *molynō*, he intentionally applies it to the faithful at Sardis who did not "defile" themselves by eating meat sacrificed to imperial cultic figures (3:4). The verb is not sexual for John; it applies rather to idolatry and the lack of resistance to that idolatry. John could craft such a connection (see 2:14, 20) because idolatry had long been imaged as improper sexuality, particularly unchastity, in Israel's history.[19]

The metaphor that accounts best for the confluence of the 144,000 as a remnant army force, the parallel between illicit sexuality and idolatry, and the rather

---

19. Aune (2:812) points to Jer 3:2; 13:27; Ezek 16:15–58; 23:1–49; 43:7; Hos 5:4; 6:10. And Beale observes, "In the OT Israel's idolatries and political and economic practices are pictured as 'harlotry' (Ezekiel 23, similarly Jer. 3:1–10; cf. Hos. 1:2), Israel's idolatry was also referred to as 'defilement' (μολύνω, μόλυνσις, and μολυσμός in Isa. 65:4; Jer. 23:15; 51:4; 1 Esd 8:80 [83E])" (740).

dysfunctional language of men undefiled by sexual relations with women—that metaphor is of holy war. Because the writers of the Old Testament considered sexuality to be such a powerful force, they instructed that it be "ritually insulated from normal life," so that "persons engaged in special occupations or missions such as the priesthood or God's army were, during the time of their service, expected to refrain from sex, not from moralistic reasons but to insulate the sacred service from other powers (Deut. 20:1–9; 23:9–10; I Sam. 21:[4–]5; [2 Sam 11:11; 1QM 7:3–6])" (Boring, *Revelation*, 169). This expectation dovetailed nicely with John's own figurative belief that in order to conquer the satanic force that expressed itself in bestial Rome, his hearers and readers must divorce themselves from any accommodation to its idolatrous expectations.

John uses the term *parthenos* (virgin) in a similarly figurative sense. He does not intend to exclude women from his portrait of the 144,000. Instead, *parthenos* describes males and females who resist accommodating ("defiling") themselves to the lures of the Roman imperial cult. Precedent for such a broad use of the term has been found by many commentators in Philo (*Cher.* 49–50), who uses the noun to refer metaphorically to God's people of both genders (e.g., Schüssler Fiorenza, *Vision of a Just World*, 88; Boring, *Revelation*, 169).

Still, at least in a twenty-first-century context, the language is disconcerting. For more than two millennia, the devaluation of both women and sexuality implied in a literal reading of the verse has borne negative consequences for women in particular and human relationships in general.[20] As we faithfully interpret and translate John's language metaphorically, we must also find ways in our public reading of the verse to transcribe not the words but the intent. A more affirming and still figuratively appropriate reading would be something like the following: "These ones are like virgins who would not be seduced by the idolatrous lures of the beast from the sea."

The second *houtoi* (these) clause identifies the 144,000 as disciples who follow (*akoloutheō*) the Lamb wherever he goes. The verb *akoloutheō* is used in the Gospels as a technical term for discipleship (Mark 8:34 = Matt 16:24 = Luke 9:23; Matt 10:38 = Luke 14:27; John 10:4; 13:36). Where does John's Lamb go? As the true and faithful witness (Rev 1:5; 3:14), he goes to such extreme lengths to resist testimony to the lordship of Rome that he is executed (5:6, 9, 12; 13:8). Through that execution, he is snatched to the throne of God (12:5). The 144,000 follow on all but one interesting phase of this journey. They follow the Lamb in his resistance, and they anticipate a future residence near the throne. However, their very status as the "sealed" or "protected" ones implies

---

20. For a critical feminist perspective on John's female imagery here and elsewhere in the book, see Pippin. For a contrasting view of feminist perspectives on John's imagery as part of a contextual study, see Blount, *Can I Get a Witness?* ch. 1.

that they will not follow the Lamb to slaughter. The trademark of their discipleship is not death, but their defiant act of witnessing resistance.

The third and final *houtoi* (these) clause identifies the 144,000 as those who were redeemed from humans (see v. 3) as firstfruits to God and the Lamb. Since the word "firstfruits" is in the climactic position, the interpretive agenda starts there. Once again John is operating figuratively. There were three kinds of offerings in the Mediterranean world: offerings of food, offerings of objects (votive offerings), and animal sacrifices (Aune 2:814). "Firstfruits" (*aparchē*) belonged to the first category (Exod 23:19; Lev 23:9–14; Deut 26:1–11). The firstfruits were the initial offerings taken from a harvest.

In fact, the firstfruits "redeemed" the remainder of the harvest for general use and consumption (Rom 11:16). John's figurative description of the 144,000 as the "redeemed" is less mysterious in light of this revelation. They act as a guarantor that many more will be gathered in the general human harvest to come (Rev 14:14–20). Such a figurative understanding coheres well with other New Testament presentations. When Paul speaks of Christ as the firstfruits in 1 Cor 15:20–23, he means that his resurrection guarantees a full harvest of eschatological resurrections. Likewise, when the apostle refers to the Spirit as firstfruits, he means that the believer's possession of the Spirit in the present is a guarantor of the full gift of eschatological salvation (Rom 8:23; 2 Cor 1:22; 5:5; cf. Eph 1:13–14). Given John's eager acceptance of the metaphor and his presentation of the 144,000 as a remnant community whose presence instills hope in their witness colleagues, it is likely that John intended this redeemed group of firstfruits not only to guarantee God's ability to protect and save those who witness to God's lordship, but also to provide tangible evidence of the coming harvest. They are the proof of what God can and will do!

**[5]** John lists lying as one of the critical vice-list acts that can thwart a person's hope for eschatological relationship with God (cf. 21:27; 22:15). The background for his language comes from Isa 53:9, where the Servant of God is described as having no deceit in his mouth. Surely, in that case, he is a model for the larger faith community. The prophet Zephaniah makes this case when he attributes the same truthfulness to the remnant of Israel (3:13). John, then, is concerned about something of much greater significance than "fibbing." The seer who appeals for a resistant witness to the lordship of Christ is more concerned with the lying, false witness that contributes to a contrary belief in the lordship of the beast from the sea. When he calls his remnant community of 144,000 blameless, then, he is thinking less about their moral purity than about their active resistance to Rome's bestial, imperial claims. It is this resistance that they model for the larger faith community. In the dangerous call to witness to the lordship of Christ, they *are* blameless: they have not accommodated themselves to the draconian lie.

14:6–11 The Gospel of Justice

> 6 Then I saw another angel flying in midheaven, with an eternal gospel to proclaim to those who inhabit the earth, that is, every nation and tribe and tongue and people, 7 saying in a foreboding voice: "Fear God and give God glory, because the hour of God's judgment has come; worship the one who made heaven and earth and sea and springs of water." 8 And another angel, a second one, followed, saying: "Fallen, fallen is Babylon the Great, who made all the nations drink from the wine of the wrath of her fornication." 9 And another angel, a third one, followed them, saying with a foreboding voice: "If anyone worships the beast[a] and its image and takes a mark on his forehead or hand, 10 then[b] he will drink from the wine of the wrath of God, poured unmixed into the cup of God's fury, and he will be tormented by fire and sulfur before holy angels and before the Lamb. 11 And the smoke of their torment rises forever and ever. Those who worship the beast and its image and take the mark of its name do not have rest day and night."

a. Although *thysiastērion* (altar) appears in A, *thērion* (beast) is attested by all other witnesses. The curious reading of Codex A ("If anyone worships the *altar* and its image") seems to have arisen out of the similarity of the two words and the proximity of *thysiastērion* in 14:18. On both internal and external grounds, *thērion* is by far the more likely original reading.

b. On the use of *kai* to introduce the apodosis of a conditional sentence as a Hebraism or Septuagintism, see Aune 2:787.

[6] With *kai eidon* (and I saw), John signals a turn to another narrative scene (see the comment on 5:1).[21] He sees "another angel." (On "another angel" as a symbolic marker for judgment, see the comments on 10:1 and 18:1.) Since the last reference to angels occurs in this flashback unit at 12:7, he may well be contrasting this angel to Michael and his cohorts at 12:7. Michael's group played an important role in securing an eschatological victory against Satan in heaven. This angel and the five who follow him will perform a similarly important task; they will set the parameters for the harvesting of humankind from the earth. Given the strong judgment orientation, it is more likely that John contrasts these six with the seven trumpet angels of chapters 8–10. Though they execute the similar task of judgment, these are different angels.

This first angel appears in flight at midheaven. The description calls to mind both the eagle flying in midheaven at 8:13 and the birds flying in midheaven at 19:17. In both those cases the flights occur in the context of God's

21. Cf. 5:6; 6:1, 8, 12; 7:2, 9; 8:2, 13; 9:1; 10:1; 13:1, 11.

graphic judgment against the idolatrous inhabitants of the earth. Such a judgment theme fits the context where a draconian force hunts the people of God and has deployed bestial sea and land forces to achieve its tactical objectives. The angel is a visible reminder that God is preparing a powerful and just response.

The angel's message sets the tone for everything else that will happen in the chapter. John says that he bears an eternal gospel; *euangelion* (gospel) is the language of good news (cf. Mark 13:10 = Matt 24:14). It is odd that the angel bears this good news in a scene saturated with strong judgment themes. But it is difficult to gauge John's understanding of the term since he uses it only here. The one other time that he uses the verb form, *euangelizō* (to proclaim the gospel), he also places it within a context of judgment (10:7). John is not using this very important term ("gospel") cynically, as the larger context of chapters 12–14 indicates. In this circumstance where the dragon, the beast from the sea, the beast from the land, and all those who ally themselves with them are persecuting the people of God, any message of a just salvation for God's people will necessarily include a corresponding note of judgment against those who have persecuted them. What is good news for God's witnesses is judgment news for those who persecute them. This is John's perspective throughout the book.

John clarifies that the gospel is preached to the ones who sit upon the earth and to every nation and tribe and tongue and people. Those who sit (*kathēmai*) upon the earth bear strong resemblance to those who inhabit (*katoikeō*) the earth at 13:8 (see also 2:13; 3:10; 6:10; 8:13; 11:10; 13:8, 12, 14; 17:2, 8). The inhabitants of the earth are presented uniformly as being hostile to the testimony of the lordship of God and the Lamb. In massaging the presentation here with a different verb (*kathēmai*, sit), John surely wants to bring them to mind while simultaneously softening his hearers' and readers' impression of them. Just as interesting, in the same chapter 13 setting, at v. 7, John identifies those who dwell on the earth with the same universal conglomeration that he uses here at 14:6: every tribe and people and language and nation. I have argued that the *kai* (and) that connects "inhabitants of the earth" and "those of every tribe and people and tongue and nation" should be read epexegetically in 13:7. That is, "those of every tribe and people and tongue and nation" further describes and clarifies "inhabitants of the earth." They will be judged because of their hostility toward God and those who have witnessed to the lordship of God and the Lamb. The same epexegetical formulation occurs in 14:6. John means to say that the gospel has gone out to "those who sit upon the earth," that is, to "every nation and tribe and tongue and people." The message is a universal one of judgment.

The descriptive nuance, however, should not be missed. John does not say "inhabitants of the earth" for the same reason that he adds the language of gospel proclamation. There is still hope for a repentant response. The 144,000 are not the only ones who have been redeemed in John's text (7:4). According to John's narration, the universal grouping of every tribe and language and people and nation has also been the object of the Lamb's successful redemptive efforts (5:9; 7:9). Indeed, the great multitude of conquering witnesses (7:14) is comprised from just this universal conglomeration (7:9). John himself is tasked with the vocation of prophesying to this group (10:11), with the knowledge that the message will deliver judgment if they do not respond appropriately (cf. 11:9). The prophetic message to fear God and give God glory (14:7)—that is, witness to the lordship of God and the Lamb—is always the same. The target audience for the prophetic message is the same. Depending upon their response, however, the message operates as either good news or judgment.

[7] The angel speaks with a foreboding tone of judgment (see the discussion of 7:2). Most recently, in this very flashback section, a foreboding heavenly voice issued a proclamation that carries the same complex nuance that John establishes here (see 12:10). There, too, the voice declared a message of salvation (for those who witness faithfully to the lordship of God and the Lamb) that morphed quickly into a pledge of judgment (against those who have persecuted God's witnesses).

Despite the change in audience, the content of the message remains constant: Fear God and render God glory. To be sure, fear of God is integrally connected to God's role as eschatological judge (15:4; 19:1–5). The reward for those who exhibit this fear will be eschatological relationship with God (11:18). The alternative is a fear of the first death, which prompts a person to accommodate to the lures and threats of Roman imperial lordship.

It is the fear of God that sparks a glorification of God. Even those who tormented the two witnesses became so frightened by God's acts of justice/judgment that they were motivated to glorify God (11:13). An appropriate fear of God can lead even where faith initially cannot go, to a right understanding of God's role as cosmic Lord.

Glory is not only due God because of God's role as judge, but also because of God's role as Creator. In this context glorification expresses itself as worship (4:9, 11). In chapter 13, humans were castigated because of their worship of the dragon and beast from the sea (13:4, 8, 12, 15). Here, the foreboding voice issues a defining corrective with a gospel message that will fall like judgment upon those who respond improperly to it.

As if to make that point explicit, the message comes to match the tone in which it is delivered; the voice declares that the hour of judgment has come. The aorist (*ēlthen*, has come) is proleptic here; it anticipates a future realization by acting as if it has already occurred. John is so sure that God will judge that he operates as if God already has. The fate of those who resist God and persecute God's witnesses is sealed.

[8] This same proleptic message of judgment is affirmed by a "second another angel." John numbers his divine figures awkwardly for a reason. He wants to

make the point that they are a part of a series of seven divine persons who on earth have taken up the battle that Michael and his cohort prosecuted in heaven (12:7). He also wants to distinguish them from the seven trumpet angels.

This second angel speaks without nuance directly to the force that has institutionalized an economic, political, social, and cultic opposition to God. Its adherents have rejected and continue to reject the call to fear God and give God glory (cf. 16:9). Though he gives it the name "Babylon the Great," he is speaking to Rome, the beast from the sea (13:1–10; cf. 1 Pet 5:13). Babylon, we know, is the name of the great imperial force that destroyed Jerusalem in 587 B.C.E., desecrated the temple, and drove much of the populace into exile. For that act of infamy, Babylon became the prototypical enemy of the people of God. Daniel 4:30 describes the arrogance of Babylon through the words of its king Nebuchadnezzar, who demanded for himself the kind of reverence due only God (Dan 3). For John, Rome reenacts Babylon's adversarial and idolatrous role. Rome is the only other force to have destroyed Jerusalem and desecrated its temple. Rome is the one imperial force that demands for itself and its emperors the devotion of lordship due only God. Because of Rome's extraordinary conceit, John applies to it the same words of judgment that Isaiah (21:9) and Jeremiah (51:7–8) assigned to Babylon. Once again using a proleptic aorist tense (*epesen*, "fallen"; see also 18:2), he declares that although it appears powerful and menacing, it has already fallen.

John uses the term "Babylon" only five other times in his entire work; in each case, he emphasizes the promise of its judgment (16:19; 17:5; 18:2, 10, 21). Even here, though, there is a contextual hint of hope. Daniel 4:27–37 suggests a transformative possibility for even Babylon if it would heed the voice of eschatological reason, repent, fear God, and give God proper glory.

The odds of that happening, though, John knows, are long. Now using imagery to which he will return in powerfully ironic ways, John establishes the passionate crime that Babylon/Rome obsessively commits. Clearly building from Jeremiah's claim that the wine of Babylon's prosperity made the world mad to imbibe it (51:7), he presses the case that Babylon/Rome has seduced all the nations to drink out of the furiously intoxicating (*thymos*) wine of her sexual illicitness (*porneia*). John speaks here about the lure of wanting to participate in the economic gluttony that Rome has established (Rev 18:3). To share in and prosper from the empire's wealth, nations are willing to "mark" themselves as patrons to its ideology and devotees of its lordship (13:16–17). The drive to be a part of Roman success/excess is a kind of madness for prosperity. It is this prosperity mania that entices the members of John's seven churches to participate in guild and trade associations, where commercial alliances can be forged and social standing advanced, but also where meat sacrificed to imperial idols is consumed. John perceives this kind of idolatrous behavior through the lens of inappropriate sexuality (see the discussion of 14:4; cf. 2:21; 9:21; 17:2, 4; 18:3;

19:2). He means to say that by selling out their devotion to the lordship of God and the Lamb in order to reap Rome's economic and social rewards, the nations have prostituted themselves to an idolatrous and false hope.

**[9–10]** The "third another angel" continues the foreboding message. The verse sets up the first half (the protasis) of a conditional statement that reflects on information already conveyed in 13:16–18. The concluding half (apodosis) of the conditional sentence begun in 14:9 is initiated with *kai*. Since v. 10 deals explicitly with those who accept the mark of the beast and therefore have rejected any recognition of God's and the Lamb's lordship, there is none of the nuance evident in v. 6. This verse is strictly about a judgment that John casts as ironic, poetic justice. He takes the very same vocabulary of passionate, intoxicating rage (*thymos*), drinking (*pinō/potizō*), and wine (*oinos*) that he has used to describe Babylon/Rome's bewitching of the nations (v. 8) and twists it into the language of God's retribution. From this point in the narrative forward, when wine (16:19; 17:2; 18:3; 19:15) and passionate rage (14:19; 15:1, 7; 16:1, 19; 19:15) appear, they will convey not idolatrous celebration but divine wrath.[22]

John sharpens the language by appealing directly to the vessel that no doubt holds this furious wine: the cup of God's wrath. The seer is drawing from plentiful Old Testament uses of the cup of wrath where God fools God's enemies by offering them an intoxicating drink that causes drunkenness, understood as judgment.[23] The wine in God's cup is much more potent than anything Babylon/Rome may have concocted. According to John, it is poured unmixed. Wine was generally mixed with spices to make it more potent. However, wine was also often diluted with water. John sees the strength of God's wine as doubly powerful, for while it was mixed with spices, it was not watered down (Reddish 278). God's wrath is at full strength.

John conveys the magnitude of his claim with the verse's concluding clause: affiliates of the beast will be tormented with fire and brimstone (sulfur) before the angels and the Lamb. The language of torment (*basanizō*) implies that this will be an eschatological punishment that, mercilessly, never ends. Whenever John employs the term, he gives it a sense of constancy (11:10; 12:2) and even perpetuity (9:5). The most telling use occurs at 20:10. There the dragon and its two minion beasts will be tormented forever in a lake comprised of the same punishing elements used here: fire and sulfur.

Fire and sulfur were traditionally understood as the instruments of divine retribution, wielded against Sodom and Gomorrah and others of God's enemies (Gen 19:24; Ps 11:6; Ezek 38:22). John maintains the practice of packaging fire and sulphur together: 9:17–18; 19:20; 20:10; 21:8.

---

22. The use of *thymos* (passionate rage) in 18:3 parallels the use in 14:8 in establishing the cause of God's wrath.

23. Pss 11:6; 75:8; Isa 51:17, 22; Jer 25:15; 49:12; 51:7; Lam 4:21; Ezek 23:31–34; Hab 2:15–16; Obad 16; Zech 12:2. Cf. Aune 2:833.

[11] John's presentation is unbearably harsh. The picture of punishment as enduring torture implied by the verb "torment" (*basanizō*) in v. 10 is reinforced in the next verse, when he declares that the smoke of the dragon's and beasts' affiliates' "torment" (noun form, *basanismos*) goes up forever. They find rest neither day nor night. The rising smoke hearkens back to the smoke of Edom's judgment rising up day and night forever (Isa 34:9–10). John is also operating from his own intratextual connections. This reflection on the rest-less day and night suffering of God's enemies is meant to parallel the heavenly praise of God that goes on without rest, day and night, at Rev 4:8. In this allusive way, the complex nuance that John introduced with his presentation of gospel as judgment at 14:6 marks its return. Salvation occurs for those who properly respond to the call to fear God and give God glory. While those who respond improperly burn in ceaseless torment, the witnesses of God and the Lamb, whom they once persecuted, are guaranteed enduring rest (v. 13; cf. 6:11).[24]

The harshness of John's picture of judgment does press one to consider how his language can be applied to contemporary twenty-first-century contexts. This language was not meant to be taken literally. The elements of fire and sulfur and the lake of fire are meant to be provocative symbols of the dis-ease that comes from eschatological separation from God. Even the language of incessant torment must be understood figuratively. After all, John is not targeting nonbelievers to get them to commit to the faith; he is targeting believers who he fears may commit apostasy in an effort to accommodate themselves to Roman economic, political, social, and cultic pressures and expectations. His fierce language is meant to dissuade them. He wants them to believe that there is a horror greater than even the worst penalty, the first death, that the Romans can surely impose. He wants his audience to see it and, through his graphic language, even feel it. It is that horror, not the first death, that they must avoid. His language is rhetorical, not literal. It is not at this point meant so much to inform as to exhort.

## 14:12–13 Model Behavior

12 Here is the nonviolent resistance of the saints, those who keep the commandments of God, that is, the faith of Jesus. 13 Then I heard a voice from heaven saying, "Write: 'Blessed are the dead who die in the Lord from now on.'" "Yes," says the Spirit, "that they might rest from their labors, for their works follow with them."

[12] As in 13:10 (cf. 17:9), the adverb "here" (*hōde*) that initiates v. 12 points both backward and forward. John means to say that what he has said previously

---

24. For a broader discussion of these cross-references, see Bauckham, *Climax of Prophecy*, 28–29.

(cf. 13:18) as well as what he will say forms the basis for the *hypomonē* ("non-violent resistance"; see the comment on 13:10) of the saints. The presentation of the 144,000 (14:1–5) encourages resistance because their presence demonstrates that God can and will protect God's own. The portrait of the gospel as a concomitant message of judgment (vv. 6–11) inspires resistance because the witnesses know that God will vindicate their efforts. The promise of harvest, both salutary and judgmental (vv. 14–20), encourages believers to resist allying with those who will be reaped as vintage.

John identifies the "saints" (see the comment on 5:8) as those who maintain the commandments of God and (i.e., which is) the faith proclaimed by Jesus.[25] The *kai* (and) is epexegetical; Jesus' faith more fully explicates what John means by God's "commandments." John is operating here much as he did at 12:17, connecting an ethical use of "keep," or "hold" (*tēreō*), with commandments, which in this context work functionally through Jesus' own witnessing behavior and the faith that drives it. The commandment of God is the expectation that believers "follow" in the witnessing way of the Lamb. The saints are those who "keep" God's commandments by living out the faith of God's Lamb (see the discussion of 12:17).

[13] The rationale for resistance is more neatly and immediately summed up in this second of John's seven apocalyptic beatitudes (1:3; 14:13; 16:15; 19:9; 20:6; 22:7, 14). In another shift to audition, John hears a voice bless witnesses who faithfully resist the threats and lures of bestial Babylon/Rome. Is the macarism an indicative or an imperative? Probably both. As an indicative, it declares that those who die in the Lord are blessed because they will rest from their labors, that is, their acts of resistant witness (6:9–11). Given the context of 6:9–11 and John's attempt in chapter 14 to encourage more such efforts so that his hearers and readers will be vindicated, one gathers the sense that by "rest from labors" John does not mean "sit back and relax," but "rest assured" that God is in charge and that God's justice will win out. The imperative sense develops from the realization that while some rest assured, others are to be about the business of fulfilling their work of witness "from now on" (see the comment on 6:11). While 6:11 highlighted rest, not work, 14:13 emphasizes, in the context of rest, that their work, their labor of resistant witness (see the pairing of work and witness in 2:2, 19), will follow them, which is to say, fulfill them. John is not expressing a theology of works righteousness where work leads to salvation; he is instead pressing the case that those who are saved must live out their salvation through their witness. That is how they are fulfilled. Verse 13 assigns a speaking role to the Spirit, who represents God's presence (see the comments on 1:4; 3:1; 4:5; 5:6).

---

25. I see the genitive operating subjectively here in the same way as in the foundational phrase "witness proclaimed by Jesus." Cf. 1:2, 9; 6:9; 12:11; 20:4. See also the "revelation proclaimed by Jesus" at 1:1.

14:14–20 Harvest Time

14 Then I looked, and behold a dazzling cloud, and seated on the cloud was one like a child of humanity. He had a golden crown on his head and a sharp sickle in his hand. 15 Then another angel came out of the temple,[a] calling with a foreboding voice to the one seated on the cloud: "Use your sickle and reap, for the hour to reap has come, because the harvest of the earth is ripe." 16 Then the one seated on the cloud swung his sickle on the earth, and the earth was harvested. 17 And another angel came out of the temple in heaven, and he also had a sharp sickle. 18 Then another angel, the one who has authority over fire, came out from the altar, and he called with a foreboding voice to the one who had the sharp sickle, saying: "Use your sharp sickle and gather the grape clusters of the vintage of the earth, because its grapes are ripe." 19 And the angel swung his sickle over the earth and gathered the vintage of the earth into the great[b] winepress of the wrath of God. 20 And the winepress was trodden outside the city, and blood flowed from the winepress as high as the bridles of horses from 1,600 stadia.[c]

a. "[Out of] heaven" (*ouranou*) appears in 051 2053 𝔐[A]; "[out of] the temple" (*naou*) is in all other witnesses. The reading *ouranou*, although slim on early manuscript support, has made its way into one branch of the Majority text tradition in Revelation. It seems to have come about as a consequence of copying continuously through the book. To this point, no angels have come out of the heavenly *naos*; they do so, however, several times from 14:15 onward (see 14:17; 15:6; cf. 14:18, where the angel comes from the altar). On the other hand, by 14:15 the reader has come to expect revelation *ek tou ouranou* (most recently, the heavenly voice in 14:2, 13). Therefore, *naou* is more likely the original reading.

b. The text reading, *ton megan* (the great), supported by (A) C P 046 051 and most miniscules (see Metzger, *Textual Commentary*, 755), is the more difficult reading and therefore probably original. John intends to describe the mammoth size of the winepress. The difficulty is that while "winepress" is a feminine noun, *megan*, the adjective intended to modify it, is offered in the masculine. The scribal adjustment *tēn megalēn* (great), supported by ℵ 1006 1841 1854 2053 *al* gig sy[ph.hmg], is the proper feminine construction and was thus surely added later. 𝔓[47] 1611 *pc* sy[h] offer a masculine genitive construction (*tou megalou*), which would then modify either God or, more likely, wrath as "great." Both adjustments attempt to correct the infelicity in John's grammar.

c. The distance varies considerably in the textual witnesses: *chiliōn hexakosiōn hex* in 2036 *pc*; *chiliōn diakosiōn* in ℵ* *pc* sy[ph]; *mille quingentis* in gig; *chiliōn hexakosiōn* in all other witnesses. The precise number of stadia that the blood flows in 14:20, while not crucial for interpretation, has nevertheless generated confusion in the textual tradition. *Chiliōn hexakosiōn hex* (1,606) probably arose from a reduplication of the prefix *hex*, while *chiliōn diakosiōn* (1,200) may reflect a concern for symbolic numerology (so Metzger, *Textual Commentary*, 755). The singular reading of the Old Latin manuscript gig, *mille quingentis* (1,500), is altogether anomalous. With NA[27] I read *chiliōn hexakosiōn* (1,600).

The harvest imagery in the final seven verses of chapter 14 is heavily debated. The core concern is whether John is presenting here the portrait of a single harvest based on the imagery from Joel 3:13, or whether he adapts the Joel material and offers first salvation (vv. 14–16) and then judgment (vv. 17–20). Given John's nuanced presentation of gospel as a message of both salvation and judgment (see the comment on v. 6), I argue that he presents a picture of the harvest that is both positive (for those who respond properly to the call to fear God and give God glory) and negative (for those who refuse).

Joel's image of a sickle reaping grapes and of treading upon them in the winepress is surely John's inspiration for the two harvests (Joel 3:13).[26] In both harvest images (vv. 14–16, 17–20), John includes the sickle and dramatically ends with the winepress and its horrific results. There is, however, a breakdown in the parallel with Joel and also with traditional harvesting images. Although the harvesting of the vineyard includes both reaping and treading, the harvesting of the grain fields that John surely implies in vv. 14–16 includes reaping but no threshing or winnowing (cf. Mark 4:29).[27] John has purposely, it seems, left off the image that would involve the judgmental separation of the proverbial wheat from the chaff. That seems to suggest, as Bauckham presses, that vv. 14–16 offer a fully salvific image of universal ingathering (cf. Mark 13:26–27; Luke 10:2; John 4:35–38).

**[14]** Once again, *kai eidon, kai idou* indicates John's move to yet another new scene ("Then I looked, and behold"; see the discussion of 5:1; cf. 6:5, 8; 13:1, 11; 14:1; 19:11). The new thing is a white cloud, occupied by a figure like a child of humanity. John has used clouds before as the wrapping for divine figures (see the discussion of 10:1). He also employs it as a metaphorical mode of heavenly transport for Christ (1:7; cf. Mark 14:62 = Matt 26:64 = Luke 22:69) and for the two witnesses (Rev 11:12). The cloud in 10:1 is particularly significant since, like the one here, it occurs in a context of judgment (cf. Matt 24:30).

There has been some debate as to whether this child of humanity figure is Christ or another of the angels who occupy Rev 14. It has been suggested, because the fourth angel (v. 15) issues an order to the one like a child of humanity, and therefore appears to be his superior, that the one like a child of humanity cannot be Christ. The objection is inconclusive. Tradition makes clear from the words of Jesus that no one, not even the child of humanity, knows the time of God's harvesting movement (Mark 13:32; Acts 1:7). It would therefore not be surprising that while operating in the field, the child of humanity would need a directive from God before proceeding to harvest. Indeed, John specifically

---

26. Cf. Aune (2:800): "While this passage [Joel 3:13] originally centers on the metaphor of the vintage harvest alone, John understood it to refer *both* to the grain harvest and to the grape harvest (קָצִיר, *qāṣîr* is normally used of the grain harvest, while בָּצִיר, *bāṣîr* is used of the vintage harvest)."

27. Bauckham, *Climax of Prophecy*, 290–96.

describes the fourth angel as coming out of the temple (v. 15). He is thus speaking for God, not for himself. Furthermore, John has developed a series of angelic presentations in the chapter and does not appear hesitant about narratively piling angels on top of each other. Had he wanted to make the one like a child of humanity "another" angel it would have been easy for him to do so, and it would have made the narrative progression much neater. Instead, he appears to suggest a central role for the one like a child of humanity by placing him in the middle of the angelic countdown, thereby highlighting not only his placement but also his role. It is he who appears to be the initiator of both phases of the harvest as they take place in the ensuing verses. His participation in the salvific grain harvest is obvious (vv. 14–16). His participation in the vintage harvest (vv. 17–20) is not as clear, but it is implied through the image of the trodden grapes because John later discloses that it was indeed Christ (as the rider of the white horse) who trod the winepress of God's fury (19:15). Finally, the identification of this child of humanity with Christ is not only consistent with the New Testament's development of the image from Dan 7:13–14 but also fits John's own labeling of the Christ in his narrative (1:13–16).

The golden crown symbolizes the lordship of the one like a child of humanity, the very truth to which his witnesses are called to testify (cf. 2 Sam 12:30; 1 Chr 20:2).[28] The sickle he holds (Rev 14:15, 16, 17, 18, 19), a curved cutting instrument, is a metaphor for his role as the one who initiates the harvests that reap the faithful from among every nation and tribe and language and people.

[15] It is the fourth "another angel" who appears out of the sanctuary of the temple and conveys God's order to the one like a child of humanity that the grain harvest should begin. His foreboding voice suggests that this harvest, like the good news itself, does not operate independently of God's justice. In support of the claim that the phrasing here supports a salvific ingathering, Caird argues that the two key terms *therizō* (to harvest) and *therismos* (harvest) never picture destruction of God's enemies in the LXX, even in passages where judgment is likened to reaping. Rather, "they are used of the ingathering of men into the kingdom of God (Matt. ix. 37f.; Mark iv. 29; Luke x. 2; John iv. 35–38)" (Caird 190).[29] Indeed, John's presentation of the harvesting imagery is consistent not only with the universal proclamation of good news (Rev 14:7) but also with the portrait of the 144,000 as a representative "firstfruits" of the universal multitude to follow, rather than an elite, exclusive company of the saved (v. 4; 7:9).

---

28. Cf. Beale (770): "The crown identifies him as king over his people, who rule with him and also wear 'golden crowns' (4:4, 10; cf. also 2:10; 3:11; 12:1). His crown also evokes kingship over his enemies (19:12)."

29. Caird points out, however, that Matt 13:24–43 "might seem to be a partial exception, since the weeds are reaped along with the wheat, and the reaping is a prelude to their destruction. But even here the object of the reaping is the storing of the crop, not the bonfire" (190).

**[16]** The child of humanity follows God's instructions and reaps the earth. As noted above, however, he does not follow up with a judgmental winnowing/threshing. Here lies the climactic movement that John narrates in the seventh seal, trumpet, and bowl. It is prefigured in this scene. The seventh act, the climactic one, belongs to the child of humanity.

**[17]** A fifth "another angel" now makes his way out of the temple sanctuary, a sharp sickle in hand. The fact that he holds the same tool as the child of humanity suggests that he will play a role in this new phase of God's final harvest.

**[18]** The sixth and final "another angel" now makes his way from the sanctuary altar. He has authority over fire. Fire is a consistent metaphor of judgment for John (3:18; 8:5, 7–8; 15:2; see the discussion of fire and sulfur as image of judgment at 14:10; cf. 9:17, 18; 19:20; 20:10; 21:8). At 8:5 the fire of the incense altar was thrown down upon the earth as an apparent answer of justice/judgment to the cries of the slaughtered saints under the altar (6:9–11). That potent image must surely be in John's mind as he envisions this sixth angel coming out from the altar with the authority of fire. When the angel commands the fifth angel to swing his sickle into motion, John's hearers and readers would not have been surprised that his voice carries the foreboding tone of judgment (see the discussion of 14:7).

**[19]** After reaping the vineyard, the angel casts the yield upon the winepress of the passionate fury (i.e., the wrath) of God. John's hearers and readers are prepared for this language by the narration at vv. 8, 10, which anticipates the actions of the Christ as depicted in 19:15. Those who have allied themselves with the dragon and the beast drink the wine of God's fury poured unmixed from the cup of divine wrath. That such language returns here is an indication of the judgmental nature of the fifth angel's actions (throwing the harvest onto the floor of the winepress), which anticipates the concluding work of the Christ (trodding the harvest underfoot). This is the judgment that awaits all who are marked with the name and number of the beast.

**[20]** The treading upon the winepress is the climactic moment of judgment. The action operates from the brutal imagery of Isa 63:1–6, where the blood of the grapes, and thus the judgment, flows freely from the press. God appears to be directly involved. Both angels come from the sanctuary and therefore act on God's orders. Furthermore, the angel's role is limited to the casting of the harvest upon the winepress. At 19:15, John makes clear that it is God's Christ who actually crushes the harvest with the passionate fury of God's wrath (cf. 14:8, 10). The end result is no less horrifying than the language of eternal torture conjured up by the vision recounted at vv. 10–11.

The action takes place outside the city. John has already used poetic irony to turn the wickedness of those who follow the beast against them. The idolatrous wine with which they have intoxicated themselves has mutated into the unmixed wine of God's anger (vv. 8, 10). Perhaps the seer is now taking yet another stab at mocking the evil that the dragon's forces have perpetrated against God's interests. The traditions maintain that Jesus was crucified, slaughtered outside the city. How deliciously just it would seem to John that not only the forces responsible for that travesty but also others who have allied themselves with those forces should meet their eschatological fate in the same place.

When it is over, so much judgment has been wreaked that John sees the land awash in a great river of blood (cf. *1 En.* 100.3). Anticipating the later shift from harvest to battle as the dominant judgment metaphor (19:11–21), John apparently mixes his metaphors so that the winepress becomes a battlefield where the riderless horses of the armies of the dragon and the beast stand bridle deep in the blood of the marked soldiers who once rode them. A literal figuring of John's 1,600 stadia would yield a span of approximately 180 miles, or 300 kilometers. John's intention, though, is not literal but figurative. Commentators note that 1,600 is the square of ten, signifying totality, multiplied by the square of four, which signifies the four corners of the earth. Whether that deciphering is what John intended, the conclusion it helps one draw certainly does correspond to his intention. "The bloodbath and terror of God's judgment affects the whole world" (Schüssler Fiorenza, *Vision of a Just World*, 91). The desperate cry for justice by the slaughtered saints of 6:9–11 has been definitively answered.

## 15:1–22:9 A Concluding Vision Cycle

### 15:1 Prelude to the Seven Bowls

Revelation 15:1 is the superscript for chapters 15 through 18; the verse simultaneously breaks the reader away from the narrative flashback in chapters 12–14 and introduces the primary theme for the material that will follow. Chapters 15 and 16 will describe the wrath of God as a series of exodus-like plagues through the metaphor of the seven bowls; chapters 17 and 18 will then detail the consequences of that wrath for imperial Babylon.

> 15:1 Then I saw another great and amazing sign in heaven: seven angels with the seven last plagues, for with them the wrath of God is finished.

[**15:1**] The *kai eidon* (then I saw) that opens the verse is John's grammatical clue that he has initiated a new narrative vision (see 5:1, 6; 6:1, 8, 12; 7:2, 9; 8:2, 13; 9:1; 10:1; 13:1, 11). This time, though, the use of this opening formula with the bracketing phrase "another sign in heaven" intentionally reminds John's hearers and readers that a previous scene has concluded. John has mentioned a "sign in heaven" only twice before (12:1–3). The chapters that followed those verses (chs. 12–14) were preoccupied with describing the lives of Christian witnesses as a perilous existence under constant threat from three bestial enemies. This third and final sign does not point back to those beasts but forward to the judgment that God will soon effect against them (chs. 15–16).

According to John, this new sign is both "great" and "amazing." The description, particularly "amazing," that is used in the entire narrative only here and in 15:3, is an intentional nod to Old Testament imagery that highlights God's activity in the world (Exod 34:10; Pss 111:2; 139:14). At 15:3, John defines that activity as justice.

The delivery vehicle for this justice will be seven "last" plagues. The plague symbolism recalls the previous trumpet scourges (9:18, 20; 11:6) and anticipates the imminent bowl horrors (15:6, 8; 16:9, 21). "Last" here is not a chronological reference; John does not mean to say that these are the last in a series of events beginning with the horrors that accompanied the breaking of the seven seals. The plagues represent the same end-time cataclysms as those recorded with the seals and trumpets, but from this third and final eschatological vantage point (see the discussion of 6:1–8). They are John's "last" look at the end.

The plagues are also "last" because God's wrath ends when they conclude. John uses *thymos* (wrath) almost exclusively as a reference to the judgment God executes against Babylon.[1] The good news is that this judgment—because believers, too, are caught up in its maelstrom—is short lived (cf. Mark 13:20). Using the same verb that Jesus called upon to signal the end of his historical life and ministry in the Gospel of John (*teleō*, 19:30), John declares that with this final revelatory barrage God's wrath, having achieved its judgment/justice objective, is finished. The (divine) passive formulation implies that it is none other than God who has extinguished it. Everything, even the horror, happens according to God's (justice) design and operates under God's control.

### 15:2–4 *A New Exodus Hymn*

In a scene that recalls the vision of the heavenly throne room in chapters 4 and 5, John observes a multitude of witnesses singing a hymn of praise to God from their station beside the sea of glass. Like the Hebrews who stood with Moses at the Red Sea and celebrated with song God's mighty acts of saving (the Hebrews) and judging (the Egyptians), so this multitude of heavenly souls commemorates God's impending plagues as acts of saving (for the believers) and judgment (for those who persecute the believers) that will transform both mythical and historical landscapes.

2 Then I saw something like a sea of glass mixed with fire, and standing beside the sea of glass with harps of God, those who had conquered the

---

1. See 14:8, 10, 19; 15:7; 16:1, 19; 18:3; 19:15. The only other use, at 12:12, refers to the dragon's wrath at being thrown from heaven as a result of God's heavenly judgment against it.

beast and its image and the number of its name. 3 And they sing the song of Moses, the servant of God, and the song of the Lamb, singing:

> "Great and amazing are your works, Lord God, the Almighty;
>   just and true are your ways,
> King of the nations!ª
> 4 Who will not fearᵇ and glorify your name, Lord?
> Because you alone are holy,
>   because all the nations will come and worship before you,
>   because your righteous judgments have been revealed."

a. God is king "of the ages" (*aiōnōn*) in 𝔓⁴⁷ ℵ*⋅² C 1006 1611 1841 *pc* vg sy saᵐˢˢ, but "of the nations" (*ethnōn*) in ℵ¹ A 051 𝔐 gig (h) syʰᵐᵍ bo; Prim. The manuscript tradition is fairly evenly split on this title of God in 15:3, between "king of *ages*" and "king of *nations*." Codex ℵ itself has been corrected from *aiōnōn* to *ethnōn* and back again. But if the external evidence is inconclusive, the internal evidence favors *ethnōn* (see Metzger, *Textual Commentary*, 755–56). It is possible that a scribe might have written *basileus tōn aiōnōn*, thinking of the similar doxology in 1 Tim 1:17 (cf. *1 En.* 9.4; Tob 13:4). Also, the immediate context is arguably better suited to the reading *ethnōn* (cf. "all the nations," *panta ta ethnē* in 15:4).

b. The awkward syntax of 15:4a has generated several variants in the textual tradition. The inclusion of *se* (you) before *ou* ("not": 𝔓⁴⁷ ℵ 1006 1841 1854 2329 *pc*) or after *phobēthē* ("fear": 051 94 1828 1859 2020 2138 and TR) is probably an effort to supply an object for the verb: "Who will not fear *you*?" The witnesses that have only *ou* (ℵ 1006 1841 2040 2065) or only *mē* ("not": 1854) arguably smooth out the more difficult emphatic negative. The reading *ou mē phobēthē* has ample manuscript support (A C P 046 1611 2053 and versions) and can readily explain the origin of the other readings (with Metzger, *Textual Commentary*, 756).

**[2]** John marks yet another scene shift with the phrase *kai eidon* (then I saw). This new episode offers a narrative interpretation of the impending plagues. Before John reveals his assessment, though, he describes a particular part of the throne room vision that has caught his attention: the sea of glass. Though John uses the word "sea" often (22 times), he only specifies a sea of glass twice, here and in the other throne-room vision at 4:6. The sea is a symbol of instability and chaos, the place where monstrous rebellion against God's authority arises (see the comment on 13:1; cf. 20:13; 21:1). At 4:6 that symbol was located in the midst of heaven, shackled—glassed over—but still undeniably present. The implication of potential danger and disruption remains with the metaphor in 15:2, but now John adds something new: the sea is "mixed with fire." The verb "mixed" is part of a passive construction that indicates God's agency. The construction should be read instrumentally. Fire, for John, is the stir stick that God uses to whip the sea into a judgmental froth.[2]

2. See 8:5, 7, 8; 9:17, 18; 11:5; 14:10, 18; 16:8; 18:8; 19:20; 20:9, 10, 14, 15; 21:8.

Prominently positioned beside the sea is an apparently vast multitude of people, who are defined by a single participial form: *tous nikōntas* (the ones who conquered). Christ, too, is described as a conqueror (5:5; 17:14). In the letters to the seven churches, Christ implored John's hearers and readers to follow Christ's model of testifying to his and his God's lordship even at the cost of his own life. He promised that those who do conquer through such witness would achieve the very reward, eschatological relationship with God, that John now glimpses (2:7, 11, 17, 26; 3:5, 12, 21). This multitude, then, is populated by believers who have witnessed as Christ implored them to do. This multitude is also the "they" of 12:11, who defeat the dragon by their association with the blood of the Lamb and by their own revolutionary testimony about the lordship of that Lamb.

"They" hold harps of God. They use those harps to accompany their singing (15:3). Twice before, John has recalled harps and their owners: 5:8, where the twenty-four elders hold them; and 14:2, where the same heavenly multitude described in 7:9–17 holds them. At 14:2–3 the multitude also uses the harps to accompany their singing. The presence of harps identifies the groups in 7:9–17; 14:2; and 15:2 as the same multitude. John's further description confirms such a conclusion. At 7:14 he observes that the members of the multitude wear robes that have been washed to a dazzling sheen in the blood of the Lamb. The dazzling effect, particularly as related to dress, is the reward for the very same revolutionary, conquering witness by which John identifies the multitude in 15:2 (cf. 2:17; 3:4–5; 18 [21]; 7:9, 13). In describing the beast, its image, and the number of its name as the objects of their conquest, John simultaneously reminds his hearers and readers of the bestial historical situation in which they now find themselves (chs. 12–14) and projects God's judgment of it (15:5–18:24) and their victory over it (cf. 12:11).

[3] "They" (the conquering multitude of 7:9–17; 12:11; 14:2; 15:2) sing an antiphonal response to the victory God has already initiated, with their witnessing assistance, and now in the bowl plagues is poised to consummate. While John's narrative is filled with hymns, the seer uses the actual vocabulary of singing (*adō*) only three times. At 5:9, the cherubim and twenty-four elders sing a new song that celebrates the Lamb's ransoming of God's people by his bloody witness. While that ransoming is often interpreted in an individual, pietistic way, John's thematic association with the exodus ransoming of the people from imperial bondage suggests an equally potent political meaning (see the comment on 5:9–10). That political sensibility is amplified by John's identification of the enemy from which the people are ransomed as Rome and its Asia Minor client governments (cf. 15:2).

In his only other appeal to the vocabulary of singing (14:3), John refers directly to the victorious multitude he reintroduces at 15:2. In chapter 14 the focus is less on the ransoming of the people than on the judgment/justice of God that will establish it. Still, the central focus that joins both prior singing episodes is celebration prompted by the realization of God's rule.

By contextually emphasizing a direct relationship between the metaphor of singing (15:3) and the plagues of wrath (15:1, 5–8), John reestablishes a focus on the realization of God's rule through the execution of God's justice/judgment. John focuses even more sharply when he identifies the sound as the song of Moses, the servant of God. The simplest concordance search yields a plethora of Old Testament verses where Moses is so designated (e.g., Exod 4:10; 14:31; Josh 1:2; 1 Kgs 8:53; 2 Kgs 21:8; 2 Chr 24:9; Neh 1:7–8; Ps 105:26; Dan 9:11; Mal 4:4). None of them is more important for John's purposes here than Exod 14:31, which designates Moses as God's servant immediately before Moses and the Israelites sing in praise of God's judgment/destruction of the Egyptian army in the sea. In other words, the song the multitude of Rev 15:3 sings is like the song Moses and the Israelites sang; it praises God's judgment, which ransoms— that is to say, liberates—God's people from those who would pursue and perse-cute them. For this reason, it is also the song of the Lamb. The connecting *kai* (and) is epexegetical; John means to say that the song of God's servant Moses is also the song of the Lamb.[3]

Still, calling this new song the song of Moses raises a problem: to what Old Testament song of Moses is John referring? Even though John envisions a sim-ilar context for the multitude's song and the Song of Moses in Exod 15:1–18, there are few grammatical and thematic parallels between the two.[4] Many scholars have noted that a better thematic comparison exists between the mul-titude's song and the one attributed to Moses and the Israelites in Deut 32:1–43. But even there the connections are quite general. Two solutions to the source problem merit mention. The first and least subscribed to is the intriguing one offered by Richard Bauckham. Pressing against the tendency to interpret Rev-elation as a book whose vision excludes all but a small chosen community from salvation, Bauckham connects the themes in this song with the universalistic perspectives of Old Testament prophetic and psalmic materials. Bauckham explains that John, following the rabbinic interpretive method of *gezerâ šawâ,* "the principle that passages in which the same words and phrases occur can be used to interpret each other," appeals in an intentionally limited way to the Exod 15 material (esp. Exod 15:11) so as to evoke the explicit image of God's almighty stature (*Climax of Prophecy,* 299). John, whose witnesses will call the God of the judging plagues the Almighty Lord (Rev 15:3), operates from a the-

---

3. The parallelism is also indicated grammatically. The subjective genitive identification of Moses ("song of Moses," not "song to Moses") prefaces and conditions a subjective genitive read-ing with regard to Lamb ("song of the Lamb," not "song to the Lamb"). Bauckham writes that the song of Moses is also the Lamb's song, "because the new exodus is a victory they have won by the blood of the new passover Lamb (cf. 7:14; 12:11)" (*Climax of Prophecy,* 297).

4. Isa 12:1–6 provides an interesting rephrasing of the Exod 15 hymn.

matic parallel between Exod 15:11 and three other Old Testament texts that also identify God as the Almighty, whose role as ultimate judge should inspire the nations to repentance. "Thus John's version of the song takes as its starting point the key verse Exodus 15:11, which is taken for granted, without being quoted, because it is the common denominator which links the passages to which allusion is made (Jer 10:6–7; Pss 86:8–10; 98:1–2). The controlling motif of this version of the song is therefore the incomparability of God" (*Climax of Prophecy*, 305).

One can hardly imagine that John, already working with such a high degree of narrative, symbolic difficulty, would impose yet even another layer of sophisticated complexity upon his hearers and readers in order to make what should be a rather simple point. The solution proposed by Elisabeth Schüssler Fiorenza is therefore to be preferred. Instead of appealing to a single text, John has, while calling upon the master image of Moses' song and all that it implies about God's majestic identity and judging behavior, based his new song upon a broad cross-section of Old Testament texts that heralds a consensus about God's almighty and salvific stature.[5]

John appeals to that almighty status explicitly in the song lyrics. The title *pantokratōr* (almighty) occurs quite often in John's hymns, especially in a context whose theme is judgment (1:8; 4:8; 11:17; 16:7, 14; 19:6, 15; 21:22; cf. LXX: Amos 3:13; 4:13). Appealing to language already introduced in 15:1, the multitude honors the works of this Almighty God as great and amazing. John's hearers and readers would certainly remember that the sign of the seven angels with the seven last plagues was also described as great and amazing (15:1). The language reaffirms what the divine passive constructions have been implying throughout the narrative: the shocking and awe-ful acts of devastation and destruction are God's way of establishing justice *for* the conquering witnesses and judgment *against* those who persecute them. The subsequent stanza of the hymn is quick to insist that these divine actions are both righteous and true. God's judgment is always God's appropriate justice meted out on behalf of God's oppressed people (cf. 16:5, 7; 19:2; Deut 32:4, 8; Ps 145:17).

---

5. Schüssler Fiorenza, *Justice and Judgment*, 137. Reddish (293) provides an excellent chart that demonstrates graphically the themes in the song of 15:3–4 with parallel Old Testament texts:

| *15:3–4* | *Parallels* |
| --- | --- |
| Great and amazing are your deeds, | Pss 92:5; 98:1; 111:2; 139:14 |
| Lord God the Almighty! | Amos 3:13 LXX; 4:13 LXX |
| Just and true are your ways, | Deut 32:4; Ps 145:17 |
| King of the Nations! | Jer 10:7 |
| Lord, who will not fear and glorify your name? | Jer 10:7; Pss 86:9, 12; 99:3; Mal 1:11 |
| For you alone are holy. | 1 Sam 2:2; Pss 99:3; 111:9 |
| All nations will come and worship before you, | Ps 86:9; Isa 2:2; 66:23; Jer 16:19 |
| For your judgments have been revealed | Ps 98:2 |

In the final words of the verse, the universalism that Bauckham worked so hard to introduce sits plainly on the surface of the narrative. John identifies the almighty judging God as the King, not of Israel or of the conquering witnesses, but of the nations (cf. Jer 10:7). Universalism is a consistent trait of the rule exercised by God and the Lamb (Rev 1:5; 17:14; 19:16); worldwide lordship belongs to God and is expressed through the exalted status of the Lamb. This confession is a direct political contradiction of the claims to global dominion made by Caesar and the empire he oversees.

[4] The emphasis on universalism continues with the question "Who will not fear and glorify your name, Lord?" When Jeremiah asked essentially the same question, he directed it not at Israel alone, but at all of the nations of the earth (Jer 10:7). John addresses the same broad audience. Among all the nations, who will not now fear this Almighty God who acts equitably in judgment and justice? Fear is an appropriate, universally available, and apparently faithful response to the recognition of God's universal sovereignty (Rev 14:7; 19:5). At 11:18 anyone who fears is rewarded with eschatological relationship with God; anyone who fights against God is judged by God's wrath. The only limits to inclusion in God's reign are self-imposed; those who refuse to fear—who refuse to give God appropriate glory and worship for God's almighty status—exclude themselves from God's ransoming presence and thereby make themselves susceptible to God's incendiary wrath.

By the manner in which he has structured this verse, John has created a synonymous relationship among showing "fear," giving "glory," and offering "worship." Showing fear and glorifying God's name are presented in parallel in the first half of the verse, as though they have the same meaning. Indeed, John's use of "glory" makes explicit reference to a theme he has to this point indicated only subtly. In the judgment context of 15:1–3, the question "Who will not fear and glorify your God?" implies an expectation of repentance for those in the nations who do not already fear and glorify. Who in one's right mind, after seeing the preliminary arrival of the plagues of almighty wrath in the form of a great and amazing heavenly sign, would not show fear and give glory, that is, repent? (See the discussion of repentance at 8:7–13 and 9:20–21.) Indeed, elsewhere John intentionally deploys the language of fear and glory to describe those who, upon seeing God's mighty acts of judgment, either do or should repent (11:13; 14:7; 16:9). John later testifies to the possibility that the nations could be included in this repentant number (21:24–26; 22:2). Significantly, at 21:24–26 that inclusion is highlighted by the image of the nations mingling their ransomed glory with the glory of God.

The rationale for fearing God/glorifying God/repenting is offered in the second half of the verse. John provides three explanatory statements, each introduced by *hoti* (because). The first reason is that only God is holy. John is clearly operating from the background of Ps 86:8–10, where the psalmist declares that because God is unique among the gods, God alone is worthy to receive glory from the nations. No doubt John has in mind the propensity of the Greco-Roman nations to surrender their praise and adulation to pagan deities, even deified humans like Caesar or a deified state like Rome. Only God is truly holy and therefore worthy, as the first half of the verse concludes, to receive glory. At 16:5, in his only other use of the term *hosios* (holy), John reaffirms that God's holiness is directly connected to God's just (righteous and true, 15:3) judgment.

The fact that all the nations will come and worship before God supplies a second reason for repentance (i.e., fearing God and giving God glory). John's appeal to Old Testament sources broadens here; his writing reminds his hearers and readers of the universal expectations of Isa 2:2; Jer 16:19; and Mal 1:11. In each of these texts, with the allusion to Ps 86, all the nations come to recognize God's sovereignty. John uses the word *ethnēs* (nations) with a similar universal emphasis: the messianic child will shepherd the nations with a rod of iron and thus lead them to repentance (see the comment on 12:5; cf. 19:15). Moreover, an angel flying in midheaven proclaims the gospel to every nation with the expectation—using the same three terms that are so crucial to the repentance theme here in 15:4—that the nations will fear, glorify, and worship God (14:6–7). Indeed, John hints that the nations would have given God proper fear, glory, and worship all along if they had not been deceived (20:3).

Third and finally, John acknowledges God as the one who orchestrates events in such a way that people will come to recognize God's majesty. The verb *ephanerōthēsan* (were revealed) is a divine passive that indicates God's agency. God revealed God's behavior as righteous acts (*dikaiōmata*), which John had already described as righteous (*dikaiai*) and true (15:3). God will enable all the nations to see what John has long understood. The result of this revelation should motivate the wayward nations' return to God in fear, glorification, and worship (i.e., repentance).

In the end, then, v. 4 provides a three-step causal rationale for the nations to repent. The nations should fear and glorify God. Why? Because in God's judgments God alone is holy, that is, just. How does one know that God is holy? Because the nations come and worship God. Why do they come and worship? Because God's just(ice) acts have been revealed. John's argument is an entirely circular one; he comes back again and again to his primary point. What was true all along (v. 3)—that God is holy, true, and therefore just—God has now demonstrated to all.

## 15:5–8 Introduction to the Seven Bowls

The bowl visions represent the third and final visualization of the end-time events that symbolize God's judgment. They are a re-presentation of the dramatic scenes already played out in the form of seven broken seals and seven blasted trumpets. From this even more devastating vantage point of the Apocalypse, John realizes that not just a third (as in the trumpet visions, 9:18, 20) but all of the earth will be decimated.

5 After this, I looked, and the temple, that is, the tent of witness in heaven, was opened, 6 and the seven angels with the seven plagues came out from the temple, clothed in clean, bright linen[a] and with golden sashes across their chests. 7 Then one of the four living creatures gave to the seven angels seven golden bowls filled with the wrath of God, who lives forever and ever. 8 And the temple was filled with smoke from the glory of God and from God's power, and no one was able to enter the temple until the seven plagues of the seven angels were finished.

a. "Stone" (*lithon*) is found in A C 2053 2062 *pc* vg[st] sy[hmg], *linoun* in 𝔓[47] (ℵ) 046 *pc* ar gig (h), and *linon* in P 051 1 1006 1611 1859 2081 it[gig, h, 61] sy[ph, h] arm *al*. This text-critical problem has caused some stir among textual critics, since its resolution is by no means simple. Westcott and Hort read *lithon*, "dressed in pure bright *stone*," adducing as a parallel the oracle against the king of Tyre in Ezek 28:13 LXX: *pan lithon chrēston endedesai*, "you were dressed in every kind of precious stone" (Hort, "Notes," WH 2:139). The UBS[4] Committee and NA[27] read *linon*, "dressed in pure bright *linen*," regarding *lithon* as a nonsensical transcriptional error, manuscript support notwithstanding (Metzger, *Textual Commentary*, 756). On the other hand, *linon*, if original, would appear only here in Revelation, which otherwise uses *byssinos*, "fine linen" (18:12, 16; 19:8, 14). In any case, *linoun* is probably secondary to *linon*.

[5] John typically uses the narrative marker *kai meta tauta eidon* (after this, I looked) to shift to a new subject area (4:1; 7:1, 9; 18:1; 19:1). This time, however, his use marks a turn back to the subject area that he broke away from after 15:1. The seer's attention was momentarily diverted by the sound of the heavenly multitude of conquering witnesses singing their affirmation of God's imminent acts of justice/judgment. Refocused, John not only returns to the heavenly sign but also instructs his readers about its origin.

The seven angels exit the sanctuary of the tent of meeting in heaven onto John's revelatory scene through an opened door. For John, "opening" language is always, even when not directly using God or the Lamb as its subject, salvation and/or judgment language (see the comment on 6:1). The passive construction ("opened") indicates God's agency; the connection of the opening with the introduction of seven plagues indicates God's coming justice/judgment. Unlike 4:1, when God opened the door to heaven so John could see inside and contemplate eschatological relationship with God in the heavenly throne room, here God opens a temple door so judgment can pour out.

The thematic relationship between the heavenly temple and God's judgment is strong with John. Except for 7:15, where the multitude of conquering witnesses worships in the temple, almost every other mention of the temple is awash with judgment imagery. Revelation 11:19 is a dramatic case in point. Connected narratively as it is with 11:1–2, it offers a temple composed of an inner and outer sanctuary, which is dramatically linked with the terrible third woe. The reference to the ark of the covenant anticipates John's description of the temple as the tent of meeting, which is where the ark resided (15:5). Angels depart the temple with the prototypical judgment tool, the sickle (14:15, 17). The temple images that follow in 15:6, 8 are integrally associated with the seven plagues. At 16:1 and 16:17, a voice from the temple initiates and then consummates God's wrath. Only at 21:22 is the mention of the temple not connected with God's wrath. That aberration is due to the fact that there God dwells directly with the people of faith and the repentant people from the nations; judgment is no longer required.

The description of the temple as no longer necessary (21:22) reminds the reader of an earlier heavenly declaration that celebrates God's decision to dwell directly with humans (21:3). The language for "dwell" is *skēnē* (dwelling, tent) in 21:3, the same term John directly associates with the temple in 15:5. In fact, the genitive form for "tent" or "dwelling" in v. 5 should be read as a genitive of apposition. The translation "the temple, that is, the tent of witness" is appropriate. John is speaking about a single heavenly edifice. In doing so, he wants to conjure yet again the image of the exodus, where the tent of meeting was so described because it was there that Moses encountered and spoke with God (Exod 33:7–11; 40:34–38; Lev 1:1–2; cf. Acts 7:44). John affirms here that this new exodus is also an expression of God's judgment against those who have persecuted God's people.

[6] This is a motion verse that serves two primary ends: it explains how the plagues will be dispersed, and it describes the seven angels who will act as the delivery vehicles. The angels exit the heavenly temple with an unmistakable intent to distribute their simmering symbols of God's wrath (15:1; 16:1). The judgment sentiment would remind knowledgeable readers of Lev 26:21, where God promised to plague the people sevenfold for their sins. Interestingly enough, in the broader context of Lev 26, God intended that the harsh judgment would inspire the people to repent. For John, the song of Moses and of the Lamb (Rev 15:2–4) appears to reckon a similar rationale for the pouring out of God's wrath; God intends repentance rather than obliteration.

The angels' dress seems to corroborate the desire for repentance. Their linen garb is priestly attire; according to Exod 28:39, the priests' vestments were to be made from such fabric. Israel's priests directed the people, even the sinful, *to* rather than away from God. Their garb is also messianic, indicating a relationship with God as intimate as that enjoyed by the one like a child of humanity. John's vision of the child of humanity at 1:13 describes someone wearing the similar uniform issue of a long robe accented with a golden sash across the chest (cf. Dan 10:5). And though John does not describe the color of the robe of the child of humanity in 1:13, the consistent presentation of heavenly attire as dazzling (white) in color suggests that, like the robes of these seven angels, the child of humanity's also dazzled (see the discussion of 3:4–5).

[7] John continues his explication of 15:1. In vv. 5–6, he explained that the angels introduced in v. 1 were God's agents, who exited the heavenly temple to execute God's justice/judgment in hope of securing the nations' repentance. Now in more dramatic detail, John describes both the angels' divine instruments and the manner in which they obtained them. The seven plagues were given to the seven angels by one of the cherubim attending God's throne (see the comment on 4:6–8). The plagues were housed in seven golden bowls. This is not the first time that John has envisioned angels and golden bowls. At 5:8, in the heavenly throne room, he saw angels with golden bowls of incense that represented the prayers of the saints. No doubt these were the same prayers that cried out for God's justice/judgment at 6:9–11 and sparked the pouring out of God's judgment fire upon the earth at 8:3–5. The contextual implications are clear: God's present judgment of wrath is integrally tied to the cries and prayers of the oppressed and executed witnesses. Those prayers motivate divine action throughout the book and perhaps represent the emotional inspiration for the book as a whole.

The term John uses for bowl (*phialē*) conjures the image of the cultic priest already initiated by the angels' linen robes (15:6). Bowls are mentioned in the Old Testament some thirty times in conjunction with priestly service at the tabernacle or temple. "The bowls were probably used to carry out the ashes and fat of sacrifices. These bowls are sometimes directly connected with 'the tabernacle of witness' (Exod. 38:23–26; Num. 4:14–15; 7:13–89) and are sometimes referred to as 'golden bowls' (1 Chron. 28:17; 2 Chron. 4:8, 21)" (Beale 806). Furthermore, "The cultic use of [*phialai*] is attested for Greek religion (Diodorus 4.49.8), where it was used primarily to pour libations of wine" (Aune 2:879). The central point in this narrative context, from both Old Testament and Greco-Roman perspectives, is that this priestly imagery reaffirms the cultic understanding of divine judgment/justice executed in the hopes of motivating repentance. The priest's goal is to broker relationship with the divine, not eliminate its possibility forever. The angels and their golden bowls of God's wrath are to be read in that light.

[8] John concludes his introductory vision of the plague cycle with a glimpse of the heavenly temple consumed by the smoke from God's glory. Smoke and related clouds are common biblical ciphers for the glorious presence of God (Exod 13:21; 40:34–35; 1 Kgs 8:10–11; 2 Chr 5:13; Isa 6:4). Indeed, sometimes, as here, cultic attendants are unable to enter the temple/tent of meeting because of that presence. The smoke is particularly reminiscent of the earlier judgment scene where the incense smoke and the prayers of God's people insti-

gate the pouring out of God's fiery wrath (8:4–5), which John has already alluded to in 15:7. Throughout the narrative, smoke conveys a sense of divine judgment (9:2–3, 17–18; 14:11; 18:9, 18; 19:3). By associating the images of smoke and temple as he does here, John makes certain that his hearers and readers understand how integrally God's glory is related to God's judgment. The relationship between the smoke and the prayers of God's people is even more provocative. Apparently God is so overwhelmed by the peoples' cries that God's passion for them takes tangible shape and overwhelms the heavenly temple like a cloud. God is so energized and agitated that this cloud will prevent anyone from entering the temple and therefore entering into God's presence until God's wrath, symbolized here by the seven plagues, has ended (see the discussion of 15:1), and the repentance that wrath seeks has been accomplished. The implication is clear: in the future, entrance—and therefore relationship with God—though now denied, is anticipated. At 21:23–26, with the glory of the Lord no longer blocking and the walls of a physical temple no longer excluding, the holy place of God, now a city, can and will be filled by the glory of the repentant nations and all the peoples who inhabit them.

## 16:1–21 The Seven Bowls of God's Wrath

### 16:1 The Command to Pour Out the Bowls

John's metaphorical presentation of God's wrath as a pouring out of seven bowls has several primary themes. First, the end-time events associated with the bowls are a re-presentation of the events previously portrayed through the metaphors of seven broken seals and seven trumpet blasts (see the discussion of 6:1–8). Second, the bowl actions affect the entire cosmos. These plagues target not only human kingdoms and the individuals who rule and populate them, but also the very four essences of creation itself: earth, water, fire, and air. Third, though utterly devastating, the plagues are God's just and appropriate response to the evil that results from the rejection of God's rule and the persecution of those who witness to that rule. Fourth, the judgment matches measure for measure the crimes that have triggered it. Fifth, the controlling image for the mayhem is the exodus event.

16:1 Then I heard a foreboding voice from the temple telling the seven angels: "Go and pour out the seven bowls of the wrath of God upon the earth."

[16:1] Chapter 16 begins with a phrase, *kai ēkousa* (then I heard), that operates in a way similar to *kai eidon* (then I looked; see the discussion of 5:1). The phrase often occurs in the text, but not as the opening to a new scene. Instead, it tends to follow up and elaborate upon an ongoing scene (1:10; 9:13;

10:4; 19:1, 6). This is particularly evident in cases where John sees something (4:1; 5:11; 6:1, 6; 7:4; 8:13; 14:2, 13; 15:5; 18:4; 21:3) and subsequently hears a voice or sound that interprets what he has just witnessed. The phrase is equally conspicuous in situations where John hears a hymn that interprets the narrative that preceded it (12:10; 16:5, 7). In this case, John hears testimony that interprets and clarifies his vision in 15:5–8.

The foreboding voice implies a tone of judgment that is consistent throughout the narrative (see the comment on 7:2) and certainly represents the mood of a text that pours out God's wrath in seven viciously lethal doses. The voice's temple origin reminds the reader of the vision of 15:5–8, which pictures the tent of meeting in heaven as the departure point for the seven angels. After the declaration in 15:8 that no one could now enter the smoke-filled temple except God, God is probably the speaker. In any event, by locating the voice in the heavenly temple, John at the least identifies the voice's command with God's eschatological intent.

God intends two specific actions. First, the angels are instructed to depart with their pestilent cargo. According to 15:6, they have already left; however, the charge to depart in 16:1 is more comprehensive. This time, apparently, the angels are to leave the temple environs completely. They are to go forth into the world and cosmos so that they can obey the second command: to shed the contents of their bowls as a representation of God's judgment. John's language is intentional and compelling. He is careful to use a verb, *ekcheō* (pour out, shed) that is exclusive to chapter 16 (vv. 1, 2, 3, 4, 6, 8, 10, 12, 17). The verb has strong cultic implications. It is often used, as here, in connection with libation bowls that contain ritual liquid offerings.[1] In fact, John deploys the verb in a very calculated, balanced way. His mechanical "pouring" narration occurs four times before and four times after its clarifying central use at 16:6. There John explains that God's enemies, working at the direction of the dragon and its beasts from the sea and land, have "shed" the blood of those who have faithfully witnessed to the lordship of God and the Lamb. The measure-for-measure punishment meted out against God's enemies begins right there. In a kind of apocalyptic lex talionis, God intends to "shed" plagues of wrath upon the earth as an appropriate judicial response to the criminal shedding of human blood (see the discussion of bowls and wrath at 15:1, 7).

### 16:2–4 The First Three Angels

2 Then the first one departed and poured his bowl on the earth, and a foul and festering sore developed on the people who had the mark of the beast

---

1. Cf. Aune: "ἐκχεῖν is also used in the LXX for the pouring out of libations of water (1 Kgdms 7:6; 2 Kgdms 23:16) or for pouring out a libation of wine, i.e., a drink offering (Isa 57:6). ἐκχεῖν is frequently used of 'shedding' blood, i.e., committing murder (LXX Jer 7:6)" (2:883).

and worshiped its image. 3 Then the second one poured his bowl on the sea, and it became like the blood of a corpse, and every living creature in the sea died. 4 Then the third one poured his bowl into the rivers and the springs of water, and they^a became blood.

a. Uncomfortable with the more difficult and probably more original third-person singular (*egeneto*, [it] became), 𝔓^47 A 1006 1611 1841 1854 2053 2329 *pc* it sy co insert a third-person plural (*egenonto*, [they] became) to match the plural subjects (rivers and springs). A smoother translation would still incorporate the third-person plural pronoun.

[2–4] The first bowl plague infects only those who have branded themselves with the mark of the beast from the sea and worshiped its image (v. 2; see the discussion of judgment against the same group at 13:15–18; 14:9–11; cf. also 19:20–21; 20:4). The effects of the plague are brutally ironic; those who marked themselves *for* the beast are now branded with gruesome sores *by* God. The particular form of the plague follows the trajectory of God's retributive modus operandi. God plagued the oppressive Egyptian humans and their animals with sores in a failed early attempt (exodus plague number six) to secure the release of the Hebrews from bondage (Exod 9:8–12). The author of Deuteronomy makes clear that the improper behavior of even the faith community can earn God's sore-plaguing wrath (Deut 28:27, 35). A return (repentance) to the proper way of faith and obedience can prompt the transformation of that wrath into safekeeping (Deut 28:1).

Though the command in Rev 16:1 was to target the earth, the second angel sheds his bowl upon the sea (v. 3). Just as with the Nile in the first exodus plague (Exod 7:17–21), the infested water turns to blood. In this more radicalized case, however, the blood is that of a corpse. The effect, though, will be the same; the mention of a corpse serves only to heighten the sense of the macabre and thus the dread. Waters turned to blood also occurred when the second trumpet angel blew his eschatological instrument (Rev 8:8). In that case, only one-third of the sea and one-third of the creatures in the sea were affected. From this final apocalyptic vantage point, the sea and every living thing associated with it dies.

More escalation occurs when the third angel sheds his bowl upon the rivers and springs of water (v. 4). With the first exodus plague still haunting the narrative background (Exod 7:17–21; cf. Ps 78:44), this new vision recalls the third trumpet plague where the star Wormwood fell from the sky and contaminated a third of the earth's fresh water (8:10–11). With this third bowl plague the metamorphosis is complete; fresh water everywhere mutates into blood.

## 16:5–7 Antiphonal Hymns in Praise of Divine Justice

Given the striking and comprehensive nature of the devastation, John, and no doubt God, must have figured that God was in danger of losing the war of public relations. What kind of crime can possibly be worthy of such total destruction? Can a God who exacts such extreme judgment be just? The questions would have moved beyond the boundary of particular crime and appropriate punishment. Given the universal scope of the second and third plagues, the potential for indiscriminate collateral damage is high. When all the waters turn to blood and all the creatures living in those waters die, every human, even the faithful witnesses, will surely be affected. Unlike the members of the heavenly army who will be protected from the cataclysms and their effects (see the comments on 7:1–8 and 14:1–5), the majority of the surviving witnesses to the lordship of God and the Lamb will suffer just like the beast servants who have persecuted them (see the discussion of 3:10). What can one say about the actions of a God who causes and allows such suffering of even the innocent?

John answers the anticipated challenge by reminding his hearers and readers of the song of Moses and the Lamb (15:2–4). There the people praised God because they believed that God's actions were the appropriate response to the evil perpetrated against God and God's people. The hymns in 16:5–7 are intentionally calculated to bring that earlier song and its message to mind. The material operates as a "judgment doxology" (cf. 19:1–2). Aune perceptively classifies it as a declarative hymn of praise that includes a judgment doxology as one of its theological motifs: "The *content* of the 'judgment doxology' . . . centers on the affirmation (in both hymns and prayers) that the divine punishments meted out by God are both just and appropriate" (2:865).[2]

5 Then I heard the angel of the waters saying, "You are just, the one who is and who was, the holy one, because you have executed these judgments;[a] 6 because they poured out the blood of saints and prophets, you also have given them blood to drink; they deserve it." 7 Then I heard the altar[b] saying, "Yes, Lord God Almighty, true and just are your judgments."

a. The phrase *tauta ekrinas* (lit., "you have judged these things") clearly refers back to the bowl plagues of the first four verses.

b. The verb *akouō* takes a genitive object. The phrase *ēkousa tou thysiastēriou* (I heard the altar) is still odd, since it appears that the altar is speaking. Some manuscripts (046 2329 *pc* ar) try to rectify the problem by inserting *ek* to suggest a partitive genitive; that is, *someone* from the altar speaks. The more difficult reading is in keeping with John's understanding that the altar can speak (see the comment on v. 7 below) and is thus to be preferred.

[5] John indicates that the hymns are an interpretive follow-up to the first three plagues when he opens vv. 5–7 with the formulaic phrase *kai ēkousa* ("then I heard"; see the comment on 16:1). An important player is speaking: the

2. Aune points to 2 Chr 12:6; Ezra 9:15; Neh 9:33; Pss 7:11; 9:4; Jer 46:28; 3 Macc 2:3.

angel who has jurisdiction over the very waters that have just been fouled by blood. John has already implied that angels were given authority over certain of the key elements of creation (fire in 14:18). This Christian narrative assertion follows from the Jewish understanding of angelic authority over nature.[3] The content of the angel's message is critical. The being assigned supervision and, one would guess, protection of the waters not only allows the violence that is done to those waters but also rules the violence to be an act of justice. In the angel's own words, God is *dikaios* (just, righteous).[4] Surprisingly, the term *dikaios* is not frequent in Revelation. At 15:3 God's destructive actions are deemed "just" because they are the legitimate response to the evil perpetrated in the earth. Those same acts are a preparatory means of salvation for those who have witnessed, which is why the witnesses simultaneously sing joyfully (15:3–4). The connection with the exodus story reminds John's readers that even though God's just acts operate on behalf of God's people, those same acts do not guarantee a life of untroubled ease. Indeed, the salvific exodus was the prelude to a long and arduous struggle in the wilderness for the Hebrew people. God's justice and the salvation it offers do not and will not come cheap.

The theme of God's just actions continues in the other two texts where John uses *dikaios* (19:2; 22:11); 22:11 confirms that the language is not exclusively about punishing the wicked but also about the justice that comes from rewarding the faithful. Here at 16:5, John makes sure that his readers recognize the connection between God's just nature and God's judging, plaguing actions (*tauta*, these things) by directly associating *dikaios* with *ekrinas* (you judged). In other words, according to the angel who had charge of the plagued waters, God has judged justly.

By describing God with the same formula he used earlier in the text ("the one who is and who was"), John demonstrates that this just God is the same God who sponsored his prophecy and cared for the well-being of the faithful (1:4, 8; 4:8). As in his use of the formula at 11:17, however, John adjusts what he says in 16:5. At 11:17, instead of formulaically declaring God as the one who is and was and will come, John substituted "because you have taken great power and begun to rule" for "will come." The dynamic had shifted. God was no longer expected; God's rule has arrived with the dramatic onset of God's judgment. So here in 16:5 God is no longer described as the coming one but as the one who has come in judgment and who is therefore "holy." The narrative context directly relates God's holiness to God's judgment; God is the holy one precisely because God is the one who judges justly. Interestingly enough, John deploys "holy one" (*hosios*) only twice, here and at 15:4, the song of Moses and

---

3. See *1 En.* 60.11–25; 61.10; 66.1–2; 69.22; 75.3; *2 En.* chs. 4–6; 19.1–4; *Jub.* 2.2; 1QH 1[9].8–13; Str-B 3:818–20. Cf. Reddish 304; Aune 2:884.

4. For Old Testament declarations that God is just, see Deut 32:4; Ps 145:17.

the Lamb to which his language of justice has already directly alluded. Moses, the Lamb, and now the angel who has charge over the waters—all three corroborate each other's testimony. God is holy, as the one who deals justice.

**[6]** The connection between judgment and crime develops explicitly from John's intentional word use. The first three angels shed (*ekcheō*) their bowls of God's wrath (see the comment on 16:1). As a result of the emptying of bowls two and three, all the waters upon the earth turned to blood (*haima*). When John states the just cause for judgment in v. 6, he appeals to exactly the same language: the accused shed (*ekcheō*) the blood (*haima*) of God's servants (cf. Ps 97:3). John describes these servants as saints and prophets. He is speaking not about the saints and prophets of old but about the very witnesses to the lordship of God and the Lamb who have been the center of his attention throughout the narrative. At 11:10, God's witnesses (11:3) are recognized as prophets. The saints play a particularly important role. At 5:8 their prayers were the ingredients of the heavenly incense the twenty-four elders carried into heavenly worship. At 8:3–4 those prayers were the cry that rose to heaven and, along with the cries of 6:9–11, provoked the execution of God's judgment. In several illustrative cases, John pairs saints with prophets as a kind of formulaic euphemism for those who risk witnessing to the lordship of God and the Lamb (11:18; 18:20, 24). In each of these texts, God's judgment is on prominent display. At 11:18 the judgment follows the lex talionis (measure-for-measure) theme to which John had already alluded in 11:1; the nations' rage would be met by God's answering rage. That same rage, which would bring judgment to God's enemies, represents the power of salvation for God's embattled people. The opposing yet constantly paired themes of salvation and judgment operate explicitly in 18:20, 24, where shed blood brings judgment upon the forces of the sea beast/whore and initiates salvation for the saints and prophets.

When John declares that God has given the forces of the beast blood to drink, he makes the lex talionis theme the metaphorical as well as the literal center of the verse. There is a cruel and bitter irony to the judgment; those who shed blood are punished by blood. There is historical precedent: the prophet Isaiah also declared that God would judge with blood those who spilled blood (Isa 49:26). The ironic balance is a reframing of the position that John has already taken: God's judgment is just. Those who spill blood are worthy (*axios*) of a punishment that uses blood as the instrument of its execution. They deserve exactly what they get. Just as God is worthy (*axios*, 4:11) of praise because of God's act of creation and the Lamb is worthy (*axios*, 5:2, 4, 9, 12) of adoration because of his witness to God's lordship even to the point of death, so human behavior is appropriately deserving (*axios*) of the divine response of judgment (here) or salvation (3:4).

**[7]** John's third use of *kai ēkousa* (then I heard) in a brief seven verses confirms that every new thing he now hears acts as a running commentary on what has been previously revealed (see the comments on vv. 1, 5). While vv. 5–6 interpret the shedding of the first four bowls as an act of justice, v. 7 affirms the previous interpretation as an accurate one. What John hears, then, is the acoustic "Amen" to the preceding hymnic declaration. This antiphonal response is also presented in the form of a hymn. The singer, though, is odd. John does not say that he hears a voice from the altar (on the distinction between sacrificial and incense altars, see the discussion of 6:9), but that the altar itself sings out (cf. 9:13, where John heard [*kai ēkousa*] the horns of the altar respond interpretively to the blowing of the sixth angel's trumpet). In almost every use of the term "altar," John attaches the theme of judgment (6:9; 8:3, 5; 9:13; 14:18). In fact, it is probably appropriate that the altar issues such an assessment since it was from under the altar (6:9) that the executed saints made their plea that God justly intervene on their behalf.

"Yes," the altar affirms, referring to the Lord God Almighty (*pantokratōr*: 1:8; 4:8; 11:17; 15:3; 16:7; 19:6, 15; 21:22), a title of respect for God's lordship (see the comments on 4:8 and 15:3) that is often packaged in the narrative, as it is in this context, with another formulaic title of lordship, "the one who is and who was" (cf. 1:8; 4:8), and with the theme of judgment: "true and just are your judgments" (cf. 19:2). John uses the adjective *alēthinos* (true) to signify the valid eschatological judge (see the comments on 3:7 and 15:3). The angel of the waters has just used the adjective *dikaios* (just) to describe God's person (16:5b). The altar uses it now to describe God's judging actions; they too are just, which in this context is to say that they are appropriate to the crimes committed. John is so certain of this and so fervently desires that his hearers and readers get the point that he frames the hymnic section with this critical adjective.

## 16:8–12 The Fourth, Fifth, and Sixth Angels

8 Then the fourth one poured out his bowl on the sun, and it was allowed to scorch humans with fire. 9 And people were scorched by an intense heat, and they cursed the name of God who has authority over these plagues, and they did not repent and give God glory. 10 Then the fifth one poured out his bowl on the throne of the beast, and its kingdom was darkened, and they gnawed their tongues in agony, 11 and they cursed the God of heaven because of their agony and sores, and they did not repent from their works. 12 Then the sixth one poured out his bowl on the great river Euphrates, and its water was dried up, in order that the way of the kings from the east might be prepared.

[8] The aim shifts, yet the target remains the same; harming the sun will hurt the stubbornly recalcitrant people of the earth. The action is broadly parallel to the disturbance caused by the fourth trumpet angel, whose disruption of the

moon and stars also precipitated chaos on earth (8:12). The result of the fourth bowl angel's actions is something akin to what happens when gasoline is poured onto an already-catastrophic fire. The contents of the bowl cause the sun to erupt into such a vicious flame that its heat scorches humans on earth. John wants to make sure his hearers and readers understand that though the angel's actions prompt the devastation, God is behind it all. Once again he turns to the divine passive (*edothē*, "it was given"; see the comment on 6:2); this sun scorching is a premeditated act of God's judgment (cf. 17:16; 18:8).

This sun plague, like the bloody transformations of the waters that preceded it, must certainly have affected God's faithful witnesses as well as those who tormented them. Revelation 7:16 appears to suggest that the faithful will be protected from the scorching of the sun. But that text refers to the heavenly multitude, those who have already assumed an eschatological relationship with God. The ones who are not scorched by the sun are those who have already been killed by the devotees of the beast (7:14). Ironically, by killing them, their enemies protected them from these end-time horrors. John has turned their greatest weapon, that of execution, into a tool of rescue in much the same way that his Christian forebears transfigured the cross from a tool of torture and execution into the mechanism that guarantees God's victory.

The believers on the earth cannot, however, escape the horror. Though they are blameless as to the cause of the judgment activity, they are still caught up in it. In the Gospel of Mark, Jesus recognized that this would happen. He opines that the end-time eschatological events will be so cataclysmic that not even believers would survive them unless God shortened their duration (Mark 13:20). The implication is clear: the faithful, too, would suffer. The promise in Revelation (and apparently Mark) is not that believers would be raptured out of such struggle but that God would give them the power (and, according to Mark, shorten the time so that they would be able) to endure it (see the discussion of 3:10).

[9] John now makes explicit what he has implied through the use of the divine passive in the previous verse: God caused the sun plague. Even those who idolatrously worship the beast as lord recognize God's agency. They are not, however, sufficiently moved by that recognition to acknowledge God's lordship. In fact, God's judgment surprisingly prompts the opposite behavior. The *kai* (and) that follows the notice of suffering from scorching heat should therefore be read in an adversative manner. "Although the devotees of the beast from the sea were scorched by the God who had authority over these plagues, they blasphemed God's name and refused to repent and give God glory."

The blasphemy against God's name is the opposite of granting God proper respect (cf. 4:11; Isa 52:5). This blasphemy, which continues unabated in Rev 16:11 and 16:21, links these obstinate ones directly with the beast from the sea, who in fighting against God on behalf of the dragon, blasphemes God and all who dwell in heaven (13:5–6; cf. 13:1; 17:3). In chapter 13, the blasphemy involves denying the lordship status of God while saluting it in the beast from the sea (cf. 13:4). It involves the same thing here; John's final comment is that the blasphemers refuse to give God appropriate glory (see the comment on 13:5–6). God's judgment is an appropriate and expected response (cf. Lev 24:16).

Blasphemy is also the opposite of the expected behavior: repentance. John's language implies, as it did at 9:20–21 (cf. also 2:5, 16, 21–22; 3:3, 19), that God expected the people to repent and render glory to God as a result of the divine eschatological activity. The plagues, then, even as a judgment tool, were not designed simply with destruction in mind but were engineered to elicit changes in loyalty and recognition of lordship. (On the connection between giving God glory and repentance, see the comments on 11:13; 14:7; 15:4.)

[10] When the fifth angel sheds the contents of his bowl, he goes exclusively after the cause of the oppression, blasphemy, and idolatry: the throne of the beast from the sea (cf. 13:1–10). No doubt this throne is the capital city of Rome, also called the great city and Babylon (16:19; 17:18; 18:10, 16, 18–19, 21). Throne language has two important nuances within John's narrative. First, there is a strong connection with the throne of Satan at 2:13. John's discussion there tied the core of Satan's work to the universal imperial cult, which had established an especially powerful presence in Pergamum. At 13:2 the dragon gives its throne to the beast from the sea. That transfer of power is represented in the image of the beast's own throne in 16:10. Second, throne language in Revelation primarily refers to God's throne, or heavenly thrones in direct relationship to it. God's throne is a euphemism for God's person and authority (see the comment on 4:2–3), just as the beast's throne is a representation of its person and authority. The use of throne imagery for both conjures the narrative picture of two kingdoms and the powerful figures who rule over them engaged in cataclysmic mortal and even supernatural conflict. The fact that the beast's throne is now targeted means that the beast's rule is targeted and about to be put to an end.

The second half of the verse confirms the end of the beast's reign through the metaphor of an imposed, fearsome darkness. There is a strong parallel with the actions that follow the blowing of the fifth trumpet (9:1–6). There the sun is darkened and the people are doomed to agony following the fall of a great star from heaven. The motif of unbearable agony accompanying great darkness has biblical precedent. At Exod 10:22–23 Moses brought a similar darkness to the land of Egypt, and Isa 8:19–22 warns that any who seek direction from a source other than God will be thrust into darkness and anguished by gloom. That is precisely what happens to the citizens of the great city here in v. 10.

[11] Verse 11 follows from v. 9 as a close parallel. John repeats here the very same themes that he initiated there. First, God is acknowledged as the force behind the plagues. Not just the darkening of the sun and bloodying of the waters but also the sending of the sores (16:2) is God's work. Second, the people,

instead of acknowledging God's lordship, blaspheme God. Third, John speaks of this blasphemy in terms of a refusal to repent (on repentance as an important theme, see the treatments in 8:7–13; 9:20–21; 11:1, 13; 15:4; 22:11).

[12] Two deadly consequences follow the actions of the sixth angel, who sheds his bowl upon the great river Euphrates and evaporates all its water. The Euphrates is a powerful water supply, whose contribution to the fertility of the area surrounding it enabled the development of great civilizations like Assyria, Babylonia, and Parthia. The drying of the river would mean the loss of a critical water source and could only be looked upon as a tremendous tragedy for both Roman and Parthian settlements. The force of that tragedy would be amplified by the fact that the Parthians might be pressed into crossing the riverbed, now dry, in search of strategic water resources on the Roman side.

Here lies the second consequence. The Euphrates River marked the eastern boundary that separated the Roman Empire from the one rival it was never able to conquer: the Parthians. Parallels with the trumpet angels continue. The blowing of the sixth trumpet (9:14–15) unleashed four angels at the Euphrates who marshaled an apocalyptic version of a Parthian Army that exacted the deaths of one-third of the human population. (See the discussion of the strategic significance of the Euphrates at 9:14–15; and the discussion of the Parthian threat and John's use of it at 6:2 and 13:3.)[5] A dry riverbed is not a strategic barrier. It becomes a roadway that allows and perhaps even invites Parthian incursions. The drying would be, at least for the Jews and Christians, a stark reminder of God's drying of the Red Sea (Sea of Reeds). This time, though, the effect of the act has a cruel, ironic twist. The drying of the Red Sea enabled the Hebrews to escape destruction in Egypt; it allowed the Hebrews to flee. The drying of the Euphrates, by contrast, provides access into Roman territory: it allows the Parthians to enter. John's grammar indicates that the development is an intentional act of judgment by God. There is significant Old Testament precedent for such a maneuver on God's part (Ps 106:9; Isa 11:15–16; 51:10; Jer 50:38; 51:36). Once again a divine-passive verb anchors the explanatory clause in the sentence. The drying occurs so that the way of crossing for the kings from the east (the Parthians and their allies) might be prepared. John's point is that God is the one who facilitates this particular preparation and encourages the devastating follow-up.[6]

## 16:13–16 An Interlude: Envisioning the Final Battle

In the previous series of seven catastrophes, an interlude has always separated the sixth and seventh movements. In 7:1–17 the presentation of the 144,000 and

---

5. Cf also Isa 41:2, 25; 46:11, where God summons forces of judgment from the east.

6. Cf. Josh 3:1–4:18, where God dried up the Jordan to allow the people of Israel to attack the idolatrous Canaanites (Boring, *Revelation*, 175).

the great heavenly multitude separates the devastations that follow the opening of the sixth seal (6:12–17) from the breaking of the seventh at 8:1. In 10:1–11:14 the presentation of the little scroll and the two witnesses separates the destructions that follow the sounding of the sixth trumpet (9:13–21) from the blasting of the seventh trumpet (11:15). A structurally similar though shorter interlude now separates the pouring out of the sixth and seventh bowls. John pauses to preview the final apocalyptic conflict the nations will be deceived into engaging. Additionally, he reminds the faithful to be prepared and instructs them on how that preparation can be achieved and maintained.

> 13 Then I saw three unclean spirits like frogs come from the mouth of the dragon, and from the mouth of the beast, and from the mouth of the false prophet. 14 For they are sign-making demonic spirits, who go out to the kings of the entire inhabited world to gather them for the war on the great day of God, the Almighty. 15 ("Behold, I come like a thief. Blessed is the one who stays alert and is clothed, in order that he might not walk around naked and people see his shame.") 16 And he gathered them to the place that in Hebrew is called Harmageddon.

**[13]** John's use of *kai eidon* (then I saw) is an indication that he has moved to a new scene in the larger bowls act (see the discussion of 5:1). The three evil powers introduced in chapters 12 (the dragon) and 13 (the beast from the sea and the beast from the land) are now acting in concert in an attempt to unleash a destructive force that is the match of God's own acts of judgment. In this text, the beast from the land (13:11–18) is for the first time given a new name: "the false prophet." That these two titles refer to the same enemy is clear from John's narration. Their identity and role are the same: by way of incredible signs, they deceive humans into acknowledging the lordship and divine status of the beast from the sea (13:12–13; 19:20; 20:10).

In this case, the deception is engineered by unclean spirits who have the appearance of frogs. The characterization of the spirits as frogs connects this disturbing development with the second plague inflicted upon the Egyptians by Moses (Exod 8:1–15; cf. Pss 78:45; 105:30). The spirits-perceived-as-frogs deploy from the mouths of the three enemies. Already the mouth of the dragon has been used to send forth weapons against God's people (Rev 12:15–16; 13:5–6). The mouth is also, though, a metaphor for the staging area from which the efforts for God's justice/salvation are launched. A sword issues from the mouth of the Lamb (1:16; 2:16; 19:15, 21); destructive power issues from the mouths of others sent to represent the reality of God's judgment (9:17–19; 11:5). The dueling mouth metaphors suggest that John is caught up in a war of words over the identity of the true Lord. The language and image of witness that he uses throughout is particularly appropriate to such a metaphor. Witnesses declare—that is to say, fight—with their words. The two sides, that of the dragon and that of God, fight it out for the allegiance of the people with what issues from their mouths: their words. The people respond with testimony: the witness of their own mouths.

John's description of the enemy as a "false" prophet is an indication that this fight is taking place within as well as outside the church communities. Prophets were recognized leaders within the Jewish and Christian communities, who exhorted proper worship and ethical behavior. Often they used signs or sign acts to demonstrate their valid relationship with the Almighty and to authenticate their message. The fact that John wants his people to be alert enough to recognize the false things these prophets say (16:15), and the opposing truth he himself presents, is an indication that these prophets potentially have as much access to his church folk as he does himself. Such a conclusion would be consistent with the content of John's urgent exhortations to his seven churches in chapters 2 and 3, where it is obvious that false prophetic figures (Jezebel, Balaam, and the Nicolaitans) encourage accommodation to the rituals and beliefs that tout the lordship of Rome and Caesar. Such a conclusion is also consistent with the wider early Christian view that false prophets operated inside as well as outside the believing communities.[7]

**[14]** The frog-appearing unclean spirits are demons. John uses the term for demons only two other times in his narrative (9:20; 18:2). On both those occasions, he relates the demonic to idolatrous worship associated with Babylon/ Rome. The relationship with Rome is confirmed by the demons' vocation. They conjure signs that have the same effect as the signs of the false prophet, to encourage worship of the beast from the sea (Babylon/Rome). These demons secure political and military alliances for the beast, alliances with the kings of the entire world. These are not the eastern kings of the Parthian Empire mentioned in 16:12; those kings were from a limited region and targeted the beast from the sea as an enemy to be destroyed. These kings represent the entire inhabited world, which draws economic, political, and even spiritual strength from relationship with Rome (see the discussions of kings at 6:15; 10:11; 13:1; cf. also 17:2, 9, 12; 18:3, 9; 19:18–19). Such accommodation with Rome is precisely what John counsels his churches against. The demonic spirits have misled these kings with their materialistic, military, and cultic signs, so that they and their kingdoms have come to believe that Rome is not only their benefactor but also their lord. For such a benefactor and lord, a client king would be

---

7. Cf. Beale (831): "Elsewhere in the NT the 'false prophet' without exception speaks falsehood *within the covenant community of Israel or the church* in order to deceive (Matt. 7:15; 24:11, 24; Mark 13:22; Luke 6:26; Acts 13:6; 2 Pet. 2:1; 1 John 4:1). This points further to the conclusion that the second beast's activity in Rev. 13:11–17 is conducted not only outside but also within the churches, which is confirmed further by 16:14–16 (especially v. 15's exhortation to saints not to compromise)."

willing to fight. The demons use their sign acts to rally these kings to just such a cause.[8]

The threat is the opposing rule of an enemy Lord, the one represented by the Lamb, whom John preaches. The demons gather the kings so that they will rise up and do battle with this God on the ultimate day of divine justice, which will bring salvation to God's faithful and judgment against those who oppress them. The demons have apparently convinced the kings that every one of God's acts of judgment is another threat against the empire that sustains them. No wonder, then, that the people and rulers who populate those kingdoms respond to these acts of judgment with fury and anger rather than repentance (16:9, 10, 20).

[15] The great day of God's rule is described as an appearance; it is a person, not merely an event. That appearance will come suddenly, just as the one like a child of humanity had already explained in 3:3. The connection between the two verses suggests that it is that same son, the Lamb, who is speaking here. The metaphor also counts against using Revelation as a kind of temporal road map whose writings are a code that, when read correctly, can predict the movement of the end of days. As Schüssler Fiorenza notes (*Vision of a Just World*, 94), John's presentation here is consistent with the presentation of God's rule as sudden, unexpected, and unpredictable (cf. Mark 13:32–37; Matt 24:42–51; Luke 12:37–40; 1 Thess 5:2–7; 2 Pet 3:10).

The third of John's seven macarisms or beatitudes (see the discussion of 1:3) follows as an antiphonal rejoinder to the declaration of the final day's shockingly sudden arrival.[9] The blessed ones in that moment will be those who have "watched." This affirmation (in the indicative mood) is also an imperative call for watchfulness on the part of those who are not already demonstrating it in their lives (see the comments on 3:11 and 22:7). This call for alertness uses the same vocabulary chosen by Jesus in the Gospel of Mark when he counseled his disciples to stay awake lest the moment of God's eschatological movement catch them unawares (13:13, 37). In John's narrative context, one prepares by dressing in dazzling clothes. One obtains dazzling clothes by witnessing (see the comments on 3:4–5; cf. 19:8). By contrast, the people who have no clothes are those whom John castigates in chapters 2 and 3, those who, like the Laodiceans, follow the advice of Jezebel, Balaam, and the Nicolaitans and accommodate themselves to the economic, political, social, and cultic practices that celebrate the lordship of Caesar and Rome (cf. 3:17). John's warning is that those who wish to find themselves in eschatological relationship with God on the last day should reject such accommodation—repent, if they are already accommodating (2:5, 16, 21, 22; 3:3, 19; cf. 9:20, 21; 16:9, 11; 18:4)—and witness to the lordship of

---

8. In Old Testament prophecies such as Zech 12–14, this gathering of the nations is accomplished by God; see Beale 835.

9. Revelation presents beatitudes in 1:3; 14:13; 16:15; 19:9; 20:6; 22:7, 14.

God and the Lamb so that they will be found witnessing whenever the one like the child of humanity returns.

**[16]** Verse 16 opens with a clarification of John's interpretation in v. 14. Though it may have appeared, to both John and the kings of the world, that it was the demonic spirits that had gathered everyone for battle on the last day, in truth God was always in charge. The seer opens the verse with a third-person singular version of the verb "to gather" (he gathered) that overrides its infinitive use in relationship to the demonic spirits in v. 14. The gathering, planned and executed by the demonic spirits, was all of God's design. The NRSV makes the reading here consistent with the interpretation at v. 14 with the translation "they [the demonic spirits] assembled." While that interpretation fits the grammar of v. 14, it is inconsistent with John's overall portrayal that everything happens by God's ultimate design. It would be perfectly consistent with the larger narrative presentation in chapter 16 for God, who gave blood to the vicious devotees who sought blood to drink (v. 6), now to give the kings of the earth the very thing they have been seeking. The assembly they seek will be the assembly they get, only it will be to their destruction.[10]

The place of assembly is called in Hebrew *Harmagedōn*. Since the term is used only here in the entire Bible, it should not attract the kind of interpretive attention that many church traditions have given it over the centuries. More than likely John has conflated two Hebrew words, *har měgiddôn,* which mean "mountain of Megiddo." "Megiddo was an ancient city that guarded the pass through the Central Highlands at the Jezreel Valley. Because of its strategic location, Megiddo was an important military site" (Reddish 312). It was the site of several notable battles in Jewish history. According to Judg 5:19, Deborah and Barak defeated the Canaanite army of Jabin there. In 2 Kgs 9:27 King Ahaziah of Judah died there while fleeing Jehu. The tragic death of the reformist king of Judah, Josiah, also occurred there during a battle with Pharaoh Neco of Egypt (2 Kgs 23:29–30; cf. 2 Chr 35:22; 1 Esd 1:29–31). Because the area was associated with significant battles in the history of Israel, it is not odd that John would locate the assembly in preparation for apocalyptic conflict there. The difficulty is that Megiddo was not actually located on a mountain but on a plain. Scholars who suggest that John is mixing his images so that the familiar name could fit into the prophetic expectations for an eschatological mountain conflict are no doubt correct.[11] In any case, what is most important to remember is that

---

10. Cf. Reddish (311): "In 16:14–15, John is drawing upon a tradition in the Hebrew Bible that envisions God gathering all the nations of the world for divine judgment (cf. Joel 3:2; Zeph 3:8; cf. Ezek 38–39, a text that John will make use of in 19:11–21)." Beale writes, "The nations are deceived into thinking that they are gathering to exterminate the saints, but they are gathered together ultimately by God only in order to meet their own judgment" (835).

11. Reddish writes, "H. B. Swete explained the designation of Megiddo as Mount Megiddo based on John's desire 'to bring the final conflict into connexion with Ezekiel 39:2, 4,' a text that

John does not intend a literal but a symbolic battle, whose result will be the realization and recognition of the lordship of God and the Lamb.

## 16:17–21 The Seventh Angel

17 Then the seventh one poured out his bowl into the air, and a foreboding voice came out of the temple from the throne, saying, "It is done!" 18 And there were flashes of lightning and rumblings and peals of thunder and a great earthquake, such as has not happened since humankind has been on the earth, so great was the earthquake. 19 The great city split into three parts, and the cities of the nations fell. And God remembered[a] to give Babylon the Great the cup of the wine of the wrath of God's fury. 20 And every island fled and no mountains were found. 21 And great hailstones, weighing about a hundred pounds, fell from heaven on the people, and the people cursed God because of the plague of the hail, because the plague was incredibly severe.

a. Literally, "Babylon the Great was remembered in God's presence," another divine passive.

[17] When the seventh angel pours out his bowl, he aims for the air, the last of the four elements that the ancients thought comprised nature (earth, v. 2; water, vv. 3, 4, 12; fire, v. 8; air, v. 17) to be targeted. A foreboding voice (see the discussion of 7:2), apparently the same one that activated the angels in 16:1, calls out as a result. That this voice from the temple belongs to God remains clear from the declaration in 15:8 that no one could enter the temple until the judgment was complete. The connection to the throne, a euphemism for God throughout the book, also indicates that God is speaking (see the comments on 4:2–3 and 7:10; cf. 7:15; 14:3).

God declares that "it is finished" (cf. 15:1; 21:6). The three-ring apocalyptic circus of breaking seals, blasting trumpets, and spilled bowls has finally reached its climactic conclusion. In the concluding chapters of his work, John will narrate that conclusion from the two angles of judgment (17:1–20:3) and salvation (20:4–22:21). The foreboding tone of the voice indicates that just now it is judgment that is on God's mind; no wonder, then, that the seventh angel's exploits introduce the devastation of Babylon/Rome, which immediately follows in chapters 17–19.

---

describes the eschatological battle against Gog of the land of Magog as a battle that will occur in the 'mountains of Israel.' This suggestion is plausible since John will make use of the Gog traditions later in the Apocalypse (20:8)" (313).

[18] The theophany package that follows God's declaration is like an eschatological exclamation point (see the comments on 4:5; 8:5; 11:19). These cosmic happenings provide the background music that accompanies the momentous movement of God's judgment and salvation into the human arena. Of particular note is the addition of the greatest earthquake ever humanly experienced. If a regular earthquake symbolizes judgment (see the comments on 6:12; 11:13), this singularly unique one clearly indicates the climactic moment of apocalyptic judgment. The language is reminiscent of Dan 12:1, which forecasts tribulation such as had never been seen (cf. Exod 9:24). In Daniel's case, though, it would be not just a day of destruction but also a day in which everyone whose name is written in the book would be saved. The imagery is as much about salvation as it is about judgment. That is the case in Revelation, too, for John will narrate the "finish" of the end time as both judgment and salvation.

[19–21] The earthquake rips the great city into three parts. John draws a critical connection between Rome and Babylon (see the discussion of Babylon at 14:8) as the great city that will be destroyed because of its refusal to recognize the lordship of God and the Lamb, as well as its persecution of those who witness to that lordship (18:10, 16, 18–19, 21; on Jerusalem as "the great city," see the discussion of 11:8).

The quake also takes out all the cities of the nations that were socially, politically, militarily, economically, and cultically allied with the great city. All who had accommodated to its delusions and practices of lordship will be consumed by the same wrath of God's judgment (see the discussion of the cup of God's wrath at 14:10; cf. 14:19; 15:1, 7; 18:19). But where that wrath is concerned, God particularly remembers Babylon/Rome because of the evil Babylon/Rome imposed upon the saints (6:9–11; 8:3–5; cf. 20:4–6).

The impact of God's presence in the force of judgment and salvation is so overwhelming that nature must flee before it (v. 20; cf. 6:14; 20:11). It is as if the geographical elements, wishing not to impede God's eschatological progress, get themselves out of God's way.[12]

The advent of huge, almost hundred-pound hailstones in v. 21 is reminiscent of the hail that falls after the sounding of the first angel's trumpet (8:7), but even more like the hailstorm that follows the seventh angel's blast at 11:19. That hail, too, followed the theophany phenomena of lightning, rumbling, thunder, and earthquake. This time the sheer magnitude of the event sets it apart. The end result, though, is unfortunately the same. Just as the Egyptian Pharaoh refused to repent in the face of God's cosmic onslaught of hail unlike anything the

---

12. Aune observes, "The motif of the disappearance of mountains is often connected in the OT and early Judaism with a theophany or the eschatological judgment, conceptions that tend to merge (Ps. 97:5; Isa 40:4; 42:15; 45:2; 54:10; Ezek 38:20; 4 Ezra 15:42), though more frequently the seismic phenomenon of the quaking of mountains is mentioned (Pss 18:7; 46:2–3; Isa 5:25; 64:1, 3; Sir 43:16)" (2:901).

Egyptians had ever before witnessed (Exod 9:13–26), so those who have accommodated themselves to the lordship of the beast from the sea refuse to repent. Indeed, they curse God instead (see the comments on 13:6; 16:9, 11). John chronicles God's response in chapters 17–19, which narrate the decisive divine judgment against the enemies of God and God's faithful witnesses.

*17:1–19:10   The Implications of God's Wrath: The Judgment of Babylon*

17:1–18   Exposing the Great City: Vision of the Woman and the Beast

John's tone, already contentious, takes a dramatic shift. The righteously indignant seer makes a vicious rhetorical turn that bludgeons women with a sweeping hammer of misogynism as it nails Rome up against the wall of civil and cultic tyranny. Following the lead of some of the most well-known and, in the first century, most oft-quoted Scriptures and prophetic figures from Israel's past, he summons the metaphor of the self-serving, other-loathing, greed-guided harlot (cf. Gen 34:31; Isa 1:21; 57:3; Jer 3:3; Ezek 16:30–31, 35; 23:44; Hos 2:5; 3:3; 4:10, 12–15; 5:3; 9:1). Even the Christian apostle Paul enlisted the striking image of the illicit and destructive prostitute (1 Cor 6:15–16). In fact, the Corinthian text has much in common with John's warning here in chapter 17. John fears that his people will destroy their relationship with Christ by accommodating themselves, through either social fear or economic lust, to a prostituting relationship with Rome (cf. chs. 2–3).

Interestingly, demonization is only necessary when one's enemy has one or several truly appealing and admirable traits. It is difficult successfully to condemn an enemy for whom your own people have sympathies and with whom they desire relationship. When logic proves insufficient for the task of turning one's followers away from such an enemy's position and back in the exclusive direction of one's own cultic and ethical directives, one can increase the persuasive odds by revealing the opponent's flaws and hyperdistorting them. John does precisely this by pointing to Rome's economic prowess, political dominance, and military supremacy, a most impressive array of imperial traits in the eyes of most Greco-Romans, and declaring that they are not marks of sovereign beauty but festering, malignant sores. These sores indicate a communicable social disease that will infest any person or people entering into intimate union with her. As beautiful as she seemed on the surface, she is, after all, a filthy, vicious whore.

The problem with the whore imagery is that, as it strikes out at Rome, it disparages women. In Revelation the patriarchal mean streak implicit in ancient Israelite and John's contemporary Christian whore metaphors becomes a misogynistic fault line capable of devouring the self-image of any woman thrown up against it. It is not just the use of the whore image that is problematic since, in this case, John uses that image to attack not women but Rome. The problem is that his use of the image privileges a male perspective on the divine and matters of human redemption in relationship to the divine. The root of evil takes on an unmistakable feminine stamp: the luscious lure of feminine sex (an image of Roman cultic and economic power) seduces the righteous male (representing the people of God) into destruction. Men, the implicit symbolic referent for the people of God, may well ally with the whore, but they are presented as victims who, unlike the woman herself, are capable of redemption if they can find it within their power to resist her. It is the female hooker, not the male "johns," who is the root of the problem. The presentation allows male perspective and image, even when chastised, far less culpability. Femininity, metaphorically speaking, is problematized at its best and demonized at its worst. Evil takes on a decidedly female shape. Sexuality is the problem, and clearly for John here, it has a female orientation.

The dysfunction represented in this portrait of the feminine takes a horrific leap forward when John narrates the destruction of Rome/Babylon as the justifiable stripping naked, devouring, and eating of this female whore. To be sure, John is speaking only metaphorically, using symbol, and not intending the torture and killing of a real woman. But commentators are right to point out that even such symbolic disparagement can have and has had disastrous effect. As Reddish concedes, "The danger of imagery such as that used in Revelation 17 is that it may be heard by some (certainly erroneously) to condone violence against women, particularly 'evil' women" (337). One can therefore only regret that John chooses the image of a female person as his operative metaphor when projecting God's judgment upon Rome. That is, however, his metaphor of choice, and in my commentary on this section I must deal with this metaphor. If I were preaching from this text, I would struggle to find another image that, while maintaining John's concern for the seductive and ultimately destructive allure of any entity that would idolatrously place its own image on a par with or in place of God, does not disparage the feminine. There ought to be a way to target the evil of empire without exposing women to such rhetorical and potentially real collateral damage.

## 17:1–2 INTRODUCTION TO THE FALL OF BABYLON

> 17:1 Then one of the seven angels with the seven bowls came and spoke with me, saying, "Come, I will show you the judgment of the great whore who sits upon many waters, 2 with whom the kings of the earth prostituted themselves and the inhabitants of the earth were made drunk from the wine of her prostitution."

[**17:1**] John's identification of his angelic guide and interpreter serves several crucial functions. First, it reminds his hearers and readers of the declaration in

1:1 that his visions would take place through the assistance of an angelic intermediary. To this point, however, he has not been explicit about the role of such a mediator. Now, and later at 21:9, he makes clear that two of the most crucial and climactic visions in the narrative are comprehensible only with this angelic assistance. Second, the connection with 21:9 initiates a parallel presentation between 17:1–19:10 and 21:9–22:9. The seductive and idolatrous dominance of the evil city is balanced against and overwhelmed by the attractive and appropriate allure of the new city that recognizes God as its power source. Third, John's clarification that this interpreting angel is one of the seven who wielded the seven bowls of God's wrath connects the angel and the vision he relates to God's end-time judgment. Indeed, the *kai* (and) that opens the verse suggests that this material is a follow-up to what has gone before. This text is describing how the end-time judgment, narrated from a global perspective with the seventh bowl (cf. 16:17–21), takes place in specific relationship to Rome. It also means to imply the reason for Rome's judgment. John deploys the noun *krima* (judgment) only in 17:1 and and two other places (18:20; 20:4). Revelation 18:20 shows that God has brokered this judgment on behalf of the witnesses who have suffered Rome's abuse (see the comments on 6:9–11 and 8:3–5).

The angel who mediates the vision of the bride city at 21:9 is also described as one who previously held one of the seven bowls of God's wrath. This narrative echo is yet another reminder that, for John, God's one moment of apocalyptic crisis engineers two distinct eschatological scenarios. The same judgment that seals Rome's doom and the destruction of all those allied with her consummates the salvation of those who have endured as witnesses to the lordship of God and the Lamb.

The instructive parallelism continues with the angel's first words: "Come, I will show you." Those words preface the introduction of the great whore and the judgment that awaits her. At 21:9, the same words present the bride in anticipation of her eschatological relationship with the Lamb. John uses the narrative strategy to present the two rhetorical women as the economic, social, and cultic competitors for the affections of hu*man*kind. Hu*man*s are drawn to both; they can only be intimate with one. The relationships are mutually exclusive.

To dissuade his hearers and readers from making the mistake of seeking the wrong relationship with Rome, John unleashes some of the most acrimonious language in his rhetorical arsenal. He appeals to the jargon of sexual immorality, to which he will return in different formulations throughout the chapter (*pornē*, *porneuō* [v. 2; cf. 18:3, 9]; *porneia* [v. 2; cf. 18:3; 19:2]). He calls Rome a whore (*pornē*); in fact, except for 19:2, he uses this description exclusively in chapter 17 (vv. 5, 15, 16). He connects the image with the name "Babylon" and the city that is Rome. At 19:2, after reminding his hearers and readers of her corrupting effect, he declares that God has judged—which is to say, destroyed—the whore, as an act of justifiable retaliation on behalf of God's people (cf. 6:9–11; 18:20).

Although John has not referred to anyone as a whore prior to 17:1, he has utilized the image of sexual immorality. In particular, he stresses that the false prophet whom he slanders with the name Jezebel leads the people into a faith infidelity akin to prostitution by allowing them to eat food sacrificed to idol gods (2:20–22). Such consumption enters them into an implicit relationship with those gods.

John's idolatrous city sits enthroned upon many waters. The reference is both literal and symbolic. As the beast from the sea, Rome literally reaches Asia Minor from the sea and would be thought of directly in relationship to it (see the discussion of 13:1). The symbolic meaning, though, is surely more important. John has in mind, as he does throughout much of chapter 17, imagery from Jer 51 (esp. 51:13). The Old Testament prophet proclaims judgment against the powerful city of Babylon, which has been destructive of God's people and has imperiously and idolatrously set itself up as an entity deserving the kind of worship due only God. John will specifically identify the whore with the name Babylon (17:5). As John certainly knows, Jeremiah described Babylon in the same way that he now envisions Rome, as a city sitting (i.e., enthroned) on many waters. Babylon literally sat on the Euphrates River. In Rome's case, the point is more theological than geographical (Boring, *Revelation*, 180). By 17:15, the whore's seating will be described as peoples, multitudes, nations, and languages. The image expands so that John's hearers and readers recognize that the great whore's/city's allure comes from her intimate and illicit relationships, her commercial and political alliances with the nations and peoples of the world, alliances that create the great wealth and power that even now seduce them.

[2] John anticipates a charge he will repeat at 18:3, though in reverse order. The kings and inhabitants of the earth have entered into a relationship that has all the trappings of a drunken orgy. The seer targets the kings of the earth first. These are the same kings who in 16:14 were deceived by demonic signs. Those signs now receive economic trappings; the kings have seen the commercial wealth of the superpower city and have been attracted to it, thinking they might share in it. Once again John is operating from a prophetic platform. Tyre, prophesied against by both Isaiah and Ezekiel for seductively luring the ancient nations and even the people of God into idolatrous political affairs, serves as the negative role model to which Rome is now compared. Beale observes, "Among all the harlot metaphors of the OT, most of which refer to Israel, the one referring to Tyre in Isaiah 23 [esp. 23:17] is the closest verbally to Rev 17:2. That Tyre is in mind here in the Apocalypse is clear from the repeated reference to the Ezekiel 26–28 pronouncement of Tyre's judgment in Revelation 18 and the specific allusion to Isa. 23:8 in Rev 18:23" (850). In a rightly ordered world, these kings would recognize God and the Lamb as their fitting ruler (Rev 1:5; 15:3; 17:14; 19:16). Yet even now, even to the end point of the book, there is hope that the kings will recognize the value of their relationship with God and

the Lamb and redemptively reengage it (21:24). Like the witnesses to the lordship of God and the Lamb, the kings of the earth owe their existence, allegiance, and affiliation to God and the Lamb. It is for this reason that their alliance with Babylon is viewed as a prostituting of themselves, and the city/power that lures them into the alliance is called a whore (17:18; 18:3, 9). It is perhaps also for this reason that the threat of judgment has always dogged them (6:15; 10:11; 19:18; cf. Ps 2:10).

The inhabitants of the earth fare no better; they too are under threat of judgment because of their prostituting alliance. Their condemnation comes as no surprise since throughout the narrative John uses the formula "inhabitants of the earth" as a euphemism for people in opposition to the lordship of God and the Lamb (see the comments on 2:13; 3:10; 13:8). They are depicted as drunk on the wine (see the discussion of 14:8) of the whore's fornication (*porneia*). Jeremiah 51:7 depicts a similar scene where the people of the world have imbibed so heavily of Babylon's economy that their lust for a greater and greater stake in her profits has driven them mad. The people of John's time have been equally greedy. They will be equally judged (8:13).

17:3–6A THE VISION OF THE WHORE AND THE BEAST

3 Then he carried me into the desert in the spirit. Then I saw a woman seated on a scarlet beast filled with blasphemous names, with seven heads and ten horns. 4 And the woman was clothed in purple and scarlet and adorned with gold and precious stones and pearls, with a golden cup in her hand full of abominations and the filth of her prostitution. 5 On her forehead was written a name, a mystery: "Babylon the Great, the mother of whores and abominations of the earth." 6a And I saw the woman was drunk from the blood of the saints and the blood of the witnesses to Jesus.

[3] The opening words in v. 3 parallel exactly John's narration at the beginning of 21:10. There, too, the angel spirits John away, but to a great and high mountain. The different destinations fit the different visions. While the desert can be and often was a place for faith's regeneration, it is also, as the abode of wild beasts and tempting demons (Mark 1:12–13; Matt 4:1; Luke 4:1–2), a place of darkness, danger, and judgment (cf. Isa 21:1–10). It retains that negative sense here; the landscape by association attracts the negative tenor of the whore John will see in it. At 21:10, on the other hand, John will see Babylon/Rome's municipal counterpart. There, from the high ground that, in keeping with a consistent biblical theme, maintains a sense of holiness, John catches a glimpse of the city of God adorned as a bride for her husband the Lamb.

The *kai eidon* (then I saw) that opens the next sentence indicates John's move to a new visionary scene (see the discussion of 5:1; cf. 5:6; 6:1, 8, 12; 7:2; 8:2,

13; 9:1). A second and concluding *kai eidon* closes this section and the vision it contains (v. 6a). The words act as a bracket that encloses this important vision of the figure who becomes the target of God's judgment activity. The target is the whore whom the angel promised to show John (17:1).

Once again the woman's posture comes into consideration. According to v. 1, she is seated on many waters. At v. 15, she will be seated on peoples, crowds, nations, and tongues. Here she is seated on a scarlet beast. The different metaphors point to the same reality. The woman, as 17:18 confirms, is the great city of Rome, enthroned upon the bestial empire whose commerce she uses to seduce the world into her idolatrous, prostituting behavior.

The beast's scarlet color identifies it immediately with both the red dragon (12:3) and the great city of Rome (18:16). An even more direct connection with bestial Rome develops from the description of seven heads, ten horns, and blasphemous names that is drawn explicitly from 13:1 (cf. 17:9), the verse that introduces the beast from the sea (see the discussion of 13:1).

Key here is the observation that the woman and the beast both seem to represent the same entity, the city of Rome. The fact that the woman rides the beast, however, suggests that they are different entities. Nevertheless, because of their parallel descriptions, I argue that John understands them to be one and the same entity, to which he gives the name "Babylon." The metaphors designate different functions of the same figure. If we were to compare Rome to a ship, we might imagine the beast as the below-decks engine room that powers the vessel and the woman as the top-deck bridge from which command decisions are made. No matter which metaphor is used (whore or beast), the same vessel is in view. As Bauckham puts it, "Chapter 17 brings the two images together: the harlot is enthroned on the seven heads of the beast (17:3, 9–10). In other words, Roman civilization, as a corrupting influence, rides on the back of Roman military power" (*Climax of Prophecy*, 343).

**[4]** John is consistent in his presentation of the woman/city as a seductive, gluttonous force. The colors of her clothing are an indication of her success and her pretension. Purple is the hue of royalty and rule, while scarlet indicates wealth.[1] A garment covered in gold, precious stones, and pearls rounds out the ostentatious ensemble. No doubt John had in mind that she literally wears her success on her sleeves. The gaudy display is also a mating maneuver. Her finery represents the wealth that has seduced the kings and inhabitants of the earth into intimate economic relationships with her. This is no ordinary street harlot; this is an expensive call girl, an alluring courtesan of the highest order. John's

---

1. See Aune 3:935. For purple, see Judg 8:26; Est 8:15; Lam 4:5; Dan 5:7, 16, 29; 1 Macc 10:20, 62, 64; 11:58; 14:43; Sir 40:4; Mark 15:17; John 19:2; *Gos. Pet.* 3.7. For scarlet/crimson, see 2 Sam 1:24; Prov 31:21; Jer 4:30; Epictetus, *Diatr.* 3.22.10; 4.11.34.

understanding of the courtesan as Rome is confirmed when, at 18:16, he narrates the same apparel adorning the great city.

The courtesan's outfit is complemented by the golden cup she holds in her hand. It holds not a liquid but the abominations and impurities of her prostituting behavior. Jeremiah 51:7 associates Babylon with a cup that makes all the world drunk. In Jeremiah's case Babylon is the cup; in Revelation, however, Babylon holds the cup in her hand. Yet the imagery of national seduction is the same.

John uses cup imagery primarily as a metaphor for divine judgment. At both 14:10 and 16:19, he narrates the cup of God's wrath. At the only other occurrence of the term, he declares that God gives to Babylon the very cup of desolation that she has mixed for others (18:6). Taken together, the images already suggest that while the call girl wields the cup in an effort to seduce and capture, God is preparing to make her elixir of abominations and impurities the means of her own punishing destruction. The punishment will not only fit the crime; the punishment will also turn out to be the crime. Her drunken paramours, juiced on the very economic and cultic orgy she has provided, will turn on her and destroy her.

[5] Despite the fact that she is an expensive call girl, John still outfits her with the trappings of a street hooker; she sports her name tattooed across her forehead. The forehead was the location of choice for the branding of ownership (7:3). At first and easy glance, everyone could see to what person or vocation someone belonged. God also marked the faithful on their foreheads. The parallel is intentional. In John's apocalyptic worldview are only two competing choices: one enlists either in God's service or in the service of the beast (cf. 13:16–17). The forehead logo brandishes the recruitment choice. Any name other than God's indicates trouble.

The whore's name is a troubling mystery. Grammatically, since all the key terms are in the same case and number, "mystery" could refer either to "name" (i.e., a name, a mystery: Babylon the Great) or "Babylon the Great" (a name: Mystery, Babylon the Great). The latter option would make the term "mystery" part of the woman's name. Since John in v. 7 determines to explain the mystery of the woman in her guise as Babylon, it is more likely that he intends the first meaning. The mystery is the name itself, and the name is Babylon the Great.

Historically, the name reminds believers of the imperial force that defeated and exiled the people of God (see the discussion of 14:8). John associates the ancient empire with Rome, the imperial force that presently threatens to lure God's people into an exile of idolatry. Using the lure of economic wealth, she has drawn kings, inhabitants of the earth, and apparently, according to John's tone in chapters 2 and 3, even many of the faithful into an idolatrous, prostituting relationship with her pagan and imperial cults. The fact that John calls her the mother of whores is a signal that Rome has successfully co-opted other cities, that is, the "children whores," into her military-economic-political complex. Their trading and diplomatic relationship with her is in truth an alliance with her idolatrous and satanic rejection of the lordship of God and the Lamb.

Contextually, at least for John, the name should be a signal to believers of God's imminent judgment. Except for this single use in chapter 17, in every situation where John exercises the name he speaks of the city's divinely orchestrated destruction (14:8; 16:19; 18:2, 10, 21). The intertextual context from which he operates portends a similarly dark forecast; much of Jer 51 is devoted to Babylon's deserved and impending judgment.

[6a] The first half of v. 6 completes the vision that introduces the whore and the beast. John uses two mechanisms to frame the section. The first is the grammatical marker *kai eidon* (and I saw), which parallels the bracketing *kai eidon* in v. 3. While the first looks forward to the vision he is about to see, the second refers back to the vision he has just seen. The second framing mechanism is the woman herself. John finishes his description of her with an added detail. She has been binging on a brew drawn from her economic, political, and cultic success: the blood of those who witness to the lordship of God and the Lamb. Though John seems to be speaking of two different groups, the saints *and* the witnesses, the *kai* (and) here should be taken epexegetically; these are the saints, *who are* the witnesses to the lordship of God and the Lamb (see the comments on 11:3, 6; 16:6 for discussions of the functional synonymy of saints, prophets, and witnesses in Revelation). At 18:24 John reiterates this ghoulish observation, this time declaring that she has consumed the blood of saints, prophets, and those slaughtered on the earth. The slaughter language is broader here than those slaughtered for their witness to the lordship of God and the Lamb. Rome's slaughtering has been much more extensive. Still, the slaughter language reminds John's hearers and readers of the "special" relationship believers have had with Rome. The woman who has their blood metaphorically in her cup has for some time now had it figuratively on her hands. The image of a refined call girl, courtesan, does not hold. As alluring as Rome is, Rome is a beast. Her preferred vintage is the blood of Christ-believers. Hope comes from the knowledge that poetic justice is imminent. The beast who craves blood will find herself choking to death on it (16:6). The slaughter and blood references imply that the judgment is God's answer to the believers' cries for justice (6:9–11; cf. 8:3–5). At 19:2 John makes that connection explicit.

17:6B–18  THE VISION INTERPRETED

6b When I saw her, I was tremendously impressed. 7 Then the angel said to me, "Why are you so impressed? I will explain to you the mystery of the woman and the beast with the seven heads and ten horns that carries her. **8** The beast that you saw was and is not and is about to rise from the abyss and go to destruction. And the inhabitants of the earth, whose names[a] were not written in the Book of Life from the foundation of the world, will be impressed when they see the beast, because it was and is not and is to appear. **9** This requires a mind with wisdom. The seven heads are seven mountains on which the woman is seated. They are also seven kings, **10** of whom five have fallen, the one is, the other has not yet come. When he does come, he must remain only a short time. **11** And the beast that was and is not, it is an eighth, but[b] is from the seven, and it goes to destruction. **12** And the ten horns that you saw are ten kings who have not yet received a kingdom, but they will receive authority as kings for one hour, with the beast. **13** They are of one mind; they relinquish their power and authority to the beast. **14** They will wage war with the Lamb, and the Lamb will conquer them, because he is Lord of lords and King of kings, and those with him are called and chosen and faithful." **15** And he said to me, "The waters that you saw, where the whore sits, are peoples and crowds and nations and languages. **16** And the ten horns that you saw and the beast will hate the whore and make her desolate and naked and devour her flesh and burn her with fire. **17** For God put into their hearts to do God's will, to have one mind and surrender their kingdom to the beast, until the words of God have been fulfilled. **18** And the woman whom you saw is the great city that has dominion over the kings of the earth."

a. A more grammatically proper rendering would offer "name" in the plural, but John uses the singular *onoma*; $\aleph$ 051 2329 2344 $\mathfrak{M}^A$ lat sy[ph] sa[mss] correct the text to the plural *ta onomata*.

b. The *kai* here is adversative: "but."

**[6b–7]** John is awestruck by what he sees. He describes his captivation with the verb *thaumazō* (to marvel). He uses it in only two other contexts, both of which detail pagan praise and worship of the beast (13:3; 17:8). Even one who despises the idolatrous excess and despotic brutality of Rome must acknowledge her power and grandeur. With the prowess of her military legions, the transnational reach of her vast commercial enterprise, and the magnificent trappings of her imperial cult, in her presence who could not help but feel awe? How could a man drawn to the worship of a Lamb not respect the towering presence of this mighty lioness?

John's guiding and apparently prescient angel immediately senses his astonishment. He offers therefore to interpret the unsettling vision of the woman and the seven-headed, ten-horned beast she rides (v. 3).

**[8]** John begins his narration of the angel's description with a relative clause formulation that he will use five times in this vision interpretation (see also vv. 12, 15, 16, 18): *ho eides* (that you saw). Initial focus is on the beast "that you saw." The threefold depiction "who was, is not, and is about to rise out of the abyss" recalls the threefold representation of God, as well as the Lamb, as the one "who was, is, and is coming" (1:4, 8; 4:8; 11:17; 16:5; the last two references do not include the third term "is coming" because by the time John deploys them, the judgment moment has narratively arrived).[2] The angel's play on the God/Lamb narration is no doubt a mocking of the beast's pretentious desire to stand itself in the place of true lordship. To be sure, the beast seemed to be all-powerful since Rome had surely built the kind of empire that could elicit awe even from a devoted Christ-follower such as John. But already the reign of the beast "is not," for with the advent of seventh seal/trumpet/bowl, God's judgment has come. Now that the judgment has arrived, the power that "was" certainly "is not" all that it thinks it is! Mockery is certain at the end of the verse when John returns to this threefold formulation, but with slightly different wording. In this rendition, the beast who "was" and "is not" is "[about] to appear." Using *parestai* (will appear), John surely conjures in most hearers' and readers' minds the root form of the verb, *pareimi*, which was used to convey the future coming (Parousia) of Christ as eschatological Lord. Bauckham notes helpfully (*Climax of Prophecy*, 435) that while John does not use the term "Parousia," he emphasizes Christ's coming by repeating the phrase "I am coming" some seven times (2:5, 16; 3:11; 16:15; 22:7, 12, 20; cf. 3:3). The beast's glorious earthly reign suggested to itself and its devotees that it had a future similar to that of eschatological lordship.

Even though it still appeared, even to John, that the awe-ful power of the beast was at its height, the angel's depiction reveals just how deceptive appearance could be. The moment the child of the woman clothed with the sun was snatched safely from the jaws of the dragon to the throne of heaven (12:5), the war was over. To be sure, the rise of the beast from the abyss (11:7) was still a terrible and threatening sight, which foreshadowed death and destruction for Christ-believers. The ultimate end of that rise, though, was not glory but destruction. John emphasizes the point at 17:11. The word he uses for destruction both there and here in v. 8 (*apōleia*) looks and sounds a great deal like *Apol-*

---

2. Aune points out that the formulation reflects "an epitaph used widely in the ancient world: 'I was not, I became, I am not. . . .' The formula occurs frequently in Latin epitaphs, 'I was not, I was born, I was, I am not; so much for that'" (3:940). He and other commentators point out that for the mockery to work, the parody must be about a person who had died and was expected to return from the dead. The reference would therefore likely have in mind the Nero-redivivus myth. But Bauckham (*Climax of Prophecy*, 435–40) argues persuasively that much more is on John's mind than Nero redivivus. That legend, which certainly controls the resurrection of the mortally wounded head at 13:3, he argues, is different from the *parousia* of the beast contemplated here. The two separate events must not be conflated. The head's resurrection speaks to the consolidation of imperial power, while the beast's parousia ends up being a threat to it (cf. 17:16).

*lyōn* ("Destroyer"), the name he earlier gave to the angel of the abyss (9:11). The imperial personification of destruction will itself be destroyed. The key emphasis here is ethical. John's hearers and readers should endure the onslaughts of the beast, resist its seductions, and witness against it because, though it looked all-powerful, it was, in truth, dead on arrival.

As for the inhabitants of the earth, these enemies of the faithful, not able to see through the interpretive lens of the angel, marvel in worship (see the discussion of v. 6b) at what they no doubt believe will be the beast's perpetual dominion.

[9] As in 13:18, the reference to wisdom suggests that only the wise mind will be able to understand what the angel has just revealed. The wise person will not lose heart and will continue to witness aggressively to the lordship of God and the Lamb because of understanding that the power that was, now is not, and rises only to its own destruction.

Less decoding is necessary for what follows because the angel provides clarity that operates from a well-established Greco-Roman tradition. The seven heads, noticed already at 13:1 and 17:3, are seven mountains upon which the woman sits enthroned. John has already alluded to the reign of the woman by noting that she sits enthroned on many waters (v. 1), which will be defined as many peoples, multitudes, nations, and languages (v. 15), and also on a beast (vv. 3, 7). Each of those symbols is, like the seven mountains, a metaphor for Rome. According to legend, Romulus, founder of Rome, built the original city on seven hills.[3] As surely as any contemporary American reader would recognize Philadelphia as "the city of brotherly love" or Chicago as "the windy city," a first-century Greco-Roman would have immediately understood a reference to "the city on seven hills" as a reference to Rome.[4]

David Aune points to a "Dea Roma" coin minted in Asia in 71 C.E., during the reign of Vespasian. He argues that depictions on coinage were generally reproductions of widely recognized art, perhaps in this case a sculpture. While on one side the coin sported the obligatory bust of the emperor, on the other was etched an image of the goddess Roma, a physical representation of the cultic praise for Rome, sitting on Rome's seven hills. Given that Asia Minor, particularly the Smyrnaeans, claimed to be the first imperial province to worship Roma, one would wager that John's readers would have immediately understood the point of John's reference (3:920–22). The woman represented Rome in all its idolatrous claims to cultic and cosmic lordship.

---

3. The hills are generally designated as the Palatine, Capitoline, Quirinal, Viminal, Esquiline, Caelian, and Aventine.

4. Cf. Beale (870): "Rome was popularly known in the ancient world as a 'city of seven hills' (e.g., Virgil, *Aen.* 6.782–83; *Georg.* 2.535; Martial, *Epig.* 6:64; Cicero, *Att.* 6.5; *Sib. Or.* 2.18; 11.113–16; 13.45; 14.108)."

More important, though, is the inference that must be drawn from John's use of such a recognizable symbol. He was not writing a cryptic document meant to be understood only by believing insiders, a document that would mislead the Romans into thinking that it was not directed at them. John used such a well-known, well-recognized symbol for a reason. It was not the case that he wanted only his followers to know that his visions of destruction were directed at Rome. He also wanted the Romans to know! In making his point so clearly and so universally, he was modeling the very nonaccommodating, challenging witness that he demanded from others. Even while in Roman exile, he speaks against Rome and declares the imminent end of Roman rule.

John's vision operates like a dream, where logical limits do not apply. In such an environment symbols can simultaneously have two different referents. Here in v. 9, the seven heads, which John has already established as seven hills, are also seven kings. The one constant that controls the image flux is the fact that all the images ultimately point to Rome. Like the seven hills, then, the seven kings are a metaphor for the empire. In this case, though, instead of referencing its cultic imperialism (the hills as related to the goddess Roma), the seven monarchs represent its political imperialism. As v. 10 will immediately clarify, they are most certainly seven Caesars.

[10] Having presented the seven heads of the beast as seven kings, John does not set out to identify them. He intends instead to establish the trajectory of their rule. The central focus is on the sixth Caesar: the one who now is. John does not identify him for two reasons. First, he is interested in the role these rulers play in the movement of God's rule into human history.[5] They represent the pinnacle of idolatrous resistance to it. Since "seven" is a number of wholeness for John, he likely understands the seven kings to represent the complete symbolization of human rule in idolatrous defiance of God's rule. Second, since the sixth is the Caesar who now rules, the hearers and readers would immediately recognize not only him but also the five who preceded him. John describes those five as having fallen. The imagery of falling alludes to violent death, like that which occurs on a battlefield, or as the result of assassination, the kind of end that many Caesars met. Unlike the eternal Lamb, their existences are transitory

---

5. John's lack of interest in the exact identities of the seven emperors has not been matched in the writings of commentators. Even though most agree that John's point is not tied to proper identification of the seven figures, numerous strategies for identifying them still abound. The problem is that, since contemporary readers no longer know the identity of the sixth emperor, they find it impossible to figure out the five who come before and the two who follow. Since it is presumed that John wrote during the reign of Domitian, one would think that calculations would begin with him. Other commentators contemplate starting at the beginning, with which emperor must have been the first of the five. But it is difficult to know which ruler was considered the first emperor: Julius Caesar, under whom the republic ended; or Octavius, under whom the empire officially began. There are also questions as to whether to include the extremely brief reigns of Otho, Galba, and Vitellius, who occupied the throne during the tumultuous years following Nero's death, 68–69 C.E.

and fragile. Why would his followers pay homage to rulers who "fall" when they have the option of worshiping the Lamb who has risen to the throne of the eternal God? The emphasis on the impermanence of Roman rule continues with the angel's explanation that the seventh king will reign for only a short time. The brevity of time is no doubt also directly related to the fact that God's judgment and the Lamb's return are so imminent.

[11] John returns to the moment of judgment when he pushes forward to the eighth and final king. If the sixth is the one who rules in John's present time, the eighth rules in that imminent moment of judgment that has already been inaugurated with the seventh seal/trumpet/bowl. Though there are different individual kings, they all represent the one beast. For this reason John describes the eighth head/king in the same way that he had earlier described the beast itself, as the one who "was" and "is not" (v. 8). John reiterates that though the beast's advent is impressive, its destruction is already assured: it is dead on arrival (DOA). He also reminds his hearers and readers that though it appears to stand apart and therefore appear impregnable, it is a part of the transient line of the seven who have come before it. It is just as fragile as they; it, too, will fall.

[12] In the second deployment of the relative clause "that you saw" (see the discussion of v. 8), John's guiding angel interprets the ten horns as ten kings who have yet to receive their kingdoms (cf. Dan 7:7–8, 20, 24). Their symbolization as horns suggests that they represent a vital source of the beast's power (on horns as symbols of power, see the comments on 12:3 and 13:1). They are to be distinguished not only from the seven Caesars, but also from the kings of the whole world at 16:14 and the kings of the earth (cf. 6:15; 17:2; 18:3, 9; 19:19). These others have already received their reigns. Like those Caesars and their client kings, though, the kings who do not yet rule represent yet another set of earthly leaders who fight against the lordship of the Lamb. It is as though the very aspiration to human lordship draws one into rebellion against the lordship of God and the Lamb. Perhaps this is John's way of saying that every human rule, because of the inclination of humans to idolize themselves and their capabilities, is on a potential collision course with God's rule.

In the case of these ten, that collision will come quickly. They will have only one hour—John's metaphorical way of saying a brief eschatological moment in the end time of God's judgment—before they are overthrown. Even at this climactic inbreaking of God's rule, they ally themselves with the authority of the beast because they do not see that the beast's rise is to its destruction (vv. 8, 11).

[13] The angel elaborates on the kings' woeful decision; they acted as if of a single mind in agreeing to delegate their potential power to the beast. John's narration will clarify that this singularity of purpose was created by God (v. 17). Just as God had once hardened Pharaoh's heart so that God could initiate judgment against Egypt, so now God drives these kings to a decision that will trigger their destruction.

**[14]** It is not surprising that the kings will declare war on the Lamb; such actions fit the pattern of those who follow the beast (cf. Dan 7:21). John has already explained that many will refrain from fighting with the beast because they perceive incorrectly that no one can fight successfully against it (13:4). Indeed, the language of a beast-directed war against the Lamb and those who follow him occurs repeatedly throughout the narrative (11:7; 12:17; 13:7; 16:14; 19:19). The occurrence in chapter 16 is particularly significant, as it narrates the gathering of an eschatological army whose engagement with the forces of the Lamb will immediately follow 17:1–19:10 (19:11–21; cf. 20:7–10).

Past victories of the beast (11:7) are not an indication of future success; in this climactic battle of the end time, the Lamb will engage directly, and the Lamb will prevail. According to 5:5, the seed of that conquest was planted long ago in the Lamb's crucifixion (5:12) and resurrection (12:5). John has always maintained that believers can participate in that victorious conquest (12:11; 15:2) through their nonaccommodating, resistant witness (2:7, 11, 17, 26; 3:5, 12, 21; 21:7).

The Lamb's victory is based in his identity as King of kings and Lord of lords (cf. Deut 10:17; Ps 136:3; Dan 2:47; 1 Tim 6:15; 2 Macc 13:4), the very title inscribed on his garment at 19:16, a scene that depicts his triumph. Verse 14 ends with the assurance that the Lamb's victory is also based in the faithfulness of those chosen and elected to witness to his lordship (cf. 12:11). The only time John applies the adjective *pistos* (faithful) to believers (2:13), he does so to describe the kind of resistant witness that testifies exclusively to the lordship of Christ and in so doing participates in Christ's victory (cf. 2:17).

**[15]** In the third deployment of the relative clause "that you saw" (see the discussion of v. 8), the interpreting angel refers to the waters upon which John saw the whore sitting (v. 1). Those waters are now defined as many peoples and crowds and nations and tongues (see the comment on 10:11). In other words, Rome sits imperially atop all the peoples of the earth. Since John primarily uses this and similar formulations as a negative representation of people who resist the lordship of God and the Lamb, he no doubt intends here to clarify that Rome not only rules the populaces of the world but has also engineered an idolatrous relationship with them. Rome has employed them in its war against the Lamb.

**[16]** In the fourth use of the relative clause "that you saw," the interpreting angel indicates that Rome's end will begin as an act of self-destruction. The forces that represent Roman resistance to the lordship of God and the Lamb will turn on themselves. Before the Lamb engages and destroys them at 19:11–21, they will engage and begin the process of destroying each other. The ten horns, which are the ten kings who have not yet received their rule, will join with the beast in hatred of the whore. It is as though the engine room that powered a ship made war on the bridge that guided it (see the discussion of 17:3). "Those who allied themselves with Rome did so because it was to their advantage. Their friendship was dependent on what it brought them. If their interests had been served better by turning on Rome, by taking what she had accumulated, then there would have been no reason for them to remain loyal" (González and González 115). Commentators correctly note that this depiction of the end is at odds with John's presentation at 18:8, where her demise is caused by plagues. Despite the narrative contradiction, however, John scores a consistent point. Rome's imminent demise is the working out of divine justice; John is just not obsessed with narrating that demise consistently.

Some of the most problematic language in the chapter occurs here. The angel relays that the kings and the beast will render the woman naked, eat her flesh, and then consume what remains with fire. John is clearly working from Old Testament imagery of God's judgment exercising itself against prostituting behavior through images of nakedness, fire, and the devouring of flesh (Lev 21:9; Jer 34:22; Ezek 16:37–41; 23:25–29, 31–34; 26:19; Hos 2:5; Mic 3:3). The most poignant reference is the recounting of the death of Jezebel, an idolatrous queen who sought to prostitute the faith of Israel with compulsory worship of Baal. Thrown from a window, she was devoured by dogs (2 Kgs 9:30–37). This misogynistic style of presentation is deeply troubling (see the introduction to ch. 17). Although it does not remove the offense, interpretation of this difficult text should not miss John's primary concern: his fear that his people will destroy their relationship with Christ through a prostituting relationship with Rome.

**[17]** The angel now finishes the thought he began at v. 13. The pact that the kings make to give their authority to the beast and then to turn against the woman with what appears to be a single mind has been inspired by God. Despite all appearances, God is in charge.

**[18]** In the final use of the relative clause "that you saw," the interpreting angel returns to the woman he promised to show John (v. 1), and whom John did see at v. 3. Explicitly, now, the angel interprets her meaning. She is the great city (see the comments on 16:19; 18:10) that has dominion over all the kings of earth. The description is as clear as the earlier one: "seven mountains on which the woman [city] is seated" (v. 9). She is Rome. But since Rome is also the beast, it becomes clear at this point that the woman and the beast are functionally synonymous metaphors. Each represents the reality of Rome's power. The woman particularly represents Rome's economic seduction; she draws people and those who rule them into an idolatrous relationship so that they refuse to acknowledge the lordship of God and the Lamb (cf. Ps 2:2).

## 18:1–24 Prophecies of the Fall of Babylon

Chapter 18, a medley of doom prophecies, really begins at 14:8. There the second of a very odd sequence of only six (as opposed to seven) angels of judgment declares that Babylon/Rome has fallen because she has caused all the nations to drink from the wine of her furiously passionate fornication. Revelation 18:1 picks up with what appears to be the climactic seventh judgment angel. He repeats the declaration of 14:8 that Babylon has fallen. Chapter 18 then fleshes out the judgment against beast and Babylon (ch. 17) that was initiated in chapter 16 after the seventh bowl was poured out (16:17–21). The entire sequence ends in 19:1–10, when the celebration anticipated in 18:20 reaches a hymnic crescendo. Revelation 17:1–19:10 thus forms a narrative of the whore Babylon's just demise. That narrative mirrors the eschatological rise of the new Jerusalem as the Lamb's bride in 21:9–22:9.

18:1–3 FALLEN, FALLEN IS BABYLON

> **18:1** After this I saw another angel with great authority descending from heaven, and the earth was lit up by his glory. **2** He cried out in a foreboding voice, saying, "Fallen, fallen is Babylon the Great. It has become a dwelling place of demons, a haunt[a] of every unclean spirit, a haunt of every foul bird, a haunt of every foul and hateful beast.[b] **3** Because all the nations drank from the wine of the wrath of her fornication, and the kings of the earth fornicated with her, and the merchants of the earth became rich from the magnitude of her luxury."

a. For the translation of *phylakē* as haunt, see BDAG 868.
b. All three "haunt" phrases likely belonged in the original text. The phrase *kai phylakē pantos thēriou akathartou* (and a haunt of every foul beast) is absent from such important witnesses as ℵ 2053 2080 vg *al* because it was omitted as a result of the repetition (cf. Metzger, *Textual Commentary*, 757).

**[18:1]** By beginning with the formulaic phrase *meta tauta eidon* (after this I saw), John signals a narrative intent to shift to a new way of thinking about a previously explored topic (see the comments on 4:1 and 15:5). Here he follows up on the chapter 17 portrayal of Babylon/Rome as the great whore. What was promised in 17:1 and forecast at 17:8 will now be narrated as a realized event. The future is so certain that it can be spoken of in the past tense.

John introduces "another" angel as the speaker. The modifier recalls 10:1, where the adjective "another" distinguished the angel from the seven trumpet angels who had appeared before him. Here, no doubt, the adjective distinguishes the angel of 18:1 from the seven bowl angels who appeared before his arrival on the narrative scene; this, then, is not the same angel who appears in 17:1. On other notable occasions, John also refers to *other* angels (7:2; 8:3). In both 7:2 and 8:3, as in 10:1, the angels appear in a context of judgment. When John introduces "another" angel, hearers and readers are right to entertain a sense of dread. John makes the judgment connection explicit with the literary relationship he establishes between this *other* angel and the *other* angels of chapter 14 (vv. 6, 8, 9, 15, 17, 18). Given John's affinity for the number "seven" as a number of completion, it is odd that in the judgment-laced chapter 14 he would offer a presentation of only six *other* angels. In effect, John compelled his hearers and readers to hold their narrative breath while the judgment initiated by these six awaited dramatic consummation some four chapters later at 18:1. Here, for the last time in the narrative, *another* angel appears; his appearance climaxes the judgment theme initiated at 14:6.

The judgment begins as a combat encounter. This *"other* angel" has great authority. At 13:2 John explained that the dragon had great authority; it ceded that authority to the beast from the sea, which chapter 17 identified as the great whore and chapter 18 names as the city of Babylon. This angel's great authority has also been leased to him by a higher power, in this case by God. As chapter 18 dawns, then, hearers and readers are presented with the angelic representative of God (v. 1) and the municipal representative of Satan (v. 2), two surrogate powers who engage each other in a proxy war on behalf of their masters. The battle, which takes place completely offstage, ends before it even properly begins; already by v. 2, Satan's representative has been laid waste. Thoroughly routed, Babylon is now ruthlessly judged.

A rationale for Babylon's judgment is implied in the final piece of the angel's description: his glory was so bright that it lit up the entire earth (cf. Ezek 43:2). The divine passive construction ("the earth was lit up") is John's way of attributing the lighting action to God (see the discussion of the divine passive in Revelation at 6:1–8; 7:2).[1] The angel's glory, like his authority, is representative. Just as the moon reflects the light of the sun but emanates no light of its own, so the angel's glory points not to the angel but to God. According to 18:7, Babylon revels in the belief that its glory is its own and reflects not God's power but its own status and strength. It is this warping sense of self-glorification that motivates the oppressive behavior for which Babylon is judged.

**[2]** While John typically uses the adjective *megas* (great) to describe an angel's great voice, the presence of *ischyros* (strong, mighty), which he applies more often to angels than to their voices (5:2; 10:1; 18:21), has the same connotation of impending judgment in v. 2. John means to say that the angel speaks in an ominous, foreboding tone (see the discussion of 7:2). Commentators apply to the intoned message an equally foreboding categorization. As Reddish puts it, "The words of the angel are similar to prophetic taunt songs, such as are found in Isaiah 23–24; 47; Jeremiah 50–51; and Ezekiel 26–27. These songs . . . announce with mockery the downfall or death of an enemy" (339).

---

1. Cf. 21:23, where God's glory is the express subject for *phōtizō* (give light). At 22:5, God is similarly the subject of the lighting action. Only in 18:1; 21:23; 22:5 does *phōtizō* occur in Revelation.

For John, Babylon's fall is simultaneously past, present, and future. Even in the present, as it appears powerful and strong, it is on its way to destruction (17:8). That destruction is described confidently with future tense verbs in 18:8–20. Here, though, John declares the certainty of that future realization through the use of aorist verbs: *epesen, epesen* (fallen, fallen).[2] The full cry, "Fallen, fallen, is Babylon the Great," is a reprisal of the macabre observation made by the second in John's series of judgment angels (14:8; see the discussion of that verse). While the angel of 14:8a shares the reason for the fall immediately in the second half of his taunt (14:8b), this seventh angel in the series inserts a more detailed description of the fall before stating its cause (v. 3). The taunt is in the details. Recalling prophetic images of divine devastation (Babylon, Isa 13:19–22; Jer 51:37; Jerusalem, Jer 9:9–11; Edom, Isa 34:11–15; Assyria, Zeph 2:13–14; cf. Bar 4:35), John declares to a Rome that is at the height of its imperial power at the close of the first century that even as it luxuriates in its military, economic, and political might, its imperial center has already become a haunted wasteland, occupied by unclean beasts and spirits.

[3] This seventh "other angel" also details the rationale for judgment that the second "other angel" announced in abbreviated form at 14:8b. Like Tyre before her (Isa 23:17), Babylon/Rome has corrupted the nations with the wine of her passion for wealth. While the angel of 14:8 says that Babylon/Rome caused the nations to drink, the angel here is more vague about the city's role. Clearly, though, because Babylon/Rome is being judged, Babylon/Rome is culpable. The implication is that Babylon/Rome has lured the nations into a relationship so addictive that they are incapable of extricating themselves from it (cf. 18:23). The metaphor for the relationship remains prostituting sexuality; the reality remains destructive economics. From chapters 2 and 3 onward, John has been warning his folk about being so desperate for economic prosperity that they could be lured into guilds and other organizations that would require the eating of meat sacrificed to pagan and imperial gods as a way of demonstrating social and political camaraderie. To buy into the economy (which John characterizes as taking on the mark of the beast), one has to buy into a recognition of lordship for pagan and particularly imperial figures, and thereby denigrate the lordship of God and the Lamb (see the comments on 2:14, 20). Economic advancement demands the exorbitant price of cultic apostasy. But it is just this economic affiliation that many come to believe they cannot survive without. This belief, heightened to an eschatological frenzy, is what John describes as a wine so passionate for material gain that the person who imbibes it will prostitute one's faith to obtain more of it.

---

2. According to Aune, "This is an example of the *perfectum propheticum*, 'prophetic perfect,' used to describe a future event with a verb in the past tense as if it had already happened" (3:985).

After his mention of the nations, this seventh "other angel" introduces two figurative groups that will play a key role in the development of Rev 18. Like the nations, the kings who rule over them have prostituted themselves. A king's true allegiance should be to the true Lord of history, the true guarantor of spiritual and economic security and success. Instead, these kings have allied themselves economically with Babylon/Rome. This illicit economic intercourse is as improper as illegitimate sex.

Babylon/Rome is finally complicit also in the corruption of merchants (see vv. 11, 15) who grew rich from but also dependent upon the luxurious splendor of the city's imperial economy. The city's wealth is as sensual as it is seductive; it captivates and controls like a magic spell (v. 23).

18:4–8 JUDGMENT FOR ARROGANT BABYLON

4 Then I heard another voice from heaven saying, "Come out of her, my people, so that you do not take part in her sins, and so that you do not share in her plagues, 5 for her sins are piled up to heaven, and God has remembered her crimes. 6 Render to her as she herself has rendered, and repay her double for what she has done; in the cup which she mixed, mix for her a double portion. 7 As she glorified herself and lived luxuriously, so give to her torment and grief. For in her heart she says, 'I sit as queen, and I am not a widow, and I will never see grief.' 8 Because of this her plagues will come in one day, death and grief and famine; she will be burned with fire, for the Lord God who judges her is mighty."

**[4]** John shifts from vision to audition with the words *kai ēkousa* (then I heard), which also mark the start of a new scene within the larger act (see the comment on 16:1). He heard another heavenly voice (see the comment on 10:4) follow up the angel's taunting. Since it immediately addresses John's hearers and readers as "my people," the voice probably belongs either to God or to Christ. Since it is unlikely that God would speak about God's own actions in the third person (18:5, 8, 20; cf. 1:8; 21:5–7, where God speaks of God's identity and behavior in the first person), the protagonist is probably Christ.

As in Isaiah (48:20; 52:11) and Jeremiah (51:45), Christ's point is clear and direct. His people must "come out" of Babylon/Rome. Because Babylon/Rome is a symbolic moniker for the entire empire and not just the city from which the empire took its name, the heavenly voice cannot be speaking literally. The political, military, religious, and economic reach of the empire is vast. As John clearly recognizes in chapters 2 and 3, the cities where his churches are located sit firmly within the imperial grasp. The heavenly voice, like John's, demands a figurative separation instead. In the Gospel of John, Christ makes a similar demand of his followers: while living *in* the imperial world, they are to find a way to not be *of* the world (John 15:19; 17:15). On a particular and limited level, this would mean refusing to eat meat sacrificed to idols in contexts that validated Greco-Roman belief in the lordship of those idols and the imperial cult they represented and supported. On a more general level, it would mean witnessing against imperial lordship by refusing to participate in the economic juggernaut that Rome had established, a significant act if Bauckham is right: "It is not unlikely that John's readers would include merchants and others whose business or livelihood was closely involved with the Roman political and economic system" (*Climax of Prophecy*, 376). Because most Greco-Romans believed that their economic and therefore social, political, and physical security were provided only through participation in this system, opting out of it would be a way of witnessing to the belief that true security comes from God alone. Only by stepping away from Rome could a believer step forward for God.

The fact, however, that Christ must make this plea is an indication that many believers were not stepping forward. When Christ says "Come out," he implies that many have already bought their way in. John makes this clear in his letters to the seven churches. Only two of those churches, Smyrna and Philadelphia, are described as impoverished. Indeed, in both cases the impoverishment seems directly linked to their fervent witness against the lordship of Rome and for the lordship of God and the Lamb (2:10; 3:10). By contrast, believers in the other churches are chastised because they have amassed wealth and prestige by accommodating themselves to doing whatever was necessary (e.g., eating meat sacrificed to idols) to participate in the Roman economy. Jezebel, Balaam, and the Nicolaitans are demonized because they not only allow but also apparently endorse such assimilation (2:14–15, 20–21). The last of the seven churches mentioned, Laodicea, was excoriated as the poster child of this "fornication" (3:17).

Still, the divine plea to come out indicates that even at this late moment, on the eve of consummate judgment, Christ extends the opportunity for repentance and therefore salvific acceptance. Eschatological relationship with God remains available if only believers would renounce their idolatrous relationship with Babylon/Rome and reestablish relationship with God. They do this by witnessing actively to the lordship of God and Christ as the only measure of present and eschatological security. The cry to "come out," then, is not only an entreaty to exit; it is also an order to engage.

[5] Babylon/Rome's sins—already introduced (v. 3), later backgrounded (v. 7), and eventually graphically listed (vv. 23b–24)—have become so quantitatively numerous and qualitatively destructive that John, no doubt working from Jeremiah's language about the historical Babylon (51:9), describes them metaphorically as a mountain reaching to the heavens. This is no prideful human erection like the Tower of Babel, however. The divine passive construction ("are piled up") indicates that God has constructed this pile of sins as

a kind of monument to momentous misdeeds. God has remembered Babylon/Rome's transgressions (cf. 16:19). And now, so will the rest of creation.

[6] There are two considerable problems of perspective in this verse. First, for the first and apparently only time in the narrative, believers are commanded by Christ to operate violently against Babylon/Rome. Second, a judgment based on works is expected (cf. 2:23), but instead of a fair measure-for-measure punishment, Christ in the role of judge apparently orders that the penalties be double the crime.

John maintains his metaphorical description of Babylon/Rome's crime; she has seduced humans into drinking from her cup (17:4; cf. also 14:10 and the responding cup of God's wrath), an idolatrous ("fornicating"), addictive mix that drugs them into a frenzied lust for economic intercourse with her. Just as the work of witnessing to the lordship of God and the Lamb will be rewarded, so will Babylon/Rome's work of defying that witness be punished (cf. Ps 137:8; Jer 50:15, 29, where Babylon was to be "repaid" for its crimes against God's people). But the punishment will be double the intensity of the crime. Is such disproportion just? According to the scriptural tradition upon which John so heavily depends, the principle of lex talionis directs that a punishment's measure shall equal the measure of the crime (Exod 21:23–25; Lev 24:17–20; Deut 19:21). The law effectively prohibited angry and vengeful victims from excessive acts of retribution. Was God above God's own limiting law? Two observations suggest a negative answer. First, the punishment actually does fit the crime; in fact, the punishment *is* the crime. Babylon/Rome's sinful work is the intoxicating cup that she mixes for others; in punishment, she is forced to drink from that same cup the very concoction that she brewed for humankind. It is quite possible, since God forces Babylon/Rome to drink from the wine cup of God's wrath (Rev 14:10; 16:19), and since the punishment is the crime, that God has commandeered her cup and deployed it now against her.

The doubling language surfaces just here; mixed in her cup is a "double portion." What, though, does this doubling language really mean? It is no doubt based on prophetic texts like Isa 40:2 and Jer 16:18, where a disobedient Israel/Jerusalem was to be doubly and justly repaid for its iniquity. There was, then, scriptural precedent for such retribution figuring appropriately rather than excessively where particularly egregious and idolatrous behavior was encountered. Beale even argues that the language of doubling should be taken to mean an intense matching of the punishment to the crime rather than an exorbitant raising of the retributive stakes. In this interpretation, Christ orders a "duplicate, twin, or matching" response rather than a literal doubling one (901).

There is still the matter of deciding to whom Christ is issuing the command to render to Babylon/Rome the violence and destruction she has rendered to others. Because Christ was clearly speaking to his people in v. 4 and there has been no explicit change of audience, one might suppose that Christ expects his believers to execute this violent reprisal. The problem with this supposition is that it counters every expectation for the believing witnesses that John has heretofore narrated. No other passage makes such a demand. In fact, believers are explicitly directed toward nonviolent forms of witnessing resistance. Nonviolent engagement is the behavior modeled by Christ, the true and faithful witness (5:9, 11; 12:5). Believers will conquer the draconian force behind the beast that is Babylon/Rome by imitating that nonviolence (12:11). Any christological expectation of witness violence in this single verse would therefore contradict the book's entire ethical superstructure. The more likely conclusion is that Christ has turned from the believing human witnesses to those like the archangel Michael (12:7) who are particularly enlisted for such purposes. Given the larger context of Revelation's overall expectations and the more specific material surrounding 18:6, there are several more likely candidates. Christ could well be addressing angels of judgment like the seven specified at 14:6, 8, 9, 15, 17, 18, since the concluding angel in this series opens the chapter's proceedings at 18:1. John has also identified ten enraged kings and the beast from the sea as the executioners who will prosecute Babylon/Rome's annihilation (17:16). Either or both of these groups are more likely than Christ's own faithful witnesses to be his intended audience. Given the development of the text, my preference falls to the kings and beast (see the discussion of vv. 11–17a below).

[7] The motif of punishment fitting the crime continues as Christ sentences Babylon/Rome to a humiliating measure of torment and grief that matches exactly the political, religious, military, and particularly economic measures she has used to celebrate her powerfully and seductively luxurious existence (the verb for living luxuriously or sensually reminds hearers and readers of the cognate noun in 18:3, *strēnos*, which was used to explain how merchants had grown rich from the power of her luxurious splendor). Self-glorification metastasizes into arrogance. In describing her own rule as a queen, she hijacks the language of royal seating (*kathēmai*) that John has used exclusively as a symbolic posture of divine rule: God's sitting on the heavenly throne (4:2–3, 10; 5:1, 7, 13; 6:16; 7:10, 15; 19:4; 20:11; 21:5); the child of humanity's sitting on a cloud (14:14–16) and on a white horse of judgment (19:11, 19, 21).[3] Babylon/Rome has already mimicked the posture by sitting enthroned on waters (17:1, 15), a beast (17:3), and mountains (17:9), but here for the first time she arrogantly defines such posturing as a ruling lordship that competes with God's.

According to the prophet Isaiah, Chaldea made a similar taunt: it sits so securely that it believes it will never be a widow or know the grief that accompanies the loss of a child (Isa 47:8; cf. Isa 14:13–14; Jer 5:12; Ezek 28:2). Clearly, John has this taunt from the prophetic literature in mind because Babylon/Rome also declares that she shall never be a widow nor know grief.

---

3. Note that the elders also sit on heavenly thrones: 4:4; 11:16.

This rabid, self-glorifying confidence in the security amassed through her polit-ical, military, religious, and economic prowess is the seedbed from which her idolatrous and murderous behavior sprouts.[4]

[8] The promised punishment will be swift. Incredibly, John's Christ inten-sifies the emotions surrounding the gruesome trumpet and bowl plagues by declaring that all of them will occur in a single day. Such a brutal concentration will heighten the sense of devastation. John's narration maintains its prophetic dependence. Just as Isaiah warned that everything Chaldea boasted about would either be lost to her or turned against her (47:9; cf. Jer 50:29, 31), so John declares that Babylon/Rome's punishment will bring the very grief and torment that she predicted she would forever avoid. True might, and therefore glory, belongs exclusively to God (cf. Jer 50:34). Christ's closing remark in this sub-section reminds John's hearers and readers that God uses might not for vindic-tive destruction but for appropriate judgment.

18:9–20 MOURNING BABYLON

9 And the kings of the earth who prostituted themselves with her and lived luxuriously with her will weep and mourn over her when they see the smoke of her burning, 10 standing far away because of the fear of her tor-ment, saying, "Woe, woe, the great city, Babylon, the mighty city, because your judgment has come in one hour."

11 And the merchants of the earth weep and mourn over her, because no one any longer buys their cargo, 12 cargo of gold and silver and pre-cious stones and pearls and fine linen and purple and silk and scarlet, and every kind of product made of scented wood, and every kind of product made of ivory, and every article of precious wood and bronze and iron and marble, 13 and cinnamon and amomum and incense and myrrh and frankincense and wine and olive oil and fine wheat flour and wheat and cattle and sheep and horses and chariots and slaves, that is,[a] human lives.

14 And the fruit which you desired has left you, and all the opulence and ostentation are lost to you, and people will never find them again. 15 The merchants of these commodities, who became rich from her, will stand far away because of the fear of her torment, weeping and mourning, 16 saying, "Woe, woe, the great city, clothed in fine linen and purple and scarlet, and adorned with gold and jewelry and pearls, 17 because in one hour such wealth was laid waste."

---

4. González and González comment, "Her pride let her believe she could do anything, that she was accountable to no one, and that led her to commit atrocities" (118–19). And Bauckham observes, "Thus John sees a connexion between Rome's economic affluence, Rome's idolatrous self-deification, and Rome's military and political brutality" (*Climax of Prophecy*, 349).

And every shipmaster and every seafarer[b] and every sailor, and everyone working on the sea, stood at a distance 18 and cried out when they
saw the smoke of her burning, saying, "What city is like the great city?"
19 And they threw dust on their heads and cried out, weeping and mourning, saying, "Woe, woe, the great city. In her all who had boats on the sea
became wealthy from her abundance. For in one hour she has been laid
waste." 20 Rejoice over her, heaven and saints and apostles and prophets,
for God has exacted justice from her on the basis of your legal claims.[c]

a. The *kai* (and) functions here epexegetically, explaining that "slaves" *are* "human
lives."

b. The reading *ho epi topon pleōn* (the one who sails for a place) is strongly supported
by A C 1006 1611 1841 1854 2030 *pm* lat, and has the added backing that it is the more
difficult reading and thus the more likely one. Its level of translation difficulty, however,
is legendary. Various manuscripts offer adjustments intended to ease the difficulty; ℵ
046 0229 2329 *pc* gig add the definite article *ton* before *topon*; 2053 2062 (sa bo) offer
*ton potamon* (the river) instead of *topon*, with "the one who sails on the river" as the
resulting translation; 051 𝔐^A offer *tōn ploiōn* (the boats) instead of *topon*, with "the one
who sails on the boats" as the resulting translation; 2073 *pc*; Prim substitute *ponton*, with
the resulting translation, "the one who sails on the sea." The various adjustments are all
clarifying changes to a very difficult original.

c. For this translation, see the comment on v. 20 below.

[9–10] In narrating the mourning that accompanies the fall of Babylon/
Rome, John's Christ operates directly from the Ezek 26–28 lamentation scenes
that surround the demise of the economic superpower that was Tyre. Christ features the groups that have the most to lose: kings, merchants, and those who
make their living from the sea. Starting with the kings, Christ initiates a formulaic pattern of mourning that, with minor variations, holds constant throughout the narration. The kings, merchants, and merchant marines grieve alike just
as they benefited in like fashion from Babylon/Rome's economic success.

First, Christ makes the subsection's central point: because their economic
triumphs are tied directly to the international economic infrastructure that
Babylon/Rome has conjured through its political and military domination, the
kings weep and mourn when Babylon/Rome is destroyed (cf. Ezek 26:16). The
kings are not only regional, client monarchs; they are also members of local
councils and of the administrative ruling elite, like the officials who governed
the Asia Minor communities where John's seven churches were located. The
language of fornication and sensual, luxurious living confirms that the issue is
primarily one of economics. Throughout the work, "fornication" has symbolized persons and communities, even believing communities, who idolatrously
sell out their recognition of true lordship (God's and the Lamb's; cf. Rev 17:2;
18:3) in order to buy into Roman (imperial) cultic and political relationships

that will guarantee access to the benefits of the Roman economy (see the comment on 18:4).[5] Christ closes the case of the kings' complicity when he follows up the language of fornication with a member of the word family that specifies the accumulation and hoarding of luxurious excess: *strēniaō* (applied to merchants in v. 7).

They also have a share in grief. John stereotypes the language here in order to build a bond of misery joining kings, merchants, and merchant marines. Repetitively, Christ declares that each group weeps (*klaiō*: v. 9, kings; vv. 11, 15, merchants; v. 19, merchant marines) and mourns (*koptō*: v. 9, kings; *pentheō*: vv. 11, 15, merchants; v. 19, merchant marines). Since John constructs this rhetorical partnership (in weeping and mourning) only here, it is clear that the links drawn among the kings, merchants, and merchant marines are intentional.

These links strengthen as the narration unfolds. Christ declares that the kings (v. 10), merchants (v. 15), and merchant marines (v. 17) all stand purposely at a distance from the city not only because her torment is so grisly but, no doubt, also because they fear that their complicity in her crimes will earn them a share of her judgment (cf. 14:11). They apparently believe that the geographical space will morph into a protective shelter that will distance them from the destructive fallout.

Watching from their designated safe zones, the three paramour groupings unleash the same chorus of despair: "Woe, woe [NRSV: 'Alas, alas'], the great city" (kings, v. 10; merchants, v. 16; merchant marines, v. 19). Even now they do not see the false nature of Babylon/Rome; even now they attach such lofty adjectives as "great." "Look," John's narration means to say, "at her greatness now!" Indeed, each reference in the Apocalypse to the city's greatness is deployed in a context that anticipates the city's destruction (14:8; 16:19; 17:5, 18; 18:2, 10, 16, 18, 19). Obviously, the adjective is used mockingly by John. The mockery bites precisely because Rome *was* a great city. Yet even in its greatness, its doom was sealed (cf. 17:8). It is the accomplishment of that doom that is lamented here. Heretofore the language of "woe" has described the forms of judgment leveled against God's enemies (8:13; 9:12; 11:14) or the persecution endured by God's people (12:12). It is poetically appropriate that the language formerly used to describe the judgment is now the language of response to it.

Responsive horror is appropriate. The anticipated barrage of plagues that was to materialize in a single day (v. 8) narrows down even further now into a single hour of that day, as lamented by kings (v. 10), merchants (v. 17), and merchant marines (v. 19). How could even a great city like Babylon/Rome endure such a concentrated dose of judgment? Yet that question is the point. The

---

5. Cf. Schüssler Fiorenza (*Vision of a Just World*, 100): "When the kings and cities of the Hellenistic world lost or gave their power to Rome, they also relinquished to the goddess Roma or to the Roman emperor the honor and cult previously paid to their local gods by Greek or Asian cities."

emphasis here is not on the timing of the judgment but on its concentration. "Day" and "hour" are eschatological terms, not chronological points. They do represent brevity, but *chronos* time is not as important as *kairos* time here. John's Christ means to say that in a single moment of end-time decisiveness (*kairos* time), all that it took Babylon/Rome so much *chronos* time to build is completely and irrevocably gone.

[11–17a] The second stanza of weeping and mourning erupts from the corner of the narrative stage where the merchants of the earth are found cringing. Like the kings, they were already introduced as mourners-in-training at 18:3. Now they are in full cry because their primary market has forever closed (cf. Ezek 27:36). Their wealth has been predicated upon Rome's voracious needs to supply its population. With the smoke of Rome's burning the only thing left of the "great" city, there is no demand for their storehouses of supply.

Notably, like the merchants who enriched themselves in commerce with Tyre (Ezek 27:7–25), these traders deal in items of luxury rather than needed staples. As Reddish observes, "The list of merchandise indicates the wealth and extravagance of Rome" (345). It also indicates the extravagant desire for wealth on the part of the merchants. Christ emphasizes this point in v. 14: in a rhetorical flourish of alliteration, he highlights the opulence (*lipara*) and ostentation (*lampra*) of this economy (cf. Bauckham, *Climax of Prophecy*, 368). Its moral decadence is placed in sharp relief by the climactic mentioning of the trade in human souls, slaves: "It is a comment on the whole list of cargoes. It suggests the inhuman brutality, the contempt for human life, on which the whole of Rome's prosperity and luxury rests" (Bauckham, *Climax of Prophecy*, 371). These are the fruits, produce blossomed from a corrupt tree of idolatrous excess, that will be pruned from the wailing merchants forever. Their fortunes, like Babylon/Rome itself, will never return. And so, with their stage brothers "the kings of earth," they stand from a distance, weep and mourn, and cry out, "Woe, woe, the great city!" because its judgment arrives in full in a single hour. Like Ezekiel describing the judgment of Tyre (LXX Ezek 26:19), John chooses the verb *erēmoō* (lay waste) to sketch the great catastrophe. In so doing, he answers a question raised by 18:6. To whom was Christ speaking when he commanded someone to render violent judgment upon Babylon/Rome? Because the verb "lay waste" occurs only in 18:17, 19 and 17:16, where the ten horns and the beast lay waste to the whore/Babylon/Rome, it seems clear that Christ was deputizing the ten horns and the beast to execute the cataclysmic judgment. They will do the deed in an hour.

Christ adds just one other detail that makes this presentation different from the presentation of the kings of the earth (the first difference is the list of luxury items): the doomed city was clothed in fine linen, purple, and scarlet and adorned in gold, precious stone, and pearl. The costume connection is unmistakable; the great whore was similarly adorned (17:4). If anyone has missed the link before, Christ now makes it crystal clear: Babylon/Rome *is* the great whore who has seduced the kings and merchants of the earth into an idolatrous mercantile tryst.

**[17b–19]** Christ concludes the mourning section by adding mention of all those who earned a living through trade by sea. This larger category would include not only those who owned and captained ships but also mariners, merchant marines, and sailors. Rome dominated the seas, eradicated piracy, and created sea lanes for more efficient and safer travel (weather remained the only consistent obstacle) of people and goods to the port in Ostia and then the approximately forty miles inland to the capital city. Many either earned a living or built a fortune because of their participation in this economic sea superstructure. The wage earner as well as the wealthy shared a stake in the idolatrous relationship that gave allegiance and gratitude for security to Rome rather than to God and the Lamb. Like the kings and merchants before them, therefore, they stand weeping and moaning as they view the smoke of the city's ruin from a distance, crying out, "Woe, woe," for the great city that will be "wasted" in a single hour.

In this parallel presentation (with the kings and merchants of the earth), Christ adds two distinctive points. First, as did passersby of more ancient cities that were judged by God for their idolatrous and disobedient behavior (Jer 22:8; Ezek 27:32), these seafarers wonder, as they look at the smoke rising from the ruins, "What city was ever like this great city?" God, obviously, is much, much greater than the greatest force earth had ever known. Second, these seafarers make their grief concrete by their behavior. Like ancient mourners who lamented the demise of Tyre (Ezek 27:30–34; cf. Josh 7:6; Job 2:12; Lam 2:10; 1 Macc 11:71), they throw dust on their heads as a sign not so much of their contrition for their involvement with Babylon/Rome as of their regret for their loss of revenue and therefore well-being.

**[20]** Christ addresses "heaven" and the believers who have stood fast behind their witness to the lordship of God and the Lamb. Unlike the "believers" who accommodated themselves to social, cultic, and particularly economic principles that put them in relationship with the beast/whore/Babylon/Rome, this categorization of saints, apostles, and Christian prophets represents all those who have actively resisted any form of accommodation (on prophets, see the comment on 10:7; on saints and prophets, see 16:6; on saints and witnesses, see 17:6; cf. 18:24). While Babylon/Rome's economic confederates mourn her destruction and grieve both their losses and their own anticipated demise, Christ counsels all faithful believers to celebrate (cf. Jer 51:48, where both heaven and earth rejoice at Babylon's destruction). The mandated joy anticipates the hallelujah chorus that will break out in 19:1–8 and formally bring the larger section that began at 17:1 to a close.

The rationale for celebration is provided in the vaguely worded second half of the verse, which is very difficult to translate.[6] The interpretive key lies in the way the larger narrative context interacts with John's particular word choices. The primary audience is composed of the believing witnesses who have remained steadfast in their faith. Since Christ specifies that audience as both "heaven" and "the saints, apostles, and prophets," we can be certain that he intends his message for both those (in heaven) who were executed because of their witness and those (still living saints, apostles, and prophets) who maintain their earthly witness even as he speaks. It is "their" judgment that God has rendered ("judged") upon Babylon/Rome. In its noun form, judgment language (*krima*) refers specifically to the executed sentence (17:1; 20:4). The verbal form is more expansive. According to 20:12, 13, God judges based on works. At 16:5 and 19:2, the work of Babylon/Rome is notably described as the persecution of God's faithful witnesses. Believers react with a responsive work of their own. At 6:9–11 (esp. v. 10), the souls of those who were executed because of their witness cry out for God's judgment of the force (i.e., Babylon/Rome) that slaughtered them and continues to slaughter their compatriots. The appeal voiced at 6:9–11 therefore serves as the motivational force for the entire Apocalypse (see the comment on 6:9–11); it provides the inspiration for God's intervention to effect justice. It is to this intervention that 18:20b speaks. It is "your cry" for judgment, then, that God has executed ("judged") upon Babylon/Rome. Elisabeth Schüssler Fiorenza's translation, therefore, while not literally precise, is the most figuratively accurate: "God has exacted justice from her on the basis of your legal claims" (*Vision of a Just World*, 99).

18:21–24 AN ANGELIC, PROPHETIC SIGN ACT

In a dramatic narrative near the end of the book of Jeremiah, the prophet issues a command to the quartermaster Seraiah, who will accompany King Zedekiah of Judah to Babylon (51:59–64). After writing in a scroll all the disasters that God had shown him would befall Babylon, Jeremiah ordered Seraiah to carry the parcel with him. Upon reaching Babylon, Seraiah was to read the scroll and then remind Yahweh that Yahweh had promised to make Babylon a desolate, deserted haunt (cf. Rev 18:2). As a sign no doubt to believers and nonbelievers alike, Seraiah was then to tie a stone to the scroll and throw it into the middle of the Euphrates River and declare that so would Babylon sink forever under the weight of the disasters God had prepared for it. In the final four verses of chapter 18, John stages an apocalyptic rendition of this prophetic event.

6. For an excellent discussion of the various options for translating the verse, see Beale 916–18.

21 Then one mighty angel took up a great stone like a giant millstone and threw it into the sea, saying, "With such violence Babylon, the great city, will be thrown, and it will never be found again. 22 And the sound of harpists and musicians and flutists and trumpeters will never be heard in you again; and no craftsman of any trade will ever be found in you again; and the sound of the millstone will never be heard in you again; 23 and the light of a lamp will never shine in you again; and the voice of bridegroom and bride will never be heard in you again; because your merchants were the elite of the earth; because all the nations were deceived by your sorcery. 24 And in her was found the blood of prophets and saints and all those who have been slaughtered on the earth.

[21] The rare appearance of a "mighty" angel signals the dawn of a highly significant narrative event that portends judgment (see the comments on 5:2 and 10:1 for discussion of the other two mighty angels). Like a melodramatic but effective prosecutor, the cherub launches his case with an attention-grabbing stunt before he offers a clarifying word. A millstone was a large, round, rolling stone connected to a horizontal beam, which was in turn attached to an animal or a human, who tugged it around the circular track of a wine or grain mill (Aune 3:1008; cf. Matt 18:6; Mark 9:42; Luke 17:2). Thrown into the sea, it would be expected to sink like the proverbial rock that it was. Babylon/Rome was the angel's proverbial case in point. He interprets his own actions with the mocking explanation that as goes the millstone, so will go the *great* city. It will not be great enough to float its way past the horrors that God has in store for it. Like a rock, having been sunk, it will rise nevermore (cf. Ezek 26:12, 21).

[22–23a] Picking up structurally from the concluding words of v. 21, and once again building from prophetic references (Isa 24:8; Jer 25:10; Ezek 26:13), the mighty angel offers a poignant, poetic presentation. Using an emphatic negative (*ou mē*), he tenders a series of subjunctive verbs coupled with the adverb *eti* (no longer, no more) to build a sorrowful feeling of tragic and permanent loss. Babylon will surely be found no more; the sounds of musicians will surely be heard no more; artisans will surely be found no more; the sound of working mills will surely be heard no more; the light of lamps will surely shine no more; the voice of brides and bridegrooms, a symbol of future family and national life, will surely be heard no more. The consistent refrain of loss reminds hearers and readers of the point made earlier: Babylon will be a deserted, haunted waste of a land (18:2).

[23b–24] And now the mighty angel explains why. He offers three reasons, the first two introduced by *hoti* (because). With the third, *hoti* is implied. First, Babylon is culpable because its merchants were the great ones of the earth. John is working here from Isaiah's depiction of the Tyre merchants as princes of the earth (Isa 23:8). This reference to greatness recalls Christ's own concern for Babylon's self-glorification (Rev 18:7).

Second, Babylon applied a kind of economic sorcery to delude the nations into believing that social security resided with it and it alone (cf. Isa 47:9). It was this misrepresentation of its own power and status that convinced even many believers like those in Pergamum, Thyatira, and Laodicea to accommodate themselves to Greco-Roman cultic loyalties and political expectations in order to advance economically. Among nonbelievers the power of such social magic was even greater still. Babylon/Rome duped all the nations into believing that idolatrous recognition of Roman gods and the imperial cult was a reasonable price to pay for a piece of its economic pie.

Finally and, given the impact of 6:9–11 on the whole of the book, more importantly, Babylon/Rome would be destroyed because it executed the prophets and saints who boldly delivered the contrary testimony that God and not Rome was the Lord of human creation and history. Indeed, Babylon/Rome was a demonic, dictatorial force so bent on the recognition of its exclusive lordship that it was ultimately responsible for the deaths of all those who had been slaughtered on the earth. The mighty angel therefore concludes that the blood of the executed, which in part sparked the motivating cry for God's intervention in 6:10 (see also 16:6; 17:6; 19:2; cf. Jer 51:49; Ezek 24:7; 36:18; Matt 23:35, 37), is the unassailable evidence that will bring Babylon/Rome down.

*19:1–10 The Hallelujah Chorus*

Chapter 19 is an odd transitional and motivational piece. The first half, a literary "hallelujah chorus," comprises vv. 1–10. These verses conclude a larger section dedicated to the judgment/destruction of the whore city Babylon/Rome that began at 17:1. As the celebratory response to that judgment, 19:1–10 anticipates the opposing twin narrative to 17:1–18:24, which is 21:9–22:9, dedicated to the commemoration of the anti-Babylon/Rome, the new Jerusalem, the bride city of the Lamb. While 19:1–4 follows up and celebrates Babylon/Rome's obliteration (17:1–18:24), vv. 5–8 prepare John's readers for the consort city to come (21:9–22:9). Verses 9–10 conclude the celebration with an angelic warning to worship only God, a command that is repeated at the conclusion of the new Jerusalem section (22:8–9). Thematically, 19:1–10 does not introduce 19:11–21:8. That section, devoted to the final battle and its aftermath, operates as a literary flashback describing the tactical battlefield maneuvers that achieved the salutary results (destruction of Babylon/Rome; rise of the new Jerusalem) described on either side of it. Those salutary results and the liturgical celebration of them have a specific literary intent. John's goal throughout has been to foster witness, that is, direct, nonviolent resistance against the religious, social, and political proclamation that Rome and Caesar are lord. Witnesses are now inspired through worship and encouraged through the visionary assurance of God's victory to continue this provocative testimony.[7]

19:1 After this I heard what sounded like the foreboding sound of a huge crowd in heaven, saying,

> "Hallelujah!
> Salvation and glory and power to our God,
> 2  because true and just are God's judgments,
> because God has judged the great whore
> who corrupted the earth with her fornication,
> and God avenged the blood of God's servants out of her hand."

3 Then a second time they said, "Hallelujah! And the smoke from her rises forever and ever." 4 Then the twenty-four elders and the four living creatures fell and worshiped God who is seated on the throne, saying, "Amen! Hallelujah!" 5 And a voice came from the throne, saying, "Praise our God, all God's servants, that is,[a] those who fear God, the small and the great." 6 Then I heard what sounded like a huge crowd, like the sound of many waters and the sound of great thunder, saying,

> "Hallelujah!
> For the Lord our God,
> the Almighty, has begun to rule.[b]
> 7  Let us rejoice and be glad
> and give God glory,
> because the wedding day of the Lamb has come
> and his bride has prepared herself;
> 8  she was given to wear fine linen, bright and clean" (for the fine linen
> represents the righteous deeds of the saints).

9 Then he said to me, "Write: 'Blessed are those who are invited to the wedding supper of the Lamb.'" And he said to me, "These are the true words of God." 10 Then I fell before his feet to worship him. But[c] he said to me, "Do not do that![d] I am a fellow servant with you and your colleagues who bear the testimony of Jesus. Worship God. For the testimony of Jesus is the spirit of prophecy."

---

7. Cf. Schüssler Fiorenza (*Vision of a Just World*, 103): "Although the prophetic rhetoric of Revelation is replete with cultic language and imagery, its social location and theological goal are not liturgical but political. Worship and praise in Revelation serve political ends and ethical decisions."

a. The *kai* (and) here is epexegetical, or explanatory. The servants *are* the ones who fear God. While A 051 0229 𝔐 latt sy bo include the *kai*, ℵ C P *pc* sa bo^(ms) omit it, perhaps fearing that its presence would suggest two different groups: servants *and* those who fear God.

b. The ingressive aorist nuance of *ebasileusas* (you began to rule) in 11:17 is repeated, using the third-person singular here.

c. An adversative *kai*: "but."

d. Literally, "do not see." For the idiomatic translation, see BDAG 578.

**[19:1–2]** John begins with a slight variation on what for him is an old literary formula. "After this," that is, following the visions of Babylon/Rome's destruction in chapters 17 and 18, he heard a heavenly, celebratory response. Though he most often accomplishes this move to a new narrative line of thought within the same overall story line with the phrase "after these things, I saw" (see the discussion of 4:1), this time he realizes the goal with a nod to what he hears. He hears a great, which is to say, a foreboding heavenly sound (see the discussion of 7:2). Because the content that follows is celebratory, the tone of judgment does not at first seem appropriate. Hearers and readers, though, must consider perspective. In Revelation, celebration and judgment are two sides of a single narrative coin.[8] Since victory for one camp can only be achieved through the destruction of the opposing camp, when the witnesses hear the sound of revelry, allies of the dragon and its vassal beasts must by definition be experiencing the noise of doom. "Hallelujah" in one camp is "woe" in the other.

The sound that is both foreboding (for allies of the dragon/beasts) *and* celebratory (for witnesses to the lordship of God and the Lamb) comes from a heavenly crowd. In Dan 10:6 the similar sound of a heavenly multitude projects from the mouth of a single figure who fits John's chapter 1 description of one like a child of humanity. In both Old and New Testament presentations, the heavenly origin of the sound is more important than the identity of its specific bearer; the tone and message are authorized by God. John does not name the crowd, making its identification difficult. Connections drawn to the multitude of Rev 7:9 are, however, intriguing. Except for a rather nondescript use of the term at 17:15, John uses *ochlos* (crowd) only here (19:1, 6) and at 7:9. The songs sung by the two crowds, which declare salvation to be an exclusive attribute of God, are also tantalizingly similar.

Before issuing its overture to salvation, however, the heavenly crowd of 19:1 begins with and focuses on the term *hallēlouia* (hallelujah).[9] The hymns of

8. Cf. Thompson, *Apocalypse and Empire*. Thompson develops a comparable view of the relationship between salvation and judgment.

9. On the meaning and background of this word, Aune writes: "The term ἀλληλουιά, 'hallelujah,' is a Greek transliteration of the Hebrew liturgical formula הַלְלוּ־יָהּ, *halĕlû-yāh*, meaning 'praise Yahweh' (occurring twenty-four times in the MT), which was taken over into Christian hymns and occurs for the first time in Christian literature in Rev 19:1–6" (3:1024).

19:1–10 are the only place where the term occurs in the entire New Testament (vv. 1, 3, 4, 6). John's chorus has its basis in the praise of the Hebrew Hallel psalms (Pss 113–118), which were sung partly before and partly after the Passover supper in commemoration of the exodus liberation (cf. also Pss 104–106; 135; 146–150). Psalm 113:1 provides a typical example: "Praise [*halĕlû*] the LORD! Praise [*halĕlû*], O servants of the LORD; praise [*halĕlû*] the name of the LORD." Use of the term also recalls Ps 104:35, where celebration erupts in response to God's judgment of sinners: "Let sinners be consumed from the earth, and let the wicked be no more. Bless the LORD, O my soul. Praise [*halĕlû*] the LORD!" Both references relate well to this context in Revelation, where the people of God are simultaneously celebrating God's judgment of a dragon-directed Babylon/Rome and the religious, social, and political liberation that judgment brings.

It is this combination of judgment and celebration that other Jewish writings associate with the Hallelujah. In 3 Macc 7:13 the people shout "Hallelujah!" because of deliverance from persecution and the judgment of apostates. In Tob 13:15–17 the streets of end-time Jerusalem shout "Hallelujah!" because the city will be rebuilt and decorated with "sapphire and emerald, and all your walls with precious stones, . . . battlements with pure gold, . . . [and] the streets . . . will be paved with ruby and with stones of Ophir." The walls and street of John's new Jerusalem are made of most of the precious metals mentioned in the Tobit account (Rev 21:18–21).

This background to the "hallelujah" also suggests its meaning as the preface to what Aune terms the judgment doxology of 19:1b–2 (3:1024). The "because" in v. 2 is the first in a series of two explicit and one implicit causal references to the reason for the celebration: God's true and just judgment (see the comments on 15:3 and 16:5–7) of Babylon/Rome in chapters 17 and 18. As Catherine and Justo González point out, "The destruction of Babylon is an act of justice, because Babylon had killed the saints, and the destruction of Babylon is the avenging of their blood" (125).

And so there is a vast throng of voices singing (cf. 19:1, 6). This heavenly crowd is no doubt the heavenly people of God. Certainly the executed souls from beneath the heavenly altar at 6:9–11 are present in this throng. They were witnesses who remained faithful and did not accommodate to the enticements or threats of the unholy trinity of dragon, beast from the sea, and beast from the land (false prophet). A series of causal statements (the first two introduced by *hoti*, because) links praise of God (to whom belong salvation, glory, and power) to the justice of God's judgments, and links the justice of God's judgments to God's judgment of the great whore who has corrupted the earth, and more specifically, to God's avenging the blood of the faithful witnesses (God's servants). The language of God's judging (*krinō*) the whore and the language of God's avenging (*ekdikeō*) the blood (*haima*) of God's servants recalls the pivotal scene of 6:9–11, where heavenly voices used the same vocabulary to appeal for the coming of justice/judgments. What the souls of the slaughtered under the heavenly altar pleaded for, heavenly voices in the hallelujah chorus celebrate as divine accomplishment. Justice has now been delivered.

The achievement of justice is God's work. Salvation (as in social and political liberation from Babylon/Rome), glory (as opposed to Babylon/Rome's attempt at self-glorification, 18:7), and power belong to God.[10] John need not elaborate on that subject because he has broached it already before (7:10). Yet the work of God's witnesses is crucial here as well. With the declaration that "God avenged the blood of God's servants out of her hand," John indicates once more that the efforts of the witnesses have made a transformative difference in connection with the divinely orchestrated salvation.[11] It is intriguing that John also integrally connected God's salvation and power to the victorious work of the witnesses at 12:10–11. The seer further develops the point in 19:10, when the voice of the angel declares that he is a fellow servant with those who hold, who keep, the testimony that Jesus himself bore—that he is ultimate Lord and ruler of human destiny. The emphasis remains on that testimony and its effect. That is why John has been declaring that the people must persevere in their resistance. They must resist because in their resistance the power of the dragon is being destroyed. Nowhere is this reality more poignant than in 16:6, where the blood of the witnesses becomes the very mechanism through which the forces that have spilled their blood will meet their demise. The hallelujah, then, is not just about what God has done; it is also about what God's people have, through faith, been continuing to do in concert with and in support of God's own activity. In bearing witness to the sovereign rule of God and the Lamb, they have been raising a contrary voice to the prevalent, powerful, and bloodthirsty opinion about the control of human history. No wonder, then, that John will define such witness as the fine, victorious linen that adorns the Lamb's bridal city (19:8).

[3] Fired up, the heavenly crowd thunders an antiphonal "Hallelujah!" to its own earlier praise shout. It is once again God's judgment that causes the celebration. As he did at 14:11, John recalls Isaiah's image of the smoke of Edom's

---

10. This term of "salvation" occurs only in 7:10; 12:10 (which is one of the other parallel texts); and 19:1. For Richard, "It means full and abundant life, and the cry that attributes salvation to God likewise has a political meaning: it is God rather than the empire that assures this *sōtería* (the empire was obligated to assure the *sōtería* of all citizens)" (138). Throughout the narrative, John describes these attributes as rightly belonging to God and the Lamb: "Salvation": 7:10 (God and Lamb); 12:10; 19:1 (God). "Glory": 1:6; 5:12, 13 (Lamb); 4:9, 11; 5:12; 7:12; 11:13; 14:7; 15:8; 16:9; 19:1, 7; 21:11, 23 (God). "Power": 1:16; 5:12 (Lamb); 4:11; 7:12; 11:17; 12:10; 15:8; 19:1 (God).

11. On the translation of the difficult phrase *ek cheiros autēs* (by her hand), Beale comments: "That John intends an allusion to 2 Kgs. 9:7 is clear because the wording is so close and because the OT figure of Jezebel the whore has been alluded to in the wider and narrower context of Rev. 19:2 (2:20; 17:16)" (928).

ruin rising forever (Isa 34:10). In Rev 14:11 punishment was inflicted upon individuals who had persecuted God's witnesses; here all of Babylon/Rome is targeted. By using the image of rising smoke, John reinforces the connection vv. 1–2 have already drawn between the witnesses' cries for justice and God's resulting judgment. At 8:4 John saw smoke rising from the incense altar with the saints' prayers, which 6:9–11 had already characterized as a petition that God avenge the blood of executed believers. The temporary rise of that smoke-borne appeal for intervention triggered the retaliation that has left Babylon/Rome a smoldering ruin, whose smoke of destruction will rise forever.

**[4]** Recalling 5:14, where the twenty-four elders (see the discussion of 4:4) and the four living creatures (see the discussion of 4:6–8a) confirm the praise of the Lamb through their own worship and an affirming "Amen!" this heavenly coterie responds to the twin hallelujahs of the crowd with an "Amen!" that validates the correctness of the praise's application to God, and then blasts a hallelujah of its own (cf. Ps 106:48). The reference to God sitting on the throne offers rationale for the praise; the God who rules in heaven (on the phrase "seated on the throne" as a euphemism for rule, see the comment on 4:2–3) has consummated that same rule on earth (see the discussion at 18:7 of Babylon/Rome's attempt to hijack the throne-rule metaphor).

**[5]** While it is all but impossible to identify the speaker of the second heavenly voice, it is clear that its heavenly location near the throne gives it an unmistakable weight of authority. It uses that authority to offer praise by demanding more of it. Its present-tense imperative, "Praise!" encourages the crowd to continue its adoration while it simultaneously prods a different crowd to get started (vv. 6–8). Using different language, the voice also models as it encourages. It responds to the hallelujahs of vv. 1, 3, and 4 and anticipates the hallelujah of v. 6 by declaring the same adoration in different wording: "The phrase Αἰνεῖτε τῷ Θεῷ ἡμῶν, 'Praise our God,' is very close to the OT formula הַלְלוּ־אֵל, *halĕlû-ēl*, 'praise God' (Ps 150:1), translated Αἰνεῖτε τὸν Θεόν in the LXX. . . . Αἰνεῖτε τῷ Θεῷ ἡμῶν is a relatively close way of rendering 'hallelujah'" (Aune 3:1028). The praise language once again recalls the celebratory injunctions of the psalms (cf. Pss 134; 135:1, 20). The voice addresses all God's servants, all who fear God (see the comments on 14:7; 15:4; cf. Ps 115:13), both small and great (cf. Rev 11:18).

**[6]** Response to the heavenly voice is immediate. Another crowd thunders a hymn of praise that is anchored by the New Testament's final "Hallelujah!" There are several reasons to suppose that this crowd is different from the one introduced in v. 1. John's use of *kai ēkousa* (and I heard) to open the verse suggests that he has switched to a different subject within the same narrative vision (see the discussion of 16:1). In this case the new subject would be a new crowd dedicated to the same narrative agenda of praise. Indeed, the lack of definite articles for "voice" and "crowd" suggests that John is not referring back to the crowd of 19:1. The adjectives used to describe the two crowds and their voices are also different. In fact, the only similarity is that both crowds cry "Hallelujah!" The linguistic connection with 11:18 provides a clue about this second crowd's identity. At 19:5 the heavenly voice addresses its praise command to all the servants, both small and great, who fear God. Verses 6–8 present their antiphonal response. At 11:18 this same grouping represents earthly witnesses to the lordship of God and the Lamb. The implication is clear: the crowd that offers hymnic praise in vv. 6–8 is the earthly counterpart to the heavenly one that sings in the first four verses.

This earthly crowd also adds a different, two-tiered rationale for the praise. The heavenly crowd sang because of God's true and just judgments, God's verdict against the whore, and God's avenging of the witnesses' blood; this earthly crowd first fittingly celebrates because, just now, following the destruction of Babylon/Rome in chapters 17 and 18, the Almighty (see the discussions of 11:17 and 15:3) God has begun to accomplish what was hymnically forecast in 11:15, 17: God's heavenly rule on earth (cf. 1 Chr 16:31; Pss 93:1; 97:1; 99:1; Zech 14:9).

[7–8] The earthly crowd's second cause for praise is more complicated. Building from Isa 61:10, where the prophet celebrates the fact that God has clothed him in garments of salvation that recall the festal clothing of bridegrooms and their brides, the choir of earthbound witnesses charge themselves ("let us") to rejoice, exult, and glorify God because the wedding of the bridegroom Lamb and his festively clothed bride has come (cf. 1 Chr 16:28; Ps 118:24). In Matt 5:12, the verbs *chairō* (rejoice) and *agalliaō* (exult, be glad) also appear together as Jesus tells followers to rejoice and be glad because the reward for their persecutions is coming. Here in Revelation, the earthly crowd celebrates the realization of Jesus' prediction.

The primary focus surely is on the wedding metaphor. The casting of Christ as a bridegroom and the people of God as the bride was well known in the early church (e.g., 2 Cor 11:2; Eph 5:25–32). At Matt 22:2, Jesus compares the reign of God to a wedding banquet that a king prepares for his son. It is this same wedding that the earthly crowd now celebrates in the only context (Rev 19:7, 9) where John deploys the term *gamos* (wedding). The Lamb is the risen, exalted Jesus. John rekindles a touch of universalism when he later reveals that the bride, as the people of God, symbolizes much more than the limited form of the church (see the comments on 5:9–10 and 15:3–4). She is the new city of Jerusalem, "the renewed world of God" (Schüssler Fiorenza, *Vision of a Just World*, 103).

John's focus on God's universal people as the divine bride takes its cue from Old Testament depictions of Israel as the bride of Yahweh (Isa 1:21; 54:1–8; Jer 2:2; 31:32; Ezek 16:8–14; Hos 2:5; cf. Eph 5:32). The reference to her prepared garments as a symbol of her readiness also has strong Old Testament foundations (Gen 35:2; Isa 52:1; 61:10; Zech 3:4; see Caird 234). John develops the metaphor for his own purposes with the language of preparation in v. 7 and an explication of what that preparation means in v. 8.

Clearly, the bride's very identity as those who witness to the lordship of God and the Lamb is a part of her preparation. John's heaviest concentration of the term *gynē* (woman, bride) appears in the corresponding chapters 12 and 17. The woman clothed with the sun, at once the people of God who give birth to the Messiah (12:1–6) and the people of God who become the followers of that Messiah (12:17), is positioned against the whore of Babylon/Rome, whose fornication disrupts all the earth. In fact, except for several literal uses of "woman" (cf. 2:20; 9:8; 14:4), John uses the word exclusively to counterpose one female metaphor for people (opposed to God) with another (witnesses for God). Here, "woman" as bridal *witness* is presented one penultimate time before its climactic and definitive presentation at 21:9. It is her witnessing that prepares her for marriage to the Lamb. No wonder, then, that this "woman" witness is also termed the Lamb's *nymphē* (bride) at 21:2, 9; 22:17.

Verse 8 describes the actual mechanics of her preparation. Using the divine-passive formulation *edothē* (it was given) that has become for John a formulaic way of presenting God as the active causal agent (see the comments on 6:2 and 7:2; cf. 6:4, 8, 11; 8:3; 11:1–2; 13:5, 7, 14–15; 16:8; 20:4), the seer clarifies that the woman is not operating on her own but through the power of God. God enables her "to be clothed" (*peribalētai*, a follow-up divine passive) in bright clean linen, further defined as the righteous deeds of the saints. Since John uses the same terminology for linen here that he uses for Babylon/Rome's luxurious cargo and the whore's dress (18:12, 16), he clearly means to counterpose the idolatrous deeds that witness to the lordship of Rome against righteous witness to the lordship of God and the Lamb. Even the description of the woman's preparation (dressing herself in fine linen), though it employs an active-voice verb ("[she] prepared herself"), implies divine agency. Beale comments, "Throughout the Apocalypse ἑτοιμάζω ('prepare') is used of events that occur *ultimately* as a result of God's decrees and not human actions (the most striking is in 21:2: 'the new Jerusalem I saw descending from heaven from God prepared as a bride'; so also 9:7, 15; 12:6; 16:12; cf. 8:6, where angels 'prepared themselves to sound')" (940). John is paradoxically mixing human initiative with divine causality. To be sure, he intends to say that the people of God have, by their acts of witnessing to the lordship of God and the Lamb under perilous circumstances, achieved both the conquest of the dragon and its forces (12:11) and the victory of eschatological relationship with God (2:7, 11, 17, 26, 28; 3:5, 12, 21). This righteous behavior does not, however, mean that humans can achieve salvation through their own merit. John means to make this point by implying that the witnessing he so celebrates has been enabled and empowered by God. The source of the strength to witness comes not from the saints themselves but from God.

Nonetheless, saints who marshal that strength into the righteous deeds of nonac-commodating resistance to the lordship claims of Caesar and Rome weave, through their resistance, the dazzling garments that John has promised all along to the faithful witnesses (see the discussion of 3:2–4). Nowhere does John make this point more clearly than at 6:11, where with the assistance of a very instruc-tive use of *edothē* (it was given), he declares that the dazzling clothing secured by the saints as a result of their faithful, resistant witness was given to (empow-ered for) them by God. What he says of the saints' dress in 6:11, he means about the woman's wedding finery here in 19:8. God does the clothing—the equipping for righteous witness.

[9] The voice that now commands John probably belongs to the angel of 17:1. It makes good thematic sense that the figure who introduced John to the vision of Babylon/Rome's destruction would preside over the vision of the resulting eschatological supper celebration. Drawing a connection between the two also makes narrative sense given that 19:9–10 operates as the closing bracket to the section that began at 17:1. It is reasonable to expect the same angel to be speak-ing in both the opening and the closing scenes. The broader narrative parallel with 21:9–22:9 offers yet another reason to believe that the same angel is speak-ing throughout. When John describes the (witnessing) bride of the Lamb (in 21:9–22:9) and also when he pictures the judgment of the (fornicating) whore of Babylon (in 17:1–19:10), he presents as emcee in both cases one of the seven angels who had the seven bowls of God's wrath. It is likely that this same angel conducts both vision sequences and is therefore present with John at the end of both visions when the overwhelmed prophet tries here, and again in the parallel scene 22:8–9, to offer to him the worship that belongs exclusively to God.

The angel gives John a simple command: he is to write the fourth of seven beatitudes chronicled throughout the book (1:3; 14:13; 16:15; 19:9; 20:6; 22:7, 14; see the discussion of 1:1–3). The blessing that envisions relationship with God as an eschatological feast is drawn from the prophetic vision of Isa 25:6–8, which was developed in early Christian circles (see Matt 8:11; Luke 13:29), particularly in the Last Supper narration, where Jesus promises to drink with his disciples at what will apparently be a messianic banquet (Mark 14:25; Matt 26:29; Luke 22:18). This macarism, like the other six in Revelation, has the same dual indicative and imperative senses (see the comment on 14:13). In this particular case, the blessing acknowledges those who have already witnessed to the lordship of God and the Lamb and have as a result of that witness con-quered (cf. 12:11). Through that conquest they have obtained the eschatologi-cal relationship with God that John describes metaphorically as an invitation to the Lamb's wedding feast. Because that wedding supper is envisioned as a place of such great eschatological joy, the macarism simultaneously goads those who have accommodated to the lordship demands of the imperial cult to "come out of Babylon/Rome" (18:4) and testify to the lordship of God instead.

In declaring the blessing, John returns to the paradox he presented with the bride's wedding garments (19:8). John wants to celebrate witness, but he does not want witnesses to believe that it is their testifying that is ultimately responsible for the eschatological relationship they seek. Believers are blessed because of their witness, but the effects of that witness are determined by God alone. To make the point, John once again resorts to a divine passive. Witnessing does not "earn" one a ticket into the wedding feast of the Lamb; witnessing creates the opportunity for one to be invited or be called (*hoi keklēmenoi*) by God into the feast. While believers' acts of witness are necessary, only God's actions are determinative.

Yet there is a problem with John's metaphorical presentation. John has introduced the bride as the people of God (vv. 7–8). Now, the people of God are suddenly the wedding guests! Can both significations hold? In John's world, as in the world of dreams and visions, they certainly can. John's presentation cannot be held to the same type of logic that governs literal narration about the "real" world. He is trying to make a single point and to do so is perfectly comfortable with mixing his metaphors, even in a conflicting way. His primary point holds whether the people of God are envisioned as the bride betrothed to the Lamb or as the guests who have been invited to the festive wedding dinner. In both cases, witnessing to the lordship of God and the Lamb establishes the opportunity for eschatological relationship. It is that witnessing and the reulting relationship that is uppermost on the seer's mind. He will use as many metaphors as necessary to demonstrate both the necessity of, and the joy that results from, that witnessing endeavor. No doubt in his mind the more ways he can find to illustrate that task, the more likely he will be to maintain some people in it and convert others to it.

John concludes the verse by declaring the words spoken here to be true. There are two possible referents: the words of the macarism, or the words extending from 17:1 through 19:10. Since the macarism is itself a climactic moment of celebration and exhortation following from the fall of Babylon/Rome, it is more likely that John intends this truth claim to refer to the entire section. Assured of the enemy's fate and the resulting celebration, believers will be more likely to witness faithfully. Despite the oppression and persecution that their testimony brings, they can trust that God will prevail and eschatological relationship with God will occur.

**[10]** Overwhelmed by all that the angel has shown him since 17:1, John positions himself to worship the messenger even though he knows full well that worship is due God and the Lamb alone (see the discussion of 3:9). The seer's inappropriate actions are mirrored in the parallel text of 22:8–9. There, too, overwhelmed by the visions that this same angel shows him of the Lamb's bride, John responds with an improper worship attempt. This phenomenon of misplaced appreciation was well known in the ancient world. "The motif of the angel who refuses worship from a seer in the context of an angelic revelation (as in Rev 19:10 and 22:9) is a *literary* motif with many parallels in apocalyptic literature, though the motif is not restricted to apocalyptic" (Aune 3:1036; emphasis orig.). Acts even records an instance where the very human Peter rebuked an appreciative believer who wanted to worship him (10:25–26). There is therefore no need to speculate as to whether John has in mind an Asia Minor angel cult. Debates about the existence of such cults and the magnitude of their following are inconclusive. One need not speculate any further than the evidence at hand. The problem is the tendency to celebrate grand visions and the figure who orchestrates them. Anything, including a heavenly directed vision, its accompanist, even the church and the faith tradition that is so integral a part of it, can become idolatrous if it is allowed to carry more freight than it should. Everything on the created planet has the same purpose: to bear witness to the lordship of God and Christ. On this functional level, humans and angels are equal partners.

The angel now equates the testimony Jesus bore, the same testimony that believers are now to bear on his behalf, to the spirit of prophecy (on the witness of Jesus Christ, see the comment on 1:2; also see the comments on 11:3, 7, 10). Prophecy is not just a matter of predicting the future. It is instead the revelation of a present truth that demands appropriate present and future behavior. The testimony and the spirit of prophecy have the same focal subject matter: the lordship of God and the Lamb. John makes this clear when he equates the language of prophecy with the material content of his own apocalyptic testimony (1:3; 22:7, 10, 18–19). He is speaking here, then, not about the Spirit of God, but about the role of human witnesses whose testimony reveals the truth about God's rule over creation and requires all humans to respond appropriately, that is, repent (see 2:5, 16, 21–22; 3:3, 19; 9:20–21; 11:13; 14:7; 15:4; 16:9, 11; 18:4). The angel makes this human dimension explicit in the parallel scene where he calls John's fellow witnesses "prophets" (22:9).

### 19:11–21:8 The Final Battle and Its Aftermath

### 19:11–16 The Rider on the White Horse

Using the preferred narrative formula for opening a new scene, *kai eidon* (then I saw), which he had first used to introduce the Lamb at 5:1, John presents a rider on a white horse—the Lamb in another, more lionlike (5:5) guise. John will deploy this formula two more times in the second half of this chapter. In each case he uses it to introduce dramatic new narrative footage: the launch of the final battle (19:17–18) and the capture of the key enemy generals (vv. 19–21). The complete section sits at the head of the entire final combat scene and its aftermath (19:11–21:8), a section that interrupts the parallel sections about the whore of Babylon (17:1–18:24), the bride of the Lamb (21:9–22:9), and the scene of heavenly praise that acts as a bridge between them (19:1–10).

This presentation of what is undoubtedly for John the Lamb's Parousia, an eschatological version of Isaiah's presentation of God as a returning warrior king (63:1–6), does not include any form of a rapture. Believers are not spirited off to a safe heavenly realm while conflict on a cosmic scale erupts on earth. Indeed, an army of apparently human believers marches forward with the Lamb, and hordes of other believers either have been executed (6:9–11; 8:3–5; 20:4) or have suffered mightily in the seal, trumpet, and bowl maelstroms that have comprised the apocalyptic run-up to this final conflict.

What this Christ Parousia does offer is a political rendering of an avenging Messiah. Commentators are right to point out that everything about this scene smacks of the white horse, diadems, title inscribed on the rider, and military imagery of the Roman triumph. The only feature missing is the chariot drawn by four horses (Aune 3:1051). John means to position the Lamb's battlefield arrival as a countertriumph, the one that will produce the ultimate and therefore (as his very name suggests) true victory and reign. Only God's triumph, executed by the Lamb, is real. Political as well as cultic loyalty is therefore due God and God alone.

It is just as clear that Christ's coming is a contemporary political rather than a future otherworldly happening. The transfiguration it promises is a historical one; the rider does not precipitate the end of the world but a re-creation of it. It is a new earth (21:1), not the end of the earth, that is promised. Witnesses participate in a reclaiming of the world for God, not an escape (i.e., rapture) from it.

11 Then I saw heaven opened, and behold, a dazzling horse, and the one seated on it is called[a] Faithful and True, and he judges and wages war in righteousness. 12 His eyes are like a flame of fire, and on his head, which has a name written that no one knows except himself, are many diadems. 13 He is clothed in a garment stained with blood, and his name is called The Word of God. 14 And the heavenly armies were following him on dazzling horses, wearing fine linen, dazzling clean. 15 From his mouth projects a sharp sword, so that he can strike the nations with it, and he will shepherd them with an iron rod, and he will tread the winepress of the fury of the wrath of God the Almighty. 16 And he has on his robe, that is,[b] at the place where the garment covers his thigh, a name written: "King of kings and Lord of lords."

a. The participle *kaloumenos* (is called) is included here by 1006 1611 1841 1854 2030 2053 2062 𝔐[K] vg[cl] sy; Ir[lat] Or. No doubt because of skittishness about the possibility that the term might lead some readers to believe that the rider was only *called* Faithful and True as opposed to *being* faithful and true, A P 051 1 2042 2081 *al* dropped the term; א replaced it, but at the wrong place, following *pistos* (see Metzger, *Textual Commentary*, 762–63).

b. The *kai* (and) here is epexegetical, or explanatory.

**[11]** Verse 11 parallels the introduction of the one seated on the heavenly throne at 4:1. In the earlier text, John saw a door opened in heaven. The divine-passive formulation implied that God did the opening. Here the same verb and passive voice indicate God's continued agency. There are two differences in the narration. First, this time all of heaven is opened (cf. Ezek 1:1; Acts 10:11). Second, the object of interest is a rider seated on a white horse (cf. 2 Macc 3:25) rather than the one seated on the throne. Posture, though, remains significant. Seated language is enthronement language (see the comments on 4:2–3 and 18:7). Just as the lordship of God was revealed through God's placement on the throne, so the Lamb's enthronement is revealed through his position on the white horse. Throne imagery reveals God's lordship as that of Ruler and Judge. The Lamb's station upon the battle horse reveals his lordship as that of the messianic conqueror who executes the judgment God has rendered. It is this latter revelation that the remaining narration of chapter 19 will confirm.

John's imagery reinforces key themes established earlier in his work. Though this horse and rider are not the same horse and rider as in 6:2 (see the discussion of that verse), the seer is certainly capitalizing on the thematic link between horses and judgment in the narration of the first four seals (6:1–8). The horse's dazzling color represents victory (see the comment on 3:2–4). It is no accident that the troops who accompany the rider sport horses of the same color (19:14). The rider's name, "Faithful and True" (cf. 3 Macc 2:9–14), is a climactic summation of descriptors previously applied to Christ: faithful witness, 1:5; the true one, 3:7; and faithful and true witness, 3:14. The implication is clear: not only did Christ faithfully declare his own and God's true lordship to the cross and beyond; as God's true Messiah, he also will faithfully execute God's judgment upon those who have fought and killed on behalf of the lordship of Caesar and Rome. "The justice meted out by the parousia Christ gives proof of his loyalty and faithfulness toward those who have kept his witness" (Schüssler Fiorenza, *Vision of a Just World*, 105).

The final phrase in the verse is an explanatory extension of the moniker "Faithful and True." By Faithful and True, John means to say that when the rider fulfills his obligations of executing judgment through war, he does so in a righteous manner (cf. Pss 72:2; 96:13; 98:9; and Isa 11:4, where God judges with righteousness). In other words, the rider acts as God acts, in ways that are commensurate with the crime (cf. Rev 15:3; 16:5, 7; 19:2; 20:13) and that procure the victory of eschatological relationship with God that was promised (2:7, 11, 17, 26, 28; 3:5, 12, 21). The rider/Lamb has not started this fight (11:7; 12:17; 13:7). He will, however, finish it (17:14). Justly.

**[12]** The rider's flaming eyes are based on Dan 10:6 and rekindle John's earlier description of Christ (Rev 1:14), who comes as judge even of believers who accommodate themselves to the lordship demands of the imperial cult (2:18: Thyatira). The many diadems further develop the imagery of rule. These symbols of kingship were previously co-opted in the narrative by the dragon and the beasts (12:3; 13:1) and commandeered by the Caesars in history, but they rightfully adorn only the crown on the head of the Christ Lamb (14:14; 19:16).

There is little doubt that John has in mind Isaiah's eschatological presentation of the holy city of Jerusalem (Isa 62:1–5). Isaiah connects the language of crown and diadem, identifying them as a single representation of God's universal lordship (62:3). In that context, Jerusalem is to God a bridal city just as the people of God are imaged as a bridal city in Rev 19:6–8. Of even more interest is the fact that Isaiah connects these images to the bestowal of a new name (62:2). Like Isaiah's vindicated Jerusalem, the diademed rider/Christ/Lamb is issued a new name. The divine-passive formulation once again points to divine agency. Based on the Lamb's true and faithful witness and the kingship he obtains as a result, God gives him a new name and promptly inscribes it on his head. Though dueling variant readings locate the inscription either on the diadems or on the rider's head, narrative clues suggest that John intends the head. Such positioning parallels nicely with the inscription of Christ's name on the forehead of his followers (14:1; 22:4) and draws an appropriate contrast to the blasphemous names on the heads of the beast from the sea (13:1).[12]

This newly accorded name is obviously not the same name, "Faithful and True," that was just mentioned in v. 11. That name was publicly stated; this new name is known only to the rider. The divine-passive formulation ("written") implies once again God's agency and suggests that God is the single exception who knows the secret of the name. This literary technique of reserving knowledge of key details to only a few is characteristic of John's work (see 14:3). Of particular interest is the new name of Christ written on the white stone given to the faithful at 2:17, which Christ himself promised to inscribe on his witnesses at 3:12. Since Paul also affirms that God will give Christ a new name exalted above every other name (Phil 2:9), the newness, if not the secrecy, of Christ's eschatological name was a part of the early tradition. The secrecy here is no doubt a metaphor of empowerment. Since the ancient world supposed that control of a person or a divinity could be exercised through the knowledge and manipulation of that person's or divinity's name (as in a magical incantation), John's imagery amounts to a declaration that Christ's lordship is beyond the

12. This reading also makes better grammatical sense of the accepted text. The participle *echōn* (having, [which] has) opens the clause introducing the written name and in this context must have *ho kathēmenos* (the one who sits) as its antecedent. The writing, then, is associated more directly with the rider than with the diadems he wears.

control of any human or power. It is his unique status and autonomy as Lord rather than any interest in deciphering his name that John wants most to impress upon his readers here.

One could argue that the secret is revealed later in this scene, when John introduces him as "The Word of God" (19:13) and then sees the inscribed name "King of kings and Lord of lords" (v. 16). Anyone familiar with the tradition cited in the prologue of the Johannine Gospel (cf. also 1 John 1) would have been surprised to learn that what had become a decidedly public metaphorical connection of Jesus to God's "Word" was now suddenly a secret. Moreover, because "name" lacks the definite article in v. 16, it is grammatically unlikely that John is referring to this secret name there either. Christ's kingship, though climactically presented in v. 16, is also not much of a secret any longer. The diadems of this immediate context illustrate the claim. The book's one revelation is that true historical and cosmic lordship belongs to God and Christ. Indeed, witness to this truth forms the book's principal ethic. The secret name cannot be related to this very public, though contested, truth. No, the matter remains one of knowledge and the control that goes with it. John wants his hearers and readers to know that even believers, faithful witnesses to the lordship of God and the Lamb, cannot parlay their righteousness into a manipulation of the Lamb's eschatological activity of dealing justice. They can know the Lord well enough to serve him, worship him, and testify about him, but they never know him well enough to control him. He will judge justly, no matter what justice requires (i.e., the plagues of the seals, trumpets, and bowls; the judgment of Christ-believers). "When they have joined all the glorious names that adoring wonder can ascribe to him, he still confronts them with an ultimate mystery" (Caird 242).

**[13]** The mystery heightens with his wardrobe. The rider wears a robe stained with blood. Given the gory narration, there are several worthy options for the source of the blood. It could be the Lamb's blood; the event of his execution is, after all, central to the work (1:5; 5:9; 7:14; 12:11). It could just as credibly be the blood of the witnesses who are executed for their testimony to the Lamb's lordship. Indeed, it is the crying out of their blood that presumably motivates divine judgment (6:10; 16:6; 17:6; 18:24; 19:2; cf. Gen 4:10). Or finally, it could be the blood of the enemies who work at the behest of the dragon and its minion beasts (14:20).

Choosing the Lamb's blood makes little narrative sense; the Lamb's blood is spilled offstage, in the crucifixion symbolized as a "snatching" that took place well before the situation now confronting the seven churches (12:5).[13] More

13. I note here that, following continued research and reflection, this conclusion represents a change in the position I offer in my book *Can I Get a Witness?* There I presented the argument that the blood was indeed the Lamb's own blood. Still, as the discussion here will soon demonstrate, the fact that it is not the Lamb's own blood does not alter the conclusion that I reached in *Can I Get a Witness?* that John depicts the Lamb as a nonviolent resister.

likely would be the blood of the witnesses, as John fears both its current and future spilling and exhorts his followers to continue testifying even in the face of such a dire circumstance. The Lamb could well be carrying a sampling of that spilled blood with him as extra motivation for the battle task at hand. The problem with this option is twofold. First, the cry of 6:9–11, renarrated in symbolic fashion in 8:3–5, provides sufficient motivation for all of the judgment/justice activity that has ensued thus far. It is difficult to believe that God would need any more motivational reinforcement just now. Second and more important, the witness blood option does not fit the narrative context. Since 17:1, John has been narrating the blood of judgment. Where the blood of believers is mentioned, it is offered exclusively as a rationale for the justice that is being wreaked. The focus throughout this extended section has been on the destruction of the whore/Babylon/Rome. When John mentions the people of God at length, he describes their postapocalyptic appearance as a bride adorned in fine and clean, not bloody, linen.

The narrative preoccupation in this part of Revelation is the final combat to consummate the acts of judgment that have already taken place. Indeed, one of those acts, pictured as the wine of God's wrath (14:10) and the subsequent treading of the metaphorical winepress that spills an immense volume of enemy blood (14:20), fits nicely with the treading of the winepress of God's wrath highlighted in 19:15. Isaiah 63:1–6, from which John is certainly working, chronicles the return of God as a warrior dressed in a garment stained with the blood of God's Edomite enemies (cf. Exod 15:3–4; Wis 18:15–16). Like John, Isaiah refers to that blood with the metaphor of a trodden winepress. This is blood judgment language. The blood on the rider's robe must therefore be the blood of those who oppose the lordship of God and the Lamb and, allied with the dragon and beasts, fight to abort it. Critics may argue that the rider has not yet gone into combat and can therefore not yet have been splattered with the blood of his enemies. To be sure, the final battle has not been engaged, but the preparatory battles chronicled in chapters 17 and 18 have already been waged and won. It is hard to imagine the decimation wrought there as a clean, bloodless kill.

It is not, however, inappropriate that hearers and readers entertain all three blood options when they read this text. In this climactic setting, the imagery of blood comes full circle, tied up as it is with the person of Christ, who with the saints (12:11) brings victory through his blood for the blood of the saints by drawing the blood of the enemy. It is that blood drawn in judgment that now stains his robe.

Caird makes the helpful point that by engaging in this bloody judgment, the Christ/Lamb/rider has not abandoned his primary role in the Apocalypse: "In turning warrior he has not deserted his original function of witness-bearing, on which all his other achievements are founded. He is armed, as we shall see in verse 15, with no other weapon than the good confession which he witnessed before Pontius Pilate (I Tim. vi. 13)" (241). His weapon *is* his witness. His witness is his word of testimony to the lordship of God and Christ. That word is the victorious sword he wields (1:16; 2:12, 16; 19:15, 21; see the comment on 12:15; cf. Wis 18:15–16). John made this case early on when he introduced the word of God, which is the testimony of Jesus (1:2; see the comment on that verse). He repeats the formulation at 1:9; 6:9; and 20:4. This word is the cutting (against the lordship claims of the imperial cult) testimony of God's and Jesus' lordship, which Jesus himself conveyed and his witnesses now proclaim. It is no wonder, then, that his name would also be "The Word of God." His witness and his name are synonymous. He is (name) what he does (witness). He is the very embodiment of the truth to which he testifies.

[14] The dazzling horse of the Lamb/Christ/rider of 19:11 is replicated here as a metaphor for victory that bears all of those who fight in league with the Christ Lamb. The identity of Christ's accompanying force is not clear. Given that the 144,000 were characterized as an army, surely they would comprise a portion of the company (see the commentary on 7:1–8; 14:1–5). Perhaps the multitude of 17:14 would also ride with him. Could the great army of witnesses chronicled at 7:9–17 make up the army's number? This seems less likely, however, since these witnesses have already retired from their battles to an everlasting repose of worship before the heavenly throne. Their fighting (i.e., witnessing) is done; their worshiping is only just beginning. It is better to focus on the battle contingent as those who still maintain the combat of witness with and for the Lamb on earth since the earth is the ground upon which the battle will take place.

For hearers and readers concerned about the violence implied by the battle imagery, it is helpful to remember that John never depicts the army actually fighting. The brawl takes place offstage. Even there, it is unclear whether John intends combat of a traditional sort. After all, the primary weapon is a sword not of steel but of God's word. Since Christ's accompanying army ride similar horses, one suspects that they also fight with a similar weapon. The combat is one of competing testimonies to competing lordships. This is a war of the Word, a war over which word, the word of whose lordship, is the true word. It is therefore on the level of testimony that the combat is waged. The army of witnesses make war by testifying to the lordship of God and the Lamb. It is this testimony that draws blood and brings down the forces of the beast (cf. 12:11). No wonder, then, that John connects the clothing of witness with the clothing of this Christ army. As 19:8 has made clear, the act of witnessing yields the dazzling dress of fine linen that characterizes a true and victorious witness. John makes the same point throughout the narrative (see the discussion of 3:2–4; cf. 6:11; 7:14; 22:14). Witnessing *is* the winning weapon.

[15] Multiple Old Testament references and allusions lie behind the metaphors John deploys in this single verse. He builds from an apparently tra-

ditional understanding of God's word (cf. Eph 6:17; Heb 4:12); the sharp sword issuing from the rider's mouth is reminiscent of Isa 49:2 and reminds John's readers of Christ's primary and most formidable weapon (see the discussion of 1:16; 2:12, 16; 19:21; also of 12:15; cf. Wis 18:15–16). He uses this sword to strike the nations. Indeed, he targets *all* the nations, even those comprised of believers (1:16; 2:12, 16). All will be judged according to their works of witness (2:2, 5, 6, 19, 23, 26; 3:1, 2, 8, 15; 20:12). For hearers and readers who are skeptical that the Lamb would initiate such apparently hostile action, it is helpful to remember that the Lamb presented in 6:16 is decisive about judgment. He remains a lion who strikes, that is, sLambs his prey with the word of God (see the excursus on ch. 5: The Lion and the Lamb).

The language of "striking" is also important because John uses it of the two witnesses who strike the earth with plagues (ch. 11). The idea behind such striking was rehabilitative, however. God's strikes, even in the plagues, were intended to motivate repentance (2:5, 16, 21–22; 3:3, 19; 9:20–21; 16:9, 11). John is clearly working here from prophetic foundations. At Isa 11:4 God intends to strike the nations with the rod of God's mouth. In this context in Revelation, the force for repentance softens the blow as John links the Old Testament imagery, particularly the Ps 2:9 image of "ruling" with an iron rod, to the symbolism of "shepherding" toward an eschatological relationship with God (see the comments on 2:27 and 12:5; cf. 11:1). Finally, the winepress as metaphor for God's judgment wrath is reminiscent of 14:19–20 (cf. 14:10), which John surely alludes to in 19:13. Both of those texts draw heavily from the image of God as a returning, victorious king in Isa 63:1–6. (On God as almighty, see the comments on 1:8; 4:8; 11:17; 15:3; 16:7.) As vicious as John's language is here, it is helpful to note that he does not invent the imagery of judgment, but works from prophetic foundations. He even manages to temper the presentation that the prophets have given him. John's God in the end is a forceful shepherd whose chief concern is the re-forming of the flock.

[16] The final name of the Lamb in this context, which is still not the revelation of the mysterious name of v. 12, is written on his garment, at the place of his thigh.[14] The divine-passive formulation suggests that God has marked him with this name. The precise location is difficult to determine since the Greek is not clear. The *kai* (and) that connects his garment with his thigh could mean either that there are two inscriptions, one on the garment and the other on the thigh, or that there is one inscription. In the latter case, the epexegetical *kai* (that is) suggests that the second half (thigh) interprets the first (garment). Even in this case, though, there are problems. Does John intend to say that the name is

---

14. Some manuscripts have changed the text to read "on the forehead." This adjustment clearly seeks to fit this text to other passages, which place the seal on the foreheads of the saints (7:3; 9:4; 14:1; 22:4) and the satanic mark on the foreheads of the enemies (13:16).

inscribed on the robe, which is at the place of the thigh, or on the thigh at the place where the robe covers it? The latter interpretation would be more in line with John's references to inscriptions written on specific persons, particularly on foreheads (7:3; 9:4; 13:16; 14:1; 22:4), throughout the narrative. Here, though, he intentionally places "garment" in the controlling grammatical position. Additionally, throughout chapter 19 he has been concerned with the garments worn by the bride, the Christ-army, and the Lamb himself. The Lamb's garment, in fact, has already been famously inscribed by blood. Given these contextual clues, John probably intends to say that the name was inscribed on Christ's garment at the place where the garment covers his thigh. Just as the garments of the witnesses are a symbol of their faithful testimony (see the discussion of 19:8), so is the Lamb's garment a testimony to the true and faithful battlefield witness he is now ready to undertake.

Even so, preoccupation with the location of the name's writing draws attention away from John's primary interest, the name itself. Everyone can and should know this name. Indeed, the entire book has been about this name. It is the proclamation of this name, and its attachment to God and the Lamb, that has provoked the draconian behavior of a Babylon/Rome determined to secure this name for itself. The name, then, is also the testimony. He, not Rome and not Caesar, is King of kings and Lord of lords, the ultimate ruler of all creation (see the discussion of 17:14). This is the testimony that Jesus himself bore. It is the witness that conquers, but also the witness that believers are persecuted for proclaiming. It is the claim that Rome tries to commandeer. It is the true witness of faithful followers (cf. 1:5; 3:14). It is a political reality drawn from a cultic claim. "Thus the parousia entails the manifestation of Christ's universal rulership" (Schüssler Fiorenza, *Vision of a Just World*, 106).

### 19:17–21  The Final Battle

17 Then I saw an angel standing in the sun, and he cried out with a foreboding voice, saying to all the birds flying in midheaven: "Come, gather for the great supper of God, 18 to eat the carrion of kings, the carrion of generals, the carrion of the powerful, the carrion of horses and their riders, and the carrion of all—both the free and the enslaved, the small and the great." 19 Then I saw the beast and the kings of the earth and their armies assembled to wage war against the one seated on the horse and against his army. 20 And the beast was captured, and with it the false prophet who performed on its behalf the signs by which he deceived those who received the mark of the beast and worshiped its image; the two were thrown alive into the lake of fire that burns with sulfur. 21 The rest were killed by the sword that projects from the mouth of the one seated on the horse, and all the birds were gorged with their carrion.

**[17–18]** The end of Babylon/Rome's claim to rule begins here. With the second of three narrative introductions to a new scene (*kai eidon*, then I saw), John communicates the aftermath of a final battle that apparently took place between scenes one (19:11–16) and two (19:17–18). Using imagery with which the martial Romans would have been well familiar, he conjures a postcombat battlefield awash in blood, strewn with human corpses. The tradition in Ezek 38–39 about the kings of the earth gathering in a doomed attempt to defeat Jerusalem is certainly in the background as John foregrounds Christ's rout of God's enemies. Of particular interest is Ezek 39:17–20. There the Lord God tells the prophet to invite the birds of the air to come and feast on the flesh and blood of the princes of the earth until they are gorged and drunk.

The macabre scene is presided over by a familiar figure. The angel standing in the sun displays the same kind of grandeur evident in 7:2, with the angel who ascended from the sun; in 10:1, with the angel whose face shone like the sun; and in 18:1, with the angel who made the earth bright with his splendor. Like the angels in 7:2 and 18:1–2, this one speaks with a foreboding voice of judgment that fits the grisly battlefield before him (see the comments on 7:2 and 10:3). Apparently operating under the same orders issued by God to Ezekiel, he invites the birds flying in midheaven. Midheaven is a locale that images judgment in both 8:13 and 14:6. Clearly, the woe that the midheavenly eagle expressed in 8:13 has come to life with a dizzying vengeance here. Indeed, this apocalyptic catastrophe could well be the realization of the mysterious third woe that John never narrates (see 9:12–21).

The instruction to the invited birds in Revelation is the same as that given in Ezekiel. John's language, however, clarifies that this is the eschatological victory meal of God first mentioned in 19:9. John is once again flipping his salvation/judgment coin. These two scenes, the marriage supper of the Lamb and the flesh feast of the birds, are one and the same event; on the back side of joy and salvation (19:10) is the judgment that brings that joy and salvation about. While the faithful partake of the bounty of God inside the wedding hall, carrion feeders gorge themselves on human remains outside. The connection has to be intentional; these two texts (19:9, 17) are the only two places in Revelation where the term *deipnon* (supper) appears. Verse 18 lists all the categories of folk whose bodies litter the battlefield. The image does not just show the broad array of categories of corpses; it also demonstrates how broad was the following of the beast. The poor as well as the wealthy, slaves as well as the great ones of the earth, fell victim to Babylon/Rome's adulterous lure. Not only did they all follow the beast; they also were so successfully seduced into placing trust in its lordship and so marked by its pretensions to power (13:16) that they were willing to fight to the death for it (cf. 6:15).

**[19–21]** The third scene in this set brings closure to the first two. John now shifts from the angel and his preoccupation with the birds to those who were vanquished. He is also flipping back and forth on the timeline. In v. 17 the angel anticipates the future, when the victory has occurred. The battle is done. But here that battle is clearly not yet. John sees the beast from the sea, the kings of the earth, and their armies *before* they become apocalyptic bird food. Still, by the time this scene closes (v. 21), the destruction by the rider on the white horse (Christ) will be just as final, just as complete.

What develops is essentially a re-presentation of the Armageddon scene (16:14–16; cf. 11:7; 17:14). Considering the gore that will follow the battle, the description of the immediate aftermath of the fight is rather mundane. John is primarily concerned with the capture of the two primary combatants. The beast from the sea and the false prophet who conjures the signs that lure humans into worshiping the beast (13:11–18) are spared being victims for the battlefield feast because an even more gruesome fate awaits. They are thrown alive into the apparent eternal torment of a lake of fire that burns with the intensity of brimstone (sulfur; cf. Num 16:33, where three figures are sent into Sheol alive). Fire has been a metaphor for judgment throughout John's work (see the comments on 8:5 and 11:5). The use of fire and sulfur as an eschatological punishment of unbearable intensity is also a previous theme (14:10–11). In fact, 14:10–11 suggests an eternal suffering rather than an immediate extermination, thus lending to this scene a severity that seems cruel and unusual even for the beast and its compatriots. If there is any doubt about the long suffering implied here, that doubt is soon eliminated when the dragon is included in the fire and the three enemies of God are said explicitly to suffer eternal torment (20:10). Death and Hades are likewise included in the fire (20:14), as are a vice parade of evil humans at 21:8. This second death is the one that John counsels his followers to avoid at any and all costs. His description of its agony certainly helps his case.

In fact, when one considers John's language in terms of rhetorical effect, one gathers a clearer picture of what he is trying to do. It is not his intent to present a real picture of the judgment. He instead intends to scare hearers and readers straight back to belief in the singular lordship of God and the Lamb. Like the plagues, the lake of fire has repentance as its primary goal. John wants both to demonstrate the vulnerability of Babylon/Rome and to encourage believers to stop accommodating to it, or never to begin to do so. This is the rhetoric of behavior transformation. Whether he believes judgment will be this cruel or not is hard to say. In any case one must challenge him for presenting such a ruthless depiction. It is a brutal vision that has little place in the Christian concept of the afterlife. But again, his point is not to depict the literal afterlife, but to envision a future that will transform present behavior. The more gruesome the depiction, the more likely it is that transformation will ensue. A people who do not trust Babylon/Rome to survive will be less likely to accommodate themselves to it, even if it promises present death to all who resist its seductive charms. After all, an even greater death remains. When given the choice of that death or eternal eschatological relationship with God, John is hoping that his hearers and readers will choose appropriately and wisely. He has certainly used every means of rhetorical persuasion at his disposal to encourage the right choice.

### 20:1–15 Aftermath of the Final Battle

Chapter 20 presents John's hearers and readers with the aftermath and consequences of the war with the beast, the kings of the earth, and their armies (19:19). While the beast (Babylon/Rome) and the false prophet (the Asia Minor puppet regimes of Babylon/Rome) are burning in the lake of fire and sulfur (brimstone), and the corpses of the kings and their soldiers are being feasted upon by winged scavengers, God's judgment/justice turns its attention to the dragon. In an alternating series of narrative presentations, John illustrates the great enemy and the people of God whom it has terrorized. Drawing again from the story line of ancient combat myths (see the introduction to ch. 12), he first depicts the dragon's imprisonment (vv. 1–3). The focus then shifts to present God's witnesses: though executed by the dragon's forces, they now ready their resurrected selves for a thousand-year rule with Christ over the same dragon-deceived earth that had once been so hostile to them (vv. 4–6). Verses 7–10 refocus on a liberated dragon, who after a thousand incarcerated years still pursues a demonic desire to destroy God's people. Following the dragon's complete defeat and eternal imprisonment, those very people of God find themselves and the rest of the human creation standing before God's great judgment throne (vv. 11–15). By keeping both characterizations in view, John never lets his hearers and readers forget the reason for God's punishing actions: the dragon's assumption of a lordship it did not deserve, and its murderous oppression of any who witnessed to the contrary lordship of God and the Lamb. The alternating presentations also reveal God's ultimate vindication of those who maintain their witness despite the draconian consequences. The seer's aim is to offer a presentation of the future that decreases present fear of the evil behind Babylon/Rome and therefore reinvigorates the ethic of resistant witness.

#### 20:1–3 SATAN, LOCKED DOWN

20:1 Then I saw an angel descending from heaven with the key of the abyss and a large chain in his hand. 2 And he seized the dragon, the ancient serpent[a] who is the devil and Satan, and bound him for a thousand years. 3 He threw him into the abyss and shut and sealed it over him, so he could no longer deceive the nations, until the thousand years were completed. After this he must be released for a short time.

a. Codex Alexandrinus (A) and a few other manuscripts offer the more difficult and no doubt original reading of the description in the nominative case. As a noun in apposition to "dragon," in the accusative case, "ancient serpent" ought to be in the accusative as well; ℵ 051 𝔐 insert just this correction.

[20:1] As he did in chapter 19, John marks the introduction of new scenes with *kai eidon* ("then I saw"; cf. 19:11, 17, 19; see the discussion of 5:1). In this case the new material builds from the narrative case established at 19:11. Together the episodes form part of a larger interlude, 19:11–21:8, that separates the parallel sections 17:1–19:10 (whore/Babylon) and 21:9–22:9 (bride/Jerusalem). Framed within this interlude section is the piece about the Lamb's Parousia as a battle and the results of that battle. The first results, the imprisonment and eternal torture of the two combat generals (beast and false prophet), were reported in 19:17–21. Chapter 20 focuses on the second result: the defeat, capture, and eternal torture of the grand strategist, the commander-in-chief of evil, the dragon.

The object in John's immediate sight is an angel sweeping down from heaven. The angel's point of origin is an indication of his authority; he comes as an agent of God. The staging is reminiscent of 10:1 and 18:1, two other texts where angels descend from heaven. In each case, the objective of their descent was judgment. In 18:1, that judgment worked out as the destruction of Babylon. Here the descending angel has the destruction of the force behind Babylon on his mind. Satan, too, can and will be judged.

The angel brings two important items with him. The first is the key to the abyss. The narration immediately reminds John's hearers and readers of an earlier angel who also possessed the key to the abyss (9:1). There are several significant differences between the two angelic characters. First, the figure in 9:1 was a "fallen" angel. This one is not thrown down but comes down, like the new Jerusalem, with a heavenly directive. Second, the angel in 9:1 held the key to the shaft of the pit, not the pit itself. Its power appears to have been more limited. Finally, the angel of 9:1 was given the key, just as the four apocalyptic horsemen were given their leave (6:1–8), for a purpose beyond and even contrary to his intent. Just as God apparently knew that the unrestrained horsemen could be counted upon to unleash a havoc that God could then use for God's own purposes, so God used the angel's predictably destructive inclinations as a way of executing judgment. God allowed his access to and release of hellish chaos. However, the angel's intentions in 20:1 are in line with God's. Instead of freeing hell from the abyss as a way of inciting judgment against the evils perpetrated on earth, this angel intends to lock away the force whose deceptions create the need for that judgment. Thus this angel also wields a chain. Before being locked up, the dragon must first be bound.

[2] The angel works quickly. For the second time the dragon (see the comment on 12:3), who would compare itself to God, is engaged and defeated not

by God, but by one of God's representatives (cf. 12:7–9). Intending to diminish the dragon even as he chronicles the danger it symbolizes, John narrates that for all its history (see the discussion of ancient names and roles at 12:9), fury, and power, God considers its defeat the kind of light work that God need not even get up from the throne to accomplish. The dragon who wants to be God does not even merit God's direct engagement.

With its chain, the angel binds the dragon for a thousand years (v. 2; for parallels on the binding of evil, see Isa 24:21–22; *1 En.* 10.4–14).[1] The thousand-year period is a symbolic time that is lengthy though still transient—nothing more. Readers and hearers of John's text should not draw more from the metaphor than John himself does. John does refer to this period of time throughout the remainder of the chapter. Most often he will apply to it the definite article (vv. 3, 5, 7), suggesting that the future uses refer back to this first reference, which does not carry the definite article. Just as interesting, though, is the fact that when he first speaks of the thousand-year rule of Christ (v. 4), he once again foregoes the article, as if in that case he is introducing the concept for the first time. Textual evidence is mixed when John again speaks of Christ's thousand-year rule in v. 6. While some manuscripts include the article, others do not. Regardless of one's decision on this text-critical question—though it makes sense that John did not intend to use the definite article in v. 6—the context confirms that vv. 4 and 6 do speak of the same thousand years. The primary question is why John does not grammatically connect the thousand years of vv. 4 and 6 with the thousand-year period of vv. 2, 3, 5, and 7 by designating them as "the" thousand years, that is, "the same" thousand years introduced as the time of the dragon's incarceration. Contextually, it seems clear that John is talking about the same period. He probably did not include the article in vv. 4 and 6 because the time period functions differently when it is viewed from the standpoint of Christ's rule. Here we once again have the two-sides-of-the-same-coin perspective on judgment and salvation that operates throughout the narrative. The thousand years will be experienced in radically different ways depending on the perspective of the person experiencing them: a prelude to salvation for those who witness to the lordship of Christ, but a harbinger of judgment for those who have aligned themselves with the dragon and its beasts. The same thousand-year period can therefore "feel" different. John tries to make this case grammatically by the way he deploys the definite article.

[3] The triple mention of the dragon's binding ("cast," "locked," "sealed") is indicative of the confidence hearers and readers should have in the incarceration of God's archenemy. It is not coming out any time soon. Not in a thousand years! And even then, not of its own power and accord. The dragon's

---

1. For other Jewish parallels, see *1 En.* 18.12–16; 21.1–10; 54.1–6; *2 Bar.* 40; 56.13; *T. Levi* 18.12; *Jub.* 5.6; 10.4–14. In the New Testament, see 2 Pet 2:4; Jude 6; cf. Mark 3:27 et par.

imprisonment prevents it from accomplishing its primary agenda: deception (see the comment on 12:15). In fact, the dragon's agenda is linked inextricably with its identity. When further introducing the dragon at 12:9 (cf. 20:2), John takes care to mention that it is the great deceiver of the inhabitants of the earth (see the comments on 2:13 and 3:10). At 13:14 (cf. 19:20), John reveals his primary concern about draconian deception; its aim is to defraud the nations into believing in the dragon's lordship and the lordship of the bestial powers that represent it. According to 20:8, 10, the dragon has not only deceived the nations of the world into believing in its lordship but also convinced them to fight for that lordship. For this thousand years, however, all such activity will cease. There are serious implications not only for the dragon but also for the composition and the future prospects of the world after the Armageddon-like battle of 19:11–21. Apparently John envisioned that huge populations survive, those who did not compose the decimated armies of the kings of the earth. A deceived people are a people who once believed correctly and might believe correctly again once the source of the deception is removed. No longer vulnerable to Satan's deceptions, they have the unfettered opportunity for a millennium to recognize God's true lordship and thereby receive an eschatological relationship with God.

Would even a thousand years, though, be enough time? Time would literally tell. After the binding, Satan must be let loose (note the divine-passive formulation) for a little while (see the discussion of "after this" at 4:1). Two questions immediately arise. Why "must" Satan be released? And why for a little while?

When dealing with the apocalyptic necessity here, it is helpful to consider it in the context of the theme of apocalyptic necessity throughout the book (see the discussion of 4:1). Revelation 1:1 and 22:6 serve as bookends enclosing the story of the whole book and, when taken with the intervening chapters, answer the question: What must happen as a result of the ongoing conflict between God and Satan? Chapter 12 sets John's contemporary scene. The dragon is in pursuit of God's people (12:17). As a result, the people cry out to God for assistance (6:9–11). The dragon and the beasts are determined, however, to maintain control (chs. 12–13). In view of the predicament of God's people, God must intervene and soon. That "must" is the book's orienting apocalyptic necessity.

The apocalyptic necessity of 20:3 fits well into this larger scenario. The dragon's pursuit of God's people is historically successful precisely because the dragon has deceived the bulk of the world's people and leaders into believing in its lordship and promoting that lordship—in part by oppressing and even executing those who profess exclusively the contrary lordship of God and the Lamb. Indeed, those who profess the dragon's lordship, and its realization in Babylon/Rome, progress so well economically, socially, and politically (cf. 18:23) that even many Christians have been deceived into accommodating themselves to the dragon's lie (cf. 2:20). To redirect God's people from such an accommodating track and to vindicate those who have refused to accommodate and have paid a steep economic, social, and perhaps physical price for that resistance, God must engage the dragon and its forces. The entire book operates from this apocalyptic premise. It is this premise that leads to Satan's incarceration. Every narrative move has been driven to this point. Satan's loosing must also be a part of this drive.

Satan is loosed to make two points. First, evil resurrects: it always comes back. The faithful must always be on guard against it. That point must be made if the faithful are always to maintain their guard. In order to make it, God must set the dragon free. But God also wants to maintain not only the appearance but also the reality of control. God therefore allows only a short time of release before God engages the dragon yet again. Evil is not stronger than God. It is always subject to some form of God's regulation. Even if things look bleak, the time of difficulty will be short. That knowledge should encourage believers to endure in their witness to God's lordship.

The second point is that resurrected evil will try to deceive even after it has been incarcerated. Even after it is clear that it is not God, when the dragon's claims to lordship ought to appear clearly bogus, it will try to deceive humans into buying into that lordship (20:8, 10). God's release of the dragon therefore provides humans with the ultimate opportunity to make the right choice. God has stacked the eschatological deck in favor of the right decision. How could anyone who knows about the dragon's thousand-year incarceration, an incarceration imposed by God, think now that the dragon's lordship was greater than God's? But God does not make the decision for humans; God respects human freedom and the right to make a choice, to act for God's lordship or against it. That freedom and the actions that result from it are recorded in the books that represent God's memory (20:12). By releasing Satan, God allows that human freedom to operate; God allows humans one final chance to make the right decision—whom will they acknowledge as Lord?—and to orient their lives accordingly. God lets Satan go so that Satan can go to a wiser people and be rejected. With the moment of final judgment looming, God offers this final, weighted opportunity for humans to choose the path that leads to life. For a little while, then, for this oddly orchestrated redemptive reason, the dragon must be set free. It is not for its sake that its freedom is allowed. It is for the sake of humankind.

20:4–6 WITNESSES, REIGNING WITH CHRIST

Now that John has introduced the first scene, which prepares for the catch and release of the dragon, he switches focus to those who have been hounded by the dragon from, narratively speaking, 12:17 on. The time frame is the same thousand-year period that he has already introduced. He has said what the dragon will be doing during that time; now he describes what God's faithful witnesses will be doing.

4 Then I saw thrones and those who sat on them were given authority to judge, that is,[a] the souls of those who had been beheaded because of the testimony of Jesus, which is[b] the word of God. They had not worshiped the beast or its image and had not received its mark upon their foreheads or on their hands. They came to life and ruled with Christ a thousand years. 5 The rest of the dead did not come to life until the thousand years were completed. (This is the first resurrection.) 6 Blessed and holy is the one who has a part in the first resurrection. Over these, the second death has no authority, but they will be priests of God and of Christ and will rule with him a[c] thousand years.

a. An epexegetical or explanatory *kai*.

b. Another epexegetical or explaining *kai*; the "word of God" and the "testimony of Jesus" are mutually defining.

c. On the matter of translating the definite article, see the comment on 20:2 above. Though ℵ 046 1611 2053 2062 2329 *pc* sy[h] include the article, its omission in A 051 𝔐 represents a better contextual reading and understanding of the material.

[4] As in v. 1, the narrative marker *kai eidon* (then I saw) signals a scene shift (see the comment on 5:1). John sees thrones and figures sitting on them (cf. Dan 7:9). While he does not identify the figures on the thrones, there is a strong contextual clue. The focus in this entire subsection is on believers who have been killed because of their testimony to the lordship of God and the Lamb. John even amplifies their importance by connecting them to the executed souls at 6:9–11, whose cry for justice and judgment motivates the book's apocalyptic activity. The entire scene is a delicious realization of poetic justice. Throughout his narrative, John has used the judicial imagery of witnessing and judgment. Those who have witnessed to the lordship of God and Christ have often, like Jesus himself, done so before the tribunal/judgment seats of Roman and Asia Minor officials. Now, when it matters most, at the ultimate judgment, the tables are turned; it is the witnesses who sit enthroned, and judgment is shown ultimately to lie in their hands. Certainly this outcome makes sense in Revelation; Christ had promised that conquering witnesses would sit enthroned with him (3:21). It also makes sense in the light of the early Christian tradition that envisioned faithful believers sharing eschatological judgment duties with Christ (Matt 19:28; Luke 22:30; 1 Cor 6:2–3).

John identifies these witnesses as the souls who have been beheaded because of the testimony of Jesus, which is the word of God (see the comments on 1:2 and 6:9). On a first reading, it appears that he is talking about a subset of those who have been executed. Beheading was only one of many forms of Roman execution.[2] Could he have intended to say that only those specifically killed in this manner would reign with Christ as judges on the heavenly thrones? That is unlikely. John's language is metaphorical rather than literal. John conjures a particularly brutal form of capital punishment here in order to continue building momentum for God's final retaliatory response of justice/judgment. His clear paralleling of this text with 6:9 indicates that he thinks of these executed souls as the same group. In fact, when the verses are set side by side, the only differences are the inclusion in 6:9 of the phrases "under the altar," "they had given," and "to Jesus," and the inverted order of the phrases "because of the word of God" and "because of the witness [to Jesus]." "Beheaded" in 20:4 is John's way of amplifying the term "executed" in 6:9.

John is not talking about another group of witnesses when he goes on to laud those who did not worship the beast (cf. 13:4) or its image or take its mark on their foreheads or hands (see 13:13–17). Appealing once again to an epexegetical, or explanatory, *kai* ("and"; see the discussion of 1:2), which uses a second clause to clarify the one that precedes it, he means to say: "the souls of those who have been beheaded, . . . who did not worship." These are the people who live and rule with Christ for the thousand years that Satan is incarcerated (vv. 1–3).

It is perhaps the Christian understatement of the last two millennia to say that this thousand-year reign with Christ has proved to be something of an interpretive problem. The less difficult problems lie with the issues of resurrection and rule that precede the talk of a thousand-year period, so it is helpful to start there. Though John does not use the language of resurrection here, he will resort to it in vv. 5 and 6 to describe this phenomenon of executed souls coming to life. Here, he appeals to the same verb *zaō* (live) that he uses to describe Jesus' resurrection at 1:18 and 2:8. It is also the same verb used in Ezek 37:10 LXX to describe the valley's dry bones as they take on a miraculous new physical life. Like Jesus, though dead, the Hebrew bones and the Christian witnesses return to life. Apparently, this is a different form of life than that enjoyed by executed witnesses as souls in heaven, for John uses the verb to distinguish between that spiritual existence and this obviously new one. This "living" is also clearly not the same kind of earthly life they enjoyed before their execution. Yet it must be a form of corporeal existence, for they enjoy this life for a thousand years on this physical earth, and they are presumably seen by and in relationship with

2. Aune suggests, since "there were several means of inflicting the death penalty under Roman law," that "it seems extremely unlikely that all of the martyrs would have been executed by decapitation" (3:1086). Rome's legal system used two forms of death penalty: *summum supplicium*, the more vindictive form, involving burning alive, crucifixion, and exposure to wild animals; and *capite puniri*, simple death by decapitation. There were two types of decapitation: by the sword and by the axe. "Provincial governors had the right to execute by sword only, not by the axe, javelin, club, or noose."

the physical humans over whom they rule. Like Jesus' own resurrection, theirs must be a bodily resurrection of some sort (cf. Luke 24:42–43; 1 Cor 15). It is with some kind of physicality that they now live. To what end? To rule (cf. Dan 7:27). With Christ. As promised (Rev 5:10; cf. 22:5).

On the thousand-year term, it is helpful to begin with the observation that too much has been made of a concept to which John gave very little attention. This interim or intermediate period between the historical and the future eschatological time occurs when John essentially merges two different Jewish eschatological traditions into a unique concept that fits his apocalyptic staging. Prophetic eschatology primarily anticipated a relationship with God that would take place within history. Aptly, for a people who had no concept of an afterlife but understood this historical existence as the place where human destiny— including, through one's progeny, the longevity of one's name and person— was worked out, the expectation for future redemption lay in the transformation of this-worldly existence into God's kingdom. In the apocalyptic theology ushered in formally in the work of Daniel and developed in many succeeding Jewish and early Christian works, however, this historical creation was understood to be so utterly corrupted that redemption could come only from beyond. The faithful anticipated the inbreaking of God's future kingdom, which would devastate the present reality and transform it into a new heaven and new earth. In John's time and, further, in John's own work, the two scenarios merge "into a scheme in which a this-worldly messiah brought this-worldly salvation during a transitional kingdom, which was then superseded by eternal apocalyptic salvation in the new world" (Boring, *Revelation*, 207). This intermediate, transitional kingdom was developed in several Jewish apocalyptic texts (see *4 Ezra* 7.26–44; 12.31–34; *1 En.* 91.11–17; *2 Bar.* 29.1–30:5; 40.1–4; 72.2–74.3), and its duration was variously measured as 40 years, 400 years, and an indefinite period. "The idea of a messianic kingdom of 1,000 years is apparently original with John" (Reddish 385). The intent, though, was symbolic rather than literal. John meant to suggest a time that, though lengthy, was transitory.

Focus on the literal span of time, however, has resulted in a fascination with millennial categories (from the Latin *mille*, thousand, and *annus*, year). Contemporary reflection falls into several basic categories. Amillennialism understands the thousand-year period to be a spiritual symbol for the reign of Christ in the church. No literal reign at the end of history is therefore anticipated. The church experiences the millennium already within history in this world. Postmillennialists believe that Christ's return will occur after a golden era of peace on earth. Human progress moves inexorably in the direction of righteousness until a moment of consummation will herald the new era. Believing the world to be too corrupt to progress toward righteousness on its own, though, premillennialists expect that Christ will first need to come and establish control and direction. Only through such divine intervention can the new era be achieved.

Dispensational premillennialists actually look to contemporary events for signs of that impending intervention by Christ.[3] Boring rightly rejects all of these speculative views as literal misreading of John's highly metaphorical language (*Revelation*, 205–6). John gave brief attention to the time period and did not expect it to receive the interpretive weight it has been accorded.

The period of Christ's rule no doubt has the same objective as the period of the dragon's incarceration. Witnesses are to see in it the truth that despite the circumstances of their oppression and even executions, God's vindication is assured. Judgment, and the justice that will come for them from that judgment, is imminent. The witnesses have only to hold on. Not only will they ultimately receive eschatological relationship with God; they also will obtain a historical, this-worldly reward that will see them rule over the very world that has persecuted and destroyed them. Still, the time period, though significant, is to be transitory. Like all of John's hearers and readers, these witnesses should focus less on the thousand years than on the new heaven and new earth to follow it. That future focus will bring even more energy to the present ethic of nonaccommodating, resistant witness to the lordship of God and the Lamb for which John appeals in Revelation. As Schüssler Fiorenza rightly points out, the focus should not be on the millennium itself, but on its function as a reward for those who have maintained their resistance to the lordship claims of draconian Babylon/Rome (*Vision of a Just World*, 108). Many contemporary churches probably spin their interpretive wheels on millennial definitions and strategies because social and political resistance too often is still too dangerous a course to undertake.

[5] John moves immediately to clarify what happens to the rest of the dead. They stay dead. This is not a punishment: their time of resurrection is also coming. This coming to life of the executed witnesses is only the first resurrection—the very designation clearly implies at least a second resurrection. It is a reward for their testimony. Since there are no other indications of such a concept in Jewish literature, it is also a concept likely developed by John himself. As Caird observes, "John seems to want the best of both worlds. He believes that the ultimate destiny of the redeemed is in the heavenly city, but he also retains the earthly paradise, the millennium. He therefore requires not one but two resurrections: the first resurrection restores the martyrs to life for their millennial reign, the second brings all the dead before the great white throne" (254).

During this thousand years, if the rest of the dead stay dead, presumably those who are already living and were not destroyed in the 19:11–21 battle stay alive. They will live under the rule of Christ and the executed, resurrected faithful. There is no rapture moment when the living faithful are taken up into a heavenly safe zone. The living faithful remain with the living unfaithful. And

---

3. For an excellent chart comparing the various millennial perspectives, see Reddish 391.

instead of being raptured out of the world, the resurrected souls are brought back to life in this world.

[6] For the second and final time in his text, John applies the word "resurrection." Those who take part in this first one are blessed and holy. In this fifth of his seven beatitudes (see the discussion of macarisms at 14:13 and 19:9), John once again presents both an indicative reality and an imperative appeal. It is easy to understand why those who rule with Christ would be considered blessed. In making that case, though, John also encourages his readers and hearers to maintain resistance even to the point where their recalcitrance might cost them their lives. Writing before the millennium, his description of the blessed state of those resurrected in the millennium serves as present ethical motivation. Everyone now should aspire, through the fact and manner of their testimony, to be a part of that first resurrection. The unique double predicate, blessed and holy (i.e., set apart), is a further reflection of the unique status of these resurrected souls. Like all the other witnesses (whose testimony did not lead to death), they are blessed. Unique among all the other witnesses and humankind in general, they experience the glory of the first resurrection.

In addition, the second death (2:11; 20:14; 21:8)—an eternal suffering that follows resurrection from the first, earthly death—has no authority over them (see the discussion of first-death and second-death cosmology in Revelation at 9:6). This does not mean that *only* they escape the second death. A final judgment awaits where others, including no doubt witnesses whose testimony did not result in their deaths, will also find eschatological relationship with God. These faithful witnesses find assurance and comfort early on, though, because the eschatological judge has already ruled in their favor.

As a way of bracketing this section, John now repeats what he has already explained at the end of 20:4: these resurrected souls will rule with Christ for the thousand years of the dragon's imprisonment. Operating with Exod 19:6 in mind (cf. Isa 61:6), John adds here the realization of a promise he had made earlier, that these kings with Christ will also be priests (1:6; 5:10; cf. 22:5). Whereas earlier he had restricted their priestly relationship to God, here he adds Christ, a further indication of his functional identification of the two. To serve one in worship is to serve the other; to witness to the lordship of one is to witness to the lordship of the other.

### 20:7–10 SATAN, THE LAST STAND

7 When the thousand years are completed, Satan will be released from his prison, 8 and he will go forth to deceive the nations that are at the four corners of the earth, Gog and Magog, to assemble them for the war. Their number is like the sand of the sea. 9 They marched up over the breadth of the earth and surrounded the camp of the saints and the beloved city. Then

fire came down from heaven and devoured them. 10 And the devil who deceived them was thrown into the lake of fire and sulfur, where the beast and the false prophet were, too, and they will be tormented day and night forever and ever.

[7] John shifts focus back to the dragon and closes out the narration of its demise that he began in vv. 1–3. He begins by corroborating what was promised in the earlier section. At the end of the thousand years, God sets Satan loose (another divine-passive construction: Satan "will be released [by God]").

[8] Apparently, the combat debacle of 19:11–21 was not enough. Even after a thousand incarcerated years to mull over the rout, the dragon, perhaps delusional, harbors the hope that it can still defeat God's forces. Once liberated, the parolee goes about doing the very thing that got it imprisoned in the first place; it tries to deceive the nations—which apparently were not completely destroyed in the first "final" battle—to join yet another ill-fated attempt to assume the lordship that belongs exclusively to God.

Earlier, John relayed that the rider on the white horse struck down the nations and shepherded them with an iron rod (19:15). That "striking down" included destruction, as 19:17–21 made clear. It apparently also included disciplining. The shepherding imagery implies that a remnant of nations remained, those who were not slain by the Word on the battlefield, together with the kings and their armies. It is these nations, scattered across John's visionary world (i.e., the four corners of the earth; on the universality implied in this image, see the comment on 7:1; cf. Isa 11:12; Ezek 7:2), that are apparently now the subject of the dragon's deceit. Despite the fact that Christ, and no doubt the resurrected souls who rule with him, have tried for over a thousand years to shepherd these nations toward an understanding of God's rightful lordship, the dragon believes it can yet change the course of their cultic, social, and political loyalties.

At this point John returns to a reliance upon Ezekiel's visions for the prosecution of his own. Having already appealed to the imagery in Ezek 37 in his presentation of the resurrection of the executed souls as an eschatological updating of the vision of the valley of dry bones (Rev 20:4–6), he now imagines the threat to that restored community to be the same one that plagued the prophet's restored Israel: Gog and Magog from Ezek 38–39. Ezekiel prophesied that a hostile nation would hound the rejuvenated people of Israel from the remotest parts of the world in the north (Ezek 38:6, 15) and would attack them in the latter days, but be utterly defeated. He identified the leader behind the invasion force as Gog, the prince of Meshech and Tubal (38:2–3; 39:1). Gog's land was called Magog. As a prophetic symbol, Gog represented one of the same truths expressed by the dragon's liberation from the abyss in Revelation: even after restoration is achieved and peace is restored, evil slogs its way back into the personal and national story. Pablo Richard's analysis is perceptive:

"Gog attacks Israel when it has returned from exile and is living in security. Gog expresses the persistence of the power of evil, a power that only God can destroy and that is continually lying in wait for God's people" (149). In Ezekiel, that threat was localized in a single national entity; in Revelation, Gog and Magog morph into dual national realities who symbolize every remaining nation from every compass point in the world. These are the forces that the dragon tries to deceive. John's identification of them as Gog and Magog suggests that they are predisposed to receive the dragon's message sympathetically.

The dragon is successful in stirring Gog and Magog to "the" war.[4] John appends the definite article to "war" because this final war effort is yet another attempt at the decisive triumph that the dragon has been plotting since it first set out against God's people (12:17). Throughout his narration John has spoken of vain attempts to prosecute *the* war (11:7; 12:17; 13:7; 16:14; 19:19). Every war effort has represented an attempt to unleash the final, decisive attack, the one that would topple God and God's forces and commandeer lordship for the dragon. With Gog and Magog's accompanying forces as great in number as the grains of sand by the sea (cf. Josh 11:4; Judg 7:12; 1 Sam 13:5; 1 Macc 11:1), this effort appears to be the most likely to succeed.

[9] Because they gather from all across the world, it makes sense for John to say that the Gog and Magog forces rally from the expanse of the earth (cf. Hab 1:6). In their maneuvering, they go "up," because their target is the elevated city of Jerusalem, to which people in Israelite and Jewish idiom always went up, never down (Ezra 1:3; Ps 122:4; Isa 2:3; Jer 31:6; Obad 21; Mic 4:2; see Aune 3:1096). Once at their target, they follow the accepted military tactics of the time; they surround the city and bring it under siege (2 Kgs 6:14; Isa 29:3; 36:1–3; 1 Macc 15:14; Luke 19:43; 21:20). Indeed, John's hearers and readers would have remembered that only two decades earlier, Rome's legions had gone up to Jerusalem, surrounded it, besieged it, and destroyed it. This visionary threat would have had a vicious ring of historical truth to it.

John describes the gathering of God's people in two ways. With "camp," he means to jog their sacred memories of Israel's exodus wanderings in the wilderness. No doubt this image was meant to convey both the brutal historical reality and the hope that promised to transform it. John's people, too, were in a wilderness, beset by the occupying force of Babylon/Rome, their destruction threatened by it. Yet even as that threat loomed, they, like the wandering faithful from their past, had visions of a promised land pervaded by the peace that comes from eschatological relationship with God. With "beloved city," he

---

4. Cf. Aune (3:1095): "The motif of the gathering of the hostile nations for an attack on Israel, and particularly on Jerusalem, is a stock motif in Jewish apocalyptic, though it is used in a variety of ways." He points to Joel 3:2; Zech 12:1–9; 14:2; *4 Ezra* 13.5, 34–35; *1 En.* 56.7; 90.13–19; *Sib. Or.* 3.663–68; 1QM 1.10–11; 15.2–3; and Lactantius, *Inst.* 7.17.10–11.

means to remind his hearers and readers that this is God's city, the place of God's temple and God's presence, the holy city (11:2; 21:2, 10, 14–16, 18–19, 21, 23; 22:14, 19), which God would one day reclaim and refashion, where God would ultimately dwell directly and intimately with God's people (21:22). Even besieged, the historical city therefore remains a defiant eschatological symbol of God's presence and God's protection.

In this particular case, God makes good immediately on the promise of that protection. God intervenes directly. John describes the victory with the familiar biblical image of fire dispatched from heaven that devours the enemies of God's people (2 Kgs 1:9–14; cf. Luke 12:49). In fact, this is the very method used by God in Ezek 39:6 to destroy the forces of Gog (cf. Ezek 38:22).

[10] Like the beast and the false prophet before him, the deceiving dragon is captured after the defeat of its forces and thrown alive with them into the lake of fire and brimstone (see the comments on 14:10–11 and 19:20; cf. Matt 25:41). John wants to make sure that his hearers and readers perceive the tie between the dragon's fate and that of the beast and false prophet. He therefore mentions them specifically. Presumably they have been burning alive in this hellhole for a thousand years by the time the dragon is thrown in with them. Now the consequence they have endured will be shared by the dragon. What 19:20 did not state explicitly, this verse does: the punishment will not be a one-time moment of apocalyptic annihilation, but eternal suffering.

This portrait of God imposing eternal suffering seems as un-Christlike a punishment as imaginable. Yet John is dealing with the twin concepts of justice and mercy/grace. For him, one cannot exist without the other. For the evil that has been perpetrated, there needs to be justice, and he conceives of it in its most undiluted form as eternal suffering in the lake of fire and sulfur (brimstone). It is important to remember, however, that this is a figurative and not a literal "lake." What John is describing is not real, physical torture but the kind of continuous, perpetual spiritual torment that he imagines must occur when a being is separated forever from the presence of God. If it is God's presence that brings vitality, peace, security, hope, and indeed "life" to the human spirit, then to be separated from that presence forever must be equivalent to a kind of eternal agony. John can think of no other way to express the force and reality of that spiritual agony than the physical one of torture. It is an inappropriate image, to be sure, for a twenty-first-century sensibility. John, however, was operating with his own and his hearers' and readers' first-century sensibilities. He was trying to think of an image that would have "teeth" for them, an image that would shock persons who were accommodating to the draconian lordship demands of Rome into resisting them and testifying in word and deed to the lordship of God and the Lamb instead. He wanted them to fear being forever separated from the presence of God. His most forceful metaphorical attempt at conveying what that separation would feel like is the lake of fire and sulfur (brimstone). A twenty-first-century effort should focus on the language of separation from God's presence and look for a contemporary metaphor appropriate to that separation, one that does not include the image of physical torture, whether eternal or otherwise.

20:11–15  WITNESSES AND EVERYONE ELSE, JUDGMENT DAY

This section is formed by two subunits, both introduced by the narrative marker *kai eidon* ("then I saw," 20:1, 4; see the discussion of 5:1). Verse 11 is a theophanic presentation of God's coming. Verses 12–15 then chronicle the results of that coming in terms of God's judgment. The complete section may well be an expansion on the judgment vision of 11:18.

> 11 Then I saw a great dazzling throne and the one seated on it, from whose presence earth and heaven fled, but[a] there was no place for them. 12 And I saw the dead—the great and the small—standing before the throne. And books were opened, and another book, which is the Book of Life, was opened, and the dead were judged by what was recorded in those books, according to their works. 13 And the sea gave up the dead in it, and Death and Hades gave up the dead in them, and all were judged according to their works. 14 Then Death and Hades were thrown into the lake of fire. This is the second death: the lake of fire. 15 And if anyone was not found recorded in the Book of Life, that one was thrown into the lake of fire.

> a. The *kai* is adversative: "but."

**[11]** Though his primary preoccupation will be with humankind before God's judgment throne, John begins with a look at the throne itself. The throne reminds hearers and readers of the first scene featuring God's throne (4:2; cf. Ezek 1:26–28; Dan 7:9). Among Old Testament references, Dan 7:9 is most important here. Like Revelation, Daniel uses the throne as a way of introducing the books of judgment that will be opened in God's presence. The role the throne plays in the process of the final judgment for John, therefore, comes directly from Daniel. The throne's dazzling color is the color of righteousness and victory (see the comment on 3:4). Its imposing size befits the stature of God as the Almighty (see the discussion of 11:17). John's description of God as the one seated on the throne is a reminder that God is the one who rules with true lordship (see the comment on 4:2).

The judgment motif is reinforced by the fleeing of earth and heaven before the presence of God (6:14; 16:20; cf. Ps 114:3–7; 2 Pet 3:7, 10, 12). Everything represented by the old earth and heaven, particularly resistance to the lordship of God and the Lamb, has no place in the coming new heaven and new earth. Recognizing this, the old heaven and old earth make a preemptive effort to save themselves by running away. Given God's universal dominance, one wonders where exactly they think they are going! There is, in fact, nowhere they can go. Their flight is a metaphor for their destruction. Since separation from God's divine presence is death, the very effort to escape God is by definition an act of self-destruction.

[12] Now that the old heaven and old earth are no longer blocking his view, John can see (*kai eidon*, "and I saw") the horde of resurrected dead, all of them, those who in life were insignificant and significant (cf. Rev 11:18; 13:16; 19:5, 8), standing before God's throne. Though he does not specify it as such, this must be for John the post-thousand-year rule "second resurrection," which his reference to the first resurrection in vv. 5 and 6 implied. In the first resurrection, only those who had been executed for testifying to the lordship of God and the Lamb obtained a spiritual, though nonetheless also corporeal, rebirth (see the discussion of 20:4). This time everybody, both righteous and unrighteous, lives again (cf. John 5:29). For some, though, the moment—and the exhilaration that no doubt went with it—will be brief.

That is because books, based on the judgment books of Dan 7:10, are opened (the divine-passive formulation indicates that God opens them). The content in these books will determine the eschatological fate of all those standing before the throne. John has already said that those in the first resurrection have a sealed fate of eschatological relationship with God. Whatever misdeeds might have been recorded about them in the books of judgment (no human would be without error!) are outweighed by the fact that they witnessed to the lordship of God and the Lamb so vigorously that their testimony cost them their lives. This truth is an indication that for John the primary ethic, the primary work, is witnessing.

For all others, however, a balance of "works" must apparently be weighed. The books are metaphors for God's remembering human behavior throughout a human lifetime.[5] Proper works-behavior is rewarded, while improper works-behavior is punished (Rev 2:2, 5, 6, 19, 22, 23, 26; 3:1, 2, 8, 15; 14:13; 18:6; 20:13; 22:12; cf. 11:18; 20:15; Ps 28:4; cf. Sir 16:12). Witnessing, no doubt, remains the primary expected behavior for which a life of eschatological relationship with God is the reward. It is this behavior that the book's entire energy has worked to secure. But other behaviors also matter, and they too are accounted for in God's memory (21:8).

Nevertheless, this possibility of a books-based "works righteousness," where a person's behavior accounts completely for that person's eschatological relationship with God or lack thereof, is tempered in this very verse by John's reference to another book, one that stands alone. This is the Book of Life

5. As Reddish notes, "The idea of such heavenly record books was widespread in the ancient Near Eastern world, including in Jewish literature (biblical and nonbiblical sources; cf. Dan 7:10; Mal 3:16; *4 Ezra* 6:20; *1 En.* 47:3; 81:1–4; 89:61–77; 90:17, 20; 98:7–8; *2 Bar.* 24:1)" (389).

(cf. Exod 32:32–33; Ps 69:28; Isa 4:3; Dan 12:1; Luke 10:20; Phil 4:3; Heb 12:23), which has already made several appearances in John's narrative (3:5; 13:8; 17:8; cf. 20:15; 21:27). In it, names are graciously written—by God (divine passive)—from the beginning of creation. Everyone whose name appears in this book will have an eschatological relationship with God (see the discussion of 13:8; cf. Dan 12:1). By joining these two books—one representing grace, the other representing works—in the same verse, John holds in positive tension these two powerful theological concepts. He recognizes the freedom that God gives to each human to make choices, and he weighs the responsibility those choices bear, but he never allows the ultimate eschatological decision to rest with anyone other than God.

**[13–14]** Verse 13 is a colorful repetition of what was just said (v. 12) except that, if taken literally, it would be chronologically out of place with v. 12. Verse 13 describes the actual resurrection whose consequences have been considered in v. 12. Before the judgment depicted in v. 12 can take place, this "second" resurrection must happen. It happens on land and sea. Sailors and others who earned their living on the sea would have been buried at sea and thus need to be distinguished from those buried on land, who after death would have found their way to the underworld of Hades (see the comment on 9:1–2). Here, as elsewhere in the book, John mentions Death and Hades together because they form a pair (see the discussions of 1:18 and 6:8). Death is the personification that apparently rules over the underworld region of Hades. Operating together, they simultaneously release the souls in their care. The point to be made here is the same point that John made in v. 12: *all* the dead are now raised. The scope of this act is universal.

Death and Hades are now cast into the second death (see discussion of first and second death cosmology in Revelation at 9:6), which is the lake of fire (20:10; see the comments on 14:10–11 and 19:20). It is now clear, given their roommates in the flames, that even when they acted in response to the Lamb's breaking of the fourth seal and the cherubim's calling voice (6:7), these forces are enemies of God yet used only to further God's purpose of judgment (cf. death as the last enemy in 1 Cor 15:26).

**[15]** The already-crowded lake of fire (i.e., second death) gets even more crowded still. What was assumed in v. 12 now comes to pass. Those whose names were not found in the Book of Life are, with the beast, false prophet, dragon, Death, and Hades, thrown into the eternal suffering that is eschatological separation from God.

## 21:1–8  A New Creation

Like his prophetic forebears, John offers future visions that have a present ethical purpose. He declares what will, or perhaps better said in this apocalyptic setting, what *must* be, so that those who hear and read his words, knowing the landscape of the future, will direct their lives in ways that conduct them toward a beneficent engagement with that future. In other words, John shows the future of an eschatological relationship with God—pictured as a new Jerusalem—and what that relationship requires so that people can act now in ways that will enable them to participate in such a relationship then. Every Jew, every Gentile—indeed, every person from every nation—is exhorted, through the hearing and reading of this vision, either to maintain a faithful life that witnesses to the lordship of God and the Lamb or to repent and begin one.

Revelation 21:1–8 divides naturally into two sections, each headlined by the voice of a divine speaker. In vv. 1–4 an unidentified voice from the heavenly throne announces God's new creation as a place devoid of pain and suffering and the tears they cause. In vv. 5–8 God then confirms the truth of that vision and distinguishes those who will participate in it from those who surely will not.

21:1 Then I saw a new heaven and a new earth. For the first heaven and the first earth passed away, and the sea was no more. 2 And I saw the holy city, new Jerusalem, descending from heaven from God, prepared as a bride adorned for her husband. 3 And I heard a loud voice from the throne, saying, "Indeed, the dwelling of God is with people, and God will dwell with them, and they will be God's peoples,[a] and God, Godself, will be with them as their God,[b] 4 and God will wipe away every tear from their eyes, and death will be no more, nor will mourning or crying or pain exist any more, because the former things have passed away." 5 Then the one seated on the throne said, "Indeed, I make all things new," and he said, "Write, for these words are trustworthy and true." 6 God also said to me, "It is done! I am the Alpha and the Omega, the beginning and the end. To the thirsty I will give freely from the spring of living water. 7 The one who conquers will inherit these things, and I will be that person's God and that person will be my child. 8 But as for the cowardly, the faithless, the vile, the murderers, the fornicators, the sorcerers, the idolaters, and all the liars, their portion is in the lake that burns with fire and sulfur, that is, the second death."

a. On the plural *laoi* (peoples), see the comment on v. 3 below. The textual evidence seems equally weighted, with P 051ˢ 1006 1611 1841 1854 2062ᶜᵒᵐ 𝔐ᴷ lat sy supporting the singular *laos*, and with ℵ A 046 2030 2050 2053 2062ᵗˣᵗ 2329 𝔐ᴬ ar; Irˡᵃᵗ supporting *laoi* (though Metzger argues a slight preference from the evidence for *laoi*; see *Textual Commentary,* 765); yet John's universal interests indicate a preference for the plural form.

b. The more difficult and therefore preferred reading includes the material rendered in brackets in NA²⁷: *autōn theos* ("[as] their God"). This reading is supported by A 2030 2050 2053 (ᵗˣᵗ 2062) 2329 *al* vg; Irˡᵃᵗ. Because the two words have the appearance of a clarification of grammar, the renderings supported by 𝔐ᴷ gig (*ho theos met' autōn estai*, God will be with them); ℵ 1 *al* sin; Aug (*ho theos estai met' autōn*, God will be with them); 051ˢ (1854) 𝔐ᴬ (*ho theos estai met' autōn theos autōn*, God will be with them as their God); and 1006 1611 1841 *pc* (*ho theos met' autōn estai theos*, God will be God with them) are due consideration.

**[21:1]** Though this is a new vision, its logic flows through events that have occurred from 19:11 forward; the combat victories secured through the deployment of God's word (cf. 19:13, 15) lead appropriately here. John makes this point structurally by introducing the section with the familiar *kai eidon* (then I saw), which he uses to launch new scenes in an ongoing narration (see the discussion of 5:1, cf. 19:11, 17, 19; 20:1, 4, 11, 12). According to 20:11, a vacuum of sorts has opened up in the cosmos. The fleeing (i.e., destruction) of heaven and earth before the oncoming presence of God created a void, which God now fills by establishing a new heaven and a new earth. Both Jewish and Christian traditions guide John as he develops his imagery now. In Isaiah, God promises the creation of a new heaven and new earth for an Israel whose hopes for a life of promise in the old earth have been dashed through the tragedy of Babylonian exile (Isa 65:17; 66:22). *First Enoch* 91.16 offers a Jewish apocalyptic example of the same expectation (see *1 En.* 45.4; 72.1; *Sib. Or.* 5.212). In 2 Pet 3:13 the author counsels weary Christ-believers to maintain their hope for a new heaven and new earth, where righteousness will reign. Paul speaks less specifically about believers as new creations in Christ at 2 Cor 5:17 and Gal 6:15.

John's intended creation, though new, will not be completely discontinuous from the one that went before it. When God declares at Rev 21:5 that God will make all things new, it is important to note precisely what the language intends. God is taking what is old and transforming it. Out of the destruction that occurs in the various plagues and battles for creation, God will weave God's new thing. The old will remain a constituent part of the new, but it will be fiercely transfigured. Boring is therefore right to say, "God does not make 'all new things,' but 'all things new'" (*Revelation*, 220). Beale appropriately directs readers to Paul's discussion of the spiritual body, which is a transfigured "new" thing established upon the image and no doubt the foundation of the "old" physical body (1 Cor 15): "Despite the discontinuities, the new cosmos will be an identifiable counterpart to the old cosmos and a renewal of it, just as the body will be raised without losing its former identity" (1040). To be sure, the resurrected body is a totally new and completely unique entity, yet it cannot be comprehended apart from a knowledge of what "body-ness" is. That comprehension finds its locus in none other than the physical body that must die so that the spiritual body might be resurrected. So, too, from the remains of the old heaven and old earth, a new heaven and a new earth, new bodily entities, are resurrected. Corporeal, they house a new city and the resurrected spiritual bodies that will now occupy it (souls; see the comment on 20:4). Catherine and Justo González make the important point that John values the physical earth in a way that must not be dismissed (137). Too eagerly, contemporary Christians profess, proclaim, and anticipate a heavenly salvation so spiritual that its ethereal existence completely separates resurrected believers from the earth and the evil its physicality allegedly signifies. John's vision, by contrast, redeems the earth as a part of God's *good* creation and as the locus of God's grand re-creation. A witness for God and the Lamb does not dream of escaping the world. A witness for God and the Lamb works with God to transform the world (see the comment on 12:11).

What is destroyed completely and irrevocably is the sea. Unlike even the archenemy dragon, the beasts from the sea and land, Death and Hades, all of whom writhe eternally in the lake of fire and sulfur (brimstone), the sea ceases to exist altogether. Perhaps this is appropriate since the sea symbolizes for John, as it did for Jewish and contemporaneous Christian literature, the chaotic source of defiance to God's sovereignty (see the discussion of 4:6–8a). According to Paul, Death was the last enemy (1 Cor 15:26). According to John's presentation here, if that statement is correct, it is correct for humans, not for God. For God, the last enemy is the one that acts as source for every other enemy. It is therefore appropriate that its demise is announced at the very moment when God's final stage in the reclamation of heaven and earth reaches its climax. In a powerful re-creation and escalation of the Genesis endeavor, God does not tame the sea by imposing land upon it; God orders the new cosmos by completely removing it.

[2] John breaks up his *kai eidon* (then I saw) opening by inserting the object of his vision between the two words. Following his sighting of the new heaven and new earth, apparently focusing more sharply this time, he locks in on a single city, the holy—and also new—Jerusalem. He will return to this initial viewing in another context at 21:10, where the countercomparison with the harlotrous city Babylon (17:1–19:10) begins (21:9–22:9). In this text, instead of using Jerusalem as a point of comparison with its narrative negative, he introduces it as the new place of living for the resurrected followers of God and the Lamb. In so doing, he highlights three of its key attributes: holy, new, and urban.

Isaiah calls Jerusalem the holy city in a context that, like this Johannine one, speaks of the beautiful garments that symbolically adorn it (Isa 52:1; cf. 48:2). Many other voices, both Jewish (e.g., Neh 11:1, 18) and early Christian (e.g., Matt 4:5) envision the municipality as a holy place. Holiness as an attribute of God, and by extension an attribute of the things and people of God, denotes radical otherness. John calls the witnesses "holy ones" or "saints" throughout Revelation because through their faithful witness they are set apart from others who either promote the lordship of Rome or accommodate themselves to it (see the comment on 5:8). To be a saint, therefore, is not to be better than others in an ethical or moral sense, but to be separated from them because of one's relationship with and activity for the holy God. In this sense holiness is an acquired trait for everyone and everything except God; it is acquired through relationship with God. As John will note, this city descends, and thus takes its characterization, from God.

Once again working from Isaiah's lead, John describes this holy city as new. As Beale observes, "Isa. 62:1–2 refers to 'Jerusalem' as that which 'will be called by a new name' at the time of its end-time glorification. This new name is then explained in Isa. 62:3–5 as signifying a new, intimate marriage relationship that Israel will have with God" (1040).

The new holy city is, finally, a city. John signals a salvific identity that is neither individualized nor spiritualized but concretized in the communal relationships that exist in an urban environment. John's view of eschatological relationship with God is not some tranquil, idyllic, one-on-one encounter in a sanctuary of eternal solitude, cloistered away from the hustling, bustling interaction with others that is so much a part of civic life on the old and apparently the new earth. Eschatological living is envisioned instead as a complex, other-connected and no doubt other-oriented relationship that brings with it all of the social and political ramifications that life in any city engenders. John's view of the future is that the believing community will find its ultimate meaning and life in urban rapport. For many contemporary Christians, this part of his vision is as scary as the segments that deal with the dragon and the plagues. Cities are inclusive, teeming, often dangerous and riotous places, where resources can be stretched to the breaking point and success—indeed, even survival—comes only when citizens work interdependently, negotiate strenuously, and compromise sincerely. Knowing all this, John believes that the city represents the most appropriate "heaven" metaphor available to him.

The seer maintains his municipal focus when he next describes the new Jerusalem as coming down out of heaven from God. This descent makes three points. First, the language of descent images judgment (see the discussion of 10:1). This scene, though, is a postjudgment scene. The imagery still fits because, for John, the reverse side of judgment has always been salvation. The two exist together. A person's or people's life choices determine whether these eschatological acts are received as judgment or salvation. Since those who will witness this descent are people whose names are written in the Lamb's Book of Life (20:15), it makes sense that the event would be experienced now as salvific. Second, the city's descent establishes the relationship with God that authorizes it and marks it as holy. Third, it is the fact that the city descends from the heavens onto the earth that establishes it as historical and this-worldly. Again it must be said, there is no rapture in the book of Revelation (see the comments on 3:10 and 19:11). Instead of believers being raptured up into the heavens, the city of God is lowered down onto the transformed earth. The ratification of the earth as a place of God's engagement and not a place from which to escape cannot be imaged in any stronger terms. Working for the transformation of the earth is important because the transformed earth is where God works even now to establish God's holy city and thus God's eschatological relationship with God's people.

God's eschatological relationship with God's people is so close that John once again resorts to the marriage metaphor to describe it (see the discussion of 19:7–8; cf. 21:9; Gal 4:26; Heb 11:16). The city, which is more a people than a place, is envisioned as a bride betrothed to the Lamb. John's use of the word *nymphē* (bride) in 21:9 and 22:17 represents the only occurrence of the word in early Christian literature (Aune 3:1121). At 19:7–8 the more neutral and common term *gynē* (woman, wife) contextually calls for the translation "wife." Once again, John works from Isaianic roots; in describing the holy city, Isa 52:1 describes the beautiful garments that adorn it, and more particularly, 61:10 speaks of God clothing Zion with garments of salvation as a bride and groom adorn themselves. The emphasis in Revelation on their bridal identity as a people develops explicitly from this language of the bride's preparation. As was explained already at 19:7–8, the dress that adorns the bride is made from the fabric of witnessing to the lordship of God and the Lamb. The people are adorned by their own triumphant witnessing! (see the discussion of 12:11). The passive formulation of the verb *hetoimazō* (prepare) reminds them, however, of a critical fact. God has given them the ability of witnessing; what they have achieved comes from God (see the comment on 19:7–8).

There is obviously a bit of symbol confusion here. If the city is the people of God, one has to wonder how the people of God can also live there. Such questions of logic mute the visionary effect that John is trying to build. Operating as he is in a dreamlike world, literal concerns like this one raise questions that the narrative does not intend to answer. What is important for John is the rhetorical effect delivered both when the city is envisioned as a place for the people of God and then when it is envisioned as the people themselves. Each image develops, rather than detracts from, the other. Interpreters reading with rather than against John will interpret each image on its own and allow them together to work as John intends.

[3] The vision turns to audition with a loud voice that speaks from the throne. The loud voice—previously experienced by those in opposition to God as foreboding—has usually signaled judgment activity (see the discussion of 7:2). Now, in these postjudgment times, it signals the salvation that is and has always been an accompanying feature of God's eschatological activity. When the voice emanates from the throne, it appears that the speaker is God. It is unlikely, though, that God would refer to Godself in the third person. This hunch is validated when God finally speaks and does so using the self-referential first-person singular (v. 5).

The throne voice declares that in this new city on the new earth, God will tabernacle, that is, "pitch God's tent," directly with God's people. In both the nominal (*skēnē*, tent) and verbal (*skēnoō*, "to tabernacle"; cf. John 1:14) forms, the language recalls God's residing with Israel during its postexodus, wilderness wanderings (as noted in the discussion on 13:6, the act of tabernacling rather than a specific place is the focus here; see also the discussion of 15:5). This is the eschatological exodus. The people have left persecution behind and exist now in direct proximity to the ultimate promise, God's presence. John has already prepared the reader for this imagery with his description of the people of God huddled as an encampment (20:9). Now God camps with the people in the new environment, where every threat has been removed.

Proximity to God implies relationship with God. John makes that relationship explicit with the clarifying words with which he finishes the verse. Appealing to numerous Old Testament witnesses (Lev 26:11–12; Ps 95:7; Ezek 37:27; Jer 31:1, 33; Zech 2:11), the throne voice declares that God will be their God and they will be God's peoples. This is covenant language. Interestingly, where the Old Testament covenant citations emphasized a single people, no doubt Israel, the throne voice turns the singular *laos* (people) into the plural *laoi* (peoples). The subtle shift in grammar signals a powerful shift in theology. What was particular has become universal (see the comments on 5:9–10 and 15:3–4). As Zech 2:11 implies and John's own vision confirms at 21:24 (cf. 5:9; 7:9; see the comment on 10:11), the nations—all peoples—will be available for participation in this eschatological covenant relationship. God will be God to all.

[4] The results of God's direct relationship with the peoples will be staggering. First, God will wipe away every tear from their eyes. The cause of tears—mourning, crying, pain, even death itself (20:14)—will be removed. This is the promise long ago foreseen by the prophets (Isa 25:8; 35:10; 65:19; Jer 31:16). It is the promise prefigured in Rev 7:17 as it introduced the springs of the water of life, which God will also address in this context (21:6). Life-giving water washes away tears. This is because, second, in the time of this life-giving water, the first, or former, things have passed away. John makes an explicit verbal connection back to 21:1, framing the resulting subsection with this critical eschatological theme. Presumably the first (former) heaven and earth were permeated with these tear inducers. When they went away, they took all of their hostilities with them.

[5] For only the second time in the entire book (cf. 1:8), God speaks (see the discussion of "the one seated on the throne" as a metaphor for God at 4:2–3). This fact alone separates this passage from the ones that surround it; vv. 5–8 form a subunit of the larger section (vv. 1–8). God personally confirms what was said about the new creation in vv. 1–4 and identifies Godself as the executor of it. Just in case there might be any confusion (i.e., with Rome), God declares that God is the one who does all this. Echoing Isa 43:19 (cf. 66:22), God is specific: "I make all things new." This general promise, though given in the present tense, is surely about the future; the specific promises that follow

occur in the future tense ("I will give," v. 6; "I will be," v. 7). Additionally, the need that God apparently feels to certify that what has been foreseen will indeed occur is an indication that it has not yet occurred. When God commands the prophet to write that these words are faithful (i.e., trustworthy) and true (see the comments on 3:14 and 19:11; cf. 22:6), God intends that the seer offer God's honor as collateral for trusting in the veracity of God's promises. God's peoples can bank on the fact that the newness that has just now been promised in God's name, and indeed in God's own words, will come true. So assured of such a future that they can converse about it in the present tense, peoples will be encouraged either to maintain or to initiate a life of appropriate witnessing, in order that they can participate positively in the future that God has promised.

[6] Having certified the validity of God's own promise, God declares, "It is done!" Here God echoes the statement of the seventh bowl angel, who declared with his actions that God's judgment is finished (16:17; cf. 15:1; John 19:30). Oddly, though, this time God chooses a plural verb, therefore literally saying, "They are done." Perhaps the change in number is a signal not just that the judgment component of God's eschatological activity has concluded but also that both partnered aspects, judgment and salvation, have in this visionary moment come to an end. Even the time of salvation will be finished when the new heaven and new earth welcome the new Jerusalem. "They" are all done. All that is left is for those who have witnessed to the lordship of God and the Lamb to reap the promised reward.

Once again, as in the previous verse, having made a provocative, sweeping claim, God finds it necessary to certify that God has the right to make it. God does so this time by appealing back to the first and only other place in the book of Revelation where God clearly speaks (1:8). There as here, God certifies the promise of Christ's imminent return by appealing to God's identity with the declaration: "I am the Alpha and the Omega" (cf. 1:17; 22:13, where Christ, in building full identity with God, identifies himself in the same way). God concludes the statement somewhat redundantly, corroborating the claim made with the first and last letters of the Greek alphabet by means of the functionally synonymous terms, beginning (alpha) and end (omega). Yet God speaks about time, not about the Greek alphabet. God is the first and the last in terms of history (cf. Isa 41:4; 44:6; 48:12). God is the first of all things and thus before all things, and is also the last of all things and thus after all things. As the only one who exists before and after history, who rules over time because God is at the beginning and end of time, God knows when the time, concerns, and objectives that drive history have come to their conclusion. When the one who is before and after all things says that all things are finished, you can believe it.

John's hearers and readers can also believe in God's specific promises about the circumstances that surround this new eschatological reality. First, God reiterates the promise made to the multitude of bloodied witnesses who throng the heavenly throne in 7:9–17, anticipating the promise that will be made to all at 22:17. These are the people who thirst for vindication (7:16) and eschatological relationship with God. To all of them, God offers the gift of the spring of living water (7:17; 22:17). While the phrase *hydōr zōēs* (water of life) can be translated either "flowing water" or "living water," the latter translation, given the context, is to be preferred. John is not speaking literally about the movement of the water but about its efficacy. This is a vision of eternal life-giving relationship, which was also imaged by the prophets as a great eschatological thirst-quenching experience (Isa 49:10; 55:1; Jer 2:13; Zech 14:8). The Gospel of John foresees Jesus as the conduit for this eternal, life-giving water (John 7:37; cf. *Odes Sol.* 30.1–2). In the Apocalypse, John connects this spring of life-giving water to the Eden-like river whose water of life runs through the heart of the new Jerusalem (22:1).

[7] God's second promise is delivered directly to the very same group that Christ targeted in each of the letters to the seven churches. In encouraging believers to maintain their witness to the lordship of God and the Lamb and to resist accommodating to the lordship designs of the imperial Roman cult, Christ addressed believers in the present with a term that describes their future designation if they remain faithful: the one who conquers (2:7, 11, 17, 26; 3:5, 12, 21; see the discussion relating "conquer" to witnessing at 5:5). Eschatological benefits were promised to those who have conquered with the hope that anticipated future reward would encourage present witness. Now it is *God's* turn to address the potential conqueror. God, too, points to the future as an inducement for appropriate witnessing behavior in the present. The one who conquers will inherit "these things," which in this context refers back to all of the eschatological benefits thus far associated with life in the new Jerusalem (vv. 3, 4, 5, 6).

The language of inheritance builds from the foundation of 2 Sam 7:14 (cf. Ezek 11:20; Zech 8:8) and prepares the way for a third promise, which echoes the throne voice's declaration that God will tabernacle directly with the peoples (Rev 21:3). God amplifies that earlier statement by declaring that any who conquer through their witness will be to God as sons and daughters. The resulting familial bond derives from the promise that God, through the prophet Nathan, made to David about the king's son Solomon. By covenant agreement, established through David's lineage, God would assume the role of Solomon's father, thus adopting him and bringing him into protective relationship. God expands the promise of such relationship, giving it an eschatological horizon and extending it to everyone; now it is not lineage but witnessing that matters.

[8] A vice list (cf. Rom 1:29–31; 1 Cor 5:9–11; 6:9–10; Gal 5:19–21; Eph 5:5; Titus 1:10, 16) follows, detailing those who will never receive the label "one who conquers." The list, which reminds hearers and readers of the one compiled at Rev 9:21 and anticipates another compiled at 22:15 (cf. 21:27), is specifically designed around the witnessing ethic that has driven John's apoc-

alyptic work. Given John's dramatic call for courageous testimony to the lordship of God and the Lamb despite the drastic consequences that such witnessing will bring, it is understandable that he headlines the list of vices with cowardice. Cowards are the ultimate accommodationists; for fear of losing social standing, economic wealth, physical well-being, and perhaps even life, they surrender their witness to God's lordship and testify to the lordship of Caesar and Rome instead. The faithless similarly have insufficient belief in the power of God to vindicate them and so cannot endure the hardships that Rome presses upon them. Idolaters and those who commit abominations are surely those who accommodate by eating the meat sacrificed to idols and thus find themselves participating in idol worship in an effort to fit in with the Roman economic and political infrastructure (17:4–5). Murderers are those who kill the witnesses in an effort to prosecute the draconian program of the beast from the sea (6:9–11; 13:15; 20:4). Fornication is a metaphor for those who idolatrously find themselves in the worship of the imperial cult when they know their singular cultic loyalty belongs to God and Christ (2:14, 20–22). Sorcerers are those who deceive others into following the forces of the dragon and the beast (18:23). Those who lie, perhaps mostly to themselves, proclaim a faith that their actions do not support (cf. 1 John 1:6).[1] Like Jezebel and Balaam, while claiming to be believers, they participate in activities that endorse the lordship of Rome instead. These are the ones who are bound for the lake of fire and brimstone, which is the second death (see the comments on 14:10; 19:20; 20:6, 14–15; cf. the discussion of first and second death cosmology in Revelation at 9:6).

Though the verbs here are in the indicative mood, John is actually issuing a vigorous appeal in the imperative mode. This is a prophetic and not a predictive vision. The seer is not describing who is already in the new Jerusalem; instead, he is using a list of the kinds of people who will never enter the eschatological city in the future in order to encourage appropriate behavior by people in the present.

### 21:9–22:9 The Implications of God's Victory: The New Jerusalem

### 21:9–14 The Introduction of the City

Verse 9 begins a new section, which characterizes the new Jerusalem as a bride (21:9–22:9). It parallels 17:1–19:10, which depicted Babylon/Rome as a whore. In John's dualistic framework, these are the only two options for responding to the claims of God's cosmic sovereignty. While the whore symbolizes rejection, the bride represents an acceptance so intimate that a marital relationship is the metaphor best suited to describe it.

---

1. The same term, *pseudēs* (liar), describes in 2:2 those who claim to be apostles, but are not. A verbal form, *pseudomai* (lie), is used at 3:9 of those who call themselves Jews but are not.

9 Then one of the seven angels with the seven bowls full of the seven last plagues came and spoke with me, saying, "Come, I will show you the bride, the wife of the Lamb." 10 And he carried me in the spirit to a great and high mountain, and he showed me the holy city Jerusalem descending out of heaven from God 11 with the glory of God. Its radiance is like a precious stone, like jasper, clear as crystal. 12 It has a great and high wall, with twelve gates. On the gates are twelve angels, and on the gates are inscribed the names of the twelve tribes of the children of Israel. 13 There are three gates on the east, three gates on the north, three gates on the south, and three gates on the west. 14 The wall of the city also has twelve foundations, and on them are the twelve names of the twelve apostles of the Lamb.

[9] The parallel with the account centering on the judgment of Babylon/ Rome (17:1–19:10) begins immediately with John's identification of the principal interlocutor, one of the seven angels with the seven bowls filled with the plagues of God's wrath. Another of those angels previously ushered the seer through his visions of the whore (see the discussion of 17:1). John does not say whether this is the same angel as the one who appeared at 17:1. In the end, it does not matter; the angel's identity (or angels' identities) is less important than his function: to introduce the key visionary object. The angel's appearance here may seem less appropriate than it did at the beginning of chapter 17. After all, it makes narrative sense to have one of the angels who poured out a bowl of God's judgment wrath upon the earth anchor the vision about the judgment/destruction of Babylon/Rome. This text, though, discloses the city that symbolizes salvation. Yet an angel connected with the bowl plagues is appropriate because John is working here with the backside of the judgment/salvation partnership. Theologically speaking, the judgment of Babylon/Rome *is* the realization of the salvific city that is the new Jerusalem. Figuratively, they happen together; they are the same climactic moment because they are different sides of the same apocalyptic act. Structurally, John makes this point by positioning the two texts in this obviously parallel fashion.

Following the grammatical presentation in 17:1 exactly, John confides that the angel spoke to him the following words: "Come, I will show you. . . ." The objects seen certainly are dramatically different. The two rhetorical women represent competing social, cultic, economic, and political lures on the affections of humankind. Humans, though drawn to both, can be intimate with only one. Relationship with one is mutually exclusive of relationship with the other.

At the time of John's writing, both these options are live. Only in the promised and envisioned future will Babylon/Rome be removed from the theological and ethical equation. In John's real time, a decision must be made. His view of how the future *will* look is meant to encourage readers and hearers to choose appropriately in favor of the woman he is preparing now to introduce.

At this point the content of the two parallel verses, 17:1 and 21:9, differs: 17:1 goes on to talk about the judgment of the whore, while 21:9 points not to judgment but to bridal existence with the Lamb. In both verses the condition of the woman is presented before the woman herself is identified. In chapter 21 the emotional content is one of joy rather than foreboding because the context is one of eschatological relationship rather than separation.

The bridal language also calls to mind John's earlier mentions of the marriage of the Lamb to the bridal city (19:7–8; 21:2). Though different vocabulary is used (*gynē*, "woman" or "wife," in 19:7–8; *nymphē*, "bride," in 21:2; 22:17), the point is the same. The city, representing the faithful witnesses as a corporate entity, will enjoy so intimate a relationship with the Lamb that they shall be to God like a child (cf. 21:7).

**[10]** John's foundation in Ezekiel's postexilic visions of restoration becomes unmistakably evident at this point, even as the seer continues to flesh out the counterparallel with his own Babylon/Rome vision (17:1–19:10). Just as the angel in 17:3 carried John away in the Spirit, so the angel here spirits John off so he can view a sharper image of the specified city. As at 17:3, and elsewhere in John's narration, movement in the Spirit is not a metaphor for escapist enthusiasm. It signals instead a prophetic inspiration that conveys information useful for making appropriate discipleship decisions (see the comment on 4:2–3). This prophetic emphasis is confirmed by the fact that John is clearly channeling Ezekiel; John's vision will serve as a prophetic reinterpretation. At Ezek 40:1–2 the Old Testament prophet is transported in the Spirit (cf. 43:5) to a high mountain, where he sees the structure of a city that he understands to be the eschatological temple.[2] Whereas in Rev 17:3 John was transported into the wilderness, a location that symbolized darkness, danger, and judgment (see the discussion of that verse), this time, like Ezekiel, he winds up on a mountaintop, where he too will soon see a city. As a location that signifies the establishment or consummation of communion with God (Gen 22:1–14; Exod 3:1, 12; Ezek 40:2; Mark 9:2; Matt 5:1; 17:1–2; Luke 9:28–29), the mountain is an appropriate setting for everything that follows.

The city John sees is the holy city, the new Jerusalem, which was already introduced as descending from heaven (21:2; see the discussion of that verse). Building from that introductory mention, John now describes the realization of that descent in detail.

**[11]** The city is possessed by the glory of God. According to 21:23, this glory is so radiant that it lights the entire municipality. No doubt John has Isaiah's prophecies in mind as he records his own. Isaiah associates the glory of God with the light of the people (58:8). Isaiah 60:1–2 then reiterates that God's glory

---

2. See Beale 1065. Transport in the spirit, by the power of the spirit, was a part of Ezekiel's commission (Ezek 2:2; 3:12, 14, 24; 11:1; 43:5). Cf. Acts 8:39.

shall be the people's light. It is, though, upon Ezekiel that John is most firmly grounded. Just before describing the vision of the eschatological city and its measurement, Ezekiel declares that the glory of God shines across the earth (Ezek 43:2). John's depiction of God's radiance also serves as a prelude to the coming narration of the city and its measurements. Indeed, John's eschatological city radiates God's glory so fiercely that it appears to shine with the dazzling sparkle of crystalline jasper. This image takes hearers and readers back to John's initial description of the heavenly throne room, where the seer also described God's glory as glistening jasper (4:3; see the discussion of 4:2–3). Other characters are briefly connected to glory (the Lamb, 5:12–13; an angel, 18:1; the kings of the earth, 21:24; nations, 21:26), yet glory is primarily an attribute of God (1:6; 4:9, 11; 7:12; 11:13; 14:7; 15:8; 16:9; 19:1, 7; 21:11, 23). John drafts a political statement by making sure not to ascribe this quality to the entity most Greco-Romans would have associated it with: imperial—and by any human standard, glorious—Rome. Rome has tried to play the role of lord of human history and, in doing so, has usurped the symbolism of the precious stones (17:4; 18:12, 16). John's point, though, is that Babylon/Rome has hoarded the currency of fool's gold. The dull recognition it has amassed through its military and economic might is nothing compared to the scintillating glory whose realization in God is so palpable that it dazzles with the awe-inspiring allure of a truly precious gem. This jasper, like the gold that John will describe later (21:18), is nothing like the rocks stockpiled in Babylon/Rome's vaults; devoid of all impurities, it is as clear as glass. Like the eschatological jewels, the glory they represent is unlike anything the world has ever seen (on the relation of crystal clarity to holiness, see the discussion of 21:22).

[12–13] In Ezekiel's vision, the citylike structure that sits atop the mountain is the eschatological temple, and it is surrounded by a wall (Ezek 40:5). He next narrates the measurements and description of that wall. John, too, starts with a description of the wall that surrounds his eschatological city. Walls represented a city's security. It was natural that a wall would be the first attribute of the city to be described. It would be seen and encountered first by any visitor or returning city resident. This particular wall would no doubt provide ample security since John describes it as great and high.

Two difficulties immediately arise from this presentation. First, since all God's enemies and the enemies of God's people have been destroyed (cf. Rev 20:15), one wonders why there would be any need for a wall. Not operating literally, John works from and for the imagination of his hearers and readers. He is trying to convey a transcendent reality for which neither he nor they have the proper words or concepts to comprehend. They have never seen an eschatological relationship with God and have no grounds upon which to fashion its look and feel. To help them conceive of it, John offers an image that is familiar to them: a great city. Great cities had great walls. To draw up the greatest city of all without walls for a marginalized people who yearned for a secure future would have been detrimental to John's narrative agenda. Its lack of realism and therefore the improbability of its claim to open up access to real vindication, peace, and security would have been problematic. John sidesteps that problem by imagining the great and secure city in the way that he knows his audience would have imagined it. He keeps the wall but transfigures it for his own unique visionary purposes. The second problem with the wall for a literally minded reader is its size. At 144 cubits, it is woefully short, given the height of the city itself. Once again, John is operating figuratively. The wall is representational and exists for symbolic purposes alone. It does not have to provide any actual security since God has already provided for that by conquering all God's enemies in the apocalyptic conflicts that have just taken place. John is merely using the wall to fulfill the expectations that his hearers and readers would have had for one. Its height is a multiple of 12 (12 times 12 = 144), which denotes completion and wholeness (see the discussion of 7:4). Despite the actual (literal) dimensions, the wall represents the complete and total (figurative) security that God's apocalyptic acts have already produced.

Just before the close of his work, the prophet Ezekiel describes the wall that surrounds his city (48:30–35). Moving clockwise through the compass points (north, east, south, west), he offers the dimensions and description of each side. Each wall measures 4,500 cubits, producing a square. Carved into each wall are three gates. On each gate is inscribed the name of one of the Israelite tribes. Though John saves the dimensions of his squared city for later (21:16), he follows Ezekiel's description of the gates in the four city walls.[3] Moving more haphazardly (east, north, south, west), he too notes that three gates are carved into each wall, and that on each gate the name of one of the twelve Israelite tribes is inscribed. Once again, the number "twelve" signifies wholeness and completion. There are sufficient gates for all who need to enter. The number "twelve," as related to the tribes, also suggests that the foundation of God's people of faith, the whole of Israel, is accounted for in the eschatological city. The restoration for which Israel has longed will be accomplished.[4]

Perhaps drawing from Isa 62:6, where God positions sentinels on the walls of Zion, John posts a guardian angel at each of the city's twelve gates. (There are no angels at the gates in Ezekiel's vision.) Since all God's enemies and the

---

3. Beale points out helpfully that John may also have the temple gates of Ezek 40 in mind here: "The multiple gates of Ezekiel's temple (ch. 40) and the twelve gates of the city listed in Ezek. 48:31–34 are merged into one group of twelve gates arranged around the one city-temple of John's vision" (1068).

4. As Aune remarks, "The association of the names of the twelve tribes of Israel with the gates of the New Jerusalem implies the realization of one of the central concerns of Jewish eschatology, namely, *the restoration of the twelve tribes of Israel*, which is repeatedly mentioned in post-exilic OT and early Jewish literature" (3:1155, emphasis orig.).

enemies of God's people no longer exist, a literal reader might wonder why guards would be needed for the eschatological city. Again, John is working imaginatively from the baseline expectations of his hearers and readers. Sentries are symbolic representations of a city's security. John graphically emphasizes this city's complete protection by retaining the metaphor. He is working for dramatic effect, not logical consistency. The visualization of angels standing guard at the city gates would have driven home the point that this city was designed and secured by God.

[14] John adds to Ezekiel's description with the notation that the 12-gated wall also has 12 foundations. The seer is updating the prophet for a particular reason, to emphasize the universalism that has been a part of his agenda throughout (see the discussion of 21:3). If the complete restoration and inclusion of the Israelite tribes is symbolized by the 12 gates, the complete inclusion of all believing Gentiles is symbolized by these 12 foundations. Noticing that each foundation stone had inscribed on it the name of one of the Lamb's 12 apostles, John follows early Christian tradition, which maintained that the eschatological city had a foundation of apostles and prophets conceived by God (Eph 2:20; Heb 11:10), with Christ as its cornerstone. The image of a city wall with Jesus' 12 apostles as foundation signifies the incorporation of the believing church into this eschatological city. The combination of the 12 tribes and the 12 apostles makes this single, critical point: the new city is founded upon and therefore open to all God's people, Jew and Gentile alike. John has used the resulting total of 24 before to express symbolically this message of inclusiveness. The 24 elders in 4:3–4 represent a similar combination of 12 and 12 that anticipates the link between Israel and the apostles here. Notably, too, in both this section and the earlier one, God's glory, symbolized by jasper, is on radiant display. John evidently joins the manifestation of God's glory, at least in part, to the universal makeup of God's eschatological community.

## 21:15–21 The Measurements of the City

15 And the one who spoke with me had a golden measuring rod to measure the city and its gates and its wall. 16 The city has four equal sides, that is,[a] its length is the same as its width. He measured the city with the rod, at 12,000 stadia; the length and the width and the height of it are the same. 17 He also measured its wall, 144 cubits, the measure of a human, that is, an angel. 18 And the foundation of its wall is jasper, while the city is pure gold, like clear glass. 19 The foundations of the wall of the city are adorned with every precious stone. The first foundation is jasper; the second, sapphire; the third, agate; the fourth, emerald; 20 the fifth, onyx; the sixth, carnelian; the seventh, chrysolite; the eighth, beryl; the ninth, topaz; the tenth, chrysoprase; the eleventh, jacinth; the twelfth, amethyst.

21 And the twelve gates are twelve pearls; each one of the gates is made out of a single pearl. The street of the city is pure gold, like transparent crystal.

a. An epexegetical or explanatory *kai* (and).

[15] John confides further that the angel of v. 9, like the "man" of Ezek 40:3, 5, came equipped for his task (cf. Zech 2:1–2). John, too, was previously given a rod (Rev 11:1–2) and told to measure the inner court of the temple as a maneuver of protection. This angel holds a qualitatively different kind of rod, however, and his actions have a substantially different objective. Reflecting the precious gems that compose the city's glory and foundation, the angel's measuring rod is made of gold. Moreover, he will not use it to measure a temple within a city but the massive eschatological city itself. It is also unclear whether this measuring is an act of protection. In addition to the fact that there is nothing and no one from which to protect the city, the narration does not explain the act of measurement in this way as it did in 11:1–2. The measuring here is no doubt instructive rather than protective. John wants his hearers and readers to get a sense not only of the city's massive size but also of its symbolic connection with the prophetic traditions that affirm God's glorious presence with the people. That connection will surface in the city's dimensions, which he is about to record. He will calibrate the city, the wall, and the gates, in that order.

[16] Like Ezekiel's city-temple, John's city is a square (see the discussion of vv. 12–13; cf. Ezek 48:16, 30–35); its length and width are equal. John, though, adds an important nuance. Like the holy of holies in the first temple, the place where Yahweh's presence was understood to reside (1 Kgs 6:19–20; 2 Chr 3:8), the new Jerusalem is also a cube; its height is equal to its length and width. The important number is 12,000. That is the scale, in the dimension of the Greek *stadion* (stadium), of the city's length, breadth, and height: "While the *stadion* was in origin a Greek measure, it was used in early Judaism and early Christianity (LXX Dan 4:12; 2 Macc 11:5; 12:9–10, 16–17, 29; Matt 14:24; Luke 24:13; John 6:19; 11:18)" (Aune 3:1161). The conversion of a *stadion* to approximately 200 yards yields a distance that the NRSV translates as 1,500 miles. While that figure gives a sense of the enormous scale of this vast municipality, I prefer a translation that maintains the more archaic 12,000 *stadia* and places the contemporary equivalent in a footnote. As hard as it is to imagine a *stadion*, John's focus lies more on the symbolically charged number "12"; once again, as with the 144,000 of 7:1–8 and 14:1–5, the seer augments the wholeness of 1,000 with that of 12 (or a multiple of it) to suggest the enormity of God's inclusiveness. The city is so massive that an innumerable multitude of God's people may stream into it and therefore into eschatological relationship with God. Symbolically speaking, the city can handle them all!

**[17–18]** The emphasis remains on the number "12" with the dimensions of the wall. Its height is 144 cubits. A cubit is generally taken as the distance between a man's elbow and the tip of his forefinger. This approximately 18-inch span, when multiplied 144 times, yields a wall (approximately 216 feet) that commentators are correct to call puny alongside a city side that is 12,000 *stadia* (1,500 miles) high. While some commentators protest that the small dimensions refer to the wall's width, John has been focused on height all along, and ancient city walls were defined in terms of height rather than width. Therefore, John, too, has height in mind.[5] The seer is less interested in literal distance than he is in the symbolism of "144" (see the discussion of 7:4). The wall represents the wholeness of God's secure provision and protection of the city. Schüssler Fiorenza believes provocatively that the imbalance is yet another way in which John highlights the inclusive nature of the eschatological city: "This enormous difference in proportion indicates that the universal cosmic salvation of the world by far exceeds that figured in the Christian community" (*Vision of a Just World*, 111).

Before he concludes the verse, John adds more confusion by the imprecise terminology he uses to describe the measurement. He says that it is the measurement of a human, which is of an angel. One would think that it would be either one or the other. John is working from and clarifying his source. Ezekiel's measuring interlocutor, upon whom John's angel is surely based, was described by the prophet as a "human." John, knowing that his hearers and readers would recognize the foundation of his own vision in Ezekiel's, uses this clumsy formulation to alert his readers to the fact that Ezekiel's "human" measurements were in reality those of an angel, too. Thus, the measurements of both cities are divinely calibrated. The measurements are therefore not only equally prophetic; they are also equally authoritative.

**[18–21]** In describing the wall, John returns to the familiar theme of jasper. Already, in v. 11, he has likened the glory of God in the city to the radiance of this rare jewel. That same glory is symbolically embedded in the city's very architectural essence. A similar radiance glows from the entire city, whose components are so breathtakingly beautiful that the city shines with the stunning vibrancy of gold so pure that it is as clear as glass (see the discussion of the theological and political meaning of this imaging at v. 11). It is not insignificant that Solomon overlaid his temple and the inner sanctuary, the places where God's presence was thought to reside, with what was no doubt a much lower grade of gold (1 Kgs 6:20–22). Surely, in the eschaton, even the holy God would

---

5. For discussion of John's focus on width rather than height, see Aune 3:1162. Beale appropriately counters that a shift to width would raise as many questions as it answers. A 216-foot base would be ridiculously insufficient for a wall 1,500 miles high (1074). It is better, instead, to focus on the symbolism rather than on the literal number.

find a place crafted out of gold so pure as to be transparent as a worthy arena in which to establish relationship with God's people.

Scanning lower, John sees that each of the twelve foundations of the wall is adorned with a precious stone. He is maintaining his focus on the city as a bride even though he has long since left the bride metaphor behind. At 21:2 he noted that the bride was adorned for her husband. He uses the same verb (*kosmeō*) to describe the city's adornment here. These two verses are the only places where he deploys the verb, an indication that the connection drawn here is intentional. John is also working from traditional roots. Isaiah envisioned the walls and gates of the city fashioned out of precious stones (54:11–12; cf. Tob 13:16). Moreover, Ezek 28:13 prepares for the linkage between precious stones and a renewed Eden, with which the vision of the new Jerusalem will conclude in chapter 22. The listing of twelve foundational stones also recalls the description of the breastpiece to be made for the high priest's vestments (Exod 28:15–21; 39:8–14).[6] The high priest, as representative of the people, particularly on the Day of Atonement, when he alone went into the cubical holy of holies to make amends for the people's sins, was to wear a breastpiece formed in a square (Exod 28:16; 39:9), no doubt fashioned to resemble the footprint of the holy of holies. Noticeably, it also resembles the footprint of John's new Jerusalem. Twelve precious stones, arranged in four rows of three stones each, were to be placed on the breastpiece. Each stone was to have engraved upon it the name of one of the twelve Israelite tribes. John alters the presentation by engraving on each foundation the name of one of the twelve apostles instead (21:14).

There is a translation question regarding whether v. 19 intends to say that the foundations were adorned with multiple jewels or that each foundation was itself a precious stone. I interpret it in the latter way because of the clues from both the biblical tradition upon which John is drawing and the literary context in Revelation. The breastpiece of the high priest and Isa 54:11–12 both suggest single jewels; the Isaiah text connected those single jewels directly to the walls and foundations. Additionally, 1 Kgs 7:10 speaks of a temple whose foundations are composed of costly stones. Even more significantly, when John turns to describing the gates, he does not anticipate that they will be covered with pearls; instead, he foresees each of them as a gigantic pearl. The imagery suggests that he is thinking of massive precious stones throughout. In the case of

---

6. Beale helpfully notes that eight of the stones listed by John are the same as those found in the Exodus accounts, "and the differently named stones in Revelation are semantic equivalents of the ones in Exodus." He further contends that John's different ordering of the stones is not evidence that the seer was not referring back to the Exodus materials "since Josephus explicitly alludes to the jewels on the high priest's breastpiece in *J.W.* 5.5.7 and in *Ant.* 3.7.5 in two other different orders" (1080). Cf. Boring (*Revelation*, 214): "Since a similar description is found in both Josephus and Philo, it is clear that John is following a tradition of interpreting the stones of the breastplate of the High Priest in this symbolic manner."

the pearls, whose textual representation here is responsible for the "pearly gates" cliché, inscriptions bear the names, and thus signal the complete restoration, of the twelve Israelite tribes (21:12).

### 21:22–27  The Glory of the City

22 I did not see a temple in the city, for the Lord God, the Almighty, and the Lamb are its temple. 23 And the city does not need the sun or the moon to illumine it, for the glory of God illumines it, and its lamp is the Lamb. 24 The nations will walk by its light, and the kings of the earth will bring their glory into it. 25 Its gates will never shut by day, for there will be no night there. 26 They will bring the glory and the honor of the nations into it. 27 But[a] nothing unclean will enter it, and no one who practices abomination and falsehood, but only those who are written in the Lamb's Book of Life.

a. The *kai* is adversative: "but."

**[22]** This verse represents John's striking departure from the Ezek 40–48 source he has been developing. In Ezekiel's orienting vision, the city structure on the mountaintop *was* the eschatological temple intended to represent the restoration of the once-exiled people (see Ezek 40:1–5; 43:1–5). Perhaps the temple's connection to the singular people of Israel was one of the reasons John has abandoned it in his more universal visionary perspective. With all peoples from every nation candidates for citizenship (see Rev 21:3, 24), perhaps the ethnic limitations attached to the Jerusalem temple were too constricting. Just as likely, perhaps even more so, John's vision is stressing that every intermediary between God and God's people, even one that has played as critical a role as the temple had played, would in this new eschatological moment become obsolete. In a reality where God pitches Godself directly in the midst of God's people (21:3) and relates to them as a father does to a child (21:7), high priests, sanctuaries, and even the holy of holies are no longer necessary. *All* of this new city, fashioned as it would be from precious gems so crystalline pure as to be transparent, would now be God's holy place. Wherever the people, the *children* of God, would find themselves in this city would be holy ground. Anywhere and everywhere they would exist within the city, they could and would meet God. Children need not find an interlocutor to speak to their parent on their behalf when that parent is in direct proximity to them. Just so, John's people would in this new Jerusalem no longer need and therefore no longer have a temple. The Lord God Almighty and the Lamb, operating together in divine concordance, would themselves serve that function. God would need no house in which to dwell, since God's glory would shroud the city like a fog. (In Ezek

43:5, God's glory engages the temple only.) God's presence is the very essence out of which this municipal edifice would be fashioned. God would be completely on the loose among God's people.

**[23]** In what is essentially a doublet of 22:5, John declares that the effect of God's direct presence in and with the city will be pervasive. The glory of God and the Lamb will have a tangible effect (see the comment on 21:11). It will become the power source that lights up the city by day and by night (cf. Isa 60:1, 19–20; Ezek 43:2; for other New Testament images of God or Christ as light, see John 8:12; 1 John 1:5). Where John's prophetic sources spoke only of God's light, John adds the lamp provided by the Lamb in order to demonstrate, as he does in 21:22, that the Lamb's divinity operates with God's own, because in the end it is God's own. Whether the sun and moon will exist in the new heaven and new earth is irrelevant because as sources of light they will themselves become irrelevant (cf. Isa 24:23). Even if they do exist, they will be overshadowed or, more appropriately said, outshone by the radiance of God and the Lamb.

**[24–27]** As John closes out the chapter, he depends as much on Isa 60 as he has earlier in the chapter depended upon the restoration visions of Ezek 40–48. The prophecy in Isa 60 retains Ezekiel's utopian dreams: "The postexilic prophet of this section of Isaiah looked forward to the renewed and rebuilt Jerusalem" (Reddish 409). Like Isaiah, John maintains a universal focus (see the comments on Rev 5:9–10; 15:3–4; 21:3). The nations, not just Israel, not just the church, will find direction from the glorious light of God and the Lamb that illuminates this city (Isa 60:3–5; cf. Dan 7:14; Zech 2:11; 8:23).[7] The nations, in other words, will walk by God's glory. With Satan no longer around to deceive them, they can see the light clearly and follow it right into the city, into eschatological relationship with God. This is only fitting since these, even though they are the populaces of the nations, are the people whose names were found to be written in the Book of Life; everyone else has either been destroyed (Rev 20:7–9), exiled (22:15), or writhes in the lake of fire (20:15).

Where once kings had brought their gifts and treasures to demonstrate homage and fidelity to Rome, now, free from deception, they bring their glory into God's city instead (cf. Isa 60:11). In v. 26 John thus repeats what he has already made clear at v. 24. The "they" he speaks of at v. 26 are certainly the kings of v. 24, since they are the only possible referent in this context. Their anticipated future behavior is a confident demonstration of true present lordship. Able to see clearly, they will no longer misappropriate their grandeur or hoard it for themselves; they will allow their grandeur to become part of the

---

7. Cf. Bauckham (*Climax of Prophecy*, 313): "It brings together the Old Testament promises for the destiny of God's own people and the universal hope, also to be found in the Old Testament, that all the nations will become God's people. The history of the covenant people—both of the one nation Israel and of the church which is redeemed from all the nations—will find its eschatological fulfillment in the full inclusion of all the nations in its own covenant privileges and promises."

city's. With the enemy kings of the earth (10:11; 16:12, 14; 17:1–2, 12, 18; 18:3, 9) now destroyed (19:18–19), the remaining kings move into the relationship with God that was always expected, where God and the Lamb are acknowledged to be the rightful ruler over all kings (1:5; 17:14; 19:16; cf. 15:3). John does not say that they bring the traditional booty that kings once brought to the Roman Caesar; rather, they bring the glory that they and their people had once refused to yield to God. John had spoken of "giving God glory" in terms of repentance (see the discussion linking glory and repentance at 15:4). These must be the repentant ones, therefore, the people who "came out of her" (18:4) in time and found their way to a recognition of the lordship of God and the Lamb and thus engaged God's moment of judgment (20:11–15) as a moment of salvation rather than destruction.

Since ancient city gates were traditionally open during the day (unless under siege or attack), it is odd that John pointedly says that the gates in the new Jerusalem will never be closed by day. The odd formulation is probably due to John's desire to emphasize the radical openness of the city (cf. Isa 60:11). There will only be day because there will be no night (cf. Zech 14:7), and thus the city will be forever open. It will never close at any part of the day because all parts of the day will be daylight (Rev 22:5), and as a result the eternal city will be eternally accessible. Perhaps, too, this part of the vision is John's way of returning to the promise Christ made to the Philadelphians, that he was even then, as John is now, setting before them doors that no one would shut (3:7–8). This vision, as a future that has not yet been realized, also offers (and requires) a present choice. Hearers and readers choose to prepare for future entrance by the way they live their present lives. John therefore sets before them two future choices, a lake whose agonizing fire will never be shut off (20:15) and a city whose gates will never be shut closed. One represents (second) death, the other (eternal) life. The exhortation is clear: by the way you witness to the lordship of God and the Lamb, choose life.

As open and inclusive as the city is, John pauses before moving on to remind his hearers and readers that so holy a place will not entertain impurity (cf. Isa 35:8; 52:1; Ezek 33:29). He has made this point more comprehensively before in the vice list of 21:8 (see discussion of that verse) and will reiterate it in 22:15. Only those whose names are in the Book of Life belong (see the comments on 3:5 and 20:12; cf. Isa 4:3).

John is writing about the future in order to exhort appropriate present witnessing behavior. Those who accommodate themselves to the lordship of Rome and therefore participate in cultic, social, political, and economic activities celebrating that lordship (abominations, 17:4–5), or who lie to (deceive) others and themselves about the truth of such behavior (e.g., Jezebel and Balaam, 2:14, 20–23)—such will never enter the city.

22:1–5  The New Life of the City

> 22:1 Then he showed me a river of living water, clear as crystal, flowing
> from the throne of God and the Lamb 2 down the center of the city's street.
> On each side of the river are trees[a] of life producing twelve fruits, each
> producing its fruit each month. And the leaves of the trees are for the heal-
> ing of the nations. 3 Nothing cursed will be found there any longer. But[b]
> the throne of God and of the Lamb will be in it, and God's servants will
> worship God. 4 And they will see God's face, and God's name will be on
> their foreheads. 5 There will no longer be a night, and they will not need
> lamplight and sunlight, because the Lord God will illumine them, and
> they will reign forever and ever.

a. Though *xylon* (tree) appears in the singular, John clearly intends multiple trees (see
the commentary on v. 2 below).
b. The *kai* is adversative: "but."

[22:1] The angel whom John introduced at 21:9 extends his promise to show
the new Jerusalem. The positioning of the river as the direct object of the verb
*deiknymi* (show) suggests that it has a functional quality on a par with the city
itself. John has used this verb throughout as a marker for key narrative images.
At 1:1, in the heading for the entire book, it was "the things soon to take place"
that were directly related to the all-important *apokalypsis* (revelation) of Jesus
Christ. At 4:1, as John opened the scene to the heavenly throne room, the significant "things" that were to happen "after this" were the verb's object. At 17:1
it was the judgment of the great whore, Babylon/Rome. At 21:9 it was the bride,
wife of the Lamb, shown to be the holy city, the new Jerusalem, at 21:10. At
22:6, in a verse that no doubt plays the role of a closing narrative footer to its
header counterpart at 1:1, the "things soon to take place" are once again the
object to be shown off. (A final participial use at 22:8 refers to the visions of
the new Jerusalem initiated at 21:9.) In each case, the verb "to show" prefaces
the introduction of a key narrative symbol, whose presence is instrumental for
understanding the overall objective of John's prophetic work. The river, as the
penultimate pairing of an accusative object with this demonstrative verb, must
therefore likewise play an important role in John's thinking about the eschatology of the end time.

The river marks the city as a new, improved, urban Eden. John builds his
case carefully. He notes that the river is composed of living water. As such, it
is a metaphor for the gift of eschatological relationship with God that humans
experienced before their expulsion from paradise. They have thirsted for its
restoration ever since (7:16–17; 21:6; 22:17). Both Jewish and Christian writings envisioned that restoration in a variety of ways. Psalm 46:4 anticipated a

river whose streams would make glad the city of God in a time of great distress. The prophet Zechariah looked to the great eschatological day when living water would flow freely from Jerusalem (14:8). The Gospel of John records Jesus' promise to the thirsty that rivers of living water would one day flow from the hearts of believers (7:37–38). Most importantly, Ezekiel offered John a vision upon which he could build his own. The prophet saw water flowing from the threshold of the eschatological temple with the superstructure of a city (47:1). Ezekiel, like John, most certainly grounded this river in the likeness of the river in Eden (Gen 2:10) that flowed out to water—that is, to give life to—paradise's garden. According to 47:8–10, Ezekiel's river flows eastward, down through desert lands, and ultimately into a sea of stagnant waters, no doubt the Dead Sea. After turning lands and waters fresh, it establishes new *physical* life in the form of swarming creatures and teeming fish.

John improves on the rivers of both Genesis and Ezekiel in two ways. First, he claims for his river a crystal clarity. No doubt he intends to mark the river with the same purity of the precious stones that characterized the city's holiness and God's glory (21:11, 22). Second, he alters the river's point of origin. The Genesis river flows out of Eden. Ezekiel's river flows from the eschatological temple. John's river flows directly from the throne of God and the Lamb. The throne, introduced in Rev 4 as the seat of authority for all creation, now acts as the lifeline for all in creation who thirst for relationship with God. The Lamb is no longer standing alongside the throne, as he was in his own introductory chapter (5:6). After building a functional identity with God (see 3:21; 7:10, 17; 14:4; 17:14; 21:22) that will climax in chapter 22, where titles associated with God fall naturally to him (22:13), he is now confirmed as ruling with God (cf. v. 3). Just as importantly, through this gift of living water he, along with God, issues eschatological sustenance, *eternal* life, to those who thirst for it.

[2] The translation of the phrase that opens v. 2 is not straightforward. Because early Greek manuscripts did not include punctuation, readers must determine from the context where to place it in contemporary translations. The phrase "down the center of its [the city's] street" may be read as completing the thought in v. 1 or as beginning the thought of v. 2. I take the phrase to conclude the thought about the river's flow. The phrase "from the throne of God and the Lamb" indicates the river's source; the paired phrase "down the center of its [the city's] street" charts its course and destination. The two pieces fit together naturally as a single thought about the river's movement that is distinct from the ensuing description of the foliage on the river's banks.

This choice of grammatical placement determines much about meaning. John speaks of the river's destination as though the city has one street, at least one primary one. He intends to say that the river flows from the throne of God and the Lamb through the middle of the city's main street, probably the same golden paved street he described at 21:21.[1] Once again he appeals to the Eden account to fill out the portrait. Genesis 2:9 speaks of abundant trees and, in particular, of a tree of life in the midst of the garden. Clearly building from the Genesis account, Ezek 47:12 speaks of trees growing on both sides of the river that flows from the eschatological temple. In conflating the two accounts, John outdoes them both. Apparently using the singular *xylon* (tree) as a collective noun, he envisions his river flanked on either side by rows of the one tree of life.[2] How else are we to take his awkward phrasing that on either side of the river there stood *a* tree of life? At least two trees are envisioned here; indeed, the allusion to Ezekiel suggests many more. Eden's garden had only one tree of life. Ezekiel's temple had many trees, but no tree of life. John's city has trees of life standing guard all along the banks of a crystal river running down the middle of a golden street. John's new Jerusalem out-Edens Eden!

Given John's presentation, it is all to be expected. Using the metaphor of washing one's clothes (i.e., those who conquer), Christ declares that those who faithfully witness to the lordship of God and the Lamb, despite the consequences, will obtain access to the tree of life (22:14; cf. 22:19). In fact, as early as 2:7, Christ promised the Ephesian church members that anyone who conquered would be given permission to eat from the tree of life in paradise. The new Jerusalem is obviously the paradise that Christ intended; it has plenty of such trees to go around.[3] This eschatological Eden is fully stocked.

So are its trees. Once again following Ezek 47:12, John observes that they bear abundant fruit (cf. *1 En.* 25.4–6). Ezekiel notes that they are always in season; because of the life-giving water flowing from the temple that nourishes them, they offer a fresh harvest every month of the year. John's trees are not only abundant; they also produce variety. The seer is careful to present that variety in terms of the number for completion: twelve. His trees are wholly sufficient. Each month will find a new fruit dangling from their branches.

John's eschatological one-upmanship continues with the trees' leaves. Ezekiel had observed that while the fruit of the trees was for food, their leaves would be for healing. So too for the trees of life in John's new Jerusalem. John, though, pointedly adds that the healing is to be for the nations. Ezekiel was

---

1. If one places the period at the end of v. 1, however, then v. 2 would begin with the phrase "into the middle of its [the city's] street." The resulting translation would therefore be something like the following: "In the midst of its street and on each side of the river is the tree of life," meaning that the street and the river run parallel to each other, with the trees between them. See Reddish 421.

2. Reddish observes, "The Greek word used here—*xylon*—is singular in form, but it is sometimes used in the singular to refer to several trees ('a forest')" (421). Aune points to collective uses of the singular *xylon* (tree) in LXX at Gen 1:11–12; 3:8; Lev 26:20; 1 Chr 16:32; 2 Chr 7:13; Eccl 2:5; Jer 17:2 (3:1177).

3. Cf. *Pss. Sol.* 14.3, where the trees of life represent believers.

interested in the healing and wholeness of a restored Israel, the ethnic people of God. John broadens God's salvific range beyond Israel to any nation whose people testify to the lordship of God and the Lamb. Not ethnicity but response to God is the decisive criterion for the eschatological relationship symbolized by the therapeutic power of the new Jerusalem's leaves. The universalism John has expressed throughout comes to a climactic crescendo here just before he brings his narrative to a close (see the comment on 21:3; cf. 21:24, 26). As he sees it, paradise—what was once the Eden in Israel's tradition—is now open to all.

[3] The new Jerusalem, however, will be closed to anything accursed. There is much discussion about what John means with his use of the term *katathema* (a person or thing under God's curse), which he deploys exclusively here. Given the proximity to the detailed vice lists (21:8, 27; 22:15) and John's explicit warning in each case that those whose lives represent such characteristics will not be allowed admittance, it is natural to assume that the seer is focused on those who are accursed because of their behavior. An unclean person surely can find no shelter in a place so holy that God dwells directly within it (see the discussion of Jerusalem as a holy city at 21:2; cf. 21:3).

Other commentators press for an alternate reading. Bauckham argues, for example, that John would not repeat the point he has already made with the vice lists. (John finds it necessary in this context to make the same point with vice lists three times [cf. 9:21]; one wonders why it is so unlikely that he would press the point home a fourth time, using a different metaphor.) Taking the word *katathema* to be functionally equivalent to *anathema* (a person or thing under God's curse), Bauckham points out that at Zech 14:11, a text John clearly seems to be alluding to here, *anathema* is used to translate the Hebrew *ḥērem*, a term that designates a sacred ban imposed by Yahweh on the enemies of Yahweh's people and rule (*Climax of Prophecy*, 316–18; cf. Aune 3:1178–79). "John has taken this to mean that the nations who dwell in the new Jerusalem, where they are healed of their idolatry and other sins by the leaves of the tree of life, will never again be subject to the destruction which God decrees for those nations who oppose his rule" (Bauckham, *Climax of Prophecy*, 317). This more positive presentation focuses on the fact that God has assembled into the city those whom God has "saved." In the end, despite the difference in nuance, the result is the same: only the righteous occupy the city.

Perhaps John also has Jer 3:17 in mind, a prophetic promise that all the nations, redeemed and no longer following their own will, will gather in apparent worship before God's Jerusalem throne. Once again combining the authority of God and the Lamb, John observes that they both hold title to the throne. Before them both, then, God's servants offer worship. John probably has in mind 7:15, the only other place where he uses this particular term for worship (*latreuō*). There the great multitude of God's witnesses worship God day and night. No doubt the same sense of perpetuity is assumed here.

[4] The worshipers before the throne of God and the Lamb possess two especially important features. First, they have the privilege and ability to see God face-to-face. The implication is that they are closer to God than even Moses, who was only allowed to see Yahweh's back as it passed by him (Exod 33:18–23). In fact, Yahweh specifically warned Moses that no one could see Yahweh's face and live (Exod 33:20). Human faculties could not safely apprehend features so holy. Yet the eschatological longing was for just this capability. The psalmist envisions the day when he will see God's face and be satisfied (Ps 17:15; cf. Ps 11:7). In the Sermon on the Mount, Jesus declares that the pure in heart are blessed precisely because they shall see God (Matt 5:8; cf. Heb 2:9). And Paul opined that though we see through a mirror dimly now, in the eschaton we will see God face-to-face (1 Cor 13:12; cf. Heb 12:14; 1 John 3:2; *Jub.* 1.28; *4 Ezra* 7.91, 98; *1 En.* 102.8).[4] As his visionary experience comes to a close, John can see this future hope already taking present form.

Second, as John has previously explained, they will carry the identifying and protecting name of God on their foreheads (see the discussion of 14:1; cf. 7:3; 9:4; 13:6; 14:9; 20:4). According to 3:12, this "branding" is the reward for those who conquer, who witness faithfully to the lordship of God and the Lamb.

[5] John closes his discussion of the new Jerusalem by reinforcing attributes that he has highlighted before. There will be no night in the city (see the discussion of 21:25). The absence of night alone would suggest that neither artificial lamp nor natural sunlight would be necessary, but John drives the point home by extolling once again that God will be their light. The seer has not only made this point already, but also depicted the glory of God and the Lamb as the energy source that fuels the eternal illumination (21:23). Finally, picking up a thread from 5:10, John affirms that these worshiping servants will rule. This reign is even more noteworthy than the already-impressive dominion of 20:4, 6. Though lengthy, the regime described in chapter 20 would last only a millennium; this one will go on forever (cf. Dan 7:18, 27).

## 22:6–9 Transition: Closing 21:9–22:5 and Initiating the Epilogue

Verses 6–9 are a bridging text. The section both closes the vision of the bridal city (21:9–22:5) and opens the epilogue (22:10–21). Because vv. 8–9 reprise the scene-closing account of John genuflecting before an angel in an ill-advised attempt at worship (19:9–10), it is appropriate to package all four verses with

---

4. As Reddish points out, "This experience of finally seeing God, of knowing God intimately and fully, is what is sometimes known as the Beatific Vision" (422).

21:9–22:5. With these verses included, the complete section (21:9–22:9) functions as a dramatic parallel to the account of the whore city, Babylon/Rome (17:1–19:10). And yet, because of the strong verbal and thematic links between the 1:1–8 prologue (esp. 1:1–3) and 22:6–7, one could make the equally compelling case that these four verses open John's closing remarks. I take the middle road. Given the strong connections to both the material in 21:9–22:5 and the prologue, it seems best to regard this material as a bridge that closes out the final narrative scene of the Apocalypse and simultaneously introduces its epilogue.

Throughout both this smaller section (vv. 6–9) and the larger unit that follows (vv. 10–21), three speakers recall the book's major themes and once more focus John's hearers and readers on the primary charge to witness to the lordship of God and the Lamb. The angel introduced at 21:9 speaks in the first two verses. John briefly reclaims center stage at v. 8, only to fade behind the voice of the angel again in vv. 9–11. Christ's voice takes charge in vv. 12–20a; then John gives the last word in vv. 20b–21. The quick movement between speakers and themes has led many commentators to the conclusion that different closing thoughts are strung together without any sense of cohesion or direction. Though this assessment has merit, it is too harsh. John uses the cacophony of remarks in this final scene to remind his hearers and readers one final, urgent time about the various matters that are important to him, and thus to them, throughout his work. A single intent prevails: to encourage witness to the lordship of God and the Lamb.

> 6 Then he said to me, "These words are trustworthy and true; the Lord, the God of the spirits of the prophets, sent God's angel to show God's servants what must happen soon. 7 'Indeed, I am coming soon. Blessed is the one who keeps the words of the prophecy of this book.'" 8 I, John, am the one who heard and saw these things. And when I heard and saw, I fell down to worship before the feet of the angel who showed them to me. 9 But[a] he said to me, "Do not do that![b] I am a fellow servant with you and your brothers and sisters, the prophets and those who keep the words of this book. Worship God!"

a. The *kai* is adversative: "but."
b. Literally, "Do not see." For the idiomatic translation, see BDAG 578.

[6] Revelation 19:9 began the conclusion to the section featuring the whore city, Babylon/Rome (17:1–19:10), with one of the guiding seven-bowl angels (17:1) attesting to the validity of the remarks made. Just so, 22:6 begins the conclusion to the structurally parallel section featuring the bride city, new Jerusalem (21:9–22:9), with one of the guiding seven-bowl angels (21:9) attesting to the validity of the remarks made. Though the angel of 22:6 is slightly

more verbose (he adds "trustworthy" to the "true" spoken by the angel of 19:9), he intends the same thought as his colleague: what has been narrated can be trusted. While the angel of 19:9 was probably verifying the message disclosed in the scene centering on judgment of Babylon, the angel here, with a view to the ensuing epilogue, focuses more broadly on the entire Apocalypse. Using familiar language, he assures his readers and hearers that they can rely on the veracity of his visions and the ideas and imperatives drawn from them (in the comments on 3:14; 19:9, 11; 21:5, see the discussion of "trustworthy and true").

The angel speaks of an abbreviated chain of revelatory transmission (God to an angel to God's servants; cf. 22:16, where another abbreviated chain is initiated by Christ) and describes the topic of that transmission as the things that must happen soon. This brief account links the unit directly to the verse that opened the Apocalypse by citing the full chain of revelatory transmission (God to Christ to an angel to John to God's servants) and describing the topic of the transmission as the things that must happen soon (1:1). This intentional connection to the opening words of the prologue, which virtually serve as a header for the entire work, suggests that John intends the angel to be verifying all of the material introduced between these two focal narrative points.

The structural move also makes several key thematic points. First, like Daniel, John celebrates that there is a God who reveals what will happen on the last day (cf. Dan 2:28). Unlike Daniel, however, who believed that the end time would be delayed (Dan 8:26; 12:4, 9), John, here at the end of the book, reinforces the apocalyptic point with which he opened it: the arrival of the final moment, when God will reveal God's intentions for all creation, is imminent. This point is so important that John not only opens his work with it; he also opens the close of his work by repeating it here and then reaffirming it in various forms four more times (22:7, 10, 12, 20).

Second, the angel bases the trustworthiness of John's Apocalypse on the God who has inspired it. In a similar way, the Old Testament seer also bases the validity of a pivotal dream and its interpretation not on the content of the dream but on the veracity of the great God who conveyed a message through it (Dan 2:45).

Third, this sovereign God connects directly to God's servants through their own spirits and so inspires them to prophetic works (on the spirit of prophecy, see the comments on 4:2–3 and 19:10). In John's context, a prophet is a servant who witnesses to the lordship of God and Christ because God has inspired testimony even in imperial circumstances that seek either to co-opt or to annihilate that testimony (see the discussion of servants as prophets at 10:7 and the treatment of witness and prophecy at 11:3). The angel therefore identifies God as the Lord God of the spirits of the prophets in the same way that God is described in the book of Numbers as the Lord God of the spirits of all flesh (16:22; 27:16). The angel and John speak here, then, not of God's Holy Spirit but of human spirits that act as conduits between the divine and the mortal, enabling the transmission of God's intent into human thought and action.[5] Working through John's spirit and the spirit of his fellow servant-prophets (22:9), God has inaugurated a "spirit of prophecy" in the churches. It is this very spirit of prophecy that has caught John up and enabled him to see what he has seen.[6] This same spirit gives a prophetic rather than an ecstatic edge to what he has conveyed. He conveys his visions for the same reason that the Old Testament prophets offered their prophecies. His primary objective is not to foretell future happenings but to exhort appropriate (i.e., witnessing) behavior in the present.

[7] To reinforce the point that God is acting soon, the angel quotes Christ: "Indeed, *I* am coming soon" (see the discussion of 3:11). If anything, John wants the point made even more fervently than does the angel. He has already quoted the same message on Christ's lips twice before (2:16; 3:11) and then restated it later in another, though just as urgent, fashion (16:15); before the chapter closes, he has Christ make the point twice more (22:12, 20). God's clinching eschatological move is not the coming of an event or even a place as magnificent as the Eden-like new Jerusalem. God's climactic move is a person. Time finds its completion in the Christ who declares through John's visions that he is the end that is coming soon. Ultimately the "things" that John says are coming soon (v. 6) are meant to be identified with and draw their significance from him. Indeed, they are to be grounded in the coming Christ as an objective and never a spiritualized reality. John does not envision an existential coming of Christ only into the hearts and spirits of humankind. In his debates with Rudolf Bultmann, Ernst Käsemann recognized that, in order to prevent the conviction of God's coming "kingdom" from devolving into exactly the kind of eschatological enthusiasm that threatened to wreck the church at Corinth, where believers felt themselves already saved through their existential encounter with the living Christ, the church must not lose its focus on that divine reign as a true, objective reality that would transform exterior reality as well as inner hearts.[7] It is this objective expectation that John certainly intends. This is why, in his climactic visions of the end, he relates Christ's coming not to personal confessions of faith but with a tangible, measurable, objective city. A real city. The Christ who comes soon comes not just to the human heart but also to the world.

5. Cf. R. E. O. White, *Biblical Ethics* (Atlanta: John Knox, 1979), 138: "Despite disproportionate attention given to Paul's teaching on the 'flesh,' there is much to show that he believed equally firmly in the 'higher' elements in human nature that were open to God, 'our Spirit' to which the Holy Spirit bears witness, 'the spirit of the man which is in him' (Romans 8:16, 1 Corinthians 2:11)." Similarly, Aune observes that "(πνεῦμα, 'spirit,' is widely used as an anthropological term for the highest faculty of human beings (1 Cor 7:34; 14:14; 2 Cor 7:1; 1 Thess 5:23)" (3:1182).

6. Revelation 1:3 and 22:9 indicate that John understands himself to be a prophet.

7. See Käsemann, esp. chs. 4 ("The Beginnings of Christian Theology") and 5 ("On the Subject of Primitive Christian Apocalyptic").

Here at the end of John's work, Christ comes with a message that reaffirms the observation and exhortation with which John began his work. Even the presentation is the same. Just as John opened his words of prophecy at 1:1 with a word about what must soon take place and followed up with a beatitude that declared blessed those who *do* and those who *will* read, hear, and keep the prophetic words (1:3; see the comment on 19:10), so he now follows up dramatic statements about the coming of Christ with a beatitude of both indicative and imperative significance (see the discussion of 14:13). This sixth in the series of seven beatitudes (1:3; 14:13; 16:15; 19:9; 20:6; 22:7, 14), like the others, functions only in part as a straightforward affirmation that all those who keep the words—who testify to the lordship of God and Christ in a world that instead proclaims the lordship of Rome—are blessed. The mere recognition of this reality also simultaneously encourages those who do not now offer such testimony to begin to do so. Through these two beatitudes, the first in the prologue (1:3) and this one in the epilogue (22:7), John at the beginning affirms and then at the end reaffirms his book's central ethical expectation. The context of apocalyptic imminence should make responding appropriately an urgent affair for John's audience.

[8–9] John now takes the stage from the angel. He does what he did earlier (1:9) and what he will soon record Christ as doing (22:16). As verification of what he has just reported, he figuratively offers his signature and, through it, his reputation as church leader (cf. 1:1, 4; 1 John 1:1–3). In this case the pronoun *tauta* (these things) refers not to the entire book, but as the second half of the verse makes clear, to the visions of the new Jerusalem. The visions have so overwhelmed him that he repeats the false step he made at 19:10, falling at the angelic messenger's feet in preparation to worship him (see the discussion of 19:10).

The angel reacts with the same alarm his predecessor displayed at 19:10. Repeating the earlier response verbatim, he cries out: "Do not do that! Worship God!" In explaining that the behavior is prohibited because he is one of John's colleagues, the angel maintains the emphasis on prophecy that has been building throughout this transitional bridge section (22:6–9) and was also central to the clarification of the testimony of Jesus in 19:10. By identifying himself as a fellow servant with John and his brothers and sisters, the prophets, the angel tacitly identifies John and his colleagues as servant prophets. The designation fits the ongoing connection between service to God and prophecy that John has established throughout his work (see the comments on 10:7 and 11:3). Fellow servants (whether angelic or not), brothers and sisters, and prophets designate a single category comprising all who are faithful Christ-believers, who respond positively to the book's primary exhortation to witness to the lordship of God and the Lamb. The *kai* (and) that joins "prophets" with "those who keep the words of this book" should therefore be understood epexegetically. The following phrase further develops the meaning of "prophets, brothers and sisters, and fellow servants." The angel intends to say, "I am a fellow servant with you and your brothers and sisters the prophets who keep the words of this book." The final point ties the angel's remarks to the beatitude of 22:7, which declares blessed (by God) those who did and would keep the prophetic words of this book.

## 22:10–21 Epilogue and Letter Closing

10 And he said to me, "Do not seal up the words of the prophecy of this book, for the time is near. 11 Let the person who is evil continue to do evil, and let the person who is impure continue to be impure, and let the person who is righteous continue to do righteousness, and let the person who is holy continue to be holy." 12 "Indeed, I am coming soon, and my reward is with me to repay everyone according to their works. 13 I am the Alpha and the Omega, the first and the last, the beginning and the end." 14 Blessed are those who wash their robes,[a] so that they may have access[b] to the tree of life and enter the city by the gates. 15 Outside are the dogs and the sorcerers and the fornicators and the murderers and the idolaters and everyone who loves and practices lies. 16 "I, Jesus, sent my angel to testify these things *to you* for the churches. I am the root and the descendant of David, the bright morning star." 17 Both the Spirit and the bride say, "Come." And let the one who hears say, "Come." And let the one who is thirsty come. Let the one who wishes take living water as a gift. 18 I testify to everyone who hears the words of the prophecy of this book: if anyone adds to them, God will add to that person the plagues described in this book; 19 if anyone takes away from the words of the book of this prophecy, God will take away that person's share in the tree of life and in the holy city, which are described in this book. 20 The one who testifies to these things says, "Surely I am coming soon." Amen! Come, Lord Jesus! 21 The grace of the Lord Jesus be with everyone.[cd]

a. Several ancient manuscripts try to define the works related to "washing the robes" more definitively by offering variant readings that build a less metaphorical case. Instead of *plynontes tas stolas autōn* ("[who] wash their robes"), which is supported strongly by ℵ A 1006 1841 2050 2053 2062 *pc* vg[st] sa; Fulg Apr, other manuscripts (𝔐 gig sy bo; Tert) offer *poiountes tas entolas autou* ([who] "do [God's] commandments"). Because the exhortation is indeed focused on works (see v. 12), either version fits nicely into the context. Given the better attestation in the manuscripts, "wash their robes" is to be preferred. Given John's penchant for symbolism, and his stress on "washing" and the relationship of that metaphor to witnessing, it also seems more likely since it fits so nicely within the literary universe he has created.[8]

8. Reddish, moreover, notes that "the two places in Revelation (12:17 and 14:12) where adherence to the commandments is mentioned, the phrase that is used is 'keeping the commandments,' not 'doing the commandments'" (427).

b. Literally, "authority over," which figuratively refers to the authorization to eat from the tree.

c. Scribal additions narrow the scope of the benediction by limiting it to the circle of Christian believers: instead of *pantōn* (all), ℵ gig substitute *tōn hagiōn* (the saints); then 051ˢ 𝔐 sy co substitute *pantōn tōn hagiōn* (all the saints); and 2030 syᵖʰ substitute *pantōn tōn hagiōn autou* (all his saints). See the commentary on v. 21 below for argument in favor of the shorter and more difficult text that is supported by A vg; Bea.

d. A concluding *Amēn* (Amen!) is inserted by ℵ 051ˢ 𝔐 vgᶜˡ sy co. The *Amēn* would supply the perfect antiphonal ending for John's entire narrative. It is for exactly this reason of rhetorical symmetry that scribes would have attached it to the manuscript. The shorter, *Amēn*-less ending supported by A 1006 1841 *pc* ar gig vgˢᵗ is thus to be preferred.

[10] Figuring to hold center stage while he has it, the angel offers a chastened John further instructions. Though John has based much of his work on Daniel and often found himself following Daniel's lead in the presentation of his own visions, he now finds that he must distance himself from his apocalyptic muse. The author of Daniel, writing pseudonymously, found himself pressed into narrating that his work had to be sealed (cf. *4 Ezra* 14.5–6, 45–46). Though the book proposes to have been written during the Babylonian exile (sixth century B.C.E.) by a famous figure of that time, it was actually penned some four centuries later (second century B.C.E.). Hearers and readers of the work would want to know why the sixth-century Daniel's prophecies took so long to be disclosed. The literary response would be clear; the author was directed to seal it (see Dan 8:26; 12:4, 9). John, writing in his own name for identifiable churches in his present, was not faced with the same dilemma. Since the exhortations developing out of his words of prophecy were intended for his contemporary believers, it made perfect sense that his work should remain unsealed. How would the urgent message to witness in the shadow of God's imminent judgment otherwise have the effect that he intended? In addition, since the end was coming soon, there were no expected future generations from which to seal his prophecies. His generations were to be the last; logically, therefore, John had to address them. The last of his mentoring angels reinforces this point by ordering him to keep his work open and accessible.

[11] The angel seems to know that John's open testimony will offer a radical opportunity for his hearers and readers. Given the lateness of the time, ultimate decisions must be made to follow the way of witnessing to the lordship of God and the Lamb, or not so witnessing. All along, John's dramatic visions have had a single intent: to shock those who were operating against God and the Lamb into testifying to and for them, while encouraging those who were already testifying to stay the difficult course. Even at the end, with the new Jerusalem already on station in the new heaven and new earth, opportunities for endurance and repentance remain. Though the angel's imperatives appear to suggest that eschatological places are already set, that the wicked are doomed beyond repair

and the righteous saved without question (cf. Dan 12:10; Ezek 3:27), nuances drawn from the context suggest an alternate reading. John's visions are future oriented, but they have not yet been realized. He is not speaking about a circumstance that has already occurred, whereby persons are locked into determined fates. Remembering that his prophecies envision the future in order to shape behavior in the present, one gains the sense that he is doing here what he has been doing throughout the new-heaven-and-new-earth cycle (see, e.g., the comment on 21:8) and indeed throughout the entire course of his narrative. As in his seven beatitudes, he is offering a declaration of reality (indicative) as a lure to motivate his ethical appeal (implicit imperative). John pictures the future in such a way that he hopes will either entice or frighten hearers and readers into making the appropriate decision to line up behind the lordship of God and the Lamb.

The plagues that accompany the opening of the seven seals, the blowing of the seven trumpets, the pouring out of the seven bowls, and the devastation that surrounds the fall of Babylon/Rome—these are all designed to shock humans to turn from the behavior that will make them subject to such judgment. The competing pictures of salvation, climactically presented in the scenes that portray a new heaven, new earth, and new Jerusalem, are designed both to invite recalcitrant humans to repent and to encourage Christ-believing humans to keep believing—and bearing witness to their convictions—no matter what the cost. The angel's comments here are a final, melodramatic way of making this same case.

The imperatives spoken by the angel ("Continue to do evil," "Continue to be impure," "Continue to do righteousness," "Continue to be holy") assure John's hearers and readers that God will certainly do what God has promised to do, that is, initiate the judgment and corresponding salvation that John has envisioned (cf. Isa 56:1). Humans must therefore make a decision. The angel's words, spoken to John but certainly intended for John's audience, functionally resemble the frustrated comments of an annoyed parent who sees her child repeatedly testing her authority by refusing to cease his misbehavior. "Keep it up! Hear!" Though a child deaf to the tones of discipline could take the apparent command literally, the parent certainly does not mean that the child should indeed keep it up. In fact, she means, and urgently so, just the opposite. A contextual appropriation of her comments indicates that she has just issued a stern warning that her child should alter his course of behavior because intervention in the form of parental judgment is imminent. The command to keep it up in such a context is in reality a last-ditch call for repentance. The angel's context is comparable; he offers a glimpse of God's imminent intervention as a means of shaking up those who are not yet living a life that witnesses in word and deed to God's lordship. "If you're doing evil, well, keep it up!" Though a hearer or reader deaf to the apocalyptic tones reverberating throughout John's book of prophecy might take the command literally, the angel means, and urgently so, just the opposite. No doubt that is why he ends his remarks by encouraging those who are already living a life of witness, as well as those who take advantage of the time that is left and start living such a life, to *really* "keep it up": persevere in acts of justice, courageous witness, and (thus) holiness, as people claimed and set apart for the realm of God.

[12] In an apparent effort to confirm everything that has been said thus far, Christ decides that it is time to speak. He verifies that the angel did not misquote him at 22:7; using exactly the same words, which he will repeat in a slightly different way in his very last comment in John's work, words to which he has appealed earlier (see the discussion of v. 7), he declares that the time of his coming is imminent. Following as it does the angel's innovative exhortation in v. 11, which was also based on a recognition that the time is near (v. 10), Christ's comment also confirms that the proximity of the end is closely related to the need for humans to comport themselves appropriately.

Christ now makes explicit his expectation for appropriate behavior when he says that he brings the realization of an eschatological relationship with God as a reward; he will repay each person according to each one's works. The larger narrative context suggests that by "works" he means witnessing to the lordship of God and Christ (cf. 2:2, 5, 6, 19, 23, 26; 3:1, 2, 8, 15). The emphasis on reward appears to suggest that he has in mind only those who live a life of appropriate witness. A broader understanding of his comments, however, suggests that he is also speaking about those who do not witness. Judgment in John's book has always, even when he has not explicitly said so, implied its opposite: salvation, or eschatological relationship with God. Whenever judgment of those who oppose God is mentioned, the realization of salvation for those who witness for God looms in the background. Conversely, when the salvation of those who witness for God is proclaimed, the reality of judgment for those who do not lurks in salvation's wake. At the end of the book, John makes this point structurally by balancing the destruction (judgment) of Babylon/Rome (17:1–19:10) against the salvific opportunity represented by the rise of the new Jerusalem (21:9–22:9). When Christ mentions the reward now, therefore, the penalty is certainly assumed (see v. 11).

The primary point is that Christ will respond appropriately to *all* human behavior. How will that response take shape? Revelation 20:12–13 describes a scene where books that record the works of all humans will be opened (cf. 2:2, 5, 6, 19, 23, 26; 3:1, 2, 5, 8; 9:20; 14:13; 16:11; 18:6). Apparently building upon a foundation in Isa 40:10, Christ declares that he will fill the role the Old Testament prophets entrusted to God (see Jer 17:10; cf. Ps 28:4; Prov 24:12). He will be the judge who determines whether a person's recorded works merit reward or punishment (for the view that this approach does not necessarily express a works righteousness, see the comment on 20:12–13).

[13] Christ immediately moves to substantiate his claim to act as eschatological judge. He requisitions titles previously applied directly (in first person)

to God (the Alpha and the Omega: 1:8; 21:6) and applies them to himself. Indeed, the explicit meaning of those titles, already appropriated in part at 1:17 and 2:8, he now fully develops as his own self-designations. Like God, he is the first and the last, the beginning and the end. What the titles revealed about God, they reveal now also about him. As the only one who exists before and after history, who rules over time because he is at the beginning and end of time, Christ, like God, can know how the time, concerns, and objectives that drive history come to their conclusion. When the one who is before and after all things says that he knows how to reward a person's works and that he will award the salvation/judgment that every human is due, John's readers and hearers can believe it.

[14] With the Apocalypse's seventh and final beatitude, Christ certifies a key narrative pronouncement: the work to which he exhorts in v. 12 is indeed the work of witness to the lordship of God and the Lamb. The verb *plynō* (wash) appears only here and at 7:14, where John describes the vast multitude of saints massed around God's heavenly throne. These are the ones who enjoy eschatological relationship with God, a direct consequence of the fact that they have washed their robes. The blood of Christ is the detergent that launders those robes to be dazzling clean. The saints are adorned with dazzling robes also in 6:11 and 7:9, there too as a metaphor for eschatological relationship with God. Earlier, though, John had specified an alternate means for acquiring dazzling robes: the saints obtain them by witnessing to the lordship of God and Christ in the imperial context where Rome greets such testimony and the persons making it with persecution, oppression, and even death (3:4–5). If these two different means of acquiring "washed" robes (3:4–5; 7:14) are both viable, then John has, narratively speaking at least, indirectly tied the blood of Christ to the act of witnessing. He makes that connection explicit in 12:11, where the act of witness and the blood of Christ together supply the weapon the saints require in order to defeat the dragon. "Washing the robes" is therefore a metaphor for witnessing, which is, in the context of chapter 22, the work that merits the reward Christ offers. Christ makes the same point more succinctly by saying that such witnesses are "blessed."

The connection of washing/witnessing to eschatological relationship is further developed through the clause that follows: "so that they might have authority over [i.e., authority to eat from] the tree of life and (so that) they might enter into the gates of the city." At 2:7 Christ promised that anyone who conquers (i.e., witnesses to the lordship of God and Christ; see the discussion of the connection between "witness" and "conquer" language at 5:5) would be able to eat from the tree of life (see the comments on 2:7 and 22:2). He makes good on that promise with the beatitude in 22:14. According to Ps 118:19–21, entry through God's gates ensures salvation. In this context, entry carries with it eternal life, since death does not exist in the city (21:4).

**[15]** It is not surprising that John's Christ would declare that sorcerers, fornicators, murderers, idolaters, and liars would be exiled outside the eschatological city. God had said exactly the same thing at 21:8, even adding cowards, the faithless, and those who commit abominations to the list of the banned. Not to be upstaged, Christ also adds a category: "dogs" will also be denied admittance. Dogs were disparaged in both Jewish and early Christian contexts for a variety of reasons, not the least of which was their tendency to scavenge and therefore eat impure things, even corpses, for food (1 Kgs 14:11; 16:4; 21:24; 2 Kgs 9:10; 9:36; in Prov 26:11 and 2 Pet 2:22 they eat their own vomit). Yet John is not concerned about literal dogs; he is speaking figuratively about unclean humans, whom he maligns by association. This tendency to denigrate undesirables by labeling them dogs was also a common feature of early Jewish and early Christian tradition (e.g., Matt 7:6; 15:26–27; Mark 7:27–28; Luke 16:21; Phil 3:2; *Did.* 9.5). The overall point that John's Christ makes by refusing "dogs" is the same point he makes with the other vice categories: those who defile themselves by accommodating to the expectations of imperial lordship, for whatever reason, are unclean and therefore unworthy of the eschatological relationship with the holy God that entry into the city symbolizes.

**[16]** John's Christ now does what John himself did at 22:8; he offers his figurative signature to validate everything that he has said and will say. Hearers and readers can trust what has just been said about the manner in which robe washing—that is, witnessing—develops an eschatological relationship with God, and how the various vices of a life that seeks cultic, economic, and political liaison with Rome destroy that relationship. Why? Because Christ is the one who makes the case. Moreover, hearers and readers can trust what will soon be said about the still-open invitations to repentance, and trust that the threats made against anyone who would dare to add to or take away from the words of John's book are real. Why? Because Christ is the one who will make them.

Christ establishes his eschatological bona fides in three ways. First, he testifies that he is the same Christ who, with God, initiated the chain of testimony that has led to John's work (see the comment on 1:1–2). The angel of 21:9, who escorted John through his visions of a new heaven, new earth, new Jerusalem, had already spoken of this chain of testimony by taking it back one step (the only one there is) beyond Christ, to God. Otherwise the angel's list of names bears a striking similarity to Christ's. In fact, both descriptions of the revelatory transmission chain operate from the foundational description at 1:1. Comparing the three chains simultaneously helps clarify some of the questions about how to translate the version of the chain that Jesus submits here.

At 1:1, the chain made the following progression: God to Jesus to an angel to John to servants and, finally, to the churches (cf. 1:4). At 21:6, although he skips several stages, the angel sticks to the same basic progression: God to an angel to servants. Given that John describes the churches as the final destination of his work (1:4), churches may be presumed to be the final stage. Christ, no doubt presuming God's presence in concert with his own (as he implies by taking God's titular designations to himself, 22:13), offers a similar progression: Christ to an angel to "you" to the churches. The commonalities at the beginning of the chain (God and Jesus) and its ending (the churches) are quite clear. The difficulty in interpretation, where 22:16 is considered, is that commentators are unsure what Christ intends with the plural pronoun "you." "I, Jesus, sent my angel to testify these things *to you* for the churches." Does he redundantly intend that "you" refer to the churches? If so, why does his grammar suggest that he considers them two separate categories? Commentators have offered many different interpretive approaches.[9]

I suggest that a comparison of this chain progression with the matching stages in the other two clarifies how the verse should be read. The first stages are constant: God/Christ, angel, John. In both 22:6 and 1:1, the stage that follows the seer John does not comprise the churches. At 1:1, John lists God's servants before he adds himself to the chain as the one who transmits the revelation to them. At 22:6, according to the angel, the angel transmits the revelation to God's servants. Because the churches are not specifically mentioned in 1:1, one could well consider that John intends servants to mean churches, or at least all the Christians in the churches.[10] It appears, though, that both in 22:16, where he specifies both "you" and "churches," and in 1:1, where the servants appear separately from the churches (mentioned in 1:4), John intends two separate categories. Servants may be members of churches, but they are, as individuals, not to be equated with the corporate entities, the churches. Indeed, that seems to be the very point that John is making by separating the "you" from "churches" in 22:16. Taken together, then, the three chains suggest the following overall progression of revelation: God to Christ to an angel to John to servants to the churches.

9. For an extensive discussion of the various interpretative alternatives, see Beale, 1143–48. (1) The "you" of 22:16 is probably the members of the seven churches addressed in 1:4. (2) "You" followed by "the churches" reflects the situation where a group in one church is first addressed in each of the seven letters (chs. 2–3) and then each letter ends by noting that it has been addressed also to the entire church. (3) "You" refers to church authorities or "prophets" like John. (4) If one reads the preposition *epi* (for, concerning) as "in," "among," so that the verse reads, "to witness these things to you among the churches" or "to you in the churches," then "you" and "the churches" are the same group. Beale favors this final option. However, Aune (3:1225) notes the grammatical problems in reading *epi* in such a way. Aune argues that in Greek it is only a remote linguistic possibility that "you" and "the churches" could refer to the same entity. This is because the presence of the preposition before "the churches" indicates that "the churches" is more remote from the action described by the verb "to testify" than is the pronoun "you."

10. See, e.g., Bauckham (*Climax of Prophecy*, 85–86): "However, it remains very uncertain whether the servants of God to whom 1:1 and 22:6 refer are the prophets rather than all Christians. The term can undoubtedly refer to all Christians (2:20; 7:3; 19:5; 22:3; and almost certainly in 11:18, where the parallel with 19:5 shows that it is not the prophets alone who are called 'your servants,' but that 'the prophets and the saints' are subdivisions of the general category 'your servants')."

Who are these servants? Like John, they are associated with the churches. Contextually, John has throughout his work tied the language of servants to that of prophets (e.g., 10:7; 11:3; cf. 11:18). Indeed, he has repeatedly reestablished that connection in inventive ways in this very chapter (22:3, 6, 9). Verse 9 forges a link between the categories of servant and prophet and suggests not only that John and the angel both fit this category but also that there is a select group of prophets who are John's direct colleagues. This depiction of a group of prophets who considered themselves leaders in and for the churches also fits John's narrative presentation. Early on, in his letters to the churches, he warns his hearers and readers in the churches about rival bands of prophets who threaten to mislead them: Balaam, 2:14; the Nicolaitans, 2:15; and the infamous Jezebel, 2:20–23. These prophets have apparently corrupted the information transmission, conveying wrong teaching about God's expectations for the churches. This literary portrait fits historical reconstructions proposed by scholars like Bauckham, who points to Acts 21:8–9, and perhaps the Christian apocalypse called the *Ascension of Isaiah*, as evidence that circles of Christian prophets did exist in Asia during the time of John's writing. "John's visionary experiences, we might suppose, would ordinarily have taken place in the context of a gathering of his fellow-prophets (probably also in the larger context of a church gathered for worship). He would relate the vision to them orally and they would later recount it to other churches" (*Climax of Prophecy*, 89).

The second way that Christ establishes his eschatological bona fides is by laying claim to an exclusive status within the Davidic genealogy. He claims to be both the root and the descendant of David. Building directly from Isa 11:1, 10, John ascribed the same designation to Christ at Rev 5:5. The allusion to Isaiah, where "root" means descendant, together with John's immediate clarification that "root" signifies "descendant," suggests that Christ does not mean the root from which a plant grows but the root that itself grows out of the Davidic plant already in place (cf. Sir 47:22). Bauckham makes the provocative point that since, according to Isa 11:10, this descendant becomes a positive signal of inclusion to the nations, John here too is expressing a universal understanding of salvation that comports well with the inclusive emphasis already established in the closing chapters of Revelation (e.g., 21:3, 24; 22:2).

Christ makes a third attempt at establishing his eschatological bona fides by laying claim to the title "bright morning star." Like the image of "root," this term has also appeared earlier in relation to Christ. Christ promised that the one who conquers (i.e., witnesses) will receive the morning star (2:28). The implication is that such witnesses will enjoy an eschatological relationship with the one who is himself the morning star. The image derives from Num 24:17, a text that foretells the promise of a messianic leader who will crush those who oppose God's people. The Jewish revolt against Rome in 132–35 C.E., led by Simon bar Kosiba, was interpreted through this messianic lens. Simon was accorded the legendary title Bar Kokhba, "Son of a Star," and presumed to be the hero who would lead God's people victoriously against the empire. This interpretation was not unique: "The text from Numbers was interpreted messianically within Judaism (cf. *T. Levi* 18.3; *T. Jud.* 24.1; and the Qumran documents CD 7.18–21; 1QM 11.6–7; 4QTest [4Q175] 9–13)" (Reddish 428). John is certainly following this line of messianic interpretation; for him, the Lamb, along with God, executes the judgment that destroys Babylon/Rome and inaugurates salvation for all who believe. Bauckham once again opens that understanding of salvation universally; he reads the star language through the lens of Isa 60:3, which understands God's light (star?) to be a beacon for the nations to find their way to the new Jerusalem (*Climax of Prophecy*, 324–25).

[17] While identifying the speaker and the message in this verse seems to be a straightforward task, identifying the target audience is a more difficult matter. Yoked to the definite article and appearing in the singular, Spirit seems here to be not the human spirits of 22:6 but the Spirit of God. Earlier in the book, John referred to this characterization with the phrase "the seven spirits." "Seven," we know, is the number that represents wholeness or completeness for John. The seven spirits together represented the complete and full Spirit of God (1:4–8; 5:6; cf. 3:1; 4:5). Referenced in the singular with the article, the Spirit is an entity who acts for God, even speaking for God as it does here (cf. 2:7, 11, 17, 29; 3:6, 13, 22 [addressing the seven churches]; 11:11; 14:13).

The bride, the focal character of the section that immediately precedes the epilogue (21:9–22:9), is even easier to identify (see the comments on 19:7–8 and 21:2, 9). She is the new Jerusalem, the city that represents the people of God. On one level, as the city of God, she invites all nations to come through her open gates and find eschatological relationship with God (21:24). On another, more complex level, as the people of God, she invites not herself, as one might think, but those of the nations who are not of the church. In other words, she appears to be inviting those who are not yet witnessing believers to become witnessing believers so that they too may enter. Here is where the interpretive difficulties arise. Most interpreters argue that the Spirit and the bride are speaking instead to Jesus, inviting him to fulfill his pledge to come soon (22:7, 12, 20).[11] If the Spirit and the bride are indeed talking to Jesus, the suggestion is that they do not believe that the Lamb, who has given his word and signed

---

11. Commentators note, for example, that the imperative verb *erchou* (Come!) is a second-person singular, suggesting that only one person is being invited: Christ. However, in the second half of the verse, where commentators agree that everyone who is thirsty is invited to come, the invitation is to all those who seek relationship with God. This plural group, though, is referenced as a single corporate entity and addressed with a singular participle and a singular imperative verb (*erchesthō*). The verb "come," as spoken by the Spirit and the bride in the singular, could therefore just as easily refer not to a single individual but to the corporate reality of those who have not yet repented as though they were a single narrative entity.

his figurative signature to it (v. 16), will honor his promise unless they intervene with an invitation. The invitation, then, is either redundant or a demonstration of a lack of faith in the Lamb. But surely the Spirit and the bride, both of whom enjoy an intimate relationship with the Lamb, trust the Lamb's word that he is coming, and coming soon. No further action on their part is necessary unless it is to encourage those who are not yet witnessing believers to repent, witness, and thus prepare themselves properly for Christ's coming. Indeed, an invitation to those who have yet to believe fits nicely with John's image of a gracious God, who even at the end extends invitations to nonbelievers to repent (see the discussion of 18:4; cf. 2:5, 16, 21, 22; 3:3, 19; 9:20–21; 11:13; 14:7; 15:4; 16:9, 11).

This open invitation continues with the ensuing clause "Let the one who hears say, 'Come.'" Of whom does Christ speak? The verb "hear" is key to answering the question. In a book of visions and auditions, one expects to have the word "hearing" crop up often (cf. 22:8). But one would probably not expect that 28 percent of the time the verb occurs, it would be tied to "doing."[12] This connection occurs especially in chapters 2 and 3, where John sets his ethical agenda. Those who hear are those who conquer. In other words, those who hear are those who have heard, repented, obeyed, and thus witness. "Those who hear," then, is another way of saying what John has already implied through his use of the term "bride." These are believers. Christ is basically repeating and reinforcing the invitation that was just extended; the people of God invite those who are not yet of God to come. Yet he has added something very important. The connection drawn between hearing and witnessing indicates *how* they can manage this necessary movement. What do they need to do to be able to come? They must become like those who invite them. They must hear. They must witness to the lordship of God and Christ.

John has already identified the thirsty (21:6; cf. Isa 55:1). This invitation continues the theme of inviting not Christ but those who desire and need eschatological relationship with him. Christ thus reinforces here what he has said earlier. The thirsty should seek entrance into the city because there resides the gift of living water (see the comments on 7:17 and 22:1).

**[18–19]** The same Christ who has already validated his remarks by putting his own person on the line in v. 16 does the same thing, using another verbal approach, just two verses later. This time, as though he is swearing himself in at a trial, he sanctions what he is about to say with the pledge "I testify." Remembering that his very name is "Faithful and True" (19:11), John's hearers and readers can certainly trust the oathlike pronouncement that follows. To everyone within the sound of his voice (and the verbal reach of John's work), he virtually commissions the sanctity of "the prophecy of this book." John is following

---

12. See Rev 1:3; 2:7, 11, 17, 29; 3:3, 6, 13, 20, 22; 13:9; 22:18.

tradition here, adopting the premise that divinely authorized works should not be altered (see Deut 4:2; 12:32; cf. 11QTemple 54.5–7). The ending to the *Letter of Aristeas* (310–311), the account of the legendary creation of the Septuagint (the Greek translation of the Hebrew Bible), is another well-known example of an inspired book ending with the prohibition against making changes to it. As commentators note over and over again, the prohibition acts as a kind of copyright in a world that had no such protective device. But putting his own work in direct line with such prohibitions, John again signals that his work has been commissioned by God. In terms of form, he utilizes the kind of curse formula that Paul also applies in some of his letters (e.g., 1 Cor 16:22; Gal 1:8–9).

The warning that follows is straightforward. John begins with a conditional sentence in which the opening clauses indicate a situation that not only might happen but is very likely to happen. He apparently has real reason to be concerned that someone might add to what he has written or take away from it.[13] In the closing clauses of both halves of the sentence come the almost mocking rejoinders. Taking a page yet again from the ancient lex talionis tradition (see the comments on 11:18; 16:1, 6; 18:6), he promises a punishment that matches the crime in kind, even if it is clearly disproportionate in terms of degree. For those who add to what John has written, Christ promises, on the basis of what is in effect his personal veracity, that God will add to them every one of the plagues that John has envisioned. Though John intends to balance the crime against the response to it, the resulting imbalance is almost laughable. The entire cosmos was unable to withstand such an onslaught; certainly any single individual would be absolutely crushed. Perhaps the horrific pain and suffering expected to attend such plagues, even more than annihilation itself, is intended. Certainly such a prospect should make any potential revisionist shudder. A corresponding response is also threatened to any who would subtract from what John has written. Christ promises that God will remove from them any stake in two of the especially precious symbols of eschatological relationship with God that John has spent the last few chapters highlighting: the tree of life (cf. 22:2) and the new Jerusalem (cf. 21:9–22:9). This final threat verifies that the earlier threat was a promise not of annihilation but of monstrous suffering. The shell of a being left in the wake of such plague-induced suffering would subsequently be doomed to the even greater suffering attached to a life of agonizing separation from God, also envisioned as eternal confinement in the lake of fire and sulfur, or brimstone (see the discussion of 20:15).

**[20]** Grounding his words in his person for yet a third time (cf. 22:16, 18), Christ identifies himself as the one who testifies to these things, in other words,

13. As Aune explains, "The textual history of other apocalypses, both Jewish and Christian, reveals that such texts were constantly being revised and modified by those who transmitted them" (3:1232).

the things he has just professed (vv. 12–19). He closes his remarks by declaring trustworthy a statement upon which John builds his exhortation to live a life that testifies to the lordship of God and the Lamb: Christ is coming soon (see the comments on 2:16; 3:11; 22:7, 12; cf. 16:15). That imminence lends urgency to all that John has said. Those who are not witnessing have little time left to repent. Those who are witnessing must continue to do so despite any persecutions, oppressions, and death that Rome might inflict.

Nevertheless, in quoting Christ here and elsewhere, and in making his own claims about the nearness of God's judgment/salvation, John was wrong. Nearly two millennia later, the moment he anticipated has yet to arrive. Commentators are right to ask whether John's chronological inaccuracy detracts from his message. First, contemporary readers of his work are right to consider that his mistake on this critical point does well imply that he was probably mistaken in other areas of his presentation. His negative presentations of women, his understanding about eternal suffering, and his depictions of God's authorization and even execution of extreme acts of violence come immediately to mind. And yet, even where his mistakes are clear, there is a potent and viable message for contemporary readers. Even in his own time, John never asked his hearers and readers to contemplate the future in order to calculate the timetable of its arrival. He did not offer his prophecies only to predict for his time or future times when God was going to act. Instead, his future-oriented visions were intended to impel his hearers and readers into appropriate contemporary action. He appealed to the imminence of God's intervention not to offer a timeline but to encourage a sense of urgency.

It is that sense of urgency—living in the present moment as though God could break into time at any moment—that carries through the ongoing centuries to sustain meaning and hope for believers in the twenty-first century. John's primary message still holds. In a world where many human and even satanic forces seem to be in control, God and the Lamb reign as Lord. No matter how powerful any country or force becomes, no matter how vast the reach of its military, political, and economic empire, God and the Lamb still reign as Lord. This enduring indicative grounds an equally enduring imperative. Those who believe in that lordship—despite seeing pretensions to lordship in people and powers, and despite enduring persecutions at the hands of those people and powers when they refuse to recognize their lordship—must continue to witness, in word and in action, to the lordship of God and the Lamb. They must do so because the Christ who is Lord, the Christ who is faithful and true, has promised that he is coming . . . soon.

Having apparently taken his cue from the heavenly hymn singers, John responds to Christ as he should, antiphonally. By crying out "Amen!" he registers his faith in the trustworthiness of what Jesus has said. In essence, he shouts, "True!"

In his penultimate statement, John acknowledges the worship setting in which it appears he expected his work to be heard. Having heard Jesus proclaim that he is coming soon, having anticipated the persecutions that will follow concerted witnessing to the lordship of God and the Lamb, John petitions Jesus to come in that very guise of Lord. It is no secret that he is operating from an early Christian formula highlighted by Paul at 1 Cor 16:22 and by the author of the *Didache* at 10.6. The *Didache* corroborates what the petition "come" suggests by positioning the petition in the context of the Lord's Supper. A eucharistic emphasis was implanted early on in the Apocalypse when Christ told the Laodiceans that he was outside, knocking on their communal door, and would indeed come in and eat with them if they stop their efforts to accommodate to the lordship claims of Rome and instead witness to the lordship of God and the Lamb. John, having just finished presenting his own written witness, now takes Christ up on his offer: "Amen! Come, Lord Jesus!" When Paul resorted to the phrase, he did not translate it. He simply transliterated the Aramaic letters of the original saying into Greek letters for his readers: *Marana tha* (Our Lord, come!).[14] One can easily imagine members of John's churches, after just listening to a reading of his work and then hearing this petition, now moving directly into the meal, where the cultic presence of the Lord would encourage participants to trust in the imminent coming of his eschatological presence.

[21] Fittingly, John closes the work he began with an epistolary greeting (1:4–6) by composing an epistolary benediction. Surely, readers in the very same Asia Minor communities where Paul had spent much of his ministry would have recognized the kind of closing greeting that the apostle used to conclude so many of his letters (see esp. 1 Cor 16:22–24, which closes with "Come, Lord [Jesus]," followed immediately by the benediction; cf. Rom 16:20; 2 Cor 13:13; Gal 6:18; Phil 4:23; 1 Thess 5:28; Phlm 25).

There is varied manuscript evidence for the wording of the final phrase of Revelation. Did John mean to wish God's grace for all the saints, all his saints, all your saints, all of us, all of you, or just all? The more specific formulations suggest that John addressed his work to the community of believers, to encourage and admonish the church alone. The more open ending, however, fits well with the universal sensibility that John has been developing throughout, but particularly here at the end (see the comments on 21:3, 24; 22:2). It is more likely that Christian scribes would have altered the open ending to specifically identify the church as John's intended audience than that they would have dropped a word so as to make the audience more universal. The more difficult open-

---

14. Though some manuscripts have *maran atha* (Our Lord has come) and others have combined the two Aramaic words into one, *maranatha*, Reddish suggests that "the contexts in 1 Corinthians, Revelation, and the Didache point toward an eschatological usage of the phrase; the *marana tha* ('Our Lord, come') is likely the correct transliteration" (431).

ended reading is therefore to be preferred. Indeed, such an open ending to the benediction matches the emphasis on divine grace at the benediction's beginning. Even at the end of time, marked with such strong literary emphasis at the end of the book, John believes that God is a gracious God who reaches out not just to the church but also to any and all who would heed the call to witness to the one revelation that this book of many visions has strained to reveal: true lordship belongs exclusively to God and Christ.

05-19-2009

# INDEX OF ANCIENT SOURCES

**OLD TESTAMENT**

**Genesis**

| | |
|---|---|
| 1:2 | 245n3 |
| 1:2–10 | 241, 245 |
| 1:11–12 | 397n2 |
| 1:21 | 243n1 |
| 1:26 | 90n8 |
| 1:30 | 215 |
| 2–3 | 52 |
| 2:2 | 31n2 |
| 2:3 | 31n2 |
| 2:8 | 397n2 |
| 2:9 | 397 |
| 2:10 | 396 |
| 3 | 234–35 |
| 3:1–16 | 225, 242 |
| 3:3 | 52 |
| 3:22–24 | 52 |
| 3:24 | 92n12 |
| 4:10 | 352 |
| 4:15 | 143 |
| 6–8 | 166n14 |
| 6:1n4 | 173n1 |
| 7 | 241n11 |
| 7:11 | 245n3 |
| 8:4 | 31n2 |
| 12:3 | 38 |
| 13:16 | 150 |
| 14:19 | 194 |
| 14:22 | 194 |
| 15:5 | 150 |
| 15:12 | 218 |
| 15:18 | 182 |
| 19:17 | 139 |
| 19:24 | 165n13, 275 |
| 19:24–28 | 184 |
| 19:28 | 175 |
| 22:1–14 | 385 |
| 22:17 | 150 |
| 26:4 | 150 |
| 28:14 | 38, 150 |
| 32:12 | 150 |
| 34:31 | 309 |
| 35:2 | 345 |
| 45:9 | 47 |
| 49 | 147n10 |
| 49:9–10 | 105 |

**Exodus**

| | |
|---|---|
| 2:15 | 232 |
| 3:1 | 385 |
| 3:12 | 385 |
| 3:14 | 33, 34, 39 |
| 4:10 | 286 |
| 4:17 | 257n8 |
| 4:22 | 47 |
| 4:30 | 257n8 |
| 5:1 | 47 |
| 7 | 211 |
| 7:8–12:36 | 166 |
| 7:15–24 | 169n18 |
| 7:17 | 47 |
| 7:17–21 | 168, 295 |
| 7:17–25 | 211 |
| 8:1–15 | 303 |
| 9:8–12 | 295 |
| 9:13–26 | 309 |
| 9:22–26 | 168 |
| 9:24 | 308 |
| 10:2 | 257n8 |
| 10:5 | 175 |
| 10:15 | 175 |
| 10:22–23 | 301 |
| 11:10 | 257n8 |
| 12 | 140, 143 |
| 12:15–16 | 31n2 |
| 13:6 | 31n2 |
| 13:21 | 189, 292 |
| 14:31 | 286 |
| 15 | 286n4 |
| 15:1–18 | 98, 286 |
| 15:3–4 | 353 |
| 15:5 | 174 |
| 15:6 | 99n2 |
| 15:11 | 249–50, 286, 287 |
| 15:12 | 99n2, 241 |
| 15:14 | 221 |
| 15:16 | 216, 216n15 |
| 16:10 | 189 |
| 16:26–30 | 31n2 |
| 16:31–35 | 60 |
| 16:32 | 232 |
| 19:4 | 225, 241 |
| 19:6 | 37, 115, 368 |
| 19:16 | 43, 160 |
| 19:16–18 | 165 |
| 19:16–19 | 86, 191n16 |
| 19:18 | 175 |
| 19:18–21 | 91 |
| 20:4 | 104 |
| 20:10–11 | 31n2 |
| 20:11 | 194 |
| 21:2 | 31n2 |
| 21:23–25 | 329 |
| 23:11–12 | 31n2 |
| 23:19 | 270 |
| 24:16 | 31n2 |
| 25:18 | 92n12 |
| 25:31–37 | 43 |
| 27:2 | 181n6 |
| 28:4 | 44 |
| 28:15–21 | 391 |
| 28:16 | 391 |

**Exodus** (*continued*)
| | |
|---|---|
| 28:39 | 291 |
| 30:1–10 | 162, 164n10, 181n6 |
| 30:11–16 | 146 |
| 30:34–38 | 113n11, 163 |
| 30:38–42 | 108 |
| 31:15 | 31n2 |
| 31:17 | 31n2 |
| 32:15 | 102 |
| 32:32–33 | 71, 374 |
| 33:7–11 | 291 |
| 33:18–23 | 399 |
| 33:20 | 399 |
| 34:6 | 74 |
| 34:10 | 283 |
| 34:21 | 31n2 |
| 35:2 | 31n2 |
| 37:17–24 | 43 |
| 37:25–26 | 181n6 |
| 38:2 | 181n6 |
| 38:23–26 | 292 |
| 39:8–14 | 391 |
| 39:9 | 391 |
| 39:29 | 44 |
| 40:5 | 181n6 |
| 40:34–35 | 292 |
| 40:34–38 | 291 |

**Leviticus**
| | |
|---|---|
| 1:1–2 | 291 |
| 2:1 | 163 |
| 2:15 | 163 |
| 4:7 | 133 |
| 6:15 | 163 |
| 10:1 | 163 |
| 13:5–6 | 31n2 |
| 13:27 | 31n2 |
| 13:32 | 31n2 |
| 13:34 | 31n2 |
| 16:11–14 | 163 |
| 16:12 | 165 |
| 21:9 | 323 |
| 23:3 | 31n2 |
| 23:8 | 31n2 |
| 23:9–14 | 270 |
| 23:16 | 31n2 |
| 23:24 | 31n2, 160 |
| 23:27 | 31n2 |
| 23:40 | 151 |
| 23:43 | 151 |

| | |
|---|---|
| 24:16 | 301 |
| 24:17–20 | 329 |
| 25:9 | 160 |
| 26 | 291 |
| 26:8 | 176n4 |
| 26:11–12 | 380 |
| 26:18–28 | 123n19 |
| 26:20 | 397n2 |
| 26:21 | 291 |
| 26:22 | 131n29 |
| 26:26 | 127 |

**Numbers**
| | |
|---|---|
| 1:2–3 | 146 |
| 1:2–46 | 146 |
| 1:16–54 | 147n10 |
| 1:49 | 148 |
| 2:33 | 148 |
| 3:14–4:49 | 146 |
| 4:14–15 | 292 |
| 7:13–89 | 292 |
| 7:89 | 92n12 |
| 8:1–4 | 43 |
| 11:6–9 | 60 |
| 14:18 | 74 |
| 16:6 | 163 |
| 16:22 | 401 |
| 16:30–34 | 241 |
| 16:33 | 358 |
| 16:46–47 | 164n10 |
| 22–24 | 58 |
| 24:14–20 | 64 |
| 24:17 | 64, 411 |
| 25 | 58 |
| 26:1–2 | 146 |
| 26:1–56 | 146 |
| 27:16 | 401 |
| 31:16 | 58 |
| 34:19–28 | 147 |
| 35:30 | 208, 208n6 |

**Deuteronomy**
| | |
|---|---|
| 1:7 | 182 |
| 2:7 | 232 |
| 2:15–16 | 232 |
| 3:24 | 250 |
| 4:2 | 414 |
| 5:8 | 104 |
| 5:14 | 31n2 |
| 8:3 | 60 |
| 10:8–9 | 148 |

| | |
|---|---|
| 10:17 | 322 |
| 11:6 | 241 |
| 11:16–17 | 211 |
| 11:25 | 216n15 |
| 12:32 | 414 |
| 15:1 | 31n2 |
| 15:9 | 31n2 |
| 15:12 | 31n2 |
| 17:6 | 208n6 |
| 18:1–5 | 148 |
| 19:15 | 208, 208n6 |
| 19:21 | 329 |
| 20:1–9 | 269 |
| 23:9–10 | 269 |
| 26:1–11 | 270 |
| 28:1 | 295 |
| 28:27 | 295 |
| 28:35 | 295 |
| 28:38 | 131n29 |
| 28:39 | 131n29 |
| 28:42 | 131n29 |
| 28:49 | 170n19 |
| 29:5 | 232 |
| 29:18 | 169 |
| 32:1–43 | 286 |
| 32:4 | 287, 287n5, 297n4 |
| 32:8 | 287 |
| 32:10 | 232 |
| 32:17 | 185 |
| 32:24 | 131n29 |
| 32:24–25 | 123n19 |
| 32:35–39 | 193 |
| 32:40 | 46, 193,193n19 |
| 32:43 | 134, 239 |
| 33 | 147n10 |
| 33:17 | 112 |

**Joshua**
| | |
|---|---|
| 1:2 | 286 |
| 1:4 | 182 |
| 3:1–4:18 | 302n6 |
| 6 | 160 |
| 6:4 | 31n2 |
| 6:5 | 160 |
| 6:15–16 | 31n2 |
| 7:6 | 335 |
| 11:4 | 370 |
| 13:14 | 148 |
| 13:33 | 148 |
| 21:4–7 | 147 |
| 24:2 | 47 |

| | | | | | |
|---|---|---|---|---|---|
| 24:7 | 232 | 12:25–33 | 148 | 16:28 | 344 |
| | | 14:11 | 409 | 16:31 | 344 |
| **Judges** | | 16:4 | 409 | 16:32 | 397n2 |
| 5 | 147n10 | 16:31 | 63 | 20:2 | 280 |
| 5:19 | 306 | 17–18 | 211 | 21:1 | 235 |
| 5:20 | 173 | 17:1–7 | 232 | 21:1–6 | 146 |
| 6:2 | 139n34 | 18:4 | 63 | 21:16 | 127n25 |
| 7:12 | 370 | 18:13 | 63 | 24:1–19 | 90 |
| 8:26 | 314n1 | 18:38–39 | 258 | 25:6–31 | 113 |
| 18 | 148 | 19:1–3 | 63 | 27:1–24 | 146 |
| | | 19:1–4 | 177n5 | 28:17 | 292 |
| **1 Samuel** | | 20:31–32 | 127n25 | | |
| 2:2 | 287n5 | 21 | 63 | **2 Chronicles** | |
| 2:9–10 | 157n2 | 22:11 | 112 | 3:8 | 389 |
| 2:10 | 191n16 | 22:19 | 88, 89n6 | 4:8 | 292 |
| 4:4 | 92n12 | 22:19–23 | 90n8 | 4:9 | 286 |
| 4:8 | 211 | 21:24 | 409 | 4:21 | 292 |
| 7:10 | 191 | 21:27 | 127n25 | 5:2 | 265n15 |
| 13:5 | 370 | | | 5:13 | 292 |
| 13:16 | 139n34 | **2 Kings** | | 7:13 | 171, 397n2 |
| 14:11 | 139n34 | 1:9–14 | 371 | 10:11 | 176n3 |
| 17:44 | 214n14 | 1:10 | 165n13, 210 | 10:14 | 176n3 |
| 17:46 | 214n14 | 1:10–14 | 258 | 12:6 | 296n2 |
| 21:4–5 | 269 | 1:12 | 165n13 | 18:10 | 112 |
| | | 1:14 | 165n13 | 22:17–18 | 146 |
| **2 Samuel** | | 2:11 | 216n16 | 35:22 | 306 |
| 1:12 | 33 | 5:19–20 | 146 | | |
| 1:24 | 314n1 | 6:14 | 370 | **Ezra** | |
| 5:7 | 265 | 7:1 | 127 | 1:3 | 370 |
| 7:8 | 220 | 9 | 63 | 2 | 146 |
| 7:14 | 382 | 9:7 | 134, 197n22, | 9:11 | 197n22 |
| 8:2a | 202n3 | | 342n11 | 9:15 | 296n2 |
| 8:2b | 202n3 | 9:10 | 214n14, 409 | | |
| 11:11 | 269 | 9:22 | 185n10 | **Nehemiah** | |
| 11:26 | 33 | 9:27 | 306 | 1:7–8 | 286 |
| 12:30 | 280 | 9:30–37 | 323 | 7 | 146 |
| 22:9 | 210 | 9:36 | 409 | 8:14–18 | 151 |
| 22:14 | 191n16 | 17 | 147n8 | 9:6 | 194 |
| 24:1–9 | 146 | 17:13 | 197n22 | 9:19 | 232 |
| | | 17:23 | 197n22 | 9:21 | 232 |
| **1 Kings** | | 19:1–2 | 127n25 | 9:33 | 296n2 |
| 5:13–18 | 146 | 19:15 | 92n12 | 11:1 | 377 |
| 6:19–20 | 389 | 21:8 | 286 | 11:18 | 377 |
| 6:20–22 | 390 | 21:10 | 197n22 | | |
| 7:10 | 391 | 21:13 | 202n3 | **Esther** | |
| 8:1 | 222, 265n15 | 23:29–30 | 306 | 8:15 | 314n1 |
| 8:6 | 222 | 24:2 | 197n22 | 8:17 | 216n15 |
| 8:10 | 189 | | | 9:2 | 216n15 |
| 8:10–11 | 292 | **1 Chronicles** | | | |
| 8:53 | 286 | 11:5 | 265 | **Job** | |
| 12:11 | 176n3 | 12:23–37 | 147 | 1–2 | 237 |
| 12:14 | 176n3 | | | 1:6 | 90n8 |
| | | | | 1:9–11 | 237 |

**Job** (*continued*)

| | |
|---|---|
| 1:16 | 165n13 |
| 2:1 | 90n8 |
| 2:4–5 | 237 |
| 2:6 | 176 |
| 2:12 | 335 |
| 3:1–26 | 177n5 |
| 3:8 | 243n1 |
| 3:21 | 177 |
| 6:8–9 | 177n5 |
| 7:15–16 | 177n5 |
| 9:26 | 170n19 |
| 11:9 | 190n15 |
| 26:6 | 179 |
| 26:12–13 | 92 |
| 28:14 | 245n3 |
| 28:22 | 179 |
| 30:6 | 139n34 |
| 31:12 | 179 |
| 36:30–32 | 91 |
| 37:2–5 | 191n16 |
| 38:7 | 173 |
| 38:16 | 174, 245n3 |
| 38:17 | 46 |
| 39:19–20 | 178 |
| 40–41 | 243n1 |

**Psalms**

| | |
|---|---|
| 1 | 31 |
| 2 | 265 |
| 2:2 | 323 |
| 2:6 | 265n15 |
| 2:6–12 | 265n16 |
| 2:8–9 | 64 |
| 2:9 | 230, 355 |
| 2:10 | 313 |
| 2:10–11 | 64 |
| 3:1–2 | 134n30 |
| 6:3 | 134n30 |
| 7 | 135 |
| 7:11 | 296n2 |
| 9:4 | 296n2 |
| 9:11 | 265n15 |
| 10:16 | 220 |
| 11:6 | 165n13, 275, 275n23 |
| 11:7 | 399 |
| 14:7 | 265n15 |
| 17:15 | 399 |
| 18:7 | 308n12 |

| | |
|---|---|
| 18:7–19 | 91 |
| 18:13 | 191n16 |
| 18:35 | 99n2 |
| 19:10 | 199 |
| 20:6 | 99n2 |
| 22:21 | 112 |
| 23:1–2 | 156 |
| 28:4 | 373, 407 |
| 29:3 | 191 |
| 31:17–18 | 157n2 |
| 33:3 | 114, 267 |
| 35 | 135 |
| 35:10 | 250 |
| 35:17 | 134n30 |
| 40:3 | 114 |
| 46:2–3 | 308n12 |
| 50:2 | 265n15 |
| 53:6 | 265n15 |
| 55 | 135 |
| 58 | 135 |
| 59 | 135 |
| 63:8 | 99n2 |
| 68:1 | 139 |
| 69 | 135 |
| 69:28 | 71, 374 |
| 71:19 | 250 |
| 71:20 | 174 |
| 72:2 | 350 |
| 74:9–10 | 134n30 |
| 74:12–15 | 92, 225 |
| 74:13 | 241 |
| 74:13–14 | 229 |
| 74:14 | 243n1 |
| 75:8 | 275n23 |
| 77:16 | 241 |
| 77:17–18 | 91 |
| 77:18–19 | 165 |
| 78:15 | 232 |
| 78:19 | 232 |
| 78:23 | 86 |
| 78:24 | 60 |
| 78:43–51 | 166 |
| 78:44 | 169n18, 295 |
| 78:45 | 303 |
| 79 | 135 |
| 79:1–5 | 214n14 |
| 79:2–3 | 214 |
| 79:5 | 134, 134n30 |
| 79:10 | 134 |
| 80:1 | 92n12 |

| | |
|---|---|
| 80:4 | 134n30 |
| 83 | 135 |
| 84:7 | 265n15 |
| 86 | 289 |
| 86:8–10 | 287, 288 |
| 86:9 | 76, 287n5 |
| 86:12 | 287n5 |
| 88:11 | 179 |
| 88:30 | 35 |
| 89:6 | 250 |
| 89:7 | 90n8 |
| 89:9–10 | 92 |
| 89:17 | 112 |
| 89:27 | 35 |
| 89:37 | 35 |
| 89:46 | 134n30 |
| 90:13 | 134n30 |
| 92:5 | 287n5 |
| 93:1 | 344 |
| 94:3 | 134n30 |
| 95:7 | 380 |
| 96–100 | 267 |
| 96:1 | 114, 267 |
| 96:11 | 239 |
| 96:13 | 350 |
| 97:1 | 344 |
| 97:3 | 210, 298 |
| 97:5 | 308n12 |
| 98:1 | 114, 267, 287n5 |
| 98:1–2 | 287 |
| 98:2 | 287n5 |
| 98:9 | 350 |
| 99:1 | 92n12, 221, 344 |
| 99:2 | 265n15 |
| 99:3 | 287n5 |
| 103:19 | 89 |
| 104–106 | 341 |
| 104:1–2 | 226 |
| 104:25–26 | 243n1 |
| 105:26 | 286 |
| 105:27–36 | 166 |
| 105:30 | 303 |
| 105:38 | 216 |
| 106:9 | 302 |
| 106:17 | 241 |
| 106:48 | 343 |
| 109 | 135 |
| 111:2 | 283, 287n5 |
| 111:9 | 287n5 |
| 113–118 | 341 |

| | | | | | | |
|---|---|---|---|---|---|
| 113:1 | 341 | **Isaiah** | | 24:19–20 | 15 |
| 113:5 | 250 | 1:9–10 | 214 | 24:21–22 | 174, 361 |
| 114:3–7 | 372 | 1:21 | 309, 344 | 24:23 | 265n16, 393 |
| 115:4–7 | 185 | 1:24 | 47 | 25:2 | 15 |
| 115:13 | 343 | 2:2 | 287n5, 289 | 25:6–8 | 346 |
| 115:17 | 157n2 | 2:3 | 370 | 25:7 | 15 |
| 118:19–21 | 408 | 2:8 | 185 | 25:8 | 156, 380 |
| 118:24 | 344 | 2:10 | 139 | 26:15 | 227, 229 |
| 118:27 | 181n6 | 2:19 | 139 | 26:17 | 227, 229 |
| 119:100–103 | 199 | 2:20 | 185 | 26:19 | 15 |
| 122:4 | 370 | 2:21 | 139 | 27 | 227 |
| 125:1 | 265n15 | 3:16 | 47 | 27:1 | 15, 92, 229, 243n1 |
| 134 | 343 | 3:24 | 127n25 | 29:3 | 370 |
| 135 | 341 | 4:3 | 71, 374, 394 | 29:6 | 138, 165, 191n16 |
| 135:1 | 343 | 5:19 | 74 | 30:8 | 43 |
| 135:15–17 | 185 | 5:25 | 308n12 | 34:4 | 100, 139 |
| 135:20 | 343 | 5:26–29 | 182n7 | 34:9–10 | 276 |
| 136:3 | 322 | 6:1–4 | 92 | 34:10 | 343 |
| 136:16 | 232 | 6:1–13 | 88, 89n6, 90n8 | 34:11 | 202n3 |
| 137 | 135 | 6:3 | 94 | 34:11–15 | 326 |
| 137:8 | 329 | 6:4 | 292 | 35:8 | 394 |
| 139 | 135 | 7:14 | 227, 230 | 35:10 | 380 |
| 139:14 | 283, 287n5 | 7:20 | 182n7 | 36:1–3 | 370 |
| 139:21 | 51 | 8:7–8 | 182n7 | 37:1–2 | 127n25 |
| 141:2 | 113, 165n11 | 8:19–22 | 301 | 40:2 | 36, 329 |
| 144 | 267 | 11:1 | 105, 411 | 40:3 | 232 |
| 144:9 | 114, 267 | 11:4 | 45, 350, 355 | 40:4 | 308n12 |
| 145:17 | 287, 287n5, | 11:10 | 105, 411 | 40:10 | 407 |
| | 297n4 | 11:12 | 141, 369 | 40:12 | 127 |
| 146–150 | 341 | 11:15–16 | 302 | 40:18 | 250 |
| 146:6 | 190n15, 194 | 12:1–6 | 286n4 | 40:25 | 74, 250 |
| 149:1 | 267 | 13:10 | 139, 170 | 40:31 | 241 |
| 150:1 | 343 | 13:19–22 | 326 | 41:2 | 302n5 |
| | | 14:12 | 173 | 41:4 | 39, 381 |
| **Proverbs** | | 14:13–14 | 330 | 41:10 | 99n2 |
| 3:19 | 81 | 14:19–20 | 214n14 | 41:25 | 142, 302n5 |
| 5:4 | 169 | 14:29–31 | 182n7 | 42:10 | 114, 190n15, 267 |
| 8:22–31 | 81 | 17:8 | 185 | 42:15 | 308n12 |
| 8:29 | 190n15 | 20:11 | 103 | 43:19 | 380 |
| 15:11 | 179 | 21:1–10 | 313 | 44:2 | 46 |
| 16:11 | 127 | 21:9 | 274 | 44:6 | 39, 46, 381 |
| 16:24 | 199 | 22:22 | 74 | 44:7 | 250 |
| 24:12 | 64, 407 | 23 | 312 | 44:9–20 | 185 |
| 26:11 | 409 | 23–24 | 325 | 44:23 | 239 |
| 27:20 | 179 | 23:17 | 312, 326 | 45:2 | 308n12 |
| 27:21 | 83 | 23:8 | 312, 338 | 45:14 | 76 |
| 30:27 | 179 | 24–27 | 15 | 46:11 | 302n5 |
| 31:21 | 314n1 | 24:1 | 15 | 47 | 325 |
| | | 24:8 | 337 | 47:5 | 157n2 |
| **Ecclesiastes** | | 24:18–23 | 138 | 47:8 | 330 |
| 2:5 | 397n2 | | | | |

**Isaiah** (*continued*)

| | |
|---|---|
| 47:9 | 331, 338 |
| 47:9–10 | 185n10 |
| 48:2 | 377 |
| 48:5 | 185n10 |
| 48:6 | 47 |
| 48:12 | 39, 46, 381 |
| 48:13 | 99n2 |
| 48:20 | 327 |
| 49:2 | 45, 355 |
| 49:10 | 156, 382 |
| 49:13 | 239 |
| 49:23 | 76 |
| 49:26 | 298 |
| 50:3 | 138 |
| 51:9–11 | 92 |
| 51:10 | 174, 302 |
| 51:17 | 275n23 |
| 51:22 | 275n23 |
| 52:1 | 345, 377, 379, 394 |
| 52:5 | 250, 300 |
| 52:11 | 327 |
| 53 | 108 |
| 53:2 | 108 |
| 53:7 | 108 |
| 53:9 | 108, 270 |
| 54:1–8 | 344 |
| 54:10 | 308n12 |
| 54:11–12 | 391 |
| 55:1 | 382, 413 |
| 56–66 | 15 |
| 56:1 | 406 |
| 57:3 | 309 |
| 57:6 | 294n1 |
| 58:8 | 385 |
| 60 | 393 |
| 60:1 | 393 |
| 60:1–2 | 385–86 |
| 60:3–5 | 393 |
| 60:11 | 393, 394 |
| 60:14 | 76 |
| 60:19–20 | 393 |
| 61:6 | 368 |
| 61:10 | 344, 345, 379 |
| 62:1–2 | 378 |
| 62:1–5 | 351 |
| 62:2 | 79, 351 |
| 62:3 | 351 |
| 62:3–5 | 378 |
| 62:6 | 387 |

| | |
|---|---|
| 63:1–6 | 281, 349, 353, 355 |
| 63:13 | 174 |
| 64:1 | 308n12 |
| 64:3 | 308n12 |
| 65:4 | 268n19 |
| 65:15 | 79 |
| 65:16 | 74, 81 |
| 65:17 | 15, 376 |
| 65:19 | 380 |
| 66:7 | 227, 230 |
| 66:7–9 | 225 |
| 66:22 | 376, 380 |
| 66:23 | 287n5 |

**Jeremiah**

| | |
|---|---|
| 1:10 | 200 |
| 1:14–15 | 182n7 |
| 2:2 | 344 |
| 2:5 | 47 |
| 2:13 | 382 |
| 3:1–10 | 268n19 |
| 3:2 | 268n19 |
| 3:3 | 309 |
| 3:17 | 398 |
| 4:5 | 170n19 |
| 4:6–13 | 182n7 |
| 4:8 | 127n25 |
| 4:13 | 170n19 |
| 4:21 | 170n19 |
| 4:29 | 139 |
| 4:30 | 314n1 |
| 5:6 | 131n29 |
| 5:12 | 330 |
| 5:14 | 210 |
| 6:1 | 182n7 |
| 6:22 | 182n7 |
| 6:26 | 127n25 |
| 7:5–11 | 185n10 |
| 7:6 | 294n1 |
| 7:25–26 | 196 |
| 8:1–2 | 214n14 |
| 8:3 | 177, 177n5 |
| 8:17 | 131n29 |
| 9:9–11 | 326 |
| 9:15 | 169 |
| 9:22 | 214n14 |
| 10:1–16 | 185 |
| 10:6–7 | 287 |
| 10:7 | 287n5, 288 |
| 10:22 | 138, 182n7 |

| | |
|---|---|
| 11:20 | 64 |
| 13:4–6 | 139n34 |
| 13:20 | 182n7 |
| 13:27 | 268n19 |
| 14:12 | 131 |
| 15:1–4 | 123n19 |
| 15:2 | 131, 253 |
| 15:16 | 199 |
| 16:4–5 | 123n19 |
| 16:4–6 | 214n14 |
| 16:10–15 | 147n8 |
| 16:18 | 329 |
| 16:19 | 287n5, 289 |
| 17:2 | 397n2 |
| 17:10 | 64, 407 |
| 20:14–18 | 177n5 |
| 21:7 | 131 |
| 22:19 | 214n14 |
| 22:8 | 335 |
| 23:5 | 105 |
| 23:14 | 214 |
| 23:15 | 169, 268n19 |
| 25:4 | 197n22 |
| 25:9 | 182n7 |
| 25:10 | 337 |
| 25:15 | 275n23 |
| 25:18 | 200 |
| 25:26 | 182n7 |
| 25:30 | 191, 200 |
| 26:5 | 197n22 |
| 29:19 | 197n22 |
| 31:1 | 380 |
| 31:2 | 232 |
| 31:6 | 370 |
| 31:16 | 156, 380 |
| 31:32 | 344 |
| 31:33 | 380 |
| 32:10 | 103 |
| 33:15 | 105 |
| 34:14 | 31n2 |
| 34:22 | 323 |
| 35:15 | 197n22 |
| 42:5 | 81 |
| 43:11 | 253 |
| 44:4 | 197n22 |
| 46–47 | 182n7 |
| 46:28 | 296n2 |
| 48:37 | 127n25 |
| 48:40 | 170n19 |
| 49:3 | 127n25 |

| | | | | | |
|---|---|---|---|---|---|
| 49:12 | 275n23 | 1:26–28 | 91, 372 | 23 | 268n19 |
| 49:22 | 170n19 | 1:27 | 189 | 23:1–49 | 268n19 |
| 49:30 | 139n34 | 1:28 | 45 | 23:25–29 | 323 |
| 49:36 | 141 | 2–3 | 101 | 23:31–34 | 275n23, 323 |
| 50–51 | 325 | 2:2 | 385n2 | 23:44 | 309 |
| 50:15 | 329 | 2:4 | 47 | 24:7 | 338 |
| 50:29 | 329, 331 | 2:8–3:3 | 198 | 25:2 | 200 |
| 50:31 | 331 | 2:9 | 99n1 | 26–27 | 325 |
| 50:34 | 331 | 2:9–10 | 100, 101, | 26–28 | 312, 332 |
| 50:38 | 302 | | 103, 190 | 26:7–11 | 182n7 |
| 50:41–42 | 182n7 | 2:10 | 99, 122 | 26:12 | 337 |
| 51 | 312, 316 | 3:11 | 47 | 26:13 | 337 |
| 51:4 | 268n19 | 3:12 | 42, 385n2 | 26:16 | 332 |
| 51:7 | 274, 275n23, | 3:14 | 385n2 | 26:19 | 323, 334 |
| | 313, 315 | 3:24 | 385n2 | 26:21 | 337 |
| 51:7–8 | 274 | 3:27 | 406 | 27:7–25 | 334 |
| 51:9 | 328 | 4:10 | 127 | 27:30–34 | 335 |
| 51:13 | 312 | 4:16 | 127 | 27:32 | 157n2, 335 |
| 51:27 | 178 | 5:2 | 168 | 27:36 | 334 |
| 51:34 | 229n6 | 5:12 | 131, 168 | 28:2 | 330 |
| 51:36 | 302 | 5:16–17 | 123n19 | 28:13 | 290, 391 |
| 51:37 | 326 | 5:17 | 131n29 | 29:3 | 229, 229n6 |
| 51:45 | 327 | 7:2 | 141, 369 | 31:8–9 | 52 |
| 51:48 | 335 | 9:2 | 44 | 31:15 | 174 |
| 51:49 | 338 | 9:4–8 | 142–43 | 32:2–3 | 229 |
| 51:56 | 125n24 | 9:11 | 44 | 32:7 | 139 |
| 51:59–64 | 336 | 10:1–22 | 92n12 | 33:3–6 | 160 |
| | | 10:12 | 93 | 33:27 | 139n34 |
| **Lamentations** | | 11:1 | 385n2 | 33:29 | 394 |
| 2:8 | 202n3 | 11:20 | 382 | 34:21 | 112 |
| 2:10 | 335 | 11:24 | 88 | 34:23 | 156 |
| 2:10–11 | 157n2 | 12:2 | 57 | 34:25 | 232 |
| 3:10–11 | 131n29 | 14:12–23 | 121 | 36:18 | 338 |
| 3:15 | 169 | 14:14 | 126 | 37 | 15, 216, 369 |
| 3:19 | 169 | 14:16 | 126 | 37:3 | 153 |
| 4:5 | 314n1 | 14:18 | 126 | 37:5 | 215 |
| 4:19 | 170n19 | 14:20 | 126 | 37:10 | 215, 365 |
| 4:21 | 275n23 | 14:21 | 121, 123n19, | 37:26–28 | 156 |
| | | | 126, 131 | 37:27 | 380 |
| **Ezekiel** | | 14:22–23 | 126 | 38 | 15 |
| 1–2 | 84 | 16:2 | 214 | 38–39 | 306n10, 357, 369 |
| 1:1 | 350 | 16:8–14 | 344 | 38:2–3 | 369 |
| 1:4 | 91 | 16:15–58 | 268n19 | 38:6 | 182n7, 369 |
| 1:4–28 | 89, 89n6 | 16:30–31 | 309 | 38:15 | 182n7, 369 |
| 1:5–25 | 92 | 16:35 | 309 | 38:17 | 197n22 |
| 1:7 | 44 | 16:37–41 | 323 | 38:19 | 138 |
| 1:13 | 91 | 16:46 | 214 | 38:19–23 | 217 |
| 1:14 | 91 | 16:49 | 214 | 38:20 | 308n12 |
| 1:18 | 93 | 17:3 | 170n19, 241 | 38:22 | 168, 275, 371 |
| 1:22 | 92 | 17:7 | 241 | 39 | 15 |
| 1:24 | 45, 91 | | | | |

**Ezekiel** (*continued*)

| | |
|---|---|
| 39:1 | 369 |
| 39:2 | 182n7, 306–7n11 |
| 39:4 | 306–7n11 |
| 39:6 | 371 |
| 39:17–20 | 357 |
| 40 | 387n3 |
| 40–48 | 202, 202n3, 392, 393 |
| 40:1–2 | 385 |
| 40:1–5 | 392 |
| 40:1–6 | 202n3 |
| 40:2 | 385 |
| 40:3 | 389 |
| 40:5 | 202, 386, 389 |
| 42:20 | 202n3 |
| 43:1–5 | 392 |
| 43:2 | 45, 325, 386, 393 |
| 43:5 | 385n2, 385, 392–93 |
| 43:6 | 86 |
| 43:7 | 268n19 |
| 43:15 | 181n6 |
| 47:1 | 396 |
| 47:8–10 | 396 |
| 47:12 | 397 |
| 47:13–48:29 | 147n8 |
| 48:16 | 389 |
| 48:30–35 | 387, 389 |
| 48:31–34 | 387n3 |

**Daniel**

| | |
|---|---|
| 1:12–15 | 55 |
| 2:28 | 30, 401 |
| 2:28–47 | 28 |
| 2:29 | 87n4 |
| 2:44 | 16, 220 |
| 2:45 | 401 |
| 2:47 | 322 |
| 3 | 258, 274 |
| 3:4 | 200 |
| 4:12 | 389 |
| 4:13–14 | 104 |
| 4:23 | 104 |
| 4:27–37 | 274 |
| 4:30 | 274 |
| 4:30–37 | 250 |
| 4:34 | 218n17 |
| 5:4 | 185 |
| 5:7 | 314n1 |
| 5:16 | 314n1 |

| | |
|---|---|
| 5:23 | 185 |
| 5:27 | 127 |
| 5:29 | 314n1 |
| 7 | 16, 84, 243 |
| 7:2 | 141 |
| 7:2–3 | 92, 245 |
| 7:3 | 213 |
| 7:3–6 | 246 |
| 7:7 | 229, 245, 246 |
| 7:7–8 | 321 |
| 7:8 | 112, 250 |
| 7:9 | 44, 70, 364, 372 |
| 7:9ff. | 84 |
| 7:9–10 | 43, 44, 91, 112 |
| 7:9–14 | 89, 89n6 |
| 7:10 | 90n8, 119, 373, 373n5 |
| 7:13 | 37, 44, 112, 216n16 |
| 7:13–14 | 38, 44, 280 |
| 7:14 | 44, 120, 220, 251, 393 |
| 7:18 | 115, 399 |
| 7:20 | 112, 229, 250, 321 |
| 7:21 | 213, 251, 322 |
| 7:22 | 115 |
| 7:24 | 112, 229, 245, 246, 321 |
| 7:25 | 205, 232, 241, 250, 251 |
| 7:27 | 115, 366, 399 |
| 8:3 | 112, 256 |
| 8:6 | 112 |
| 8:8 | 112 |
| 8:10 | 173, 230 |
| 8:15–17 | 188n14 |
| 8:18 | 45 |
| 8:19 | 193 |
| 8:20 | 112 |
| 8:26 | 193, 401, 405 |
| 9:6 | 197n22 |
| 9:10 | 197n22 |
| 9:11 | 286 |
| 10:2–9 | 188n14 |
| 10:5 | 44, 292 |
| 10:6 | 44, 45, 189, 340 |
| 10:13 | 233 |
| 10:15–21 | 44 |
| 10:21 | 103, 233 |

| | |
|---|---|
| 11:30–39 | 155 |
| 11:36 | 250 |
| 11:44 | 155 |
| 12 | 154, 194 |
| 12:1 | 77, 233, 308, 374 |
| 12:1–2 | 71 |
| 12:1–4 | 154 |
| 12:2 | 222 |
| 12:4 | 103, 401, 405 |
| 12:5 | 190 |
| 12:5–9 | 187 |
| 12:5–13 | 188n14 |
| 12:7 | 193, 205, 232, 241 |
| 12:9 | 103, 401, 405 |
| 12:10 | 155, 406 |
| 12:12–13 | 31 |

**Hosea**

| | |
|---|---|
| 1:2 | 268n19 |
| 2:5 | 309, 323, 344 |
| 3:1–4:2 | 185n10 |
| 3:3 | 309 |
| 4:10 | 309 |
| 4:12–15 | 309 |
| 5:3 | 139, 309 |
| 5:4 | 268n19 |
| 6:10 | 268n19 |
| 8:1 | 170n19 |
| 9:1 | 309 |
| 11:1 | 232 |
| 11:10 | 191 |
| 13:5 | 232 |
| 13:7–8 | 131n29 |

**Joel**

| | |
|---|---|
| 1:6 | 179 |
| 2:1 | 160, 175 |
| 2:1–11 | 182n7 |
| 2:2 | 179 |
| 2:3 | 168 |
| 2:4 | 179 |
| 2:4–5 | 179 |
| 2:10 | 138, 139, 175 |
| 2:11 | 140 |
| 2:15 | 160, 175 |
| 2:20–25 | 182n7 |
| 2:29 | 177 |
| 2:30 | 168 |
| 2:31 | 175 |
| 3:1 | 177 |
| 3:2 | 306n10, 370n4 |

| | |
|---|---|
| 3:13 | 279, 279n26 |
| 3:15 | 170, 175 |
| 3:16 | 138, 191 |

**Amos**

| | |
|---|---|
| 1:2 | 191 |
| 1:6 | 47 |
| 1:9 | 47 |
| 1:11 | 47 |
| 3:7 | 29 |
| 3:8 | 191 |
| 3:13 | 220–21, 287, 287n5 |
| 4:10 | 167 |
| 4:13 | 220–21, 287, 287n5 |
| 5:7 | 169 |
| 5:18–29 | 15 |
| 5:20 | 170 |
| 7:1 | 182n7 |
| 7:7–9 | 202n3 |
| 8:2 | 15 |
| 8:2–3 | 157n2 |
| 8:9 | 170 |
| 8:10 | 127n25 |

**Obadiah**

| | |
|---|---|
| 16 | 275n23 |
| 21 | 370 |

**Jonah**

| | |
|---|---|
| 1:9 | 190n15 |
| 2:6 | 174 |
| 2:20–22 | 19 |
| 3:5–8 | 127n25 |
| 4:3 | 177n5 |
| 4:8 | 177n5 |

**Micah**

| | |
|---|---|
| 1:4 | 138 |
| 2:3 | 47 |
| 3:3 | 323 |
| 3:5 | 47 |
| 4:2 | 370 |
| 4:7 | 265n16 |
| 5:12–6:8 | 185n10 |
| 7:18 | 250 |

**Nahum**

| | |
|---|---|
| 1:5 | 138 |
| 1:6 | 140 |
| 1:14 | 185n10 |
| 3:1–4 | 185n10 |

**Habakkuk**

| | |
|---|---|
| 1:6 | 370 |
| 1:8 | 170n19 |
| 2:15–16 | 275n23 |
| 2:20 | 157n2 |

**Zephaniah**

| | |
|---|---|
| 1:14ff. | 160n6 |
| 1:14–15 | 140 |
| 1:14–16 | 160 |
| 1:16 | 160 |
| 2:13–14 | 326 |
| 3:13 | 270 |
| 3:8 | 306n10 |

**Zechariah**

| | |
|---|---|
| 1:3 | 47 |
| 1:4 | 47 |
| 1:7–17 | 121 |
| 1:12 | 134 |
| 1:14 | 47 |
| 1:16 | 47, 209 |
| 1:17 | 47 |
| 1:18–21 | 112 |
| 2–3 | 209 |
| 2:1–2 | 389 |
| 2:1–5 | 202, 202n3 |
| 2:5 | 202 |
| 2:11 | 380, 393 |
| 2:13 | 157n2 |
| 3–4 | 208 |
| 3:1 | 237 |
| 3:4 | 345 |
| 3:8 | 105, 209 |
| 4 | 209 |
| 4:2 | 43, 91, 112 |
| 4:2–3 | 209 |
| 4:3 | 43 |
| 4:6 | 43 |
| 4:10 | 112 |
| 4:11–14 | 209 |
| 4:14 | 43, 209 |
| 6:1–8 | 121, 141 |
| 6:5 | 141 |
| 6:7–8a | 124n22 |
| 6:9–14 | 208 |
| 6:11 | 55 |
| 6:12 | 105 |
| 6:14 | 55 |
| 8:8 | 382 |
| 8:23 | 393 |

| | |
|---|---|
| 9:14 | 160 |
| 12–14 | 305n8 |
| 12:1–9 | 370n4 |
| 12:2 | 275n23 |
| 12:10 | 37, 38 |
| 13:9 | 168 |
| 14 | 151 |
| 14:2 | 370n4 |
| 14:5 | 139 |
| 14:7 | 394 |
| 14:8 | 382, 396 |
| 14:9 | 344 |
| 14:11 | 398 |

**Malachi**

| | |
|---|---|
| 1:11 | 287n5, 289 |
| 3:2 | 140 |
| 3:2–3 | 83 |
| 3:16 | 373n5 |
| 4:4 | 286 |

**NEW TESTAMENT**

**Matthew**

| | |
|---|---|
| 2:13–15 | 232 |
| 4:1 | 313 |
| 4:5 | 377 |
| 4:19 | 249 |
| 5:1 | 385 |
| 5:8 | 399 |
| 5:12 | 344 |
| 7:6 | 409 |
| 7:15 | 256, 304n7 |
| 8:11 | 346 |
| 8:23–27 | 92n11 |
| 9:37f. | 280 |
| 10:5–6 | 147n9 |
| 10:28 | 55 |
| 10:32 | 72 |
| 10:38 | 269 |
| 11:15 | 51 |
| 11:21 | 127n25, 209 |
| 13:9 | 52 |
| 13:24–43 | 280n29 |
| 13:43 | 52 |
| 14:17–19 | 176n4 |
| 14:24 | 389 |
| 15:26–27 | 409 |
| 16:19 | 74 |
| 16:24 | 249, 269 |
| 17:1–2 | 385 |

**Matthew** (*continued*)

| | |
|---|---|
| 17:2 | 45, 70, 189 |
| 18:6 | 337 |
| 18:16 | 208n6 |
| 18:18 | 74 |
| 19:28 | 147n8, 364 |
| 20:2 | 127 |
| 20:21 | 99 |
| 21:5 | 265 |
| 22:2 | 344 |
| 22:2–9 | 60 |
| 22:44 | 99 |
| 23:35 | 338 |
| 23:37 | 338 |
| 24 | 154 |
| 24:11 | 304n7 |
| 24:14 | 272 |
| 24:15–16 | 139 |
| 24:15–31 | 77 |
| 24:21–22 | 176 |
| 24:23–25 | 258 |
| 24:24 | 304n7 |
| 24:29 | 139, 170 |
| 24:30 | 37, 216n16, 279 |
| 24:31 | 160, 160n6 |
| 24:42–44 | 69 |
| 24:42–51 | 305 |
| 25:1–13 | 129 |
| 25:33–34 | 99 |
| 25:41 | 234, 371 |
| 26:26 | 198 |
| 26:29 | 346 |
| 26:52 | 254 |
| 26:64 | 99, 216n16, 279 |
| 28:3 | 70 |
| 28:4 | 45 |

**Mark**

| | |
|---|---|
| 1:12 | 205 |
| 1:12–13 | 313 |
| 1:17 | 249 |
| 3:27 | 361n1 |
| 4:9 | 52 |
| 4:23 | 52 |
| 4:29 | 279, 280 |
| 4:35–41 | 92n11 |
| 6:38–41 | 176n4 |
| 6:39 | 130 |
| 6:47–51 | 92n11 |
| 7:27–28 | 409 |

| | |
|---|---|
| 8:34 | 249, 269 |
| 9:2 | 385 |
| 9:2–8 | 266 |
| 9:2–13 | 211n10 |
| 9:3 | 70 |
| 9:42 | 337 |
| 10:37 | 99 |
| 12:36 | 99 |
| 13 | 154 |
| 13:7–20 | 77 |
| 13:10 | 272 |
| 13:14 | 139 |
| 13:19–20 | 176 |
| 13:20 | 283, 300 |
| 13:21–23 | 258 |
| 13:22 | 304n7 |
| 13:24–25 | 139, 170 |
| 13:26 | 216n16 |
| 13:26–27 | 279 |
| 13:32 | 279 |
| 13:32–37 | 305 |
| 13:37 | 305 |
| 14:12 | 110 |
| 14:25 | 60, 346 |
| 14:62 | 37, 99, 216n16, 279 |
| 15:17 | 314n1 |
| 16:5 | 70, 99 |

**Luke**

| | |
|---|---|
| 1:11 | 99 |
| 1:12 | 216n15 |
| 1:15–17 | 211n10 |
| 1:65 | 216n15 |
| 1:68–79 | 147n9 |
| 2:29–32 | 147n9 |
| 4:1–2 | 313 |
| 4:25 | 211 |
| 4:25–26 | 211n10 |
| 6:26 | 304n7 |
| 7:11–17 | 211n10 |
| 7:33–34 | 129 |
| 8:8 | 52 |
| 8:22–25 | 92n11 |
| 9:13–16 | 176n4 |
| 9:23 | 249, 269 |
| 9:28–29 | 385 |
| 9:29 | 70 |
| 9:54 | 258 |
| 10:1 | 208 |

| | |
|---|---|
| 10:1–24 | 208n6 |
| 10:2 | 279, 280 |
| 10:13 | 127n25, 209 |
| 10:18 | 173, 179 |
| 10:19 | 173, 208 |
| 10:20 | 71, 374 |
| 11:28 | 31 |
| 11:40 | 103 |
| 12:6 | 176n4 |
| 12:8 | 72 |
| 12:37–40 | 305 |
| 12:39–40 | 69 |
| 12:49 | 371 |
| 12:52 | 176n4 |
| 13:29 | 346 |
| 14:27 | 269 |
| 14:35 | 52 |
| 16:21 | 409 |
| 17:2 | 337 |
| 17:37 | 170 |
| 19:43 | 370 |
| 20:42 | 99 |
| 21 | 154 |
| 21:20 | 370 |
| 21:20–21 | 139 |
| 21:26 | 139 |
| 21:27 | 216n16 |
| 22:7 | 110 |
| 22:18 | 346 |
| 22:30 | 147n8, 364 |
| 22:69 | 37, 99, 279 |
| 23:27–30 | 177n5 |
| 23:30 | 139 |
| 24:13 | 389 |
| 24:42–43 | 366 |
| 24:51 | 216n16 |

**John**

| | |
|---|---|
| 1:14 | 380 |
| 1:29 | 108 |
| 1:36 | 108 |
| 1:47 | 147n9 |
| 2:1–10 | 129 |
| 4:35–38 | 279, 280 |
| 5:29 | 373 |
| 5:43–47 | 147n9 |
| 6:19 | 389 |
| 7:37 | 382 |
| 7:37–38 | 396 |
| 8:12 | 393 |

| | | | |
|---|---|---|---|
| 8:17 | 208, 208n6 | 20:7 | 43 |
| 8:30–47 | 54n2 | 20:31 | 49 |
| 8:44 | 54n2 | 21:11 | 47 |
| 10:4 | 269 | 21:8–9 | 411 |
| 11:18 | 389 | 24:1 | 176n4 |
| 11:52 | 147n9 | 26:14–23 | 147n9 |
| 12:15 | 265 | | |
| 13:36 | 269 | **Romans** | |
| 15:19 | 328 | 1:3 | 105 |
| 17:15 | 77, 328 | 1:7 | 20, 34 |
| 18:33–19:16 | 36 | 1:24–31 | 185n10 |
| 19:2 | 314n1 | 1:29–31 | 382 |
| 19:30 | 283, 381 | 8:16 | 402n5 |
| 21:15 | 108 | 8:23 | 241, 270 |
| | | 8:27 | 64 |
| | | 8:34 | 99 |
| **Acts** | | 9–11 | 147n9 |
| 1:7 | 279 | 9:33 | 265 |
| 1:9 | 216n16 | 11:13–26 | 150 |
| 2:14–21 | 147n9 | 11:16 | 270 |
| 2:20 | 138 | 11:26 | 265 |
| 2:25 | 99 | 16:20 | 416 |
| 2:33 | 99 | | |
| 2:34 | 99 | **1 Corinthians** | |
| 4:24 | 134, 194 | 1:3 | 20, 34 |
| 5:5 | 216n15 | 2:11 | 402n5 |
| 5:31 | 99 | 5:7 | 110 |
| 6:5 | 51n1 | 5:9–11 | 382 |
| 7:44 | 291 | 6:2–3 | 364 |
| 7:55 | 99 | 6:9–10 | 382 |
| 7:56 | 99 | 6:15–16 | 309 |
| 8:32 | 108 | 7:34 | 402n5 |
| 8:39 | 385n2 | 8–10 | 10, 59 |
| 10:11 | 350 | 10:19–20 | 185 |
| 10:25–26 | 348 | 12:13 | 143n5 |
| 13:6 | 304n7 | 13:12 | 399 |
| 13:13 | 7 | 14:14 | 402n5 |
| 13:48 | 218n17 | 14:19 | 176n4 |
| 14:13 | 110 | 15 | 366, 376 |
| 14:18 | 110 | 15:20–23 | 270 |
| 15:20 | 185n10 | 15:26 | 374, 377 |
| 15:28–29 | 64 | 15:52 | 160, 160n6 |
| 16:14–15 | 9, 62 | 16:2 | 43 |
| 18:12–16 | 54n2 | 16:22 | 414, 416 |
| 18:19–21 | 49 | 16:22–24 | 416 |
| 19:8–10 | 49 | | |
| 19:17 | 216n15 | **2 Corinthians** | |
| 19:23–41 | 49 | 1:2 | 20, 34 |
| 19:31 | 257 | 1:22 | 143n5, 270 |
| 19:35 | 49, 53 | 5:5 | 270 |
| 20:6 | 176n4 | 5:17 | 376 |

| | | | |
|---|---|---|---|
| 7:1 | 402n5 | | |
| 11 | 50 | | |
| 11:2 | 344 | | |
| 12 | 50 | | |
| 12:2–4 | 192n17 | | |
| 12:4 | 268 | | |
| 13 | 50 | | |
| 13:1 | 208n6 | | |
| 13:13 | 416 | | |
| | | | |
| **Galatians** | | | |
| 1:3 | 20, 34 | | |
| 1:8–9 | 414 | | |
| 3:7 | 150 | | |
| 3:29 | 147n9, 150 | | |
| 4:26 | 379 | | |
| 5:19–21 | 185n10, 382 | | |
| 6:15 | 376 | | |
| 6:16 | 147n9, 150 | | |
| 6:18 | 416 | | |
| | | | |
| **Ephesians** | | | |
| 1:13 | 143n5 | | |
| 1:13–14 | 270 | | |
| 2:11–22 | 147n9 | | |
| 2:20 | 388 | | |
| 4:30 | 143n5 | | |
| 5:5 | 185n10, 382 | | |
| 5:18 | 129 | | |
| 5:25–32 | 344 | | |
| 5:32 | 344 | | |
| 6:17 | 355 | | |
| | | | |
| **Philippians** | | | |
| 1:2 | 20, 34 | | |
| 2:9 | 351 | | |
| 3:2 | 409 | | |
| 4:3 | 71, 374 | | |
| 4:14 | 41 | | |
| 4:23 | 416 | | |
| | | | |
| **Colossians** | | | |
| 1:15 | 81 | | |
| 1:18 | 52 | | |
| 2:1 | 81 | | |
| 3:1 | 99 | | |
| 3:5 | 185n10 | | |
| 4:12–13 | 81 | | |
| 4:13 | 81 | | |
| 4:15 | 81 | | |
| 4:16 | 81 | | |

**1 Thessalonians**

| | |
|---|---|
| 1:1 | 20, 34 |
| 1:3 | 50 |
| 4:16 | 160, 160n6 |
| 4:17 | 216n16 |
| 5:2–4 | 69 |
| 5:2–7 | 305 |
| 5:23 | 402n5 |
| 5:28 | 416 |

**2 Thessalonians**

| | |
|---|---|
| 1:8 | 165n13 |
| 2:9 | 258 |

**1 Timothy**

| | |
|---|---|
| 1:17 | 284 |
| 3:6 | 237n9 |
| 3:8 | 129 |
| 5:19 | 208n6 |
| 6:13 | 29, 36, 110n7, 354 |
| 6:15 | 322 |

**Titus**

| | |
|---|---|
| 1:10 | 382 |
| 1:16 | 382 |

**Philemon**

| | |
|---|---|
| 3 | 20, 34 |
| 25 | 416 |

**Hebrews**

| | |
|---|---|
| 1:3 | 99 |
| 1:12 | 139 |
| 1:13 | 99 |
| 2:9 | 399 |
| 4:12 | 45, 355 |
| 8:1 | 99 |
| 9:1–4 | 222 |
| 10:12 | 99 |
| 10:28 | 208n6 |
| 11:10 | 388 |
| 11:12 | 150 |
| 11:16 | 379 |
| 12:2 | 99 |
| 12:14 | 399 |
| 12:22 | 265 |
| 12:23 | 71, 374 |

**James**

| | |
|---|---|
| 1:1 | 147n9 |
| 5:17 | 211 |

| | |
|---|---|
| 5:19–20 | 211 |

**1 Peter**

| | |
|---|---|
| 1:19 | 108 |
| 2:6 | 265 |
| 2:9 | 147n9 |
| 3:22 | 99 |
| 5:8 | 237n9 |
| 5:13 | 274 |

**2 Peter**

| | |
|---|---|
| 2:1 | 304n7 |
| 2:4 | 361n1 |
| 2:15 | 58 |
| 2:22 | 409 |
| 3:7 | 372 |
| 3:10 | 69, 305, 372 |
| 3:12 | 372 |
| 3:13 | 376 |

**1 John**

| | |
|---|---|
| 1 | 352 |
| 1:1–3 | 403 |
| 1:5 | 393 |
| 1:6 | 383 |
| 3:2 | 399 |
| 3:12 | 110 |
| 4:1 | 50, 304n7 |

**Jude**

| | |
|---|---|
| 6 | 361n1 |
| 9 | 233, 237n9 |
| 11 | 58 |

**Revelation**

| | |
|---|---|
| 1 | 88, 189, 236, 340 |
| 1–2 | 68n4 |
| 1–3 | 84, 86, 88, 264 |
| 1–4 | 159 |
| 1–11 | 245, 259, 263 |
| 1:1 | 5, 29, 30, 37, 40, 41, 87, 88, 141, 277n25, 310–11, 362, 395, 401, 403, 409, 410, 410n10 |
| 1:1–2 | 7, 27–31, 36, 42, 409 |
| 1:1–3 | 27–32, 40, 77, 155, 238, 346, 400 |
| 1:1–8 | 20, 27–39, 400 |

| | |
|---|---|
| 1:2 | 5, 28, 29, 36, 40, 75, 110n6, 132, 154, 242, 254, 277n25, 348, 354, 364, 365 |
| 1:3 | 7, 30, 31–32, 33, 38, 47, 69, 70, 77, 88, 93, 110n6, 199, 242, 277, 305, 305n8, 346, 348, 402n6, 403, 413n12 |
| 1:4 | 5, 29, 30, 33–35, 38, 39, 40, 43, 45, 46, 64, 74, 91, 94, 112, 157n1, 159, 212, 215, 221, 256, 277, 297, 318, 409, 410, 410n9 |
| 1:4–6 | 20, 33, 416 |
| 1:4–8 | 29, 32–39, 40, 66, 94, 112, 191, 241, 412 |
| 1:5 | 5, 29, 33, 34, 35–37, 38, 46, 52, 56, 57, 58n3, 67, 69, 71, 105, 106, 110, 115, 252, 269, 288, 312, 350, 352, 356, 394 |
| 1:5–6 | 44, 109–10, 116 |
| 1:5b | 46 |
| 1:5b–6 | 38 |
| 1:6 | 37, 38, 42, 55, 81, 116, 147n9, 197, 342n10, 368, 386 |
| 1:7 | 33, 37–38, 44, 51, 81, 85, 216, 279 |
| 1:8 | 33, 34, 38–39, 46, 94, 95n14, 212, 221, 287, 297, 299, 318, 327, 355, 380, 381, 408 |
| 1:9 | 5, 28, 29, 30, 40–42, 44, 49, 52, 53, 55, 62, 69, 75, 87, 105, 132, 154, 211, 237, 238, 242, 254, 255, 277n25, 354, 403 |

| | | | |
|---|---|---|---|
| 1:9–20 | 20, 39–40 | 2:1–7 | 20, 48–52, 75, 77 |
| 1:9–3:22 | 20, 39–84, 84 | 2:1–11 | 237 |
| 1:10 | 45, 87, 88, 142, 160, 161, 215, 293 | 2:1–3:22 | 20, 47–84, 218 |
| 1:10–11 | 42–43 | 2:2 | 30, 48, 49–50, 55, 62, 66, 68, 82, 254, 277, 355, 373, 383n1, 407 |
| 1:10–12 | 43 | | |
| 1:10–13 | 192n18, 216 | | |
| 1:11 | 20, 33, 45, 47, 53, 100, 192 | 2:2–3 | 62 |
| 1:12 | 35, 45, 49 | 2:3 | 50, 57, 68, 250, 254 |
| 1:12–13 | 43–44, 47, 87 | 2:4 | 36, 50–51, 58, 62, 63 |
| 1:12–18 | 47 | | |
| 1:12–20 | 48, 62 | 2:5 | 51, 59, 63, 64, 69, 69n5, 69n6, 70, 77, 82, 185, 218, 301, 305, 318, 348, 355, 373, 407, 413 |
| 1:13 | 35, 49, 291, 292 | | |
| 1:13–16 | 280 | | |
| 1:14 | 44, 187n13, 189, 210, 351 | | |
| 1:14–15 | 62 | 2:6 | 50, 51, 58, 68, 355, 373, 407 |
| 1:15 | 44–45, 187n13, 189 | | |
| 1:16 | 5, 10, 45, 49, 57, 66, 98, 100, 159, 173, 175, 187n13, 189, 210, 226, 227, 241, 303, 342n10, 354, 355 | 2:7 | 36, 42, 51–52, 55, 60, 64, 65, 71, 72, 79, 80, 84, 106, 215, 238, 253, 285, 322, 345, 350, 382, 397, 408, 412, 413n12 |
| 1:17 | 45–46, 52, 53, 67, 100, 112n10, 152, 220, 381, 408 | 2:8 | 43, 46, 47, 53, 67, 67n2, 141, 159, 192, 247, 365, 408 |
| 1:18 | 33, 37, 46, 53, 67, 67n2, 74, 130, 142n2, 174, 177, 365, 374 | 2:8–11 | 20, 52–55, 74, 91 |
| | | 2:9 | 48, 53–55, 66, 68, 73, 75, 82, 83, 154, 235 |
| 1:19 | 43, 53, 86, 87n5, 192 | | |
| 1:19–20 | 47 | 2:10 | 37, 46, 49, 61, 77, 78, 80, 123, 154, 178, 280n28, 328 |
| 1:20 | 35, 43, 45, 49, 53, 66, 98, 100, 141, 159, 169, 173, 227 | 2:10–11 | 11, 41n5, 55, 117n18, 227 |
| 2 | 21, 30, 37, 43, 47, 49, 68, 110, 115, 154, 155, 167, 185, 304, 305, 315, 326, 327, 410n9, 413 | 2:10–21 | 239 |
| | | 2:11 | 36, 42, 52, 71, 106, 141, 178, 215, 222, 238, 253, 258, 260, 285, 322, 345, 350, 368, 382, 412, 413n12 |
| 2–3 | 59, 88, 90, 117n17, 129, 153, 170, 203, 225, 236, 238, 258, 263, 309 | 2:12 | 5, 10, 43, 45, 47, 57, 141, 159, 192, 241, 354, 355 |
| 2:1 | 43, 44, 47, 49, 51, 66, 100, 141, 159, 173, 192, 227 | 2:12–17 | 20, 56–60, 261 |

| | | | |
|---|---|---|---|
| 2:13 | 5, 21, 36, 46, 48, 50, 52, 57–58, 62, 64, 66, 68, 69, 75, 77, 78, 105, 110, 132, 134, 177, 179, 235, 250, 252, 257, 272, 301, 313, 322, 362 | | |
| 2:14 | 29, 50, 59, 61, 63, 180, 241, 268, 326, 383, 394, 411 | | |
| 2:14–15 | 328 | | |
| 2:14–16 | 51, 58–60, 63 | | |
| 2:15 | 50, 58, 59, 63, 411 | | |
| 2:16 | 5, 10, 45, 51, 59, 63, 64, 69n5, 70, 77, 116, 185, 210, 241, 250, 301, 303, 305, 318, 348, 354, 355, 402, 413, 415 | | |
| 2:17 | 36, 42, 49, 52, 60, 71, 79, 80, 106, 215, 238, 250, 253, 285, 322, 345, 350, 351, 382, 412, 413n12 | | |
| 2:18 | 43, 44, 47, 61, 62, 141, 159, 189, 192, 210, 351 | | |
| 2:18–29 | 20, 60–65, 130, 261 | | |
| 2:19 | 36, 48, 50, 62, 66, 68, 254, 277, 355, 373, 407 | | |
| 2:20 | 63, 225, 235, 241, 268, 326, 342n11, 345, 362, 410n10 | | |
| 2:20–21 | 180, 328 | | |
| 2:20–22 | 312, 383 | | |
| 2:20–23 | 29, 50, 394, 411 | | |
| 2:21 | 59, 69n5, 185, 195, 218, 274, 305, 413 | | |
| 2:21–22 | 301, 348, 355 | | |
| 2:21–23 | 63–64 | | |
| 2:22 | 10n2, 59, 69n5, 37, 185, 305, 373, 413 | | |
| 2:23 | 49, 61, 130, 177, 329, 355, 373, 407 | | |
| 2:24 | 67n3, 235 | | |

**Revelation** (*continued*)
2:24–25  64
2:25  57, 70, 78
2:26  36, 42, 52, 106,
238, 242, 285, 322,
345, 350, 355, 373,
382, 407
2:26–27  242
2:26–28  64–65
2:26–29  32
2:27  202, 203, 230,
249, 355
2:28  71, 173, 345,
350, 411
2:29  52, 65, 215, 253,
412, 413n12
3  21, 37, 43, 47, 49,
50, 110, 115, 154,
155, 167, 185, 304,
305, 315, 326, 327,
410n9, 413
3:1  34, 43, 47, 48, 49,
66–67, 68, 112, 141,
157n1, 159, 173, 192,
215, 227, 250, 256,
277, 355, 373,
407, 412
3:1–6  20, 65–72
3:2  67–69, 137, 355,
373, 407
3:2–4  49, 83, 90, 115,
123, 346, 350, 354
3:2–5  135, 150
3:3  32, 51, 59, 67,
69n5, 69–70, 75,
185, 217, 218, 242,
301, 305, 318, 348,
355, 413, 413n12
3:4  68, 70–71, 90, 91,
95, 96, 104, 105,
106, 114, 268,
298, 372
3:4–5  136, 155, 285,
292, 305, 408
3:5  36, 42, 49, 52, 78,
91, 100, 106, 141,
226, 238, 252, 253,
285, 322, 345, 350,
374, 382, 394, 407
3:5–6  71–72

3:6  52, 72, 215,
253, 412, 413n12
3:7  43, 46, 47, 76, 134,
141, 159, 174, 192,
196, 299, 350
3:7–8  49, 73–75,
122, 394
3:7–13  20, 54, 72–79, 218
3:8  32, 37, 48, 50, 57,
69, 76, 78, 87,
87n2, 196, 242, 250,
355, 373, 407
3:8–10  78
3:9  36, 37, 75–76, 235,
347, 383n1
3:10  32, 57, 69, 75,
76–77, 122, 134,
176, 217, 242, 252,
254, 257, 272, 296,
300, 313, 328,
362, 378
3:11  30, 55, 57, 59, 64,
70, 77–78, 91, 93,
280n28, 305, 318,
402, 415
3:11–12  227
3:12  36, 42, 52, 60, 62,
80, 106, 156, 187,
203, 238, 250, 265,
285, 322, 345, 350,
351, 382, 399
3:12–13  78–79
3:13  52, 79, 215, 253,
412, 413n12
3:14  5, 29, 37, 43, 47,
58, 71, 74, 81,
105, 106, 110, 115,
120, 141, 152, 159,
192, 269, 350, 356,
381, 401
3:14–22  20, 79–84
3:15  48, 66, 355,
373, 407
3:15–16  82
3:17  55, 82, 83,
305, 328
3:18  71, 83, 115, 135,
150, 210, 226,
281, 285
3:18–19  83

3:19  59, 69n5, 185,
218, 301, 305, 348,
355, 413
3:19–22  83–84
3:20  37, 111, 122, 413n12
3:21  36, 42, 49, 52, 62,
106, 238, 285, 322,
345, 350, 364,
382, 396
3:22  52, 84, 215, 253,
412, 413n12
4  84, 112, 114,
283, 396
4–5  84–85
4–19  110
4:1  37, 43, 47, 75,
75n10, 86, 86–88, 87,
87n2, 103, 122, 140,
149, 160, 161, 172,
180, 216, 290, 294,
324, 340, 350,
362, 395
4:1–2  186, 192n18
4:1–8a  85–93
4:1–11  20
4:1–5:14  84–120
4:1–11:19  20
4:1–22:5  84
4:1–22:9  20, 84–404
4:2  37, 40, 88, 89,
215, 372
4:2–3  42, 88–89, 99, 112,
151, 232, 267, 301,
307, 330, 343, 350,
380, 385, 386, 401
4:2b–8a  84
4:3  89, 186, 189,
256, 386
4:3–4  388
4:4  55, 71, 89, 89–91,
94, 96, 105, 135,
150, 152, 153, 220,
226, 227, 267,
280n28, 330n3, 343
4:5  34, 66, 91, 112,
123, 159, 165, 191,
210, 215, 223, 256,
277, 308, 412
4:6  89, 90, 103, 241,
245, 284, 284

| | | | | | | |
|---|---|---|---|---|---|---|
| 4:6–8 | 213, 292 | 5:5–6 | 117 | 5:13–14 | 120 |
| 4:6–8a | 92–93, 107, 123, | 5:5–7 | 84 | 5:14 | 76, 81, 93, 96, |
| | 152, 245, 267, | 5:6 | 34, 37, 52, 66, 91, | | 112n10, 152, 220, |
| | 343, 377 | | 99n1, 107, 107–12, | | 249, 343 |
| 4:8 | 34, 39, 89, 95n14, | | 109, 112, 116, 126, | 6 | 102, 124, 125, 130, |
| | 96, 157n1, 221, 276, | | 132, 151, 152, 157n1, | | 137, 139, 140, 141, |
| | 287, 297, 299, 318, 355 | | 211, 214, 215, 216, | | 142, 159, 163 |
| 4:8–11 | 95 | | 229, 231, 238, 245, | 6:1 | 99n1, 102, 122–23, |
| 4:8b | 84 | | 246, 247, 252, 256, | | 157, 176, 191, 245, |
| 4:8b–11 | 84, 93–95, 105 | | 264, 265, 269, 271n21, | | 271n21, 282, 290, |
| 4:9 | 33, 46, 67n1, 93, | | 277, 282, 313, 396, 412 | | 294, 313 |
| | 96, 153n, 193, 273, | 5:6–7 | 231 | 6:1–8 | 121–31, 137, 141, |
| | 342n10, 386 | 5:6–10 | 106–16, 114 | | 141, 144n7, 151, 153, |
| 4:9–10 | 84, 142n2, 227 | 5:7 | 108, 112, 119, 330 | | 161, 164, 187n12, |
| 4:10 | 33, 67n1, 76, 91, | 5:8 | 93, 100, 112–13, | | 189, 191, 212, |
| | 96, 112n10, 152, 220, | | 113n12, 152, 164, | | 215, 283, 325, |
| | 227, 249, 280n28, 330 | | 220, 251, 277, 285, | | 350, 360 |
| 4:11 | 37, 70, 84, 96, 120, | | 292, 298, 377 | 6:1–17 | 157 |
| | 153n, 221, 256, 273, | 5:8–12 | 84 | 6:1–8:1 | 20, 120–57, 166, |
| | 298, 300, 342n10, 386 | 5:8–14 | 267 | | 188, 189, 198, 219 |
| 5 | 84, 100, 101–2, 111, | 5:9 | 5, 19, 29, 36, 38, | 6:1–8:5 | 194n20 |
| | 114, 117, 141, 142, | | 52, 70, 96, 100, | 6:2 | 37, 91, 99n1, |
| | 143, 188, 189, 194, | | 102, 104, 106, 111, | | 123–26, 124, 126, |
| | 194n20, 198n23, 226, | | 114, 126, 150, 200, | | 130, 135, 171, 175, |
| | 238, 283, 355 | | 214, 221, 238, 247, | | 179, 182, 202, 250, |
| 5:1 | 43, 98, 99, 99–104, | | 251–52, 264, 266, 267, | | 300, 302, 345, 350 |
| | 100, 101, 101n3, 102, | | 269, 273, 285, 298, | 6:2–8 | 131 |
| | 103, 104, 122, 141, | | 330, 352, 380 | 6:2a | 126, 130 |
| | 170, 173, 186, 188, | 5:9–10 | 38, 84, 113–16, | 6:3 | 102, 121, 126, 130 |
| | 190, 193, 194n20, 198, | | 114, 116, 120, 285, | 6:3–4 | 126 |
| | 245, 264, 271, 279, 282, | | 344, 380, 393 | 6:3–8 | 124 |
| | 293, 303, 313, 330, | 5:9–14 | 95 | 6:4 | 109, 125n23, 131, |
| | 348, 360, 364, 372, 376 | 5:10 | 37, 55, 96, 147n9, | | 135, 171, 202, |
| 5:1–2 | 102 | | 366, 368, 399 | | 229, 345 |
| 5:1–5 | 98–106 | 5:11 | 89, 93, 96, 99n1, | 6:4a | 124n22 |
| 5:1–14 | 20 | | 141, 152, 183, | 6:4b | 124n22 |
| 5:1–8:1 | 189, 190, 193 | | 294, 330 | 6:5 | 37, 99n1, 102, 121, |
| 5:2 | 70, 95, 98, 99n1, | 5:11–12 | 119–20, 152 | | 123, 127, 138, 208, |
| | 100, 101, 102, 104, | 5:11–12a | 84 | | 264, 279 |
| | 114, 141, 142, 188, | 5:11–14 | 119–20 | 6:5a | 130 |
| | 236, 298, 325, 337 | 5:12 | 36, 37, 52, 70, 104, | 6:6 | 127–30, 141, 294 |
| 5:3 | 99, 100, 105, 120, | | 106, 120, 126, 142, | 6:7 | 102, 121, 130, 374 |
| | 173, 227 | | 152, 152n11, 153n, 214, | 6:7–8 | 130–31 |
| 5:3–4 | 104–5 | | 247, 252, 256, | 6:8 | 37, 46, 99n1, 121, |
| 5:4 | 70, 99, 100, | | 261, 269, 298, | | 123, 124n22, 125n23, |
| | 105, 298 | | 322, 342n10 | | 130, 131, 135, 171, |
| 5:5 | 37, 98, 100, 102, | 5:12–13 | 96, 386 | | 177, 202, 213n13, |
| | 105, 109, 112, 114, | 5:12b | 84 | | 245, 250, 254, 264, |
| | 116, 147, 238, 285, | 5:13 | 33, 37, 231, 330, | | 271n21, 279, 282, |
| | 322, 348, 408, 411 | | 342n10 | | 313, 345, 374 |

**Revelation** (*continued*)

6:9    5, 28, 75, 90, 102, 109, 111, 126, 131, 132, 154, 163, 163n9, 203, 211, 214, 231, 237, 238, 277n25, 299, 354, 364, 365

6:9–11    3, 50, 52, 71, 96, 97, 97n16, 113, 125, 131–32, 135, 137, 138, 139, 158, 162, 163, 164, 165, 174, 178, 181, 183, 194, 205, 228, 231, 239, 242, 247, 251, 255, 277, 281, 292, 298, 308, 311, 316, 336, 338, 341, 342, 343, 349, 353, 362, 364, 383

6:10    57, 72n9, 74, 77, 97n16, 134, 142, 215, 252, 257, 272, 336, 338, 352

6:10–12    115

6:11    30, 41, 49, 90, 111, 125n23, 132, 137, 150, 171, 195, 202, 254, 276, 277, 345, 346, 354, 408

6:12    37, 99n1, 102, 127, 138, 170, 175, 208, 211, 217, 245, 271n21, 282, 308, 313

6:12–17    137, 140, 142, 151, 153, 158, 177, 303

6:13    139

6:14    100, 139, 308, 372

6:15    139, 259, 304, 313, 321, 357

6:16    139, 330, 355

6:16–17    125, 221

6:17    111, 140, 144, 215

7    140, 141, 157, 162, 260, 266

7:1    86, 93, 140–41, 142, 290, 369

7:1–3    140–44, 141, 142, 151, 153, 181, 182, 266

7:1–8    141, 145, 149, 157, 158, 186, 204, 204n5, 205, 265, 296, 354, 389

7:1–17    140–56, 302–3

7:2    43, 67n1, 99n1, 102, 104, 125n23, 141–42, 151, 161, 164, 170, 171, 187n12, 188, 189, 190, 202, 212, 215, 216, 220, 236, 245, 259, 271n21, 273, 282, 294, 307, 313, 324, 325, 340, 345, 357, 379

7:3    102, 142–44, 144, 176, 315, 355n14, 356, 399, 410n10

7:4    144–47, 149, 205, 260, 266, 294, 387, 390

7:4–8    144–48, 145, 146, 227

7:5–8    145, 147–48, 227

7:6    147

7:8    147

7:9    37, 38, 71, 86, 111, 135, 149–51, 150, 151, 156, 200, 226, 245, 251, 266, 271n21, 273, 280, 282, 285, 290, 340, 380, 408

7:9–10    231

7:9–11    220

7:9–12    95, 96

7:9–13    90

7:9–14    91, 115

7:9–17    144, 145, 148–56, 149, 157, 158, 176, 186, 204, 205, 266, 268, 285, 354, 382

7:10    142, 151–52, 307, 330, 342, 342n10, 396

7:11    76, 89, 93, 112n10, 152, 159, 220, 249

7:12    81, 152–53, 152–53n11, 261, 33, 342n10, 386

7:13    71, 96, 153, 226, 285

7:13–14    11, 41n5, 117n18, 135, 238

7:14    33, 42, 77, 149, 153–55, 154, 226, 266, 273, 285, 286n3, 300, 352, 354, 408

7:15    155–56, 203, 215, 290, 307, 330, 398

7:16    175, 300, 382

7:16–17    156, 395

7:17    156, 230, 231, 380, 382, 396, 413

7:22    215

8    162, 169

8–10    271

8:1    101, 102, 122, 157–58, 157n3, 303

8:1–6    189, 195

8:2    43, 159, 159–62, 160, 161, 170, 189, 196, 202, 245, 271n21, 282, 313

8:2–6    158–66

8:2–11:18    120

8:2–11:19    20, 158–223

8:3    125n23, 133, 162–65, 163n9, 188, 203, 204, 299, 324, 345

8:3–4    113, 113n12, 138, 298

8:3–5    157n1, 158, 161–62, 163, 164, 166, 174, 175, 181, 183, 194, 292, 308, 311, 316, 349, 353

8:4    164, 165–66, 343

8:4–5    293

8:5    91, 123, 133, 138, 163n9, 165, 191, 203, 204, 217, 223, 281, 284n2, 299, 308, 358

8:5–8    210

8:6    160, 161–62, 172, 345

8:7    130, 161, 168, 172, 175n2, 211, 284n2, 308

| | | | | | | | |
|---|---|---|---|---|---|---|---|
| 8:7–8 | 281 | 9:12–21 | 357 | 10:3–4 | 123, 200 |
| 8:7–13 | 38, 51, 166–71, | 9:13 | 112, 133, 133, 161, | 10:4 | 49, 143, 192–93, |
| | 288, 302 | | 162, 163, 163n9, | | 192n18, 199, 202, |
| 8:8 | 161, 168, 172, 211, | | 164n10, 172, 181, | | 294, 327 |
| | 284n2, 295 | | 183, 204, 293, 299 | 10:4–7 | 192–97 |
| 8:8–9 | 168–69, 169n18 | 9:13–21 | 180–86, 303 | 10:5 | 100, 187, 189, |
| 8:9 | 132 | 9:13–11:13 | 219 | | 193, 202 |
| 8:10 | 161, 168, 172 | 9:14 | 160, 180 | 10:5–6 | 193–96, 205 |
| 8:10–11 | 169–70, 173 295 | 9:14–15 | 181–83, 302 | 10:6 | 33, 67n1, 142n2, |
| 8:10–12 | 139 | 9:15 | 183, 217, 345 | | 193, 195, 196 |
| 8:11 | 250 | 9:16 | 145 | 10:7 | 29, 161, 172, |
| 8:12 | 161, 170,172, | 9:16–19 | 183–84 | | 177, 185n11, 196–97, |
| | 175, 300 | 9:17 | 165, 191, 281, | | 212n12, 222, 272, 335, |
| 8:13 | 57, 67, 67n3, 77, | | 284n2 | | 401, 403, 411 |
| | 99n1, 142, 160, 161, | 9:17–18 | 210, 275, 293 | 10:8 | 100, 101, 122, |
| | 170–71, 172, 215, 218, | 9:17–19 | 303 | | 190, 198 |
| | 236, 245, 271, 271n21, | 9:18 | 165, 171, 211, 247, | 10:8–9 | 101 |
| | 272, 282, 294, 313, | | 281, 283, 284n2 | 10:8–10 | 189, 190, 197 |
| | 314, 333, 357 | 9:19 | 141 | 10:8–11 | 193, 197–201, 201 |
| 9:1 | 74, 99n1, 125n23, | 9:19–21 | 144n7 | 10:9 | 100, 101, 101n4, |
| | 139, 161, 169, 172, | 9:20 | 67n3, 69n5, 76n11, | | 122, 190, 199 |
| | 173, 174, 181, 212, | | 185, 211, 247, 283, | 10:9–10 | 198–99 |
| | 245, 271n21, 282, | | 304, 305, 407 | 10:10 | 100, 101, 101n4, |
| | 314, 360 | 9:20–21 | 38, 49, 51, 167, | | 190, 199, 202 |
| 9:1–2 | 46, 171, 172–75, | | 185n11, 218, 252, | 10:11 | 81, 197, 199, |
| | 173, 179, 187n12, | | 288, 301, 302, 348, | | 199–201, 200, 202, |
| | 196, 374 | | 355, 413 | | 203, 207, 215, 218, |
| 9:1–6 | 301 | 9:21 | 69n5, 274, 305, | | 232, 249, 252, 273, |
| 9:1–11 | 180 | | 382, 398 | | 304, 313, 322, |
| 9:1–12 | 172–80, 181, | 10 | 100, 101, 102, 188, | | 380, 394 |
| | 182, 218 | | 188n14, 189, 195, | 11 | 43, 111, 197, 199, |
| 9:1–21 | 171–86, 189, | | 197, 198n23, 199, | | 201, 202, 208, 213, |
| | 202, 250 | | 200, 201, 202, 215, 232 | | 215, 218, 219, 220, |
| 9:2 | 121, 122, 165, | 10:1 | 38, 44, 45, 101, | | 231, 232, 242, |
| | 212, 245 | | 104, 175, 186–89, 187, | | 245, 355 |
| 9:2–3 | 293 | | 188, 202, 216, 226, | 11–13 | 233 |
| 9:3 | 125n23, 165, 206 | | 245, 271, 271n21, 279, | 11–14 | 218–19 |
| 9:3–5 | 171, 175–77, 252 | | 282, 324, 325, 357, | 11:1 | 38, 51, 76, 133, |
| 9:4 | 102, 130, 141, 143, | | 360, 378 | | 163, 163n9, 202–4, |
| | 173, 355n14, 356, 399 | 10:1–3 | 186–91 | | 207, 209, 211, 218, |
| 9:5 | 125n23, 275 | 10:1–11 | 186 | | 230, 231, 249, 250, |
| 9:6 | 55, 177–78, 183, 197, | 10:1–11:13 | 186–218 | | 252, 298, 302, 355 |
| | 239, 258, 374, 383 | 10:1–11:14 | 162, 303 | 11:1–2 | 125n23, 171, 197, |
| 9:7 | 91n9, 345 | 10:2 | 98, 100, 101, | | 201–5, 203, 205, 206, |
| 9:7–10 | 178–79 | | 101n3, 101n4, 122, | | 208, 209, 211, 214, |
| 9:8 | 184, 191, 345 | | 189–90, 193, | | 215, 222, 260, 291, |
| 9:10 | 141, 197 | | 194n20, 198 | | 345, 389 |
| 9:11 | 173, 176, 179–80, | 10:3 | 142, 190–91, 196, | 11:1–13 | 186, 194n20, |
| | 212, 245, 250, 319 | | 200, 202, 223, | | 198n23 |
| 9:12 | 37, 86, 171, 180, 333 | | 236, 357 | 11:1–19 | 201–23 |

**Revelation (*continued*)**

11:1–15:4 198n23

11:2 194, 203, 204–5, 206, 208, 239, 249, 371

11:2–3 214, 215, 232, 250

11:3 29, 138, 157n3, 194, 206, 207–9, 209n8, 218, 222, 252, 298, 316, 348, 401, 403, 411

11:3–13 206–18

11:4 111, 209

11:5 210, 212, 284n2, 303, 358

11:5–6 208

11:6 206, 207, 208, 210–11, 218, 247, 252, 283, 316

11:6–7 207, 222

11:7 52, 174, 207, 208, 211–13, 217, 219, 222, 233, 242, 245, 250, 251, 260, 318, 322, 348, 350, 358, 370

11:7–9 11, 41n5, 117n18

11:7–10 213

11:7a 210

11:8 207, 214, 217, 308

11:9 38, 157, 194, 200, 214–15, 216, 219, 239, 249, 252, 273

11:10 57, 77, 207, 215, 216, 219, 222, 272, 275, 298, 348

11:10–11 215–16

11:11 111, 157, 194, 215, 216, 217, 412

11:11–13 212

11:12 87, 87n3, 142, 192n18, 215, 216–17, 218, 220, 279

11:12–13 236

11:13 38, 51, 65, 67n3, 138, 208, 217–18, 220, 252, 273, 288, 301, 302, 308, 342n10, 348, 386, 413

11:13a 218

11:14 37, 78, 171, 219, 333

11:15 33, 161, 172, 220, 221, 236, 303, 344

11:15–18 95, 97, 161, 236

11:15–19 196, 208, 217, 219–23, 222, 231

11:16 76, 112n10, 152, 249, 330n3

11:16–17 220–21

11:17 5, 34, 39, 95n14, 220, 221, 287, 297, 299, 318, 340, 342n10, 344, 355, 372

11:18 29, 67, 134, 139, 196, 200, 221–22, 249, 250, 273, 288, 298, 343, 344, 372, 373, 410n10, 411, 414

11:19 91, 122, 123, 138, 165, 168, 191, 203, 217, 222–23, 224, 263, 291, 308

12 31, 47, 55, 179, 198n23, 213, 219, 223, 225, 226, 227, 229, 231, 236, 238, 245, 303, 345, 359, 362

12–13 260, 362

12–14 21, 224, 245, 259, 263, 264, 265, 272, 282, 282, 285

12:1 91n9, 175, 224, 224–27, 225, 226, 228, 233, 280n28

12:1–3 282

12:1–6 223, 224–32, 233, 236, 240, 345

12:1–17 20, 213, 223–42

12:1–14:20 20, 223–82

12:1–22:5 198n23

12:2 227–28, 229, 233, 275

12:2–6 227

12:3 37, 112, 126, 224, 225, 228–30, 246, 314, 321, 351, 360

12:4 139, 225, 229n5, 230, 232, 240

12:5 5, 19, 38, 62, 64, 203, 227, 230–31, 238, 239, 240, 240n10, 242, 249, 252, 265, 289, 318, 322, 330, 352, 355

12:6 157n3, 194, 205, 208, 215, 224, 227, 232, 234, 239, 240, 241, 242, 250, 345

12:7 160, 225, 226, 229n5, 233–34, 234, 237, 250, 271, 274, 330

12:7–9 173, 187n12, 223, 232–35, 236, 239, 361

12:7–10 226

12:8 234

12:9 229n5, 234–35, 237, 240, 241, 242, 361, 362

12:10 41, 116, 142, 151, 192n18, 221, 236–37, 238, 273, 294, 342n10

12:10–11 131, 223, 342

12:10–12 98, 118, 131, 135, 235–39

12:11 5, 11, 30, 36, 41n5, 42, 52, 75, 106, 115, 117, 117n18, 132, 145, 150, 155, 178, 210, 211, 212, 212n11, 226, 228, 231, 234, 236, 237, 237–39, 238, 239, 240, 248, 252, 255, 263, 265, 266, 277n25, 285, 286n3, 322, 322, 330, 345, 346, 352, 353, 354, 377, 379, 408

12:12 171, 187n12, 223, 239, 283n1, 333

12:13 150, 173, 225, 229n5, 240

12:13–17 223, 240–42

| | | | | | |
|---|---|---|---|---|---|
| 12:14 | 157, 194, 205, 208, 215, 227, 232, 239, 240–41, 250 | 13:7 | 38, 52, 125n23, 171, 200, 213, 233, 245, 250, 251–52, 254, 260, 272, 322, 345, 350, 370 | 14:1 | 37, 60, 79, 102, 111, 123, 143, 250, 259, 263, 264, 264–66, 279, 351, 355n14, 356, 399 |
| 12:15 | 45, 241, 354, 355, 362 | | | | |
| 12:15–16 | 303 | 13:8 | 19, 57, 71, 72, 76n11, 77, 100, 214, 215, 247, 252–53, 257, 261, 269, 272, 273, 313, 374 | 14:1–5 | 111, 143, 145, 146, 204, 263, 263–70, 266, 277, 296, 354, 389 |
| 12:16 | 91n9, 122, 229n5, 234, 241 | | | | |
| 12:17 | 5, 32, 47, 55, 67n3, 69, 212n11, 225, 226, 229n5, 230, 232, 233, 234, 235, 237, 241–42, 250, 277, 322, 345, 350, 362, 363, 370, 404n8 | | | 14:1–20 | 21, 263–82 |
| | | 13:9 | 52, 253, 413n12 | 14:2 | 45, 123, 191, 192n18, 264, 266–67, 278, 285, 294 |
| | | 13:10 | 42, 49, 62, 126, 253–55, 254, 258, 259, 266, 276, 277 | | |
| | | | | 14:2–3 | 267, 285 |
| | | | | 14:3 | 93, 114, 266, 267–68, 270, 285, 307, 351 |
| 12:18 | 243, 256 | 13:11 | 99n1, 112, 229n5, 256–57, 258, 264, 271n21, 279, 282 | | |
| 12:18–13:18 | 20, 242–63 | | | 14:3–4 | 115 |
| 13 | 8, 16, 31, 55, 213, 219, 229, 233, 234, 235, 241, 242, 243, 245, 248, 252, 260, 262, 263, 272, 273, 301, 303 | | | 14:4 | 145, 225, 268, 268–70, 274, 280, 345 |
| | | 13:11–17 | 304n7 | | |
| | | 13:11–18 | 255–63, 303, 358 | 14:5 | 270 |
| | | 13:12 | 57, 67n1, 76n11, 77, 177, 215, 247, 257, 272, 273 | 14:6 | 38, 57, 77, 167, 170, 188, 200, 251, 271–73, 272, 275, 276, 279, 325, 330, 357 |
| 13:1 | 92, 112, 213, 243, 245–46, 247, 250, 256, 260, 264, 271n21, 279, 282, 284, 301, 304, 312, 314, 319, 321, 351 | | | | |
| | | 13:12–13 | 303 | | |
| | | 13:12–17 | 72n9 | 14:6–7 | 185n11, 218, 289 |
| | | 13:12–18 | 257 | 14:6–11 | 271–76, 277 |
| | | 13:13 | 169n17, 187n12, 210, 224n1, 257–58, 305 | 14:7 | 76, 142, 217, 236, 263, 273, 280, 281, 288, 301, 342n10, 343, 348, 386, 413 |
| 13:1–3 | 213 | | | | |
| 13:1–10 | 229, 243–55, 274, 301 | 13:13–17 | 365 | | |
| | | 13:14 | 57, 67n1, 77, 125n23, 171, 215, 224n1, 235, 247, 258, 272, 362 | 14:8 | 188, 200, 273–75, 275n22, 281, 283n1, 308, 313, 315, 316, 323, 324, 325, 326, 330, 333 |
| 13:2 | 229n5, 246, 301, 325 | | | | |
| 13:3 | 109, 126, 177, 244, 247–49, 249, 252, 257, 261, 302, 317, 318n2 | | | | |
| | | 13:14–15 | 345 | 14:8a | 326 |
| | | 13:15 | 125n23, 171, 215, 258–59, 273, 383, 76n11 | 14:8b | 326 |
| | | | | 14:9 | 76n11, 142, 143, 188, 236, 259, 275, 325, 330, 399 |
| 13:4 | 76n11, 212, 229n5, 249–50, 252, 257, 273, 301, 322, 365 | 13:15–18 | 295 | | |
| | | 13:16 | 100, 143, 259–60, 266, 355n14, 356, 357, 373 | | |
| 13:5 | 125n23, 171, 208, 215, 232, 250, 254, 258, 260, 263, 345 | | | 14:9–10 | 275 |
| | | 13:16–17 | 259, 274, 315 | 14:9–11 | 260, 295 |
| | | 13:16–18 | 275 | 14:10 | 139, 184, 210, 221, 276, 281, 283n1, 284n2, 308, 315, 329, 353, 355, 383 |
| 13:5–6 | 301, 303 | 13:17 | 115, 250, 260–61 | | |
| 13:6 | 50, 75, 122, 244, 250–51, 309, 380, 399 | 13:18 | 261, 261–63, 277, 319 | | |
| | | 14 | 263, 266, 277, 279, 285, 325 | 14:10–11 | 263, 281, 358, 371, 374 |

**Revelation** (*continued*)
14:11      76n11, 165, 250,
           259, 276, 293,
           333, 342, 343
14:12      32, 56, 57, 69,
           217, 242, 254, 263,
           266, 276–77, 404n8
14:12–13                276–77
14:13      31, 34, 43, 49,
           66, 67, 137, 178,
           192, 215, 236, 263,
           276, 277, 278, 294,
           305n8, 346, 368, 373,
           403, 407, 412
14:14      37, 38, 91, 123,
           125, 227, 263,
           264, 279–80,
           351, 396
14:14–16   216, 263,
           279, 280
14:14–20   270, 277,
           278–82
14:15      142, 188, 203,
           217, 236, 278, 279,
           280, 291, 325, 330
14:16      280, 281
14:17      188, 203, 278,
           280, 281, 291,
           325, 330
14:17–20   263, 279, 280
14:18      133, 142, 163,
           163n9, 188, 204,
           210, 236, 271, 278,
           280, 281, 284n2,
           297, 299, 325, 330
14:19      275, 280, 281,
           283n1, 308
14:19–20                355
14:20      278, 281–82,
           352, 353
15         162, 219, 282
15–16                   283
15–18                   282
15–22      259, 263
15:1       159, 162, 211,
           212n12, 224, 247,
           275, 282–83, 286,
           287, 290, 291,
           292, 293, 294,
           307, 308, 381

15:1–3                  288
15:1–16:21               21
15:1–22:9   21, 282–404
15:2       52, 99n1, 106, 111,
           238, 241, 245,
           250, 261, 266,
           267, 281,
           284–85, 322
15:2–3                  267
15:2–4                  162, 267,
           283–89, 291, 296
15:3       38, 39, 95n14,
           114, 221, 283,
           284, 285, 285–88,
           286, 289, 297, 299,
           312, 341, 344, 350,
           355, 394
15:3–4     287n5, 297, 344,
           380, 393
15:3b–4                  98
15:4       38, 51, 76, 250,
           273, 284, 288–89,
           297, 301, 302, 343,
           348, 394, 413
15:4a                   284
15:5       37, 86, 122, 203,
           222, 290–91, 294,
           324, 380
15:5–6     162, 292
15:5–8     286, 289–93, 294
15:5–18:24              285
15:5–19:10              159n4
15:6       44, 203, 211,
           247, 278, 283,
           291–92, 294
15:7       33, 67n1, 142n2,
           275, 283n1, 292, 293,
           294, 308
15:8       165, 203, 211,
           212n12, 247, 283,
           292–93, 294, 307,
           342n10, 386
16         169, 219, 282,
           293, 324
16:1       142, 159, 203, 236,
           275, 283n1, 291,
           293–94, 295, 296,
           298, 299, 307, 327,
           343, 414
16:1–20    166, 293–307

16:1–21                 120
16:2       76n11, 259, 260,
           294, 295, 301, 307
16:2–4                  294–95
16:3       67, 132, 168, 294,
           295, 307
16:3–4                  211
16:4       169, 294,
           295, 307
16:5       34, 134, 221, 287,
           294, 296–98, 297,
           299, 318, 336, 350
16:5–6                  299
16:5–7     95, 97, 295–99,
           296, 341
16:5b                   299
16:6       11, 41n5, 70n7,
           117n18, 134, 168,
           294, 298, 306, 316,
           335, 338, 342,
           352, 414
16:7       39, 95n14, 133, 163,
           163n9, 167, 181, 204,
           221, 287, 294, 296,
           298–99, 350, 355
16:8       125n23, 171, 175,
           210, 284n2, 294,
           299–300, 307, 345
16:8–9     167, 170
16:8–12                 299–302
16:9       51, 69n5, 185, 211,
           218, 247, 274, 283,
           288, 300–301, 305,
           309, 342n10, 348, 355,
           386, 413
16:10      294, 301, 305
16:11      51, 69n5, 185, 218,
           300, 301–2, 305,
           309, 348, 355,
           407, 413
16:12      142, 182, 200,
           294, 304, 307,
           345, 394
16:13      99n1, 229n5, 241,
           256, 303–4
16:13–16                302–7
16:14      39, 200, 221,
           224n1, 258, 287,
           304–5, 306, 312,
           321, 322, 370, 394

| | | | | | | |
|---|---|---|---|---|---|---|
| 16:14–15 | 306n10 | 17:3 | 40, 88, 99n1, 112, | 17:16 | 112, 210, 213, |
| 16:14–16 | 304n7, 358 | | 126, 213, 215, 225, | | 229, 246, 300, |
| 16:15 | 31, 32, 69, 70, | | 229, 232, 244, 246, | | 311, 318, 318n2, |
| | 242, 277, 304, | | 250, 301, 313–14, | | 322–23, 330, |
| | 305n8, 305–6, | | 316, 319, 322, 323, | | 334, 342n11 |
| | 318, 346, 402, | | 330, 385 | 17:17 | 212n12, 321 |
| | 403, 415 | 17:3–6a | 313–16 | 17:18 | 200, 214, 225, |
| 16:16 | 306–7 | 17:4 | 126, 225, 226, 272, | | 301, 313, 314, |
| 16:17 | 142, 203, 236, | | 274, 314–15, 329, | | 318, 333, 394 |
| | 291, 294, 307, 381 | | 335, 386 | 18 | 217, 282, 312, |
| 16:17–21 | 307–9, 311, 324 | 17:4–5 | 383, 394 | | 323, 324, 325, |
| 16:18 | 123, 138, 165, | 17:5 | 58, 143, 250, 274, | | 327, 336, 340, |
| | 191, 217, | | 311, 312, | | 341, 344, 353 |
| | 223, 308 | | 315–16, 333 | 18:1 | 86, 187, 271, |
| 16:18–21 | 91 | 17:6 | 11, 41n5, 99n1, | | 290, 324–25, |
| 16:19 | 139, 214, 221, | | 117n18, 134, 316, | | 325n1, 330, 357, |
| | 274, 275, 283n1, | | 335, 338, 352 | | 360, 386 |
| | 301, 315, 316, | 17:6–7 | 225 | 18:1–2 | 188, 357 |
| | 323, 329, 333 | 17:6a | 314, 316 | 18:1–3 | 324–27 |
| 16:19–21 | 308–9 | 17:6b | 319 | 18:1–24 | 323–38 |
| 16:20 | 305, 308, 372 | 17:6b–7 | 317 | 18:2 | 142n1, 274, 304, |
| 16:21 | 168, 187, 211, | 17:6b–18 | 316–23 | | 316, 325–26, |
| | 247, 283, 300, 308 | 17:7 | 112, 213, 229, 246, | | 333, 336 |
| 17 | 8, 198n23, 282, 309, | | 315, 319 | 18:3 | 58, 83, 200, 274, |
| | 310, 311, 312, 314, | 17:8 | 57, 71, 72, 72n9, | | 275, 275n22, |
| | 316, 323, 324, 325, | | 77, 100, 174, 212, | | 283n1, 304, 311, |
| | 340, 341, 344, 345, | | 215, 221, 244, 244n2, | | 312, 313, 321, |
| | 353, 384 | | 245, 250, 272, 317, | | 326–27, 328, 332, |
| 17–19 | 263, 307, 309 | | 317–19, 318, 321, 322, | | 334, 394 |
| 17:1 | 159, 310–12, 311, | | 324, 326, 333, 374 | 18:4 | 192n18, 211, 247, |
| | 312, 314, 319, 322, | 17:9 | 213, 225, 229, 246, | | 294, 305, 327–28, |
| | 323, 324, 330, 335, | | 247, 261, 276, 304, | | 329, 333, 346, |
| | 336, 338, 346, 347, | | 314, 319–20, | | 348, 394, 413 |
| | 353, 384, 385, | | 323, 330 | 18:4–5 | 36n4 |
| | 395, 400 | 17:9–10 | 314 | 18:4–8 | 327–31 |
| 17:1–2 | 200, 310–13, | 17:10 | 320–21 | 18:5 | 327, 328–29 |
| | 394 | 17:11 | 17, 249, | 18:6 | 49, 64, 315, |
| 17:1–18 | 309–23 | | 318, 321 | | 329–30, 373, |
| 17:1–18:24 | 338, 349 | 17:12 | 112, 200, 213, | | 407, 414 |
| 17:1–19:8 | 171n20 | | 229, 246, 304, | 18:7 | 328, 330–31, 333, |
| 17:1–19:10 | 21, 309–48, | | 318, 321, 394 | | 338, 342, 343, 350 |
| | 311, 322, 324, | 17:13 | 321, 323 | 18:8 | 130, 134, 177, |
| | 346, 347, 360, | 17:14 | 52, 106, 117, 213, | | 210, 211, 247, |
| | 377, 383, 384, | | 250, 285, 288, 312, | | 284n2, 300, 323, |
| | 385, 400, 407 | | 322, 350, 354, 356, | | 327, 331, 333 |
| 17:1–20:3 | 307 | | 358, 394, 396 | 18:8–20 | 326 |
| 17:2 | 57, 58, 77, 139, | 17:15 | 200, 213, 311, | 18:9 | 33, 58, 165, 200, |
| | 215, 272, 274, 275, | | 312, 314, 318, | | 293, 304, 311, |
| | 304, 311, 312–13, | | 319, 322, | | 313, 321, 333, 394 |
| | 321, 332 | | 330, 340 | 18:9–10 | 332–34 |

**Revelation** (*continued*)

18:9–20            331–36

18:10              171n20, 214, 217,
                   274, 301, 308,
                   316, 323, 333

18:11              115, 327, 333

18:11–17a          330, 334–35

18:12              126, 290,
                   345, 386

18:13              113n12, 132

18:14              132, 334

18:15              83, 327, 333

18:16              126, 171n20, 214,
                   226, 290, 301,
                   308, 314, 315,
                   333, 345, 386

18:17              217, 333, 334

18:17b–19          335

18:18              165, 214,
                   293, 333

18:18–19           301, 308

18:19              83, 171n20,
                   214, 217, 308,
                   333, 334

18:20              30, 50, 134, 239,
                   298, 311,
                   327, 332

18:20b             336

18:21              104, 188, 214,
                   274, 301, 308,
                   316, 325, 337

18:21–24           336–38

18:22–23a          337

18:23              200, 214, 235,
                   312, 326, 327,
                   362, 383

18:23b–24          328, 337–38

18:24              11, 41n5, 109,
                   117n18, 126, 134,
                   188, 214, 247,
                   298, 316, 335, 352

19                 47, 350, 356, 360

19:1               86, 142, 236, 290,
                   294, 340, 341,
                   342n10, 343,
                   344, 386

19:1–2             151, 296, 343

19:1–4             95, 97, 338

19:1–5             273

19:1–6             340

19:1–8             335

19:1–10            324, 338–48,
                   341, 349

19:1b–2            341

19:2               11, 41n5, 117n18,
                   134, 275, 287,
                   297, 299, 311,
                   316, 336, 338,
                   341, 342n11,
                   350, 352

19:3               33, 165, 293,
                   341, 343

19:4               76, 81, 93, 112n10,
                   152, 220, 249, 330,
                   341, 343

19:5               288, 344, 373,
                   410n10

19:5–8             95, 97, 338

19:6               39, 45, 123, 191,
                   221, 266, 287,
                   294, 299, 340,
                   341, 343

19:6–8             343, 344, 351

19:7               225, 342n10, 344,
                   345, 386

19:7–8             78, 225, 347,
                   379, 385, 412

19:8               125n23, 226, 290,
                   305, 342, 345,
                   346, 347, 354, 356

19:9               31, 43, 192, 277,
                   305n8, 344, 346,
                   357, 368, 400,
                   401, 403

19:9–10            41, 338, 346, 399

19:10              29, 45, 76, 89,
                   112n10, 113, 152,
                   207, 212n11, 220,
                   237, 342, 348,
                   357, 401, 403

19:10c             28n1

19:11              37, 58, 122, 123,
                   124, 134, 191,
                   250, 264, 279,
                   330, 350, 351,
                   354, 360, 376,
                   378, 381,
                   401, 413

19:11–13           115

19:11–15           145

19:11–16           38, 116,
                   348–56, 357

19:11–21           5, 282, 306n10,
                   322, 362, 367, 369

19:11–21:8         21, 338,
                   348–83, 360

19:12              44, 60, 210,
                   246, 280n28,
                   351–52, 355

19:12–13           250

19:13              71, 226, 352,
                   352–54, 376

19:14              90, 145, 226,
                   266, 268, 290,
                   350, 354

19:15              5, 39, 45, 64,
                   140, 200, 203,
                   210, 221, 230,
                   241, 249, 275,
                   280, 281, 283n1,
                   287, 289, 299,
                   303, 353, 354–55,
                   369, 376

19:16              71, 246, 250,
                   288, 312, 351,
                   352, 355–56, 394

19:17              142, 170, 175,
                   236, 271, 357,
                   358, 360, 376

19:17–18           259, 348, 357

19:17–21           356–59, 360, 369

19:18              139, 313, 357

19:18–19           200, 304, 394

19:19              99n1, 321, 322,
                   330, 359, 360,
                   370, 376

19:19–21           348, 357–59

19:20              67n1, 76n11, 184,
                   210, 224n1, 235,
                   243, 256, 258,
                   259, 260, 275,
                   281, 284n2, 303,
                   362, 371, 374, 383

19:20–21           295

19:21              5, 45, 67n3,
                   210, 241, 303,
                   330, 354, 355, 358

20                 47, 195, 212, 253,
                   335–36, 359,
                   360, 399

| | | | | | |
|---|---|---|---|---|---|
| 20–21 | 184–86 | 20:10–11 | 234 | 21:7 | 106, 322, 381, |
| 20–22 | 198n23, 263 | 20:11 | 308, 330, | | 382, 385, 392 |
| 20:1 | 74, 173, 174, 187, | | 372–73, 376 | 21:8 | 178, 184, 185, 210, |
| | 212, 213, 245, 360, | 20:11–15 | 359, 372–74, | | 222, 275, 281, |
| | 364, 372, 376 | | 394 | | 284n2, 358, 368, |
| 20:1–3 | 359–63, 365, 369 | 20:12 | 49, 67, 100, 101, | | 373, 382–83, 394, |
| 20:1–15 | 359–74 | | 102, 122, 253, | | 398, 400, 406, 409 |
| 20:2 | 229n5, 234, | | 336, 355, 363, | 21:8–9 | 399 |
| | 360–61, 362, 364 | | 373–74, 376, 394 | 21:9 | 159, 211, 247, |
| 20:2–3 | 130 | 20:12–13 | 64, 134, 407 | | 311, 345, 379, |
| 20:3 | 86, 143, 174, | 20:12–14 | 222 | | 383, 384–85, 389, |
| | 195, 196, 212, | 20:12–15 | 372 | | 395, 400, 409, 412 |
| | 212n12, 213, 235, | 20:13 | 46, 49, 67, 178, | 21:9–10 | 225 |
| | 245, 289, 361–63 | | 245, 284, 336, 350, | 21:9–11 | 400 |
| 20:4 | 5, 28, 75, 125n23, | | 373, 374 | 21:9–14 | 383–88 |
| | 132, 143, 171, 212, | 20:13–14 | 46, 130, 374 | 21:9–22:5 | 399–400 |
| | 213, 242, 259, 260, | 20:14 | 178, 284n2, 358, | 21:9–22:9 | 21, 311, 324, |
| | 277n25, 295, 311, | | 368, 380 | | 338, 346, 349, |
| | 336, 345, 349, 354, | 20:14–15 | 210, 383 | | 360, 377, 383, |
| | 361, 364–67, 365, | 20:15 | 71, 100, 252, | | 383–404, 400, 407, |
| | 368, 372, 373, 376, | | 284n2, 373, 374, | | 412, 414 |
| | 377, 383, 399 | | 378, 386, 393, | 21:10 | 40, 88, 187, |
| 20:4–5 | 67, 67n2 | | 394, 414 | | 215, 313, 371, |
| 20:4–6 | 11, 41n5, 116, | 21 | 156, 385 | | 377, 385, 395 |
| | 117n18, 131, 308, | 21:1 | 15–16, 92, 158, | 21:11 | 89n7, 342n10, |
| | 359, 363–68, 369 | | 241, 245, 245, | | 385–86, 390, |
| 20:4–22:21 | 307 | | 284, 349, | | 393, 396 |
| 20:4a | 131 | | 376–77, 380 | 21:12 | 227, 392 |
| 20:4b–6 | 131 | 21:1–4 | 375, 380 | 21:12–13 | 386–88, 389 |
| 20:5 | 67, 67n3, 212n12, | 21:1–8 | 374–83, 380 | 21:12–14 | 146 |
| | 361, 365, 367–68 | 21:2 | 78, 99n1, 113, | 21:12–20a | 400 |
| 20:6 | 31, 55, 178, 222, | | 187, 345, 371, | 21:13 | 142 |
| | 260, 277, 305n8, | | 377–79, 385, 391, | 21:14 | 30, 38, 50, 227, 391 |
| | 346, 361, 365, 368, | | 398, 412 | 21:14–16 | 371 |
| | 383, 399, 403 | 21:3 | 37, 38, 156, 251, | 21:15 | 389 |
| 20:7 | 130, 187n12, | | 291, 294, 375, | 21:15–16 | 202 |
| | 212, 212n12, 213, | | 379–80, 382, 388, | 21:15–21 | 388–92 |
| | 247, 361, 369 | | 392, 393, 398, | 21:16 | 227, 387, 389 |
| 20:7–9 | 393 | | 411, 416 | 21:17–18 | 390 |
| 20:7–10 | 322, 359, 368–72 | 21:4 | 156, 178, 380, | 21:18 | 386 |
| 20:8 | 15, 76, 235, 307n, | | 382, 408 | 21:18–19 | 89n7, 371 |
| | 362, 363, 369–70 | 21:5 | 37, 43, 192, 330, | 21:18–21 | 341, 390–92 |
| 20:9 | 36, 187, 210, 212, | | 376, 379, 380–81, | 21:19 | 89n7, 391 |
| | 258, 284n2, | | 382, 401 | 21:20 | 89n7 |
| | 370–71, 380 | 21:5–7 | 327 | 21:20b–21 | 400 |
| 20:9–10 | 210 | 21:5–8 | 39, 375, 380 | 21:21 | 227, 371, 397 |
| 20:10 | 33, 184, 235, 243, | 21:6 | 39, 156, 307, 380, | 21:22 | 39, 78, 95n14, 99n1, |
| | 256, 275, 281, 284n2, | | 381–82, 382, 395, | | 156, 203, 209, 221, |
| | 303, 358, 362, 363, | | 408, 409, 413 | | 223, 287, 291, 299, |
| | 371–72, 374 | 21:6a | 33 | | 371, 386, 392–93, 396 |

**Revelation** (*continued*)
21:22–27        392–94
21:23        175, 325n1,
    342n10, 371, 385,
    386, 393, 399
21:23–26        293
21:24        38, 313, 380,
    386, 392, 393,
    398, 411, 412, 416
21:24–26        288
21:24–27        393–94
21:25        399
21:26    38, 386, 393, 398
21:27        100, 252, 270,
    374, 382, 398
22        391, 396, 408
22:1        30, 231, 382,
    395–96, 397n1, 413
22:1–5        395–99
22:2        38, 52, 227,
    288, 395, 396–98,
    397n1, 408, 411,
    414, 416
22:3        396, 398–99,
    410n10, 411
22:4        60, 102, 143,
    250, 259, 265,
    351, 355n14,
    356, 399
22:5    33, 37, 116, 175,
    325n1, 366, 368,
    393, 394, 399
22:6        28, 29, 30, 32,
    87, 362, 381,
    395, 400–402, 410,
    410n10, 411, 412
22:6–7        400
22:6–9        399–404,
    400, 403
22:7    7, 31, 32, 47, 69,
    70, 77, 93, 100,
    242, 277, 305,
    305n8, 318, 346,
    348, 401, 402–3,
    404, 407, 412, 415
22:8    5, 30, 40, 112n10,
    152, 220, 395,
    409, 413
22:8–9    41, 45, 113, 199,
    338, 346, 347, 403–4

22:9        29, 32, 69, 100,
    207, 237, 242,
    348, 348, 402,
    402n6, 411
22:10    5, 7, 32, 47, 70,
    77, 93, 100, 143,
    193, 348, 401,
    405, 407
22:10–21    21, 30, 399,
    400, 404–17
22:11    38, 51, 297, 302,
    405–7, 407
22:12        49, 70, 77, 93,
    318, 373, 401,
    402, 404, 407,
    408, 412, 415
22:12–19        415
22:13    39, 46, 52, 381,
    396, 407–8, 410
22:14    31, 49, 155, 214,
    277, 305n8, 346,
    354, 371, 397,
    403, 408
22:15    270, 382, 393,
    394, 398, 409
22:16        7, 28, 29, 30,
    40, 63, 64, 105,
    169, 173, 401, 403,
    409–12, 410, 410n9,
    413, 414
22:17    32, 34, 215, 345,
    379, 382, 385,
    395, 412–13
22:18    7, 47, 100, 211,
    247, 413n12, 414
22:18–19    348, 413–14
22:18–20        77
22:19    7, 47, 100, 214,
    371, 397
22:20    70, 77, 81, 93,
    318, 401, 402,
    412, 414–16
22:21    20, 34, 416–17

**SEPTUAGINT
AND APOCRYPHA**

**Baruch**
4–5        147n8
4:35        326

**1 Esdras**
5        146
8:80        268n19
9:8        218n17
29:31        306

**2 Esdras**
4:35–36        137n33
13:40–47        147n8

**Judith**
7:30        176n4
8:9        176n4
8:15        176n4

**1 Kingdoms**
7:6        294n1

**2 Kingdoms**
23:16        294n1

**1 Maccabees**
1:20–24        251
3:25        216n15
6:1–5        251
7:18        216n15
10:20        314n1
10:62        314n1
10:64        314n1
10:89        44
11:1        370
11:58        314n1
11:71        335
13:36–37        96n15
13:51        150
14:43        314n1
15:14        370

**2 Maccabees**
1:14–17        251
2:4–8        60, 222
3:24        216n15
3:25        350
10:6–7        151
10:7        150
11:5        389
12:9–10        389
12:16–17        389
12:22        216n15
12:29        389
13:4        322
14:4        96n15

**3 Maccabees**
| | |
|---|---|
| 2:3 | 296n2 |
| 2:9–14 | 350 |
| 7:13 | 341 |

**Sirach**
| | |
|---|---|
| 16:12 | 373 |
| 18:1 | 46 |
| 39:25–40:9 | 123n19 |
| 39:29 | 168 |
| 39:30 | 176 |
| 40:4 | 314n1 |
| 43:16 | 308n12 |
| 47:22 | 411 |

**Tobit**
| | |
|---|---|
| 2:3–8 | 214n14 |
| 12:15 | 160n5 |
| 13:4 | 284 |
| 13:15–17 | 341 |
| 13:16 | 391 |

**Wisdom of Solomon**
| | |
|---|---|
| 10:19 | 174 |
| 12:3–6 | 185n10 |
| 13:10–19 | 185 |
| 16:9 | 175, 176 |
| 16:22 | 168 |
| 18:14–16 | 157n3 |
| 18:15–16 | 353, 354, 355 |
| 18:21 | 165n12 |

**PSEUDEPIGRAPHA**

*Apocalypse of Abraham*
| | |
|---|---|
| 31.1 | 160 |

*Ascension of Isaiah*
| | |
|---|---|
| 4.2–14 | 249n4 |

*Assumption of Moses*
| | |
|---|---|
| 3.1 | 182n7 |

*2 Baruch*
| | |
|---|---|
| 3.7 | 158 |
| 6 | 182n8 |
| 24.1 | 373n5 |
| 29.1–30:5 | 366 |
| 29.3–4 | 243n1 |
| 40 | 265n16, 361n1 |
| 40.1–4 | 366 |
| 56.13 | 361n1 |
| 63 | 147n8 |

| | |
|---|---|
| 67 | 147n8 |
| 72.2–74.3 | 366 |
| 78–87 | 147n8 |

*1 Enoch*
| | |
|---|---|
| 1–36 | 16n4 |
| 9.4 | 284 |
| 10.4–14 | 361 |
| 14.8–16.4 | 89n6 |
| 18.12–16 | 361n1 |
| 20.1–7 | 160n5 |
| 21.1–10 | 361n1 |
| 21.7 | 173n1 |
| 25.4–6 | 397 |
| 37–71 | 16n4 |
| 39.1–40.10 | 89n6 |
| 40 | 160n5 |
| 40.7 | 237n9 |
| 45.4 | 376 |
| 46.1 | 44 |
| 47.3 | 373n5 |
| 47.4 | 137 |
| 54.1–6 | 361n1 |
| 54.6 | 160n5, 233n8 |
| 56.5–8 | 182n8 |
| 56.7 | 370n4 |
| 60.7–11 | 243n1 |
| 60.11–25 | 297n3 |
| 61.10 | 297n3 |
| 66.1–2 | 297n3 |
| 71.1–17 | 89n6 |
| 71.8–9 | 160n5 |
| 71.10 | 44 |
| 72–82 | 16n4 |
| 75.3 | 297n3 |
| 81.1–3 | 103 |
| 81.1–4 | 373n5 |
| 81.5 | 160n5 |
| 83–90 | 16n4 |
| 85–90 | 16n4 |
| 86.3 | 173 |
| 88.3 | 173 |
| 89–90 | 16n4 |
| 89.61–77 | 373n5 |
| 90.6–12 | 112 |
| 90.13–19 | 370n4 |
| 90.17 | 373n5 |
| 90.20 | 373n5 |
| 90.21–22 | 160n5 |
| 90.37 | 112 |

| | |
|---|---|
| 91–105 | 16n4 |
| 91.11–17 | 366 |
| 91.11–18 | 16n4 |
| 93.1–3 | 103 |
| 93.1–10 | 16n4 |
| 98.7–8 | 373n5 |
| 100.3 | 282 |
| 102.8 | 399 |
| 103.1–3 | 103 |
| 106.5–6 | 44 |
| 106.19 | 103 |
| 108.3 | 71 |

*2 Enoch*
| | |
|---|---|
| 4–6 | 297n3 |
| 19.1–4 | 297n3 |

*4 Ezra*
| | |
|---|---|
| 2.38 | 143n3 |
| 2.40 | 143n3 |
| 4.33–37 | 134n30 |
| 4.35–37 | 137 |
| 6.5 | 143n3 |
| 6.20 | 373n5 |
| 6.23 | 160, 160n6 |
| 6.39 | 158 |
| 6.47–52 | 243n1 |
| 7.26–44 | 158, 366 |
| 7.30 | 157n2 |
| 7.91 | 399 |
| 7.98 | 399 |
| 9.38–10.57 | 227n2 |
| 12.31–32 | 105 |
| 12.31–34 | 366 |
| 13.5 | 370n4 |
| 13.25–38 | 210 |
| 13.25–52 | 265n16 |
| 13.32–38 | 225 |
| 13.34–35 | 370n4 |
| 14.5–6 | 405 |
| 14.45–46 | 405 |
| 15.42 | 308n12 |

*Greek Apocalypse of Ezra*
| | |
|---|---|
| 4.36 | 160 |

*Jubilees*
| | |
|---|---|
| 1.20 | 237n9 |
| 1.27 | 160n5 |
| 1:28 | 265n16, 399 |
| 1.29 | 160n5 |
| 2.1–2 | 160n5 |

*Jubilees (continued)*
2.2                297n3
2.18               160n5
5.6                361n1
10.4–14            361n1
15.27              160n5
17.15–16           237n9
18.9–12            237n9
23.11–21           77
23.23              214n14
30.18–20           209n9
31.14              160n5
48.15–18           237n9

*Letter of Aristeas*
310–311            414

*Odes of Solomon*
30.1–2             382

*Psalms of Solomon*
2.25               229n6
2.30–31 [26–27]    214n14
14.3               397n3
15.6               143
15.9               143
17.28–31           147n8
17.40              147n8
17.42–43           83

*Sibylline Oracles*
1.324–30           261
2.18               319n4
3.634–46           214n14
3.663–68           370n4
4.150–57           17
4.175–77           17
5.38–47            17
5.158–61           173
5.212              376
8.88               17
8.193–201          17
11.113–16          319n4
13.45              319n4
14.108             319n4

*Testament of Dan*
6.1–6              237n9

*Testament of Judah*
24.1               412
24.5               105

*Testament of Levi*
3.5                160n5
3.5–6              164n10
5.1                89n6
5.6                237n9
8.2                160n5
18.12              361n1
18.3               412

*Testament of Moses*
2.3–9              147n8
8.1                77

**DEAD SEA SCROLLS**

*CD (Damascus Document)*
CD 7.18–21         412

*Hodayot*
*(Thanksgiving Hymns)*
1QH 1[9].8–13      297n3
1QH 4[12].21       209n9
1QH 18.24–29       209n9
1QH 21.9–14        209n9

*Milḥamah (War Scroll)*
1QM 1.2            148
1QM 1.10–11        370n4
1QM 2              147n8
1QM 2.2            148
1QM 7.3–6          269
1QM 7.14           160
1QM 11.6–7         412
1QM 15.2–3         370n4

*Pesher Habakkuk*
*(Habakkuk Commentary)*
1QpHab 13.1–4      157n2

*Testimonia*
4QTest (4Q175) 9–13   412

*Temple Scroll*
11QTemple 54.5–7   414

**PHILO**

*Cherubim*
49–50              269

*Joseph*
25                 214n14

*Moses*
1.95               167

**JOSEPHUS**

*Against Apion*
2.83–84            251

*Jewish Antiquities*
2.14.1             167
3.7.5              391n6
6.99               139n34
6.116              139n34
12.272–75          139n34
12.421             139n34
14.429             139n34

*Jewish War*
1.307              139n34
3.376–78           214n14
3.380–84           214n14
4.314–18           214n14
5.5.7              391n6
5.33               214n14
6.370              139n34

**RABBINIC LITERATURE**

BABYLONIAN TALMUD
*Berakot*
46a                237n9

*Yoma*
20a                237n9

TOSEFTA
*Sanhedrin*
13.10              147n8

**GRECO-ROMAN
LITERATURE**

CICERO
*Epistulae ad Atticum*
6.5                319n4

DIO
66.23.1            169

DIO CHRYSOSTOM
*To the People of Rhodes*
*(Or. 31)*
84                 71n8

**DIODORUS**
4.49.8 292

**EPICTETUS**
*Diatribai*
3.22.10 314n1
4.11.34 314n1

**EUSEBIUS**
*Ecclesiastical History*
3.39.4 6
3.39.5–7 6
7.25.14 7
7.25.7–8 7

**HESIOD**
*Theogony*
319–24 184n9

**HOMER**
*Iliad*
6.181–82 184n9

**IRENAEUS**
*Againsgt Heresies*
5.30.3 8

**JUSTIN MARTYR**
*Dialogue with Trypho*
81.4 6

**LACTANTIUS**
*The Divine Institutes*
7.17.10–11 370n4

**MARTIAL**
*Epig.*
6.64 319n4

**PLINY**
*Epistulae*
6.16.11 169
10.96–97 11

**POLYBIUS**
31.9 251

**SUETONIUS**
*Nero*
49 248

**VIRGIL**
*Aeneid*
6.782–83 319n4

*Georgica*
2.535 319n4

**EARLY CHRISTIAN
LITERATURE**

**APOSTOLIC FATHERS**
**2 Clement**
3.2 72

*Didache*
9.5 409
10.6 416
14.1 43
16.6 160

**SHEPHERD OF HERMAS**
*Similitude*
6.3.6 218n17
8.6.3 218n17
*Vision*
2.1.4 190
2.8.1–2 190

**NEW TESTAMENT
APOCRYPHA**

*Gospel of Peter*
3.7 314n1

# INDEX OF SUBJECTS

Abaddon, 179
abyss, 173–74
    functionally identical to the sea, 245
    key to, 360
    language of, 212
accommodation
    rejecting, in favor of eschatological rela-
        tionship with God, 305–6
    strong influence of, during writing of Reve-
        lation, 8–11
adelphos, indicating nonhierarchical relation-
    ship of witness, 41
afterlife, depiction of, 358–59
Aland, Barbara, 22
Aland, Kurt, 22
Almighty One, significance of title, 221
altars
    imagery of, 158, 163–64
    linked to judgment, 133, 164, 299
    singing, 299
    speaking their inanimate minds, 181
Amen, significance of, 81, 152–53, 343
amillennialism, 366
Ancient of Days, 44
angels, 141–43, 271–74
    appearing in context of judgment, 271,
        324–25
    authority over fire, 281
    descending from heaven, 360
    disgraced and deposed, linked to fallen
        stars, 173
    dispatched to carry out catastrophe, 173
    fallen, 173–74, 181–82
    fellow-servants in the faith, 41
    given certain authority over nature, 297
    harvesting humankind from the earth,
        271–72
    holding back the four winds, 141
    holding keys to the abyss, 173–74
    involved in harvesting, 280, 281
    mighty, 101, 104–5, 187–91, 337
    priestly assignment of, 162

roaring like a lion, 190–91
on summation of John's message, 400–404,
    406
anger, in Revelation, 1–2
Antiochus IV Epiphanes, 250–51
Antipas, 57–58, 105
Apocalypse Now and Then (Keller), 18–19
apocalyptic, 14–20
    beatitudes found in mode of, 31
    presented through travel scenarios, 84
apocalyptic theology, 366
apokalypsis, narrative importance of term,
    27–28
Apollyon, 179
apostles, false, 50, 51
archery, Rome's legions never mastering,
    125
ark of the covenant, 222–24
Armageddon, re-presentation of, 358
Artemis, temple of, 68
audition, 144, 277, 327, 379
Aune, David
    on Lamb image, 109
    on the writing of the scrolls, 103

Babylon. See also Rome
    clothing of, at time of doom, 334–35
    crime of, 329
    culpability of, 326–27, 337–38
    encompassing woman and beast, 314
    fall of, introducing, 310–13
    final battle of, 357–59
    heavenly voice demanding figurative
        separation from, 327–28
    judgment against, 312, 327–31, 325
    mourning, 332–36
    passionate crime committed by, 274–75
    posturing as a ruling lordship, 330–31
    promise of its judgment, 274
    prophecies of the fall of, 323–38
    smoke of, climbing into the sky, 165
    towering sins of, 328–29

Balaam, 58, 59
  as false apostle, 50
  in Numbers, 65
  prophetic work of, challenged, 30
  spiritual prostitution of, 9–10
Bauckham, Richard
  on the new Jerusalem, 398
  on the song of Moses, 286–87
Beale, G. K., on the scroll's seals, 102–3
beast
  as apocalyptic cipher for Rome, 213
  associated with the dragon, 212–13
  blasphemous names on heads of, 246
  boastfulness and blasphemousness of, 250–51
  calculating the number of, 261–62
  dead on arrival, 318–19, 321
  as dragon's prime minion, 242–43, 246
  end of reign, 301
  under God's ultimate control, 250
  identity of, 213
  inferior to the Lamb, 264
  imperial heads of, 247
  John asking his hearers and readers to pre-
    pare for, 253–54
  linked with dragon and Rome, 212–23, 246,
    314
  mark of, 259–61, 295
  mocking, through worship of, 263
  parodying the Lamb, 247–48, 249–52
  pretentiousness of, mocked, 318
  resurfacing before final victory, 212
  tormented forever, 275–76
  worship of, 249, 252, 263
beast from the land, 256–58, 303, 304
beast from the sea, 244–48, 254
  followers of, refusing to repent, 308–9
  throne of, 301
beatitudes, 31–32, 277, 305, 368, 403, 408
believers
  blessed because of their witness, 347
  established as reign of priests to God, 37
  excommunication of, in Philadelphia, 75
  as faithful witnesses, 36
  firmly planted in God's presence and care,
    78–79
  given power to endure judgment activities,
    300
  linking salvation of, and judgment of those
    who persecute them, 151
  persuaded by false prophets' tactics, 259

public declaration of, 41–42, 46
  as a reign of priests, 115–16
  responding to Babylon's destruction, 336
  rewards for, 71–72
  still standing at heavenly altar, 136
  ultimate fate of, 149–56
  unprotected, after measuring of the temple,
    204
*biblaridion*, 101, 190
*biblion*, 100
black, significance of, 127, 138
black church tradition, identifying with Old
  Testament view of God, 135
blasphemy, 300–302
blessedness, importance of, 31–32
blood, 211
  Christ's, 37, 42, 408
  of faithful witnesses, God avenging, 341–44
  of the Lamb, washing in, 91, 115, 136,
    153–55, 226, 285
  plague of hell and fire, mixed with, 168
  power of, 98
  significance of, 36, 115
  waters turning to, 168, 295–98
  on the white horse rider's clothing, 352–53
  woman consuming, 316
Boesak, Allan, 3–4, 135, 116
Book of Life, 71–72, 78, 373–74
  exclusion from, 252–53
  function of, 253
  other books being opened prior to, 253
Book of Watchers, 173n1
bowls. *See also* seven bowls
  introduction of, paralleling introduction of
    the trumpets, 162
  related to priestly service, 292
breath of life, 215
bride
  identified as new Jerusalem, 412
  preparation of, 345
  representing acceptance, 383
  representing new city of Jerusalem, 344
brimstone, 358
brothers and sisters, testifying to Christ's
  lordship, 237–39

Caesar, 134
  lordship of, 41, 54, 93, 94, 145, 304, 305,
    346, 350
  sixth, 320–21

Caird, G. B., on John's approach to the millennium, 367
Callahan, Allen, 35
celebration, linked to judgment, 340, 341–42
censers, 162–63
census, purpose of, 146
Chaldea, 330
cherubim
  in praise of the Lamb, 113
  in the throne room, 92–95, 96
child of humanity, 44–45, 87, 279–80
  clothing of, 291–92
  holding keys to Death and Hades, 130, 174
  holding the key of David, 134, 174
  involved in harvesting, 281
  relation of, to first horseman, 125–26
Christ. *See also* Jesus
  as the Alpha and Omega, 39, 407–8
  as the Amen, 81
  bestowing triple new name on believers, 79
  as bridegroom, 344
  as child of humanity, 44. *See also* child of humanity
  coming of, 20, 59, 77–78, 349
  coming like a thief in the night, 69–70
  commanding violent action against Babylon, 329–30, 334
  concerns about Pergamum, 58
  conquering action of, 109
  controlling experience of death, 215
  counseling believers to celebrate Babylon's destruction, 335–36
  dangers of allegiance to, 11–13
  demanding firm stance of believers, 82
  endorsing ethic of defiant witness, 51–52
  expectation of, for people's appropriate behavior, 407
  as faithful witness, 109, 110
  holding the key to David's eternal kingdom, 74–75
  holding the keys of Death, 46
  human destiny lying with, 45
  as the holy and true one, 74
  laying claim to title of bright morning star, 411–12
  linked with God, 44, 64
  as Lord, 38, 85, 236–37
  lordship of, beyond control of any human or power, 351–52
  modeling role of resistant witness, 69

  offering reward for witnessing, 84
  period of his rule, 367
  physical description of, 44
  pleading for separation from Babylon, 328
  positioning himself within Davidic genealogy, 411
  praising Ephesians' witness work, 50
  promising authority over the nations, 64
  response of, to human behavior, 407–8
  role of, in the Apocalypse, 353–54
  self-identification of, 40, 45–46, 49, 53, 57, 62, 66, 81
  sentencing Babylon to torment and grief, 330–31
  shining face of, 45
  significance of his resurrection, 46
  as son of God, 62
  validating his case, 409–15
  word of, indistinguishable from God's word, 75
Christ-believers. *See* believers
Christ's faith, 57
Christianity, polarity within, 4
Christians
  accommodating themselves to Greco-Roman life, 9–11
  no wholesale persecution of, during Domitian's reign, 11–12
*chronos*, use of, in Revelation, 195
city. *See also* Jerusalem, new
  envisioned as a bride, 379, 391
  as the people of God, 379
  representing heaven metaphor for John, 378
city of God, lowered onto earth, 378–79
civil rights movement, 255
clothing
  dazzling, linked to conquest, 70–71, 91, 96. *See also* dazzling *listings*
  linked to resistant witness behavior, 70, 71, 90–91
  related to eschatological relationship with the divine, 70, 71
  of the rider on the white horse, 352–53
  significance of, in Revelation, 226
clouds
  conveyance upon, 216
  as metaphor for God's presence, 188–189
  significance of, 38, 279, 292–93

Collins, John J., defining "apocalypse," 14, 15–17
combat myths, ancient, 243, 358
*commune Asiae*, 257
completion, numbers representing, 153n. *See also* seven; twelve
confession, identified with witnessing, 13, 75
conquest
    identified with witnessing, 52, 106, 408
    linked to dazzling clothing, 70–71, 91, 96
    linked to God and Christ, 37
cosmic woman
    appearance of, 224–25
    attire of, 226
    considering active role of, 228
    identity of, 225, 226–27
    intimately involved with God, 227
    messianic son of, 230, 231
    representative of God's intention for humankind, 226
    representing the church, 232
    re-visioned as the church, 240
cosmos
    divine rolling up of, 139
    vacuum in, 376
counterapocalyptic perspective, 18–19
creation, new, 375–83
crime, linked with judgment, 298
crowns
    linked with conquest, 91
    significance of, 55, 94n13, 227
    symbol of eschatological life, 78
cultic propaganda, in Thyatira, 62
cup imagery, metaphor for divine judgment, 315

Daniel, book of
    apocalyptic imagery in, 16–17
    John distancing himself from, 405
    Revelation's reliance on, 84
Daniel, on God being in control of history, 16
darkness, unbearable agony accompanying, 301
Day of Atonement, use of censer and incense during, 162n7
dazzling clothing, 226, 285
    linked to conquering witness to Christ's lordship, 150, 154
    reward of, 135–36
    as symbol of conquest, 70–71, 91, 96

dazzling/white, 292
    as euphemism for witness, 155
    result of witnessing, 354
dazzling/white horse, signifying God's judgment, 123–25
Dea Roma coin, 319
death
    different layers of, 55, 177–78
    harbingers of, Old Testament parallels to, 131
    leading to eschatological relationship with God, 239
    measure of control regarding, 177
    preferable to life, 177
    second, 368, 374
Death, personification of, 130, 374
death penalty, two forms of, in Roman legal system, 365n2
deities, threefold formulation for celebrating, 34, 38–39
demonization, tactic of, 309
demons
    appearing as frogs, 304
    gathering kings to battle God, 305
    related to idolatrous worship, 304
descent motif, 187, 378
desert, negative sense of, 313
destruction
    moving people toward salvation, 2–3
    by thirds, 166–71
diadems, 229–30, 246
Dionysius of Alexandria, 7
discipleship, Jesus' linking of, to present tribulation, 154
dispensational premillennialism, 367
divine passives, indicating God's design, 2, 122, 125, 139, 164, 166, 170, 171, 175, 181–83, 189, 247, 250, 258, 283, 300, 325, 345, 350, 351
dogs, disparaging of, 409
Domitian, 8–9
    edict of, following great famine, 128–29
    fondness of, for Apollo, 179–80
dragon
    appearance of, in the sky, 224–25
    associated with the beast, 212–13
    deception of, 362–63
    defeat of, 234–35
    description of, 229, 237

fate of, linked to beast and false prophet,
371
introduction of, 229
last stand of, 369–72
linked to serpent in garden of Eden and
bestial forces of Rome, 234–35
looking for reinforcements from the sea,
243–55
metaphor for satanic force behind imperial
power, 229
never on a par with God, 226
no hope of destroying the church, 242
role of, balanced against Michael, 233
seeking out cosmic woman's other children,
240, 241–42
significance of, 228
tormented forever, 275–76
treatment of, after the final battle, 359–74
using his mouth for assault, 241
worship of, 249
dragon's war, 223–42
drought, related to repentance, 211

eagle
imagery of, reinforcing judgment theme,
170–71
wings of, significance of, 240–41
earthquake, 165, 191
as part of final judgment, 308
significance of, 138, 217
economic advancement, John warning against,
10, 41, 62, 260, 326–27
elders
offering advice on worthiness to break the
scroll's seals, 105
positive response of, to God's reign, 221
in praise of the Lamb, 113
in the throne room, 90–91, 94–95
emperor worship, 9
end time
coming like a thief in the night, 69
earliest thinking of, 15
endurance, as the faith of the saints, 254
Ephesians
becoming a policing community, 51
demonstrating nonviolent resistance, 50
testing false apostles, 50
Ephesus, letter to, 49–52
eschatological living, 378
eschatological temple, 386–87

eternal life, reward of, 52
Euphrates River
angels positioned together at, 182
drying up, 302
significance of, for Jewish people, 182
Eusebius, 6–7
evil
acting as God's judgment tool, 174–75
hatred of, 51
resurrection of, 363
exodus
eschatological, 380
imagery of, used for judgment, 166, 168,
175
Ezekiel, book of
apocalyptic scenes in, 15
Revelation's reliance on, 84
Ezekiel, ordered to prophesy against enemies
of God and God's people, 200

faith, related to endurance, 254–55
Faithful and True, as name for rider on the
white horse, 350–51
faithful witness, guaranteeing direct access to
God, 216–17. *See also* witness
falling, imagery of, 320–21
false prophets, 58, 256–59
beast from the land designated as, 303, 304
operating inside and outside believing
communities, 304
famine, 127–30
fear
falling upon enemies of God's people, 216
from human associates of the beast,
217–18
Festival of Booths, 151, 156
fifth angel, 141–43
final battle, aftermath of, 359–74
fire
element of divine retribution, 210, 275,
276, 281
flaming torches, significance of, 91
lake of, 358
metaphor for God's spirit, 210
plague of, 184
stopping satanic forces, 212
thrown onto the earth, as symbol of divine
wrath, 165
first death, 55
*First Enoch*, 16, 17

firstfruits
  harvesting imagery consistent with, 280
  interpretation of, 270
flashback, use of, 158, 213, 231, 245, 260,
  264, 338
foreboding sound, from heaven, 340, 341
foreboding voice, 294, 307, 325, 357. *See also*
  great voice
foreheads
  God's protective mark on, 142–43, 146,
    173, 265–66, 399
  marking of, 259–60, 315, 356
  names inscribed on, 351
  significance of, 100, 102
fornication, symbolism of, 332–33
four horsemen, 121–31, 141
four winds, destructive potential of, 141
freedom, human, 374
frogs, unclean spirits appearing as, 303, 304
"from the foundation of the world," interpretation of, 252–53
fulfillment, related to time, 137
future, commitment to, 17–18

gematria, 261–262
God
  as the Almighty One, 39, 220–21, 287–88
  as Alpha and Omega, 34, 381
  blaspheming the name of, 300–302
  challenge to, to vindicate God's people,
    113–14
  changing future based on human behavior,
    19
  climactic move of, presented as a person,
    402
  clouds as metaphor for presence of,
    188–89
  communicating to humans through
    designated intermediaries, 29–30
  connection between wrath and judgment of,
    222
  in control of history, 16, 34, 171
  controlling experience of death, 215
  creating a people of faith, 227–28
  creator of heaven, earth, and sea, swearing
    upon, 193
  deciding satanic forces' access to humanity,
    174
  destroying the whore (Rome/Babylon), 311
  destructive actions of, deemed just, 297–98

  determining who has relationship with, 72
  encouraging witness to, in final accounts,
    400
  escape from, as act of self-destruction, 373
  eschatological relationship with, eternal
    nature of, 155–56
  establishing new heaven and new earth, 376
  faithfulness of, regarding God's promises,
    196
  fear and glorification of, 273, 288–89
  fleeing from the presence of, 139
  as force behind the plagues, 301
  full-strength wrath of, 275
  giving the authority to torture, 176
  harshness of punishment, 134–35
  identified as one who is, was, and is com-
    ing, 34
  judgment of, executed through fifth angel,
    142–43
  as just judge in control, 124–25
  key attributes of, 152–53
  language for, pitted against dragon lan-
    guage, 212
  linked with Christ, 37, 44
  as Lord, 85
  making all things new, 380–81
  not fighting directly, 226
  offering gift of living water, 382
  operating by proxy, 201
  orchestrating the trumpet blasts, 161
  parodying of, 247–48, 249–52, 256, 259
  quotations from, 39
  reign of, 220, 236
  responsible for punishing judgments, 168,
    169
  rule of, 297, 305
  salvation, power, and glory belonging to,
    342
  seeing the face of, 399
  self-imposed limits on inclusion in reign of,
    288
  separation from, as eternal agony, 371
  speaking, 380–81
  as temple in new Jerusalem, 155–56
  transcending and controlling human
    history, 34
  transfiguring new creation out of destruc-
    tion, 375
  ultimate victory belonging to, 250
  violence of, 2–4

withstanding the wrath of, 140
worship of, 85, 95–96, 98, 298
gods
  animating images of, 258
  rejection of, implying resistance to the
    state, 62
Gog, 369–70
golden bowls, in the throne room, 113. *See
    also* seven bowls
gospel, placed in context of judgment,
    272–73
grace, 34, 374
grammar
  errors in, purposeful use of, 58n3
  skewed, to make intertextual point, 33, 35
grand visions, celebrating, becoming idola-
    trous, 348
Great Day of the Lord, inauguration of, 140
great voice, 43, 104, 142, 216. *See also* fore-
    boding voice
Greco-Roman culture, spiritual activity in,
    political implications of, 53–54
green, John's use of color, 130

Hades, 46, 130, 374
hailstones, at final judgment, 308
half, significance of, 157
Hallel psalms, 341
hallelujah, in hymns of resistance, 97
hallelujah chorus, 338–44
Hanson, Paul, 15
Harmagedon, 306. *See also* Armageddon
harps, 285
  signifying praise for realization of God's
    rule, 267
  in the throne room, 113
harvest imagery, 279–82
hearing
  connection with keeping, 32
  related to conquering and witnessing, 412
heaven
  lifting a hand toward, symbolism of, 193
  opening of, 350
  rotting away, 139
  silence in, 157–58
heavenly council, modeling throne room ethic,
    89–90
heavenly voice, with message of salvation and
    judgment, 266, 273
heavenly war, 233–36, 239–42

heavenly worship, as model for adoration by
    humans, 85
history, deterministic and pessimistic view
    of, 18
holiness
  acquired through relationship with God,
    378
  denoting radical otherness, 377
holy city, as eschatological symbol, 371. *See
    also* Jerusalem, new
holy war, 269
horns, 229–30
  significance of, 112, 246
horse
  dazzling/white, signifying God's judgment,
    123–25
  killing-machine versions of, 183–84
  white, rider on, 348–56
hour, indicating imminent arrival of God's
    judgment, 217
humans
  affairs of, already determined, 17
  rule of, colliding with God's rule, 321
  singled out for destruction, 173
  used to reveal mysteries of the dream
    world, 28
hymns
  explaining God's victory, 235–39
  for a new exodus, 285–86
  of thanksgiving, 220–21

"I am" declaration, 46
idolatry, wormwood used as punishment for,
    170
Ignatius, 53
imminence
  linked with judgment, 78
  theme of, 30
imperial cult, seeming to come alive and
    speak, 258
incense, 158
  eighth angel offering, before blasting of
    trumpets, 162–65
  inserted into account of trumpets, 161
  not typically associated with atonement, 164
  offering of, in ancient Israel, 163
  pleasing to humans and deities, 165n11
  related to judgment, 164
  related to prayers, 113, 164–65
  role of, in Jerusalem temple, 113

"inhabitants of the earth," 72n9, 76–77, 134, 215, 252–53, 272–73, 313
inheritance, significance of, 382
"in the spirit," significance of phrase, 88–89
interludes, separating sixth and seventh movements of catastrophes, 302–3
Irenaeus, 8
iron rod, symbolism of, 64
Israel
    creation of new heaven and earth for, 375
    representing the universal church, 147
    tribal listing of, 147–48

jasper, 390–91
Jeremiah, commanded to prophesy against the earth's inhabitants, 200
Jericho, walls of, falling, 160
Jerusalem. *See also* Jerusalem, new
    as bridal city, 351
    citizenship in, significance of, 187
    eschatological presentation of, 351
    holy, new, and urban, 377–78
    possessed by God's glory, 385–86
    temple of, altars in, 132
Jerusalem, new, 375
    closed to anything accursed, 398, 409
    coming out of heaven from God, 378
    commemoration of, 338
    glory of, 392–94
    introduction of, 383–84
    measurement of, 389–91
    new life of, 395–96
    openness of, 394
    represented as the bride to Christ's groom, 344–45
    trees in, 397–98
    wall surrounding, 386–88
    worship in, 398–99
Jesus. *See also* Christ
    blood of, linked to conquest and Christian witness, 155
    connection to God's Word, 352, 354
    conveying revelation to the angel, 30
    crucifixion of, response to, 19
    death as act of witness, 110–11
    death not linked to atonement, 109–10
    as faithful witness, 29, 36
    rationales for human praise of, 36
    revealing of, 27–28
    as ruler of entire human realm, 36

set up as messianic middleman, 28
    witness of, linked to word of God, 28
    witness proclaimed by, 35–36
Jezebel, 58
    as false apostle, 50
    prophetic work of, challenged, 30
    spiritual prostitution of, 9–10
    at Thyatira, 63–64
John (author of Revelation), 7–8
    commanded not to write, 192–93
    commanded to write, 43, 47, 53, 88, 192
    depending on Hebrew tradition for his visions, 262
    describing work as prophecy, 32
    different understandings of death, 177–78
    exile of, 42
    falling before angels in worship, 112–13
    falling prostrate, 45
    improper worship attempt of, 347–48, 403–4
    invited into heavenly throne room, 86–87
    measuring the temple, 201–5
    misogyny of, 10–11, 309–10
    narrating two witnesses, 208–12
    petitioning Jesus to come, 416
    poor grammar of, 35
    preoccupied with women's primary roles, 225
    prophetic spirit of, 88–89
    recommissioned to task of prophecy, 199–200
    reinforcing imminence of end time, 401–2
    repentance as primary goal of rhetorical style, 358
    reserving knowledge of key details to a few people, 351
    seeing the lost ark of the covenant, 222–23
    self-identification of, 30, 33, 40–41
    significance in namings by, 58, 63
    unorthodox presentation of narrative time, 195–96
    using language figuratively, 268
    viewing cities as appropriate heaven metaphor, 378
    visions of, meant to exhort appropriate present behavior, 402
    wrong in his sense of urgency, 415
John (presbyter), 6

John, son of Zebedee, 6
Johns, Loren, 11, 12
    on expectation of persecution, 41
    on rhetorical force of Lamb symbolism,
        109–10
Jonah, 19
Judaism
    brokering concessions regarding worship of
        non-Greco-Roman deities, 54
    eschatological traditions, two strains of, 366
    history of, three developmental periods in,
        for apocalyptic thinking and writing,
        15–17
    intra-Jewish conflict, 54
judgment
    altars related to, 133, 163
    based on works, 329
    climactic conclusion of, 307–9
    flip side of, as eschatological life lived with
        God, 222
    foreboding voice related to, 142, 357
    as good news, 171–86
    image of, 44
    intended to motivate one toward
        repentance, 291
    linked to celebration, 340, 341–42
    linked to crime, 298
    linked to imminence, 78
    linked to salvation, 362, 407
    mediated by mighty angel, 187
    sackcloth related to, 127
    scales related to, 127
    silence related to, 157
    universal nature of language related to,
        200–201
judgment doxology, 296, 341
justice
    call for, 3
    as God's activity in the world, 283

Käsemann, Ernst, 19–20, 402
keeping, connection with hearing, 32
Keller, Catherine, 18–19
key, imagery of, important to John, 174
King, Martin Luther, Jr., 117
kingdoms, unauthorized, 96
kings
    mourning Babylon, 333
    owing position to God and the Lamb, 313
*koinon*, 257

Lamb
    battlefield arrival of, 349
    battling with the dragon, 230
    blood of, linked to believer's witness, 115
    call to act in manner of, 111–12
    completed conquest of, 238
    encouraging witness to, in final accounts,
        400
    executing judgment, 139–40
    execution of, 269
    eyes and horns of, 112
    as faithful witness, 106, 109
    final name of, 355–56
    holding vulnerability and conquest in
        tension, 116–18
    intertextual history of term, 108–9
    introduction of, 264
    kings declaring war on, 322
    marriage of, to bridal city, 385
    as Messianic Rider, 124
    as motivating factor for faith, 256–57
    new song sung in celebration of, 266–67
    Parousia of, 349
    proclaiming lordship, 5
    as rider on a white horse, 348–49
    role of, in the Apocalypse, 353–54
    Scroll of Life of, 101–2
    second hymn to, 119–20
    self-sacrifice of, 5
    as shepherd, 156
    shift in focus to, from the lion, 108, 114
    souls connected to, 132
    standing, 110–12, 264–65
    as temple in new Jerusalem, 155–56
    victory against the beast, 322
    wedding of, 344–45
    withstanding the wrath of, 140
    worshiping Lordship of, 98
    worthiness of, 95–96, 112–15, 119–20,
        247–48, 298
lampstands, seven, 43
Laodicea, letter to, 80–84
Last Judgment, preparatory build-up to, 120
learning, tied to resistance, 268
*Letter of Aristeas*, 414
letter writing, Hellenistic conventions of,
        adapted, 33–34
lex talionis, 221, 294, 298, 329, 414
liberation, as appropriate theme for
        Revelation's intent, 166

lightning, 165–66, 191
lion, significance of, 190–91
lion/Lamb imagery, 116–17
little scroll, 101–2, 188, 189–90, 194–95, 197–201
locusts, 141, 143, 171, 175–77
  compared to horses, 178–79
  representing an army of demons, 179
Lord, identifying, 84–85. *See also* Christ; God; Jesus
love
  connected to works, 50–51
  as primary motivation for salvation/vindication, 36
lying, thwarting hope for eschatological relationship with God, 270

macarism, 31–32, 69, 70, 305, 346
Magog, 369–70
manna, hidden, 60
Mark, Gospel of, apocalyptic tendencies in, 19
marriage, as metaphor for God's eschatological relationship with God's people, 379
*martyria*, 211–12
*martys* (witness), 13, 28–29
Martyr, Justin, 6
meanness, in Revelation, 1–2
meat, sacrificed, eating of, 58–59, 63
Megiddo, 306
merchant marines, mourning Babylon, 333, 335
merchants, mourning Babylon, 333, 334
Messianic Rider, 124
Michael
  balanced against the dragon, 233–34
  perpetual battle with Satan, 237
midheaven, 170, 271–72, 357
mighty angels, 101, 104–5, 187–91, 337
millstone, thrown into the sea, to mock destruction of Babylon, 337
moon, bloody, 138
morning star, related to Christ, 64–65
Moses, as servant of God, 286
Mount Vesuvius, 169
mouth, dueling metaphors for, 303–4
myriad, significance of, 183

*naos*, as object of measurement, 203
nations
  shepherded toward repentance, 203

responding with rage, to God's reign, 221
necessity, theme of, 30–31
Nero, 8
  depicted in one of the beast's heads, 248–49
  linked to 666 (and 616), 262
  personifying imperial Rome, 261–62
Nero redivivus, 248–49
new life, following Type A death, 178
new song, significance of, 114
Nicolaitans, 9–10, 50, 58, 59
nonviolence
  power of, 4
  as response of God's people, 16–17
nonviolent resistance, 37
  Antipas as ultimate representative of, 58
  Ephesians demonstrating, 50
  expected of Christ-believers, 42
  referring to witnessing activity, 49–50
  rewarding of, 76–77
  sword as metaphor for, 45

Old Testament, universalistic perspectives in, regarding prophetic and psalmic materials, 286
olive oil, protection of, during famine, 128–30
the 144,000, 144–48, 265–70, 277
open door, 75n10, 76, 86–87
"opening" language, 122, 157, 290
*opistograph*, 103

palm branches, 150–51, 156
palm fronds, symbolism of, 96–97
Papias of Hierapolis, 6
Parousia, 38, 349
Parthia, 125
Parthians, 184, 302
Patmos, 9–10, 42
patron deities, groups' alignment with, 59
Paul, in Ephesus, 49
peace, offer of, 34
people of God
  as both bride and wedding guests, 347
  nonviolent role of, 16–17
Pergamum, letter to, 56–60
persecution
  endurance and conquering of, 77
  expectation of, 41, 117–18
  from hostility between Smyrna church and Jewish neighbors, 53–54
  linked to reign, 42

for witnessing to Christ's lordship, 53, 236–37

Peter, having custody of the heavenly keys, 74

Philadelphia
  impoverished state of, 328
  ironic naming of, 73
  letter to, 73–79
  witnesses in, heavenly door opened to, 86–87

physical body, Roman celebration of, 136

plagues
  connecting witnesses with Moses and Elijah, 210–11
  designed to elicit changes in loyalty, 301
  dispersal of, 291
  God acknowledged as force behind, 301
  understood as inducement to repentance, 167

Pliny the Younger, 11–12

political theology, narrative poetics of, 243

politics, mixed with religion, 9

Polycarp, 53, 54

postmillennialism, 366

posture, importance of, 350

power, synonym for reign of God, 236

prayer
  incense linked with, 113
  related to judgment, 164

premillennialism, 366

present, commitment to, 17–18

priests, goal of, to broker relationship with the divine, 292

proper names, anarthrous treatment of, 73

prophecy
  practices of, John exhorting from churches, 209
  primary objective of, 32
  related to witness, 207–8, 211
  as revelation of present truth demanding appropriate behavior, 348

prophetic eschatology, 366

prophetic spirit, 42

prophets
  circles of, during John's time, 411
  common promise among, 196–97
  false, 58, 256–59
  God revealing divine intent to, 29

punishment
  God's, harshness of, 134–35
  unending torture of, 275–76

red, John's use of color, 126

Reddish, Mitchell G.
  on Lamb image, 109
  on the writing of the scrolls, 103

redemption
  linked with sin, 36–37
  morphing into prophecy for judgment, 200

religion, mixed with politics, 9, 34

repentance, 63–64
  call for, 1–2
  drought related to, 211
  expected action following judgment, 166–67
  God expecting, from the faithful and from recalcitrants, 218
  lack of, 184–85
  language of, 59
  rationale for, 288–89
  response to God's forgiving love, 51
  sackcloth signifying, 209
  striking linked to, 355

resistance
  active ministry of, 118
  encouraged by the presence of the 144,000, 277
  learning tied to, 268
  part of God's strategy, 254–55

resistant witness. *See also* witness
  fulfilling nature of, 277
  of Lamb's followers, 98

rest, unending, 276

resurrected body, 376–77

resurrection
  first, 367–68, 373
  second, 367, 373, 374
  significance of, 46

retribution, final, 137–40

revelation, defining, 28

Revelation
  anger and violence in, 1–5
  authorship of, 5–8
  binary dualism in, 3
  dating of, 8
  epistolary greeting of, 32–39
  final phrase of, varied evidence for, 416–17
  genre of, 14–20
  grammar skewed in, to make intertextual point, 33, 35
  hymns of, as songs of resistance, 95–98
  literary approach of, 13–14

Revelation (*continued*)
longest allusion to Old Testament passage
in, 156
manuscripts of, 22–23
as metaphor of salvation and judgment, 102
narrative time in, 21–22
outline and structure of, 20–22
presentation of God's judgment in, based on
Zechariah and Ezekiel, 121
presented as a letter, 20
prohibiting alterations to, 414
prologue of, 27–32
prophetic intent of, 7–8, 10–11, 21–22
rapture not present in, 2, 77, 122, 349, 378
revelation of, 13–14
similar language at opening and closing of,
87–88, 416–17
social setting of, 8–14
structural parallels between prologue and
epilogue, 30
urgency of, 32, 415–16
visions of, intended to be perceived as happening simultaneously, 21
worldwide targets for destruction in,
168–69
Richard, Pablo, 34, 217
rider on the white horse, 348–56, 369
right hand, as symbol, 99–100
river, marking new Jerusalem as new,
improved, urban Eden, 395–97
robes
dazzling, 90–91, 96, 135–36, 150–51,
153–55, 226, 285
washing, significance of, 135–36, 226, 285,
408
Rome. *See also* Babylon
affiliation with, sin tied to, 37
claiming to be sole provider of salvation,
151–52
control of the seas, 335
demonization of, through whore imagery,
309–10
end of, beginning with act of self-destruction, 322–23
end-time judgment specifically related to,
311
God acting against, 34
historical symbol for mythical abyss, 213
John counseling churches against
accommodation with, 304

metaphors for, 319–20
opposition to, in hymns, 96
placement on the sea, symbolic meaning of,
312
relating sexual immorality to, 311
woman and beast both representing, 314
rumblings, 165–66, 191

sackcloth, 127, 138, 208–9, 226
saints, as those who keep God's
commandments, 277
salvation
available to all, 253
explicit use of term, 151
linked to judgment, 362, 407
political aspect of, 151–52
positional display of, 99
synonym for reign of God, 236
unable to achieve through human merit,
345
salvation/vindication, 36–37
Sardis
letter to, 65–72
worthiness of remnant at, 104, 105
Satan
connected with demon locust ruler, 179
last stand of, 369–72
locked down, 360–62
perpetual battle with Michael, 237
release of, necessity of, 362–63
role of, in heaven, 237
scales, related to judgment, 127
Schüssler Fiorenza, Elisabeth
on the liberating aspects of the death of
Christ, 115
song of Moses based on cross-section of OT
texts, 287
on transformation of redemption into
sociopolitical idea, 116
Scroll of Life, 101–2
scrolls. *See also* little scroll; Scroll of Life;
seven-sealed scroll
determining who is worthy to break the
seals on, 104–6, 107–8, 114
eating, 101, 197, 198–99
John's use of, in writing Revelation,
100–102
representing knowledge and control of
history, 120
sealed, Old Testament accounts of, 103

sea
  ceasing to exist, 377
  functionally identical to the abyss, 245
  significance of, 92, 241, 245, 284
sea of glass, 92, 266, 284
seals
  of the living God, 142–43
  opening, symbolizing judgment and salvation, 122–23
  seven opening of, 120–57
  on scrolls, significance of, 102–3
seals, trumpets, and bowls texts, as different viewings of same events, 163, 166, 168, 176, 189, 219, 293
second death, 55, 258–59
secrecy, as metaphor of empowerment, 351
Seraiah, 336
serpent, associated with Satan, 235
servant-prophets, 401, 411
  God revealing divine intent to, 29
  revealing God's intent to the churches, 29
servants, revelation transmitted to, 410–11
seven, significance of, 31, 33, 91, 102, 112, 191, 246, 262, 412
seven angels
  as archangels from Jewish literature, 160
  blowing trumpets and pouring out God's wrath from bowls, 159–60
  with seven plagues, 162
seven bowls
  first three plagues of, 295
  fourth, fifth, and sixth angels pouring out, 299–302
  God's command to pour out, 293–94
  housing plagues, 292
  introduction to, 289–93
  prelude to, 282–83
  primary metaphorical themes of, 293
  seventh angel pouring out, 307–9
seven churches
  characterized as lampstands, 35
  command to write to, 43
  common structural format of letters to, 47–48
  enticed by prosperity mania, 274–75
  as final stop for the revelation, 29
  letters to, 47–84, 106, 154
  as target audience, 33–34
seven heads, in whore of Babylon vision, 319
seven kings, symbolism of, 320–21

seven lampstands, signifying churches, 43
seven-sealed scroll, 96, 102–3, 188
seven seals, opening of, 120–57
seven stars, as patron angels of the seven churches, 45, 47
seven thunders, 191, 192–97
seven trumpets, sounding of, 158–223
sex, refraining from, 268–69
sexual immorality, 311–12
shepherding
  activity of, 203
  relating to conquering and witnessing, 230–31
signs, 224n1, 257–58
silence, in heaven, 157–58
Simon bar Kosiba, 411–12
sin
  linked with redemption, 36–37
  tied to affiliation with Rome, 37
singing
  celebratory, 266–67
  linked to the plagues of wrath, 286
  references to, 285–86
sixth Caesar, 320–21
slaughter, 154
  not previously considered expiatory, 109–10
  term's significance, 126
slaughtered Lamb (*sLamb*), as action verb, 117, 238, 355
slaughtered souls, 131–37, 164
slaughter language, with whore of Babylon, 316
smoke
  plague of, 184
  pouring from door of the abyss, 175
  related to wrath and judgment, 165
  significance of, 292–93, 342–43
Smyrna
  impoverished state of, 328
  letter to, 53–55
social body, dissonance with witness body (soul), 136
song of the Lamb, 114
song of Moses, 114, 286–88
song of Moses and the Lamb, 296, 298
soul, John's use of term, 132
soul force, 136–37
souls, slaughtered, 131–37
Spirit, movement in, significance of, 385

spirits, seven, symbolizing God's expansive power, 34–35
spiritual activity, political implications of, 53–54
stadion, 389
standing, significance of, 111, 216, 265
stars
    controller of, having ultimate power, 45
    equated with angels and representing churches, 227
    as metaphors for angels, 173
    patron angels of the seven churches, 45, 47
stones, precious, imagery of, 391–92
Strathmann, H., 28–29
striking, significance of, 355
struggle, referring to witnessing activity, 49–50
suffering, eternal, 358, 371–72
sulfur, 275, 276, 358
sulfur/brimstone, plague of, 184
sun, significance of, 226
sun plague, 299–300
sword, death by, 254
synagogue of Satan, 54, 73–74, 75–76

taunt songs, 325
tears, cause of, removed, 380
temple
    described as no longer necessary, 291
    eschatological, 386–87
    God opening sanctuary of, 222
    heavenly, thematically related to God's judgment, 290–91
    as the Lord God and the Lamb, 78
    measuring, 163, 201–5
    in new Jerusalem, comprising Lord God and the Lamb, 155–56
    postexilic reconstruction of, 209
theophanies, 43, 91, 191
    accompanying God's judgment and salvation moving into human arena, 308
    of God's coming, 372–73
    intent of, 165–66
    series of, unleashed, 223
Third Isaiah, apocalyptic literature in, 15–16
thousand-year period, 361, 365–67
threefold formulation, for celebrating deity, 34, 38–39, 94
throne room
    attendees in, and position of, 107–8

decor of, 43
description of, 89–94
God inviting John into, 86–87
imagery of, common to biblical and apocalyptic texts, 89
material about, in Daniel and Ezekiel, 84
praise scene in, after redemption of the multitude, 152
thrones, significance of, 301, 307, 343, 350, 372–73
throne voice, signaling salvation, in postjudgment times, 379–80
thunder, 165–66, 191
    mystery of the seven, 192–97
    symbolism of, 123, 191
Thyatira
    letter to, 61–65
    witness of believers at, 62
time, completion of, 402
torture, God's complicity in, 176–77. See also suffering, eternal
Trajan, 12
tree of life, 397
tribes, 38
tribulation
    great, horde of people moving through, 149–56
    linked to witness and sacrifices, 155
    present, Jesus linking to discipleship, 154
    resulting from actions early in Revelation, 88
trisagion, 94
trumpets
    blasting of, occurring simultaneously with breaking of the seals, 158–59, 161–62
    change in, matched by change in sensory perception, 181
    final blast of, 196
    first four, 166–71
    imagery of, 158
    interlude in account of, 186–218
    introduction to, 158–66
    liked to exodus plagues, 171–72
    related to punishments, 166, 168–71
    seventh, 219–23
    significance of, 97, 160–61, 172–73
    twelve, significance of, 90, 146, 227, 387–90
    two witnesses, Revelation's story of, 208–18
Type A death, 177–78, 183
Type B death, 178

Tyre
  demise of, 332, 335
  as negative role model to which Rome is
    compared, 312

understanding, linked to wisdom, 261
universalism, as exercised by God and the
  Lamb, 288, 289
universe, three-tiered understanding of, 104

verbs, passive, in Revelation, 2. *See also*
  divine passives
vice list, 382–83
violence
  God's, justification for, 3–5
  in Revelation, 2
Volf, Miroslav, 4–5

wall, surrounding the new Jerusalem, 386–88
war, language of, in battle of dragon and cosmic woman, 233–34
washing. *See also* robes
  connected to eschatological relationship, 408
  as euphemism for witness, 155
water, bloody transformation of, 168, 295–98,
  300
wedding supper, as eschatological celebration,
  346
white, as divine color, 70–71, 348–56
white stone, offered to Pergamum believers,
  60
whore of Babylon
  clothing and appearance of, 314–15
  devouring of, 323
  emerging from the abyss, 174
  as mother of whores, 315–16
  name of, 315–16
  posture of, 314
  synonymous with the beast, 323
  vision of, interpreted, 317–23
whore and the beast, vision of, 313–16
whore imagery, 309–10
wild animals, destruction by, 131
wilderness
  cosmic woman fleeing to, 240–41
  as place of refuge, 232
wine, protection of, during famine, 128–30
winepress, imagery of, 279, 281–82, 353, 355
wisdom
  linked to understanding, 261

mode for beatitudes, 31
witness
  believer's, linked to Lamb's blood, 115
  believers urged to, 32
  bridal, 345
  effect of, on one's apparel, 91, 354
  effecting conquest, 42, 105–6
  facade of, Sardis church engaged in, 67–68
  faithful, guaranteeing direct access to God,
    216–17
  as focus of tribulation language, 154–55
  goal of, 106
  God determining effects of, 347
  holding to, 69
  inspired through worship, 338–39
  Jesus' death as act of, 110–11
  leading to eschatological victory, 212
  leading to hostility, 55
  as primary theme, 27
  proclaimed by Jesus, 35–36
  purchase related to, 115
  related to prophecy, 207–8, 211
  renewed call to, 204–5
  as resistance, 269–70
  results of, 242, 345–46
  reward for, 97, 156, 382
  risks of, 254
  story of two witnesses, 208–18
  stressing the testimony of the past, 239
  willingness to, 248
  working to transform the world, 377
witnesses
  as conquerors, 285
  efforts of, making a difference in salvation,
    342
  executed, coming to life, 365–66
  expected to act in the spirit of
    prophecy, 89
  reigning with Christ, 364–68
woe package, four horsemen as part of, 124
women, John's demonization of, 10–11,
  309–10
word of God, linked to witness of Jesus
  Christ, 28
works
  connected to judgment, 49
  connected to witnessing to the lordship of
    God and Christ, 49
  linked with grace, 72
  love connected to, 50–51

works (*continued*)
  rewarded and punished, 373
works righteousness, 373–74
wormwood, 169–70, 295
worship
  blended with politics, 9, 97
  improper attempts at, 347–48, 403–4
  perpetual, 155
worthiness, 104–6, 298
  earned through endeavor, 70–71

of the Lamb, 95–96, 112–15, 119–20,
    247–48, 188, 298
  linked to conquest, 106
wrath
  cup of, 275, 281
  finishing of, 283
  plagues of, linked to singing, 286

Zealots, 201n1
Zion, understanding of, 265